Collective Bargaining and Industrial Relations

The Irwin Series in Management

and

the Behavioral Sciences

L.L. Cummings and E. Kirby Warren
Consulting Editors

Collective Bargaining and Industrial Relations

From Theory to Policy and Practice

Thomas A. Kochan
Alfred P. Sloan School of Management
Massachusetts Institute of Technology

Harry C. Katz
New York State School of
    Industrial and Labor Relations
Cornell University

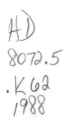

Second Edition

1988

IRWIN
Homewood, Illinois 60430

To Kathy, Andrew, Sarah, Samuel, Jacob, and Benjamin Kochan
and to Jan and Ariel Katz

© RICHARD D. IRWIN, INC., 1988

All rights reserved. No part of this publication may be
reproduced, stored in a retrieval system, or transmitted, in any
form or by any means, electronic, mechanical, photocopying,
recording, or otherwise, without the prior written permission of
the publisher.

Acquisitions editor: William R. Bayer
Developmental editor: Wendy L. Campbell
Copyediting coordinator: Joan A. Hopkins
Production manager: Carma W. Fazio
Compositor: Publication Services, Inc.
Typeface: Times Roman
Printer: Arcata Graphics/Kingsport

ISBN 0-256-03025-1

Library of Congress Catalog Card No. 87-082179

Printed in the United States of America

1 2 3 4 5 6 7 8 9 0 K 5 4 3 2 1 0 9 8

Preface

The first edition of this book was designed to serve as a graduate level text on collective bargaining and industrial relations. A collateral objective was to integrate economic, behavioral, and institutional research to develop a model of collective bargaining and industrial relations. That objective seemed appropriate for the time because an analytical framework was needed to organize and summarize the emerging work in the field.

In the eight short years since the publication of the first edition in 1980, the world of industrial relations has changed in fundamental ways, requiring substantial changes in the approach, scope, and content of this second edition. Again, our approach is to draw on recent research to provide the conceptual and empirical foundations for introducing students to contemporary practice. But this time we have superimposed on the previous model the three-tier model of strategic choice that we have been developing with our colleagues over the past several years in our studies of the changes taking place in U.S. industrial relations.

Our approach builds on the growing realization that collective bargaining cannot be isolated from decisions made well *above* the bargaining table, at the level of top management and labor strategy making, nor from developments *below* the bargaining table, at the workplace where individual workers interact with one another and their supervisors and adjust to changes in technology, markets, and the organization of work. This new model retains the basic assumptions and much of the analytical content of the framework used in the first edition, but it goes on to focus more directly on how the strategic choices of management, labor, and government decision makers influence the process and results of bargaining. Human resource management practices in the nonunion sector also are more prominent in this edition than in the first because they are becoming increasingly important in stimulating change in the established collective bargaining practices.

Our goal in this edition is to use recent research to introduce both graduate and undergraduate students to the changing nature of contemporary collective bargaining and industrial relations. We use a variety of examples throughout the book to illustrate how these changes are being played out in key bargaining relationships. Thus, in contrast to the first edition, our emphasis here is less on presenting new findings or on stimulating further research and more on translating recent research into appropriate teaching materials. To further aid in this effort, we use italics each time a key concept is introduced or defined.

A book like this owes a deep debt of gratitude to all the members of the industrial relations research community who have provided the raw materials for us to draw upon. We especially want to thank our colleague Robert B. McKersie for his leadership, inspiration, and contributions to our collaborative work. We also wish to thank the following people who provided research assistance along the way: Jeffrey Arthur, John Chalykoff, Joel Cutcher-Gershenfeld, Jeffrey Keefe, Adam Lerner, Kirsten R. Wever, and Louise Waldstein. Michelle Kamin and Jackie Dodge handled the task of processing innumerable drafts and revised drafts into final form.

We received very helpful comments on selected chapters from Trevor Bain and James Dworkin. Peter Feuille diligently read the entire manuscript and made what seemed like an endless number of suggestions for improvement. The only thing that saved our friendship with Pete is that all of his comments and suggestions were right on the mark. We appreciate the care and effort put into all those reviews.

Finally, a very special word of appreciation is due Wendy L. Campbell. Wendy not only served as our editor throughout all stages of this project but also provided many of the ideas for how to organize and communicate our abstract material to our intended audience. She brought to this project a rare combination of substantive expertise in industrial relations, professional editing skills, and a real concern for the student's needs and interests. Her willingness to take on these tasks made this project possible.

We dedicate this book to the members of our families. They have had to cope with seemingly endless hours of watching us stare at words on a screen and accept on faith that someday a book would emerge. We thank them for their patience and support thoughout it all.

Thomas A. Kochan and Harry C. Katz

Contents

CHAPTER 1

A Model of Collective Bargaining and Industrial Relations

Industrial relations is a broad, interdisciplinary field of study and practice that encompasses all aspects of the employment relationship. The field includes the study of individual workers, groups of workers and their unions and associations, employer and union organizations, and the environment in which these parties interact. Within this broad field industrial relations professionals have historically given special attention to relations between labor and management. In the United States this focus further translates into a special interest in collective bargaining as a system for governing labor-management relations. This is because U.S. public policy has identified bargaining as the preferred process for setting the terms and conditions of employment and for structuring interactions between labor and management at the workplace.

To analyze collective bargaining, industrial relations researchers draw on a wide variety of theories and data from economics, history, law, political science, international studies, and the behavioral sciences. Box 1–1 outlines how our field has drawn on these diverse disciplines to address specific topics in industrial relations. We will follow this tradition in this book by making liberal use of theories and evidence from a variety of disciplines. To make effective use of this material, however, we need to develop a more specific model of collective bargaining and industrial relations activities. The purpose of this chapter is to introduce the model we will use throughout the book.

A MODEL OF COLLECTIVE BARGAINING

Like other models of industrial relations ours emphasizes the relations among three key *actors*—management, labor, and government. [1] We use

1

BOX 1–1
Industrial relations as an interdisciplinary field of study

Academic discipline	*Industrial relations topics within the discipline*
History	Labor history
	history of trade unions
	history of labor movements
	history of the working class
	History of industrial organizations
	Economic history
Economics	Labor market theory and industrial relations theory
	Labor market studies
	labor supply
	labor demand
	labor mobility and turnover
	wages and fringe benefits
	income distribution
	productivity
	technological change
	Government macroeconomic policies
	wage-price policies
	policies on union-management relations; pensions, retirement, and social security; unemployment, job creation, and skills improvement; health, safety, disability, and other working conditions; discrimination; and immigration
Law	Laws governing union-management relations in the private and public sectors and the topics listed above under macroeconomic policies
Political science	Employers, unions, and workers in politics (lobbying)

---

the term *management* to refer to those individuals or groups responsible for promoting the goals of employers and their organizations. In fact this term encompasses at least three groups: (1) owners and shareholders of an

BOX 1–1 *(continued)*

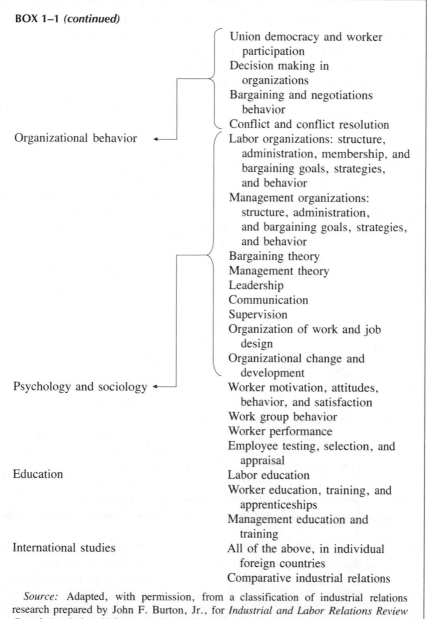

Organizational behavior

- Union democracy and worker participation
- Decision making in organizations
- Bargaining and negotiations behavior
- Conflict and conflict resolution
- Labor organizations: structure, administration, membership, and bargaining goals, strategies, and behavior
- Management organizations: structure, administration, and bargaining goals, strategies, and behavior

Psychology and sociology

- Bargaining theory
- Management theory
- Leadership
- Communication
- Supervision
- Organization of work and job design
- Organizational change and development
- Worker motivation, attitudes, behavior, and satisfaction
- Work group behavior
- Worker performance
- Employee testing, selection, and appraisal

Education

- Labor education
- Worker education, training, and apprenticeships
- Management education and training

International studies

- All of the above, in individual foreign countries
- Comparative industrial relations

Source: Adapted, with permission, from a classification of industrial relations research prepared by John F. Burton, Jr., for *Industrial and Labor Relations Review Cumulative Index, Volumes 1–39, 1947–1986,* comp. Brian Keeling and Wendy L. Campbell. Greenwich, Conn.: JAI Press, in press.

Note: The brackets and arrows above indicate topics that are also a part of the next discipline listed.

organization, (2) top executives and line managers, and (3) industrial relations and human resource staff professionals who specialize in managing relations with employees and unions. The term *labor* is equally broad and encompasses (1) employees and (2) the unions that represent the employees. Finally *government* is meant to encompass (1) the local, state, and federal political processes, (2) the government agencies responsible for passing and enforcing public policies that affect industrial relations, and (3) the government as a representative of the public interest. Government leaders also play an important role by setting the political climate for labor-management relations. Presidents Kennedy and Johnson, for example, took an active interest in labor-management relations, and union leaders had considerable influence over labor policy during their administrations. By contrast, union leaders have been granted little influence and labor policy has played a more limited role in the Reagan administration.

Figure 1–1 lays out the structure of the model we will use throughout this book. The model is driven by the *goals and expectations* the three actors have for collective bargaining. How the parties go about achieving their goals is described by what we will refer to in the model as the *institutional structures and processes* of collective bargaining. It is through these structures and processes that the parties interact and make choices that, together with forces in their environment, determine the extent to which their goals are met.

Our framework departs somewhat from most previous approaches to analyzing this subject. The study of collective bargaining has traditionally focused on the *process* and *outcomes* of negotiations and the *administration* of the bargaining agreement. In explaining variations in these aspects of bargaining, scholars have paid closest attention to (1) the structural characteristics of bargaining (for example, whether the agreement covers a single plant or a whole industry); (2) the organizational characteristics of unions and employers (for instance, whether the union represents workers with different skills, needs, and interests, or workers who are fairly homogeneous; whether the company is geographically concentrated or spread out; and whether its operations are limited to one product line or vertically integrated); and (3) the general features of the external environment (such as the state of the overall economy, the extent of foreign competition, or the pace of technological change). In recent years, however, changes in collective bargaining practices have led both researchers and practitioners to argue that this traditional approach is too narrow and no longer describes the basic forces driving and shaping union and management behavior. The framework we have developed is therefore broader and more dynamic in its depiction of collective bargaining activities. In particular, it emphasizes the range of options management, labor, and government policymakers have in responding to environmental changes (such as increased competition or changes in technology), rather than treating technology or competitive pressures as overriding constraints.

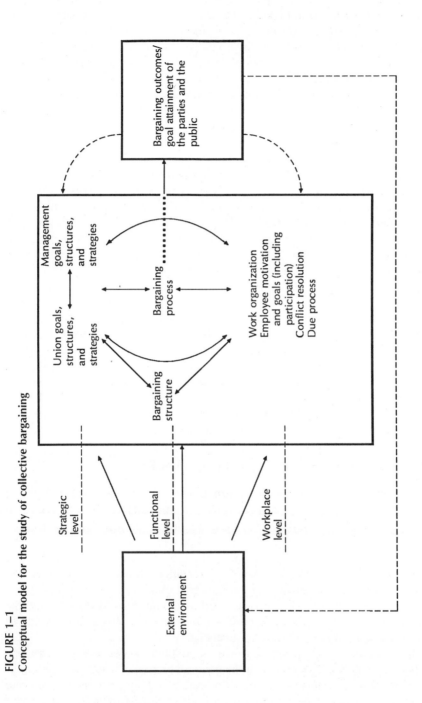

FIGURE 1–1
Conceptual model for the study of collective bargaining

The model depicted in Figure 1–1 starts, as do most traditional treatments of this subject, with consideration of the environmental context of collective bargaining. It then turns to the internal features of the bargaining system. Here we draw on much of our recent work by adopting a *three-tier approach* to depict the institutional structure of industrial relations within a firm. [2] The top tier, the *strategic,* comprises the strategies, values, structures, and other organizational features that influence collective bargaining and industrial relations. Here we ask questions such as how business strategy affects industrial relations; for example, we might compare a business strategy that emphasizes product differentiation and innovation against one that seeks to minimize labor costs. The middle tier, the *functional* or collective bargaining level, represents the actual process and results of contract negotiations. Discussions of strikes, bargaining power, and wage determination feature prominently here. The bottom tier, the *workplace,* illustrates the activities in which workers, their supervisors, and their union representatives engage in administering the labor contract and adjusting to changing circumstances and new problems on a daily basis. A typical question we ask at this level, for example, is how the introduction of employee participation programs has changed the day-to-day life of workers and supervisors.

It is through the joint effects of the environment and the actions of the parties within this three-tier institutional structure that collective bargaining either meets the goals of the parties and the public or comes up short. Since the ultimate question in any study of the collective bargaining system is whether it is effective—that is, the extent to which it meets the goals of the parties and the public—we start our discussion of the framework with an overview of these goals. Before doing so, however, let us set forth the basic assumptions guiding our approach.

BASIC ASSUMPTIONS OF INDUSTRIAL RELATIONS

The primary thread running through industrial relations research and policy prescriptions is that labor is more than a commodity, to be exchanged in the open competitive market like other, nonhuman market goods, and more than a set of human resources, to be allocated to serve the goals of the firm. Instead, because workers bring their own goals, expectations, and aspirations to the workplace, industrial relations must also be concerned with how the policies governing employment relations, and the work itself, affect workers and their interests, as well as the interests of the firm and the larger society. Thus, we take a *multiple interest* perspective on the study of collective bargaining and industrial relations.

This perspective requires that we be explicit about the relationships between the goals of workers and the goals of employers. A critical assumption underlying industrial relations research is that there is an *inherent conflict of interest* between employees and employers. That conflict arises out of the clash of economic interests between workers seeking job and income security and employers looking to promote efficiency and organizational effectiveness. Because this conflict of interests is viewed as inherent in the structure of the employment relationship,[3] overt conflict is viewed as a logical outgrowth of a system that seeks to allow the parties to pursue their pluralistic goals. *Thus, conflict is not viewed as pathological.* Conflicts should be limited in scope and frequency, however, since (1) the goals of the parties are interdependent, that is, neither party can achieve its goals without the other, and (2) the parties share a number of common goals as well. The essence of an effective employment relationship is therefore one in which the parties both successfully resolve issues arising from their conflicting interests and successfully pursue joint gains in cases where they share common interests.

Collective bargaining is only one of a variety of mechanisms for resolving conflicts and pursuing common interests at the workplace. In fact, as we will note later in this chapter and throughout the book, collective bargaining competes with these alternatives. Not all employees, for example, perceive deep conflicts with their employers or want to join unions. In dealing with their employers, some workers prefer individual over collective actions or representative processes. Others exercise the option of *exit* (quitting a job) when dissatisfied with employment conditions rather than choosing to *voice* their concerns, individually or collectively.[4] The role of public policy is therefore not to require unionization and collective bargaining for all workers, but to provide a fair opportunity for workers to choose whether collective bargaining is the means *they* prefer to resolve conflicts and pursue common interests with their employer.

GOALS OF THE PARTIES TO COLLECTIVE BARGAINING

Goals and goal attainment drive the discussions in this book. The key question to ask of any industrial relations system is whether the system is meeting the goals of the parties to it. Thus, we must also ask how we know when the system is performing effectively. In answering this question, we must hearken back to the primary function of the U.S. industrial relations system and ask: Is the system successfully balancing the conflicting goals of the parties?

These questions, with few exceptions, have not been systematically addressed by collective bargaining researchers in the past.[5] Indeed, many have argued that collective bargaining has too many diverse and conflicting interests, is too dynamic and situation-specific, or simply is too complex an institution to conform to any social scientist's conception of "good" and "bad," "effective" or "ineffective." But the public, and in recent years the federal government and the parties themselves, is demanding a more satisfactory response to these queries. The public has always listened with bewilderment to rhetoric about the value of "free" collective bargaining when forced to absorb the social and economic costs of a long strike. A Gallup poll in 1967 found, for example, a majority of union members and nonmembers alike favored limiting strikes to 21 days.[6] Other polls have demonstrated the public's approval of compulsory arbitration as a substitute for strikes that might impinge on public health and safety. Similarly, the federal government began to take a more active role in setting employment standards in the 1960s and 1970s; policymakers themselves had grown disenchanted with the strategy of leaving the substantive conditions of employment solely to the province of collective bargaining or to the workings of the market.

By the late 1970s and early 1980s federal deregulation of such industries as airlines, trucking, communications, and banking signaled a policy shift toward promoting greater *efficiency* in product markets. In turn, labor markets were then open to stiffer competition and thus greater influence from market forces. In effecting deregulation, government decision makers had little or no concern for the potential effects of the new policies on collective bargaining or union-management relations. In fact, the effects have been profound. In the airline industry, for instance, almost all the workers have had to take deep wage cuts. In-flight workers at Republic Airlines gave up 23 percent of their pay in 1983; certain pilots at Western Airlines took pay cuts of close to 40 percent in 1984, as did many workers at Eastern Airlines in 1985. All of these labor concessions resulted from dramatic increases in competitive pressures in industry. This experience illustrates an important feature of the environment of collective bargaining that should be kept in mind as we evaluate its performance: Collective bargaining, as a political and social institution, must compete for support with other economic policy institutions and political values. Indeed, as we will show in Chapter 2, only in the 1930s—a rare moment in American labor history—did policymakers specifically endorse collective bargaining as a key policy objective and specify its use as an instrument for achieving broad economic and social progress. Since the 1930s policymakers have continued to endorse collective bargaining in their political rhetoric, but only rarely have they taken any concrete steps to strengthen the role and functions it is expected to serve. Thus, collective bargaining must compete for support in a political and social environment that historically has granted it little encouragement.

We will argue that labor and management will find it very difficult indeed to make collective bargaining perform effectively at the workplace if unions and collective bargaining are not afforded a high degree of acceptance, legitimacy, and support in the society at large. The vast majority of U.S. employers have resisted unionization of their employees and therefore have often been only reluctant participants in collective bargaining. Managers tend to evaluate the performance of collective bargaining by comparing it with the nonunion alternatives in terms not only of their relative effects on the economic competitiveness of the firm but also of their effects on the employer's control, power, and flexibility in managing the workplace.

The growing sophistication of human resource management strategies and the increasing competitive pressures from nonunion sectors of the domestic and international economy have induced more and more top corporate managers to scrutinize the performance of their labor relations functions. Most top executives no longer hold the view that labor relations is an element of corporate affairs that is outside their control. Instead, as we will show in later chapters, they are taking direct action to integrate their labor relations strategies with their business strategies. For example, firms in the steel, auto, aerospace, and retail industries have worked with unions to modify labor relations practices in order to make new investments in plant and equipment pay off. In the airline industry one firm (Continental) declared bankruptcy in order to cut wages by 50 percent and transform the company into a low-cost, bargain-fare carrier.

As workers have become better educated, they too have become more vocal in expressing their goals and needs. They have initiated further pressure on the bargaining system, namely, that it become more responsive to their individual concerns for better working conditions, more say on how to do their jobs, and so on. Moreover, as noted earlier, collective bargaining is not the only means employees have for asserting their interests at work. Labor market competition for workers with scarce skills or abilities, government policies that protect workers' individual rights, and employers' human resource policies—all these serve as alternatives to collective bargaining in the eyes of workers. Thus, since workers as well as employers evaluate the performance of collective bargaining against its alternatives, these comparisons should be an explicit part of any analysis of collective bargaining.

Trade-offs among Conflicting Goals

Since many of the goals of the major actors—workers and their unions, employers, and the public or the government—conflict, we cannot specify a single overriding effectiveness criterion for collective bargaining. Focusing on any single one of these goals would destroy the effectiveness of collective bargaining as an instrument for accommodating the multiple interests of workers and employers in a democratic society. Unions could not survive or effectively represent their members, for example, if employers were completely free to suppress or avoid unionization. Likewise, employers could not compete effectively in global or domestic markets if collective bargaining constantly produced wages or other conditions of employment that increased costs above what the market would bear. Thus, we need to examine collective bargaining from the standpoint of each of the actors and to recall that collective bargaining is, by definition, an institution designed to achieve a *balance* among a number of these conflicting goals. In practice, collective bargaining reflects the parties' ongoing search for more effective ways to pursue those goals which they have in common.

Specific Indicators of Performance

Our framework for evaluating collective bargaining, to be useful, must identify specific indicators of how well collective bargaining is serving the varied goals and expectations of the parties and the public. We also need to identify which of these goals fall within the province of the collective bargaining relationship.

On the labor side we will examine the impact of bargaining both on objective indicators of such things as wages, benefits, and safety conditions and on more subjective measures of job satisfaction. We will also examine the effects of a number of recent union-management experiments and other innovations designed to improve the overall quality of working life (QWL) or employment security. Many of these recent initiatives have expanded the traditional agenda of collective bargaining. It is by analyzing these various indicators that we can begin to develop a well-rounded assessment of the effectiveness of collective bargaining from the standpoint of the individual worker.

On the management side we will examine the effects of collective bargaining on labor costs, productivity, profits, product quality, the degree of managerial control, managerial flexibility in altering workplace operations, the predictability and stability of labor relations processes, and various personnel concerns, such as turnover, motivation, and performance. All of these are specific indicators of the extent to which collective bargaining aids or hinders employers' quest for competitiveness in the product market.

Identifying the goals of the public and the government is a more difficult task. The National Labor Relations Act, the basic law governing most private sector bargaining relationships, and its amendments specify maintaining industrial peace and union democracy as basic public policy objectives. In addition, we need to examine the effects of collective bargaining on economic policies to control inflation and reduce unemployment and on policies to provide adequate labor standards, such as safety and health, equal employment opportunity, and income security. In light of contemporary concerns over new technology, we will pay special attention to the effects of collective bargaining on the introduction and use of technology.

Finally, since a free labor movement is important to any political democracy, we need to examine the effects of collective bargaining on the security, strength, and administration of labor organizations. That is, we need to assess whether the current mix of public policies and private actions produces a bargaining system that enhances and strengthens democracy at the workplace and in the society at large.

EXPLANATORY VARIABLES IN THE FRAMEWORK

Let us return now to Figure 1–1 and track the key environmental features and tiers of the institutional structure of bargaining that, respectively, serve as independent and intervening variables [7] in the framework presented in this book.

The Environment

The characteristics of the external environment are the initial set of explanatory variables to enter the framework. Analysis of almost any labor problem begins with an examination of its economic dimensions. Likewise, our framework begins by examining the macroeconomic and microeconomic features of product and labor markets that can affect the behavior of the parties and the conduct and outcomes of collective bargaining. The external environment also includes the political, social, technological, demographic, and public policy contexts of bargaining relationships. For example, is the public at large favorably inclined toward unions? Do the provisions of typical collective bargaining contracts adequately address the needs of women in the work force, of youths, of the elderly? Is the government enforcing the existing labor laws? We will link these aspects of the external environment to the goal attainment of the parties by tracing both their direct effects and their indirect effects on the strategies, structures, and processes of the parties.

Finally, we assign a crucial role to history as an explanatory variable. Most change in any social institution is incremental; that is, the range of choices open to the parties at any time depends on the strategies implemented previously. As we will see later, only when pressure for change reaches a critical threshold do the parties break from past patterns and introduce fundamental changes in their roles and relationships. As we will show, this is exactly what has happened in many bargaining relationships in recent years.

Institutional Features

We examine the values, strategies, processes, and practices through which the parties interact at the three tiers of the institutional structure of the industrial relations system: the strategic tier, the functional tier, and the workplace tier. As shown in Figure 1–1, the institutional arrangements at these three levels play an intervening role in our framework. On the one hand, they must be responsive to the pressures the parties face in their external environment and therefore must be amenable to change over time as external conditions change. At the same time, these institutional features of the bargaining system are not completely determined by external environmental forces. The parties retain a considerable degree of discretion or *choice* in shaping their bargaining systems. These choices, their interrelationships, and their consequences need to be explored and understood to appreciate fully how collective bargaining works.

Our analysis of these internal characteristics of collective bargaining starts with the structure of collective bargaining. *Bargaining structure* refers to the scope of employees and employers covered or in some way affected by the terms of a labor agreement. For example, are a number of different employers involved in the agreement or is there just one? Does a given company bargain with one union or many? Does a given union represent workers with diverse or homogeneous skills or interests? The structure of bargaining in the United States is often described as highly decentralized. The U.S. Bureau of Labor Statistics estimates (no exact census has ever been attempted) somewhere between 170,000 and 190,000 separate collective bargaining agreements exist in this country. Yet this number may overstate the actual degree of decentralization of bargaining, since an informal process known as *pattern bargaining* often operates to tie separate agreements together so that a change in one leads to similar changes in others within the same firm, region, or industry. For instance, the United Auto Workers union, which represents workers in both the auto parts and the auto assembly sectors, has commonly tried to extend the contract improvements in assembly plants of the major auto manufacturers to the parts-producing plants owned by other companies. As we will see, the strength of these patterns varies considerably over time; however, pattern bargaining remains an important feature of contemporary collective bargaining.

For collective bargaining to work effectively, the formal structure of bargaining and the informal pattern bargaining arrangements must be well matched to the external environment and to the strategies and needs of the parties. Two examples of cases where such patterns became difficult to maintain are the rubber tire and airline industries. The technological shift from bias-ply to radial tires in the 1970s made many of the older rubber plants obsolete, which led to a breakdown of bargaining patterns in the late 1970s. Deregulation, rising fuel costs, and heightened competition in airlines led some carriers to break with contract patterns as early as 1982, and by the mid-1980s the patterns had completely eroded. Both of these examples illustrate the impact of environmental changes on the structures of collective bargaining. In Chapter 4 we will explore how the structures of bargaining have undergone considerable change in those settings where the environment and the strategies of the parties have been changing most dramatically. In this way we will demonstrate the important links between bargaining structure and other concepts in the framework.

Values, Goals, Strategies, and Organizational Structures

Next our analysis turns to the key values, goals, strategies, and structural characteristics of management and labor organizations. We present these as the top tier of the three-tier model of highly interdependent activities within a given bargaining relationship. Traditionally, most treatments of the organizational characteristics of unions and employers have focused on a rather narrow conception of the internal management structure for labor relations or on union wage objectives and internal politics. We take a much broader approach by stressing the importance of the underlying values, goals, and strategies that guide the long-run direction of U.S. private and public enterprises and the deep-seated values and principles that guide the strategies of U.S. union leaders. For instance, is a given company's top management content to work with its union(s) over the long run, or is it fundamentally committed to devoting its resources to nonunion pursuits and operations? Is a given union leadership committed to maintaining a distanced and adversarial posture in negotiations, or is it interested in exchanging new forms of flexible work organization for greater control over the design of the production process? Indeed, as the parties themselves have come to explore these questions more fully in recent years, they have brought about significant changes in industrial relations practice.

Having an accurate understanding of the links between basic business strategies and the consequences of collective bargaining is crucial for anyone who wants either to interpret or to participate in the bargaining process. The same is true for the roles played by the values and strategies union leaders choose for representing their members. We will explore the nature and effects of these and other organizational features of union and management organizations in Chapters 5 through 7.

The Process and Outcomes of Negotiations

The middle tier of activity within a bargaining relationship encompasses the heart and soul of the process. The functional tier has traditionally served as the center of attention in the study and practice of union-management relations. It is the arena in which the formal contract *negotiations process* takes place and the terms and conditions of the labor agreement, or, as we will often refer to them, the *outcomes* of bargaining, are established and periodically modified. Of this level of the model, we will ask the following main questions:

1. How can the dynamics of the negotiations process be described and explained? Here we will examine the behavior of the parties to negotiations through the complete cycle of negotiations, starting with the presentation of opening offers and demands and proceeding through the signing of the final agreement.
2. What causes strikes to occur in some negotiations and not in others and to vary in frequency and intensity over time and across industries?
3. What alternative mechanisms for resolving disputes are available and under what conditions are they effective? Here we examine the processes of mediation, factfinding, arbitration, and other impasse resolution procedures.

Most, but not all, of the outcomes of the negotiations process are codified in the collective bargaining agreement. Figure 1–2 exhibits the range and complexity of the substantive terms and conditions of employment that are covered in many contemporary labor contracts. This list illustrates that most of the agreements address, at the very least, the following sets of issues: (1) wage and fringe benefit levels, payment systems, and administration; (2) job and income security; (3) physical working conditions; (4) selected personnel management and plant operation practices; and (5) union and management rights, responsibilities, and relations. Nonetheless, the scope and content of bargaining agreements in the United States vary widely. Since contract provisions define the rights and obligations of each of the parties, they furnish a starting point for assessing how well the interests of workers, employers, unions, and society are faring at the workplace.

Recently, a number of companies and unions have moved to simplify the rules contained in their agreements, as part of their efforts to lower costs and increase flexibility in the management of human resources. We will therefore address both the historical growth in the complexity of bargaining agreements and the more recent efforts to streamline some of the work rule provisions.

FIGURE 1–2
Standard provisions in collective bargaining agreements

Establishment and administration
of the agreement

Bargaining unit and plant supplements
Contract duration and reopening and
    renegotiation provisions
Union security and the checkoff
Special bargaining committees
Grievance procedures
Arbitration and mediation
Strikes and lockouts
Contract enforcement

Functions, rights, and responsibilities

Management rights clauses
Plant removal
Subcontracting
Union activities on company time
    and premises
Union-management cooperation
Regulation of technological change
Advance notice and consultation

Wage determination and administration

Rate structure and wage differentials
Incentive and bonus plans
Production standards and time studies
Job classification and job evaluation
Individual wage adjustments
General wage adjustments during the
    contract period

Plant operations

Work and shop rules
Rest periods and other in-plant time
    allowances
Safety and health
Plant committees
Hours of work and premium
    pay practices
Shift operations
Hazardous work
Discipline and discharge

Paid and unpaid leave

Vacations and holidays
Sick leave
Funeral and personal leave
Military leave and jury duty

FIGURE 1–2 (*continued*)

Job or income security	*Employee benefit plans*
Hiring and transfer arrangements	Health and insurance plans
Employment and income guarantees	Pension plans
Reporting and call-in pay	Profit-sharing, stock purchase, and
Supplemental unemployment	thrift plans
benefit plans	Bonus plans
Regulation of overtime, shift work, etc.	
Reduction of hours to forestall layoffs	
Layoff procedures, seniority, recall	
Worksharing in lieu of layoff	*Special groups*
Attrition arrangements	Apprentices and learners
Promotion practices	Handicapped and older workers
Training and retraining	Women
Relocation allowances	Veterans
Severance pay and layoff benefit plans	Union representatives
Special funds and study committees	Nondiscrimination clauses

Source: Adapted from Joseph W. Bloch, "Union Contracts—A New Series of Studies," *Monthly Labor Review* 87 (October 1964): 1184–85.

Administration of the Bargaining Agreement

Since collective bargaining agreements have no effect on individual workers until they are put into practice, another important set of industrial relations activities is the interaction of workers, supervisors, and local union representatives at the workplace on a day-to-day basis.

The grievance and arbitration procedures in almost all labor agreements are traditionally viewed as the centerpiece of the contract administration process in the United States. Some view grievance arbitration as *the* most significant innovation of the U.S. industrial relations system. But although the grievance and arbitration processes play central roles in the daily administration of the employment relationship, we must go beyond the operational features of these formal processes to examine how well collective bargaining is performing as an overall system for dispensing industrial justice and managing workplace conflicts. The contract administration process in general, and the grievance arbitration process in particular, have been undergoing significant change with the growth of external laws governing health and safety, equal employment opportunity, and other matters that influence the rights of individuals and add to the responsibilities of both unions and employers.

The management of conflict and the delivery of due process are only two of several generic activities that occur on a continuous basis at the workplace. Two others are the motivation, participation, and supervision of individual workers and the structuring of work into jobs, groups, or teams. These ongoing activities have received a great deal of recent attention and will be taken up as part of our discussion of processes for managing change in union-management relationships.

Change in Union-Management Relations

Collective bargaining relationships are not static but exist in environments that constantly exert pressure on the parties to revise existing practices and conceptions about their appropriate roles. Although these pressures are seldom welcomed, even the most entrenched bargaining relationships are periodically subject to either external or internal pressures that dictate the need for a change. One of the most obvious forms of change is the implementation of new technologies. Changing technology or changes in market conditions periodically force the parties to modify the terms of the labor contract to avoid losing jobs to competitors. Similarly, changes in the attitudes and expectations of workers may create internal pressures on union and management leaders, for example, to improve the quality of working life and the degree of participation afforded workers and supervisors. Finally, intense pressure to improve productivity and product quality has renewed the interest of many employers in the tasks of managing change and innovation.

Yet collective bargaining, like any other institution in society, rarely responds quickly to pressure for change. Furthermore, changes are not always neutral or beneficial to all the parties. Giving rank-and-file workers more say over their jobs, for example, often reduces the power and status of supervisors. Thus, the dynamics of union-management change and the factors that facilitate or impede this change process serve as another important part of the bargaining system. Indeed, the task of managing change and innovation in bargaining relationships may be the single biggest challenge facing labor and management today. Although this topic will surface throughout our analysis, Chapter 13 is devoted specifically to it.

THE BROADER CONCERNS OF U.S. LABOR POLICIES

A major assumption underlying our approach is that collective bargaining is a limited institution, one that is not capable of solving all of the industrial relations, economic, or social problems that surface in an employment relationship. Yet most U.S. labor policies have been targeted at the unionized sector of the labor force. The NLRA states that collective bargaining is the preferred method of setting the terms and conditions of employment in the United States and that the thrust of U.S. labor policies is to promote the orderly development and conduct of that method. Events of recent decades, however, have gradually come to challenge this basic premise. We are in a time, therefore, that requires continual assessment of the roles collective bargaining is expected to serve and constant evaluation of the impact of collective bargaining on the actors in the system and on society relative to the alternatives for performing its functions.

Since less than one-fifth of the U.S. labor force is now represented by trade unions, to regulate employment conditions the government will need to go beyond the simple process of promoting collective bargaining and will have to establish supplementary policies. In some instances public policies preempt collective bargaining by creating alternative means by which labor-management conflicts and issues can be addressed. The critical challenge for policymakers is to supplement policies that promote unionism and collective bargaining with other initiatives that do not threaten the survival and security of those institutions. Consequently, after covering the components of the framework outlined above, we will examine the changing role and status of collective bargaining in the broader context of national labor, employment, and human resource policies.

SUMMARY

This brief overview of our model of collective bargaining and industrial relations sets the stage for the remainder of the book. The framework outlined here adopts the premise that a complex social or economic system can be best understood by first standing back and conceptualizing its major components and then examining in detail each component and its interconnections with other parts of the system. Thus, we view collective bargaining as a complex social system made up of environmental forces, institutional features, outcomes, and change—all driven by the goals and expectations of the parties. With this framework in mind, we can begin to examine its historical development and then go on to look more closely at its detailed parts.

Notes

1. See John T. Dunlop, *Industrial Relations Systems* (New York: Holt, 1958).

2. For a summary of the theoretical and empirical research on which this model is based, see Thomas A. Kochan, Harry C. Katz, and Robert B. McKersie, *The Transformation of American Industrial Relations* (New York: Basic Books, 1986).

3. For two exceptions to this statement see Milton Derber, W. E. Chalmers, and Milton Edelman, "Assessing Union Management Relations," *Quarterly Review of Economics and Business* 96 (November 1961): 27–40; and Jeanne M. Brett, "Behavioral Research on Unions and Union Management Systems," in *Research in Organizational Behavior*, vol. 2, ed. Barry Staw and L. L. Cummings (Greenwich, Conn.: JAI Press, 1979), 177–214.

For two sociological views of the employment relationship that adopt this perspective see Rolf Dahrendorf, *Class and Class Conflict in an Industrial Society* (London: Routledge and Kegan Paul, 1959); and Alan Fox, *A Sociology of Work in Industry* (London: Collier-Macmillan, 1971).

4. See Albert O. Hirschman, *Exit, Voice, and Loyalty: Responses to Declines in Firms, Organizations, and States* (Cambridge: Harvard University Press, 1970).

5. Derek C. Bok and John T. Dunlop, *Labor and the American Community* (New York: Simon and Schuster, 1970), 20.

6. For a summary of public opinion data on this topic, see Donald E. Cullen, *National Emergency Strikes* (Ithaca, N.Y.: New York State School of Industrial and Labor Relations, Cornell University, 1968), 12–20.

7. An intervening variable is a special type of explanatory variable in a theory, one that occupies an intermediate position in the causal relationship between independent and dependent variables. An intervening variable is caused by one or more independent variables and in turn causes variations in one or more dependent variables. For example, in the series $X \rightarrow Y \rightarrow Z$, X is an independent variable, Y is an intervening variable, and Z is a dependent variable.

CHAPTER 2

Historical Evolution of the U.S. Industrial Relations System

We have defined collective bargaining as one means for organized groups of workers and their employers to resolve their conflicting interests and seek agreement over issues in which they have common interests. It is by no means, however, the only way to conduct industrial relations or to set and administer the terms and conditions of employment. Indeed, in the long history of work and of industrial society, collective bargaining is only a recent arrival. Moreover, like any institution it has had to adapt over its history to changing times, to the changing values and expectations of the people it is expected to serve. This chapter will explore the evolution of industrial relations in the United States and place the arrival and development of collective bargaining in a historical perspective. In doing so, the discussion will illuminate both the dynamic, adaptive character of collective bargaining and its still-tenuous position in the U.S. industrial relations system.

As a point of departure, we will explore the ways in which different societies have historically addressed issues of employment and examine the nature of the U.S. industrial relations system that developed from these various historical systems.

THE ROOTS OF INDUSTRIAL RELATIONS

Over the centuries attitudes toward work have undergone drastic changes. Those changes reflected not only economic and political philosophies, but also cultural and religious values as they evolved in the larger society.

The early Greeks viewed work as a most unpleasant activity, a form of drudgery to be relegated to the lower classes and avoided by the aristocratic or leisure classes. [1] With the development of Christianity, this view was

19

to change. Catholic scholars of the Middle Ages, such as Thomas Aquinas, looked upon work as being instrumental to a healthy soul. Later, Lutheranism, and then Calvinism, further extolled the value of work, as a virtue in itself and as a necessity to a full and complete life. Under what came to be known as the Protestant ethic of the eighteenth century, work was viewed as a means of serving God. This descendant of Aquinas's philosophy was at least partly responsible for the development of the concept of the *work ethic* in modern society;[2] in fact, Tilgher argues that the Protestant ethic in general, and Calvinism with its emphasis on discipline in particular, laid the moral foundation for the discipline and division of labor required by the modern industrial system.[3] These religious teachings also provided the moral basis for the technological requirements of industrialization and for the hierarchical structure of modern organizations.

But although these philosophies may have provided the moral justification for the emerging factory system of the late 1800s, not all workers were able easily to adjust their work habits to fit the stringent time and disciplinary requirements of industrial work. Labor historians have noted, for example, that managers in the early mills and factories of New England had to impose strong discipline and extensive socialization on immigrants and other first-generation factory workers to make them adapt to the new work system.[4] Box 2–1 excerpts one of the most famous moral and disciplinary codes, one imposed by a New England employer in the early 1800s. Box 2–2 contains a description of working conditions at a southern mill at the turn of the last century.

The first groups of workers to challenge such employer initiatives effectively by joining together and demanding improved wages were skilled craftsmen such as shoemakers and printers. Although records show that the 1700s did witness associations of masters and merchants who sought to eliminate unfair competition and stabilize prices, most sources cite the union of Philadelphia shoemakers organized in 1792 as the first modern trade union in the United States.[5] It was from the actions of this union that a famous 1806 trial produced the *criminal conspiracy doctrine* governing labor union activity; this common law doctrine was to dominate court decisions until the 1840s.

Employment relationships during those early years of industrialization in this country were governed solely by the common law traditions carried over from Great Britain. That is, neither any constitutional provision nor any state or federal statutes explicitly addressed the rights of workers or the obligations of employers. It was left to the courts to develop their own prescriptions of the rights and responsibilities of the parties to employment contracts.[6] But though these judicial theories were modified slightly, from the American revolution to the mid-1800s, common law rule generally translated into few enforceable contractual or implied rights for individual employees and, in fact, into outright hostility toward collective action by labor organizations. During that period state and local courts treated unions as criminal conspiracies impinging on industrial workers' "freedom" to contract with an employer.

Then, in the celebrated 1842 case of *Commonwealth* v. *Hunt*, Judge Shaw broke from the criminal conspiracy doctrine by applying the theory of the means justifying the ends. Henceforth, unions per se were not illegal, but instead the courts had to assess whether unions had abused their power or violated the constitutional rights of workers or private property holders in taking any given action.[7] Thus, by the late 1800s judges had generally turned from restricting unions' rights to exist to issuing injunctions limiting the ability of unions to strike, picket, or boycott employers. At the turn of the century, therefore, the accepted doctrine still provided little encouragement or protection of workers, unions, or the process of collective bargaining.

BOX 2–1

GENERAL REGULATIONS
To Be Observed by Persons Employed by The
LAWRENCE MANUFACTURING COMPANY

1st. All persons in the employ of the Company, are required to attend assiduously to their various duties, or labor, during working hours; are expected to be fully competent, or to aspire to the upmost efficiency in the work or business they may engage to perform, and to evince on all occasions, in their deportment and conversation, a laudable regard for temperance, virtue, and their moral and social obligations; and in which the Agent will endeavor to set a proper example. No person can be employed by the Company, whose known habits are or shall be dissolute, indolent, dishonest, or intemperate, or who habitually absent themselves from public worship, and violate the Sabbath, or who may be addicted to gambling of any kind.

2d. All kinds of ardent spirit will be excluded from the Company's ground, except it be prescribed for medicine, or for washes, and external applications. Every kind of gambling and card playing, is totally prohibited within the limits of the Company's ground and Board house.

3d. Smoking cannot be permitted in the Mills, or other buildings, or yards, and should not be carelessly indulged in the Board Houses and streets. . . .

Lowell, Massachusetts, 21 May 1833.

Source: William Cahn, *A Pictorial History of American Labor* (New York: Crown Publisher, 1972), 49.

BOX 2–2
Southern cotton mill towns of the 1800s

The cotton mill village was like one big white family closed off to the external world. Rows and rows of white clapboard houses lined dirt roads leading to the mill, while the mill owner lived some distance away in a mansion.

Workers, mostly women and children, labored sixteen hours a day for wages that were just enough to pay rent on their mill houses and their bills at the general store. Mill workers survived primarily on food grown in their own gardens. Mill owners not only encouraged child labor, they insisted upon it. Some mill villages provided schools, but most did not, and the majority of this first generation of mill workers grew up illiterate. The church was usually built on land owned by the mill which also provided its financial support. Thus sermons frequently followed the theme of hard work, deprivation, and suffering as the path to salvation.

Source: Victoria Byerly, *Hard Times Cotton Mill Girls: Personal Histories of Womanhood and Poverty in the South* (Ithaca, N.Y.: ILR Press, 1986), 12.

LABOR AS AN ECONOMIC COMMODITY

As workers adapted to the industrial system, and with the rise of mass, urban society, moralistic views of work and the suppressive legal doctrines of common law gradually gave way to the "rational" analysis of the functions labor serves in an industrial society. In particular, the economic theories of Adam Smith, David Ricardo, Thomas Malthus, John Stuart Mill, and Alfred Marshall became the predominant modes of conceptualizing the role of labor in society during the late 1800s. This school of thought emphasized identifying the "natural laws" of *classical economics* that shaped the conditions under which labor and capital interacted in an employment relationship. Although the various classical economists disagreed on numerous points in their theories, they all viewed *labor as a commodity*, that is, as any other factor of production. Like other commodities, labor was subject to the laws of supply and demand, and therefore these economists saw little need to develop any special system for governing employment relationships. Nor did they see any justification for special treatment of workers adversely affected by the workings of market forces. Instead, the classical economists shared the view that in the long run the "invisible hand" of the competitive market would work in the best interests of the largest numbers of workers and society.

MARX AND THE WEBBS

Although the labor-as-commodity view may seem harsh and insensitive today, it served as the dominant influence on U.S. public policy until well into the 1930s. Nonetheless, it had come under attack much earlier from a host of intellectuals and social reformers. Karl Marx was one of the most vocal and influential critics. Rejecting the application of classical economic theory to labor, [8] he disavowed the notion that the working class should bear the painful consequences of the market system. Simply stated, Marx argued that the pain and injustice of the poverty, exploitation, and alienation inflicted on workers by the capitalistic system would eventually lead to the revolutionary overthrow of the system. He believed that workers would eventually develop a *class consciousness* that would pave the way for revolution and the ultimate solution to their problems—a Marxian economic and social system.

Marx supported trade unions in their struggles for higher wages, but he believed they should simultaneously pursue the ultimate end of overthrowing the capitalistic system. Later, Lenin was also critical of the tendency of trade unions to focus exclusively on short-term economic struggles and reform politics. He believed that gradualistic strategies for change, by working within capitalistic institutions, tended to reinforce rather than challenge the existing order. Lenin therefore stressed the necessity of pursuing revolutionary political objectives along with economic goals. He assigned to the Communist party the task of developing and mobilizing such revolutionary consciousness. [9]

Marxist concepts met with hostile treatment from U.S. employers and other groups that dominated local and national politics. From the earliest efforts at unionization among the shoemakers in Philadelphia to the present day, labor organizations that have attempted to adopt Marxist or other leftist ideologies or strategies have faced strong resistance in the employment, legal, and political systems and have failed to garner a significant following within the American labor force. Nevertheless, a number of dynamic and energetic advocates of labor's cause urged workers to organize and fight for improved working conditions, even in the face of employer and government resistance. Among the most colorful of these was "Mother Jones," whose exploits are described in Box 2–3.

Historians continue to debate whether the lack of a Marxist or socialist labor movement in the United States is a reflection of the legal and political suppression these movements have endured historically or simply a reflection of the fundamental lack of class consciousness among the nation's rank-and-file workers. The fact is, however, that radical labor movements have never survived long enough to become an influential actor in the U.S. industrial relations system. [10] Instead, their role has been to serve as a threat to employers at various junctures, such as in the early years of this century. In turn that threat convinced employers to accept more moderate brands of U.S. unionism. [11]

During the last decade of the nineteenth century Sidney and Beatrice Webb, two British economists and social reformists, joined Marx in his critique of the commodity approach to treating labor. [12] Their reaction

---

BOX 2–3
"That's No Lady, That's Mother Jones"

During the late 1800's and early 1900's, when gunfire and bloodshed often accompanied workers' attempts to form unions, a sweet-faced old woman known only as Mother Jones tramped over most of the country's coalfields to encourage miners to organize and strike.

Mother Jones looked like a kindly grandmother. A mere 5 feet tall and weighing less than 100 pounds, she generally wore a genteel, lacetrimmed, black dress and a Victorian bonnet. But while Mother Jones appeared gentle, her words and actions were as hard as life in the mines.

In 1917–18, 87-year-old Mother Jones told a group of striking West Virginia miners, "You goddamned cowards are losing this strike because you haven't got the guts to go out there and fight and win it. Why the hell don't you take your high-power rifles and blow the goddamned scabs out of the mines?"

The miners loved Mother Jones; mine owners, police, and many less radical union leaders looked forward to her death. She was arrested and jailed several times, once for allegedly conspiring to commit murder, stealing a machine gun, and attempting to blow up a train with dynamite. When she died at the age of 100, the priest who delivered her eulogy said, "Sometimes she used methods that made the righteous grieve . . . but her faults were the excesses of her courage, her love of justice, the love in her mother's heart."

She, like today's feminists, preferred the word "woman" to "lady."

"No matter what your fight, . . . don't be ladylike! God Almighty made women and the Rockefeller gang of thieves made the ladies."

Source: Quoted from *200 Years of American Worklife* (Washington, D.C.: U.S. Department of Labor, 1977), 104, 108.

---

to the classical economists was couched within a theory of Fabian socialism, however, rather than Marxism. They agreed with Marx on the need for special strategies to ameliorate working conditions and increase wages by expanding the bargaining power of workers vis-à-vis their employers. But they broke ranks with Marx in their belief that a gradual evolution, rather than a revolution, would transform society. Consequently, they viewed trade unions as a means of representing the interests of workers through the strategies of *mutual insurance, collective bargaining,* and *legal enactment.* [13]

The work of the Webbs contributed to the development of industrial relations as we know it today in at least three ways. First, their normative values helped to challenge the authority of the classical economic theorists in shaping British policies toward labor. The Webbs were active and highly visible advocates of laws designed to eliminate the deplorable employment and living conditions of British working men, women, and children. Second, they were the first to develop a theory of trade unionism and the collective bargaining power of workers and employers. Finally, they based their ideas and policy prescriptions on empirical research. In their studies of trade unions and "factory legislation," they presented historical analyses of observed effects rather than deductive theories or "laws" of classical economics. As we will see, all three of these important contributions (or challenges to the classical economic and Marxian paradigms) were adopted by the intellectual architects of the U.S. industrial relations system, the institutional economists.

THE RISE OF INSTITUTIONAL ECONOMICS

Institutional economics, which rejected the classical economic analysis of labor, provided many of the intellectual underpinnings of the national labor policies that emerged in the United States in the twentieth century. John R. Commons, the person most deserving of the title Father of U.S. Industrial Relations, identified the essence of institutional economics as "a shift from commodities, individuals, and exchanges to transactions and working rules of collective action." [14] Commons was a student of Richard T. Ely, one of the early social reformist economists. Like the Webbs Ely severely criticized the theories and the abstract methods of the classical economists, [15] yet Commons was a reformist of moderate dimensions compared to the Marxist or even the non-Marxist socialist critics. Commons followed a middle path by rejecting the economic determinism of classical economics, on the one hand, and the followers of the utopian solutions of the Marxists and other socialists, on the other. Instead, he and his fellow institutionalists placed great value on negotiations and on compromise among the divergent interests of labor, management, and the public. This approach reflected these economists' pluralistic view of industrial society.

There were, however, some interesting similarities in the views of Commons, Marx, and the Webbs. Like Marx and the Webbs Commons and other institutional economists rejected the view of labor as a commodity, for two fundamental reasons. First, all of the institutionalists saw work as being too central to the interests and welfare of individual workers, their families, and their communities to be treated simply as just another factor of production. [16] Because of the centrality of work, labor does not behave like an inanimate factor of production and does not respond in an undifferentiated fashion to the forces of the market. In short, as Marx argued, labor as a factor of production cannot be separated from labor as a human being with individual motivations, needs, and goals.

Second, the institutionalists also echoed the Webbs and the Marxist theorists by arguing that under conditions of "free competition" most individual workers deal with the employer from a position of unequal bargaining power. In the vast majority of employment situations, that is, the workings of the market tilt the balance of power in favor of the employer. A selection from Beatrice Webb's classic essay on the economics of factory legislation in Britain, shown in Box 2–4, amply illustrates this argument and points up the differences the institutionalists had with the classical economists.

These two assumptions—that labor required protection from the workings of the competitive market and that unions could materially improve the conditions of the worker—naturally led to the two basic labor policies advocated by these early American scholars: legislation protecting the rights of workers to join unions; and legislation on such workplace issues as safety and health, child labor, minimum wages, unemployment and workers' compensation, and social security. [17] In addition to making scholarly contributions, therefore, the institutionalists served as early advocates of the social and legislative reforms that were to become the centerpiece of the New Deal labor policy.

The work of the institutionalists reflected a number of other, more implicit assumptions about the nature of industrial society and of relations between workers and their employers. Their championing of protective labor legislation and union organization implied an acceptance of the belief that an *inherent conflict of interests* exists between workers and their employers. Commons and his followers shared this basic assumption with Marx and the Webbs. But unlike either Marx or the Webbs, they did not believe the root of this conflict of interests lay in the nature of capitalism. The means for dealing with it, therefore, was through worker organization, union-employer accommodation, and periodic conflict resolution—all strategies for working within the capitalistic system.

Selig Perlman's *A Theory of the Labor Movement* more precisely differentiated between Commons's "Wisconsin School" and the European socialist theorists. [18] Perlman explained workers' attitudes and behavior as dominated by their need for job security. Later, Jack Barbash extended the Commons-Perlman framework by proposing that at the core of labor problems was the clash between the *job security* interests of workers and the organizational *efficiency* or effectiveness needs of employers. [19] Furthermore, unlike the utopian socialists these institutionalists argued for the need to recognize the legitimacy of both worker and employer interests in industrial society and therefore argued for continuous accommodation of these interests. Their philosophy thus represented a middle ground between the classical economists, on the one hand, and the Marxists and socialists, on the other. By accepting the fundamental legitimacy of the employer's role in a capitalistic or a socialistic system as being responsible for representing the interests

---

BOX 2–4
Beatrice Webb on the balance of power between employee and employer

If the capitalist refuses to accept the workman's terms, he will, no doubt, suffer some inconvenience as an employer. To fulfill his orders, he will have to "speed up" some of his machinery, or insist on his people working longer hours. Failing these expedients he may have to delay the delivery of his goods, and may even find his profits, at the end of the year fractionally less than before. But, meanwhile, he goes on eating and drinking, his wife and family go on living, just as before. His physical comfort is not affected: he can afford to wait until the labourer comes back in a humble frame of mind. And that is just what the labourer must presently do. For he, meanwhile, has lost his day. His very subsistence depends on his promptly coming to an agreement. If he stands out, he has no money to meet his weekly rent, or to buy food for his family. If he is obstinate, consumption of his little hoard, or the pawning of his furniture, may put off the catastrophe; but sooner or later slow starvation forces him to come to terms. And since success in the higgling of the market is largely determined by the relative eagerness of the parties to come terms—especially if this eagerness cannot be hidden—it is now agreed, even on this ground alone, "that manual labourers as a class are at a disadvantage in bargaining."

Source: Mrs. Sidney Webb, ed., *The Case for Factory Acts* (London: Grant Richards, 1901), 8–9.

---

of the consumer and the producer, the institutionalists were more conservative than the socialists and more liberal than the classical economists.

THE EVOLUTION OF BUSINESS UNIONISM

The moderate views of the institutionalists were also compatible with the form of trade unionism that had evolved and was to prove most enduring in the U.S. environment. Although a variety of reformist organizations attempted to organize workers and build political coalitions among such groups as workers, advocates for women's rights, and anti-monopolists, it was the American Federation of Labor (AFL), founded in 1886, that overcame the opposition of employers and the courts to build a membership able to survive the ups and downs of business cycles. Led by the former cigar maker Samuel Gompers for all but one year between 1886 and his death in 1924, the AFL espoused a *business unionism* philosophy, best expressed by Gompers when he said, "The trades unions pure and simple are the organizations of the wage workers to secure their present material and practical improvement and to achieve their final emancipation." [20]

Business unionism cut a compromise between the broad reformist goals but passive strategies (such as opposition to strikes) of the Knights of Labor and the radical political ideals and tactics of the International Workers of the World. The AFL strategy, specifically, was to organize craft workers into exclusive unions; rely on collective bargaining with employers to achieve improved wages and working conditions and to protect the status of the trades; and pursue a limited political course in which labor would help its friends and punish its opponents but would eschew any permanent political alliances or long-term political or social objectives. Although an active and colorful debate continues today among labor historians over whether this is the *only* form of unionism that could have survived and sustained the support of a large number of American workers, for our purposes it is sufficient to note that it was the AFL unions that did survive and that constituted the core of the U.S. labor movement from the late 1800s until the debates over the New Deal labor policies began in the early 1930s. It was the business unionism philosophy and collective bargaining strategies of the AFL that the intellectual and political advocates of the New Deal policy sought to protect and encourage through federal legislation.

One of the guiding principles of the AFL was that workers should be organized into separate *craft unions*. That is, each trade, such as carpenters, printers, machinists, and the skilled trades within large manufacturing firms, was to have *exclusive jurisdiction* or rights to organize workers engaged in these occupations regardless of the industry or firm in which they were employed. As the organization of production moved from small job shops to large-scale mass production, however, the vast array of semiskilled and unskilled production workers were left without any viable basis for organizing. The emphasis on craft organizing made it difficult to counter the power of large-scale industrial corporations. For example, in 1919 a strike against the steel industry was called by 24 different unions with jurisdiction over different craft groups. The strike ultimately failed in part because of the inability of these unions to coordinate their efforts. By the early 1920s, therefore, a number of union leaders and socialists were urging the formation of new *industrial unions* that would organize all production and maintenance workers in a given industry regardless of their skill level or craft. Since this approach to organizing would cut into the jurisdictions of many established craft unions, it was opposed vigorously by Gompers, by his successor as president of the AFL, William Green, and by other AFL union presidents.

The debate between the advocates of AFL craft unions and the advocates of industrial unionism came to a head at the AFL convention in 1935. It was at this convention that John L. Lewis, president of the United Mine Workers and a leading spokesman for industrial unionism (see Box 2–5), lost a crucial vote on the issue of granting charters to unions in the auto and rubber industries; landed a famous punch on the nose of "Big Bill" Hutcheson, president of the Carpenter's Union; and then stormed out of the convention and established the Committee for Industrial Organization. Later

---

BOX 2–5
John L. Lewis: The leader and his strategy

No labor leader played a more important or colorful role in history from the 1930s to the 1950s than John L. Lewis. His skill in capturing the changed political climate of the Roosevelt administration is illustrated by the following handbill used in organizating coal miners in the 1930s.

> The United States Government Has Said LABOR MUST ORGANIZE. . . . Forget about injunctions, yellow dog contracts, blacklists, and the fear of dismissal. The employers cannot and will not dare to go to the Government for privileges if it can be shown that they have denied the right of organization to their employees. ALL WORKERS ARE FULLY PROTECTED IF THEY DESIRE TO JOIN A UNION.

Organize John L. Lewis did—5 million American workers into industrial unions in the major mass production industries of the nation in about 4 years.

. . .

Lewis was the son of a Welsh immigrant coal miner. He went to work in the coal mines at 14 and his quick mind, strong personality, and gift for oratory soon won him election to Illinois union posts. In 1920 Lewis became president of the United Mine Workers of America. From that time until his death in 1960 he pursued the course of organizing the unorganized and representing workers in collective bargaining and political affairs with the vigor and style that is nicely captured in the following excerpt from one of his speeches:

> I have never faltered or failed to present the cause or plead the case of the mine workers of this country. I have pleaded your case from the pulpit and the public platform; in joint conferences with the operators of this country; before the bar of state legislatures; in the councils of the President's cabinet; and in the public press of this nation—not in the quavering tones of a feeble mendicant asking alms, but in the thundering voice of the captain of a mighty host, demanding the rights to which free men are entitled.

Source: Quoted from *200 Years of American Worklife* (Washington, D.C.: U.S. Department of Labor, 1977), 142, 150.

---

this group changed its name to the Congress of Industrial Organizations (CIO). Through the leadership of Lewis and the efforts of the CIO, industrial unions formed and successfully organized large numbers of blue-collar workers in steel, autos, rubber, and other manufacturing industries.

Although the CIO enlisted a large number of socialists as union organizers and in general projected a more militant image in collective bargaining than did many of the AFL unions, the rival federations shared a commitment to the use of collective bargaining as the central means of achieving economic gains for their members. In this way the strategies of both the AFL and the CIO unions fit well with, and benefited greatly from, the labor policies enacted during the New Deal.

THE NEW DEAL LABOR POLICY

The election of Franklin D. Roosevelt in 1932, and the economic and social crises caused by the Great Depression (described in Box 2–6), gave rise to a new era in federal labor policy. Roosevelt introduced a series of new governmental programs designed to bolster citizens' purchasing power and assist workers and the poor to cope with their economic hardships. The new programs included unemployment insurance, job creation, social security, and the minimum wage. Roosevelt's program became known as the New Deal. A critical part of the New Deal agenda was enactment of a new labor policy that was consistent with the principles advocated by the institutional economists and the AFL and CIO leaders. The cornerstone of the new national labor policy was the National Labor Relations Act (NLRA) of 1935, also known as the Wagner Act after its chief legislative sponsor, Senator Robert F. Wagner of New York.

BOX 2–6
The Great Depression

People perceived the Great Depression in different ways. Some looked at it dramatically, as did British economist John Maynard Keynes when he compared the situation in Europe and on the American continent to the Dark Ages. Others looked at it simply, like the 14-year old Appalachian boy in Chicago who said, "See, I never heard that word 'depression' before. They would all just say 'hard times' to me."

The bare facts of the situation are eloquent enough. By early 1933 unemployment had increased to about 13 million—about 25 percent of the labor force. A third of these people were between the ages of 16 and 24. Hourly wages were down 60 percent. Industrial output was down by about half. On the farm, income was off by two-thirds, tenancy had doubled. 1 of every 4 farms was being foreclosed, and 500,000 farm families were living at the starvation level. A million transients were on the road, including 200,000 young people.

Unemployed autoworkers marched on the closed River Rouge Ford plant in Dearborn, Michigan, and four of them were shot by notorious "security guard" Harry Bennett and his thugs.

Former professionals and skilled tradespeople demonstrated potato papers and patent medicines in store windows and sold apples on street corners to the tune of a popular song, "Brother Can You Spare a Dime?" which reflected the desperate times.

A huge band of jobless veterans encamped in Washington and were routed in a needless show of military force which involved future war heroes named MacArthur, Eisenhower, and Patton.

Source: Quoted from *200 Years of American Worklife,* 140–41.

Although we will provide a more complete discussion of the nature and evolution of the New Deal industrial relations system later in this chapter and throughout the book, we should note here both how important and how unique a period the 1930s was for the development of collective bargaining. It was important because it explicitly *encouraged* collective bargaining—by establishing the right of employees to organize themselves into unions, by setting the standards for union elections, and by specifying certain unfair labor practices of employers. It was unique because, as labor historian Irving Bernstein has argued, the Wagner Act was passed at "the most favorable possible moment," or as John Dunlop later remarked, at the "apogee of the New Deal," when political support for improving the economic conditions of the nation's workers was at its historic high watermark. [21] An aide to Senator Wagner, reflecting back on this period, noted that the Wagner Act could probably not have been passed at any other time in American political history. [22] Lewis and his CIO colleagues were quick to capitalize on this changing political and legal environment by, among other things, imploring workers to join unions with slogans such as "The President Wants You to Organize!" (See also Box 2–5.) It was in this new environment that the autoworkers in Detroit and rubber workers in Akron were able to stage successful sitdown strikes to gain collective bargaining contracts. This wave of unrest and show of newfound power convinced many employers in the steel industry and others that unions and collective bargaining were now here to stay and forces to contend with in new ways.

Thus, the intellectual foundation for the U.S. collective bargaining system evolved only gradually as the institutionalists learned from and later championed the early experiments of labor and management. And it took a fundamental shift in the political balance of power, an economic and social crisis (the Depression), and a public perception that worker interests were severely disadvantaged by prevailing management policies to achieve a legislative endorsement of collective bargaining as the cornerstone of national labor policy.

THE ROLE OF MANAGEMENT IN INDUSTRIAL RELATIONS

Although the intellectual forerunners of industrial relations may have laid the foundation for U.S. labor policy and the role of trade unions in the society, they had little to say about the strategies and policies of management except to exhort managers to accept unions and collective bargaining as legitimate partners in modern employment relationships. For example, in an essay titled "Right and Wrong in Labor Relations" William Lieserson advised management to recognize the futility of resisting unionization. [23] Limited as they were, these arguments had little practical effect on management philosophies, strategies, or personnel practices. To understand the evolution of management's role as the designer of workplace conditions, we need to examine how conditions in the economic and political environment of the industrializing nation interacted with employer resistance to unionism and gave rise to scientific management, welfare capitalism, the human relations movement, and then finally to the professionalization of the industrial relations and human resource management functions within modern corporations.

"If a man is dissatisfied, it is his privilege to quit." [24] This oft-quoted statement of a steel industry executive during the famous strike in McKees Rocks, Pennsylvania, in 1909 captures the prevailing philosophy of U.S. employers and their response to worker unrest in the years before World War I. Company executives asserted their rights as owners or protectors of private property to treat labor as a commodity and to oppose challenges to their authority by unions. Their assertions took the form of appeals to the courts and, if necessary, to the local or state police forces.

This managerial philosophy made the shop floor, ruled by the foreman, the central arena of industrial relations activity. Hiring, firing, and general supervision of labor were all controlled by the foreman. He had almost unlimited opportunities to treat workers arbitrarily, discriminatorily, or even harshly; and as a result turnover rates among both skilled and unskilled workers were high. In 1913, prior to Henry Ford's decision to raise wages to five dollars a day, annual turnover in auto plants averaged 370 percent![25] Despite the adverse consequences of the *drive system* (as the foreman-controlled workplace was called), it was not seriously challenged as the appropriate way to manage the work force until around the time of World War I, when the combination of tight labor markets, government pressure for wartime production, and a rising threat of unionization led a large number of firms to establish personnel departments. [26] As we will see, it was these increased external pressures, along with an emerging set of new managerial theories, that gave rise to explicit personnel and industrial relations policies, first, within the large, highly visible firms and, later, within their smaller competitors. Throughout the search for a management policy toward labor, one value held constant: Unions capable of directly challenging management authority were to be avoided.

Scientific Management

The first important step toward establishing a professional personnel management function within the firm came with the introduction of *scientific management* to industry. Although the ideas behind the scientific management movement can be traced as far back as the mid-1800s, it was Frederick Taylor's widely recognized efforts to promote these ideas in the first two decades of the twentieth century that gave them their broadest diffusion. Scientific management blended economic incentives and industrial engineering techniques to produce the "one best way" for organizing work. By tying the individual worker's wages to output, it was assumed, the interests of the worker—economic rewards—and the interests of the firm—productivity—could be made compatible. Management's function was to design the jobs, supervise, and compensate the work force so as to eliminate any potential conflict of interest between workers and the employer. Industrial engineering principles (such as time and motion studies) and incentive wages were the basic strategies employed to this end.

These ideas stood in direct contradistinction to those of the advocates of collective bargaining. Instead of seeing conflicts of interests as an inherent part of the employment relationship, advocates of scientific management argued that appropriate task designs and wage systems could eliminate the sources of conflict between workers and employers. Because the optimal work system was to be determined through "scientific" engineering studies, there was no role for bargaining and therefore no need for union representation. [27] It is easy to see why proponents of the scientific management movement and those of the union movement carried on an extended war of words over the first several decades of the 1900s. [28] But the most important lasting effect of the scientific management movement was not its campaign against unionism but its advocacy of industrial engineering principles and a narrow division of labor in organizing work. This form of job design and work organization gradually became the standard means for organizing work in the mass production industries and the form of work organization the industrial unions would inherit when they came into existence in large numbers starting in the 1930s. [29]

Welfare Capitalism and Human Relations

By 1920 a competing model of worker performance and workplace systems, one that stressed the social significance of work and *work groups,* had gained popularity. Whereas the theory behind scientific management was that productive workers would be well compensated and therefore satisfied, the *human relations* and *welfare capitalism* proponents reversed the causal argument. They believed that satisfying workers' needs would produce high levels of productivity. This view was popularized by the famous Hawthorne experiments at Western Electric. The scientific management and human relations schools shared a common belief, however: that by following their principles employers could eliminate conflict with workers, thereby obviating workers' need for union representation.

As the basic tenets of human relations gained in influence over the 1920s, the decade witnessed a gradual expansion of personnel departments. The departments centralized and standardized many of the functions previously controlled by the foreman. Hiring, firing, discipline, promotion, and compensation policies were developed and administered by the personnel staff. Foremen, in turn, were trained to follow the rules embodied in these policies. Coinciding with the growth of progressive personnel policies during and after World War I was an aggressive *open shop movement* that actively sought to discourage unionization through company-controlled employee representation programs and an expansion of pension, welfare, and profit-sharing programs.

Also hand in hand with the growth of progressive personnel policies during the 1920s came a corresponding growth in suppressive anti-union practices such as industrial espionage, blacklisting union members or supporters, strike breaking, and contracting private police forces to disband picket lines. [30] Company-controlled unions were set up in a number of chemical, oil, and other large firms. This mixture of progressive and suppressive policies to avoid unions was highly successful. Union membership fell from approximately 5.8 million members in 1921 to fewer than 2 million members in 1931. But the deep recession of 1921–23 and the stagnation of manufacturing employment later in the decade foreshadowed the erosion of managerial commitment to progressive employment policies and standards that was to come with the Great Depression in the 1930s.

Thus, as an abrupt shift in the economic, political, and social environment occurred with the election of Franklin Roosevelt as President in 1932, policymakers faced an unprecedented set of choices. The high degree of trust and confidence the public had placed in the personnel management and human relations policies of the major corporations had been broken by the massive layoffs and sustained unemployment of the Depression. Labor unrest was rising, in both its frequency and its intensity. Encouraged by the passage of the National Industrial Recovery Act (NIRA) in 1933, Section 7(a) of which declared the rights of employees to self-organize, workers began organizing in greater numbers and strikes increased. By 1934 union membership and strike activity had returned to the levels reached in the years immediately following World War I. [31] But in 1935 the Supreme Court ruled the NIRA unconstitutional. The stage was set for the crucial public policy debate the ultimate outcome of which was the New Deal industrial relations system.

THE NEW DEAL INDUSTRIAL RELATIONS SYSTEM

The Wagner Act did not constitute a completely new or untried way for resolving labor and management conflicts. Instead, the act embodied many of the principles and practices that had demonstrated their fit with American political values and with the practices of many unions and companies, for example, those in railroads, clothing, and other industries that had developed ongoing relationships in the years before the Depression. The new law also codified many of the policies that had been recommended and pursued by the National War Labor Board in World War I and the National Labor Board that had been established under the now-defunct NIRA. It also served to endorse the moderate and pragmatic form of business unionism and collective bargaining that had been promoted by the AFL. Nonetheless, the law was not passed without vocal and vociferous opposition from employer groups; and it was not until it was ruled constitutional by the Supreme Court in 1937, in the *Jones & Laughlin* case, [32] that most firms began to revise their managerial practices in recognition of the fact that a new era in the history of U.S. industrial relations had begun.

Indeed, it was not the law alone that produced the transition to what we will refer to as the *New Deal industrial relations system*. Instead, this turning point in industrial relations was brought about by the confluence of (1) the shift in political power that accompanied the Depression and the election of the Roosevelt administration, which created the support needed to enact legislation in favor of worker and union rights to bargain; (2) a shift in the strategy of the labor movement away from the craft union and voluntarist model of the AFL under Gompers to the *industrial unionism* model of organizing and representing workers promulgated by the CIO; and (3) the passage of a law that provided a stable and seemingly permanent foundation for collective bargaining. As we noted earlier, this was indeed a unique confluence of events. These forces set in motion the gradual diffusion and institutionalization of a collective bargaining system that was to prove durable for almost 50 years.

Let us now examine the New Deal industrial relations system in the light of our three-tier model of the strategic, functional, and workplace levels of industrial relations practices.

The Functional Level: Collective Bargaining as the Cornerstone

The enactment of the NLRA signaled the choice of the middle tier of activity as the preferred forum for labor and management jointly to address and resolve their differences. Once a majority of workers indicated, either by voting in an election or by some more informal means, that they wanted to be represented by a union, management was required by the law to negotiate in good faith with that union over wages, hours, and working conditions. The act was specifically designed to foster industrial peace, first, by replacing violent conflicts over union recognition with orderly election and certification procedures and, second, by lending a degree of permanence to the union's right to represent the employees. Employers could no longer terminate their recognition of a union during recessions. Instead, their duty to bargain with a union continued indefinitely and would end only if the workers voted to decertify their union or if the plant or establishment moved or went out of business.

The Strategic Level: Management Acts and the Union Reacts

Although the Wagner Act produced no great change in the ideology of management, it did force a more pragmatic acceptance of unions in those firms and industries caught up in the mass union-organizing drives that took place in the decade following the passage of the act and the shift to an industrial unionism strategy by the labor movement. Indeed, management rights to make strategic business decisions were left intact by the NLRA. As collective bargaining evolved, the principle "management acts and workers and their unions react" became its key doctrine. [33]

Leaving strategic business decisions to management fit not only management's desire for control over the key decisions on resource allocation in the firm, but also the still-prevailing business unionism philosophy of the labor movement. Even the supporters of industrial unionism did not break with the view that unions should not seek to participate directly in managerial decision making or to gain control of private enterprise. Instead, unions sought to preserve their independence in order to advocate their members' interests more effectively through collective bargaining. This philosophy was part and parcel of the labor movement's moderate agenda for political and social reform. Labor had no ultimate political goal of overthrowing the capitalist system but rather sought to improve workers' living standards gradually by promoting expansion of the social welfare system of unemployment and workers' compensation, social security, minimum wages, and health and safety laws. Thus, at the strategic level the New Deal system coincided with the prevailing values of both the parties themselves and the American public.

The Workplace Level: Job Control Unionism

The arrival of established rules for collective bargaining did not produce a revolutionary new system for organizing work. The principles of scientific management and industrial engineering had gained the full acceptance of most employers, who were convinced of the need to rationalize the structure of jobs and the division of labor among workers. What collective bargaining did do was to codify many of the existing work systems within the labor contract, make them enforceable through the grievance procedure, and strengthen the role of seniority as a decision rule for allocating scarce job opportunities among workers. [34] In so doing, institutionalized collective bargaining laid the foundation for what has been referred to as *job control unionism*. Job control unionism is characterized by detailed and often highly complex contracts that outline workers' rights and obligations on the job, the structure of jobs and promotion ladders, and the rates of pay corresponding to each job. The contracts also specify seniority rules that govern the order in which workers are to be laid off in the event of temporary or permanent work force reduction.

Job control unionism served to meet the immediate needs of both management and labor. Labor reaped greater uniformity and fairness in workplace administration and thereby overcame much of the arbitrary power previously exercised by foremen. Management, in turn, achieved the work force stability necessary to take advantage of growing market opportunities. Government policymakers came to value the industrial peace this system provided during World War II, and therefore they actively promoted further acceptance of grievance arbitration as a means for interpreting and enforcing contracts on a day-to-day basis.

THE EVOLUTION OF THE NEW DEAL SYSTEM

The principles and practices that came to be part of the New Deal system gradually diffused throughout U.S. industry as union membership expanded from 3.5 million in 1934 to 17 million, or approximately 35 percent of the nonagricultural labor force, by the mid-1950s. Although the fifties proved to mark the peak of union penetration in the private sector economy, the New Deal principles continued to evolve and dominate collective bargaining up to at least the early 1980s. Within this long evolution, however, several distinct stages of development can be identified.

The 1940s: Institutionalization of Basic Principles

The exigencies of World War II demanded that labor and management maximize production of the goods needed to support the war, while avoiding both strikes and wage and price inflation. To help achieve these objectives, the Roosevelt administration established the National War Labor Board (WLB) in January 1942. The WLB was a tripartite agency, composed of neutrals who chaired boards of inquiry that included representatives of labor and management. Although the agency lacked any legal enforcement power, the tripartite structure, the national commitment to the war effort, and the implicit threat of more direct legislative intervention gave the "recommendations" of the agency considerable influence. From 1942 to 1945 the WLB succeeded in helping to settle over 20,000 labor-management disputes. [35]

In carrying out this role, the board also used its offices to promote wider acceptance of many of the principles and practices of collective bargaining that would take hold in U.S. industrial relations and extend well beyond the immediate postwar period. Among the key practices advanced by the WLB were grievance arbitration, union security arrangements known as maintenance of membership (see Chapter 11), payroll deduction of union dues (otherwise known as dues checkoff), the use of industry and regional wage comparisons in the setting of wages, and gradual expansion of the bargaining agenda to include an array of fringe benefits such as vacations, sick leave, and holiday pay. In fact, many of the actual contracts the board wrote remained in effect, with minor changes, throughout the postwar era.

In addition to its substantive role in helping to gain acceptance and institutionalization of these aspects of collective bargaining, the WLB served as a training ground for many of the leading mediators, arbitrators, and government advisors who would later shape the evolution of collective bargaining in the decades that followed the war. Those professionals shared a deep commitment to the principles of *"free" collective bargaining,* that is, that industrial democracy and free enterprise capitalism could best be achieved through negotiations and enforcement of labor agreements by the parties themselves, with as little government intervention as possible. George W. Taylor, chairman of the WLB and a leading teacher and neutral after the war, described his and his colleagues' views as follows:

> One conclusion invariably emerges whenever and wherever "the labor problem" is subjected to impartial analysis. It is: collective bargaining must be preserved and strengthened as the bulwark of industrial relations in a democracy. This is just another way of saying that organized labor and management should settle their own differences by understanding, compromises, and agreement without government interference. A rare unanimity of opinion exists about the soundness of collective bargaining as the most appropriate means for establishing conditions of employment. [36]

In this respect, this generation of WLB scholars, teachers, and neutrals carried on the tradition of John R. Commons and his fellow institutional economists.

After the war ended and the WLB was disbanded, a surge of strikes overtook the nation, as illustrated in Box 2–7. In 1946 more production time was lost because of strikes than in any year before or since. The strike wave, along with a general swing toward a more conservative political climate and a switch to Republican control of the Congress, led to the passage of the Labor Management Relations Act, known as the Taft-Hartley Act, in 1947. The act's amendments to the NLRA did not fundamentally alter the principles and practices that were already developing in collective bargaining; but it was designed to strengthen management's power at the bargaining table by limiting the union's rights to boycott the employer and by establishing a detailed set of rules governing the union's obligation to bargain in good faith. It also designated the rights of the government to intervene in strikes that constituted national emergencies. All of these changes reflected a shift in the public's view. Unions were perceived as too powerful, and it was thought that their use of the strike should be limited in some way.

Given this turn in the political environment, employers might have attempted, as in previous periods of labor history, to break from their union relationships. The collective bargaining model had become sufficiently entrenched, however, and unions were viewed as sufficiently strong that a rebalancing of labor-management power occurred instead.

Throughout the 1940s managements at the larger unionized firms had taken steps to strengthen and professionalize their industrial and labor relations staffs. The postwar strike wave further elevated the importance of trained professionals who could help stabilize labor-management relations by establishing formal procedures for negotiating and administering labor contracts. As these large, influential firms adapted to collective bargaining, they served as bellwethers for smaller organizations. [37] By 1952, 70 percent

BOX 2–7
The postwar strike wave

With the end of the war, the expected strike wave began. . . . Forty-three thousand oil workers struck in twenty states on September 16th (1945). Two hundred thousand coal miners struck September 21st. . . . Forty-four thousand Northwest lumber workers struck, seventy thousand Midwest truck drivers, forty thousand machinists in San Francisco and Oakland. East Coast longshoremen struck for nineteen days, flat glass workers for 102 days, and New England textile workers for 133 days. . . .

When G.M. failed to respond to a union offer to have all issues settled by arbitration if the company would open its books for public examination, 225,000 workers struck on November 21st. . . . On January 15th, 1946, 174,000 electrical workers struck. Next day 93,000 meatpackers walked out. On January 21st, 750,000 steelworkers struck, the largest strike in United States history. At the height of these and 250 lesser disputes, 1,600,000 workers were on strike. On April 1st, 340,000 soft-coal miners struck. . . . The first six months of 1946 marked what the U.S. Bureau of Labor Statistics called the "most concentrated period of labor-management strife in the country's history," with 2,970,000 workers involved in strikes starting in this period.

Source: Jeremy Brecher, *Strike!* (San Francisco: Straight Arrow Books, 1972), 227–28.

of the executives who responded to a survey of large firms indicated that the personnel and industrial relations functions were as important to the success of the firm as were the production, finance, and marketing functions. Moreover, 80 percent of the respondents stated that contract negotiation was one of the most important personnel activities within the firm.[38] Thus, the rise of powerful unions had produced a managerial response to professionalize labor-management relations.

Unions, too, faced and made a number of key strategic choices in the 1940s that had an important bearing on the shape of collective bargaining and industrial relations in subsequent years. For one thing, the immediate postwar years witnessed a great deal of internal union conflicts over the role of Communists in the labor movement. The net results of these battles were that the CIO expelled several Communist-dominated unions (such as the United Electrical Workers) and some individual unions (such as the United Auto Workers) purged Communist party members from leadership positions.

The 1946 and 1948 rounds of bargaining in the auto industry best illustrate the choices union leaders made that were to affect the long-term development of collective bargaining. During the 1946 Autoworkers strike against General Motors, Walter Reuther, head of the General Motors department of the union, called on GM to "open the books" and proposed limiting the UAW wage demands in return for a pledge by GM not to raise prices. If that demand had been accepted, it would have represented a major transformation of collective bargaining by expanding union influence over to strategic management issues. But as a result of his demand, Reuther came under heavy criticism from Philip Murray, president of the CIO. Murray urged Reuther to accept the more conventional steel industry wage pattern and to stay out of the managerial decision-making process in order to maintain labor's independence from management. Reuther eventually dropped his proposal and negotiated a conventional wage settlement.

Then, in the 1948 bargaining round GM proposed a multiyear contract with a wage formula that was tied to productivity and cost-of-living increases. This wage formula was later to become a standard not only in the auto industry but in other industries as well. Thus, by choosing not to press for inroads into managerial prerogatives and instead centering attention on formulas for improving wages and for gradually expanding the scope of issues covered under the contract, the parties in this industry—and many others—were following the practice encouraged by the early administrators of the Wagner Act and nurtured by the members of the War Labor Board. The New Deal system of industrial relations had become firmly embedded in the private practices of labor and management. As we will see, developments in collective bargaining over the following three decades represented only marginal or incremental adjustments to this system, adjustments made in response to equally marginal or gradual shifts in the balance of power between labor and management.

The 1950s: A Return to Hard Bargaining

By this time few differences remained in the bargaining agendas or organizing strategies of AFL and CIO unions. As a result these two federations merged in 1955 to become the AFL–CIO. The merger allowed the member unions to focus their energies more directly on extending and expanding the wage and benefit concepts introduced in collective bargaining in the 1940s.

The early years of the 1950s therefore saw these collective bargaining principles and wage formulas and patterns spread throughout the major firms and unions in key sectors of the economy: steel, coal, rubber, meat packing, and transportation. In addition to the widespread diffusion of pattern bargaining, the *scope of bargaining* continued to expand to take up such topics as supplementary unemployment benefits, pensions, severance payments for workers dislocated by technological change or plant closings, and a variety of other fringe benefits and working conditions. [39] But near the end of the decade a harder line in collective bargaining came on the stage as firms sought to limit any further expansion of the scope of bargaining or the influence of unions.

The most visible example of this harder line was General Electric's policy that came to be known as *Boulwarism* after Lemuel Boulware, the architect of the policy and GE's vice president of industrial relations. [40] Boulwarism was a management strategy for regaining the initiative in bargaining by polling workers to determine their interests and goals and then making one "firm and final" offer in negotiations with the union that reflected the financial condition of the firm and the results of the worker surveys. Although this approach (described in more detail in Chapter 8) was eventually ruled by the NLRB to have violated management's obligation to bargain in good faith, it signaled the determination of management to limit union influence.

By 1959 a similar hard line had appeared in contract negotiations at U.S. Steel that resulted in a 116-day strike over management's right to change work rules. Similar strikes over what some authors have labeled a return to management's hard line were staged in the late 1950s in railroads, airlines, electrical products, and other industries. Nonetheless, although these management responses were significant, the dominant trend in collective bargaining during the 1950s continued to be the gradual institutionalization of the postwar principles governing wage determination and contract administration. Only a few firms exhibited the initial signs that an alternative—a nonunion managerial strategy—was beginning to emerge on a trial-and-error basis. This alternative was to gain momentum in the turbulent social environment and cyclical industrial growth of the 1960s.

Management's tougher stance paralleled a decline in labor's public image and political influence. In the late 1950s a series of Congressional hearings highlighted corruption within the Teamsters and other unions. The culmination of the Congressional debates over internal union affairs was the passage of the Labor-Management Reporting and Disclosure Act as an amendment to the NLRA. As spelled out in more detail in the next chapter's Table 3–3, Landrum-Griffin, as the act is called, established reporting and disclosure requirements for union finances, specified the rights of individual union members, and imposed a duty on union leaders to represent their members' interests fairly.

The 1960s: Rank-and-File Unrest

The 1960s were marked by strong economic growth, stimulated by tax cuts and the government purchases to support the Vietnam War, as well as social upheavals, brought forth by the civil rights movement, urban riots, and widescale protests over continued expansion of that war. The resulting tight labor markets and general environment of protest fed employee militance at the workplace, exemplified by a growing number of contract demands, wildcat strikes during the term of the contract, and rank-and-file rejections of contracts negotiated by their union leaders. [41] At the same time, unions were beginning to reap success in organizing large numbers of public sector workers. We will discuss the development of collective bargaining in the public sector in detail in Chapter 14. For now it is sufficient to note that the explosive growth of union membership among public employees during the 1960s carried bargaining to a setting where the employer was also the government. Thus, the 1960s were years of great challenge to management and union leaders alike. In the private sector the parties struggled to cope with pent-up pressures and conflicts at the workplace and in local unions, while in the public sector labor and management searched for principles to guide the extension of collective bargaining to this new terrain.

Meanwhile, stimulated by governmental research and development expenditures to support the effort to catch up with the Soviet Union in the space race, the demand for white-collar, technical, and managerial employees expanded rapidly. What later came to be known as the "high technology" industries were born and flourished. These forces had two effects on collective bargaining. First, the power and status of personnel and human resource management professionals grew as they were charged with satisfying the needs and aspirations of these highly skilled and educated employees. The role of these professionals was further expanded by passage and enforcement of new governmental regulations covering the workplace, as, for example, in equal employment opportunity.

Second, the high-technology organizations were structurally different from the traditional industrial organization. Their new approaches to motivating and managing the work force made it more difficult for unions to establish a foothold. These developments will be discussed in more detail in Chapters 6 and 7. For now suffice it to say that the late 1950s and early 1960s marked a turning point for union membership levels in the private sector. From 1957 to today growth in union membership has not kept pace with increases in the size of the labor force. This has resulted in a steady decline in the percentage of the labor force that is unionized, from roughly 33 percent to 35 percent in the 1940s and 1950s to less than 18 percent by 1986.

The 1970s: Stability and Atrophy

The 1970s may go down in American labor history as one of the least distinguished in the history of collective bargaining. As the economic pressures to change collective bargaining intensified, labor and management continued following the principles and the patterns of behavior developed in the earlier years. Management became preoccupied with holding the line against any further union gains in bargaining. And labor leaders seemed to push no further than preserving the gains they or their predecessors had achieved in collective bargaining and legislation in the previous decades. Granted, interest in issues such as productivity improvement and the quality of working life (QWL) began to surface in labor-management discussions. But little more than isolated and limited experimentation actually occurred. For example, the Ford Foundation and the National Commission on Productivity and the Quality of Work sponsored several highly visible QWL demonstration projects to try to generate innovation around these issues, but they garnered little interest from labor and management practitioners.

Government policymakers as well were stymied, caught in a political stalemate between labor and management, as evidenced by the failure of Congress and a Democratic President to pass modest labor law reforms in 1978. [42] No party—labor, management, or government—successfully initiated any bold advance in bargaining practice, yet each seemed quite effective in constraining the actions of the others. For example, despite pressures from mounting foreign competition and domestic nonunion competition, union workers' wages grew more rapidly throughout the 1970s than did nonunion wages, thereby expanding the union labor cost differential and further eroding employment in unionized firms and industries.

In the steel industry, for instance, the parties negotiated an "experimental negotiating agreement" (ENA) in 1972 that provided an automatic annual escalation in wage rates in return for a no-strike agreement. The ENA was designed to overcome the boom-and-bust employment cycle that had troubled previous contract negotiations, as buyers of steel stockpiled inventories as a hedge against a strike. By 1979, as a result of three contract settlements negotiated under the ENA, the wages of the steelworkers covered under the ENA had grown from 120 percent of the average wages in manufacturing in 1970 to 160 percent of the 1979 average. The auto industry allowed a similar wage expansion, from 132 percent of the manufacturing average in 1970 to 155 percent in 1979. [43] More generally, rapid inflation in the 1970s encouraged unions to negotiate cost-of-living adjustment (COLA) clauses. Whereas 26 percent of contracts covering 1,000 or more workers had COLA clauses in 1970, 61 percent of all major agreements had COLA clauses by the end of the decade. [44] The net result of these developments was that the union-nonunion wage differential grew from between approximately 10 percent and 15 percent in the 1960s to between 20 percent and 30 percent by the end of the 1970s. [45]

More specific evidence of the status quo orientation of management during this period will be discussed in Chapter 7. For now suffice it to say that during this decade industrial relations professionals continued to emphasize the goals of labor peace and stability, while pressures for change continued to mount. As a result, they became more defensive and isolated from other managers within many corporations, and their influence with top executives began gradually to erode. It was not, however, until a dramatic shift in the environment took place in the early 1980s that these mounting pressures suddenly propelled the parties into an era of fundamental change and adjustment in collective bargaining.

The 1980s: Experimentation and Change

Since throughout this book we will be making comparisons between current practices and the way collective bargaining worked before the 1980s, we will provide here only a brief preview of the developments that began unfolding in the early years of this decade. The election of Ronald Reagan as President reflected a strong conservative shift in the political climate of the country. This shift, and its implications for unions, was vividly illustrated early in his administration when he fired and permanently replaced members of the Professional Air Traffic Controllers Union (PATCO) in August 1981.

PATCO had been engaging in an illegal strike over the terms of a new collective bargaining contract. Although the President's actions were directed at employees of the federal government, those actions and the support they received from the public sent a strong message to many employers that the labor movement had lost not only much of its political power but also the public's support. Many observers believe the government's response and the eventual demise of PATCO at once sparked and solidified the resolve of private and other public employers to seize the initiative in negotiations.

The deep economic recession of 1981–83 further mobilized many employers to sidestep or even abolish collective bargaining as it had evolved in the first three decades following World War II. Box 2–8 summarizes the story of the Greyhound bus line, which illustrates this trend. The rise in the value of the U.S. dollar against foreign currencies further reduced the competitiveness of U.S. producers that operated in foreign markets. Massive layoffs in key, highly unionized sectors resulted, reaching deep into union ranks and thereby cutting off unions' primary source of bargaining power. Thus began the era of *concessionary bargaining*.

BOX 2–8
The Greyhound Bus Company and the Amalgamated Transit Union

The Amalgamated Transit Union (ATU) represented the drivers at the Greyhound Bus Company, but not at Trailways. In 1983 Greyhound drivers went on strike, refusing to grant the carrier extensive labor concessions. In any case, the strike ended with substantial concessions, allowing Greyhound to gain a competitive edge over Trailways.

Three years later, as the concessionary contract was about to expire, management demanded further concessions, which the union refused to accept. The company threatened to sell its bus business unless the union acceded to the cuts; and when the union still refused to make concessions, management carried through on its threat. The new owners first elicited further deep concessions from the workers and then sold off stations, allowing station agents to become independent contractors.

Many observers view the story of Greyhound and the ATU as one of the bitterest labor losses of the decade.

Note: For more on this case see "If Anyone Won the Strike, Greyhound Did," *Business Week,* 19 December 1983, 39–40.

At the same time, new forms of employee participation and new concepts of how to organize work, along with somewhat more halting efforts by a few unions to exert more influence over strategic management decisions, were making their appearance at the workplace. But the rate of decline in union membership not only continued during the 1980s, it accelerated. By 1985 the labor movement publicly acknowledged the depth of its membership crisis and called on its leaders and members to consider a variety of new strategies that might produce a resurgence in union membership and union effectiveness at the collective bargaining table and in political affairs. [46]

Although these pressures did not hit all bargaining relationships with equal force, their cumulative effects posed fundamental challenges to the basic principles underlying the New Deal industrial relations system. We can highlight the most significant challenges by briefly reviewing the changes that were wrought in the key principles of the New Deal model at the functional, workplace, and strategic levels of industrial relations activity.

In collective bargaining the advent of concessionary bargaining signaled a breakdown in the ability of the parties to take wages out of competition through the use of wage comparisons, centralized bargaining structures, and pattern bargaining. Because of the growing penetration of foreign imports, the gradual expansion of domestic nonunion competition, and the more sudden competitive pressures brought about in industries that were deregulated in the late 1970s and early 1980s, many unionized firms found they could no longer pass on labor cost increases to customers and find their cost increases matched by their competitors. To achieve a fundamental break with the wage formulas and pattern bargaining practices of the New Deal model, employers took aggressive new initiatives to (1) decentralize bargaining structures, (2) communicate more directly (not through the union) with rank-and-file workers to convince them to accept wage reductions, and (3) in general search for ways to link wages more directly to the economic conditions of their specific enterprises. In turn, to accomplish these initiatives, many firms took power and control away from their labor relations professionals and increased the role of line executives and human resource management professionals in the collective bargaining process.

At the workplace two divergent developments challenged the dominant job control model of work organization and day-to-day administration. First, the pressures to increase productivity and product quality led to a major effort on the part of some companies and unions to experiment with various forms of worker participation under such labels as quality of working life, employee involvement, quality circles, or labor-management participation teams. These experiments were designed to overcome the adversarial climate of the workplace and to give individuals and small groups of employees more direct involvement in solving production problems.

Second, many employers sought to introduce greater flexibility in the design of work organizations to overcome what they viewed as the overly rigid and costly work rules that had grown up over the years under the job control model. Their drive for greater flexibility reflected not only the cost pressures of the deep recession but also shifts in market structures and the development of new technologies that required greater adaptability in work arrangements. In some cases management used concessionary bargaining to achieve changes in work rules. In others the various workplace participation activities were gradually expanded to encompass alterations in work design. Regardless of the means used, the result was new principles of flexibility at the workplace that departed dramatically from the detailed contractual specifications that were central to the job control model.

To achieve these changes in bargaining and at the workplace, equally fundamental departures from the New Deal principles needed to occur at the strategic level of managerial and union practice. We already mentioned that a shift in power occurred within the structure of management in many firms as line managers and executives took more active roles in the decisions and functions traditionally controlled by labor relations staff. This was only part of a larger process of more closely integrating the industrial relations strategies of the firm with its underlying business strategies and objectives.

Substantial strategic level changes have occurred in those select bargaining relationships in which management could not unilaterally move away from the New Deal industrial relations principles without granting some significant quid pro quo to the union. In that situation management needed to involve union leaders more directly in the firm's strategic business affairs. In some cases this took the form of sharing more detailed business and financial data with the union's leaders. In many cases implicit or explicit "strategic bargains" were negotiated, whereby management pledged new investment dollars or made employment security commitments in return for wage concessions, work rule modifications, or totally new industrial relations practices. In others union leaders were granted ongoing formal or informal roles in high-level managerial discussions; and in cases of extreme financial crisis, as faced several airline, trucking, and steel companies, union representatives were granted seats on the board of directors. The precise form union involvement took is of less import than the fact that each of these examples departs from the New Deal principle that it is management's job to manage and the union's job to negotiate only over the effects of management's decisions.

The nature and extent of these changes varied considerably across the range of bargaining relationships in different industries and firms. By no means were they universal; they probably are not prevalent; and they may not prove to be lasting features of collective bargaining. But their net impact has been to challenge seriously the dominance of the New Deal principles. More practically, those firms and unions that took the lead in introducing and experimenting with these changes posed a new set of strategic choices, not only for themselves but also for management and labor leaders elsewhere who, facing the same economic pressures, could not help but ask whether they should adopt them in their own settings.

Thus, the 1980s have been a critical period of experimentation and new strategic choices for management, labor, and government decision makers. All three of these actors must now decide which of the new ideas deserve to be institutionalized and which of the New Deal principles and practices remain valid and useful today and for the future. The environmental and organizational factors that will influence these choices and the expected consequences of different strategies will occupy a great deal of our attention as we explore contemporary collective bargaining in more detail in the chapters that follow.

SUMMARY

The episodic history of collective bargaining and industrial relations traced in this chapter should point out an important fact that will be helpful to bear in mind as we explore current practices in the chapters ahead. Only during a few relatively short periods of time could future trends and developments in collective bargaining be accurately predicted by extrapolating from existing patterns of behavior. Incremental changes in the status quo did provide a good prediction for the relatively stable years of the 1950s and the 1970s. But the open shop movement, the growth of welfare capitalism, and the dominance of the AFL's craft union strategy during the 1920s did not anticipate the arrival of industrial unionism and the enactment of the New Deal model in the 1930s. The language of the NLRA and the bargaining strategies of labor and management in the 1930s did not predict the expansion of the bargaining agenda and the diffusion of grievance arbitration and other contract administration principles fostered by the War Labor Board in the 1940s. After a gradual expansion and extension of these new principles in the 1950s, labor experienced a resurgence of management opposition at the bargaining table near the end of the decade and a rise in rank-and-file unrest in the 1960s. Finally, the status quo bargaining in the 1970s was followed by the fundamental changes in the New Deal model principles of the 1980s.

The lesson is clear. Relations between labor and management are highly dynamic and adapt over time to changes in the environment and in the organizational strategies, values, and structures that dominate within their organizations. Moreover, if we look back in history to the period preceding the 1930s, we can see that collective bargaining is an institution that gained acceptance in American society only recently and then only as part of a larger set of economic and social reforms. To understand the future directions of collective bargaining and industrial relations, we therefore need to explore how different forces in the environment interact with the values, strategies, and structural features of the parties to the bargaining relationship.

Suggested Readings

A useful anthology of classic writings on industrial relations is:

Kerr, Clark, and Paul D. Staudohar, eds. *Industrial Relations in a New Age*. San Francisco: Jossey-Bass, 1987.

A range of different interpretations of labor history and the history of industrial relations in the United States can be found in:

Brody, David. *Workers in Industrial America: Essays on the Twentieth Century Struggle*. New York: Cambridge University Press, 1982.

Harris, Howell. *The Right to Manage*. Madison: University of Wisconsin Press, 1983.

Jacoby, Sanford M. *Employing Bureaucracy*. New York: Columbia University Press, 1985.

Lens, Sidney. *The Labor Wars: From the Molly Maguires to the Sit-Downs*. Garden City, N.Y.: Doubleday, 1973.

Rayback, Joseph G. *A History of American Labor*. New York: Macmillan, 1966.

Salvatore, Nick, ed. *Seventy Years of Life and Labor: An Autobiography of Samuel Gompers*. Ithaca, N.Y.: ILR Press, Cornell University, 1984.

For discussions of the origins and legislative history of the NLRA and the subsequent history of the National Labor Relations Board, see:

Gross, James A., ed. "The NLRA: A Symposium," *Industrial and Labor Relations Review* 39 (October 1985): 5–75.

For a recent analysis of the evolution of technology and its implications for work organizations, see:

Piore, Michael J., and Charles T. Sabel. *The Second Industrial Divide*. New York: Basic Books, 1984.

Notes

1. A. Tilgher, *Work: What It Has Meant to Men Through the Ages* (New York: Harcourt Brace, 1930). See also Alan Fox, *A Sociology of Work in Industry* (London: Collier-Macmillan, 1971), 3–7.

2. Max Weber, *The Protestant Ethic and the Spirit of Capitalism* (London: Allen and Unwin, 1930).

3. Tilgher, *Work*.

4. Herbert Gutman, *Work, Culture, and Society in Industrializing America* (New York: Alfred A. Knopf, 1975), chap. 1.

5. Neil W. Chamberlain and James W. Kuhn, *Collective Bargaining,* 3d ed. (New York: McGraw-Hill, 1986), 6–8.

6. Sanford M. Jacoby, "The Duration of Indefinite Employment Contracts in the United States and England: An Historical Analysis," *Comparative Labor Law* 5 (Winter 1982): 85–128.

7. *Commonwealth (Mass.)* v. *Hunt,* 45 Mass. 4 (Metcalf) III, 1842.

8. See for example, Karl Marx, "Wage Labor and Capital," reprinted in *The Marx-Engels Reader,* ed. Robert C. Tucker (New York: W.W. Norton, 1978), 203–19.

9. V.I. Lenin, "What Is to Be Done?" reprinted in *Selected Works,* Lenin (Moscow: Progress Publishers, 1975), 92–234.

10. For a radical critique of the U.S. labor movement's failure to develop a strong class consciousness among the nation's workers, see Stanley Aronovitz, *False Promises: The Shaping of American Working Class Consciousness* (New York: McGraw-Hill, 1973).

11. See James Weinstein, *The Corporate Ideal in the Liberal State, 1900–1918* (Boston: Beacon Press, 1968).

12. Sidney and Beatrice Webb, *Industrial Democracy* (London: Longmans, 1897).

13. Ibid., 559.

14. John R. Commons, *Institutional Economics: Its Place in the Political Economy* (New York: Macmillan, 1934), 162.

15. Joseph Dorfman, *The Economic Mind in American Civilization* (New York: Viking Press, 1949), 169.

16. For a thorough discussion of the philosophies of the major economic theorists of the late 1800s and early 1900s see Dorfman, *The Economic Mind.*

17. For a discussion of the policies advocated by the early institutionalists and ultimately passed in the wave of New Deal legislation, see Joseph P. Goldberg, Eileen Ahern, William Haber, and Rudolph A. Oswald, *Federal Policies and Worker Status Since the Thirties* (Madison, Wis.: Industrial Relations Research Association, 1977).

18. Selig Perlman, *A Theory of the Labor Movement* (New York: Macmillan, 1928).

19. Jack Barbash, *The Elements of Industrial Relations* (Madison: University of Wisconsin Press, 1984).

20. Samuel Gompers, *Seventy Years of Life and Labor: An Autobiography,* ed. Nick Salvatore (Ithaca, N.Y.: ILR Press, Cornell University, 1984).

21. John T. Dunlop, "The Legal Framework of Industrial Relations and the Economic Future of the United States," in *American Labor Policy,* ed. Charles J. Morris (Washington, D.C.: Bureau of National Affairs, 1987), 2.

22. Leon H. Keyserling, "The Wagner Act after Ten Years," cited in Dunlop, "The Legal Framework," 2.

23. William Lieserson, *Right and Wrong in Labor Relations* (Berkeley: University of California Press, 1938).

24. David Brody, *Steelworkers in America: The Nonunion Era* (Cambridge: Harvard University Press, 1960), 78.

25. Sanford M. Jacoby, *Employing Bureaucracy* (New York: Columbia University Press, 1985), 31–32. For a discussion of the turnover rates and the power of foremen in the auto industry before the formalization of personnel policies at

Ford, see David Halberstam, *The Reckoning* (New York: William Morrow, 1986). See also Daniel Raff and Lawrence Summers, "Did Henry Ford Pay Efficiency Wages?" photocopy (Cambridge: Department of Economics, Harvard University, 1986).

26. Jacoby, *Employing Bureaucracy,* 99–133. See also James N. Baron, P. Devereaux Jennings, and Frank R. Dobbin, "Mission Control?: Some Evidence on the Development of Personnel Systems in U.S. Industry," photocopy (Stanford: Graduate School of Business, Stanford University, 1986).

27. Edwin Locke, "The Ideas of Frederick W. Taylor: An Evaluation," *Academy of Management Review* 7 (January 1982): 14–24.

28. For a good discussion of the debate, see Milton J. Nadworny, *Scientific Management and Unions* (Cambridge: Harvard University Press, 1955).

29. Michael J. Piore and Charles T. Sabel, *The Second Industrial Divide* (New York: Basic Books, 1985).

30. For a discussion of employers' labor relations practices in the 1920s, see Irving Bernstein, *The Lean Years* (New York: Houghton Mifflin, 1972), 144–89.

31. Jacoby, *Employing Bureaucracy,* 224.

32. *NLRB* v. *Jones & Laughlin Steel Corp.,* 301 U.S. 1 (1937).

33. For a discussion of the origins of this principle, see Robert F. Hoxie, *Trade Unionism in the United States* (New York: Appleton and Company, 1920).

34. Jacoby, *Employing Bureaucracy,* 243–53.

35. See *Termination Report of the War Labor Board* (Washington, D.C.: GPO, 1946).

36. George W. Taylor, *Government Regulation of Industrial Relations* (New York: Prentice-Hall, 1948), 1.

37. James N. Baron, Frank R. Dobbin, and P. Devereaux Jennings, "War and Peace: The Evolution of Modern Personnel Administration in U.S. Industry," *American Journal of Sociology* 92 (September 1986): 350–84.

38. *The Personnel Executive: His Title, Function, Staff, Salary, and Status* (Washington, D.C.: Bureau of National Affairs, 1952). See also John T. Dunlop and Charles A. Myers, "The Industrial Relations Function in Management: Some Views on Its Organizational Status," *Personnel* 31 (1955): 406–13.

39. For a description of these provisions, see the U.S. Department of Labor, Bureau of Labor Statistics series of publications called *Characteristics of Major Collective Bargaining Agreements* (Washington, D.C.: Bureau of Labor Statistics, 1979). See also *Basic Patterns in Union Contracts* (Washington, D.C.: Bureau of National Affairs, 1984).

40. Herbert N. Northrup, *Boulwarism* (Ann Arbor: Graduate School of Business, University of Michigan, 1964).

41. William E. Simkin, "Refusal to Ratify Contracts," in *Trade Union Government and Administration,* ed. Joel Seidman (New York: Praeger, 1970), 107–48.

42. D. Quinn Mills, "Flawed Victory in Labor Law Reform," *Harvard Business Review* 53 (May-June 1979): 99–102.

43. Harry C. Katz, *Shifting Gears* (Cambridge, Mass.: MIT Press, 1985), 13–48.

44. Robert Ferguson, *Cost of Living Adjustments in Union-Management Agreements* (Ithaca, N.Y.: New York State School of Industrial and Labor Relations, Cornell University, 1977). See also Wallace E. Hendricks and Lawrence M. Kahn, "Wage Indexation in the United States: Prospects for the 1980s," in *Proceedings of the Thirty-Seventh Annual Meeting, December 28–30, 1984,* ed. Barbara D. Dennis, 413–19 (Madison, Wis.: Industrial Relations Research Association, 1985).

45. For a review of this evidence see Richard B. Freeman and James L. Medoff, *What Do Unions Do?* (New York: Basic Books, 1984).

46. AFL–CIO Committee on the Evolution of Work, "The Changing Situation of Workers and Unions," report (Washington, D.C.: AFL–CIO, February 1985). The report is discussed in more detail in Chapter 5.

CHAPTER 3

The Environment of Collective Bargaining

$\mathbf{T}$ he process and outcomes of collective bargaining are heavily influenced by the economic, public policy, demographic, social, and technological contexts of the bargaining relationship. The reader will recall that Figure l–l, our conceptual model of collective bargaining, begins with these broad environmental influences—the subject of this chapter.

As we saw in the previous chapter, the environment surrounding collective bargaining over the 1960s and 1970s, although changing, did not lead management and labor to initiate fundamental changes in the nature of bargaining that had developed and matured over the 1940s and 1950s. But, as explained in Chapter 2, the rapid environmental transformations of the later 1970s and 1980s began to have an enormous influence on collective bargaining as labor and management were forced to respond to threatening new forms of economic competition and the shift in national politics to conservative public policies and ideologies. Both changes—economic and sociopolitical—played a crucial role in the wave of "concessionary" bargaining that began in the early 1980s. Our analysis will focus primarily, therefore, on the effects of the recent environmental changes, with an eye not only toward providing an understanding of current collective bargaining practice but also toward highlighting the role the environment always plays in collective bargaining. Before examining these recent events, however, we first need a conceptual understanding of the role played by the various environmental influences on labor relations.

CONCEPTUAL FRAMEWORK

We use as a framework an extension of the model proposed by John Dunlop. Dunlop classified the industrial relations environment into three main influences: (1) the *economic* context, (2) the *technological* context, and (3) the *locus of power* in the larger society. [1] Dunlop included in that third category, which refers mainly to the public policy contexts of the bargaining system, the role played by the ideology of the larger society as a critical part of the overall *social* and *political* contexts of collective bargaining. We will address social factors separately below, and we will further extend Dunlop's model by considering *demographic* influences. The changing characteristics of the labor force have always had a major effect on all aspects of industrial relations.

The external environment provides both incentives and constraints to labor and management in their efforts to meet their bargaining goals and the expectations of the work force. On the other hand, the parties to collective bargaining also seek to mold their environment to better serve their needs. Thus, although we have presented the environmental context as the first set of influences in the analysis of a collective bargaining system, those influences are not entirely outside the control of the parties. For example, since the 1920s, many textile, apparel, and other small, soft-goods employers have migrated from the Northeast to the South, partly (if not primarily) to take advantage of a more favorable economic environment (lower labor costs) for business and a less hospitable social and political environment for trade unions. More recently, many U.S. manufacturing firms have opened production facilities overseas or established joint ventures with foreign producers, thereby helping to create an economic environment of sluggish employment growth in their industries. Thus, these firms have directly shaped the economic environment for collective bargaining in their industries.

The parties' ability to influence their environment is even more pronounced in the case of public policy because, quite simply, organized labor and management are the prime lobbyists influencing the public policies that regulate their own behavior. It is good to keep in mind, therefore, that in the long run the environment is to some extent influenced by the parties. It is only in the short run (and for the purposes of simplifying our presentation here) that we can view the environment as being external to and relatively fixed for the parties.

THE ECONOMIC CONTEXT

Economic pressures, constraints and incentives, have a critical influence on all of the other components of the collective bargaining system, shaping both bargaining processes and bargaining outcomes. Economic factors can be separated into the macro (economywide) and the micro (those relevant only to a specific bargaining relationship). A common thread joins the macro- and microeconomic factors, however: Both exert much of their influence through their effects on the bargaining power of each of the two parties.

Bargaining power can be defined simply as the ability of one party to achieve its goals in bargaining in the presence of opposition by another party to the process. This definition is useful in any analysis of industrial relations because it focuses attention on the various sources of power that are at work in a collective bargaining relationship. A key assumption throughout this chapter, and indeed the book as a whole, is that the power held by the union and the employer in any bargaining pair is directly determined by environmental, structural, and organizational factors.

Microeconomic Forces

The bargaining power enjoyed by a union is most critically the result of the union's and its members' ability to withdraw their labor, usually (though not always) through a strike. [2] Thus, workers are more likely to win higher wages and other gains the more they are willing and able to sustain a strike. Moreover, strikes, once undertaken, are more likely to succeed the greater the costs of the strike to the employer. Holding other things constant, then, the simplest measure of bargaining power is the amount of strike leverage each party holds.

Strike leverage. The relative degree to which workers and the employer are willing and able to sustain a strike is their *strike leverage.* More specifically, to measure each party's leverage, we need to know what costs a strike would impose on each party and what alternative income sources each party has to offset any costs induced by a strike. Figure 3–1 diagrams the principal determinants of the parties' strike leverage: workers' ability to harm production, sales, and profits; and management's ability to find alternative means to maintain production, sales, and profits.

Once a strike has begun, the first indicator of workers' bargaining power is the degree to which the strike has impaired production. Workers who succeed in actually halting production because there are no readily available labor substitutes—supervisory employees, employees in or from another plant, strike breakers, or automated equipment—have, obviously, the greatest possible strike leverage, or economic bargaining power. In

FIGURE 3–1
Determinants of management and union strike leverage

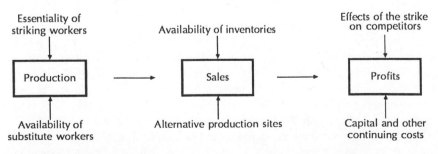

other words, these workers are *essential* to the production process. Craft workers, who are typically very difficult to replace because of their skills, are in many cases a prime example of labor having significant strike leverage. For example, the high skill levels of electricians and repair machinists help explain why they earn so much more than production workers in the auto, steel, and textile industries.

The power of a striking work group is tempered, however, if the halt in production does not lead to a reduction in sales. Employers can sever, or at least weaken, the link between production and sales if inventories are high or if alternative production sites can produce or quickly shift to production of the goods in short supply. We should note, however, that all of these determinants of leverage are influenced by the bargaining structure and by the extent to which other workers at the site join or support the strike.

Finally, even if production and sales are stopped by a strike, the firm may not necessarily witness a serious decline in profits, the third determinant in Figure 3–1. For example, firms with relatively high ongoing capital expenses have a harder time withstanding a loss of income caused by a strike. This helps explain why construction workers, who can temporarily halt costly construction projects, have so much bargaining power. In contrast, firms facing a strike that also shuts down all the competitors' operations have an easier time withstanding strikes, since their lost sales and profits may be largely postponed rather than permanently forgone.

Outside of the immediate economic environment of the firm depicted in Figure 3–1, strike leverage is also affected by the degree to which either the workers or the employer can draw on or generate alternative income sources during a strike. Obviously, workers in unions that offer ample strike benefits can better afford to stay out on strike than those in other unions, other things equal. Likewise, firms that have substantial savings or alternative income sources (such as from other lines of business) can more easily absorb the costs of a strike. Later in this chapter we discuss how the recent growth in employers' nonunion operations has improved their strike leverage through this channel.

A second set of factors beyond the microeconomic environment of the firm is the attitudes of union members and management personnel. Workers' feelings of solidarity with one another have a great deal to do with whether picket lines will be honored; and pent-up frustrations held by either management or labor will influence workers' willingness to stay out on strike. In brief, strikes are highly emotional undertakings, and, as discussed in detail in Chapter 8, their immediate causes and the form they take depend on numerous factors, not simply the microeconomic environment.

Nonetheless, strike leverage, as determined by the microeconomic environment, in turn determines whether the workers are *able* to press for a higher wage settlement or other more advantageous contractual provisions. But higher wages often bring cuts in employment, and unions thus have to, and do, consider the employment effects of their actions as well as the direct wage gains. For example, autoworkers at Chrysler Corporation lowered their wage demands in the 1980 bargaining round because they feared that any higher wage payments by Chrysler would push the company into bankruptcy. The trade-off between wages and employment, which is summarized by economists as the elasticity of the demand for labor, is therefore the second microeconomic influence we will examine.

Marshall's conditions. In his seminal analysis of labor and management bargaining power, Alfred Marshall argued that unions are most powerful when the *demand for labor* is highly *inelastic,* that is, when increases in wages will not result in significant reductions in employment in the unionized sector. [3] Marshall further proposed *four basic conditions* under which the demand for union labor would be inelastic: (1) when labor cannot be easily replaced in the production process by other workers or machines; (2) when the demand for the final product is price inelastic; (3) when the supply of nonlabor factors of production is price inelastic; and (4) when the ratio of labor costs to total costs is small. [4] Let us address each of these conditions in turn.

The first condition, *workers' being difficult to replace,* depends on the production technology. The more difficult it is to replace workers with machines, the less apt the workers will be to fear their displacement. This condition, along with Marshall's second condition concerning the inelasticity of demand for the final product, is consistent with another well-established hypothesis regarding the extent of union penetration into any given product market. As early as 1916, in his famous essay on the Philadelphia shoemakers, John R. Commons pointed out the importance to unions of taking wages out of competition by organizing the entire product market. [5] He showed that once transportation systems had improved, making it feasible for employers to manufacture products wherever labor was cheapest and then transport the products to the highest price markets, unions found it necessary to organize competing employers in these various locations.

The basic principle here is that the more successful unions are at organizing workers who could function as substitutes for existing union labor, the less likely will increases in wage costs in the unionized portion of the market result in employment shifts from the union to the nonunion sector. Employees in the unionized sector are similarly affected by the extent to which consumers can shift their demand to the nonunion sector, a factor called the *elasticity of product demand*.

The problem for the union is even more acute if the employer has nonunion plants that produce the same products in other locations. Wage increases imposed in one plant will lead to employment declines for union labor if production is then shifted to the nonunion sites.

Examples of the importance of union coverage of the relevant product market are numerous. Textile unions in the United States, for example, have historically been weak because of their inability to organize their entire industry. The U.S. Bureau of Labor Statistics reports that in 1980 less than 18 percent of the domestic textile industry was organized by unions and covered under a collective bargaining contract. [6] Similarly, in industries easily entered by new firms, unions must find ways not only of covering the existing employers, but also of controlling access to the industry. Simply stated, the failure to control entry in the face of increasing wages in the existing industry will encourage the entrance of new employers that put a premium on their ability to remain nonunion. This has been the historical experience in the residential construction industry and more recently has been the case in other areas of the construction industry as well. Although unions in construction do exert some control over the supply of labor to the union jobs (through hiring halls, apprenticeship programs, and quasi closed-shop arrangements), the new firms have recently demonstrated a strong resolve to find ways to remain nonunion. Consequently, unions in the construction industry have been losing an increasing proportion of the market to nonunion employers. In Chapter 5 we cite statistics on the recent growth of nonunion operations in a number of industries, and in Chapters 6 and 7 we describe how strategic choices by employers have influenced this expansion of the nonunion sector.

In the longer run union coverage can also erode as the employer develops substitute products. In the longshoring industry, for example, the containerization of cargo has resulted in more of the loading tasks' being performed away from the docks, often by nonunion labor, and has led to a severe reduction in the demand for longshoremen.

This mobility of capital can also pose a long-term threat to the union's control over the product market. As noted earlier, the movement of the textile and apparel industries from New England and New York City to the South reduced the percentage of those industries unionized. An extension of this same principle is the threat raised by foreign imports that become more attractive to domestic consumers as wages in the domestic unionized economy rise. The auto, apparel, steel, and electrical appliance industries are all recent cases in point.

Unions can try to limit the ease with which management can introduce new technology by raising the costs of substituting other factors of production for union labor, but they face a dilemma in that strategy. Collectively bargained constraints on technological change may keep unions from losing employment, but slowing the rate of technological change may also constrain the rate of productivity growth, limiting the longer run potential for wage increases.

Marshall's third condition, that an *inelastic supply of other factors* of production should increase union power, is based on the fact that if it is expensive to increase investments in these other factors to economize on union labor, unions will be able to push up wages without fear of employment cutbacks. Whereas Marshall's first condition concerns the degree to which it is technologically feasible to substitute machines or other factors for unionized labor, his third condition concerns the costs to the firm of increasing its use of alternative factors.

Marshall's fourth argument was that unions are more powerful when labor costs represent only a small proportion of total costs. This condition has often been restated as *the importance of being unimportant;* that is, an employer is less likely to resist union pressure if a given wage increase affects only a very small proportion of the total cost of the product. Thus, a small craft unit, such as the skilled maintenance employees in a plant, is often less likely to meet management resistance to its wage demands than would a broad bargaining unit that represents all production and maintenance employees. This condition is not as applicable to the case of employers that have to consider the "spillover" effects of a settlement negotiated with one small unit on the rest of the firm's work force.

One bargaining pair that well demonstrates the importance of being unimportant is that in the public sector. Labor costs for local government often run between 60 percent and 70 percent of budget, and in some jurisdictions occupations such as firefighters run as high as 90 percent of budget. Thus, when local government officials seek to control total budget costs, they take a very hard line in collective bargaining because the wages and salaries of public employees represent their largest controllable cost.

All of the Marshallian conditions are based on the assumption that workers and unions are concerned about the employment effects of wage increases. To the extent that union members are willing to accept a slow rate of growth in employment or a decline in union jobs as a trade-off for higher wages, the sources of power discussed above are less important. Perhaps the classic example of this strategy was the United Mine Workers of America (UMW) in the 1940s. UMW President John L. Lewis had adopted a strategy of pursuing high wage increases while giving employers a free hand to invest in labor-saving technology. The result was that, though mine workers' wages increased, employment in the industry declined sharply throughout the 1940s and into the 1950s. Despite this decline the union's leaders did not soften their demands for ever higher wages. Here, the UMW's considerable strike leverage was a more critical determinant of its bargaining power than the *wage-employment trade-off.*

In fact, the industrial relations community has long engaged in a heated debate over the role the wage-employment trade-off actually plays in collective bargaining. Arthur Ross argued that political factors rather than employment consequences shape trade union wage policy; he also claimed that workers' wage demands are heavily influenced by their making comparisons with the wages of other workers or unions (by "orbits of coercive comparisons"), a practice that gives union leaders some leeway in defining their wage goals. [7] John Dunlop had a very different view of trade union wage policy, attesting that unions do consider the employment consequences of their wage demands and that they may even use the maximization of the wage bill as a guide to their evaluation of the wage-employment trade-off. [8]

Recent concessionary bargaining rounds offer evidence that unions and workers do consider these employment effects, particularly when the effects entail the possibility of a plant closing. But wage-bill maximization or some other sort of optimization process is too simple a model to capture all of the complexity involved in the collective bargaining process. For example, as Ross asserted, political factors do appear to play an important role in shaping whether and the extent to which employment is a concern in wage bargaining. As we discuss in more detail in Chapter 12, workers' willingness to accept concessions and what they win in exchange for those concessions are affected by a host of factors, including business and union strategies.

Industry concentration. A number of other microeconomic influences have been hypothesized as important in determining the power each party brings to the bargaining table. Perhaps the most widely discussed of these is the degree of concentration in an industry. *Industry concentration* is a measure of the monopoly power of the largest employers in the industry and is normally measured by the percentage of total industry sales or shipments controlled by the four largest employers in the industry. Economists who approach the study of wage determination from a perspective of competitive market theories say there is no theoretical basis for expecting greater union bargaining power in the concentrated industries except as a consequence of the elasticity of demand for the final product. Yet a good deal of evidence supports the existence of a relationship between concentration and wage levels within the manufacturing sector. [9] Furthermore, a number of studies have found that industry concentration and the percentage of the industry organized by unions together have an important impact on the power of the union. [10]

The effects of concentration can be understood better in the light of some of the ideas of bargaining theorists such as John R. Hicks. Hicks stated that market forces simply set the upper and lower limits on the wage bargain. The more competitive the industry, the less *discretion,* or "bargaining space," or "range of practical bargains," is available to the union and management negotiators. [11] Set by competition in the labor market, the lower limit or the *floor* on wages is the wage level required to attract workers of the quality and skill level necessary to perform the job. The upper limit or the *ceiling* is set by competitive conditions in the product market. Wages cannot be pushed up beyond the point at which the employer cannot sell the product. In a perfectly competitive industry the lower and upper limits should coincide; and as the industry moves away from conditions of perfect competition, the distance between the two limits widens. Thus, as the industry becomes more concentrated and employers have more discretion over the price of the final product and therefore over the price of labor, there is more opportunity for the union to seek higher wages. In other words, in the short run, market constraints in concentrated industries play a lesser role in dictating the level of wages or the amount of increase in wages that the consumers will tolerate than they do in competitive industries.

Thus, industry concentration at best provides the economic *potential* for union power; it provides the short-run insulation from competitive market forces that is essential to union power. Conversely, in a highly competitive market unions must develop some other strategy for increasing the range of discretion in wage setting.

Profits and productivity. Two other microeconomic factors that have some effect on the bargaining power of unions are the rate of profit and the rate of productivity growth in the industry or of the employer. Both profits and productivity affect the ability of the employer to absorb an increase in wages. Nevertheless, the evidence for a precise effect of profits and productivity on wages is somewhat mixed. Although a number of authors have found the two to be critically important explanatory variables, others have found they have little or no consistent effect. These differing results illustrate an important fact that must be remembered in analyzing bargaining power. Although profits and productivity certainly are components of employer wage policies and influence the objectives employers bring into the bargaining process (see Chapter 7), they are only two among many off-setting influences on the balance of power in collective bargaining. Thus, although the empirical evidence does not suggest that profits and productivity have been dominant factors, they cannot be discounted either. Indeed, profits and productivity may become a more important determinant of wages in the future as markets become more competitive and leave unions with little power to link wages to national or regional patterns.

Macroeconomic Forces

The macroeconomic environment affects bargaining outcomes through a number of channels. The state of the labor market is most crucial, mainly because of its effects on bargaining power. A union's strike leverage, for example, depends in part on the availability of jobs—both for the striking workers and for their spouses or other family members who might help support the strikers. The higher the unemployment rate, the less likely striking workers or family members will be to find substitute employment and the more likely the family members normally employed will be on layoff.

Three sets of governmental policies influence the macro economy and the labor market and thus, indirectly, the results of collective bargaining. As shown in Figure 3–2, these are aggregate monetary policies, aggregate fiscal policies, and incomes policies. In turn, these policies affect, and are affected by, the aggregate rates of wage and fringe benefit increases

FIGURE 3–2
Simplified macroeconomic model of collective bargaining

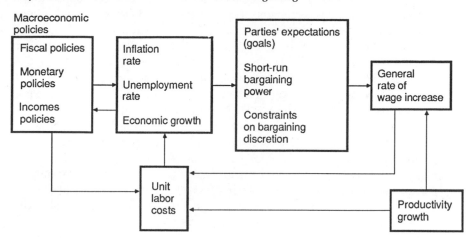

negotiated in previous years. The figure shows, in a simplified model, the ways in which these macroeconomic policies are linked to the results of collective bargaining and, in turn, are affected by the results of bargaining.

More specifically, the macroeconomic policies influence the overall condition of the economy by affecting rates of inflation, unemployment, and economic growth. These in turn influence the collective bargaining process in three important ways. First, they influence the expectations and goals of the parties; second, they have an important impact on the bargaining power of unions and employers; and third, they set constraints on the range of discretion that union and management negotiators have at the bargaining table.

Union and management expectations. The overall condition of the economy, but especially the rate of inflation, shapes the expectations and goals of the parties entering bargaining. If the inflation rate is high and workers anticipate it will continue to be high over the life of the new contract, they will pressure their union leaders to seek large wage increases at the bargaining table or risk a contract rejection if they do not adjust their own expectations and settlement targets upward. This effect has been demonstrated in unions' changing interest in cost-of-living adjustment (COLA) clauses over the course of this century.

COLA clauses first appeared in union contracts shortly after World War I, a highly inflationary period. [12] By the late 1920s, however, when prices had stabilized, interest in COLA clauses virtually disappeared, not to reemerge until World War II. In 1948 General Motors Corporation and the United Automobile Workers (UAW) negotiated in their national agreement the first

COLA clause to cover a significant number of workers nationwide. Within ten years approximately 50 percent of all workers covered under major collective bargaining agreements (those covering 1,000 or more workers) had escalator clauses in their contracts, but that percentage fell to a low of only one-fifth of all such workers by 1966 as unions adjusted their demands to a period of relative price stability. Again, in the mid-1970s steep inflation rates brought a renewed interest in the clauses, and by 1976 around 59 percent of workers covered under major collective bargaining agreements had COLA clauses. This oscillation continued into the 1980s, which have witnessed a sharp decline in inflation rates and in both the use of COLAs and the scope of those still in existence. Whereas COLA payments had accounted for 33.7 percent of effective wage adjustments in major collective bargaining agreements in 1981, they accounted for only 15 percent of those wage adjustments in 1983. [13] Thus, variations in the rate of inflation influence both the content and the magnitude of the expectations that workers and union leaders bring into the bargaining process.

Bargaining power.   One of the most widely accepted hypotheses concerning macroeconomic effects on bargaining power is that unions' power increases as the business cycle moves toward full employment. Conversely, the power of unions declines during periods of falling product demand and rising unemployment. The factors at work here include those discussed earlier regarding striking workers' need for alternative income sources and employers' vulnerability to strikes when product demand is high or increasing. During periods of slack demand employers may, in fact, welcome a strike because they can then lower their inventories and use the strike as a substitute for layoffs.

This connection between macroeconomic conditions and bargaining power is supported by evidence that the aggregate rate of wage increase in the economy responds directly to changes in the cost of living and to fluctuations in the business cycle: Wages rise in times of rising inflation, and they fall in times of falling employment levels. Nevertheless, declines in product demand and increases in unemployment have been shown to have a weaker downward effect on collectively bargained wage increases than on wage increases in the nonunion sector. [14] Unions tend to aggressively resist wage cutting, making it harder for union employers than nonunion employers to cut wages or to moderate the pace of wage increases during recessionary periods. The fact that union wage rates are often set in multiyear agreements (labor contracts in trucking and the auto industry, for example, have traditionally been three years in duration) makes union wages less responsive than nonunion wages to changing economic conditions. In addition, as will be seen later, the effects of labor market forces on the results of collective bargaining in the short run are very unevenly distributed across industries. Thus, although high aggregate unemployment rates affect the more competitive sectors of the economy and some occupational groups quickly and harshly, other less competitive industries, including some of the major strongholds of unionism, are less quick to be affected by aggregate unemployment rates.

This lesson was vividly illustrated by the efforts of the Nixon administration to reduce the rate of wage increases by increasing the rate of unemployment over the years 1969–71. Although the administration's macroeconomic policy (to tighten the money supply and lower the rate of government spending) did slow economic growth and increase unemployment, it was not successful in lowering the aggregate rate of wage increases negotiated in major collective bargaining agreements. This led to the decision to institute policies more directly targeted at wage inflation, namely, the wage and price controls of 1971–73.

Incomes policies. Of the three sets of macroeconomic policies in our model, incomes policies, when in force, place the most direct constraints on the discretion of union and management negotiators. Although incomes policies designed to limit precisely the size of wage and price increases have not been used in the United States in recent years, they had important effects on collective bargaining in earlier periods.

Wartime administrations from World War I through the Korean War instituted tripartite boards that used various techniques to stabilize wages. Between 1962 and 1966 the Kennedy and Johnson administrations formulated a set of *wage-price guideposts,* advisory or voluntary limits union and management negotiators were asked to observe. In general, the guideposts recommended that wage increases be limited to the average long-term increase in the rate of productivity growth for the economy as a whole, initially specified as 3.2 percent. The guideposts were replaced by a more informal, case-by-case system of intervention known as *jawboning,* whereby the President or his advisors privately negotiated with company and union officials to moderate their price and wage increases. Obviously, the administration could jawbone on only a very selective basis, essentially only with the largest unions and employers.

The first two years of the Nixon administration, 1969–70, brought a return to hands-off incomes policies. By 1971, however, administration advisors' concern over wage escalation in construction brought about the establishment of the Construction Industry Stabilization Committee, a tripartite group that reviewed wage increases and later used its authority to reject increases it found were out of line. Later that year, in August, domestic and international economic conditions led the Nixon administration to impose the strongest and most direct form of incomes policies: *wage and price controls.* The first "phase" of the controls consisted of an economywide wage-price freeze, in effect from 15 August to 13 November 1971, followed by a two-year period of gradually loosening controls. Phase II limited the size of wage increases to 5.5 percent (with greater discretion for fringe benefit increases), and Phase III gradually decontrolled specified sectors of the economy. These wage and price controls were the first in peacetime during this century.

The next experience with a formal incomes policy came in 1978. After several years of monitoring wage and price trends, President Carter announced a "voluntary" set of *guidelines* backed up by the threat that the government would refuse to purchase goods or services or to provide any grants or contracts to employers that exceeded the wage or price standards.

In the light of these different forms incomes policies have taken, it is easy to conclude that their impact on collective bargaining agreements was greatest when the controls were formal and precisely defined and when they were strictly enforced. It would be a mistake to assume, however, that the existence of controls either automatically reduced the aggregate rate of increases in wages and compensation costs to the target levels in the short run or reduced the longer run rate of wage and benefit increases. In fact, the record of incomes policies on both these scores is at best mixed. Although the guideposts of 1962–66 and the controls of 1971–74 did lower the rate of wage increase while they were in effect, strong *catch-up effects* followed their demise. Catch-up wage increases were especially strong in 1974 and 1975 because the rate of price increases had continued to rise during the period of wage controls. Thus, the controls probably had their greatest effect on delaying the timing of wage increases, at least for those unions that were strong enough to demand and achieve catch-up increases after the controls had been lifted. Obviously, such catch-up effects are likely to be stronger if prices continue to rise throughout the period of wage restraint.

The Reagan administration has made no recourse to incomes policy. Not only is the administration ideologically opposed to governmental regulation of wage bargaining (and many other economic affairs), but it has faced no pressure to institute controls because the economy has been characterized by a marked drop in the rate of inflation.

Effects of bargaining on macroeconomic performance. The analysis of the macroeconomics of collective bargaining cannot close without attempting to identify how bargaining outcomes in turn affect the economy itself. Bargaining outcomes not only illustrate the success of the macroeconomic policies designed to curb inflation and unemployment, but they also add a dynamic component of feedback to our framework: They influence the economic context for future collective bargaining negotiations and set the cycle of events in motion again.

The effects of collective bargaining settlements on the economy are complex, only partly understood, hotly debated by economists, and, as shown in Figure 3–2, moderated by a number of other economic conditions. Basically, the model suggests that increases in bargained wages will lead to increases in unit labor costs (the cost of labor for one unit of production) only to the extent that they exceed increases in productivity. The effect of unit labor cost increases on inflation, unemployment, and economic growth will, in turn, depend on the monetary, fiscal, and incomes policies of the federal government, as well as other economic conditions. These basic propositions are discussed in more detail below.

Both Albert Rees and George Hildebrand have argued that negotiated wage increases that exceed the rate of productivity increase of unionized workers have little effect on inflation. [15] They claimed that if an aggregate increase in wages in the unionized sector exceeds productivity, product demand will shift to the nonunion sector, which in turn will shift employment from the union to the nonunion sector. Under most conditions the resulting wage increases of nonunion workers will be modest because in the long run their supply will gradually increase. This view holds that although some unions may increase wages at an inflationary rate (wage increases greater than productivity increases), in a competitive economy these inflationary increases will be offset by adjustments in the quantity of goods demanded and the number of workers employed in the union and nonunion sectors.

Even though union workers receive higher wages than their nonunion counterparts, the differential does not necessarily produce inflation. For union wage increases to lead *directly* to inflation, the union-nonunion wage differential would have to be ever widening. Although the differential did widen during the 1970s, it narrowed in the early 1980s; and in any case it has historically not been ever increasing.

A more significant way in which unions might cause the inflation rate to rise is through the slower response of union wages than nonunion wages to changing economic conditions. A number of studies have shown that wages in the unionized sector (or in highly unionized industries) respond less to increases in unemployment than wages in the nonunion sector (or in industries with a low rate of unionization). [16] Thus, traditional strategies for reducing the rate of inflation by increasing the rate of unemployment and thereby holding down wage increases may be less effective for union wages than for nonunion wages.

Both of the above effects are limited to the impact of unions on wages in the unionized sector. Since unions represent less than 20 percent of the labor force, an increase in union wages will not be very inflationary unless union wage increases spill over to nonunion wages. Whether they do spill over to the nonunion sector has been widely debated, but there is little empirical evidence of the magnitude of this effect at an aggregate level. To the extent that they do spill over, however, the impact of union wage increases on inflation is increased.

Some observers have argued that all of these direct economic effects of unions on wages are less important in the overall wage-price inflationary spiral than are the political lobbying efforts of unions. For example, if the competitive market hypothesis outlined above is accurate, the wage-price spiral will continue only if the government pursues expansionary monetary or fiscal policies, or both. An expansionary policy encourages enough economic growth to occur to allow the reemployment of any workers displaced by inflationary wage increases. Although the labor movement is certainly not the only lobbying group that supports expansionary monetary and fiscal policies, its support is a critical supplement to its more decentralized strategies to achieve individual wage and benefit agreements. Without an adequate rate of expansion and economic growth, collectively bargained wage increases would exert a great toll on the employment opportunities of unionized members of the labor force.

The labor movement also supports a wide range of other economic and social policies that supplement its collective bargaining efforts. Again, it has been argued that many of these policies lead to a greater inflationary pressure than do the individually bargained wage increases. Some observers suggest, for example, that the union movement's support of full-employment policies, minimum wage legislation, prevailing wage legislation such as the Davis-Bacon Act and the Walsh-Healey Act, various income transfer policies such as unemployment compensation, workers' compensation, and social security all adds to the inflationary pressures in the economy. Yet the effects of these policies on the economy as a whole are very unclear. And even if these policies were shown to contribute to inflationary pressures, many observers would counter that these pressures are well worth the benefits provided by the policies.

The macro record, 1974–86. A brief review of the economy's macroeconomic performance since 1974 provides a useful background for understanding recent collective bargaining developments, while also illustrating the role macroeconomic policies and conditions play in bargaining. We start in 1974 because it was the year of a major recession and the start of a period of enormous swings in the performance of the U.S. economy.

In 1974 and 1975 the economy entered the worst recession it had faced since the Great Depression. Unemployment rates rose from 4.9 percent in 1973 to 5.6 percent in 1974 and to 8.5 percent in 1975. Although wage increases slowed somewhat from their previous rates to rates of 8.2 percent in 1976 and 7.8 percent in 1977, wages continued to increase at rates substantially above those of the 1950s and 1960s, even in the face of very high unemployment rates.

Moreover, the rates of wage increases throughout the period consistently outpaced increases in productivity, resulting in relatively high rates of unit labor cost increases in the mid- (and late) 1970s. Thus, the results of collective bargaining over this period helped to nudge the inflation rate upward from the cost side.

What does this macroeconomic history tell us about the interrelationships between collective bargaining and economic policy? First, over the 1970s wage increases in collective bargaining appear to have become more sensitive to price increases and less sensitive to the aggregate unemployment rate. Closer examination of this trend confirmed the price responsiveness of bargaining but also clarified the unemployment effects. Although the wage increases were less sensitive to rises in aggregate unemployment, increases in the unemployment rates of prime-age men (who make up the preponderance of union members) still exerted a moderating effect on wage increases. [17] This evidence clearly suggests that a given increase in prices brought about a greater increase in wages under collective bargaining in the 1970s than it did in the 1950s and 1960s. One reason for this is the growth in the COLA clauses in major contracts described earlier.

Recession and higher unemployment rates did eventually curb wage increases and the inflation rate by 1977, but these came with enormous social costs caused by the sharp increases in the unemployment rate. Then, in 1978 the U.S. economy suffered another price shock when oil prices jumped once again. As Table 3–1 shows, by 1979 the inflation rate had risen to 13.3 even in the face of a 5.8 percent unemployment rate. The voluntary wage and price guidelines in force at the time had yielded few results. In 1979 wage increases in major collective bargaining agreements averaged 7.4 percent, and yet workers were frustrated by their loss in real income, the result primarily of the transfer of income from the United States to the oil-producing nations. Rank-and-file workers demanded more from their union leaders, demands reflected in a high contract rejection rate.

By early 1980 the economy had begun to slide into another recession, which then deepened after the Federal Reserve Board sharply curtailed the money supply in an effort to check inflation. The economy's struggle to absorb the higher oil prices and subsequently other rising prices, along with the policy decisions of the Federal Reserve Board, led the nation into an even worse recession that that of the 1970s; the nation's unemployment rate rose to 10.8 percent in December 1982.

Facing major layoffs and receiving the blame for continuing low productivity growth, unions were in poor stead. Even as the economy began to edge its way out of its slump, union leaders considered 1982 their most disastrous year since the Great Depression as the scope and frequency of concessionary bargaining grew. In a number of industries the effects of the macroeconomic recession were compounded by employment losses sustained under the rising tide of imports. For the economy as a whole, imports and the balance of trade were emerging as major macroeconomic problems. Rising import shares and burgeoning federal budget deficits raised interest rates and attracted into the country substantial foreign monetary flows, which in turn worsened the balance of payments.

The events of the 1970s and 1980s, particularly the rising oil prices, the growing penetration of imports in several key manufacturing industries, and the large trade deficit, carried the issue of the international economy straight to collective bargaining agendas. In terms of bargaining power, international economic linkages limit the gains unions achieve by

TABLE 3–1
Macroeconomic history, 1964–85

Year	Inflation rate[a]	Unemployment rate[b]	Wage increase in major collective bargaining settlements[c]	Productivity increase (output per month hour)[d]	Unit labor cost increase[e]	Contract rejection rate[f]	Incomes policy
1964	1.2%	5.2%	3.2%	3.9%	0.59%	8.7%	Guideposts
1965	1.9	4.5	3.8	2.5	1.0	10.0	Guideposts
1966	3.4	3.8	4.8	2.1	3.5	11.7	Guideposts
1967	3.0	3.8	5.6	2.3	3.2	14.2	Jawboning
1968	4.7	3.6	7.4	2.6	4.8	11.9	None
1969	6.1	3.5	9.2	−0.5	5.1	12.3	None
1970	5.5	4.9	11.9	0.3	6.5	11.2	None
1971	3.4	5.9	11.7	3.0	2.8	9.9	Controls
1972	3.4	5.6	7.3	3.2	3.4	10.1	Controls
1973	8.8	4.9	5.8	1.8	5.5	9.6	Controls
1974	12.2	5.6	9.8	−2.2	11.9	12.4	Decontrol
1975	7.0	8.5	10.2	1.8	7.8	11.2	None
1976	4.8	7.7	8.2	2.6	5.6	9.8	None
1977	6.8	7.1	7.8	1.5	6.2	11.5	None
1978	9.0	6.1	7.6	0.8	7.7	11.9	Guidelines
1979	13.3	5.8	7.4	−1.6	11.2	11.9	Guidelines
1980	12.4	7.1	9.5	−0.4	10.9	10.7	Guidelines
1981	8.9	7.6	9.8	1.0	8.4	8.9	None
1982	3.9	9.7	3.8	−0.6	8.3	n.a.	None
1983	3.8	9.6	2.6	3.4	1.3	n.a.	None
1984	4.0	7.5	2.4	1.6	1.6	n.a.	None
1985	3.8	7.2	2.3	−0.0	3.9	n.a.	None

[a] Consumer price index. Taken from *The Economic Report of the President,* various years. The data are calculated from January to December.
[b] The data are taken from U.S. Department of Labor, Bureau of Labor Statistics, *Handbook of Labor Statistics* (Washington, D.C.: GPO, January 1986).
[c] The data are from *Current Wage Developments,* March 1983 and March 1986. The figures represent wage adjustments in all industries for the first year of a contract.
[d] The data are from U.S. Department of Labor, *Handbook of Labor Statistics.* The figures represent the output per hour of all workers in the nonfarm business sector, with quarterly data at seasonally adjusted annual rates.
[e] The data are from ibid. The authors calculated the annual percentage change based on the index.
[f] The data are from Federal Mediation and Conciliation Service, *Annual Report of the Federal Mediation and Conciliation Service,* various editions (Washington, D.C.: GPO). The FMCS no longer kept these data after 1981.

organizing a large share of the domestic labor and product markets. Foreign workers had become a major competitive threat to organized labor in the United States because it is very difficult for unions to take wages out of competition when goods and investments easily move across national borders. Perhaps the growth of multinational companies is the modern-day equivalent of the competitive menaces faced by the Philadelphia shoemakers Commons described so well.

Although the economy recovered, according to many indicators, from 1983 through 1986, serious questions remained regarding its long-run health. Bluestone and Harrison have asserted that the layoffs and other labor force dislocations associated with the recession of the early 1980s were in fact part of a deindustrialization of the U.S. economy, a process triggered by the heightened mobility available to capital. [18] Piore and Sabel agreed that the economy was in the midst of a fundamental transformation, but in their view the transformation entailed a shift away from mass production methods and toward more flexible manufacturing, a switch induced by advances in microelectronics and the increased volatility of the economy as a whole. [19] We will have more to say about each of these claims in later sections of this chapter.

The broad economic forces discussed above and diagrammed in Figure 3–2 are useful for explaining the aggregate average and long-run behavior of the collective bargaining system and its effects on the national economy. It is necessary to start with this larger picture, if only to be constantly reminded that the collective bargaining system still operates in and is influenced by a competitive economic system that is only partially controllable by governmental policies or by the actions of private decision makers. Although much of our later discussions of more micro levels will identify ways unions and employers modify the impact of these competitive market and governmental policy forces, these forces must be considered in the context of their prevailing toll in the longer run.

Together macroeconomic and microeconomic forces act as one major set of determinants of the outcomes of collective bargaining and affect the development of structural and strategic means to moderate their influence. The factors described in the remainder of this chapter either supplement the economic forces or serve as the mechanisms through which the economic forces are translated into actual results in the collective bargaining system.

THE PUBLIC POLICY CONTEXT

Before passage of the National Labor Relations Act (NLRA, or Wagner Act) in 1935, the economic environment was the dominant external force affecting collective bargaining. Without a comprehensive policy framework regulating union-management relations, and facing general hostility from the courts, unions had to rely almost solely on their economic power to obtain recognition for bargaining and favorable contracts from employers. By promoting and regulating collective bargaining, the Wagner Act brought another set of external conditions to bear on the parties that served in part to moderate the economic power advantage enjoyed by either party. And in the years since its passage, other federal and state laws have exerted an increasingly important influence on the practice of collective bargaining, although their influence is often indirect. It has been argued, for example, that as the federal government has increased its influence in the labor market through health and safety or pension regulations, workers' interest in joining unions has waned because, as a result, unions have less to offer workers. Consequently, we need to examine the role or functions of public policy, how that role has been changed over the years, and how public policy affects the behavior of unions and employers and the process and results of collective bargaining.

In a series of essays delivered in 1959 Archibald Cox cited four principal concerns of national labor policy: union organizing, negotiating collective bargaining agreements, administering bargaining agreements, and handling internal union affairs. [20] In addressing these concerns, the cornerstone of U.S. labor policy remains the NLRA of 1935, the amendments in the Taft-Hartley Act of 1947, and the amendments in the Landrum-Griffin Act of 1959. The provisions of those acts are summarized in Table 3–2. As stated in the preamble to the NLRA, its purpose is to promote the orderly and peaceful recognition of unions and the use of collective bargaining as a means for establishing the terms and conditions of employment. The Taft-Hartley amendments added a list of unfair labor practices for unions and turned the NLRA into a detailed and comprehensive code of conduct for collective bargaining; the Landrum-Griffin amendments added provisions governing internal union affairs and sought to define the rights of union members vis-à-vis their union organizations and leaders.

Although the amended NLRA, the administrative decisions of the National Labor Relations Board, and the Supreme Court decisions interpreting the law remain as the central core of policies governing private sector collective bargaining, three major supplements to this body of law have added to the policy environment since Cox wrote his essays. First, over 30 states have passed collective bargaining legislation governing employees of state and local governments, and the U.S. Congress codified the procedures governing collective bargaining by federal employees that were embodied in Executive Orders handed down since 1962. In the 1970s California extended bargaining rights and procedures similar to those in the NLRA to farm workers. Most of the state laws, and to a slightly lesser extent the federal policies, are modeled after the principles set forth in the NLRA, but they differ considerably in the procedures specified for implementing the principles. Thus, collective bargaining principles underlying the NLRA have been extended to additional sectors of the economy besides the private sector.

Second, since the 1960s national labor policy has shifted away from a concern to promote the process and procedures of collective bargaining toward a concern to regulate the substantive terms and conditions of employment. And third, over the 1970s and 1980s public policy changed to reemphasize competitive markets by deregulating key industries such as transportation and communications. Although deregulation was not motivated by labor

TABLE 3–2
The major features of the National Labor Relations Act, as amended

Act	Section	Provisions
National Labor Relations Act (NLRA; Wagner Act) 1935	1	*Findings and policy:* an endorsement of collective bargaining, worker self-organization, and selection of representatives.
	2	*Definitions:* of employer, employee, labor organization, unfair labor practice.
	3–6	*National Labor Relations Board:* its establishment, authority, funding, and structure.
	7	*Rights of employees:* includes rights to self-organize and select representatives for bargaining.
	8	*Unfair (employer) labor practices:* prohibits interference with employee's section 7 rights.
	9	*Representatives and elections:* majority's selection is exclusive bargaining representative. Board can define appropriate unit, certify employee representative.
	10	*Prevention of unfair labor practices:* Board can issue cease and desist orders, take "affirmative action, including reinstatement of employees with or without back pay."
	11–12	*Investigatory powers:* the NLRB can issue subpoenas, examine witnesses, etc. Refusal to obey may result in court contempt proceedings.
	13–16	*Limitations:* act does not limit the right to strike.
Labor Management Relations Act (LMRA; Taft-Hartley Act) 1947 (amendments to NLRA)	2	*Definitions:* added *supervisor, professional employee, agent.*
	3	*National Labor Relations Board:* expanded from three to five members.
	7	*Rights of employees:* to refrain from activities listed in section 7.
	8	*Unfair labor practices:* creates 8(b), Unfair Labor Organization Labor Practices.

TABLE 3–2, continued

Act	Section	Provisions
	9	*Representatives and elections:* separate standards for professional employees, craft groups, guards. Expanded and defined election procedure.
	Title II	*Conciliation of labor disputes:* in industries affecting commerce; national emergencies.
	Sec. 301	*Suits by and against labor organizations.*
Labor Management Reporting and Disclosure Act (LMRDA; Landrum-Griffin Act) 1959 (amendments to LMRA)	Title I	*Bill of rights of members of labor organizations:* includes freedom of speech and assembly, protection from dues increase without vote, and improper disciplinary action.
	Title II	*Reporting by labor organizations:* provides for reporting of officers' names, provisions for members' rights, annual financial statements.
	Title III	*Trusteeships:* defines reasons for trusteeships; provides for reports on all trusteeships.
	Title IV	*Elections:* guarantees regular local and national (and/or international) elections by secret ballot of all members in good standing.
	Title V	*Safeguards for labor organizations:* Officials' Fiduciary Responsibility, requires bonding for all individuals who handle funds or property.

policy concerns, it has had sizable effects on the process and outcomes of collective bargaining, as we shall see.

The Evolution of U.S. Labor Policy

American policies on collective bargaining can be classified into four categories, which correspond roughly to four different time periods: (1) the common law approach, 1800–1890; (2) the business law approach, 1890–1931; (3) the labor law approach, 1932–1959; and (4) the social and economic policy approach, 1960 to the present. Table 3–3 outlines the four approaches and the laws and court decisions that shaped them.

The common law approach. Before there was any constitutional or statutory framework for regulating labor-management relations, the earliest policy statements on the subject appeared in the decisions of state courts. The period from approximately 1800 to 1890 is often referred to as the common law era because the state courts relied on interpretations derived from British common law to regulate the conduct of unions and employers. The first landmark case among these decisions was the 1806 Philadelphia *Cordwainers'* case, in which the court ruled that efforts by unions or other combinations of workers to raise wages were illegal per se. In other words, unions were viewed as a form of "criminal conspiracy." This doctrine changed after the 1842 decision in *Commonwealth* v. *Hunt* in Massachusetts. There the court attempted to distinguish between legal and illegal means for achieving unions' ends; unions had a right to exist but were prohibited from using coercive pressures to achieve their goals.

Throughout this period the courts viewed unions with hostility and suspicion. They had trouble fitting the idea of unions and collective activity into a constitutional system and a dominant political ideology that emphasized individual action and freedom of contract, property rights, and laissez-faire capitalism. Thus, the ability of workers to engage in collective action in pursuit of their goals was severely limited. In addition, the statutory void meant that jurisdiction was basically confined to local or state courts; there was little or no federal involvement in labor relations during this time.

The business law approach. Passage of the Sherman Anti-Trust Act in 1890 signaled a new approach: the beginnings of federal regulation of union activity. Under the antitrust approach, labor was treated as a commodity to be regulated in a manner similar to other factors of production. That is, unions were viewed as labor market monopolies to be limited as other combinations or conspiracies aimed at restricting free trade in product markets. Thus, a law designed to regulate business became the predominant framework for regulating unions and collective bargaining. Also during this time courts began widespread use of injunctions to discourage strikes and other forms of union pressure against employers.

Throughout this period the courts were able to play a dominant role in constraining unions because they could now use a federal statute, rather than common law, to justify their decisions. The continued hostility or, at best, indifference of policy toward unions and collective bargaining reflected the weakness of labor as a political force in society and the dominance of business and agricultural interests. It also reflected the prevailing social ideology, advanced by leading industrialists, management, and economic theorists, that placed a premium on individual effort, achievement, and freedom. At the same time, however, industrialization and the growth of the factory system had called forth popular demands for a legitimation of union activity. Thus, the need for a statutory framework, along with the supremacy of business as a political force, produced a labor policy based on business law. This period therefore vividly illustrates the impact of political and social values and power on the content of public policies toward labor.

TABLE 3–3
Overview of major developments in U.S. labor policy

Period	Date	Event	Description
Common law approach	1806	*Cordwainers'* case	A combination of workers seeking a wage increase is a criminal conspiracy.
	1842	*Commonwealth v. Hunt*	Unions are lawful. Combinations of workers are allowed as long as lawful means are used to gain lawful ends. Courts still hostile to unions.
Business law approach	1890	Sherman Anti-Trust Act	"Every combination . . . or conspiracy in restraint of trade or commerce among the several states . . . is hereby declared to be illegal." Used by employers seeking injunctions for union activity.
	1894	*Debs* case	A famous use of the injunction. Eugene Debs jailed for refusing to obey a court back-to-work order in the American Railway Union strike.
	1906	*Danbury Hatters* case	Union boycott of goods in violation of the Sherman Act. Union is assessed triple damages.
	1912	Lloyd-LaFollette Act	Public employees are allowed to request raises from Congress. Postal workers may organize, but not strike.
	1914	Clayton Act	"Labor is not a commodity," but courts continue to find union acts illegal.
	1926	Railway Labor Act	Railway workers are allowed to organize and bargain collectively.
Labor law approach	1932	Norris-LaGuardia Act	Federal courts are severely restricted in issuing injunctions against unions; yellow-dog contracts "shall not be enforceable."
	1933	National Industrial Recovery Act	Workers are extended the "right to organize and bargain collectively through representatives of their own choosing . . . free from interference, restraint, or coercion of employers" (Sec. 7a).

	1935	*Shechter Poultry* case	Supreme Court decision: NIRA is held unconstitutional.
	1935	NLRA (Wagner Act)	Establishes organizing rights, unfair (employer) labor practices, and the National Labor Relations Board.
	1935	Social Security Act	Includes OASDHI (old age, survivors, disability, and health insurance) and OAA (old age assistance).
	1947	Taft-Hartley Act	Amends the NLRA. Adds unfair union labor practices, Sec. 8(b).
	1959	Landrum-Griffin Act	Establishes a bill of rights for union members. Requires financial disclosing by unions. Lists guidelines for trusteeships and elections.
Social and economic policy approach	1962	Executive Order 10988	Encourages public sector bargaining. Requires maintenance of management rights. Orders added by Kennedy in 1963, Nixon in 1969 (Executive Order 11491). Followed by passage of state laws giving employees of local and state governments the right to bargain.
	1962	Wage-price policies	Guideposts 1962–66; controls 1971–73; guidelines 1978–79.
	1964	Civil Rights Act, Title VII	Unlawful for employer or union to discriminate on the basis of race, color, religion, gender, or national origin.
	1970	Occupational Safety and Health Act	Establishes standards for safety and health; Occupational Safety and Health Administration.
	1972	Supplementary Security Income Act	Effective January 1, 1974. Replaces OAA of 1935 Social Security Act.
	1974	Employee Retirement Income Security Act (ERISA)	Establishes minimum standards for private pension plans.
	1978	Mandatory Retirement Act	"Age Discrimination in Employment Act." Outlaws mandatory retirement rules for workers up to age 70.

In their review of the evolution of labor policies Brown and Myers pointed out three deviations from the business law approach. [21] First, the Lloyd-LaFollette Act of 1912 gave postal employees the right to organize. Second, during World War I the National War Labor Board adopted a policy statement asserting the right of workers to organize into unions and bargain collectively. And third, the Railway Labor Act, passed in 1926, was the nation's first law to endorse the process of collective bargaining in the private sector. It gave railway employees the right to organize and to bargain collectively. All three of these deviations represented pragmatic adjustments in the prevailing policy, deviations designed to address specific pockets of union power. The already existing postal service and railroad unions had sufficient power to obtain legislation legitimizing the positions they had obtained through their economic and political power. Similarly, wartime production needs placed the existing unions in a position to impose severe costs on society. Thus, employers during the first World War agreed not to break those unions that already existed, setting the stage for a greater acceptance of unionization in later decades.

The labor law approach.   A major shift in policies regulating union-management relations took place in the 1930s with passage of the Norris-LaGuardia Act of 1932 and the NLRA in 1935. The former limited the use of the labor injunction, and the latter protected the rights of private sector employees to unionize and bargain collectively with their employers. The NLRA marked the first public acknowledgment of the need to have specific *labor* legislation for regulating industrial relations activities. Instead of building on common law or business law theories as in the past, the legislation passed from 1930 to 1959 was aimed directly at promoting and regulating the process of collective bargaining and, as such, recognized the need for principles and practices that were suited particularly to this segment of the economic and social system. Thus, the NLRA elevated the status of collective bargaining to new heights of legitimacy in society. From an institution that was once viewed as a criminal conspiracy and then as a form of monopoly, collective bargaining was transformed into the preferred mechanism for determining wages, hours, and other terms and conditions of employment.

The explicit support for unionization and collective bargaining embodied in the NLRA reflected the major shift in public attitudes toward business caused by the Great Depression. But in pragmatic terms it also granted unions a power they had never known in their dealings with employers. The 1947 Taft-Hartley amendments to the NLRA were an attempt to reverse that shift somewhat by providing countervailing rights and powers to employers and to society. The 1959 Landrum-Griffin amendments more finely calibrated the balance of power between the parties by limiting the power of union leaders over the rank-and-file. All of these laws, however, shared the same underlying objective, namely, to promote or regulate a process of collective bargaining as the cornerstone of national labor policy.

Throughout the 1960s and 1970s this *labor law approach* remained the preferred means for regulating collective bargaining and union-management activity. Collective bargaining rights were extended to federal employees through Executive Order 10988 in 1962 and to a majority of state and local government employees through state legislation over those two decades. Although those extensions made several exceptions to specific provisions in the NLRA, most notably in restricting public employees' right to strike, they carried through the basic principle of promoting independent collective bargaining.

The pattern by which those public sector statutes developed further illustrates how the larger economic and political environment influences public policy. The first states to legislate bargaining rights for public employees were the highly industrialized, highly unionized, and more ideologically liberal states of the Northeast and upper Midwest, which also had higher per capita expenditures on public services. [22] The more rural, ideologically conservative states of the South and the Rocky Mountain region have been slow to follow suit.

Amendments to the NLRA continued to be introduced in Congress. The most salient example of these was the Labor Law Reform bill of 1978, which passed the House of Representatives but then died in the Senate. This bill would have speeded up the procedures for union representation elections, imposed stronger penalties on violators of labor laws, and expanded the membership of the National Labor Relations Board by two members. In many respects, therefore, the labor law approach continues to drive U.S. labor policies.

The economic and social policy approach. Beginning around 1960, however, a competing approach to labor policy began to develop, incrementally and in many ways unintentionally. We call it the *economic and social policy approach* because it departs from the premise that specific legislation promoting or regulating the collective bargaining process should serve as the cornerstone of labor policy. The legislation of the last two decades, as well as the increasing role of the federal executive and judicial branches in labor relations, signifies an effort to manage an array of economic and social conditions through direct regulation of the terms and conditions of employment. For example, the experimentation with wage-price guideposts over the years 1962–1966 and wage-price controls in the early 1970s represented efforts by the federal government to have a direct influence on wages. Similarly, Title VII of the 1964 Civil Rights Act represented an effort to influence employers' allocation of job opportunities within the firm and thus gave the government a hand in workplace decisions on promotion, transfer, seniority, and other terms of employment. The same can be said about the

Occupational Safety and Health Act (OSHA) of 1970 and the Employee Retirement Income Security Act (ERISA) of 1974. Thus, the 1960s and the 1970s witnessed a shift away from a labor policy approach that focused on regulating the process of collective bargaining by balancing the power of the two major actors to a focus on direct regulation of the workplace and, again, perhaps unintentionally, the outcomes of bargaining. A byproduct of this shift was a tripling of the number of regulatory programs administered by the U.S. Department of Labor. [23]

In a sense these policies that directly determined workplace conditions are more similar to the approaches taken before the 1930s than they are to the labor law approach because they were designed not to promote collective bargaining as the means for deciding on workplace conditions but to promote certain economic and social concerns. This approach includes an ambivalence toward collective bargaining as an institution. As Brown and Myers speculated in 1962, perhaps the labor law era that began in the 1930s was simply an aberration or a temporary deviation from American society's long-standing skepticism toward unions and collective bargaining. Whether one accepts their view or not, the incremental legislative initiatives governing the workplace have definitely added up to a serious challenge to the primacy of collective bargaining envisioned by the framers of the NLRA in 1935.

A return to competitive market policies. The expansion of federal policies governing employment conditions came to an end by the late 1970s. Since then the conservative political trend first evident in the Carter administration and then more obvious in the Reagan administration produced a range of policies that emphasized competition in product markets at the micro and macro levels of the economy.

Important developments at the micro level include deregulation of the transportation and communications industries. As discussed earlier, unions have trouble keeping wages out of competition and maintaining their penetration of any industry in the face of entry by new competitors. This has certainly been the case in the trucking industry since passage of the Motor Carrier Act of 1980, which reduced the regulation of industry pricing and entry by the Interstate Commerce Commission. In the airline industry deregulation in 1978 spurred the growth of nonunion carriers and concessionary bargaining in the unionized airlines. In the communications industry deregulation has led to both a growth in the share of telecommunications markets that are served by nonunion companies such as MCI and the breakup of a national bargaining structure in the former Bell Telephone System.

At the macro level the commitment of the Reagan administration to free trade and floating exchange rates has sparked heated debates over trade policy as the nation faces huge trade deficits and a loss of employment in those industries most threatened by foreign competition and imports. The increasing internationalization of the U.S. economy has also raised questions whether the labor law framework adopted in the 1930s is still appropriate.

A return to the jungle? Another serious challenge to the traditional NLRA system of labor regulation comes from within the labor movement itself. Several labor leaders have begun to speculate whether labor unions would be better served if the NLRA were repealed and the parties returned to a variant of the public policy environment that prevailed before the 1930s. Lane Kirkland, AFL–CIO president, has stated, "If by boycotting the [NLRB] one could divest oneself of the jurisdiction of the Board and go to the law of the jungle, I think that would be an option worth considering and I think we might very well be better off." [24] Although this option has not been pursued by the ranks of union leaders or members, it is noteworthy because it stands in dramatic opposition to the position traditionally held by U.S. labor leaders, who have been among the staunchest supporters of the NLRA.

This questioning of the ongoing value of the NLRA has arisen from union leaders' frustration with both the current administration of the law and the union record of achievement in recent years, particularly in representation elections. Labor leaders (and others) argue that NLRB decisions and representation elections now come about only after enormous delays—caused in part by the lack of commitment to the original purposes of the NLRA exhibited by some NLRB members. The delays are also alleged to be the result of employer practices, such as the filing of numerous challenges and requests for postponement, which only serve to thwart the original intent of the NLRA for timely and fair elections. Overall, these critics argue that NLRA enforcement procedures operate to the advantage of management and against the original purposes of the law.

Labor leaders are also frustrated by the meager success unions are now having in representation elections and by the more general decline in union membership. They blame their lack of success on the current administration of the NLRA and stepped-up "union avoidance" tactics on the part of management. And so they speculate whether unions and workers would be better served by a return to *the law of the jungle* than by a continuation of current practices.

The Multiple Roles of Labor Policy

In many respects we have come full circle in the evolution of U.S. labor policy and find ourselves once again facing the task of balancing multiple objectives in designing a labor policy suited to the needs of both the parties and the economy. There are signs of a serious debate beginning over whether major modifications should be made to the national labor laws. As this debate proceeds, the multiple objectives of labor policy will have to be considered. At least four partly conflicting objectives will be of greatest concern.

First, because the laws governing labor-management relations affect the bargaining power of the parties, one of the major functions of public policy is to foster a balance of power among workers, unions, employers, and the government. As the British legal scholar Otto Kahn-Freund observed, statutes governing labor relations emerge because common law does not adequately take into account disparities in the power of the different parties. [25] The same can be said for the market system. Thus, the major shifts in public policy that have occurred since the 1800s all reflect efforts to modify, in one way or another, the power of one or more parties to the employment relationship.

Second, public policy choices reflect the prevailing ideology in the society and the distribution of political power among interest groups. Consequently, although one goal of the law is to attain a balance of power, any law will inevitably reflect the existing distribution of power among the parties. As it is commonly put, "The lion tends to get the lion's share of the benefits." In other words, the political nature of the policymaking process makes it difficult for policy to carry out its power-balancing function. In the United States this truism translates into a balance in favor of management, but one advantage of this aspect of policymaking is that it keeps the collective bargaining system in tune with the prevailing political ideology.

A third objective of labor policy is to specify how much the parties should be left to themselves or, in other words, how much weight should be given to "free" collective bargaining. As discussed further in Chapter 8, free collective bargaining has received much praise in this country on the grounds that the parties themselves know best their own particular problems and needs. At the same time, however, pursuit of other social and labor policy objectives has often meant the introduction of constraints and bounds on collective bargaining. The critical issue here is the set of trade-offs associated with relaxing or extending the autonomy of the parties.

Finally, the government is not simply a mediator of conflicting interests in collective bargaining. Instead, it has an important stake in labor policy as an employer of approximately one-sixth of the total labor force and as the subsidizer of a sizable quasi-public sector comprising railroads, hospitals, public utilities, and other industries. Thus, another important function of public policy is to assert the goals of the government as an actor in the industrial relations system.

In some cases these various objectives conflict, while in others they support one another. Where they conflict, the debates over new policies will have to address the trade-offs involved in balancing the objectives— an ever more crucial and difficult task in today's complex, changing, and interdependent society.

THE DEMOGRAPHIC CONTEXT

Few theories of collective bargaining make explicit reference to the importance of worker characteristics. Yet over the past decade the changing nature of the labor force has caused many to question whether collective bargaining is obsolete. We therefore need to examine the nature of those changes and explore their implications for collective bargaining.

Changes in the demand for and supply of workers have profound effects on all aspects of industrial relations, including collective bargaining. A framework for tracing the effects of demographic shifts on a collective bargaining system is presented in Figure 3–3. Changes in the characteristics of workers or jobs can, over an extended period of time, be expected to influence the needs, attitudes, and expectations of workers. These, in turn, may influence the individual's propensity to join unions and willingness to accept the jobs offered. Once a match between individual and job is made and the worker becomes a member of a union (or is covered under a collective bargaining agreement), a process of adjustment takes place in which the worker may attempt to change aspects of the job that do not meet his or her original expectations or needs. [26] One avenue of change is that of influencing union goals in collective bargaining.

Thus, the first stage of the model depicted in Figure 3–3 proposes that (1) changes in the demographic mix of a work force produce changes in workers' needs, expectations, and attitudes and upset the balance between job characteristics (such as the compensation system, job design, working conditions, and worker autonomy) and worker expectations; and (2) changes in this balance lead workers to seek changes in the collective bargaining goals of unions. The second stage of the model then proposes that, to the extent that unions adapt their goals in bargaining to accommodate their members' changing needs, and to the extent that unions are successful in

FIGURE 3–3
The effects of demographic change on collective bargaining

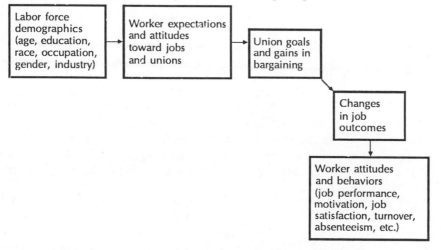

achieving change in the job outcomes or characteristics of concern, the employment system adjusts in ways that produce higher levels of worker performance, more favorable worker attitudes toward their jobs and their unions, and lower rates of turnover, absenteeism, drug and alcohol abuse, and injuries and illnesses, among other things.

Although there is little theory or empirical evidence to support this model directly, we can safely hypothesize that the faster the demographic makeup of a work force, union, or bargaining unit changes, the more difficulty the union and the employer will have in adjusting to change. Unions are not designed to adapt well to individual or subgroup differences within their constituencies. The very purpose of a union is to pursue the common goals of its members through the exercise of collective power. Thus, the more rapid the demographic changes, and the more heterogeneous the union constituency becomes, the greater the potential for internal conflict and the more difficulty the union will have in trying to establish bargaining priorities. Furthermore, it is unlikely that newly hired, younger workers will have an effective political base to influence the existing, often older, union leadership. Note the same problem faces women, racial minorities, or any other new groups that move into union jobs. Until they can establish an effective political base, or exert enough pressure on existing union leaders, their particular needs are not likely to be given as high a priority as they might desire.

The posture of employers in collective bargaining may reinforce the delayed response to changes in a bargaining unit, since most changes in bargaining goals mean additions to the existing bargaining agreement. For example, adding a day care center or more flexible work schedules for working mothers represents an additional provision in the contract that has costs associated with it, something employers may resist in negotiations.

Labor Force Trends

Since World War II the U.S. labor force has grown at an unprecedented rate, largely as a result of the postwar "baby boom." The labor force of the 1980s mirrors the movement of the baby boom cohort into its prime working years (25–54). The labor force is expected to grow at a slower rate from 1985 to 1995 than it did in the previous ten years because baby boomers will no longer be entering the labor force but rather traveling through it. In fact, a slowdown in the growth of the labor force began in the late 1970s as the last of the boomers entered the labor force. In 1978 and 1979 the labor force grew by 3.2 million people, whereas in 1984 and 1985 it grew by only 1.9 million. [27]

As this trend continues, the median age of the labor force will change accordingly. The median age peaked in 1960 at 40.5 and remained relatively constant until the first of the baby boomers entered the labor force in 1970, at which time it declined significantly. The median age was 39.0 in 1970 but had fallen to 34.8 by 1982. By 1995 it is projected to have risen again, up to 37.6, reflecting the aging of the baby boomers. In 1984 two-thirds of the labor force was at its prime working age (25–54); by 1995 three-quarters will be in that range. By the turn of the century this generation will be nearing retirement and producing strains on private and public retirement systems.

These general patterns mean that in the short run unions and employers will be faced with a younger work force than ever before. Employers will therefore continue to have the dual task of socializing these new entrants into the demands of industrial and organizational life and adapting their own practices to motivate and train the young workers. Not all industries are equally affected by the influx of young workers. Those industries or regions that are growing are more likely to attract younger workers and therefore experience a significant shift in the age distribution of their work forces than those that are declining and experiencing outmigration. [28]

As the baby boom cohort moves through its prime working years, workers will be in sharp competition for jobs at the higher levels of careers and occupations. Several observers have predicted that this competition will find its voice in greater workplace conflicts and a heightened demand for union representation. They argue, in essence, that these will be years of mounting frustration as workers realize that their aspiration for upward mobility may not be attainable. The process of readjusting either promotional ladders and compensation practices or the expectations of workers is expected to yield intensified industrial conflict. And job seekers born during the birth rate slump of the 1960s and 1970s will face a tight labor market for entry-level positions across a wide variety of occupations. The resulting upward pressure on wages at the entry level could create a ripple effect on wages throughout the remainder of the occupational distribution. At the same time the mid- to upper-level workers and their families will be in their peak consumption years when their income demands will be greatest. Over the longer run, 1995 and beyond, the problems of an aging population will become increasingly important and the *dependency ratio*, the ratio of those not in the labor force to those in the labor force, will increase—posing difficult problems indeed for all the actors in the industrial relations system.

Women in the Labor Force

The growing number of working women is the most significant labor force development of the last 15 years. In 1970 one-half of all women participated in the labor force; in 1985, 70 percent of women between the ages of 25 and 44 worked, and that fraction was expected to rise beyond 80 percent by 1995. [29] The general trend can largely be explained by women's changing marital status, educational attainment, and career expectations.

One component of the trend has been the increased participation in the labor force of women with young children. Women have been taking less time off from work for child rearing: In 1985, 60 percent of all mothers had entered the labor force before their youngest child was four years old; and about half of all mothers with infants one year old or younger were in the labor force, as compared to 39 percent in 1980 and 31 percent in 1975. Consequently, working mothers have begun to challenge employers and unions to meet their social needs. They pose a particular challenge because the propensity to work has been greater among the more highly educated women. Between 1975 and 1984 the labor force participation rate for female college graduates ages 25 to 64 rose from 61 percent to 78 percent. In 1985 the college-educated labor force was 38 percent women, whereas in 1970 it was 32 percent. Thus, in addition to being a growing component of the labor force, women may well become a vocal component. Their increasing numbers and their increasing education, militancy, and consciousness of women's issues may pressure employers and unions to change their postures toward female workers. Finally, women may present a new focal point for union-organizing campaigns.

In the 1970s there were modest declines in the degree of segregation by gender across jobs and occupations. In 1970 more than half of all men worked in occupations that had 10 percent or fewer women, but by 1980 only 37 percent of all men worked in such occupations. Over the same period there was a significant change in the share of women working in occupations that had 10 percent or fewer men. Perhaps the most significant distributional change in the 1970s was the increase in female managers — from 18 percent of all managers in 1970 to 31 percent in 1980.

Educational Attainment

The educational attainment of workers has been steadily increasing over the past century and continues to do so. In 1970 the median number of years of school completed for all workers was 12.4, or just slightly beyond a high school degree; by 1983 the median had risen to 12.8, or nearly a full year past a high school degree. [30] In 1970, 66.4 percent of all workers had graduated from high school, and 12.9 percent had graduated from college. In 1984 those figures had risen to 80.6 percent and 20.9 percent, respectively. Thus, the labor force of the future will, on average, be more highly educated and therefore should be somewhat more productive.

There is, however, an important caveat to consider in projecting the overall "quality" of the labor force. High rates of teenage unemployment (18.6 percent in 1985), high dropout rates from high schools (16 percent for whites, 19 percent for blacks in 1981), and the poor quality of education offered in urban and, particularly, in poor urban areas all suggest that a large number of new entrants in the labor force over the next decade will have little work experience, few skills, and a low potential for adapting to the rigors of organizational life. [31] Teenagers who grow up in areas with few or no jobs, high rates of crime, and poor schools will pose significant challenges to managers and union leaders of the future. Past experience has shown that it is difficult indeed for employers to reverse the effects of these liabilities.

These two separate educational patterns pose different but equally challenging problems to future managers and union leaders. The more highly educated workers may be less tolerant of authority, seek more involvement on their jobs, and demand more career development opportunities, while the educationally disadvantaged will require more remedial training to mold them into more literate, trainable, and motivated participants in the labor force.

Occupational and Industry Trends

As the supply characteristics of the U.S. labor force have been changing, so has the occupational and industry demand for labor. The most obvious trends in the occupational distribution since 1960 have been the growth of the white-collar sector and the decline of the blue-collar sector. Over half of the labor force is now classified as white-collar; in 1960 that proportion was 43 percent. As Table 3–4 shows, as of 1983 the percentage of the labor force employed in service-producing jobs was 74 percent, whereas the percentage employed in goods-producing jobs was only 26 percent.

These major shifts in industry demand over the last 25 years have profound implications for collective bargaining. The portion of the labor force employed in manufacturing jobs—the traditional stronghold of unions—declined from 31 percent in 1960 to 20.5 percent in 1983. Furthermore, manufacturing industries have been steadily migrating from the Northeast and Midwest toward the western and southern states. From 1960 to 1983 the share of all U.S. manufacturing employment located in the Northeast declined from 33.2 percent to 24.6 percent, while in the South it rose from 22.0 to 30.8 percent and in the West, from 11.7 to 16.2 percent. [32] These industry and occupational trends document the movement of jobs away from

TABLE 3–4
The relative size of industrial sectors in the United States, 1983

Year	All service-producing	All goods-producing	Manufacturing only	Government only
1919	52.6%	47.4%	39.4%	9.9%
1940	59.1	40.9	33.9	11.6
1960	62.3	37.6	31.0	15.4
1983	74.0	26.0	20.5	17.6

Source: U.S. Department of Labor, Bureau of Labor Statistics, *Handbook of Labor Statistics* (Washington, D.C.: GPO, June 1985).

Note: The percentages represent workers as a percentage of the total nonagricultural labor force.

the most unionized industries and regions to industries and areas where unions have traditionally been less successful in organizing workers.

There has also been a significant increase in the share of employment in part-time jobs. In 1963, 10.7 percent of all employees worked part-time; by 1984 that figure had grown to 13.7 percent. The percentage of employed youths 16 to 19 years old who worked on a part-time basis rose from 37.8 percent in 1963 to 50.2 percent in 1984. [33]

As part-time work has grown, so has the number of jobs being performed at home. Home-based occupations have grown in ranks partly in response to advances in information technologies that make it possible to perform production tasks at home while in communication with a business or businesses out of the home. This is especially true of several data-processing occupations. At this time, however, there are no reliable aggregate estimates of the percentage of the labor force involved in home-based jobs. Both part-time workers and home-based workers are difficult to reach with union-organizing drives.

The increase in the number of service and part-time jobs has spurred an intense debate. Bluestone and Harrison and others believe that the growth in these jobs represents a long-term deterioration in the health of the U.S. economy and signals a process of deindustrialization. They further argue that these shifts in job composition go hand-in-hand with an emerging bifurcation in the income structure. The better paying jobs such as skilled trades, steel, and auto production jobs, they claim, are disappearing and are being replaced by lower paying service jobs. [34]

On the other side of the debate stand analysts such as Robert Lawrence who hold that the growth in the number of service and part-time jobs has been a response to the availability and desires of workers who want and are skilled for those jobs. [35] These observers see this as a sign of health in the U.S. economy and compare the job growth in the United States over the 1970s to the sluggish employment growth in Europe over the same period. Lawrence and others on this side of the debate claim there is no evidence of a bifurcation in the income distribution. [36] There is a middle position in this debate, as well, with some disclaiming any deindustrialization but at the same time pointing to many persistent problems in the U.S. labor market. [37]

This debate subsumes both a disagreement over what the facts are and a disagreement over how the facts should be interpreted. Yet the debate is crucial to the future of the labor market because the issues at stake are of enormous importance. For if one decides that the labor market is relatively healthy, there is little reason to seek government policies to alter the outcomes in that labor market, and vice versa. Furthermore, any answer to the question whether deindustrialization or a bifurcation in the income structure is taking place will affect government policy toward collective bargaining and many other labor market institutions.

Whatever the outcome of this academic debate, the shift to greater part-time, service sector, and home-based employment has two indisputable implications for collective bargaining and union organizing. First, since part-time workers have looser attachments to a single employer than others (they are often only temporarily employed), union organizing among them is more difficult and probably requires nontraditional techniques. It is not surprising that the labor movement has vigorously criticized the growth of temporary and home-based work. It is unlikely, however, that labor's opposition will have any effect on the growth occurring in these types of employment relationships. Thus, to organize these workers, the labor movement will need to develop organizing and representational strategies that are tailored to their particular needs. One strategy that has been discussed within labor's ranks is to provide associate member status or individual forms of representation to these workers. [38] Other solutions may be developed outside the United States since the growth in temporary, part-time, and home-based work is a problem confronting labor movements all over the globe.

Second, in negotiating contracts, unions that represent workers in the lower paying, service occupations cannot rely solely on traditional strategies of taking wages out of competition and threatening to strike. The ease of entry into service occupations and industries, the low level of skill required, and the ease of replacing striking workers all make it difficult for unions to acquire bargaining leverage through traditional means. Not surprisingly, several unions that represent service workers have been experimenting with strategies outside the workplace designed to build support for their demands and broaden their power in the larger community. These unions also tend to emphasize training, career development, and other strategies to upgrade the skills, productivity, and labor market status of their members.

A Demographic Profile of Union Members

A more complete discussion of the demographic characteristics of union members appears later, in Chapter 5. At this point it is important simply to reiterate the differences between union members and nonmembers and the trends in the labor force that were summarized above. The average union member is more apt to be working in industries, occupations, and regions in which the demand for labor is either declining or growing at a slower pace than elsewhere in the economy. In addition, women, whose labor force participation is increasing rapidly, are underrepresented in the unionized sector.

What do these differences imply for collective bargaining? First, the challenge to unions as organizations is obvious. Their traditional constituency — male, blue-collar, manufacturing, mining, construction, and transportation workers living in the Northeast or North Central regions — is declining in significance; and the types of workers, regions, occupations, and industries that have traditionally posed the greatest difficulties for unions are growing in importance and size. Second, current union members are on average older and less well educated than the new entrants to the labor force. To the extent that worker attitudes, goals, expectations, and perceptions of unions vary systematically by education and age, unions may have difficulty adjusting to the demands of a younger, more vocal constituency. Finally, although specific data on union membership by age of plant are not available, we can infer from the data summarized above that unionized plants are likely to be older and less efficient than the newer, more technologically advanced plants that have opened in the weakly unionized regions of the country. Thus, the growth of the Sunbelt region at the expense of the Northeast and upper Midwest is demanding ever more creative solutions by union and management leaders alike to address competitive pressures and the productivity gaps that exist between union and nonunion plants.

In short, the demographic context of collective bargaining influences the constituency of unions, the expectations and attitudes union members and workers in general have toward their jobs, and the human capital (skills, abilities, and educational levels) workers bring to the job. These factors, in turn, influence the substantive goals and priorities of the parties in collective bargaining, workers' and employers' satisfaction with the outcomes of bargaining, and ultimately, change in the union-management relationship.

At the very least, the demographic changes now taking place will modify the constituency of collective bargaining in future decades. Unions may or may not succeed in organizing this new constituency and integrating these workers as active and committed members of their organizations. If unsuccessful, they will see their membership as a percentage of the labor force continue to decline. If successful, they will face pressures for change—both within their own organizations and at the bargaining table. Moreover, a broadening of the locus of unionism will inevitably lead to more diversity in organizing and representational methods. In any event, it is clear that any analysis of collective bargaining must account for the demography of the labor force.

THE SOCIAL CONTEXT

What is the image of the union movement in the eyes of the American public? Is the society supportive of or hostile to unions? From time to time these questions have been the subject of a good deal of speculation and rhetoric. Ups and downs in the rate of union growth, in the labor movement's effectiveness in politics, in the policies of employers in collective bargaining, and in the loyalty and commitment of members to their unions have all been attributed at least in part to the public image of the labor movement—an image that varies considerably by region and over time.

Polls that ask only a single-item question regarding unions have consistently shown a decline in the public's image of unions over the last 20 years. Gallop polls, for example, show a decline from 71 percent in 1965 to 58 percent in 1985 in the share of the population that "approves" of labor unions. An accurate portrait of the public's contemporary views of unions, however, requires distinguishing among three different attitudes the public holds toward unions, namely, their attitudes toward (1) union leaders, (2) the political or social roles played by unions, and (3) the role of unions in representing workers' interests at the workplace.

Union Leaders' Public Image

Polls consistently have shown that the American public holds union leaders in low esteem, and the public's confidence in union leaders (and business leaders) has fallen to even lower levels in recent years. In Harris polls taken between 1966 and 1985, only 15 percent of the public, on average, indicated they had a "great deal of confidence in union leaders." [39] (Only 24 percent indicated a great deal of confidence in the leaders of major companies.) Another striking finding of these polls is that the confidence ratings of leaders of business, labor, and eight other institutions (churches, government, professions, and so on) all declined, on average, from a high of 49 percent in 1966 to 27 percent in 1985. But, although skeptical of union leaders, the American public has continued to express strong approval of the *functions* unions perform in representing worker interests.

Dual Images of Union Activity

Table 3–5 presents the responses of a 1977 national sample of workers to a series of questions designed to gauge their beliefs about U.S. trade unions. Analysis of these responses indicated that the questions could be grouped into two separate categories. Six questions clustered together into a category that has been labeled a *big labor image* of the U.S. labor movement. These questions asked respondents the extent to which they agreed or disagreed with six statements to the effect that the labor movement exerts a powerful influence over others in society.

Between 70 percent and 80 percent of the respondents agreed with the statements that unions exert a strong influence over who is elected to public office, what laws are passed, how the country is run, and their members. Just over two-thirds of the respondents agreed that unions are more powerful than employers and that union leaders are more interested in obtaining benefits for themselves than for their union members. Thus, a large majority of workers see unions as big, powerful institutions in society. Together, these interrelated beliefs suggest that the big labor image of the trade union movement is shared by a large majority of U.S. workers.

TABLE 3–5
U.S. workers' beliefs about trade unions (N = 1,515)

"Big labor" image	Strongly agree	Agree	Neither agree nor disagree	Disagree	Strongly disagree
Influence who gets elected to public office	37.5%	46.0%	1.8%	12.7%	1.1%
Influence laws passed	24.0	56.6	3.8	14.4	1.2
Are more powerful than employers	24.8	41.6	6.2	25.4	2.0
Influence how the country is run	18.1	53.4	4.8	21.7	1.9
Require members to go along with decisions	18.5	56.0	3.9	20.1	1.6
Have leaders who do what's best for themselves	22.8	44.7	6.4	24.0	2.1
Instrumental image					
Protect workers against unfair practice	20.5	63.0	3.4	11.2	2.0
Improve job security	19.2	61.0	2.8	14.5	2.5
Improve wages	18.9	67.6	3.2	8.7	1.7
Give members their money's (dues') worth	6.9	38.5	6.3	36.9	11.3

Source: Thomas A. Kochan, "How American Workers View Labor Unions," *Monthly Labor Review* 102 (April 1979): 15–22.

These results are consistent with earlier opinion poll data. In a 1941 survey, for example, 75 percent of the respondents said union leaders had accumulated too much power, and in 1950, 62 percent agreed with this statement. Questions asked about union leaders in four polls between 1942 and 1965 consistently showed that the public held union leaders in lower esteem than business leaders, religious leaders, government officials, and college professors. [40] The data from the 1977 survey once again documented the public's skeptical view of union leaders. Although differences in the wording of the questions in the earlier polls preclude exact comparisons, the similarity of the responses suggests that there has been little change in the views of the political role played by the U.S. labor movement. There simply is little public identification with the political or social actions of the labor movement. When these responses were analyzed to determine whether any subgroups of workers had more positive or negative views of labor in politics, it was found that those most likely to agree with the six statements were older workers and white-collar workers; those most likely to disagree with the statements were union members, southerners, women, racial minorities, and public sector workers. These variations across demographic, regional, and occupational groups were small, however, in light of the general uniformity of worker responses to the questions. The big labor image is evidently a belief shared by a majority of workers across most, if not all, demographic, industrial, regional, and occupational groups. Measured in this way, then, the social climate for the *political* activities of trade unions appears to be somewhat unreceptive and perhaps even downright hostile.

The remaining four questions listed in Table 3–5 queried whether unions are instrumental and helpful in improving the working lives of their members. Over 80 percent of the respondents agreed that unions improve the wages and job security of their members and represent their members effectively against unfair employer practices. The respondents were almost equally divided, however, over the question whether unions provide their members with their money's worth. Again, these data are consistent with previous polls, which had shown that despite the negative political image of the trade union movement, 60 percent to 70 percent of the respondents approved of unions in general and believed in the right of workers to join unions of their own choosing.

Thus, while only a minority of the public seems to identify with the political activities of trade unions, the majority does accept the legitimacy of unions as a means for protecting the economic and job-related interests of workers. This latter set of beliefs has been interpreted as a strong endorsement by the public of the institution of collective bargaining.

The public's continued support of the functions unions perform was further documented in two more recent surveys. A 1984 Harris poll reported that 69 percent of a national sample disagreed with the statement that only blue-collar workers need unions. Similarly, other surveys conducted by the Opinion Research Corporation found that 64 percent of a national sample disagreed with the statement that "unions are no longer needed in this country."[41]

These survey data indicate that U.S. workers have a dual image of trade unions. On the one hand, the majority of workers see unions as big, powerful institutions in society that exert significant control over political decision making and elected officials, as well as over employers and union members. The majority also take a skeptical view of union leaders' personal motivations. On the other hand, an equally large majority of workers see unions as being helpful or instrumental in improving the working lives of their members. Still, however, the public is about equally divided over whether the benefits provided by unions are greater than the costs of union membership. Furthermore, although those who see unions as powerful political institutions are less likely to see unions as instrumental in improving the lives of their members, these are by no means mutually exclusive images. Instead, the majority of U.S. workers apparently hold both of these views. Evidently, then, most U.S. workers are skeptical of the political activities of trade unions but accepting of their collective bargaining activities. Thus, their general view of labor unions in the broader society does not seem to interfere with their evaluation of how well unions function as representatives of their members in collective bargaining.

It should be noted, however, that workers may not interpret the political role or power of unions as a negative attribute. Fiorito's analysis of these same data revealed a positive correlation between the respondent's assessment of the political influence of unions and that individual's propensity to join a union. [42]

Perhaps the most surprising finding from the analysis of these data is that these views vary little across regions of the country. Giving the lie to the stereotype of the anti-union southern worker, southern respondents perceived unions as effective in representing worker needs in collective bargaining. In addition, southerners rated the political power of unions slightly lower than did northeasterners. Overall, therefore, these data suggest that the social environment for collective bargaining in this country is still quite favorable, even if Americans do not look with favor on unions' political activities.

These national survey data do not do justice, however, to regional and urban-rural variations in the actual climate for unions and the collective bargaining process. While the attitudes of individual workers in the South may be becoming more like the attitudes of workers elsewhere, community and state leaders in many locations continue to tout their area's favorable "business climate," lack of constraining labor legislation, and lower rates of unionization, in efforts to attract new industry. Furthermore, states with right-to-work laws are concentrated in the South and the Rocky Mountain states, and the majority of the states that have not passed legislation granting public employees the right to bargain are in the South. Thus, there is some indirect evidence that the social climate for unions continues to vary somewhat across state lines. On the other hand, even within the "strong union" or highly unionized states, considerable variation exists in the climate for collective bargaining. Within New York, for example, tremendous differences in the resistance to unions exist between the rural and generally conservative areas and the metropolitan areas of New York City, Buffalo, Syracuse, and Albany. States like Wisconsin and Michigan differ in an analogous fashion between their industrialized and rural areas. These differences in social climate should be kept in mind as an important external component of a collective bargaining system.

THE TECHNOLOGICAL CONTEXT

We cannot leave our discussion of the environmental contexts of collective bargaining without discussing the role of technology as an environmental determinant of behavior in union-management relationships. All observers of industrial relations believe that technological change had a major role in workers' early efforts to look to unions and collective bargaining as a way to alter their employment conditions; and all observers of the current scene believe that ongoing technological changes will have huge effects on future employment conditions. Yet, in the face of this agreement, many still disagree over how and why technology influenced early unionization and what current technological changes imply for the future of industrial relations.

Both Karl Marx and John R. Commons believed that workers were spurred to join unions by technological change, the shift from craft systems of production to the hiring of wage labor, and the rise of the modern factory system. But they disagreed sharply over exactly why changes in technology and the organization of work had that effect. To Marx the critical event was the chasm that capitalism and capitalist methods of production opened up between workers and the owners of the means of production. That chasm, according to Marx, would inevitably result in a worsening of working conditions, a profit crisis, and the emergence of a revolutionary class consciousness among workers. Followers of Marx went on to argue that it was the *loss of control* that workers experienced as a result of the shift in production methods and ownership that led them to form unions. To those observers collective bargaining was, and is, a continuing battle between workers and managers over control of the production process. Harry Braverman built on this argument and claimed that technological change typically leads to a lowering of the skills required in jobs *(deskilling)* as part of this battle for control. [43]

Commons, on the other hand, observed that the shift in production methods was itself a product of an expansion of the market brought about by urbanization and new transportation methods. To Commons, as the market expanded and the organization and ownership of production changed, workers came up against a host of competitive menaces in the form of "bad wares," greenhands, and prison or child labor (various forms of lower wage labor). Workers then turned to unions to protect themselves and improve their standard of living. Commons and his students such as Selig Perlman argued that unions and workers sought *income and job security* rather than control of the production process. [44] Thus, although Marx and Commons differed sharply over the interpretation of unions' objectives, both saw the rise of capitalism as the spur to unionization.

To Kerr, Dunlop, Harbison, and Myers it was the process of *industrialization* and not capitalism per se that brought forth the changes in the relationship between workers and employers that in turn led to unionization. [45] They argued that modern technology produced a uniformity in the rules governing relations between workers and employers. Collective bargaining and contractually negotiated rules were a logical way to formalize and structure the rules required in modern industry. Given this framework, specific technological changes are important within collective bargaining because they result in changes in the relative bargaining power held by management or labor. In this regard the industrialization thesis is closer to Commons than to Marx.

Beyond these broad debates over the role of technology research has analyzed the specific consequences of different forms of technological change.

Joan Woodward found that the characteristics of labor-management relations varied among small batch, mass production, and continuous process technologies. [46] Specifically, she found greater pressure on supervisors and employees and ultimately greater workplace conflict in the mass production technologies than in the other two. Moving to the level of the individual, a good many writers have argued that worker attitudes, especially job satisfaction and alienation, are influenced by the nature of the technology. [47] Here the arguments usually focus on the effects of mass production technology and its routine, repetitive, and often boring work. At least one study has clearly documented that employees in highly routinized assembly-line jobs report lower job satisfaction and employee motivation than employees with more discretion in their jobs. [48] Others have observed that technology affects the nature of the work setting and the amount of interaction that employees have on their jobs, and thus work group cohesion. Still others have shown that the nature of the technology influences the strategic position of employees in the production context and therefore is an important source of bargaining power for a work group. [49]

The recent expansion in the use of microelectronic technology has reignited the debate over the effects of technological change. As noted earlier in this chapter, Piore and Sabel argue that industrial society is now in the midst of a major shift from mass production to flexible specialization, a shift that has far-reaching effects on labor-management relations. According to Piore and Sabel, industry is shifting to flexible manufacturing in response to the heightened environmental volatility and uncertainty reflected in sharp macroeconomic business cycles and unstable markets. In the face of this market instability, production volumes and mixes must be rapidly adjusted, thereby making computerized machinery attractive because it can be reprogrammed. Employment systems are influenced by this shift in production methods because managers are demanding that their work organizations also become more flexible. Furthermore, according to Piore and Sabel, flexible production techniques work best if workers' skill levels are raised as work processes are restructured to link the design and execution of work tasks; in the process the work organization moves away from hierarchical and Tayloristic practices.

In this new debate the rebutters to Piore and Sabel maintain that the new technology is being used to wrestle control away from the work force and to deskill workers now just as it allegedly was in the past. [50] These observers see little evidence of a shift away from the hierarchical forms of work organization. In fact, modern proponents of the deskilling thesis argue that much of the concessionary bargaining of the 1980s has been over management efforts to increase the pace of work and use new technology to weaken workers' bargaining leverage and skills. The deskilling thesis proponents also predict that new technology will lead to significant employment displacement and unemployment.

A number of behavioral scientists believe that new technologies serve to "unfreeze" existing practices and open up a variety of options for reconfiguring the organization of work, career ladders, compensation criteria, and other aspects of the employment relationship. [51] According to this view there is no single effect of technology; rather, its effects depend on the choices made by decision makers and the way the new technology is implemented. A large body of research on the implementation of new technology suggests that the active involvement of the user of a technology encourages more successful adoption of the technology. There also is evidence that organizations and workers gain more from new technology when they have been involved in the early managerial and engineering decisions about the design and use of the technology. If these hypotheses are correct, union and worker involvement in both the strategic decisions concerning technology and the workplace implementation of new technology could serve the long-term interests of workers, managers, and unions. New technology thereby offers another example of an environmental pressure extending industrial relations activity above and below the traditional, middle tier of industrial relations.

Obviously, without ongoing advances in technology, productivity will not rise and wages will stagnate. But on the other hand, changes in technology threaten workers' job security, often alter the balance of bargaining power between labor and management, and thus have the potential for disrupting labor-management relations. Management of technological change is therefore one of the most challenging problems facing practitioners. And worker reactions to new technologies and to resulting changes in industrial relations practices warrant considerably more attention by scholars and students as well. Thus, there are practical as well as theoretical reasons for improving our theories and empirical research on the role of technology in industrial relations. At this point perhaps the best we can say is that technology is important, but the specific ways in which technology affects skill levels, employment, and collective bargaining have yet to be understood.

RECENT ENVIRONMENTAL PRESSURES ON COLLECTIVE BARGAINING

Recent changes in the environment of collective bargaining form a major theme of this book, and so at this stage we will only preview some of these changes in closing our discussion of the environment of collective bargaining.

In the early 1980s a number of changes in the environment placed unions at a distinct disadvantage. The macroeconomic recession of 1980 to mid-1983 brought with it a large number of layoffs and a sharp rise in the unemployment rate. These events were exacerbated by increases in foreign competition and imports, which had been threatening a number of industries in the 1970s and some industries, such as textiles and garments, for even longer. The net effect of these macroeconomic and trade developments was sharp and prolonged employment declines. Between 1980 and 1984, the Bureau of Labor Statistics estimated, approximately 2 million jobs were lost in manufacturing; of those, slightly more than half were the jobs of union members. [52] Employment in many industries dropped from previous peak levels, in most cases attained in 1979, to recession lows, in most cases reached in 1983: Declines over that period were 44 percent in the steel industry, 48 percent in the farm machinery industry, 50 percent in copper mining, and 39 percent in the auto industry.

Unions had faced sharp employment declines before, during previous recessions. What made the declines of the early 1980s so severe was their scale and their duration. Plant closings and the threat of further closings convinced many workers that these employment declines signaled a more permanent shift in the economic environment than was true in earlier recessions. Many unions feared that unless they agreed to concessionary modifications in their existing and new contracts, they would face even more substantial job cutbacks.

Unions also faced new competition in the form of growing numbers of domestic nonunion firms. In industries such as construction, trucking, textiles, and mining the share of nonunion production had risen substantially. Furthermore, even in traditional strongholds of unionism such as steel and autos, nonunion firms were entering the industry. Nonunion competition became an even greater threat as employers became more willing and able during strikes to shift production to nonunion sites. As a result, unions became less able to take wages out of competition, and as predicted by our earlier theoretical discussion, their bargaining power declined significantly.

Economic pressures were only part of the story, however. The labor movement in general entered the 1980s to encounter a conservative swing in political ideology that found its outlet in local bargaining and national public policies. As the public grew warier of unions, strikers found their picket lines crossed by fellow workers and less support for strikes in the broader community. The latter result was perhaps most evident in President Reagan's firing of the striking air traffic controllers in 1980. Many observers have commented that this action served to legitimize employers' already harder line in bargaining and gave an example to those other employers of ways they could resist union demands. When unions sought recourse through the NLRB or the courts to block such management practices as the movement of operations to other sites or the abrogation of collective bargaining contracts during bankruptcy reorganization, they received little help.

The economy, public policy, ideology, and, as we saw earlier, demography had all taken a turn that would hamper the efforts of organized labor. And yet, in the face of all these environmental pressures, the union movement was exhibiting some signs of innovation and adaptation. As discussed in more detail in later chapters, concessionary bargaining in some firms and industries led to a broadening of the bargaining agenda and increased union involvement in managerial decision making. As we discuss in Chapter 12, the form and extent of concessionary bargaining was heavily shaped by union and business strategies. Moreover, the mid-1980s found the labor movement engaged in serious soul-searching, as illustrated in the 1985 AFL–CIO report on potential new organizing and representational strategies. [53] Before we can understand the roots and implications of these many changes under way in collective bargaining, however, we first need a more complete theoretical understanding of the bargaining system.

SUMMARY

This chapter introduced the chief external influences on collective bargaining. Together these environmental forces provide the starting point for understanding the behavior of the other parts of the bargaining system, for evaluating how well it is performing, and for prescribing changes in the system. Ultimately, not only the level of performance but, indeed, the survival of collective bargaining as an institution, will depend on its ability to adapt to the changing characteristics of its environment. If our interpretation of the environmental influences is accurate, the magnitude of this challenge is now increasing. Economic pressures on the U.S. collective bargaining system have steadily grown since foreign competition and persistently high unemployment became threatening in the 1980s. Public policy is not only challenging the status and priorities assigned to collective bargaining, but also placing new expectations on the bargaining system for the achievement of goals that may be inconsistent with the goals of union members and management. The social context has come to play an important role during negotiations and strikes. Furthermore, the demographic context poses serious organizing challenges for union leaders, productivity and motivation problems for managers, and an intensified challenge for arbitrators, mediators, and the NLRB. Finally, technological change and changing structures of employment portend far-reaching modifications in work organization and employment patterns.

Suggested Readings

For a detailed discussion of how the economic context influences bargaining power, see:

Freeman, Richard B. *Labor Economics*, 2d ed. Englewood Cliffs, N.J.: Prentice-Hall, 1979.
The role of incomes policies in the macroeconomic environment is discussed in:

Weber, Arnold R., and Daniel J. B. Mitchell. *The Pay Board's Progress*. Washington, D.C.: Brookings Institution, 1978.

A classic discussion of the evolution of U.S. labor policy is:

Cox, Archibald. *The Law and National Labor Policy*. Los Angeles: Institute of Industrial Relations, University of California, 1960.

A seminal treatment of the relationship between technology and work organization is:

Blauner, Robert. *Alienation and Freedom*. Chicago: University of Chicago Press, 1964.

Notes

1. John T. Dunlop, *Industrial Relations Systems* (New York: Holt, Rinehart & Winston, 1985).

2. Workers can also withdraw their labor through more informal actions, such as a "rulebook" slowdown, the "blue flu," and other means of slowing production.

3. Alfred Marshall, *Principles of Economics,* 8th ed. (New York: Macmillan, 1920), 383–86.

4. Others have pointed out that for a low labor cost ratio to act as a source of power, as Marshall hypothesized, the elasticity of demand for the final product must be greater than the elasticity of substitution of nonlabor inputs in the production process. See Richard B. Freeman, *Labor Economics,* 2d ed. (Englewood Cliffs, N.J.: Prentice-Hall, 1979), 67–71.

5. John R. Commons, "American Shoemakers, 1648–1895: A Sketch of Industrial Evolution," *Quarterly Journal of Economics* 25 (November 1919), reprinted and revised in *A Documentary History of American Industrial Society,* vol. 3, ed. John R. Commons (New York: Russell and Russell, 1958), 18–58.

6. U.S. Department of Labor, Bureau of Labor Statistics, *Earnings and Other Characteristics of Organized Workers,* bulletin 2105 (Washington, D.C.: GPO, 1980).

7. Arthur M. Ross, *Trade Union Wage Policy* (Berkeley: University of California Press, 1948).

8. John T. Dunlop, *Wage Determination Under Trade Unions* (New York: Macmillan, 1944).

9. Bruce T. Allen, "Market Concentration and Wage Increases: U.S. Manufacturing 1947–1964," *Industrial and Labor Relations Review* 21 (April 1968): 353–65.

10. See, for example, Daniel S. Hamermesh, "Market Power and Wage Inflation," *Southern Economic Journal* 39 (October 1972): 204–12. Also see Henry Farber, "Union Bargaining Power and Wages," master's thesis (Ithaca, N.Y.: Cornell University, 1974).

11. John R. Hicks, *The Theory of Wages,* 2d ed. (London: Macmillan, 1963), 136–58. See also A. C. Pigou, *Economics of Welfare,* 4th ed. (London: Macmillan, 1938), 451–61; or John R. Commons, *Institutional Economics: Its Place in Political Economy* (New York: Macmillan, 1934), 311.

12. Robert Ferguson, *Cost of Living Adjustments in Union-Management Agreements* (Ithaca, N.Y.: New York State School of Industrial and Labor Relations, Cornell University, 1976), 12.

13. Wallace E. Hendricks and Lawrence M. Kahn, *Wage Indexation in the United States: Cola or Uncola?* (Cambridge, Mass.: Ballinger, 1985).

14. Daniel J. B. Mitchell, *Unions, Wages, and Inflation* (Washington, D. C.: Brookings Institution, 1980), 113–62.

15. Albert Rees, *The Economics of Trade Unions* (Chicago, University of Chicago Press), 101–4; George H. Hildebrand, "The Economic Effects of Unionism," in *A Decade of Industrial Relations Research,* ed. Neil Chamberlain, Frank C. Pierson, and Theresa Wolfson (New York: Harper & Row, 1958), 107.

16. See, for example, Farrell E. Bloch and Mark S. Kuskin, "Wage Determination in the Union and Nonunion Sector," *Industrial and Labor Relations Review* 31 (January 1978), 183–92.

17. Michael Wachter, "The Changing Cyclical Responsiveness of Wage Inflation," *Brookings Papers on Economic Activity,* vol. 1 (Washington, D.C.: Brookings Institution, 1976), 115–59.

18. Barry Bluestone and Bennett Harrison, *The Deindustrialization of America* (New York: Basic Books, 1982).

19. Michael J. Piore and Charles F. Sabel, *The Second Industrial Divide* (New York: Basic Books, 1984).

20. Archibald Cox, *The Law and National Labor Policy* (Los Angeles: Institute of Industrial Relations, University of California, 1960).

21. Douglas V. Brown and Charles Myers, "Historical Evolution," in *Public Policy and Collective Bargaining,* ed. Joseph Shister et al., 1–27 (New York: Harper & Row, 1962).

22. Thomas A. Kochan, "Correlates of State Public Employee Bargaining Laws," *industrial Relations* 12 (October 1973): 322–37.

23. John T. Dunlop, "The Limits of Legal Compulsion," *Labor Law Journal* 27 (February 1976): 67.

24. In "AFL–CIO Will Oppose Collyer Nomination as Board Counsel," *Daily Labor Report,* 9 May 1984, A-4.

25. Otto Kahn-Freund, *Labour and the Law* (London: Stevens and Sons, 1972), 2.

26. For a general model of the work adjustment process that traces a similar path, see Lloyd H. Lofquist and Rene V. Dawis, *Adjustment to Work: A Psychological View of Man's Problems in a Work Oriented Society* (New York: Appleton-Century-Crofts, 1969).

27. All these figures come from various issues of *Special Labor Force Reports,* U.S. Department of Labor, Bureau of Labor Statistics.

28. See, for example, Henry S. Farber, "Individual Preferences and Union Wage Determination: The Case of the United Mine Workers," *Journal of Political Economy* 86 (October 1978): 923–42.

29. U.S. Department of Labor, Bureau of Labor Statistics, *Handbook of Labor Statistics* (Washington, D.C.: GPO, 1985).

30. All the data on the median number of years of education are from U.S. Department of Labor, Bureau of Labor Statistics, "Education Attainment of Workers, March 1982–83," bulletin 2191 (Washington, D.C.: GPO, April 1984).

31. Data regarding dropout rates are from U.S. Department of Commerce, Bureau of the Census, *Current Population Survey,* series P-20, no. 373.

32. These percentages are derived from data in U.S. Department of Labor, Bureau of Labor Statistics, *Handbook of Labor Statistics,* December 1983 and June 1985 editions (Washington, D.C.: GPO).

33. See Ronald G. Ehrenberg, Pamela Rosenberg, and Jeanne Li, "Part-Time Employment in the United States," paper presented to the conference "Employment, Unemployment, and Hours of Work," Berlin, Germany, 17–19 September 1986.

34. Bluestone and Harrison, *Deindustrialization.*

35. Robert Z. Lawrence, *Can America Compete?* (Washington, D.C.: Brookings Institution, 1985).

36. See, for example, Neal Rosenthal, "The Shrinking Middle Class: Myth or Reality," *Monthly Labor Review* (March 1985): 3–10.

37. See, for example, Paul Osterman, *Employment Futures* (New York: Oxford University Press, forthcoming).

38. AFL–CIO Committee on the Evolution of Work. *The Changing Situation of Workers and Their Unions* (Washington, D.C.: AFL–CIO, February 1985).

39. These data are discussed more fully in Thomas A. Kochan, Harry C. Katz, and Robert B. McKersie, *The Transformation of American Industrial Relations* (New York: Basic Books, 1986): 215–18.

40. See Derek Bok and John T. Dunlop, *Labor and the American Community* (New York: Simon and Schuster, 1970), 11–17.

41. James L. Medoff, "The Public's Image of Labor and Labor's Response," photocopy (Cambridge: Harvard University, 1984).

42. Jack Fiorito, "Union Voting and Politics," in *Proceedings of the Thirty-Eighth Annual Meeting, December 28–30, 1985, New York*, ed. Barbara D. Dennis, 270–78 (Madison, Wis.: Industrial Relations Research Association, 1986).

43. Harry Braverman, *Labor and Monopoly Capital* (New York: Monthly Review Press, 1984).

44. Selig Perlman, *A Theory of the Labor Movement* (Philadelphia: Porcupine Press, 1979 reprint of 1928 edition).

45. Clark Kerr, John T. Dunlop, Frederick Harbison, and Charles A. Myers, *Industrialism and Industrial Man* (Cambridge: Harvard University Press, 1960).

46. Joan Woodward, *Industrial Organization: Theory and Practice* (Oxford: Oxford University Press, 1965).

47. See, for example, Robert Blauner, *Alienation and Freedom* (Chicago: University of Chicago Press, 1964). See also *Work in America: Task Force Report for the Secretary of Health, Education, and Welfare* (Boston: MIT Press, 1971).

48. Denise M. Rousseau, "Technological Differences in Job Characteristics, Employee Satisfaction, and Motivation: A Synthesis of Job Design Research and Sociotechnical Systems Theory," *Organizational Behavior and Human Performance* 19 (1977), 18–41.

49. See, for example, Leonard R. Sayles, *The Behavior of Industrial Work Groups* (New York: Wiley, 1958); James W. Kuhn, *Bargaining and Grievance Settlement* (New York: Columbia University Press, 1961); or C. Frederick Eisele, "Organization Size, Technology, and Frequency of Strikes," *Industrial and Labor Relations Review* 27 (July 1974), 560–72.

50. See David F. Noble, *Forces of Production* (New York: Oxford University Press, 1986); and Harley Shaiken, *Work Transformed* (New York: Holt, Rinehart & Winston, 1984).

51. Richard Walton, "Work Innovations in the United States," *Harvard Business Review* 57 (July/August 1979): 88–98; Barry Wilkinson, *The Shopfloor Politics of New Technology* (London: Heinemann Educational Books, 1983); Stephen Barley, "Technology, Power, and the Social Organization of Work," *Research in the Sociology of Organizations,* ed. Samuel B. Bacharach and Nancy DiTomaso (Greenwich, Conn.: JAI Press, forthcoming).

52. Paul O. Flaim and Ellen Sehgal, "Displaced Workers of 1979–83: How Have They Fared?" *Monthly Labor Review* 108 (June 1985): 6.

53. AFL–CIO Committee on the Evolution of Work, *The Changing Situation.*

CHAPTER 4

Structures for Collective Bargaining and Organizational Governance

In its broadest sense the structure of collective bargaining outlines the arena in which labor and management are expected to interact, negotiate, and solve problems. A bargaining structure must therefore be judged by its effectiveness as a means for the parties to engage each other in decision making on the issues that affect their vital interests. Because the middle tier of industrial relations activity has been the preferred arena for joint decision making by labor and management since the New Deal, most discussions of bargaining structure have focused on the rules and other factors influencing the choice of a negotiation unit and, in turn, on the unit's effects on the process and outcomes of bargaining.

We will follow this convention in this chapter; but we will take a broader approach to studying the structure of bargaining, since recent developments in industrial relations have been broadening the scope of interactions between labor and management to encompass interactions well below and well above the level of formal contract negotiations. We will ask both how traditional bargaining structures are changing as labor and management seek to adapt to changes in their environments and whether the structures of bargaining embedded in the New Deal model facilitate or impede effective employee and union involvement in the governance of modern work organizations.

THE TRADITIONAL DEFINITION OF BARGAINING STRUCTURE

Bargaining structure has traditionally been defined as the *scope* of the employees and employers covered or affected by the bargaining agreement.

Specifically, the *formal structure* of bargaining is defined as the *bargaining unit* or the *negotiation unit*, that is, the employees and employers that are legally bound by the terms of an agreement. The *informal structure* is defined as the employees or employers that are affected by the results of a negotiated settlement, through either pattern bargaining or some other nonbinding process. The most recent U.S. Bureau of Labor Statistics estimate is that between 180,000 and 194,000 separate bargaining agreements exist in the United States. That estimate has been comparably high since the 1940s, and the U.S. system of collective bargaining has therefore always been viewed as highly *decentralized*. That is, most labor contracts in this country cover members of one local union at a single employment site.

In contrast, bargaining in many European countries, such as West Germany and Sweden, has traditionally been more centralized, with more contracts covering entire industries or broad regions and with a stronger role for employer associations than for individual firms. [1] In recent years, however, many European employers have been arguing for greater decentralization of bargaining to allow individual firms the latitude to adjust to their particular economic circumstances. [2] As we will see, many U.S. employers are pressing for even further decentralization of the formal and informal structures of bargaining in this country, as well.

In Chapter 1 we listed the structure of bargaining as an important intervening variable in our model of the collective bargaining system. The choices made in designing a bargaining structure are not independent but are constrained by the need to match the structure of bargaining to the environmental and organizational conditions in which negotiations will take place. Indeed, as shown in Figure 1–1, we view the structure of bargaining as the initial and primary determinant of all the internal features of a bargaining system.

It is important to recognize that decisions concerning the structure of bargaining are highly influenced by the structure of union and management organizations themselves and by unions' and employers' strategies and goals. It is much less obvious precisely what the cause-and-effect relationships are. Nonetheless, a change in any one of these—the structure of bargaining, the structure or goals of management, or the structure or goals of the union—is likely to trigger a change in the other two.

For example, in reviewing the development of the highly centralized bargaining structure in the West German automobile industry, Streeck noted that it was the centralization of German employers before World War II that produced the initial structure. Because unionism and collective bargaining, along with other democratic institutions, were supressed during the Hitler era, a new collective bargaining system had to be established after the war. The German unions favored reestablishing centralization because it complemented both the new, more streamlined and centralized industrial union structure and the common, or *solidarity*, wage structure the unions favored. [3]

Similarly, in the United States the gradual centralization of managerial decision-making power within AT&T that occurred from the 1940s through the 1970s led, first, to the merger of many of the independent unions of telephone workers into the Communications Workers of America (CWA), a national union, and, then, to the development of a centralized, nationwide contract and bargaining structure. But, later, the 1984 divestiture of AT&T into regional telephone and service companies forced a return to the company-by-company bargaining structure. [4] Because the evolution of the Bell System–CWA bargaining structure illustrates many of the points we have to make about this topic, we will draw on it quite extensively in this chapter. Box 4–1 provides a chronology of the structure of bargaining between these parties as it evolved over the past 50 years.

BOX 4–1
The evolution of a bargaining structure: AT&T and the CWA

1885	AT&T incorporated to provide long-distance service linking the separate Bell Telephone companies.
1937	Bell System employee associations sever ties with the telephone companies to form a federation of local unions, the National Federation of Telephone Workers (NFTW).
1940	First collective bargaining agreement signed between New York Telephone Company and a local of the NFTW.
1940–44	Separate agreements signed with other Bell System companies; NFTW membership grows from 45,000 in 1939 to 170,000 in 1945.
1942–45	Telephone workers included in wage pattern set by "Little Steel" formula established by the War Labor Board.
1946	NFTW threatens to call a national strike against AT&T Long Lines in an effort to achieve a national pattern. Contract settled with intervention by the U.S. Secretary of Labor, with AT&T agreeing to use the agreement as a pattern for the settlements with the Bell System companies. In 1946 difficulties in negotiating a national agreement serve as an impetus for NFTW to reorganize for more centralized control of the union.
1947	Communications Workers of America (CWA) formed as a successor union to the NFTW. Some Bell System employees are represented by the International Brotherhood of Electrical

---

BOX 4–1 *(continued)*

Workers (IBEW); others remain in independent unions. Lack of union solidarity causes pattern bargaining to break down.

1950–70　The CWA takes gradual steps toward national bargaining. Some cluster bargaining and pattern bargaining take place throughout the Bell System. In 1965 COLA clauses are added to all Bell agreements.

1971　The CWA and IBEW call their first national strikes against the Bell System.

1974　National bargaining is established. The national agreement signed covers wages and benefits; local supplements cover specific working conditions and a portion (.4 to .6 percent) of the wage increase.

1984　AT&T divestiture. Seven regional holding companies are established to provide local telephone service.

1986　A national agreement is signed with AT&T after a brief strike by the CWA. Separate contracts are negotiated with the regional companies, with the CWA following a pattern bargaining strategy and the companies stressing their individual needs and conditions.

Sources: Information adapted from Marianne Koch, David Lewin, and Donna Sockell, "The Determinants of Bargaining Structure: A Case Study of AT&T," in *Advances in Industrial and Labor Relations,* vol. 4, ed. David Lewin, David B. Lipsky, and Donna Sockell (Greenwich, Conn.: JAI Press, in press); Wallace E. Hendricks, "Telecommunications," in *Collective Bargaining in American Industry,* ed. David B. Lipsky and Clifford B. Donn, 103–34 (Lexington, Mass.: Lexington Books, 1987).

ALTERNATIVE STRUCTURAL DESIGNS

Negotiations cannot take place until a bargaining representative has been duly certified as the exclusive representative of the employees. Normally, this requires that a union win a representation election (although an employer may voluntarily recognize a union if the union can demonstrate that it represents a majority of the employees involved). Our discussion of the formal structure begins, therefore, with a description of the criteria commonly considered in the choice of an election unit. The election unit serves as the basis for the bargaining unit—and for the broader policy issues concerning union recognition, the establishment of a new bargaining relationship, and the termination of recognition and representation. Box 4–2 provides the context for this discussion by outlining the stages that occur in a typical union-organizing and election process.

The Election Unit

The *election unit* is the group of employees that the National Labor Relations Board (NLRB) (or the appropriate state agency with jurisdiction over the employees involved) determines is covered under the statute and is eligible to vote in the certification election. Two main decisions must be made to define the appropriate election unit. First, the range of employees to be included must be decided. This involves choosing between craft (a specific occupation) and industrial (for example, all the blue-collar production and maintenance workers within an organization); and between employees at one plant or location and employees at multiple plants or job sites. Second, the issue of who functions as a supervisor or manager must be decided because, since the passage in 1947 of the Taft-Hartley amendments to the National Labor Relations Act (NLRA), supervisors have been excluded from coverage under the act.

The scope of the unit. Since the composition of the electorate can influence the outcome of the election, the scope of the unit is often a hotly contested issue. Quite simply, the union will seek an election unit that maximizes its ability to win the election, and the employer will seek a unit that minimizes the union's chances of winning. The NLRA states the fundamental objective in choosing an election unit should be to insure employees "the full freedom in exercising the rights guaranteed by this act."

The NLRB and the state and local boards normally consider the following general criteria in deciding on the appropriate election unit: (1) the community of interests among the employees, (2) the potential effects of alternative units on stability in the labor-management relationship, (3) the need to provide sufficient freedom of choice to professional and skilled employees, and (4) the history of bargaining or the employer's decision-making structure. This fourth criterion is useful in resolving disputes between the parties over whether certain employees should be excluded because they perform supervisory or managerial functions.

Craft severance has historically been one of the most controversial issues the NLRB has had to address in making these decisions. Although Section 9(b)(2) of the Taft-Hartley Act was designed to limit the NLRB's ability to allow craft workers in a larger production and maintenance unit, the board has consistently rejected petitions to exclude craft workers from the large industrial units found in manufacturing industries, such as rubber, steel, and autos. Indeed, the board has argued that the interdependence between

BOX 4–2
Steps in the union-organizing and and representation election process

1. Interested employees seek out a union to learn their rights and gain help in organizing, *or* a union seeks out a group of employees in order to explain their rights and explore their interest in organizing.

2. The union builds support for organizing among the employees and solicits their signatures on authorization cards.

3. When sufficient cards are signed to indicate substantial employee support, the union asks for recognition as the bargaining agent for the employees. If at least 30 percent of the employees have signed cards, the union can petition for an NLRB certification election. If over 50 percent of the employees have signed cards, the union can ask the employer for recognition, or, if this is refused and serious unfair labor practices are committed by the employer, the union can ask the NLRB for certification. If the employer does not voluntarily recognize the union, either party can petition for an NLRB certification election to determine whether the union has majority support.

4. The NLRB investigates to determine whether an election should be held. The board considers the issues of whether it has jurisdiction, whether there is sufficient interest among the workers, and whether there is already a bargaining agent or there had been an election within the past 12 months. Most importantly, the NLRB determines the appropriate bargaining unit.

5. If the NLRB finds that the conditions for an election have been met, it orders that one be held. Procedures of varying formality are used, depending on the level of disagreement between the parties. Expedited procedures can be used if the union has engaged in organizational or recognitional picketing.

6. With the election date set, campaigning on both sides intensifies. Restrictions apply to both union and management behavior during this period, in an attempt to maintain "laboratory conditions," that is, to allow the workers to make free, uncoerced choices.

7. Representatives of the NLRB conduct a secret-ballot election. An individual's right to vote can be challenged by the union, management, or the NLRB. If there are more than two choices on the ballot and no option receives a majority vote, a runoff election will be held between the two choices that received the most votes.

8. If the union wins the election, and following any objections or appeals, the NLRB certifies the union as the exclusive bargaining agent for the employees. The employer has the obligation to begin negotiating a first contract. If the employer wins the election, there can be no further election for 12 months.

craft workers and production workers in these industries warrants a single comprehensive unit. [5] The board has been somewhat more willing to grant professional employees a separate bargaining unit. Again, Section 9(b) of Taft-Hartley prohibits the NLRB from including professional employees in a bargaining unit with nonprofessional employees unless the professionals decide by a majority vote to be included in a larger, more comprehensive unit.

The spread of bargaining to hospitals and the public sector has raised a number of new and complex questions concerning election and, ultimately, bargaining unit choices. Hospitals, for example, exhibit a wide range of fine distinctions among various professional and quasi-professional employees and vast differences in the nature of the tasks each group performs. Should registered nurses, practical nurses, and nurses' aides all be included in a single unit, or should they be separated into three distinct units for the purposes of a representation election? In general, hospitals illustrate that the more complex and differentiated the technology or the skills required in the jobs performed and the more occupational distinctions that exist in an organization, the more difficult is the task of choosing an appropriate election unit. The NLRB resolved these questions initially by establishing separate units for each of the following: registered nurses, other professional employees, technical employees such as practical nurses and laboratory specialists, business office and clerical employees, and service and maintenance employees. Later decisions, however, favored fewer and broader units by distinguishing professional and technical employees from administrative and support personnel.

Changes in technology can render previous unit determination decisions obsolete by modifying how the work is performed, thereby raising the question whether the new jobs created should be excluded from the existing unit. Computer-aided design (CAD) serves as one example of just such a technological change. CAD can transfer drafting, model making, and other similar jobs from their traditional place within blue-collar production and maintenance units to the purview of design or manufacturing engineers, who traditionally have been either nonunion or in a separate engineers' union and bargaining unit. In one aerospace company we have been studying, for instance, conflict has arisen over whether members of the machinists' union or members of the professional engineers' union should be given the work of maintaining the thousands of computers used in the firm. Box 4–3 illustrates another such dispute that was ultimately resolved by an arbitrator. In this case robots took over some of the tasks traditionally performed by blue-collar workers, and the issue was in part who should be given the job of bringing the robots on line and adapting their specifications to perform specific jobs.

These examples illustrate an important feature of the structure of bargaining in the United States. Because so much rests on the definition of the

BOX 4–3
Arbitrating over technological change

The Issue

Did the company violate the collective bargaining agreement when it assigned certain machining and fixturing work on robotics to non–bargaining unit personnel? If so, what shall be the remedy?

The Facts

The grievant and other bargaining unit personnel did fixturing work on production technology referred to as Robot No. 1. They did similar work for a while on Robots No. 2 and No. 3, but then this assignment stopped in 1984. In December 1983 the company formed a new department called Advanced Automation and Technology, and the fixturing work, what the company calls "development work," was given to non–bargaining unit engineering personnel assigned to the new department.

The Arbitrator's Discussion

In establishing the Advanced Automation and Technology department, the company made a major change that affects the allocation of work that previously had been done by tool room personnel. . . . In a world of changing technology and methods specific duties and responsibilities may shift within an organization. The issue in this case arises because of a shift from earlier technology (that is rather standard and can be adapted in a straightforward manner by bargaining unit personnel) to new technology that requires considerable experimentation by engineers and technicians.

And so we have a situation where an organizational change has shifted the function of preparing production technology, but it is not clear whether the new skills and duties that are involved belong in the bargaining unit or elsewhere in the organization. *Given the grey area that is involved in this dispute, it would be desirable for the parties to establish principles to guide the allocation of work.*

The Arbitrator's Decision

Given the fact that the union has not established conclusively that fixturing work for robotic technology belongs to the bargaining unit, it was not a violation of the collective bargaining agreement when the company assigned certain machining and fixturing work to non–bargaining unit personnel.

Nonetheless, given that the establishment of the Advanced Automation and Technology department represented a major decision with important consequences for the bargaining unit, . . . the parties are directed to negotiate in good faith over the effects of this change.

Source: Arbitration decision of Robert B. McKersie in the case of Northrup Corporation and United Auto Workers Local 1596, 1 July 1986. Adapted and used with permission of the arbitrator.

boundary of the units, many fine legal distinctions have been drawn over the years; and the parties often rely on these legalistic NLRB or arbitration rulings to modify the boundary to fit changing technologies or organizational practices. If, as we fully expect, these issues become more common in the future as new technologies and new ways of organizing work are adopted, the parties may need to find better ways of resolving the issues than through arbitration or NLRB precedents. As the arbitrator quoted in Box 4–3 observed, it is generally preferable for the parties to develop their own principles for handling these issues as they arise, rather than to rely on an arbitrator to devise a viable solution after the fact.

The Japanese industrial relations system and some European systems may be better suited to respond to changing technologies than the U.S. system because they include both blue- and white-collar workers within the same union and the same election or bargaining unit. In Japan, for example, *enterprise unions* represent all blue- and white-collar workers within a single firm. In Germany, most industrial unions include both the blue- and the white-collar workers employed within a company and an industry. In Great Britain, on the other hand, a tradition of not only separate blue- and white-collar unions but also a greater reliance on craft unions makes this problem potentially more troublesome than it is in our country. Thus, we can expect that those industrial relations systems that make fine distinctions among election and bargaining units are more likely than others to face difficulty in adapting to the new technologies now spreading across industries.

Exclusion of supervisors and managers. The 1947 Taft-Hartley amendments excluded supervisors in the private sector from coverage under the NLRA. Section 2(11) of the amendments defines a supervisor as an employee:

> having authority in the interest of the employer, to hire, transfer, suspend, layoff, recall, promote, discharge, assign, reward, or discipline other employees, or responsibly to direct them, or to adjust their grievances, or effectively to recommend such action, if . . . such authority is not of a merely routine or clerical nature, but requires the use of independent judgment.

Thus, a supervisor is defined in terms of the duties the employee performs and the power the employee has to make key personnel management decisions or to exercise independent judgment. [6]

The Taft-Hartley exclusion of supervisors rested on the argument that if supervisors were allowed to unionize, they would become less loyal to management and less committed to the goals of their employer; become less effective in handling grievances, the disciplinary problems of subordinates, and other responsibilities; experience greater role conflicts; be less likely to cross a picket line when rank-and-file workers strike; and depend on the support of the rank-and-file union for their bargaining power.[7] Plainly, some of the opposition to supervisory bargaining reflects a belief that management deserves a set of loyal representatives of its own interests. The actual legislative rationale for this policy, however, rested on assumptions about the responsibilities supervisors had (outlined in Section 2[11]) at the time Taft-Hartley was enacted.

Two questions are immediately obvious. First, are the roles and powers of today's supervisors still the same as they were assumed to be in 1947? And second, would the negative organizational consequences hypothesized by the congressional majority in 1947 actually result if supervisors were given the right to organize? Since the public sector treatment of supervisors is, in fact, different from the Taft-Hartley approach, we can look for answers to these questions in the experience in this sector.

Those arguing for public sector supervisors' right to bargain point to the distinct managerial structure in the public environment. They argue that, unlike in the private sector, where supervisors are assumed to have the authority to make independent judgments on the critical personnel functions noted in the law, in the public sector those functions are more centralized in the form of civil service commissions and rules. Moreover, they argue, there are many more levels of supervisors in the public sector hierarchies, and thus many individuals with the title of supervisor do not serve as bona fide supervisors as defined in the law.[8] Some have also argued that the community of interests in economic issues between supervisors and their subordinates is greater in the public than the private sector. Others claim that public sector supervisors perform duties similar to private sector supervisors and therefore should be covered under similar laws. Consequently, most state laws do not *exclude* public sector supervisors from collective bargaining. Some laws, however, require supervisors to form separate bargaining units from rank-and-file employees.

More recently this question has become the focal point of a debate over the rights of college faculty members to unionize and bargain. In a test case decided in 1980 the Supreme Court ruled that the faculty at Yeshiva University had managerial responsibilities and therefore excluded them from coverage under the NLRA.[9] The Court reasoned that because the faculty members were involved in hiring, promotion, course assignment, and a variety of other managerial decisions affecting wages, hours, and working conditions, they fit the definition of *supervisor* embodied in the law. Thus, Yeshiva had no legal obligation to recognize a union of faculty members; and collective bargaining with faculty members in this university, as well as in several others, ended. Although many observers have criticized the logic of the Yeshiva ruling, and although the NLRB has subsequently found faculty members at several other universities to be eligible for coverage under the law, the debate over this question has recently intensified. The question now is whether the supervisory or management exclusion contained in the law is outmoded and in conflict with contemporary efforts to encourage greater decentralization of and employee participation in managerial decision making. [10]

Box 4–4 presents excerpts from an important discussion paper the U.S. Department of Labor issued to stimulate debate over this question. Schlossberg and Fetter, the authors, strongly argue that the supervisory-

---

BOX 4–4

Excerpts from "U.S. Labor Law and the Future of Labor-Management Cooperation"

More and more large and progressive companies are embracing labor-management cooperative programs tailored to the particular needs of their operations. . . . The Department of Labor supports and encourages the adoption of such cooperative efforts between labor and management. Yet such arrangements do not fit easily within the framework of labor and related statutes that evolved out of the confrontation and industrial conflict of the 1930's. For example, the Supreme Court, construing the legislative intent of the National Labor Relations Act (NLRA), wrote in a 1981 decision that "Congress had no expectation that the elected union representative would become an equal partner in the running of the business enterprise. . . ." More recently, two pace-setting labor-management agreements involved in GM's Saturn project were challenged as unfair labor practices. These charges were dismissed, but the mere possibility of their full prosecution has the potential to deter parties from attempting dramatic and innovative cooperative initiatives in the future.

The Department of Labor, therefore, has embarked on a study of labor laws and practices that may inhibit improved labor-relations. . . . The ultimate goal of the study is to reach consensus on policy recommendations for interpretation of modification of the laws so that they support both the ingredients and the goals of labor-management cooperation rather than conflict with them.

. . .The laws as applied embody certain concepts that may not reflect practical arrangements that make sense in the real world of dealings between labor and management. For example, in its 1980 decision under the NLRA involving Yeshiva University, the Supreme Court . . . concluded that the faculty members were "in effect, substantially and pervasively operating the enterprise." Therefore, as managerial employees, they were not covered under the Act. This conclusion, unfortunately, could jeopardize a desired method of operation . . . and, if extended beyond the educational setting, could cast doubt on the most innovative features of other cooperative agreements such as those in the steel and auto industries, among others.

Source: Stephen I. Schlossberg and Stephen M. Fetter, "U.S. Labor Law and the Future of Labor-Management Cooperation," executive summary (Washington, D.C.: U.S. Department of Labor, June 1986).

nonsupervisory distinctions found in the law are no longer compatible with the labor policy objective of encouraging employee participation and labor-management cooperation.

This issue will continue to stimulate debate in the years ahead. If the existing policy is not updated, an increasing percentage of the labor force is likely to be legally barred from collective bargaining coverage on grounds that were not anticipated when the framers of the Taft-Hartley amendments wrote the provisions excluding supervisors. Until such time as the policy is revised, practitioners and policymakers alike would benefit from more detailed study of the consequences of union representation, collective bargaining, and other forms of participation in organizational governance for "supervisors" and "managers."

One such study has been undertaken: an empirical analysis of the effects of supervisory bargaining rights on fire departments. [11] The analysis compared the job performance levels and the degree of management identification of unionized and nonunionized fire officers. Performance data for over 1,600 officers in 700 departments were obtained by surveying the fire chiefs and a sampling of officers. The results showed that the unionized officers were neither more nor less identified with the top management of the department than their nonunion counterparts. Instead, both union and nonunion officers were able to separate their roles as supervisors from their roles as employees. For example, the officers identified more with the goals of top management on such issues as discipline and the enforcement of rules, and they identified more with the goals of rank-and-file workers on such issues as wages and economic fringe benefits. There was also no consistent evidence that unionized officers performed less effectively than nonunionized officers. Interestingly, the vast majority of the fire officers surveyed preferred to be unionized.

The empirical results from this study of fire officers are not presented here to suggest that there would be no negative consequences for management if supervisors in all occupations and industries were allowed to bargain collectively. The unique nature of firefighting work likely provides a stronger bond or community of interests between rank-and-file workers and fire officers than would be found in any other public or private sector organization. Nonetheless, at least some of the fears regarding the consequences of supervisors' unionizing have not been realized among this particular group. Again, only further research into these consequences can settle the question.

In summary, first-line supervisors and middle managers are caught in an untenable predicament. On the one hand, changes over the years in technology, organizational decision-making processes, and personnel policies have reduced their power and status. [12] And as organizations continue to engage in experiments to give rank-and-file employees more influence over their jobs, supervisors' power and influence are even further reduced. On the other hand, they remain unprotected by the law if they engage in collective efforts to improve their conditions of employment. As we have seen, the changing role of supervisors and middle managers in large firms poses a serious challenge to the assumptions and doctrines that have guided U.S. labor policy for the past three decades.

The Conduct of Representation Elections

The central objective of public policies regulating union representation elections is to assure that employees are able to exercise free choice, untrammeled by false promises or information, threats of reprisals or promises of benefits, or misuse of economic power by the employer or the union. [13] To carry out this objective, the NLRB (and most state labor boards) attempts to establish "laboratory conditions" for the election process. A good deal of scholarly and political controversy in recent years has centered on whether the labor board is actually insuring free choice in elections; whether its detailed approach to regulating union and employer campaign conduct is achieving laboratory conditions; and, more broadly, whether the entire election process is working according to the original legislative intent.

Since 1974, labor unions have won slightly fewer than half of all the elections conducted. This figure has declined steadily since 1964, when unions won 61 percent of all the representation elections held. [14] In large, multiplant companies unions have had trouble even securing enough signed authorization cards to certify to the board that an election should be held. (Before the NLRB will schedule an election, at least 30 percent of the election unit must have signed an authorization card indicating they would like an election to be held.) Thus, most recent organizing successes have been in relatively small election units. A critical question in the debate over the policies governing these elections is whether the poor organizing record of the labor movement reflects some deficiency in the labor policies or simply the inability of the labor movement to attract workers into unions.

In 1977 and 1978 labor law reform bills were introduced in Congress. Vigorously supported by the labor movement and just as vigorously opposed by employer groups, the bills would have imposed harsher penalties on labor law violators; required stricter time limits on the election process, in order to avoid the delays that unions believe cost them votes; and provided more effective remedies for victims of unfair labor practices. Although the bills met an early death (H.R. 8410 passed in 1977, but its companion, S. 2467, died in a filibuster in 1978), the debate continues over the performance of the nation's labor policies. Advocates of reform often argue that the existing penalties for unlawful behavior by employers are too weak and the procedures for remedying unfair labor practices and for holding representation elections are too protracted.

Although few could marshal much empirical evidence in the debate over the reform bills, subsequent research has shown that delays do cost unions votes in these elections. Roomkin and Juris, for example, found a significant negative relationship between the median number of days from the initial petition to the election and the percentage of elections won by unions between 1952 and 1972. [15] Using published NLRB data, Prosten found that the proportion of union victories drops by approximately 2.5 percent for each month of delay in the election. [16] Another part of his study found that even among those unions that won a representation election, 22 percent failed to negotiate an initial contract with the employer and an additional 13 percent failed to negotiate a successor agreement to the first contract. Thus, more than one-third of the unions that won a representation election failed to develop and maintain a successful collective bargaining relationship with the employer. More recent studies have demonstrated that nearly 40 percent of first contract negotiations fail to produce an agreement and that illegal employer behavior during the election campaign (a signal of aggressive employer opposition to bargaining) further reduces the probability that a first contract will be settled. [17]

Another empirical study of NLRB election regulation practices paid particular attention to whether election campaigns are overregulated. In the 1970s Getman, Goldberg, and Herman studied more than 30 election campaigns and concluded that the illegal campaign tactics of employers and unions had little effect on either individual voting or election outcomes. [18] They therefore argued that the board should expend less effort in regulating campaign conduct (specifically, by investigating the accuracy of campaign statements; promises of benefits; or threats by either party). Instead, the authors proposed reforms that would deter employers' anti-union strategies carried out before the campaign. The authors argued that precampaign strategies may be a more important determinant of how employees respond to a union-organizing drive than the tactics used by either party during the actual campaign.

Our own analysis of data from a 1983 Conference Board survey reinforces and extends this conclusion that employer opposition or resistance to union organizing before the start of an election campaign significantly reduces the likelihood that a union can win the election. In the survey firms that placed a high priority on the labor relations goal of avoiding future unionization were twice as likely to win representation elections as those firms that placed a lower priority on union avoidance. Specifically, firms with a union avoidance strategy lost only 18 percent of the elections held in their organizations between 1975 and 1983, whereas firms that did not specify union avoidance as their top labor relations priority lost 38 percent of the elections held. [19]

The Conference Board survey data pointed up an even more important feature of contemporary union organizing. In new facilities opened by the firms surveyed, relatively few new union members were recruited through the normal election processes if management opposed the unions' efforts. Instead, the best predictors of the ability of unions to organize new facilities were, first, the lack of an employer strategy of union avoidance and, second, the presence of a dominant union in the firm. Our interpretation of these results is that it takes a large and strong union capable of engaging management at the strategic level of decision making to neutralize employer opposition to new union organizing. This is definitely not a feature of the election or union recognition process envisioned in the NLRA, but as we will see, it is one of the most controversial issues in labor-management relations today.

Indeed, the loss of confidence in election procedures has led several unions to adopt more aggressive *corporate campaigns* and other tactics designed to achieve employer neutrality and thereby increase the chances of organizing new workers. Corporate campaigns involve a variety of union efforts to bring public, financial, or political pressures to bear on top management. In its extensive corporate campaign against the J.P. Stevens Company in the late 1970s, the Amalgamated Clothing and Textile Workers Union (ACTWU) waged a successful national boycott of Stevens products, threatened to withdraw the union pension funds from banks that had officers on Stevens' board, and eventually, after almost a decade of effort, negotiated its first contract with the company in 1981. Similar efforts have been mounted in recent years in attempts to organize the operations of such firms as Beverly Nursing Homes and Litton Industries.

Most of the campaigns have been accompanied by strategies designed to influence the target firm indirectly by pressuring individuals or other firms that do business with or have interlocking directorates with the firm. Unlike the other forms of union-management interactions at the strategic level, corporate campaigns tend to have very specific, short-term objectives, namely, to continue the pressure on the firm only as long as it takes to change the company's policies and achieve the specific organizing or bargaining objectives of concern. Although the record of these efforts is mixed, their increasing use by the labor movement attests to the unfairness labor leaders perceive and the frustrations they have experienced with the election process as it has been administered by the NLRB.

The Getman, Goldberg, and Herman study led to considerable debate and controversy, both in public policy circles and among legal and empirical researchers. [20] The NLRB, for example, has twice reversed its policies regarding regulation of campaign statements: first abandoning the policy of detailed regulation, and then reinstating the policy. Each time, members of the board used the results found by Getman and his colleagues to justify their opinions. [21] In recent years reanalysis of the Getman data [22] and other analyses of data on NLRB elections and initial contract negotiations have yielded a range of evidence suggesting that, although Getman, Goldberg, and Herman may have been correct in arguing that the NLRB is incapable of distinguishing between legal and illegal employer conduct, employer strategies both before and during election processes significantly reduce the probability that a union will win an election. Moreover, it also appears that employer opposition significantly reduces the chances that a union that wins a representation election will be successful in negotiating a first contract. [23] Finally, in a broad survey of evidence from the studies conducted in recent years, Freeman and Medoff noted that over the 1970s there was a fivefold increase in the number of workers illegally discharged for union-organizing activity. Further, they concluded that this increased level of employer opposition accounted for as much as 40 percent of the decline in union victories in representation elections. [24] This evidence has led legal experts to suggest various labor law reforms designed to speed up the election process and to overcome protracted managerial resistance. Box 4–5 summarizes a number of these recommendations.

In sum, although further research is needed on these issues, any future policy debate over the procedures governing representation elections will

---

BOX 4–5
Selected proposals for reforming representation election procedures

1. Provide unions with rights of access to employees for campaign purposes equal to the access enjoyed by employers.

2. Stop attempting to regulate statements by employers or unions made as part of election campaigns.

3. Speed up the enforcement of current rules governing elections, and strengthen the penalties imposed on violators of the law by:
   a. using court injunctions to stop and/or remedy serious violations of the law, such as discriminatory discharges during campaigns;
   b. reinstating employees quickly, in time to allow union supporters to return to employment *before* the campaign is over and the vote is held;
   c. allowing employees or the union to sue for civil damages in cases of an employer's willful violation of an employee's rights; and
   d. lifting the constraint on the amount of the settlement available to an employee in cases where employer conduct exhibits a consistent pattern of illegal behavior. (Under current law a court can only award a settlement equal to the wages lost by an employee since the time of discharge).

4. Conduct speedy elections, with a very short time allowed for campaigning.

5. Strengthen the ability of a union to strike to achieve a first contract by eliminating the ability of an employer to permanently replace strikers and by allowing other workers to boycott the goods of an employer on strike.

6. Require arbitration of first contracts if an impasse occurs.

Sources: Paul C. Weiler, "Milestone or Millstone: The Wagner Act at Fifty," in *Arbitration 1985: Law and Practice,* ed. Walter J. Gershenfeld, 37–67 (Washington, D.C.: Bureau of National Affairs, 1986); Charles J. Morris, *American Labor Policy: A Critical Appraisal of the National Labor Relations Act* (Washington, D.C.: Bureau of National Affairs, 1987).

benefit from taking into account at least the following general conclusions from the empirical research conducted since the 1978 debate over labor law reform:

1. Legal and illegal employer opposition before and during organizing drives has increased over the past 15 years.
2. Delays in completing elections and employer opposition before and during election campaigns and initial contract negotiations significantly reduce the probability that the union will win the election or successfully establish a new bargaining relationship.

New Experiments with Voluntary Recognition

Employers' voluntary recognition of a union and their neutrality in elections held in newly opened establishments have declined relative to their prevalence in the 1940s and 1950s. Nonetheless, these stances of management's not only remain important features of many bargaining relationships, but in recent years they have become more common topics of discussion in labor-management circles. Several examples of cases where voluntary recognition has been the pattern will illustrate its pivotal role in contemporary collective bargaining.

Xerox Corporation has a bargaining relationship with ACTWU that dates back to the 1930s. Because Joseph Wilson, the company's founder, believed strongly in the value of a positive labor-management climate and relationship, the company has historically remained neutral or unopposed to ACTWU's representing Xerox production and maintenance workers when the company opened new plants. (Yet it is still the union's responsibility to seek and achieve recognition, either through an election or by presenting management with evidence that a majority of the workers have signed cards authorizing the union to represent them.) Partly as a result (and partly, perhaps, as a cause), relationships between the union and the company have been quite cooperative and innovative over the years. Xerox and ACTWU have been pioneers in introducing a variety of forms of employee participation and work organization redesign into their manufacturing bargaining units. Recently, the parties extended their participation efforts to joint discussions of where to build a new plant and how to design its work system.

The history of union recognition and its relationship to the existing bargaining units at General Motors Corporation is equally instructive. In the early 1970s GM opened a number of new, nonunion plants in the South and was successful in keeping them nonunion despite United Automobile Workers (UAW) efforts to organize them. But in its 1976 negotiations with the company, the UAW insisted that GM agree to remain neutral in future organizing efforts in the new plants, and the union prevailed. Then in 1979 the parties agreed to an "accretion" clause, which provided that any new plants opened that did work traditionally done by UAW members would automatically be included in the bargaining unit and represented by the union. The union achieved these provisions by making it clear to the company that the UAW could not continue to cooperate with GM in expanding QWL and other joint activities in existing sites if the company was determined to fight the union over union representation rights in the new facilities.

In 1985 GM and the UAW took this process one step further by jointly planning the design of the labor-management relationship and the work system to be included in a new division of the corporation created to build small cars. The agreement governing this new Saturn Division raised serious objections from conservative, anti-union groups. They argued that the agreement violated the NLRA because it established union recognition before employees had been hired and therefore did not give the new employees an opportunity to vote for or against union representation. Although the NLRB rejected this argument and allowed the recognition to stand, this chain of events represents another departure from the election procedures called for in the law.

The Xerox and GM cases illustrate a development in contemporary collective bargaining that is still the exception rather than the rule but that is nonetheless likely to be the subject of continuing experimentation and debate. Union leaders are increasingly arguing that the price for their continued cooperation and flexibility in existing bargaining relationships is that management provide unions an effective opportunity to benefit from new investments and to represent employees in new establishments. Management likewise often takes the position that its acceptance of the union in new establishments is contingent on the union's accepting a new role in the relationship—one demonstrating greater flexibility in the organization of work and a sustained commitment to greater employee participation and labor-management cooperation. Thus, one of the key strategic choices facing labor and management in the future is whether to continue the highly contested representation election process at the risk of limiting union-management cooperation in existing as well as future relationships or to agree to accept voluntary recognition of the union in return for a different type of union-management relationship. The Saturn agreement is only the most visible of several that might become a model for those who make the latter decision.

Another innovative solution to a novel recognition case involved a union in Ohio that sought to represent migrant farmworkers employed by tomato and cucumber growers. The Campbell Soup Company, the major purchaser of the produce, was also a party to this case since the union believed Campbell had a good deal of influence over the growers. For several years, the union, the Farm Labor Organizing Committee (FLOC), had sponsored a nationwide boycott of Campbell's products in an effort to pressure the company into insisting the growers abandon their opposition to the farmworkers' attempts to organize. Finally, in 1985 the parties selected a commission of labor experts to mediate the conflict. After a year of study and mediation, the commission handed down a decision on the terms of employment for workers employed by the growers—including specified procedures for determining whether the FLOC should (or did, in fact) represent the workers of a particular grower. [25]

Types of Bargaining Units

Bargaining units in the United States exhibit a wide variety of structures. Recall that we define bargaining structure as "the scope of employees and employers covered or affected by the bargaining agreement." For our purposes, then, we can identify the two primary characteristics of a bargaining structure as: the scope of employee or union interests represented in the unit, which we will classify as *narrow* or *broad*; and the scope of employer interests represented in the unit, which are classified as *centralized* or *decentralized*.

Figure 4–1 illustrates this classification of bargaining structures in matrix form. The horizontal axis of the matrix depicts the breadth of employee interests. As in the case of an election unit, a narrow bargaining unit might include only those craft, skilled, or professional employees within one narrow occupational class. Police, firefighters, teachers, plumbers, and airline pilots are examples of occupations typically represented in narrow, craft units. A broad unit, on the other hand, might include all the production and maintenance employees in an organization. The broad unit is the most common type found in the manufacturing sector.

The vertical axis of Figure 4–1 depicts the range, or the degree of centralization, of employer interests in the bargaining unit. A unit representing

FIGURE 4–1
The four main types of bargaining units, with industrial and occupational examples

	Employer interests covered	
Employee interests covered :	Centralized	Decentralized
Narrow	Airlines Construction trades Hotel associations Interstate trucking Longshoring Railroad crafts	Federal employees Firefighters Police officers Printing and publishing Teachers

Broad	Automobiles
	Coal mining (underground)
	Electrical machinery
	Farm equipment
	Paper
	Retail food
	State government
	Steel
		Chemicals
		Oil refineries
		Public utilities
		Many small
		    manufacturing
		    plants and
		    industrial unions

only one plant or establishment is an example of a decentralized bargaining unit, whereas a multiplant, single-employer bargaining unit is a more centralized unit. The units found in the auto, rubber, telephone, copper, and oil industries are examples of the latter structure. In these industries employers with more than one plant negotiate a single contract covering employees in all their plants as opposed to having a separate contract for each plant. In most cases these *master agreements* are supplemented with local agreements that cover those working conditions specific to a given plant. The most centralized units are the multiemployer bargaining units. In industries such as construction, longshoring, underground coal mining, hotels, railroads, and (in some cities) hospitals, employer associations negotiate contracts covering a number of different employers either within a given locality (such as all of the voluntary hospitals in New York City) or within an industry (such as those coal producers that are members of the Bituminous Coal Operators' Association).

A more detailed classification of the degree of centralization in collective bargaining structures is presented in Table 4–1. Listed there, for the years 1961 and 1975, are the percentages of major bargaining agreements (those with 1,000 or more employees) negotiated in (1) single-employer, single-plant, (2) single-employer, multiplant, and (3) multiplant units. The table demonstrates that the majority of manufacturing industries negotiate in the single-employer structures, whereas the majority of nonmanufacturing industries negotiate in multiemployer structures.

The data in Table 4–1 are also useful in comparing the prevalence of the different structures in 1961 and in 1975. In general, little changed over the intervening years. Thus, although there was a growth in centralization from the passage of the Wagner Act to the 1960s, at least for major bargaining units, bargaining structures were generally stable from 1960 through the 1970s.

Unfortunately, comparable data on the distribution of formal structures of bargaining in the 1980s do not exist, and so we cannot provide an exact profile of contemporary bargaining structures. Nonetheless, there is ample evidence to conclude that both the number of agreements and the number of workers covered under centralized structures have declined to a considerable extent. Industries as diverse as steel, trucking, coal, and rubber have all experienced reductions in the percentage of the industry's work force covered by centralized bargaining structures. If we also consider data on the declining extent of pattern bargaining, the movement toward greater decentralization looks even more profound.

The steel industry provides the most vivid example of this decline. At the beginning of the 1970s the ten largest steel companies negotiated as a group (although formally each company signed a separate contract). But by 1982 the number of companies that participated in the industry association had shrunk to eight; and by 1986 the association had disbanded, and bargaining with the seven remaining firms began to take place on a company-by-company basis. Although the settlements that resulted carried through many

TABLE 4–1
The distribution of bargaining unit types in major agreements, 1961 and 1975

Industry/ Type of unit	Percentage of agreements		Percentage of workers	
	1961	1975	1961	1975
Manufacturing	60.3	53.8	52.4	53.1
Single-employer, single-plant	25.4	25.8	11.0	13.2
Single-employer, multiplant	22.6	17.9	29.7	29.3
Multiemployer	12.2	10.1	11.6	10.6
Nonmanufacturing	39.7	46.2	47.6	46.9
Single-employer, single-plant	2.9	3.3	1.4	1.5
Single-employer, multiplant	13.4	9.9	11.4	10.1
Multiemployer	23.5	33.0	34.0	35.3
	———	———	———	———
Total	100.0	100.0	100.0	100.0
All industries				
Single-employer, single-plant	28.3	29.1	13.5	14.7
Single-employer, multiplant	36.0	27.8	41.1	39.5
Multiemployer	35.7	43.1	46.6	45.8
	———	———	———	———
Total	100.0	100.0	100.0	100.0
Number of agreements	1,733	1,514		
Number of workers			8,308,000	7,069,750

Sources: For 1961 data, "Major Union Contracts in the United States, 1961," *Monthly Labor Review* (October 1962): 1137; U. S. Department of Labor, Bureau of Labor Statistics, *Characteristics of Major Collective Bargaining Agreements, July 1, 1975,* bulletin 1957 (Washington, D.C.: GPO, 1977), 12. For 1975 data, David B. Lipsky; unpublished data used with his permission.

Note: A major collective bargaining agreement is defined as one covering 1,000 or more workers.

of the common features of the earlier ones, significant variations across the agreements were introduced—variations in wages, fringe benefits, profit sharing, work rules, and the extent of employee participation in management decision making.

Among the nonmanufacturing industries trucking and coal mining have witnessed major reductions in both the number of firms and the number of workers covered by multiemployer or industrywide contracts. In communications (as noted in Box 4–1) the national contract of the 1970s covering all Bell System employees gave way to greater decentralization following AT&T's divestiture of the regional telephone companies in 1984.

Thus, although we lack precise estimates of the magnitude of decentralization in bargaining that has occurred in recent years, we have no doubt that the stability that characterized bargaining structures in the two decades before 1980 has ended. For a better understanding of why these changes have occurred, we now turn to a discussion of the factors that influence the parties' choice of a bargaining structure.

DETERMINANTS OF BARGAINING STRUCTURES

The major forces affecting the degree of centralization in formal bargaining structures are illustrated in Figure 4–2. Centralization can take the form of either multiemployer bargaining (as is more common in nonmanufacturing industries) or single-employer, multiplant bargaining. Centralization can

FIGURE 4–2
A model of the main forces affecting centralization in bargaining structures

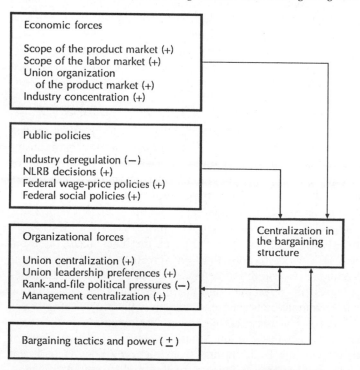

Note: The plus (and minus) signs indicate whether the variable has a positive (or negative) effect on the degree of centralization.

also occur more informally through pattern bargaining arrangements. We need to distinguish how different factors lead to each form of centralization; but first, we will outline a number of the common factors that affect the degree of centralization.

Economic Forces

The choice of an appropriate bargaining unit depends heavily on the nature of the product and labor markets in which the union and the employer operate. [26] As pointed out in Chapter 3, unions will seek to take wages out of competition by organizing as much of the product market as possible and by insuring that equal wages are paid to workers performing the same work within the relevant market. One of the primary mechanisms for insuring that wages are taken out of competition is to expand the formal or informal bargaining structure to correspond with the scope of the market. But to achieve a high degree of centralization, unions usually must first organize a large proportion of the product market and then successfully maintain union coverage over time—a tall order.

As noted in Chapter 3, in his famous essay on the Philadelphia shoemakers John R. Commons described the effects of the product market expansion that had come about in the early 1800s because of improved transportation. [27] As it became possible for nonunion shoemakers outside the Philadelphia area to transport their products into the Philadelphia market and sell them at a low price, the bargaining power of the unionized shoemakers in Philadelphia was weakened. It therefore became important for the Philadelphia shoemakers to organize their fellow shoemakers from the surrounding areas and to see them covered under the same wage agreement to equalize the price of labor.

A similar product market effect holds for localized industries with a large number of competitive employers. Unions of construction workers, for example, have a strong incentive to equalize the wage costs among competitive bidders on the same project. Thus, in the construction industry bargaining tends to occur on a multiemployer basis in local, regional, or national markets depending on the geographic distribution of the employers that will bid on specific projects. The structure of bargaining in residential or small-scale commercial construction tends to be localized, since few construction companies will move their operations to a distant location for only small jobs. Highway construction firms, on the other hand, often bid on contracts across a wider region, therefore creating stronger pressures for regional bargaining. Construction contracts for large industrial facilities such as power plants, oil refineries, and chemical plants are often bid on by national or international construction companies; therefore, some issues affecting the labor costs of these large projects are negotiated either on a specific project-by-project basis or on a national level, with coalitions of national unions or with the Building and Construction Trades Department of the AFL–CIO. Furthermore, as the size of the product market changes, pressures to change the structure of bargaining inevitably result.

Nonetheless, we must note that the percentage of the market for unionized construction work has declined in the 1980s; and as it has, more and more individual contractors have been resisting areawide or multiemployer contracts and seeking instead single-employer agreements. [28] In some cases area or regional union-management committees have been established to negotiate simplified contracts that eliminate cross-jurisdictional conflicts among craft unions. Both of these developments indicate how pressures from nonunion competition in the product and labor markets can produce pressures to alter traditional bargaining structures. The most common trend is for increasing nonunion competition to lead to greater decentralization of formal bargaining structures and to a weakening of pattern bargaining by making it more difficult for unions to take wages out of competition.

Unionized employers also have a major stake in making the bargaining structure responsive to the market structure in order to regulate the competition. The apparel industry is perhaps the best example: Employers have come to depend on the stability the apparel unions have historically provided to their highly competitive industry. To the extent that the apparel unions are unsuccessful in equalizing competition over wages by establishing a common rate for common work, those employers paying higher rates will lose business to the lower wage competitors. In an industry like apparel, where labor costs are a significant component of total costs, unionized employers are likely to be receptive to a union that can equalize wage costs and thus stabilize product market competition.

Public Policies

Another crucial determinant of bargaining unit structures is the NLRB's approach to structuring election units and to resolving disputes between employers and employees trying to modify the election unit or change an established bargaining unit. Unit determination decisions made by the NLRB in the initial representation election, along with rulings on unfair labor practices regarding efforts by one or both parties to change the bargaining unit, have major effects on the structure of bargaining. For example, for a number of years throughout the 1960s the unions representing General Electric (GE) workers attempted to engage in *coalition bargaining* but met with strong resistance from the company. The NLRB was faced with the decision whether to allow employees of multiple unions to sit at the negotiating table when the contract with only one union was under discussion. The board's decision to allow the unions to do so helped them move toward full coalition bargaining with GE. Other influential board decisions have been made on whether the employer can withdraw from the multiemployer bargaining unit after having given proper notice before the start of negotiations or only after an impasse has been reached.

Some have argued that the NLRB has exhibited a strong preference for larger bargaining units and thus has aided in the trend toward greater centralization. George W. Brooks has been one of the most articulate critics of the board's preference for large production and maintenance bargaining units and against craft severance. [29] He argues that the preference for centralization reduces employees' free choice among alternative unions and makes it impossible for individual members to influence effectively the direction of their unions. This, in turn, he believes, produces undemocratic and unresponsive unions. At the heart of this critique is the view that the NLRB has placed too high a priority on maintaining stability and predictability in collective bargaining at the expense of union democracy, employees' free choice, and representational effectiveness. Whether one agrees with this critique or not, NLRB decisions have no doubt encouraged greater centralization in the structure of collective bargaining.

A number of other government policies influence the structure of bargaining—if only indirectly. It has often been argued, for instance, that federal wage and price guidelines or controls encourage the trend toward centralization. That is, wage policies that are developed and enforced at the national level create pressures for centralized bargaining to influence these policies. There is little empirical evidence to date, however, that the wage-price guideposts of the 1960s, the formal wage-price controls of 1972–74, or the Pay Board of 1979 and 1980 had any lasting effect on bargaining structures. Nonetheless, the impetus for centralized bargaining in the steel industry has been traced to National War Labor Board (WLB) efforts to develop a national wage policy. The WLB has also been cited as a factor promoting the move toward companywide bargaining in the meat-packing industry. [30]

By far the most significant effects of government policy on bargaining structures have come in recent years from the deregulation of product markets in trucking, airlines, and communications. In all of these cases, the effect of deregulation has been to open the industry to new entrants that start on a nonunion basis, pay wages and benefits below the unionized rates in the industry, and, in turn, put pressures on unionized firms to seek new labor contracts that will allow them to tailor their wages and other labor contract terms in ways that will meet the new competitors. As a result, firms in all three of these industries are attempting to decentralize their bargaining structures.

In trucking, for example, before industry deregulation in 1980 the Teamsters had negotiated a national master freight agreement covering "over the road" (intercity) truck drivers. Essentially all the major trucking companies that hauled freight between cities or across the country were covered by this single, national contract. After deregulation, however, the influx of new, nonunion firms and small, independent contractors in the full-truckload portion of the industry—and intense price competition among the firms that remained highly unionized (essentially the "less than truckload" businesses that required large networks of terminals)—led to considerable decentralization. Several full-truckload companies broke out of the master freight structure and negotiated separate contracts with different wage payment and pension arrangements. Another set of firms negotiated separate employee stock ownership plans (ESOPs) in an effort to lower labor costs and restructure their operations. Still other firms that failed to adapt to deregulation went bankrupt or left the trucking business.

In the airline industry the effects of deregulation on the formal structure of bargaining have been less obvious. Nonetheless, the strong form of pattern bargaining that characterized negotiations across American, United, Northwest, and other major airlines before the 1980s has given way to a more varied pattern of company-specific adjustments, including two-tier wage agreements (that is, wage settlements that lower the starting pay rates of future hires), changes in hours worked, wage cuts, profit-sharing plans, ESOPs, and employee memberships on company boards of directors. [31]

There are yet more examples of public policies affecting bargaining structures. Efforts to force construction unions and employers to negotiate affirmative action programs have had a centralizing effect on some aspects of negotiations. For example, in the late 1960s the Philadelphia plan and other "hometown" plans were negotiated by bringing together occupational groups and employer associations in an effort to set goals and timetables for bringing more minorities into the construction trades.

Government efforts to encourage equal employment opportunities or to achieve other equal rights objectives have introduced other pressures for change in existing bargaining structures. A court decision enforcing a desegregation plan for the Wilmington, Delaware, school district required a consolidation of bargaining units covering teachers in the eleven school districts affected by the order. Again, the direction of this pressure has been to extend the range of employees and employers covered in a bargaining unit.

The examples of the effects of wage-price policies, industry deregulation, and government efforts to implement equal employment opportunity policies all illustrate how the government influences the structure of bargaining in a variety of ways beyond the express purview of the NLRB. As a general proposition, the more active the federal government is in economic and social planning and intervention, the more it will encourage further centralization of the structure of bargaining. Conversely, the more government policy promotes competition or deregulation of product markets, the greater the pressures to decentralize bargaining structures.

Organizational Forces

In addition to these economic and governmental forces, the internal organizational characteristics of employers and unions themselves have generated pressures to broaden the bargaining unit. In particular, the growth of large corporations and the increased centralization of managerial decision making over key policy issues have led unions to seek to expand the structure of bargaining. A fundamental principle underlying their efforts is that unions will attempt to expand the structure of negotiations to the level where the effective or critical management decision makers are involved.

AT&T, for example, has historically centralized its industrial relations policy making in its corporate headquarters in New York. In the 1950s and 1960s, however, the Communications Workers of America (CWA) still bargained separately with each state affiliate of the Bell System. Consequently, throughout the 1960s the union sought to bring about a more centralized or national bargaining arrangement. Although CWA succeeded in negotiating a national contract in 1974, the breakup of the Bell System into regional telephone companies in 1984 forced a return to decentralized bargaining at the regional company level. But since AT&T remained a company of national scope with a centralized management, bargaining on behalf of AT&T employees remained centralized at the national level.

On the other hand, management may attempt to counter union centralization with a centralization of managerial decision-making power. In the 1950s James R. Hoffa, president of the Teamsters, moved to consolidate his own power within the union by centralizing the structure of bargaining for the over-the-road truckers. As Hoffa's drive succeeded, employers moved to reorganize their own decision-making functions into a national truckers' association. Thus, the structure of bargaining for over-the-road truckers developed partly as a function of the preferences of a union leader for increasing his power within the union. But again, as the Teamsters lost market share to nonunion firms in the 1980s, pressure to decentralize bargaining to the company level led to a decline in the power of the management association.

Union structure and politics also affect the degree of centralization in bargaining. For one thing, the higher the percentage of employees organized by a single union within a firm or an industry, the higher the probability that the union will be able to convince an employer or a set of employers to bargain on a centralized basis. For example, in the steel, auto, rubber, and aerospace industries—each organized by one dominant union—most or all the workers in the major firms are covered by a single contract covering multiple plants in the company. But these are the exception in manufacturing. The more common pattern there is for a multiplant firm to deal with a variety of different unions and to bargain on a plant-by-plant basis.

In settings where no single union dominates in representing a firm's employees, the Industrial Union Department (IUD) of the AFL–CIO has attempted to coordinate bargaining. The success of this coordinated bargaining, however, depends to a great degree on the ability and the willingness of the different unions to work together and maintain the support of their rank-and-file. Long-standing coordinated bargaining arrangements can be found in the electrical products, glass, and machinery industries and in a number of highly diversified conglomerates such as General Electric, Pittsburgh Plate Glass, and Textron. In 1987 the IUD coordinated some 80 such contracts with its affiliated unions.

Other internal union pressures have acted as a brake on the trend toward centralization. Weber argued that "representational factors"—the need to maintain a community of interests, to avoid including too many diverse employees who do not share a common interest—help keep bargaining decentralized. [32] The best examples of these representational factors are in the public sector, where a good deal of bargaining occurs on both a decentralized and a craft basis. For example, even though the wages and benefits of police and firefighters are often similar, if not identical, there is very little joint police-firefighter bargaining in U.S. municipalities. The rivalry between these two groups and their history of separate organizations preclude formal coordinated or coalition bargaining in many cities, except in extreme crises.

Finally, union leaders' opposition to consolidated bargaining units or to formal union mergers acts as an additional constraint on the centralization of negotiations. The reasons for this are very simple. Any consolidation of negotiating units or unions means that some leaders are going to lose influence, status, and perhaps even their jobs. Consolidation increases competition for higher level union positions. When two unions merge, only one person can be the president of the new organization. It is difficult to negotiate mergers unless the two unions are blessed with a situation in which one of the established leaders is of advanced age and therefore can simply retire with dignity and financial security. The same problem characterizes consolidating bargaining structures in the bottom tier of the industrial relations model, since centralizing bargaining within a union means that local union leaders lose some of their influence, while the hand of the national union leadership gains strength. Local leaders, therefore, tend to resist these structures.

Tactical Considerations

Because the structure of bargaining has a crucial influence on the bargaining power of the parties, much of the jockeying for particular structures can only be understood as efforts by one or both parties to gain a tactical advantage at the bargaining table. For example, the efforts of unions to institute coalition bargaining in electrical equipment and other industries arose out of the unions' interest in maximizing their bargaining power and their ability to impose strike costs on the employers in those industries. Thus, the tactical or bargaining power advantages that each party believes it can reap from certain structures influence all of the debate and conflict over bargaining units.

Although unions were the driving force behind the coalition bargaining movement of the 1960s, it should not be inferred that unions always gain (and employers lose) a tactical advantage in larger or more centralized bargaining structures. In construction, local service industries (such as hotels, restaurants, laundries, and local truck haulers), and in some cases local hospitals, employers have found it to their advantage to form associations and bargain in multiemployer units. Consolidating the bargaining function allows employers to avoid being *whipsawed* by local union leaders who compete with one another by negotiating a bargain that is not only equal to but in some ways better than the ones previously negotiated. If carried to an extreme, whipsawing is never ending, since those unions whose contract settlements are improved upon are then under political pressure to catch up. Many observers argue that the many different unions in the airline industry were able to follow this whipsawing model until the late 1970s. Association bargaining in highly competitive local industries that may comprise a number of small and relatively marginal firms also helps to stabilize competition and partially insulate individual firms from the pressure of a strike, since all the competitors suffer equally when a strike occurs.

We will return to the question of the effects of the formal structure of bargaining on union power in Chapters 7 and 11, which examine management wage policies and the outcomes of bargaining. For now, suffice it to say that the structure of bargaining is an important tactical weapon that plays a role in the balance of power in collective bargaining.

The Nature of the Issue

It should be noted that even within centralized bargaining structures many issues are negotiated on a local basis. That is, in most cases the master agreement negotiated at the centralized level covers only broad issues, ones that are universal in scope, such as wage rates and fringe benefits. Issues that are either company- or plant-specific, such as safety and health conditions, seniority provisions, production standards, shift changes, and overtime distribution, are often left to more decentralized levels of the bargaining structure. James W. Kuhn proposed that the structure of bargaining extends even further down to the departmental or informal work group level, where individual supervisors and work groups often negotiate unwritten side agreements or in fact ignore certain provisions of the contract. He termed this activity *fractional bargaining*. [33] Indeed, one of the most important developments of the 1980s has been to push more issues down to the decentralized levels. In companywide structures such as in autos and steel, variations in work rules are now more prevalent than in the past. And within all structures, variation within bargaining units is more and more the case as QWL and other means of employee involvement take place at the level of the work group or team.

The Case of Multiemployer Structures

Although most of the general forces driving centralization or decentralization noted above apply to both companywide and multiemployer structures, a few more specific factors can be identified that increase the likelihood of the latter form's emerging as a stable bargaining structure. The vast majority of multiemployer bargaining structures found in the United States involve regional associations of relatively small employers that compete within a single industry and bargain with a single union. The pattern is widespread in retail foods, hotels, and specialized local construction.

The common factors leading to the development of these local multiemployer structures, therefore, are that (1) the product and labor markets are local or regional in scope, (2) the employers are small and highly competitive, and (3) a single union has organized a large proportion of the workers in those markets. Under these circumstances it serves the interests of both the employers and the union to negotiate a single regional agreement to stabilize wage competition. But where these product and labor market conditions are present but no single union has been successful in organizing a high proportion of the local labor force, employers can be expected to resist forming an association to bargain as a group.

Consider, for example, how bargaining structures in the retail food industry differ between Los Angeles and Boston. In Los Angeles the United Food and Commercial Workers (UFCW) and the Teamsters represent employees of firms holding approximately 94 percent of the market share. [34] Most of the major food chains are members of the Southern California Food Association and negotiate a single contract with the unions. In Boston, however, only one of the major food chains (the Stop & Shop Company) is unionized. This firm negotiates separate contracts with the UFCW and the Teamsters.

Two recent empirical studies suggest these patterns apply to the relatively few multiemployer bargaining structures found in manufacturing as well. Hendricks and Kahn have shown that multiemployer structures in manufacturing were more probable in the more highly competitive (less concentrated) industries with high labor costs where a single union had organized a relatively high proportion of the employees. [35] And Beaumont, Thomson, and Gregory have produced remarkably similar findings for British manufacturing as well. [36]

THE CONSEQUENCES OF ALTERNATIVE STRUCTURES

Unfortunately, although an enormous amount has been written about the choice of different structures, there is little systematic empirical evidence about their effects. Consequently, the discussion in this section will introduce only a few of the most widely held beliefs about the major advantages and disadvantages, or consequences, of each of the four types of units depicted in Figure 4–1.

Narrow, Decentralized Units

Narrow, decentralized units have often been criticized for hampering the parties' ability to adapt to technological change. These structures place perhaps their greatest constraint on management's ability to reassign workers to different jobs as the technology or the product mix changes. Consider, for example, the history of the craft unions in the railroad industry.

Before 1970 bargaining in the railroad industry was done on a craft basis. There were some 17 craft unions of "nonoperating" employees (those who work in the train yards or the offices rather than on the trains). For example, machinists, boilermakers, sheetmetal workers, railway clerks, and other craft employees each had their own separate union organization. Fourteen of these craft unions bargained as a coalition over some terms and conditions of employment, but the jurisdiction of each nonetheless remained clearly defined. In addition, five "operating" crafts—firemen, switchmen, brakemen, conductors, and engineers—bargained separately.

Over the last 30 years the railroad industry has suffered a general decline in demand because of increased competition for passenger traffic from the airline and auto industries. In its freight business the industry faced similar competitive pressures from intercity trucking. Moreover, the rapid adoption of the diesel locomotive in the period from 1945 to 1960 changed the overall technology of the industry considerably. The diesel allowed for longer trains with heavier loads, required less maintenance, and eliminated the need for the fireman on the engine crew. As a result of these and other technological and market changes, railroad employment declined from 1.2 million in 1950 to 343,000 in 1985, according to recent Bureau of Labor Statistics estimates.

Unfortunately, the craft jurisdictions in railroads—developed early in this century—made it difficult to negotiate transfers of employees across the craft lines or to merge seniority lists. The issue of the fireman, for example, was not resolved until after the firemen's union merged with three other operating crafts to form the United Transportation Union (UTU) in 1969. This merger allowed the UTU to negotiate the transfer rights of the firemen and meant that the union members' jobs could be saved while this craft faded into history. The important point here is that it is unlikely this kind of adjustment to technological change could have been negotiated without the change from a craft structure to a quasi-industrial union and bargaining structure. To this day, however, work rules, staffing levels, and craft distinctions remain controversial issues in railroad bargaining. [37]

Other examples of the effects of narrow, decentralized bargaining structures can be found in the printing and local construction industries. In printing computerized typesetting has all but eliminated the need for the work traditionally falling within the jurisdiction of the International Typographical Union (ITU). It is not surprising, therefore, that this union searched for candidates for merger over the past decade. In 1986 the search ended, with the ITU merging with the CWA. The ITU is thus another example of one of the major disadvantages of narrow, craft units: They make the task of adjustment to technological change more difficult and slower than it is under broader bargaining units.

One of the chief criticisms of the narrow and decentralized forms of bargaining units found in the local construction industry has been that they lead to a variation on the whipsawing discussed earlier in this chapter.

A modified form of whipsawing can occur in bargaining with a single employer. For example, an employer with a large number of different bargaining units can whipsaw the unions by seeking to negotiate a contract with the weakest unit first and then to force that pattern on the other bargaining units. Or the unions can hold back and wait until the strongest unit has negotiated a contract and then attempt to spread its terms to the weaker units. In either case, whipsawing in narrow units has the effect of destabilizing bargaining. Even if the effects of whipsawing on bargaining outcomes are indeterminate, the threat of multiple strikes against the same employer can pose serious problems. This has been a particular concern in the hospital industry, which came under the extension of NLRA in 1974.

Narrow, decentralized units often also suffer from the same problem as that facing the CWA in its efforts to centralize bargaining in the telephone industry. Decision-making power on the employer's side is often more centralized than the narrow unit structure. This is clearly the pattern in the public sector, in both municipal and state jurisdictions. For example, although police, firefighters, white-collar workers, and blue-collar workers almost always negotiate separate contracts with city governments, the government's control over major wage and fringe benefit decisions lies not in each of the departments that correspond to this unit structure but rather in the hands of the mayor and the city council. Thus, a good deal of rivalry over the allocation of scarce economic resources often develops in municipal bargaining. Furthermore, because the separate units are often subject to different impasse resolution procedures, city management often has trouble coordinating bargaining across these units and in engaging in systematic, long-term financial planning. (Indeed, labor and management officials in New York were able to save that city from bankruptcy in the 1970s precisely because they were able to devise and implement financial plans that covered all bargaining units.) The same is often true in state government, where the critical financial decisions are made by the governor and the state legislature. Over the years, therefore, the parties have moved toward greater centralization of bargaining at the state level. Some cities (New York, for example) have also reduced fragmentation by consolidating bargaining units. [38]

Despite the number of disadvantages we have cited for narrow, decentralized units, these units have one very important advantage: They maximize the community of interests among the employees covered by the contract. Because the constituencies of these units are relatively homogeneous, unions should experience less internal conflict in choosing bargaining priorities or in making trade-offs in negotiations. The same is true on the employer side of the table. Since only one employer, and often only one organizational level within the employer organization, is involved, fewer intramanagement conflicts and power struggles are likely to arise in using this structure.

Of all the bargaining structures the decentralized unit gives individual employees and the managers of the establishment or agency the greatest control over their representatives at the bargaining table and provides the highest probability that the terms of the settlement will be responsive to employee concerns. Consequently, this type of unit serves as an attractive alternative if the structure of decision making on the employer side is decentralized; if a strong community of interests exists among a group of craft or professional employees; and if the countervailing disadvantages of lessened stability or adaptability to changing technology do not outweigh these important advantages.

Narrow, Centralized Units

Many of the same problems of adaptability to technological change exist within the narrow, centralized bargaining unit. In addition to these problems, however, this unit sacrifices the major advantage of the craft unit; that is, maximizing the community of interests among the constituencies involved. For these reasons relatively few of these types of units exist. The centralized unit adds into the bargaining process multiple hierarchies of decision making and sometimes multiple organizations. The multiple impasses that result in bargaining with separate units on a companywide or industrywide basis work against the concern for stability in labor-management relations as well. The railroad industry (in recent years) and the airlines are good examples of this problem. It is not surprising that some of the most difficult bargaining problems and intractable disputes arise in these kinds of bargaining structures.

The main advantage of this type of unit is its ability to promote and enforce professional standards or rules of conduct among members of a specific occupation. The recent experiences of airline pilots represent a good case in point. After several years of concessionary bargaining and company mergers in this industry, the Air Line Pilots Association (ALPA) took steps in 1985 to limit the carriers' demand for further concessions by requiring the national union's approval of new contract terms negotiated in individual airlines. ALPA also began to offer more technical assistance and advice to individual units affected by airline mergers. [39]

Broad, Decentralized Units

The major advantage of broad, decentralized units is their closeness to the workplace. The community of interests and employee participation benefits of unionism and collective bargaining are more likely to be realized under this type of structure than under the more centralized structures.

On the other hand, this bargaining structure often suffers from not being centralized enough to engage management at the locus of its decision-making power. This problem is one unions fear most these days, as corporations move products and technologies from one plant to another.

Increasingly, multiplant firms are making new investments in individual plants contingent on the local union's willingness to modify work practices and other contract terms. Although this approach to reinvestment can enhance the employment security of the workers in a given plant, if uncoordinated by a national union, it can lead to a continuously downward spiral of wages. Local unions in the meat-packing industry have experienced this problem throughout the 1980s. The bitter strike of Hormel employees in Austin, Minnesota, over the years 1984–86 (see Figure 12–2) is only one of many such cases.

Thus, the broad, decentralized unit fits best in small manufacturing operations, single-plant employers, and employer subsidiaries that have the requisite autonomy in business strategies, labor relations policies, and operating decisions and that have a local or regional product market or nontransferable products.

Broad, Centralized Units

The broad, centralized structures represent the most complex form of collective bargaining. Here the community of interests and employee participation objectives are traded for increased union bargaining power and for improved chances of the union's taking wages out of competition. Obviously, these structures bring more diverse interests into the bargaining process and internalize many of the conflicts within the union and management organizations that would otherwise be reflected in conflicts *between* unions and employers. Thus, of the four structures these broad-constituency, centralized structures are likely to produce the greatest degree of intraorganizational conflict. They also are likely to require the greatest degree of shared decision-making power among groups within the different units. The 1977 negotiations between the International Association of Machinists and Aerospace Workers (IAM) and Lockheed Aircraft Corporation are illustrative.

Lockheed has several plants in southern California and a large facility in Marietta, Georgia. At the same time as the IAM contracts expired for the units in Marietta and in Sunnyvale, California, the union was also negotiating a new contract with Boeing Aircraft Corporation. A strike was in progress at Boeing when the contract deadline with Lockheed arrived. William Winpisinger, the international union president, favored delaying a strike against Lockheed to await the settlement at Boeing. But the local leaders in the Sunnyvale plant lost control of the membership, and momentum for a strike built. Contrary to Winpisinger's wishes, the Sunnyvale local went out on strike. To avoid internal dissension and embarrassment, the IAM president withdrew his request to delay the strike and called a strike against all Lockheed plants. Workers at the Marietta plant declined to strike, but nine days later they acceded to pressures from Winpisinger. As he stated at the time, "We explained [to the Marietta local] that you can't do that. . . . Either we are going to be a union or we are going to be out of business." [40]

As local union members and their leaders become more highly educated and vocal, the task of mustering a unified front is likely to become harder to manage. As a representative of the top IAM leadership put it, "Workers are brighter. They want part of the decision making. They question more. Guys are not going to accept things blindly today. Remember, the colleges are apathetic today, but in the work force you've got the product of the 1960s, people weaned on challenge." [41] In short, we have here an example of the trade-off between a union's quest for greater bargaining power and the internal conflicts engendered by a broad, centralized, and complex structure.

Although broad, centralized bargaining structures present the most complex problems of coordination and intraorganizational conflict resolution, they confer a number of compelling advantages on unions and on employers operating in national product markets with centralized decision making. In contrast to narrow bargaining units, the broad units with centralized decision making are better able to adapt to technological change and to support innovative job security protections for workers. [42] Since they carry with them a larger pool of workers, employers can more easily and effectively engage in long-term human resource planning.

There are advantages to these structures in other areas of industrial relations as well. For example, the costs of new fringe benefits can more easily be absorbed in large organizations. Greater professionalism in decision making on the part of both management and union—made possible by centralized, professional staffs—can increase the probability of achieving other innovations in collective bargaining. Furthermore, the parties have the luxury of being able to try out experiments in selected locations before extending untested approaches to the entire bargaining unit.

Thus, the challenge to unions in these structures is to develop mechanisms for reducing the extremes in the trade-off between the goal of maintaining a strong, cohesive union with sufficient bargaining power to inflict meaningful costs on the employer and the goal of participating in longer term strategic discussions with upper management while at the same time maintaining local union support and solidarity. For large employers that engage in centralized decision making, the challenge is to coordinate the firm's overall labor relations and human resource policies, while at the same time allowing local managers sufficient autonomy and flexibility to handle local workplace issues.

PATTERN BARGAINING: THE EFFECTS OF INFORMAL BARGAINING STRUCTURES

The consequences of any formal structures of bargaining are often blurred by the effects of pattern bargaining. *Pattern bargaining* is an informal means for spreading the terms and conditions of employment negotiated in one formal bargaining structure to another. It is an informal substitute for centralized bargaining aimed at taking wages out of competition.

Students of collective bargaining first began noticing the importance of pattern bargaining after World War II. The WLB had encouraged the development of pattern settlements, first, by attempting to fashion a national wage policy and, second, by making comparisons between proposed wage settlements and other industry, area, and national settlements a prime criterion for deciding wage disputes. The WLB's concern for making traditional or historical wage differentials among workers subject to "inequity" adjustments further reinforced the practice of making comparisons with other settlements an accepted wage-setting principle. [43] We do not mean to attribute all of the roots of pattern bargaining to the WLB, however. Even before centralized bargaining appeared, and in some cases before unions themselves, steel companies, among other concentrated industries, tended to adjust their wages in tandem by following the lead of a principal firm—in the case of steel, the U.S. Steel Corporation. [44] In any event, the principles developed by the WLB helped to legitimate and diffuse the practice of pattern bargaining.

Although there are no precise empirical estimates of the number of employees who are affected by some form of pattern bargaining, a 1977 Conference Board survey of bargaining in 668 of the largest unionized firms in the private sector found the settlements of large units do spill over to many other workers, both within and outside the firm. On average, the employers responding to the survey estimated that the pattern established in their largest bargaining unit affected approximately two and one-half times as many employees outside the unit and within the firm, and another four times as many workers outside the firm but within the region or industry. [45] We can conclude, therefore, that pattern bargaining is an important phenomenon among the major bargaining units in this country.

Some observers have argued that pattern bargaining has become insignificant in the 1980s. [46] This may be an overstatement, but there is strong evidence of greater variability in recent collective bargaining settlements across and within industries and even among different locations within the same firm. Moreover, as we will demonstrate in Chapter 12, the economic returns to unions from pattern bargaining seemed to decline in the early 1980s. We unfortunately lack any hard data on how much weaker pattern bargaining became; only additional experience and analysis will tell us whether the decline in the scope and effects of pattern bargaining will be lasting or temporary.

Interindustry Pattern Bargaining

From time to time economists who would like to see labor and management follow simple principles that link wage adjustments to macroeconomic trends look to Japan's "Spring Wage Offensive" as a model. During this annual bargaining process a tremendous amount of information sharing and discussion takes place among government, management, and labor leaders over economic trends and prospects for the coming year. Out of these discussions often emerges a general view of what the overall rate of wage increase should be for the next year. Then, individual companies and their unions "separately" negotiate increases that are consistent with this general expectation. [47]

The extreme diversity and decentralization of union and nonunion work places across the United States make this stylized version of Japanese practice impractical here. Yet over the years there have been periods when something that approaches an interindustry if not a national pattern has been visible.

Some interindustry pattern bargaining was evident, for example, in the major bargaining rounds of the decade following World War II. In the early 1960s authors of two separate studies divided the manufacturing sector into what were termed "key" and "nonkey" industries. [48] The key industries tended to be the highly unionized, more concentrated, heavy durable goods industries. The studies showed that wages in those key industries moved in identifiable cycles of bargaining in the postwar-to-1960 period and that average unemployment and profits for all those industries together were better predictors of the size of wage adjustments than were the specific economic conditions in each industry. From these results the authors concluded that interindustry pattern bargaining was a prominent feature of the collective bargaining system throughout the period in question. Yet the results also indicated that the national pattern settlements were limited to a subset of the most highly unionized, centralized, and concentrated industries in the country.

The most recent studies of the strength of national pattern bargaining have concluded that, although wage interdependence continues to exist among unionized industries, interindustry wage imitation was not as strong in the 1960s or 1970s as in the earlier bargaining rounds. Moreover, the industries participating in and moving out of the "national pattern" were not the same ones from one round to the next. [49] For example, a post hoc analysis of wage movements between 1965 and 1977 showed that the rubber industry dropped out of the national pattern and then rebounded to exceed the pattern settlements in 1976, whereas over-the-road trucking joined the pattern in the mid-1960s and, some might argue, set the pattern between 1970 and 1979 (by being the first major contract negotiated in the three bargaining rounds during that decade). Other entrants to the national patterns were the coal and telephone industries. But any semblance of a national pattern or a set of key bargains that cut across industries disappeared in the 1980s.

These examples illustrate the difficulty of using the *national* pattern setting–following process for either theoretical understanding or policy development. There is little evidence of sustainable national or interindustry pattern bargaining in this country. Furthermore, it is unlikely that any serious discussion of interindustry or national pattern bargaining will reappear in the forseeable future given the diversity of union and nonunion wage-setting processes.

Intraindustry Pattern Bargaining

Perhaps the form of pattern bargaining most closely identified with the New Deal model of industrial relations is the intraindustry variety. This form has become prevalent because it is one means for stabilizing competition over wages within industries or product markets. In addition, the existence of dominant unions within an industry facilitates the spread of negotiated patterns from one employer to another. The trade-off between meeting the pattern settlement and reaching a settlement that is responsive to the specific economic conditions of the firm and the industry is not necessarily a problem if the firms in the industry are similar in their size, ability to pay, and productivity. Yet, as we will see, this form of pattern bargaining has also withered in the 1980s.

In his classic study of intraindustry pattern bargaining in the auto industry, Harold Levinson pointed up a number of conditions under which deviations from the pattern settlement are found. [50] First, he noted that pattern following had declined considerably between 1946 and 1957. Second, he found that deviations from the pattern settlement were more likely in smaller firms, in firms that were less closely associated with the auto industry, and in firms with a severe inability to pay. He also concluded that union representatives gave virtually no consideration to wage-employment trade-offs until a "crisis point" was reached and the firm could document that a "clear and present danger" was associated with meeting the auto industry pattern. Only under these conditions were the union negotiators willing to agree to less than the pattern settlement. Unions in large firms were also strongly opposed to any deviation from the pattern. Their failure to achieve the pattern settlement with the larger firms would have severely threatened their ability to spread it to their smaller units. On the other hand, unions in the large firms were frequently willing to negotiate some productivity trade-offs to lower the costs of spreading the wage pattern.

The Levinson study suggests there is often a conflict between the national union's goal of spreading a wage pattern across an industry and the employer's goal of negotiating a settlement that reflects the firm's specific situation. Levinson found that this conflict is greater when national unions try to spread patterns across companies facing diverse economic conditions.

A number of problems result from overextending a pattern settlement to firms or to different parts of an industry that are unable to absorb its costs. Overextension is likely to reduce employment opportunities for the pattern-following employees, encourage the entrance of new competitors into the industry, and ultimately reduce the ability of the union to take wages out of competition—the original purpose of pattern bargaining.

In moderation, however, pattern bargaining serves an important set of functions in a collective bargaining system. It reduces the number of strikes, since it not only serves as a standard for the acceptability of a proposed wage settlement, but also helps to establish norms of equity among workers. It begins to play a dysfunctional role when it is overextended or when the terms of the pattern bargain conflict with the economic interests of employers and rank-and-file union members and with the larger society's concerns for price stability.

TOWARD A BROADER CONCEPT: ALTERNATIVE GOVERNANCE STRUCTURES

The formal and informal structures of collective bargaining in the United States have proven to be quite adaptable to the tremendous changes in the environment and the changing organizational needs of labor and management in the past 50 years. Yet if the trend toward greater experimentation with interactions above and below the formal negotiations process continues, more flexibility may be required in the future. Since labor and management in this country are only tentatively experimenting with these broader types of interactions at this point, we cannot draw on a conclusive body of research to specify what these new structures will be and how they will serve and be served by existing bargaining arrangements. Indeed, the need for further debate and discussion on this question is precisely the reason the U.S. Department of Labor issued the paper on the future of labor law excerpted in Box 4–4. In concluding this chapter, therefore, we will draw on models already in place in the industrial relations systems of other countries to point up a few possibilities the parties in this country might choose from. First, however, we should clearly state why some observers believe the structural concepts and arrangements embedded in the New Deal industrial relations system now need to be supplemented or modified.

The Current Structures: Problems and Challenges

Recall that the basic function of a collective bargaining structure is to provide a stable forum for labor and management to decide on issues affecting their vital interests. The New Deal legislation specified the negotiations process as the preferred forum and established a set of rules and election procedures governing the establishment of a bargaining relationship and rules governing the conduct of the parties in negotiations (doctrines governing the duty to bargain in good faith, the scope of bargaining, and so forth). A central hypothesis emerging from industrial relations research and practice in the 1980s is that critical decisions and activities affecting the vital interests of labor and management are under way well above negotiations, at the strategic level of decision making, and well below negotiations, at the workplace. Another hypothesis advanced in recent years is that unless the parties broaden the scope of their joint interactions to these levels, the U.S. industrial relations system will fail to meet its competitive challenges and fail to respond to the needs of the labor force. While a good deal of the experimentation now under way may be demonstrating the value of broadening the scope of interactions between the parties, public policymakers and private practitioners have not yet determined whether or how to diffuse these experiments to more settings.

The Department of Labor discussion paper does a good job of outlining a number of the structural features of the New Deal system that may be inappropriate in the current environment. We have cited many of these already in this chapter and so will only briefly outline them here.

First, new technologies, along with new forms of employee participation and work organization, are eroding the demarcation between workers and supervisors specified in the NLRA. What is needed is some means of encouraging participation and representation that cuts across traditional boundaries among bargaining units and beyond the boundary drawn by the NLRA.

Second, the scope of bargaining is limited by law to discussion of wages, hours, conditions of employment, and the *effects* of strategic managerial decisions that set these terms and conditions of employment. Yet effective representation requires early participation in the planning and analysis of multiple strategic choices involving such complicated matters as new investments, new technology, and new organizational designs. Further complicating these choices is the fact that assessing them requires knowledge of highly sensitive technical and economic data—data that must be kept confidential to protect the competitive advantage of the firm. The process of labor-management interaction can therefore be neither open to broad dissemination nor highly adversarial in nature. Instead, forums for consultation and joint planning are needed that promote information sharing, broad exploration of options without making firm commitments, and thorough analysis of the costs and benefits of different options—without risking public disclosure. The concept of managerial prerogatives that has evolved under the NLRA impedes these types of processes. Moreover, the involvement of labor representatives in these types of forums at the strategic level broadens their role and strengthens their power—two things that most U.S. employers have been and still are reluctant to do.

Third, participation at the workplace establishes another, often parallel structure to the traditional union and management structures for administering contracts. The exclusive role of the union steward or committee representative as the communications link between manager and worker and as the guardian of uniformity in contract administration is challenged by any direct involvement of workers. Workers from multiple bargaining units, nonunion workers, and supervisors in the firm must participate jointly and cooperatively if these processes are to succeed. Yet the tight boundaries drawn into our legislation regarding bargaining units and the differential rights and protections afforded those covered by collective bargaining and those excluded as supervisors or managers make joint participation by these different workers and occupational groups difficult.

Other, more specific problems with the existing bargaining structures will be noted in the chapters ahead, as we explore in more detail how the parties are, in fact, adapting their organizational practices and structures to accommodate these new forums for governing the workplace.

Foreign Alternatives

Despite the paucity of tried and true alternative structures for workplace governance in the United States, we can look beyond our borders to a variety of very different structures in other countries. Let us examine briefly just two such alternatives.

As noted earlier, the Japanese model of industrial relations rests on the *enterprise union*, which represents *all* blue- and white-collar workers within a firm and thereby avoids the boundary problems that arise under U.S. labor law and practice. Moreover, informal processes of consultation and participation in major strategic decisions are part of the informal norms and customs of management; [51] no formal structural arrangements for strategic or workplace-level consultation or participation are mandated by law. Some unions have, however, negotiated formal written policies that specify management's duty to provide notice of such impending issues as technological change. Finally, a good deal of participation, training, and flexibility in work organization, along with strong employer commitments to employment continuity, are embedded in the day-to-day administration of the workplace. [52]

The West German model (followed, to some degree, in several other European countries as well) takes a more formal approach to workplace decision making. At all work sites, the law requires that *works councils* composed of blue- and white-collar workers be established to advise management and, in some cases, to decide major issues affecting working conditions, such as new technology, layoffs, and safety and health practices. At the strategic level of decision making, *codetermination* law provides workers with formal representation on the board of supervisors (a body generally, but not exactly, analogous to American boards of directors). Again, because West German unions represent both blue- and white-collar workers within a given industry and firm, the industrial relations system faces fewer of the boundary problems of the U.S. system.

We do not present these two models as solutions that could be directly imported to the U.S. industrial relations system. Instead, we offer them simply as reminders that alternative governance systems do exist and should be more carefully examined for their applicability and adaptability to the U.S. context. We will continue to do so as we explore how labor and management are practicing both the traditional collective bargaining activities and new forms of interaction at the workplace and the strategic levels of industrial relations.

SUMMARY AND CONCLUSIONS

The structure of bargaining should fit both the nature of the external environmental (particularly the economic) conditions facing the parties and the organizational strategies and structures of the unions and employers involved. More generally, the task of a governance structure is to insure that employees and employers have an effective opportunity jointly to decide on issues that affect their vital interests. Failure to adequately match the structure to its external environment and organizational conditions will not only undermine this task but also engender other problems in the organization.

For example, overcentralization of the bargaining structure can result in:

1. heightened intraorganizational conflicts;
2. the inability of individuals to influence decisions and a loss of the industrial democracy and employee participation benefits of trade unionism and collective bargaining; and
3. the increased probability of major strikes that in turn may impose severe costs on the safety and well-being of a larger segment of the citizenry and, consequently, increase public pressure for governmental intervention.

Overreliance on pattern bargaining risks:

1. the imposition of wage settlements that are not responsive to the employer's particular economic conditions and may, therefore, threaten the firm's and the employees' economic security; and
2. reinforcement of an inflationary spiral by establishing a floor on wage settlements.

Reliance on too narrow or too decentralized a structure in the face of environmental and organizational characteristics that call for a more centralized or broader bargaining structure can result in:

1. difficulties in adapting to technological change or reductions in the demand for labor;
2. imbalance in the bargaining power of the parties;
3. imbalance between the level at which bargaining occurs and the level at which critical management (or, in some cases, union) decisions are made;
4. less innovation in bargaining and fewer opportunities for experimentation with new ideas;
5. more difficulty for a union in taking wages out of competition;
6. whipsawing; and
7. difficulties in eliminating internal inequities among employee groups within a given employer and, in general, more problems of administrative coordination for employers.

Failure to develop supplementary structural forums for consultation and participation above and below the level of the formal negotiations may limit:

1. the ability of workers and union representatives to influence major decisions affecting their interests until after those decisions are made;
2. diffusion and institutionalization of workplace processes designed to provide individual workers with opportunities to participate in task-related decisions and to contribute fully to enhancing their individual, group, and organizational performance; and
3. the opportunity of workers traditionally excluded from coverage under the NLRA to participate or be represented in the forums and policy-making processes governing their employment relationship.

Bargaining and governance structures therefore play a crucial role in the work organization's adaptation to changing environments, changing organizational needs, and changing needs for representation of individual workers. The contingent nature of all the decisions necessary to design a bargaining structure and other governance arrangements implies that no single structure suits all situations or all times. Moreover, any single structural arrangement involves a number of difficult trade-offs among competing objectives; and it also affects the overall distribution of power among the parties to an employment relationship.

Debates over the most effective bargaining structures and governance arrangements will therefore continue in the industrial relations community. The task for public policymakers and for labor and management is to design structures that are both responsive to current needs and yet flexible enough to allow the parties to innovate and adapt to change as time goes on. As we now turn to the strategies, structures, and internal operations of labor and management organizations, we will gain a better understanding of how well the present structural arrangements are working.

Suggested Readings

For discussions of the legal issues involved in bargaining structure, see:

Lewin, David, Thomas A. Kochan, Peter Feuille, and John T. Delaney. *Public Sector Labor Relations: Analysis and Readings,* 3d ed. Lexington, Mass.: Lexington Books, 1987, chap. 3 [for the public sector].

Morris, Charles J., ed. *The Developing Labor Law,* 2d ed. Washington, D.C.: Bureau of National Affairs, 1983 [for the private sector].

One of the most important books on the structure of bargaining remains:

Weber, Arnold R., ed. *The Structure of Collective Bargaining.* Chicago: Graduate School of Business, University of Chicago, 1964.

Three classic case studies of pattern bargaining are:

Alexander, Kenneth. "Market Practices and Collective Bargaining in Automotive Parts," *Journal of Political Economy* 69 (February): 15–29.

Livernash, E. Robert. *Collective Bargaining in the Basic Steel Industry.* Westport, Conn.: Greenwood Press, 1961.

Seltzer, George. "Pattern Bargaining and the United Steelworkers." *Journal of Political Economy* 59 (August): 319–31.

For studies of bargaining structures and conduct in different industries, see:

Lipsky, David B., and Clifford B. Donn, eds. *Collective Bargaining in American Industry.* Lexington, Mass.: Lexington Books, 1987.

Somers, Gerald G., ed. *Collective Bargaining: Contemporary American Experiences.* Madison, Wis.: Industrial Relations Research Association, 1981.

Notes

1. See Industrial Democracy in Europe Working Group, *European Industrial Relations* (London: Oxford University Press, 1980).

2. Ben C. Roberts, ed., *Industrial Relations in Europe* (London: Croom Helm, 1985).

3. Wolfgang Streeck, *Industrial Relations in West Germany: A Case Study of the Car Industry* (New York: St. Martin's Press, 1984).

4. Marianne Koch, David Lewin, and Donna Sockell, "The Determinants of Bargaining Structure: A Case Study of AT&T," in *Advances in Industrial and Labor Relations,* vol. 4, ed. David Lewin, David B. Lipsky, and Donna Sockell (Greenwich, Conn.: JAI Press, in press).

5. See *Mallenkrodt Chemical Works,* 162 NLRB 387 (1966).

6. Charles J. Morris, ed., *The Developing Labor Law* (Washington, D.C.: Bureau of National Affairs, 1971), 204.

7. National Labor Relations Board, *Legislative History of the Labor Management Relations Act* (Washington, D.C.: GPO, 1947), 400–410.

8. Stephen L. Hayford and Anthony V. Sinicropi, "Bargaining Rights Status of Public Sector Supervisors," *Industrial Relations* 15 (February 1976): 44–61.

9. *NLRB* v. *Yeshiva University,* 444 US 672 (1980).

10. James P. Begin and Barbara A. Lee, "Collective Bargaining Rights of Professionals," *Industrial Relations* 25 (Winter 1987). See also Barbara A. Lee and Joan Parker, "Supervisory Participation in Professional Associations: Implications of *North Shore University Hospital,*" *Industrial and Labor Relations Review* 40 (April 1987): 364–81.

11. Hoyt N. Wheeler and Thomas A. Kochan, "Unions and Public Sector Supervisors: The Case of Fire Fighters," *Monthly Labor Review* 12 (December 1977): 44–48.

12. Leonard A. Schlesinger and Janice A. Klein, "The First Line Supervisor: Past, Present, and Future," in *Handbook of Organizational Behavior*, ed. J. Lorsch (Englewood Cliffs, N.J.: Prentice-Hall, 1984).

13. *Sewell Mfg. Co.*, 138 NLRB 66, 69–70 (1962).

14. National Labor Relations Board, *NLRB Annual Report* (Washington, D.C.: GPO, 1985).

15. Myron Roomkin and Hervey Juris, "Unions in the Traditional Sectors: Mid-Life Passage of the Labor Movement," in *Proceedings of the Thirtieth Annual Meeting, December 28–30, 1977,* ed. Barbara D. Dennis, 212–22 (Madison, Wis.: Industrial Relations Research Association).

16. Richard Prosten, "The Longest Season: Union Organizing in the Last Decade, a/k/a, How Come One Team Has to Play with Its Shoelaces Tied Together?" in *Proceedings* (ibid.), 240–49.

17. William N. Cooke, *Union Organizing and Public Policy: Failure to Secure First Contracts* (Kalamazoo, Mich.: W.E. Upjohn Institute for Employment Research, 1985).

18. Julius G. Getman, Stephen B. Goldberg, and Jeanne B. Herman, *Union Representation Elections: Law and Reality* (New York: Russell Sage Foundation, 1976).

19. Thomas A. Kochan, Harry C. Katz, and Robert B. McKersie, *The Transformation of American Industrial Relations* (New York: Basic Books, 1986), 78.

20. A summary of the debate is in Stephen B. Goldberg, Julius G. Getman, and Jeanne M. Brett, "The Relationship Between Free Choice and Labor Board Doctrine: Differing Empirical Approaches," *Northwestern University Law Review* 79 (November 1984), 721–35.

21. See *Shopping Kart,* 228 NLRB 190 (1977), and *General Kait of California Inc.,* 239 NLRB 101 (1978).

22. William T. Dickens, "The Effect of Company Campaigns: *Law and Reality* Once Again," *Industrial and Labor Relations Review* 36 (July 1983), 560–75.

23. Cooke, *Union Organizing and Public Policy.*

24. Richard B. Freeman and James L. Medoff, *What Do Unions Do?* (New York: Basic Books, 1984), 233–39.

25. "Commission Report," report of the joint commission established by the Campbell Soup Company and the Farm Labor Organizing Committee, 19 February 1986, in the authors' possession.

26. Arnold R. Weber, "Stability and Change in the Structure of Collective Bargaining," in *Challenges to Collective Bargaining,* ed. Lloyd Ulman, 13–36 (Englewood Cliffs, N.J.: Prentice-Hall, 1967).

27. John R. Commons, "American Shoemakers, 1648–1895: A Sketch of Industrial Evolution," *Quarterly Journal of Economics* 25 (November 1919), reprinted and revised in *A Documentary History of American Society,* vol. 3, ed. John R. Commons, 18–58 (New York: Russell and Russell, 1958).

28. Herbert R. Northrup, *Open Shop Construction* (Philadelphia: University of Pennsylvania Press, 1975).

29. George W. Brooks, "Stability Versus Employee Free Choice," *Cornell Law Review* 61 (March 1976): 344–67.

30. See Ralph Helstein, "Collective Bargaining in the Meat Packing Industry," in *The Structure of Collective Bargaining,* ed. Arnold R. Weber, 151–77 (New York: Free Press of Glencoe, 1961).

31. Peter Cappelli, "Competitive Pressures and Labor Relations in the Airline Industry," *Industrial Relations* 24 (1985): 316–38.

32. Weber, "Stability and Change," 18–20.

33. James W. Kuhn, *Bargaining and Grievance Settlements* (New York: Columbia University Press, 1962).

34. This percentage is based on private survey data collected by the Joint Labor-Management Committee in the retail food industry.

35. Wallace E. Hendricks and Lawrence M. Kahn, "Determinants of Bargaining Structure in U.S. Manufacturing Industries," *Industrial and Labor Relations Review* 35 (January 1982): 181–95.

36. P. Beaumont, A.W.J. Thomson, and M.B. Gregory, "Bargaining Structure," *Management Decision* 18, no. 3 (1980): 114.

37. For a thorough discussion of technological change in the railroad industry, see Harold M. Levinson, Charles M. Rehmus, Joseph P. Goldberg, and Mark L. Kahn, *Collective Bargaining and Technological Change in American Transportation* (Evanston, Ill.: Transportation Center, 1971).

38. Between 1968 and 1977 the number of bargaining units in New York City declined from 400 to 97. *Annual Report to the Office of Collective Bargaining in the City of New York*, 1977, p. 10.

39. Kirsten R. Wever, "Changing Union Structure and the Changing Structure of Unionization in the Post-Deregulation Airline Industry," *Proceedings of the Thirty-Ninth Annual Meeting, December 28–30, 1986, New Orleans,* ed. Barbara D. Dennis (Madison, Wis.: Industrial Relations Research Association, forthcoming).

40. *New York Times*, 7 December 1977, A-11.

41. Ibid.

42. Thomas A. Kochan and Richard N. Block, "An Interindustry Analysis of Bargaining Outcomes: Preliminary Evidence for Two-Digit Industries," *Quarterly Journal of Economics* 91 (August 1977): 442.

43. National War Labor Board, *Termination Report of the War Labor Board* (Washington, D.C.: GPO, 1946).

44. George Seltzer, "Pattern Bargaining and the United Steelworkers," *Journal of Political Economy* 59 (August 1951): 322.

45. Audrey Freedman, *Managing Labor Relations* (New York: Conference Board, 1979).

46. Audrey Freedman and William Fulmer, "Last Rites for Pattern Bargaining," *Harvard Business Review* 60 (March-April 1982): 30–48.

47. Kazutoshi Kashiro, "Development of Collective Bargaining in Post-War Japan," in *Contemporary Industrial Relations in Japan*, ed. Taishiro Shirai, 205–58 (Madison, Wis.: University of Wisconsin Press, 1982).

48. Otto Eckstein and Thomas A. Wilson, "The Determination of Money Wages in American Industry," *Quarterly Journal of Economics* 75 (August 1962): 370–414; John E. Maher, "The Wage Pattern in the United States," *Industrial and Labor Relations Review* 15 (October 1961): 1–20.

49. See Robert J. Flanagan, "Wage Interdependence in Unionized Labor Markets," *Brookings Papers on Economic Activity*, vol. 3 (Washington, D.C.: Brookings Institution, 1976), 635–81. See also Daniel J.B. Mitchell, "Union Wage Determination: Policy Implications and Outlook," *Brookings Papers on Economic Activity*, vol. 3 (Washington, D.C.: Brookings Institution, 1978).

50. Harold M. Levinson, "Pattern Bargaining: A Case Study of the Automobile Industry," *Quarterly Journal of Economics* 74 (May 1964): 296–317.

51. Taishiro Shirai, "Characteristics of Japanese Management and Their Personnel Policies," in *Contemporary Industrial Relations in Japan*, ed. Shirai, 369–84.

52. Takeshi Inagami, *Labor-Management Communications at the Workshop Level* (Tokyo: Japan Institute of Labor, 1983).

CHAPTER 5

Union Strategies for Representing Workers

$\mathbf{A}$ union's primary function as an organization is to represent workers' interests. In carrying out that function, union leaders address a number of decisions on representational strategies. They must decide how much of their resources and energy to devote to organizing new members and how they will structure their internal organization to represent the existing members. They also make strategic decisions on the form of collective bargaining and other representational activities they will pursue. In recent years these questions have come to have renewed significance—even among well-established unions—as leaders have had to address whether and how to include involvement in strategic management or workplace issues as part of their representational strategy. In the face of an increasingly complex and often adverse bargaining environment unions have been forced to reassess two critical decisions: the extent to which they will pursue political and legislative issues; and the appropriate mix of federal, state, and local political or legislative activity they will pursue.

The organization of this chapter follows from this list of strategic options. We first examine the aggregate growth and membership of trade unions. The chapter then examines internal union structures for collective bargaining and focuses on the relationship between union structure, internal union democracy, and bargaining effectiveness.

We then discuss the extent to which unions have traditionally emphasized collective bargaining at the expense of other possible representational strategies and whether their traditional policies are meeting the expectations and needs of today's workers. Whether workers want to join a union and what they want their unions to achieve for them are heavily influenced by workers'

149

attitudes toward their work, their employer, and unions in general. We review the evidence on workers' attitudes and consider the linkages between contemporary workers' attitudes and the representational choices facing unions in the United States.

Our analysis of union representational strategies recognizes that unions are internally complex organizations and that a wide variety of factors shapes decision making within unions. We also recognize that no union has total discretion over strategic issues. Instead, the strategies unions employ to improve their bargaining effectiveness are constrained by other components of the bargaining system, as outlined in Figure 1–1. An understanding of unions as strategic actors, therefore, serves as an important building block in our comprehension of the overall industrial relations system.

UNION GROWTH AND MEMBERSHIP CHARACTERISTICS

Before exploring the factors influencing the growth of the labor movement, let us examine a brief profile of current patterns and recent trends in union membership. Recent data are of particular importance because they reveal a significant decline in union membership and illuminate some of the organizing and representational problems unions confront.

No single historical data series consistently tracks union membership over the twentieth century. Piecing together several different data sources does, however, provide a reasonably clear picture. Figure 5–1 plots union membership as a percentage of the nonagricultural labor force over the years 1930–85. As shown in the figure, union membership peaked during World War II and again in the mid-1950s, at around 35 percent. In 1960 approximately 31 percent of the nonagricultural labor force was unionized.

These overall figures mask, however, major differences in union membership trends between the public and the private sectors. Table 5–1 reports union membership data by industry from 1930 to 1985. Although the percentage of manufacturing employees unionized declined from 42.4 percent in 1953 to 24.8 percent in 1985, the percentage of government employees in labor unions rose over the same period from 11.6 percent to 35.8 percent. Thus, the explosion of unions in the public sector during the 1960s and 1970s stands in stark contrast to the decline in private sector unionization. Unionization in the service sector followed a different pattern. As Table 5–1 shows, the percentage of service workers unionized rose from 9.5 percent in 1953 to 13.9 percent in 1975 but then fell to 6.6 percent in 1985.[1]

The Loci of Union Membership

Before examining in more detail these membership declines and explanations for the declines, it is informative to look more closely at the loci of union membership. *Union density* (also called *union penetration*) levels show a remarkable diversity depending on the occupational, regional,

FIGURE 5–1

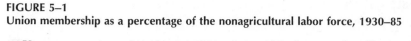
Union membership as a percentage of the nonagricultural labor force, 1930–85

Sources: Reprinted, by permission, from Thomas A. Kochan, Harry C. Katz, and Robert B. McKersie, *The Transformation of American Industrial Relations,* p. 31. ©1986 by Basic Books. The 1985 figure is from *Employment and Earnings,* February 1987.

Note: The September 1985 figure is the percentage of employed wage and salary workers in all industries, private and public, who were union members. In 1980, this figure was 23.0 percent.

and personal characteristics of union members. In 1984 New York and Michigan had the highest union densities in the nation, with, respectively, 39 and 37 percent of their labor forces organized.[2] At the other end of the spectrum were North and South Carolina—with less than 10 percent of their labor forces organized—and Texas, Florida, and South Dakota, with union densities of less than 15 percent.

Just as the majority of union members are concentrated in a handful of states, a majority of members are concentrated in a handful of large unions. Table 5–2 shows that in 1983 the five largest unions in the country were the Teamsters; the National Education Association; the United Food and Commercial Workers; the United Automobile Workers; and the American Federation of State, County and Municipal Employees (AFSCME). These five unions accounted for 31.6 percent of all union members in the country; and the ten largest unions accounted for almost half (48.1 percent) of all union members. Analysis of these data reveals there has been *no* sizable increase in the degree of membership concentration by union over the last half-century.

TABLE 5–1
Union membership by industry, 1930–85

Year	Total nonfarm	Manufacturing	Government	Services
1930	12.7%	7.8%	8.5%	2.3%
1935	13.5	16.4	9.0	2.6
1939	21.2	22.8	10.8	6.0
1940	22.5	30.5	10.7	5.7
1947	32.1	40.5	12.0	9.0
1953	32.5	42.4	11.6	9.5
1966	29.6	37.4	26.0	n.a.
1970	26.9	38.7	31.9	7.8
1973	28.5	38.8	37.0	12.9
1975	28.9	36.0	39.5	13.9
1977	26.2	35.5	38.0	n.a.
1980	23.2	32.3	35.0	11.6
1983	20.7	27.8	36.7	7.7
1984	19.4	26.0	35.8	7.3
1985	18.0	24.8	35.8	6.6

Sources: Figures through 1980 are from Leo Troy and Neil Sheflin, *Union Sourcebook* (West Orange, N.J.: Industrial Relations Data and Information Services, 1985). Data for the years 1983–85 are from U.S. Department of Labor, Bureau of Labor Statistics, *Employment and Earnings,* January 1985 and January 1986.

Recent research has shown that national union characteristics play a role in union success in certification elections. More specifically, unions with greater internal democracy, less centralized bargaining, lower strike activity, and larger size have greater success in organizing both blue- and white-collar workers than other unions.[3]

The two fastest growing unions in the country since 1970 (where growth did not occur through merger) have been public sector unions. Between 1970 and 1983 AFSCME gained approximately 409,000 members (plus an estimated 206,000 members of the Civil Service Employees Association, which affiliated with AFSCME in 1978), and the American Federation of Teachers nearly tripled in size. In addition, after 1970 the Service Employees (SEIU) and Communications Workers (CWA) gained large numbers of new members.

Union organizing successes have also varied by occupation. Table 5–3 presents estimates of the percentage of employees in major occupational groups that were members of trade unions in 1970 and 1980. Whereas 39 percent of blue-collar workers were organized in 1980, only 15 percent of the white-collar workers were union members. Within blue-collar ranks the highest levels of organization were in the semiskilled occupations (operatives and transport equipment operators), followed by the skilled crafts.

TABLE 5–2
Membership in individual unions, selected years

Union	Number of members (in thousands)			
	1983	1979	1960	1939
Teamsters	1,616	1,975	1,481	442
National Education Association	1,444	1,594	0	0
Food and Commercial Workers	1,203	892	364	66
Auto Workers (UAW)	1,026	1,520	1,136	165
State, County and Municipal (AFSCME)	955	942	195	27
Electrical Workers (IBEW)	869	922	690	136
Steelworkers (USW)	694	1,205	945	225
Carpenters and Joiners	678	727	757	215
Service Employees (SEIU)	644	597	269	62
Communications (CWA)	578	523	269	71
Machinists (IAM)	540	735	687	178
Laborers	461	537	443	158
Teachers (AFT)	457	452	56	32
Operating Engineers	436	452	282	58
Hotel and Restaurant	344	398	435	221
Municipal and local (independents)	329	320	0	0
Plumbers	329	338	261	61
Garment Workers (ILGWU)	303	396	393	202
Clothing and Textile (ACTWU)	251	316	273	240
Paperworkers	234	269	0	0
Postal Workers	226	263	0	0
Musicians (AFM)	219	274	260	127

Source: Leo Troy and Neil Sheflin, *Union Sourcebook* (West Orange N.J.: Industrial Relations Data and Information Services, 1985).

Service workers were less organized (16 percent). Since 1970 the percentage of skilled craft workers organized has declined, while union membership in the blue-collar service occupations has risen. Among white-collar workers professional and technical occupations were the most organized, at 22.7 percent, in 1980. Many of the unionized workers in those occupations were in the public sector, such as public school teachers. Only 7.6 percent of managers and administrators and 4 percent of sales workers were organized. Union organization of white-collar workers increased from 9.8 percent to 15.3 percent between 1970 and 1980, with the largest gains among professional and technical workers. Although unions still have not penetrated very deeply into the white-collar occupations, white-collar unionists are accounting for an increasing percentage of all union and association members.

Union membership levels also vary by demographic characteristics. In 1985, 22.1 percent of all men and 13.2 percent of all women were members of unions.[4] Since 1970 the number of female union members has increased

TABLE 5–3
Union membership, by occupation, 1970 and 1980

Occupational classification	1970	1980
Blue-collar workers	39.3%	39.1%
Craft and kindred workers	42.7	38.9
Operatives, except transport	40.4	40.0
Transport equipment operatives	n.a.	44.6
Nonfarm laborers	28.9	33.1
Service workers	10.9	16.2
White-collar workers	9.8	15.3
Professional and technical	9.0	22.7
Managers and administrators	7.5	7.6
Clerical	13.1	16.3
Sales workers	4.9	4.1
All occupations	20.4	n.a.

Sources: 1970 data are from the Current Population Survey of March 1970. 1980 data are from Courtney D. Gifford, *Directory of U.S. Labor Organizations, 1982–1983 Edition* (Washington D.C.: Bureau of National Affairs, 1982.)

by almost 10 percent, while the figure for men has decreased by about 6 percent. It is important to note that although women are still less prevalently represented by unions than men, the numbers as a percentage of all union and association members have been rising since 1970: Women made up 25 percent of all members in the mid-1970s.

Blacks and other minorities are slightly more likely to be members of unions than are whites. Bureau of Labor Statistics (BLS) estimates for 1985 indicated that 24.3 percent of all blacks and other minorities were union members, whereas 17.3 percent of all whites were. Union representation among blacks was up from 21 percent in 1970 but down from 27 percent in 1975. The net increase apparently reflects a growing movement of minority workers into the more highly unionized sectors of the economy.

Recent Membership Declines

By 1984, the BLS estimated, union membership among the total nonfarm labor force had fallen to 19.4 percent from its 1953 peak of 33 percent. The 1984 estimate most comparable to the earlier BLS measures obtained from surveys of national unions put the figure slightly lower, at about 18 percent. The declines were especially pronounced between 1980 and 1984, when the most highly unionized industries were hit hardest by the effects of the 1981–82 recession, by the declining competitiveness of U.S. manufactured goods on world markets, and by the economic and organizational restructuring under way within these industries. As Table 5–2 shows, from 1979 to 1983

FIGURE 5–2
Union membership as a percentage of wage and salary workers, by selected industries, 1970–84

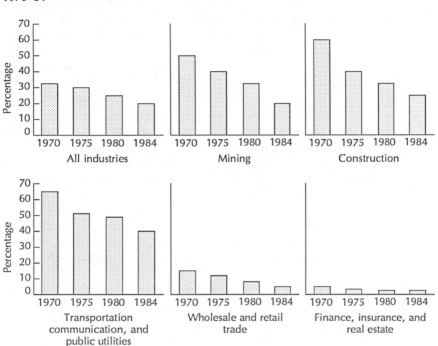

Source: Reprinted, by permission, from Thomas A. Kochan, Harry C. Katz, and Robert B. McKersie, *The Transformation of American Industrial Relations*, p. 50. ©1986 by Basic Books.

the Steelworkers lost 511,000 members; the UAW, 494,000 members; and the Machinists, 195,000 members.

Although these numbers demonstrate the seriousness of the decline in unionization, they conceal an even more important characteristic of recent unionization patterns, one we uncovered in several industry case studies we conducted. Over the 1960s and 1970s a significant nonunion sector emerged in virtually every industry we examined. Figure 5–2 illustrates the decline in the percentage of workers unionized from 1970 to 1984 in several key industries. For some industries such as petroleum refining (not shown), where union membership had declined from approximately 90 percent of all blue-collar workers in the early 1960s to roughly 60 percent in the 1980s, the change is not surprising, given the tradition of independent unions, decentralized bargaining, and elaborate personnel policies that bore the imprint of the industry's dominant founders. But the decline has also been dramatic in industries that have historically been viewed as strongholds of unionism such as mining, construction, and trucking.

In underground bituminous coal mining the nonunion sector has grown from virtually nothing to some 50 percent of the industry. Major companies are now operating completely nonunion mines, often in the heart of United Mine Workers territory, such as Kentucky and West Virginia. In construction nonunion shops have begun to arise even among large commercial operations. During the 1950s and 1960s open-shop construction companies had moved into residential and light commercial construction, but unionized companies continued to dominate the important, heavy construction sector. Starting in the 1970s, however, the situation changed; increasingly, major office buildings and large industrial sites are being built by nonunion labor. Overall, between 1975 and 1984 nonunion operations have grown from approximately 50 percent to 75 percent of all construction work. Over-the-road (intercity) trucking presents a similar picture. Since its deregulation in 1980 the industry has experienced a sharp transformation. Approximately 20 percent of the large, unionized carriers went into bankruptcy and were replaced by smaller, independent, and generally nonunion companies.

At the company level, data from a number of highly visible firms further illustrate this general trend. In the early 1960s General Electric had 30 to 40 nonunion plants, but by the mid-1980s that number had roughly doubled as a result of the new, nonunion plants that had gone into operation in the sixties and seventies. The drop in the percentage of workers organized at GE has not been as great as these figures might suggest, however, since the newer plants are smaller (often dedicated to producing a particular component), usually employing only about 500 to 1,000 workers. Companies such as Monsanto and 3M have seen a drop in the representation rate for their production and maintenance workers—from approximately 80 percent to 40 percent or less. Similarly, some of the major companies in the auto parts industry, such as Dana, Bendix, and Eaton, have developed sizable nonunion sectors. The most complete transformation has occurred at Eaton, where as of the early 1980s the only unionized operation to remain was at its main facility in Cleveland. Its other unionized plants had been closed down, and all the new plants opened are, to date, nonunion.

CAUSES OF RECENT UNION MEMBERSHIP DECLINES

Declines in union membership, as we have seen, have been widespread. Yet at the same time, those declines have varied in degree, timing, and location; as we shall see, they also varied in their causes. Figure 5–3 illustrates our view of the key forces that have interacted to produce growth in the nonunion sector since 1960.

Structural Changes in the Economy and the Labor Force

Employment opportunities in occupations, industries, and regions where unions had failed to make significant inroads burgeoned in the years after

FIGURE 5–3
The emergence of nonunion employment relationships since 1960

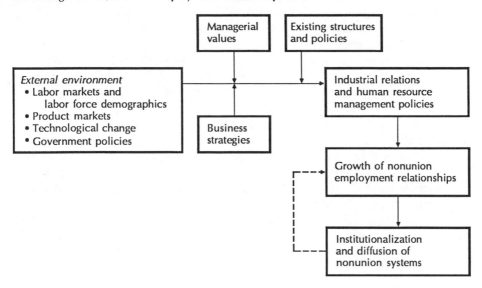

1960. Labor supply and labor demand grew in white-collar occupations, in the South, and in the service sector; and women began working in much greater numbers than before. Management in the United States had historically opposed unionization of white-collar, professional, and middle management employees much more adamantly than it had its blue-collar employees, and this fact alone goes a long way toward explaining how the relatively greater expansion of these occupations contributed to the growth of the nonunion sector.

One study has investigated the extent to which the labor force would have been organized in 1977 if there had been no change in the demographic, occupational, regional, and sectoral mix of jobs that existed in 1953.[5] The results of the regression analysis suggest that, taken together, these structural changes accounted for approximately 40 percent (3.9 of 9.4 percentage points) of the decline in the labor force unionized between the mid-1950s and the late 1970s. The greatest portions of that decline were attributed to shifts from blue- to white-collar occupations, from the North to the South, and from manufacturing to the service sector; each of these shifts accounted for about 1.0 to 1.2 percentage points of the decline. The growth in the proportion of women in the labor force, on the other hand, accounted for only about 0.5 percentage points of the decline.

It would be incorrect to infer from these results, however, that the union declines that resulted from these structural shifts occurred independent from management or union influences. The shift in employment to the South reflected, in part, management's decision to take advantage of the region's labor costs—lower than those prevailing in the more highly unionized North—and managers' belief that the social and political climate of the South reduced employers' vulnerability to unionization. Similarly, while employment opportunities were shifting to the service sector, unions did not follow suit by reallocating their organizing resources to take advantage of that shift. For example, the director of the AFL–CIO Department of Organization and Field Services recently noted that since 1974 only 22 percent of union representation elections have been in the service sector, where, based on its growth and size, he believes 70 to 80 percent of union elections should be.

Thus, although changes in the structure and composition of the economy explain an important part of the decline in unionization, a more complete account requires an examination of the interactions of external economic changes and organizational policies. These interactions involve the interplay among changes in product markets, business strategies, and management values (as shown in Figure 5–3), and they are discussed in more detail in Chapter 6.

Union-Organizing Difficulties

Some of the recent decline in unions' probability of succeeding in organizing attempts can be traced to declining incentives to unionize, and some, to the more intensive legal and illegal tactics management has recently used to defeat unions in elections. These assertions are borne out by data from national studies of union-organizing activities and outcomes and by some of the data from the Conference Board survey.

An analysis of overall trends in union election activity since 1950 showed that between 1960 and 1980 the number of elections held as a percentage of the labor force, the number of workers voting in those elections, and the unions' win rate in the elections held all declined.[6] As a result of these declines the annual percentage of eligible workers in the labor force that became newly organized fell from about 1 percent in 1955 to about 0.2 percent in 1980. That 1980 rate of new union organizing produced less than half the number of new union members that would have been needed just to offset the number of workers who left unions because they were leaving the labor force.

A more recent analysis of the effects of the declining returns to representation elections further helps place these numbers in perspective. In their 1985 study of these issues Dickens and Leonard concluded that "even if unions had continued to win representation rights for the same percentage of voters in certification elections [over the years 1960–80] as they did in 1950–54, their share of employment would still have fallen over [the later] period nearly as much as it actually did."[7] The authors further noted that union coverage would still have fallen even if unions had won 100 percent of all the elections held since 1950. Thus, a broader set of factors than just declining success in elections must be responsible for the decline in unionization over the past quarter-century.

Conference Board data have helped to round out that broader set of causes.[8] Of the firms that faced representation elections between 1978 and 1983, 80 percent won the election; that is, in only 20 percent of the cases did the union succeed in its organizing attempts. Union win rates were particularly low in those firms that assigned a high priority to union avoidance. Specifically, unions won only 17.6 percent of the elections held in firms that placed a high priority on union avoidance, whereas in firms that did not have that priority unions won twice as many elections, or 37.9 percent. Thus, a corporate strategy of union avoidance has a significant effect on the results of union-organizing efforts in a given plant or location.

Moreover, a regression analysis of changes in union membership in those firms showed that even if the union win rate had doubled or tripled, the new members gained would not have offset the losses incurred due to the previously discussed broader environmental and organizational forces causing membership declines. These data therefore reconfirm what the national trends suggest: Not only are unions faring poorly in the elections that are being held, but changing the outcomes of those elections would still not be enough to reverse the pattern of declining membership that has taken hold over the past 25 years. Chapter 4 contained a discussion of the controversy over how much of unions' poor showing in representation elections is the result of either legal or illegal employer practices during election campaigns.

Union Decertification

Unions gain members through winning union representation elections; they lose members through decertification elections. The 1947 Taft-Hartley amendments to the NLRA prescribed election procedures for decertifying a union. The decertification elections held since Taft-Hartley have been far fewer than the representation elections; but in recent years their number has been increasing, and unions have been losing an increasing percentage of these contests. The first year after passage of Taft-Hartley, for example, witnessed 97 decertification elections, or only 3 percent of the 3,822 representation elections held that year. That percentage held steady throughout the 1950s and 1960s but began creeping upward in the 1970s; by 1983 the ratio had risen to 21 percent.

Most of the decertification elections held have been in small units. Moreover, one study has shown that the smaller the unit, the most likely unions are to lose the decertification election.[9] The most common explanation for these findings is that unions find servicing small units costly and therefore may pay inadequate attention to them. And although losing a decertification election hurts the local union, decertifications have accounted for only a small fraction of the post-1950 decline in trade union membership. In the late 1970s only .23 percent of all union members voted in a decertification election.[10]

MODELS OF UNION GROWTH

Researchers have long been trying to explain the growth and decline in trade union membership throughout history, not simply since the most recent decline. Most of the theoretical and empirical research on this topic concurs with Dunlop's argument that trade union growth can best be understood by considering a variety of environmental factors.[11] Researchers from different academic disciplines have focused on different aspects of the environment, but most have considered the effects of the (1) economic, (2) political or social, and (3) legal or public policy contexts. Others have examined the effects of changes in industry and labor force composition. Another group of researchers has argued that though these environmental factors are important, various organizational characteristics and strategies of unions and employers must also be added to a model of the determinants of union growth. The theoretical and empirical support for each of these arguments will be discussed below.

Environmental Determinants

Economic influences. Most researchers who focus on the environmental determinants of union growth and decline begin by speculating about economic influences. Commons was one of the early theorists; he argued that unions would grow during economic prosperity and decline during economic downturns.[12] His argument rested on the theory that as labor markets tighten, workers will more aggressively pursue their goals and employers will less aggressively resist collective efforts by their employees. With the higher profit rates that accompany prosperity, employers have less incentive to resist unionization. The empirical basis for the Commons argument can be found in the experiences of the U.S. trade union movement in the latter half of the nineteenth century. Union fortunes (in terms of both membership and the numbers of national unions) rose and fell in sync with changes in the business cycle throughout that period.[13]

The most systematic empirical study of aggregate trade union growth in the United States strongly confirms the positive relationship between the business cycle and union growth in the years between 1900 and 1960.[14] Although several people have argued about whether increasing prices, increasing profits, or the tightening of labor markets is the underlying cause of union growth during periods of economic expansion, it is probably correct to assume that all three factors contribute to union growth. So far, efforts to identify the primary cause of union growth during economic upswings have been neither conclusive nor convincing. It is likely that the relative importance of these specific economic conditions fluctuates over time; and so there may not be one, generalizable cause to identify.

Although the business cycle clearly affects union growth, it is important to note that much of the growth in U.S. labor unions took place in only a few significant spurts. As Figure 5–1 shows, unionism flourished during the late 1930s and the early and mid-1940s. Public sector unionism also grew in a spurt, starting in the early 1960s.

Political and social influences.   In an effort to explain those spurts political scientists and social theorists have contended that the political and social climates are the primary determinants of union growth.[15] Citing the Great Depression and the two world wars to support their contentions, they point to the fact that the most dramatic increases in union growth have come during times of major social upheavals. In particular, they point to the favorable political climate of the New Deal period and the social upheavals caused by the wartime economy as giving workers the reasons to turn to unions.

Economists have responded to these assertions by noting that during each of the periods identified by the social and political theorists, the appropriate combination of economic variables appeared to account for part of the union growth that occurred. They concede, however, that additional environmental factors beyond the economy may contribute to union growth and thus help account for the seemingly isolated spurts in union growth. Ashenfelter and Pencavel attempted to measure the effects of these political and social determinants with two variables: first, as a measure of the political climate, the percentage of Democrats in Congress in each year; and second, a measure of the severity of the most recent economic recession or depression. Regarding the latter, the authors predicted that at times of major depressions worker grievances would escalate, and the demand for union membership would therefore increase. Their results suggested that only in periods of very severe depression and in years when the political climate had shifted considerably in favor of the labor movement did union growth increase.[16] Although one can question the validity of their two measures of political and social climate, Ashenfelter and Pencavel's findings suggest that at least part of the explanation for union growth in the mid-1930s and perhaps as well during the two world wars is workers' response to the social and political events of the time. Overall, however, the existing longitudinal research offers only weak evidence linking social and political events to union growth spurts.

A cross-sectional study of differences in union membership among the states gives a clearer picture of political and social determinants of unionization. As noted earlier in this chapter, union membership is highly concentrated in the industrialized states of the Northeast and upper Midwest. The southern states have the lowest levels of union membership in the nation. After controlling for economic differences across these states, Moore and Newman found that the percentage of voters in the state who voted Democratic in the 1964 presidential election (a measure of the degree of support for a "liberal" candidate) was a good predictor of the unionization rate in the state.[17] Thus, political and social environmental variables may help explain the variations in union membership by state at a given time.

One of the most hotly debated questions about union growth and decline is the role of the legal environment or public policy. Some observers believe it was not the effects of the Great Depression but the encouragement to collective bargaining given by the NLRA of 1935 that led to the proliferation of unions in the late 1930s. These observers are joined by others who aver that as long as right-to-work laws (laws making it illegal to require employees to join unions as a condition of employment) remain in force in 19 states, those states will remain sparsely unionized. The debate over the Labor Law Reform bill in the mid-1970s (see Chapter 3) illustrated the intensity of the beliefs that public policy influences union growth. Finally, the growth of public sector unions in the 1960s and 1970s closely corresponded with passage of state legislation protecting the rights of public employees to unionize and to bargain collectively.

Unfortunately, it is not entirely clear which was the cause and which the effect in those public sector developments. On the one hand, union membership has grown fastest in states that have passed legislation. On the other hand, an already favorable political climate, the existence of a strong potential for organizing, and, in some cases, the beginnings of union organization in the public sector all contributed to the passage of the state laws in the first place. Thus, it is probably safest to conclude that in the public sector the passage of legislation is both partially a cause and partially an effect of union growth.[18]

This simultaneous or reciprocal causality in the relationship between public sector unionization and legislation plagues the analysis of all efforts to sort out the independent effects of public policy variables on union growth in general (and on many other aspects of collective bargaining as well). Consequently, we cannot answer conclusively whether passage of the NLRA was the primary, or only a secondary, cause of the rate of union growth experienced after 1935.

There is some more casual evidence to suggest that, though favorable public policies may not necessarily be the primary cause of increases in union membership, public policies that protect the rights of unions and workers to organize and that also provide procedures for union recognition *stabilize* union membership by making it more difficult to decertify a union once it has been recognized as the exclusive bargaining representative. Three sets of data support this hypothesis.

First is evidence on the ups and downs and ultimately the demise of the Foreman's Association of America (FAA) between the late 1930s and passage of the Taft-Hartley Act in 1947. During that time the law vacillated on whether foremen could be members of trade unions and whether they were protected under the Wagner Act. The FAA formed in 1941 under the protection of an NLRB ruling. But in 1947 Taft-Hartley specifically excluded foremen from coverage under the law. Subsequently, the FAA faded into oblivion.[19]

Second, earlier evidence gathered by Ulman showed that between 1860 and 1929 the ratio of union failures to new union formations increased during periods of economic recessions and declined during periods of prosperity.[20] That is, unions emerged during booms and disbanded during declines. But after passage of the NLRA unions were better able to survive cyclical economic downturns.

A third example is the experience of the United Farm Workers of America (UFW) in California. In the late 1960s the UFW claimed at least 55,000 members and had signed collective bargaining contracts with a number of major growers. As those initial contracts expired, however, the growers signed contracts with the Teamsters rather than continue their relationship with the UFW. By 1974 membership in the UFW had fallen to below 6,000.[21] In 1975 California passed legislation establishing procedures for union representation elections. That legislation assured that once a union was certified as the exclusive bargaining representative, it could not easily be raided by another union or ignored by the employer.[22] By 1977 the UFW had grown to 12,000 members. It has since held steady at that figure,[23] illustrating, again, how union fortunes may rise and fall in the absence of protective legislation, but stabilize in the presence of such legislation.

In summary, it is clear that an analysis of the environmental determinants of union growth must consider the roles of the economic, political, social, and legal contexts. Although the empirical evidence is strongest in support of the business cycle as an important determinant of union growth over the long term, there is also enough industry-specific evidence to require us to add legal, social, and political determinants to our analysis if we expect to successfully explain why unions have grown at different rates during different times.

Any theory that focuses exclusively on the environmental determinants, thus is not likely to provide a full explanation of unionization. Not all industries are unionized during union growth spurts, nor are all firms within an industry, nor even all plants within a firm. We therefore also must consider the organizational strategies and characteristics of unions and employers as additional factors in the growth and decline of unions. The next section examines organizational factors within the labor movement and their impact on union growth. Chapters 6 and 7 will discuss managerial strategies for industrial relations and their consequences for union growth.

Organizational Determinants

In contrast to the highly empirical methodologies employed in research on the environmental determinants of union growth, most of the literature on the organizational determinants is impressionistic. In assessing union organizations, the research has focused on the labor movement's "missionary zeal," or level of commitment to organizing new workers. A number of critics of the movement have argued that labor no longer approaches the task of organizing new workers with the same enthusiasm or commitment as that which characterized the organizing drives of the 1930s.

At least two authors have taken this argument a step further by suggesting that the resources unions allocate to union organizing vary in direct proportion to the incentives local union leaders have to expand their organizations.[24] This proposition rests on the assumption that there is little incentive for local unions to allocate resources to organizing if adding new members has no bearing on their existing members' bargaining power. Similarly, union leaders with well-established constituencies and a firm basis of political support may see little personal advantage to organizing new workers who could possibly erode that support. Thus, there is likely to be wide variation in the resources that unions are willing to allocate to organizing activities. Voos has outlined a variety of benefits and costs of union-organizing activity.[25]

Ironically, unions may also be the victims of their own earlier success. As noted in the previous section of this chapter, and as Freeman and Medoff have contended, it was unions' success—measured by the growing gap between union and nonunion workers' wages in the 1970s—that at least in part spurred the subsequent growth in nonunion firms and heightened managerial opposition to unions during representation elections.[26] If this hypothesis is true, it rates as the cruelest catch-22 facing the labor movement. On the one hand, unions must be effective in increasing wages and improving conditions of employment for their existing members if they hope to attract new members (as will be argued in the next section). On the other hand, if successful, they risk boosting labor costs to a level that will price unionized labor out of the market and increase management's incentive both to expand the firm's nonunion operations and to vigorously oppose union-organizing drives. Unions therefore walk a tightrope between two no man's lands: one encompassing unions that fail to attract new members, and the other inhabited by unions facing threatening nonunion competition. Compounding this challenge is the fact that it is not easy for union leaders to assess where the boundaries of those two lands lie, that is, what the point of diminishing returns is for any given wage demand.

Most of the aggregate analyses of union growth have failed to conceptualize adequately the factors that influence individual workers to support unionization. Clearly, this failure limits the power of the aggregate models to explain the results of specific union elections or specific individuals' decision to unionize. In the next section we examine a model of the decision of *individual* workers to join unions.

THE INDIVIDUAL DECISION TO JOIN TRADE UNIONS

If the central argument of the preceding section is accurate, that is, if changing environmental conditions will make it more difficult for unions to maintain, much less expand, their membership base, then an understanding of individual workers' motivation to join or reject unions is indeed important. If the labor movement is to continue as an important social and economic force in American society, it will have to be attractive to contemporary and future members of the labor force. This means that the labor movement not only will have to understand the factors motivating workers to join unions, but also will have to develop strategies to influence those motivations.

As mentioned in Chapter 2, the trade union movement in the United States has been characterized by theorists, social critics, and union practitioners themselves as following a *business unionism* philosophy. That is, unions have been viewed as pragmatic organizations determined to do whatever is necessary to improve the economic and social conditions of their members in the short run. Samuel Gompers once elaborated, "Trade unions not only discuss economic and social problems, but deal with them in a practical fashion calculated to bring about better conditions of life today."[27] This philosophy has produced a labor movement that avoids identifying with any overarching political or social ideology and instead focuses on improving members' conditions of employment through collective bargaining.

U.S. business unionism has engendered in workers a natural response: a very pragmatic approach to the decision to support unionization. The motivation to unionize arises out of the worker's unmet expectations or dissatisfaction with the job or work environment and his belief that unionism affords a useful means for reversing those conditions. But at the same time, the worker must also believe that the potential benefits of unionism will outweigh the costs. Workers' decision whether to join a union and their desires regarding appropriate union objectives thus are shaped by workers' attitudes toward their work, the employer, and the union or the union movement.

Evidence from a number of studies shows that for workers to express a preference for unionizing they must (1) be deeply dissatisfied with their current job and employment conditions, (2) believe that unionization can be helpful or instrumental in improving those job conditions, *and* (3) be willing to overcome the generally negative stereotype of unions held by the population as a whole. A 1984 Harris poll conducted for the AFL–CIO, for example, indicated that workers who were dissatisfied with their pay, job security, on-the-job recognition, and promotional opportunities were more likely, by some 40 percentage points, to express a preference for unionizing than workers who were satisfied with those aspects of their jobs.[28] Respondents' belief that a union would be helpful or instrumental in improving their working conditions increased the probability of voting for unionization by another 21 percentage points, while a negative image of unions reduced the willingness to organize by about 24 percentage points.

These results strongly suggest that all three beliefs listed above must exist for a union to have a 50–50 or better chance of successfully organizing a given election unit. In other words a majority of the workers in the election unit must hold these three views in order for a union to win a representation election.

Yet most U.S. workers do not hold these views. In fact, in 1984 only about one-third of the nonmanagerial labor force sampled by Harris expressed a willingness to vote union if offered the opportunity to do so. This is not surprising, since in response to other questions in the survey, more than 80 percent of the nonunion sample expressed general satisfaction with their jobs and less than a majority of nonunion workers judged unions could materially improve their wages, working conditions, or degree of participation and recognition.

Even so, however, one-third of the nonunion respondents did view unionization as a vehicle for improving specific job conditions and would want a union to represent them, if given the opportunity. Not surprisingly, those workers who expressed the most interest in unionization were minorities, women, and low-wage workers. Econometric evidence has demonstrated that the dominant effect of unions has been to improve the wages, benefits, and general working conditions of lower wage, lower skilled workers who lack individual labor market power and mobility.[29] Thus, although the Harris survey revealed a mixed market for unions, their problem is not a lack of workers interested in membership. Instead, the challenge for unions is how to translate the individual interest into majority support within a specific work unit.

UNIONS' REPRESENTATIONAL STRATEGIES

Once a union has gained the right to represent a given group of workers it must choose a strategy that will produce tangible success in meeting the goals and objectives of those workers. Traditionally, unions have focused their efforts primarily on the bread-and-butter issues of wages, hours, and working conditions. Recently, however, their members have demanded greater influence in addressing such workplace issues as the organization of work and managers' strategic decisions. As a result, unions in the 1980s have begun to develop new representational strategies.

Workers' Views of Their Jobs: Recent Evidence

Survey data on workers' values collected over the 1970s and 1980s from a large number of work sites consistently demonstrated that although workers continued to place a high value on pay and benefits, their concerns for career advancement, challenging work, and effective supervision began to take on higher value as they moved up the organizational hierarchy.[30]

Our own research evaluating employee participation programs has significant parallels to those findings. The data presented in Table 5–4 indicate that across five different work sites the majority of blue- and white-collar respondents wanted "some" or "a lot" of say in both traditional bargaining issues, such as pay and the grievance procedure, and workplace issues concerning how their job was to be done. Between 83 and 95 percent of the workers indi-

TABLE 5–4
Workers' interest in participation, by issue of concern

Issues	Blue-collar workers				White-collar professionals
Workplace issues	Case 1	Case 2	Case 3	Case 4	Case 5
The way the work is done— methods and procedures	83%	83%	91%	87%	95%
The level of quality of work	83	78	88	87	96
How fast the work should be done—the work rate	72	70	81	76	85
How much work people should do in a day	55	43	64	61	70
Who should do what job in your group or section	46	57	51	83	61
Collective bargaining and personnel issues					
When the work day begins and ends	50	33	63	65	76
Pay scales or wages	67	78	82	73	92
Who should be fired if they do a bad job or don't come to work	39	38	39	35	42
Who should be hired into your work group	35	23	32	37	45
Handling complaints or grievances	67	70	72	59	79
Who gets promoted	39	27	42	41	48
Strategic and management issues					
The use of new technology on your job	69	70	68	77	79
Management salaries	27	22	13	41	22
Hiring or promotions to upper management	27	8	25	31	44
The selection of your supervisor	42	18	39	52	58
Plant expansions, closings, or new locations	45	22	51	70	40
The way the company invests its profits or spends its money	46	52	41	43	32

Source: Reprinted, by permission, from Thomas A. Kochan, Harry C. Katz, and Robert B. McKersie, *The Transformation of American Industrial Relations,* p. 212. ©1986 by Basic Books.

Note: The figures indicate the percentage of respondents who said they wanted "some say" or "a lot of say" in the issue.

cated an interest in gaining a say in the way the work is done, with the highest degree of interest in such issues expressed by white-collar professionals. Interestingly, the survey respondents generally expressed less interest in gaining control over hiring, promotion, discipline, or discharge decisions.

These findings suggest that unions can no longer focus their representational strategies exclusively on traditional bargaining issues; they can no longer ignore workers' desires for more say in the nature of their work. At the same time, however, these data suggest that workers are unlikely to favor representational strategies or participation programs that stress workplace and task-related issues at the expense of, or as a substitute for, adequate pay, benefits, or due process.

Our survey also found that workers had relatively little interest in participating in broader managerial decisions concerning such issues as investment, plant location, or management salaries. This finding is consistent with data from other surveys of workers in both the United States and European countries. There was one exception to this pattern, however. Across the work sites surveyed two-thirds to over three-quarters of the respondents indicated they wanted some or a great deal of say in new technology used on their jobs.

Thus, workers in the United States appear to approach involvement in strategic issues in their traditionally pragmatic fashion. They are interested in broadening their involvement in strategic issues when that involvement may help them attain their job and career objectives. As we discuss later, in Chapter 13, these pragmatic goals of the U.S. worker have played a critical role in the course of worker participation programs.

An Evaluation of Unions' Strategies

How do current union members evaluate the performance of their organizations? For a comprehensive picture we need to look at both overall evaluations of union performance and evaluations of union activities at the workplace, collective bargaining, and strategic levels of the industrial relations system. In two recent national surveys union members have given largely positive ratings of their union representation overall. In the 1984 Harris survey mentioned earlier 75 percent of the union members responding indicated they were satisfied or very satisfied with their unions. And in the 1982 National Longitudinal Survey of adult men union members gave an even stronger endorsement of unionism in general. When asked how they would vote if a union representation election were held on their current job, 87 percent said they would vote to continue union representation.[31]

Data from five of our case studies of worker participation programs, summarized in Figure 5–4, present a more detailed breakdown of members' evaluations of their union's performance. Of the three categories of issues—workplace, collective bargaining, and strategic—respondents in all five cases rated their union highest on its performance in addressing traditional

FIGURE 5–4
Members' ratings of their union's performance in handling selected
workplace, collective bargaining, and strategic issues
(percentage rating = percentage of members rating it "good" or "very good")

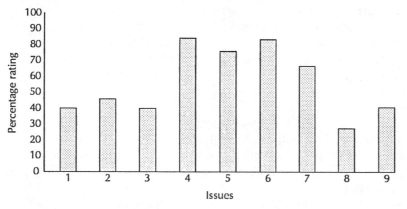

Issues

Source: Thomas A. Kochan, Harry C. Katz, and Nancy R. Mower, *Worker Participation and American Unions: Threat or Opportunity?* (Kalamazoo, Mich.: W.E. Upjohn Institute for Employment Research, 1984), 120–21, table 4–5.

Note: 1 = Say on how to do their job (40 percent)
2 = Making the job more interesting (46 percent)
3 = Improving productivity (40 percent)
4 = Getting good wages (84 percent)
5 = Getting good fringe benefits (76 percent)
6 = Protecting workers from unfair treatment (83 percent)
7 = Handling grievances (69 percent)
8 = Getting workers a say in how the business is run (27 percent)
9 = Representing worker interests in management decision making
(41 percent)

collective bargaining issues. Ratings on both workplace and strategic issues were consistently lower. For example, 84 percent of the respondents rated their union as "good" or "very good" at "getting good wages"; 76 percent, at "getting good fringe benefits"; 83 percent, at "protecting workers from unfair treatment"; and 69 percent, at handling grievances. In contrast, only 40 percent of the respondents gave their union good or very good ratings on its gaining workers "a say on how to do their jobs"; 46 percent, on "making their jobs more interesting"; and 40 percent, on improving productivity. Ratings were even lower on the strategic issues: Only 27 percent rated the union good or very good at gaining workers a say in how the business was run; and only 41 percent approved of their union's ability to represent worker interests in managerial decision making.

Performance ratings on the strategic and workplace issues varied significantly depending on whether the respondents had been directly involved in a worker participation process, the scope of that participation effort, and the nature of the union's role in the process. Specifically, further analysis of our data and the cases themselves showed that the union members who were active in the participation programs under way in two of the cases gave more favorable ratings to union performance on workplace and strategic issues than their counterparts in the other cases. In these two cases the union played an active role in initiating and administering these processes, and the QWL processes went beyond a narrow focus to address key concerns about employment security, work organization, and issues traditionally reserved for management. It is not surprising, therefore, that these two unions also received higher overall effectiveness ratings from their members than did the other three unions in the sample. These results imply that just as workers' expectations of their jobs and their employers have expanded in recent years, so have union members' expectations of their unions.

Thus, we can expect a continued demand for traditional collective bargaining, direct employee participation at the workplace within union and nonunion employment settings, and greater participation or representation on strategic management issues in situations where workers perceive a tangible link between strategic management decisions and their own goals and interests.

Union Leaders' Roles in Shaping Strategies and Priorities

Although there is ample room for more systematic analyses of the influence of members' priorities on unions as they prepare for negotiations, it is clear that the actual bargaining demands of unions reflect more than just an averaging of their members' preferences. Several factors combine to produce the complex process by which union leaders arrive at their bargaining objectives.

First, in addition to considering the preferences of their members, union leaders must evaluate their objectives in light of the probability that they can be attained. Unrealistic or unattainable goals must be discarded during prenegotiation planning sessions or early on in negotiations.

Second, individual union members have varying political influence within the union. Older or more skilled workers, for example, may be more politically influential than other members. Thus, the objectives ultimately selected may reflect some workers' goals more than others'. The successful union is likely to have active members who express their goals and lobby on their own behalf to have their goals accepted.

Third, union leaders must also be concerned about the long-run survival and power of the union and must take steps to preserve those interests. There is always the risk that union leaders will emphasize union security at the expense of member preferences.

Finally, it should be recognized that a central job for union leaders, like all leaders, is to *lead*! Union leaders must be able to weigh the strategic options, make decisions, and secure the ongoing support of their members for those decisions.

In recent years union leaders have been forced to decide how far they are willing to extend bargaining beyond its traditional agenda. The ongoing strategic choices leaders make on this issue will have a profound effect on the nature of U.S. unionism and its future. Recognizing the crucial need for longer run strategic planning, a number of unions such as the Communications Workers, the Bricklayers, the Steelworkers, and the Auto Workers have created committees to examine alternative strategies for the future. This sort of planning is likely to become a more common part of trade union administration in the future.

ALTERNATIVE UNION STRATEGIES: THE 1985 AFL–CIO REPORT

One example of the union movement's recent consideration of new strategies is the 1985 report of the AFL–CIO Committee on the Evolution of Work.[32] The committee stresses the need (1) to develop more effective means for allowing organized workers to resolve—as individuals—the problems on their jobs and (2) to provide more individual membership options for those workers who are unable to establish (or uninterested in establishing) a formal collective bargaining relationship with their employer. The basis of these recommendations can be seen in the Harris poll conducted for the committee and in the committee's analyses of the growing number of workers who have only temporary or short-term attachments to a single employer.

For example, approximately 20 percent of the employed labor force work in part-time jobs. In addition, a small but growing number hold temporary jobs, are consultants or independent contractors, or work for temporary-help agencies and thus are not attached to a single employer. This is clearly an increasingly important segment of the labor force. Moreover, the lack of deep and stable attachment to any given employment relationship poses difficulty for both the traditional union-organizing model and the innovative or high-commitment human resource management model. Thus, one objective of the AFL–CIO Committee on the Evolution of Work was to identify alternative strategies and processes for representing these workers and nonunion workers in general. The question the committee asked was: Is there interest among unorganized workers in some alternative form of representation?

Nonunion workers in the Harris poll conducted for the AFL–CIO committee were about evenly divided in their responses to a question concerning whether workplace problems are better resolved by going to the employer as individuals or collectively. Specifically, 45 percent of the nonunion workers indicated a group response was more effective, while 43 percent indicated an individual response was better. About 12 percent either were not sure or had no opinion. Younger, lower wage, and less skilled workers were more likely to express a preference for the group response, whereas older, higher wage, managerial, professional, and sales employees tended to prefer the individual response. These data imply that interest in both individual and group expression is stronger than the preference for traditional union representation. (Recall that only about one-third of the nonunion sample expressed a willingness to unionize.)

Further evidence of interest in alternative forms of representation was found when respondents were asked whether they were interested in receiving more individualized benefits and services that could transfer with them across jobs and employers. Majority support for such benefits and services as health insurance, labor market information, legal services, and consumer discounts is understandable, given the increasing mobility of the labor force and employers' increasing preference for part-time, temporary, contract, and other flexible (nonpermanent) hiring and employment relationships. The support voiced for these types of services led the AFL–CIO committee to recommend experimentation with an associate-membership option that would allow individual workers to join unions and receive individual benefits even if no collective bargaining unit existed at their place of employment. It is clear that we will see some experimentation along these lines in the future. The question remains, however, whether the labor movement or any single employee organization can develop stable and effective strategies for providing these more individualized benefits and services.

UNION STRUCTURES FOR COLLECTIVE BARGAINING

For a union to pursue its goals effectively in the collective bargaining process, it must adapt its organizational structure to meet the requirements of the process. A major theme underlying the model of the collective bargaining system presented in Chapter 1 is that a close interrelationship exists among union structure, management structure, and the bargaining structure. In turn, all three of these components of the bargaining system must be adapted to fit the external environment. It is not surprising, then, that the merits of alternative structural configurations of unions have been much debated among students and practitioners of trade unionism and collective bargaining. The structure of a union not only is important to its success in collective bargaining, but it also directs the internal distribution of power and influence among union decision makers. This section will briefly describe the main structural characteristics of unions in the United States and the factors that make for differences in union structures. It will also review the debate over the consequences of different structural arrangements for internal union democracy and union effectiveness in bargaining.

The Structure of the Labor Movement

Most students of the U.S. labor movement agree that the national union is the key body and the center of power within most trade unions. Let us begin, however, by describing how the national union fits into the larger structure of the overall labor movement.

The structure of the AFL–CIO, the dominant labor federation in the United States, is diagrammed in Figure 5–5. The supreme governing body of the AFL–CIO shown in the official structure is the biennial convention. Between conventions, however, the federation is run by the president of the AFL–CIO, with assistance from the Executive Council. The president has traditionally been the major source of power in the federation—with significant influence over the Executive Council and the membership—because he has the authority to interpret the constitution between meetings of the Executive Council and because he manages the federation staff.

It is important to understand that the two primary roles of the AFL–CIO are to promote the political objectives of the labor movement and to assist the component unions in their collective bargaining activities. The federation itself has no formal authority over the collective bargaining activities of its member unions and only rarely becomes directly involved in them. In recent years, however, the Building and Construction Trades Department and the Metal Trades Department of the AFL–CIO have played a more active and direct role in collective bargaining in selected construction projects and in the federal sector, respectively. Similarly, the Industrial Union Department has played a key supporting role in some coalition bargaining efforts in a number of industries. More generally, the staff departments of the federation offer extensive research and technical support to individual unions or groups of unions experiencing common problems. In addition, competing unions turn to the federation to arbitrate their jurisdictional disputes.

The Structure of National Unions

The starting point for any analysis of union structure is the jurisdiction of a union. Union jurisdiction determines the range of workers who can be legitimately organized by the union. As noted in earlier chapters, unions are commonly described as either craft or industrial. A *craft union's* jurisdiction is limited to workers in a specific trade (such as painters, electricians, or carpenters) or profession (for example, teachers, nurses, baseball players, and firefighters). An *industrial union's* jurisdiction typically encompasses all employees in an industry (such as, steel, autos, and coal mining). The early U.S. unions were craft unions organized within local labor markets. From its formation in 1886 the AFL firmly adhered to the craft union principle as the cornerstone for organizing skilled workers. But as labor markets and product markets broadened with transportation improvements and the growth of mass production industries, the need to expand union jurisdictions became evident. Markets began to cross state lines, and unskilled workers became a significant part of the labor force, raising serious challenges to the appropriateness of the narrow, craft-based organizations. In 1935 advocates of industrial unionism, led by John L. Lewis, president of the United Mine Workers, split with the craft union advocates in the AFL and formed what became in 1937 the Congress of Industrial Organizations (CIO). As the

FIGURE 5–5
The structure of the AFL–CIO

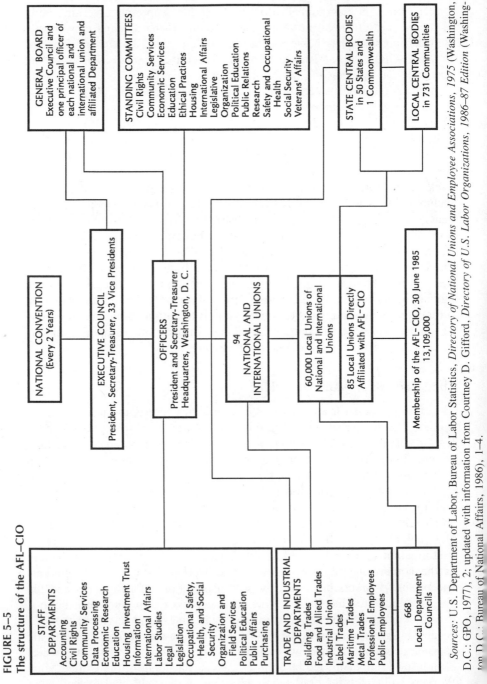

174

Sources: U.S. Department of Labor, Bureau of Labor Statistics, *Directory of National Unions and Employee Associations, 1975* (Washington, D.C.: GPO, 1977), 2; updated with information from Courtney D. Gifford, *Directory of U.S. Labor Organizations, 1986–87 Edition* (Washington, D.C.: Bureau of National Affairs, 1986), 1–4.

large industrial unions grew, corporations and markets continued to expand, and centralized bargaining became more popular—all of which helped to establish the national union as the central, or most powerful, structure in most industrial unions.

There appears to be general, though not total, agreement on these reasons why bureaucratization of unions has taken place. There is less agreement, however, on the consequences of these structural developments for unions as organizations and for their effectiveness in collective bargaining. Empirical studies by Edelstein and Warner and by Anderson of internal union democracy have suggested that the more complex (and bureaucratic) the structure of a union, the less control its members have over decision making within the union.[33] These two studies also found, however, that structural complexity increased the closeness of votes in union elections and the number of candidates vying for open positions.

Union and Worker Involvement in Negotiations

The most important union activity is the negotiation of a collective bargaining agreement. In this section we review a typical chronology and common procedures followed by unions and workers during the negotiation of a collective bargaining contract. The procedures used by management in preparing for negotiations are discussed in Chapter 6.

In negotiations with management the union is represented by a negotiating committee. The makeup of the union's negotiating committee varies across unions, although it typically includes some union officers, support staff (such as members of the local or the national union's research staff, or both), and elected worker representatives. Often the leaders of the union's negotiating committee are the highest elected officers of the union covered by the collective bargaining agreement under negotiation. Some unions, such as local construction or trucking unions, tend to rely on hired *business agents* to lead their negotiations.

The negotiating committee will meet a number of times before the start of negotiations to formulate the union's list of demands and to begin to establish expectations regarding what the union can feasibly win in negotiations. The negotiating committee will have already solicited from the members information on their demands and expectations, either directly through membership meetings called to discuss the upcoming negotiations or in some cases through polls or caucuses held among the membership. In the UAW, for example, representatives elected from the local unions meet in a convention and vote on bargaining resolutions during preparations for the triannual companywide bargaining in the auto industry (members are also consulted during the negotiation of plant contracts that supplement the companywide agreement).

The negotiating committee also receives information and advice from the national union's research staff during its preparations for bargaining.

The information provided typically covers the financial performance of the company, forecasts of the future performance of the company and the economy, and summaries of recent settlements in other, comparable unions or the wage and benefit improvements received by similar unorganized workers (such as unorganized workers in the same city, firm, or industry).

If the union comes to an impasse with management during the negotiations and is considering going on strike over its unresolved disputes with management, two steps occur. In local contract negotiations the union's constitution typically requires the local to seek authorization for the strike from the national union, an important process because among other things it enables striking workers to receive strike benefits from the national union's strike fund. A union considering a strike also typically will poll its members. The strike vote serves a dual purpose: it tells the union leadership whether the union's members support such an action, and it also helps rally the workers around the purpose of the strike.

When an agreement is reached between the union's negotiating committee and management's representatives, the union proceeds through its *contract ratification* procedures. Here there is much variation in the exact procedures used by different unions. Some unions first send a proposed agreement to a council made up of lower level union officers, for example, a council of local union officers when a companywide agreement is negotiated (as in the steel and auto industries). Union constitutions typically also require that the workers covered by a negotiated agreement vote on any proposed settlement. There are some notable exceptions to this pattern, however. For instance, until the 1970s coal miners represented by the United Mine Workers did not have the right to vote on new contracts negotiated by their national union leaders with management's industrywide association. But in the usual case workers must approve contract settlements, thereby providing a mechanism for participatory democracy in this critical aspect of union decision making.

Internal Administrative Adjustments

Contemporary U.S. trade unions find themselves in a difficult structural dilemma. On the one hand, a number of environmental pressures lead them to centralize power, to rely more on professional experts, and to formalize their procedures to cope effectively with the complexities of the collective bargaining process. On the other hand, these same procedures required for bargaining make it more difficult for the rank-and-file to maintain internal union democracy. The centralization of power is likely to increase the probability that dissident groups will become alienated from or disenchanted with the union's leadership, to give rise to factionalism from below, and to encourage the use of repressive tactics from above to suppress internal dissent. These internal consequences, in turn, can initiate a decline in the vitality of the trade union that ultimately leads to oligarchy, stagnation, or corruption. The essence of the dilemma, therefore, is that while centralization may be needed to perform effectively in bargaining (at least in unions with broad product markets and centralized bargaining structures) *at any given time,* the longer centralization is maintained in the absence of an effective political process, the less effective the union is likely to become. Contemporary trade unions are highly complex organizations that can no longer rely on grass-roots or town meeting forms of democracy to survive, but at the same time they must develop ways to maintain an effective political process within a complex bureaucratic structure.

How can large, complex unions address this dilemma? Strauss has suggested one solution: to foster the development of occupational or other interest groups that are given a say in the union's decision-making process.[34] An example is the UAW's creation, in the early 1970s, of a skilled trades conference that has been given special opportunities to promote its interests within the union. Gamm has proposed that national union executive boards be elected on a regional, rather than on an at-large, basis, as is the practice in the majority of national unions.[35] These suggestions are consistent with Lipset, Trow, and Coleman's proposition that just as interest groups become a necessary component of political democracy when the town meeting form of participation and democratic action loses significance, so too does union members' direct participation in critical union decisions give way to interest group representation.[36] When the requirements of bargaining force decision making to become more centralized and when a larger array of interests must be accommodated, democratic procedures for satisfying the various interests within the union become all the more critical.

The need for less individualistic forms of representation brings about a corresponding need for systematic means of soliciting upward communications—in the form of opinions, grievances, and suggestions—from the rank-and-file and from local representatives to the decision makers, as well as means for decision makers to communicate their activities and decisions back to the members. Union leaders are becoming obliged to adapt the sophisticated techniques of modern communications to promote democracy and members' identification with the organization, just as employers are doing. Thus, we find unions using such techniques as satellite hookups and television advertising to communicate to, and on behalf of, their members.

The vitality of an organization depends not only on its organizational structures, processes, and practices, but also on the leadership abilities of its officers. Union democracy cannot be maintained over time unless highly qualified local union leaders are recruited and given opportunities for development, upward mobility, and career advancement. Lipset, Trow, and Coleman observed over 30 years ago a key source of vitality and democracy in the International Typographical Union was its ability to attract the most able and highly motivated of its members into union service and politics.[37] One of the reasons talented members sought union positions was their belief that their participation would be rewarded with upward mobility. Unfortunately, we know little about how today's union members view careers in the labor movement or how successful today's unions are in attracting their most promising members into active union roles. There is little evidence that unions have systematic plans in place for recruiting members into leadership positions, or that they pay much attention to career planning once a promising leader is identified.

No effort has been made in this section to present a comprehensive theory of union democracy. Instead, we have simply taken the position that the key to democracy in contemporary unions lies in their internal political processes and particularly in their ability to adapt modern administrative and communications techniques to overcome the oligarchic features of the now-complex union structures. In the long run the leaders' ability and willingness to do so will dictate both union democracy and union effectiveness.

Unions as Administrative and Service Agencies

Are unions experiencing the costs of increasing complexity and bureaucracy without any concomitant gains in administrative effectiveness? Consider, for example, the following indictment of the administrative performance of trade unions:

> Judged by contemporary standards of administration, the typical international union leaves much to be desired. Little effort is devoted to systematic research and long-range planning. Careful procedures for budgeting and resource allocation are virtually unknown. The methods for selecting, training, and motivating officials are often haphazard and not well designed to elevate the ablest, best-trained men to union office. The process of communication up and down the union hierarchy does not produce the information required for formulating and implementing effective policy. And the structure of the union is often ill-adapted to the programs of the organization.[38]

If this assessment is still accurate, it provides further support to the critics of union bureaucracy. But as we have seen, the solution does not lie in a return to smaller, less complex union organizations.

For example, a study of the performance of union-management safety and health committees concluded that the administrative performance of the unions studied fell short of what would have been necessary if those committees were to make significant long-term contributions to improved workplace safety and health. The authors' recommendations for improving union administration, however, all called for changes that could be viewed as *increasing* the complexity of the union structure, namely, (1) greater centralization of safety and health efforts within the national union; (2) greater use of staff specialists at the local, intermediate, and national levels of the union; (3) greater coordination of the committee activities in different plants and locals; (4) greater use of planning, reporting, and evaluation procedures to monitor the performance of the committees in different plants; and (5) more long-term research on health and safety hazards at a centralized level of the labor movement.[39]

The administrative performance of unions is likely to become an increasingly important dimension of overall union effectiveness in the future, given the complexity of union-management problems and rank-and-file expectations for greater involvement in union decisions and better communications from their leaders. This dimension of union effectiveness deserves to be added to the more traditional list of union growth, goals, structure, and internal democracy as subjects of concern in trade unionism and collective bargaining.

Union Mergers: Consolidating Union Structures

One goal of the AFL–CIO merger in 1955 was to promote greater rationalization of union structures through mergers and consolidation of member unions. Indeed, George Meany and Walter Reuther, then leaders of the AFL and CIO, respectively, expected the original 135 unions in the new federation to be reduced to approximately 50.[40] Although the number of unions in the AFL–CIO now stands at 95, there were 85 mergers between 1960 and 1983.[41]

Proponents of union mergers cite the administrative benefits that accrue from greater economies of scale and the organizing and bargaining benefits from reduced interunion competition and rivalry. More specifically, small unions that lack the financial resources and professional expertise needed to adequately service union members can be absorbed into larger, more richly endowed organizations. Reducing competition among unions in the same industry or occupation can free up resources previously used in fighting with each other to improve collective bargaining or political efforts. And finally, unions whose traditional occupational or craft jurisdictions have eroded can concentrate on helping their members adjust to the changing environment by protecting their job security and expending less of their effort on ensuring the institutional survival of the union.

Critics of merger activity, on the other hand, posit that mergers do not necessarily reflect the rational consolidation of outmoded union jurisdictions. Instead, they say, some mergers are simply opportunistic or expansionist in nature and arise out of union leaders' desires for greater memberships, larger treasuries, more stable jobs for themselves, and increased status and power within the labor movement. Critics also question whether mergers increase unions' administrative or collective bargaining effectiveness. They stress the negative consequences of large-scale unions for membership control and union democracy.[42]

Some mergers do provide grist for the critics' mill. Consider, for example, whether rationalization results from the merger of such organizations as the Pottery and Allied Workers and the Seafarers (a liaison that lasted but two years) or the Cigar Makers and the Retail, Wholesale and Department Store Union. Other visible examples of opportunistic or expansionist mergers are the Teamsters' absorption of the Brewery Workers, the Laundry, Dry Cleaning and Dye House Workers, the American Communications Association, and the Allied Independent Unions; and the Steelworkers' absorption of the Mine, Mill and Smelter Workers, the Stone and Allied Products Workers, and District 50, Allied and Technical Workers (heavy and highway construction, as well as manufacturing, service, and other industries).

Chaison developed an interesting model of union merger activity, one that considers the relative strength of the motivation to merge vis-à-vis the barriers to merger. He also observed that many of the recent union mergers involved absorptions of small, public employee unions or unions with narrow jurisdictions operating in declining industries.[43]

Nevertheless, in the face of the recent drops in membership a number of unions entered financial crises and drastically cut back the size of their staffs. Thus, just as the workers in declining industries were facing layoffs, so were a number of union staff members. Some unions responded by merging in an effort to regain bargaining strength and staff economies through the creation of a larger union. For example, in 1979 the Meat Cutters and Butcher Workmen joined with the Retail Clerks to form the United Food and Commercial Workers International Union. In 1980 the Aluminum, Brick and Clay Workers merged with the Glass and Ceramic Workers to form the Aluminum, Brick and Glass Workers International Union.

One comes away from an examination of this record of union mergers with a mixed evaluation. On the one hand, some of the mergers did seem to fit the rationalization pattern expected and encouraged by AFL–CIO leaders. On the other hand, some of the occupations or jurisdictions that could benefit the most from union mergers, such as construction, have yet to witness any significant merger activity. Furthermore, there is no clear evidence that the anticipated benefits of union mergers have in fact been realized. For example, some of the unions that merged at the national level have not consolidated at the local level. Others simply merged their existing professional staffs into a single organization, with little or no reduction in administrative costs. Finally, no studies have yet determined whether improved administrative service or greater bargaining effectiveness has been achieved through mergers.

We can expect that changes in technology, along with the rising administrative costs of running an effective union, will continue the pressure for union mergers. At the same time, however, the political problems associated with merging two or more autonomous, and often rival, organizations into one body (with, obviously, only one president) will continue to limit the rate of mergers. Critical questions that must be addressed are: Do mergers produce the improved administrative and bargaining service they promise? Do they enhance unions' and their members' ability to adapt to technological change? And do those benefits result without also yielding losses in union membership control and internal union democracy? These are questions worthy of greater attention by both researchers and practitioners who hope to evaluate the consequences of further mergers and decide whether to promote or oppose additional mergers among U.S. unions.

UNIONS AND POLITICS

The U.S. labor movement, as mentioned earlier, has historically devoted the bulk of its efforts to collective bargaining as opposed to political action; that is, it has followed the business unionism approach. Few would quarrel with this characterization, especially in light of the extensive political activities pursued by unions in other countries. For one thing, the U.S. political system has lacked the labor party found in a number of European countries. For another, U.S. unions, with few exceptions, have not identified themselves with a socialist political platform, another characteristic common among many European labor movements. But, these observations notwithstanding, researchers continue to debate how fully business unionism is an appropriate characterization of U.S. labor movement history, and contemporary unionists also continue to debate the proper role of unions in U.S. politics.

The debate over the business unionism label arises in part from the fact that U.S. unions have historically played an important role in the nation's political affairs. At the national level they have been active and fairly successful supporters of numerous welfare programs such as social security, medicare, and Aid to Families with Dependent Children, and they were strong supporters of the 1964 Civil Rights Act. Unions also have been ardent and, again, successful supporters of federal legislation to protect and improve employment conditions. Here the list of federal programs includes the minimum wage, the Occupational Safety and Health Act, the Davis-Bacon procedures, and various pension regulations. AFL–CIO unions play an active role in the preparation for and debates surrounding federal legislation through the activities of the federation's Committee on Political Education (COPE).

Unions also remain an effective force in mobilizing voters in the United States. In the aftermath of Ronald Reagan's sweeping victory over Walter Mondale in the 1984 presidential election, the popular press was quick to question the vitality of labor's political clout because the AFL–CIO had formally endorsed the losing candidate at an early stage in the Democratic presidential primary process. But it should be remembered that exit polls by the major television networks found that 53 percent of union voters in the 1984 election did vote for Mondale. Furthermore, Mondale won 88 percent of the votes of AFL–CIO members registered as Democrats, and as a group union members voted in greater numbers than most other demographic groups.[44]

U.S. unions are also active in state and local politics, both in the preparation of legislation and in the election of government officials. A number of state COPE organizations and a number of local unions are very active in state and local affairs.

The debate among researchers concerns the significance of labor's political activity as compared to its collective bargaining activity and the factors that have shaped labor's political activity. Was political action only a limited supplement to labor's search for job security, and was that action largely forced upon labor by the political activists involved in promoting the New Deal? Or were U.S. workers not unlike their European counterparts—fully in possession of demands for social equality and political reform—but subject to much greater resistance to those demands from management and the courts?

The ongoing debate among the ranks of the U.S. labor movement concerns the appropriate mix between collective bargaining and political activities. As Chapter 3 pointed out and as shown further in the membership declines discussed in this chapter, the current environment is posing a serious challenge to U.S. labor organizations. Some union leaders blame their election losses on NLRB decisions; some blame membership declines on the sluggish macro economy and its effects on the historical strongholds of U.S. unions; others cite burgeoning imports and dwindling exports as causes of employment decline, and some of these observers blame the trade deficit on unfair international trade policies; still others blame these same trade policies for recent shifts in manufacturing jobs overseas.

All of these issues involve matters of national policy. Their increasing importance has led some unionists to call for a reorientation of labor's strategy away from its traditional emphasis on collective bargaining and toward political action as the preferred means to labor's ends. Labor leaders such as Douglas Fraser (former president of the UAW) have periodically vented their frustration with recent policy changes by expressing interest in an independent labor party. The Solidarity Day marches in Washington on Labor Day in 1983 and 1984 brought together a wide range of political interest groups under labor's leadership and served as yet another expression of labor's interest in heightened political activity.

Nonetheless, however frequent or well-publicized these calls for political activism may be, they have not been taken up in any significant or widespread way. Despite all its recent problems the labor movement in the United States has yet to make a fundamental change in its political orientation or activity. Changes may come in the future, of course, but they would require a major break, not only from recent trends but from the long history of labor's involvement in U.S. politics.

SUMMARY

The union membership figures reported at the beginning of this chapter highlight one of the central challenges facing unions today. Unions' share of the U.S. labor force has declined substantially over the last ten years, a decline even more alarming given the inroads nonunion firms have achieved in many industries that were once bastions of union organization. Responsible for this decline have been innovative human resource and union avoidance policies nonunion firms have adopted, structural shifts in the economy and labor force, the effects of recession and industrial decline, and unions' unproductive and, in some cases, only feeble efforts to counteract these and other developments.

Yet the outlook for the labor movement is not completely gloomy. The benefits of the human resource innovations that serve as a partial alternative to unionization have diffused to only a limited number of U.S. workers. And many workers lack the long-term attachment to an employment relationship that is needed to make the participatory processes embedded in the new human resource management models work. We are referring here to the growing numbers of temporary, part-time, or flexible-contract employees and to the growing numbers of professionals who hold a greater attachment to their occupation than to their employer.

At the same time, although workers remain suspicious of union leaders and labor institutions, they also appear to be attracted to a representational system that addresses workplace and strategic issues when those issues have a direct influence on their employment security and working conditions. These unmet needs for workplace and strategic representation have led unions and the AFL–CIO to begin to rethink some of their basic strategies. But whether lasting and deep changes in unions' representational strategies follow and whether these changes are linked to a new union political strategy remain to be seen.

Suggested Readings

For a classic discussion of the factors influencing union growth and union structures for bargaining, see:

Ulman, Lloyd. *The Rise of the National Trade Union*. Cambridge: Harvard University Press, 1958.

For a thorough rendering of the factors contributing to union decline in the United States, see:

Dickens, William T., and Jonathan S. Leonard. "Accounting for the Decline in Union Membership, 1950–1980." *Industrial and Labor Relations Review* 38 (April 1985): 323–34.

For insights into where the AFL–CIO may be heading in its future bargaining and organizing strategies, see:

American Federation of Labor–Congress of Industrial Organizations, Committee on the Evolution of Work. "The Changing Situation of Workers and Their Unions," report. Washington, D.C.: AFL–CIO, February 1985.

Notes

1. We must caution that the source of data on the service sector changed after 1980, making comparisons over the years in question only tentative.

2. Courtney D. Gifford, *Directory of U.S. Labor Organizations, 1982–83 Edition* (Washington, D.C.: Bureau of National Affairs, 1982).

3. Cheryl L. Maranto and Jack Fiorito, "The Effect of Union Characteristics on the Outcome of NLRB Certification Elections," *Industrial and Labor Relations Review* 40 (January 1987): 225–40.

4. U.S. Department of Labor, Bureau of Labor Statistics, *Employment and Earnings* (Washington, D.C.: GPO, January 1986).

5. Henry S. Farber, "The Extent of Unionization in the United States," in *Challenges and Choices Facing American Labor*, ed. Thomas A. Kochan, 15–43 (Cambridge: MIT Press, 1985).

6. Richard B. Freeman, "Why Are Unions Faring Poorly in NLRB Representation Elections?" in *Challenges and Choices,* ed. Kochan, 45–64.

7. William T. Dickens and Jonathan S. Leonard, "Accounting for the Decline in Union Membership, 1950–1980." *Industrial and Labor Relations Review* 38 (April 1985): 332.

8. Thomas A. Kochan, Robert B. McKersie, and John Chalykoff, "The Effects of Corporate Strategy and Workplace Innovations on Union Representation," *Industrial and Labor Relations Review* 39 (July 1986): 487–501.

9. James B. Dworkin and Marian Extejt, "Why Workers Decertify Their Unions," photocopy (West Lafayette, Ind.: Purdue University, 1978).

10. Dickens and Leonard, "Accounting for the Decline," 326.

11. John T. Dunlop, "The Development of Labor Organizations: A Theoretical Framework," in *Insights Into Labor Issues*, ed. Richard A. Lester and Joseph Shister, 175 (New York: Macmillan, 1948).

12. John R. Commons, *A Documentary History of American Industrial Society*, vol. 5 (Cleveland: Arthur H. Clark, 1911), 19. See also Leo Wolman, *The Ebb and Flow in Trade Unionism* (New York: National Bureau of Economic Research, 1936).

13. Lloyd Ulman, *The Rise of the National Trade Union* (Cambridge: Harvard University Press, 1958), 4–6; Harry A. Millis and Royal E. Montgomery, *Organized Labor* (New York: McGraw-Hill, 1945), 12–165.

14. Orley Ashenfelter and John H. Pencavel, "American Trade Union Growth, 1900–1960," *Quarterly Journal of Economics* 83 (August 1969): 434–48.

15. For a review of these arguments, see Woodrow L. Ginsberg, "Union Growth, Government, and Structure," in *A Review of Industrial Relations Research,* vol. 1 (Madison, Wis.: Industrial Relations Research Association, 1970), 207–60.

16. Ashenfelter and Pencavel, "American Trade Union Growth."

17. William J. Moore and Robert J. Newman, "On the Prospects for American Trade Union Growth," *Review of Economics and Statistics* 57 (November 1975): 438–45.

18. Richard B. Freeman, "Unionism Comes to the Public Sector," *Journal of Economic Literature* 24 (March 1986): 42–86; Gregory Saltzman, "Bargaining Laws as a Cause and Consequence of the Growth of Teacher Unionism," *Industrial and Labor Relations Review* 38 (April 1985): 335–51.

19. Charles P. Larrowe, "A Meteor on the Industrial Relations Horizon: The Foreman's Association of America," *Labor History* 2 (Fall 1961): 259–94.

20. Ulman, *The Rise of the National*, 6.

21. Sam Kushner, *Long Road to Delano* (New York: International Publishers, 1975).

22. Joseph R. Grodin, "California Agriculture Labor Act: Early Experience," *Industrial Relations* 15 (October 1976): 275–94.

23. Courtney D. Gifford, *Directory of U.S. Labor Organizations, 1986–87 Edition* (Washington, D.C.: Bureau of National Affairs, 1986), 62.

24. Monroe Berkowitz, "The Economics of Trade Union Organizing and Administration," *Industrial and Labor Relations Review* 7 (July 1954), 575–92; Richard N. Block, "A Theory of the Supply of Union Representation and the Allocation of Union Resources," photocopy (East Lansing: Michigan State University, 1978).

25. Paula Voos, "Union Organizing: Costs and Benefits," *Industrial and Labor Relations Review* 36 (July 1983): 576–91.

26. Richard B. Freeman and James L. Medoff, *What Do Unions Do?* (New York: Basic Books, 1984).

27. Samuel Gompers, *Labor and the Common Welfare* (New York: Dutton, 1919), 7.

28. These data are discussed more fully in Thomas A. Kochan, Harry C. Katz, and Robert B. McKersie, *The Transformation of American Industrial Relations* (New York: Basic Books, 1986), 215–18.

29. Henry S. Farber and Daniel H. Saks, "Why Workers Want Unions: The Role of Relative Wages and Job Characteristics," *Journal of Political Economy* 88 (April 1980): 349–69.

30. See, for example, Graham L. Staines and Robert P. Quinn, *The 1977 Quality of Employment Survey* (Ann Arbor: Survey Research Center, University of Michigan, 1978).

31. Stephen M. Hills, "The Attitudes of Union and Nonunion Male Workers Toward Union Representation," *Industrial and Labor Relations Review* 38 (January 1985): 179–94.

32. American Federation of Labor–Congress of Industrial Organizations, Committee on the Evolution of Work, "The Changing Situation of Workers and Their Unions," report (Washington, D.C.: AFL–CIO, February 1985). Note that another alternative strategy is the corporate campaign, discussed in Chapter 4.

33. J. David Edelstein and Malcolm Warner, *Comparative Union Democracy: Organization and Opposition in British and American Unions* (New York: Halsted Press, 1976); John C. Anderson, "A Comparative Analysis of Local Union Democracy," *Industrial Relations* 17 (October 1978): 278–95.

34. George Strauss, "Union Government in the U.S.: Research Past and Future," *Industrial Relations* 16 (May 1977): 241.

35. Sara Gamm, "The Election Base of National Union Executive Boards," *Industrial and Labor Relations Review* 32 (April 1979): 295–311.

36. Seymour M. Lipset, Martin A. Trow, and James S. Coleman, *Union Democracy: The Internal Politics of the International Typographical Union* (Glencoe, Ill.: Free Press, 1956), 13–16.

37. Lipset, Trow, and Coleman, *Union Democracy*.

38. Derek C. Bok and John T. Dunlop, *Labor and the American Community* (New York: Simon and Schuster, 1970), 186.

39. Thomas A. Kochan, Lee Dyer, and David B. Lipsky, *The Effectiveness of Union-Management Safety and Health Committees* (Kalamazoo, Mich.: W.E. Upjohn Institute for Employment Research, 1977), 86.

40. Arthur Goldberg, *AFL–CIO: Labor United* (New York: McGraw-Hill, 1956), 229.

41. Gifford, *Directory, 1986–87,* 1–4.

42. For a generally critical view of union mergers see George W. Brooks and Sara Gamm, *The Causes and Effects of Union Mergers,* report to the U.S. Department of Labor (September 1976).

43. Gary N. Chaison, *When Unions Merge* (Lexington, Mass.: D.C. Heath, 1986).

44. Those exit polls were reviewed in *Daily Labor Report,* no. 232, 3 December 1984: D1–D5.

CHAPTER 6

Management Strategies and Structures for Collective Bargaining

In Chapter 1 we introduced management as one of the major actors in the industrial relations system. In this chapter we assess how responsive the system is to management goals. An understanding and appraisal of management as a bargaining organization is another essential building block in the study of the U.S. collective bargaining system because management practices play a dominant role in shaping the pattern of labor relations in this country. As noted in the previous chapters, unions tend to be defensive organizations, that is, they react to management's policies and seek to protect the interests of their members against any adverse effects of management actions. Thus, by understanding the current philosophies, structures, goals, and practices of management, we can gain a good deal of insight into the future of labor relations in this country.

The material presented in this chapter will draw heavily on a 1977 Conference Board survey of labor relations practices in 668 of the largest private sector unionized firms in the country and on a follow-up survey conducted in 1983.[1] In 1977 those firms employed approximately 9,260,000 workers, of which approximately 4,250,000, or 44 percent, were unionized. Table 6–1 lists the primary industries with which the responding firms in 1977 were affiliated. Although the 1983 survey yielded a smaller sample (409) than the earlier one, the industrial compositions of the two samples were quite similar. Whenever we make comparisons between the two samples, we rely on data from the sample of 243 firms present in both surveys.

Our framework presented back in Figure 1–1 serves as the starting point for analyzing the tremendous variation that exists in the policies, struc-

TABLE 6–1
Primary industry of the firms responding to the 1977 Conference Board survey

Primary industry of the firm	Number of firms in the survey
Mining; oil and gas extraction	11
Construction	15
Food processing and tobacco	55
Textiles	9
Apparel	11
Lumber and wood products	10
Furniture	8
Paper	25
Publishing	17
Chemicals	47
Petroleum and coal products	16
Rubber and plastics	11
Leather, footwear, luggage	1
Glass, clay, stone products	25
Primary metal refining	32
Fabricated metals	34
Machinery	60
Electrical equipment	49
Transportation equipment	29
Instruments	21
Miscellaneous manufacturing	16
Transportation	26
Communications	14
Electric and gas utilities	71
Retail and wholesale trade	49
Miscellaneous	6
Total	668

Note: It is becoming increasingly difficult to identify the primary industry of a corporation, as conglomeration brings many different lines of business under one management. This table is particularly subject to such misplacement, because it includes many large businesses.

tures, and practices of different management organizations. As shown in the model, management's choices and decisions are partly constrained by the external environment, the structure of collective bargaining, and the characteristics of the unions with which they deal. Beyond these external determinants of management policies, however, lies a good deal of organizational discretion. Within the organization labor relations policies are shaped in various ways by (1) managers' basic values toward human resource management and toward unions, (2) by the types of business strategies the organization uses to compete in its markets, and (3) by the structure and dynamics of management decision making.

Consequently, we will begin our analysis by placing the management of industrial relations in a broader organizational and strategic perspective. As we will show, this is especially important to an understanding of contemporary industrial relations practices since many of the changes in collective bargaining in recent years were introduced at management's initiative, reflecting changes in these organizational and strategic variables. Before beginning that analysis, however, we will make several more general points about management's role in industrial society and in a collective bargaining system.

THE ROLE OF MANAGEMENT IN INDUSTRIAL RELATIONS

Management is the driving force in any advanced industrial relations system. Management is responsible for efficiently allocating scarce organizational resources. Efficiency is valued not only as an important organizational goal, but also as a societal goal. To achieve these goals, management is expected to make rational decisions so that all of the organization's human and financial resources are put to their most productive uses.[2]

The Role of Business Strategy

Not all firms choose to pursue their goals in the same way. In addition to the variation in practices required by the differences in external environments reviewed in earlier chapters, firms must decide precisely how to compete within each of their markets or business units. Although there is no definitive typology of business strategies, for our purposes we can distinguish between the effects on industrial relations of two different competitive strategies: a strategy to supply the *lowest cost* product or service; and a strategy to supply a product or service that is high in quality, technologically innovative, or some other way *differentiated* from the product or service of competing firms, thereby allowing the firm to sell it at a premium. The latter strategy, much more than the former, requires ready adaptability to changing technologies, market conditions, and consumer tastes.

The priorities given to different business strategies can vary systematically over the course of a business or product life cycle. In the early or growth stages of a product line or business, management faces strong pressures to get the product to the market. Those pressures tend to translate into pressures on human resource and labor relations professionals to minimize labor turnover and maximize labor peace. Recall that in the post-Depression years of rapid economic growth, industrial relations professionals rose to power largely because their efforts were deemed crucial in achieving labor peace (by developing working relationships with union leaders and uniform policies for administering day-to-day relationships at the workplace). In later, more mature stages of a product life cycle, when market demand has leveled off or is declining, the goals of cost control and productivity improvement, product improvement and flexibility in the use of human (and capital) resources increase in importance.

Given the rudimentary state of empirical research linking concepts from business strategy to human resource and industrial relations strategy, our statements here might best be regarded as working hypotheses rather than broadly agreed upon facts. Nonetheless, throughout this book we will find much support for these propositions because they are instrumental in explaining recent changes in management practice. In fact, linking business strategy and industrial relations policies is one of the critical tasks senior executives are calling on contemporary industrial relations professionals to perform as a normal part of their role in the organization.

The Role of Managers' Values

Human resource or industrial relations strategies are not determined solely by external forces and the demands of business strategies. Instead, the values held by top organizational executives serve as filters through which potential policies or options must pass. Thus, the expressed or implicit values or ideology of management toward unions and toward workers more generally influences the choice of industrial relations policies and practices of the firm as well.

It must be recognized that employers in general are reluctant participants in collective bargaining. As will be discussed in more detail later, the vast majority of employers would prefer to be nonunion. Most, therefore, participate in bargaining only if they are compelled to do so by law (that is, a union has been duly certified as the exclusive bargaining agent of their employees) and if the union is powerful enough to force the employer to bargain and keep the employer from withdrawing from the relationship. This basic (and rather obvious) point must be kept in mind when trying to explain management behavior in collective bargaining.

HISTORICAL AND CONTEMPORARY STRATEGIES TOWARD UNIONIZATION

Much of American labor history is a documentation of bloody organizing struggles and attempts by management to reduce the incentive for employees to join unions. Although the level of bloodshed has declined and the strategies used to oppose unionization have become more subtle over the years, management's vigorous opposition to unions is as strong now as ever. Brown and Myers aptly described the sentiments of perhaps the majority of U.S. management executives in an article written in the mid-1950s:

> It may well be true that if American management, upon retiring for the night, were assured that by the next morning the unions with which they dealt would have disappeared, more management people than not would experience the happiest sleep of their lives.[3]

Yet, even given the tenacious hold of this sentiment, some firms place a lower priority on remaining nonunion than others. Some employers have been pragmatic enough to recognize that in their situation either it is impossible to avoid unionization or the costs of attempting to avoid unions outweigh the potential benefits; these employers have therefore been less aggressive in resisting unions.

Thus, the intensity of employers' resistance to unionization, as well as the strategies they use to remain nonunion, has varied across firms and over time. Our task here is to trace the evolution of management philosophies toward unions and to identify the tactics used to carry these philosophies out in different firms and at different times.

The Historical Evolution of Two Union Avoidance Strategies

In Chapter 2 we noted that as early as the 1920s two different strategies were used by employers to avoid unions: the direct *union suppression* approach (actively resisting any organizing drives); and the indirect *union substitution* approach (removing the incentives for unionization). It was predominantly the larger companies that used the union substitution strategy (although many used both strategies simultaneously). In 1932, for example, 118 companies employing 1,000 workers or more accounted for 97 percent of all employees covered under employee representation (company union) plans.[4] It therefore seems that the strategies used to avoid unionization are to some extent a function of the firm's financial resources or market constraints. If a firm can afford the specialized personnel and employee relations staffs necessary to implement the strategy, it will also use the most sophisticated management techniques it can afford. Those firms unable to absorb these expenses of the more sophisticated approach will oppose unions by using the direct suppression strategies.

To what extent do these same patterns hold today? Although systematic evidence on this is obviously hard to find, the same approaches are still apparent, and they seem to be distributed in the same systematic pattern as they were in the earlier decades. In the early 1970s, for example, the labor movement singled out the southern textile industry in general, and the J.P. Stevens Company in particular, as the symbol of the direct suppression approach to avoiding unionization.[5]

A number of environmental and organizational conditions appear to increase the probability that the employer will choose the direct approach to union avoidance. Among these are the presence of a hostile social and political environment toward unions; employment of low-wage or unskilled workers who have few labor market alternatives; an abundant supply of alternative workers; low recruitment and training costs; a low-profit, highly competitive industry; smaller firms; the lack of a professional personnel staff; and a willingness to litigate union challenges through administrative and judicial channels. Although numerous examples can be found of firms that fit this profile, there is no way to measure precisely how many firms actively oppose unions through hard-line, suppressive tactics. As noted in Chapter 4, however, some evidence suggests that the use of union suppression tactics has increased in the past 20 years. For instance, the number of employees illegally discharged by employers during organizing campaigns increased tenfold from 1960 to 1975.[6] Thus, management's use of suppressive tactics against union activists is not merely an artifact of pre–New Deal labor history but a feature of contemporary industrial relations that has actually been growing.

At the same time, some firms continue to reduce the incentives to unionize, by employing contemporary tools of personnel and organizational behavior. Recall our proposition (in Chapter 5) that many workers reluctantly turn to unionization only after they have exhausted all other means to influence employer policies. It is therefore not surprising that firms try to use positive personnel policies to meet employee needs before workers become frustrated enough to turn to a union. Although many firms that institute sophisticated personnel policies do not do so solely, or even primarily, to avoid unions but rather to motivate, satisfy, and more effectively supervise their employees, the fact is that the effect is to lessen the incentive to unionize.

A representative profile of the contemporary strategies used to reduce the incentives to unionize would include most if not all of the following: (1) wages and fringe benefits equal to or greater than those paid comparable workers in the local labor market; (2) a high rate of investment per worker in such employee programs such as training and career development; (3) extensive efforts to stabilize employment and avoid layoffs as much as possible; (4) advanced systems of organizational communications and information sharing; (5) informal mechanisms for, or encouragement of, participation in decision making about the way work is to be performed; (6) development of a psychological climate that fosters and rewards organizational loyalty and commitment; (7) rational wage and salary administration, performance appraisal, and promotion systems that reward merit but also recognize seniority; (8) a nonunion grievance procedure (usually without binding arbitration); (9) location of new production facilities in rural areas or areas only sparsely unionized; and in some cases (10) the use of employee selection devices that weed out workers who are or might be pro-union.[7] All of these policies are aimed at retaining workers who are satisfied with their economic rewards, the intrinsic aspects of their jobs, and their ability to influence decisions having to do with their work. Again, as shown in Chapter 5, these are exactly the conditions that reduce the incentives to join unions.

Data from the Conference Board survey demonstrate that these strategies have, in fact, been highly successful in avoiding unionization. Firms that actively pursued the policies described above and that had a policy of resisting unionization were nearly 100 percent successful in avoiding unionization in the new facilities they had opened in recent years.[8]

These types of personnel policies are not only compatible with a business strategy of rapid growth, they are instrumental in its execution. A key question therefore arises: How many of the companies that adopt these personnel policies during periods of high growth will remain committed to them as they move farther into their product life cycles and experience slower growth and greater cost competition?

We cannot answer this question conclusively, but our own research suggests that those firms that have embedded these personnel policies deep within the value system or culture of the organization are unlikely to abandon them quickly or easily.[9] Both the ongoing usefulness of the policies in managing human resources and the fear that abandoning them will lead to unionization will likely sustain managers' commitment to them even when the organization faces slower rates of market growth and profit. On the other hand, it is unlikely that we will see as much innovation in the human resource policies of these firms as in the past, and we can expect to see smaller firms' commitment to the more costly policies erode as they come to face sustained competition in their markets.

Among the best known examples of mature companies that continue to apply some or all of these practices successfully (they have remained nonunion) are IBM, Eastman Kodak, Digital Equipment, Motorola, DuPont, and Michelin Tire. Two companies that have been relatively successful using these strategies in more competitive environments and with lesser skilled work forces are Marriott Hotels and Sears Roebuck.[10] An increasing number of construction contractors, and even a few relatively new coal mines, have embarked on these strategies in recent years. Moreover, there is an ample supply of behavioral science consultants who specialize in helping companies develop policies to stay nonunion. In all respects, therefore, the union substitution strategy is alive, well, and growing in popularity in organizations with the financial and professional resources necessary to support it.

In sum, companies with sophisticated personnel systems are most likely to be those that enjoy an environment of growth, high profits, large-scale operations, and employees with sufficient skills and training to warrant the investments in human resource management required. Furthermore, they must have highly trained personnel staffs to monitor effectively employee attitudes and the wages, benefits, and personnel practices of other firms.

Although we can safely use these examples and theoretical arguments to propose that the strategy management chooses to avoid unionization is at least partly a function of its economic environment and business strategies, we cannot specify precisely how tightly these factors limit the discretion of the firm. Management ideology or values clearly play an important role as well. Moreover, many of the sophisticated personnel policies have moved beyond the experimental stage and are now "state of the art," that is, they have taken on a life of their own. Thus, they may survive even in the face of changing market conditions and business strategies.

Nor is there always a clear distinction between the union substitution and union suppression strategies. As noted above, some companies overtly pursue both at the same time, but in other firms a thin line often separates the two. For example, how much direct but covert suppression of union organizing goes on in the large, high-growth organizations that employ the union substitution approach? Some evidence suggests, quite a bit. Box 6–1 describes what happened to one worker who showed an interest in organizing in a firm that is well known for its use of progressive personnel policies.

BOX 6–1
Union avoidance in action—at Texas Instruments,
if you're pro-union, firm may be anti-you

"It's like '1984'," says one worker as he waits for a machine in the lobby to read his badge and unlock the entrance door. "Big Brother is always watching for spies and for invaders from the union."

I am an invader of a different sort, a reporter who worked on the plant's electronics assembly line for three weeks to get a first-hand look at what labor unions say is one of the most calculated and effective antiunion operations in the country. The company didn't know I was a reporter when it hired me, and it has since strenuously objected to the way in which the story was obtained.

Texas Instruments—or TI—is the third largest nonunion company in the United States, after International Business Machines and Eastman Kodak. It earned $116.6 million last year—20% more than in 1976. In 1977, the company sold more than $2 billion of computers, calculators, semiconductors and other electronic products, ranging from digital watches to guided missiles. More than 45,000 employees work in the company's 15 U.S. plants.

. . . The company made its feelings about unions clear to me and the other new "TIers"—as we're called—during our first hour of orientation. A TI-produced videotape told us that unions were detrimental and were unnecessary for progress. An orientation booklet warned us that we might be approached by union organizers and asked to sign a union card. "We encourage you to do as a large majority of TIers all over the U.S. have done," the booklet ends, "and reject the union attempts to organize."

"Don't you mess with unions, girl," advises my assembly line's tough, kind group leader and a TI employee for 10 years in Dallas and Austin. "That's the one thing that'll put you out the door faster'n what you come in. If TI finds out you're even bending that way, well, you won't progress at TI.

BOX 6–1 *(continued)*

You'll be the first one laid off. They'll put you somewhere you can't make no trouble."

My casual conversations in which I express pro-union views trouble a few co-workers so much that they begin to avoid me. "Please don't talk to me on break anymore," one nervous fellow worker says. "If the company finds out I'm listening, I'll get fired."

Employee fear seems to be a major part of TI's antiunion defense system. TIers have heard how the company feels about unions, and they have also heard that TI swiftly terminates offenders.

To test TI's reputed union alarm mechanism, I tell [my group leader] a made-up story that I have been approached by another worker in the parking lot and asked to sign a union card. [She] immediately tells her supervisor, and a day later she mentions to me that she has already been questioned about her report by "higher-ups." "They called me on the carpet about it," she says. "They just always like to know where they stand, so's they can take action if they have to."

My plan was to work at the plant for a month, but by the end of my third week, my pro-union comments were so well known that I was referred to by some workers as "that union chick from Detroit."

Abruptly, right before Independence Day weekend, my supervisor pulled me from the assembly line and escorted me to the office of the chief of security at the Austin plant. [He] charged me with a "very serious, serious offense"—falsifying my application by omitting the fact that I am a college graduate. He has me sign a two-page document he has handwritten in my name, which explains that I falsified my application in order to obtain a job.

"You see how it works?" said one older colleague after hearing I had been fired. "They got you fair and square. Probably all of us here got something to hide."

Source: Reprinted with permission of *The Wall Street Journal,* Dow Jones and Company, Inc., 1978. All rights reserved.

The Intensity of Management's Opposition to Unions

In the Conference Board survey industrial relations executives were asked to indicate which labor relations function was more important in their company: remaining as "nonunion as possible" or achieving the most favorable bargain possible with their existing unions. In 1977, 31 percent of the firms responded that remaining as nonunion as possible was the more important function of the two. The majority of the firms with fewer than 40 percent of their employees organized assigned top priority to avoiding further union organizing; the majority of those that were more unionized gave priority to bargaining with their existing unions.

Among these same firms in 1983, however, 45 percent indicated avoiding further unionization was their top priority. Thus, the number of firms assigning a higher priority to union avoidance than bargaining increased by 14 percentage points over the six intervening years. One reason for this increase was that unions were losing members during those years, and it therefore became more *feasible* for firms to adopt an active union avoidance strategy.

Interviews with labor relations executives in the firms included in the survey provided further information on the differences in the importance that firms attach to remaining nonunion. The interview data both reinforce and extend the correlational results. One executive from a major brewery indicated that he took for granted that any new plants opened by his company (two major new facilities had been opened in the previous five years) would be organized by the union that had contracts in the existing plants. This company had not opposed unionization since it had lost the early organizing battles of the 1940s and a single union emerged as dominant in the industry. In 1970 the company had agreed to shift from single-plant agreements to a national master agreement with local supplements. The company agreed to this shift with full knowledge not only that all new plants would be organized by the same union, but also that they would be brought under the master contract.

Another highly successful company that has been organized by a single union for over 30 years has developed a very cooperative bargaining relationship and does not actively oppose organization of its new facilities by the union. On the other hand, this same company strongly opposes any organization of white-collar employees and therefore attends to their needs and expectations for participation as part of its efforts to reduce the incentive to unionize.

These two examples illustrate another factor that the survey data show influences whether a union avoidance strategy will be used by a firm: the degree of centralization in the structure of bargaining. Those firms that deal with a single union in a companywide bargaining structure are less likely than others to resist unions vigorously in any newly opened facilities. In these bargaining relationships the dominant union has the leverage needed to engage top management decision makers at the strategic level of the firm—the level where the basic decision is made on whether to resist or to recognize a union. If a union cannot reach this level of managerial decision making, the firm will most likely adopt a union avoidance strategy.

The history of the United Auto Workers and General Motors is the most obvious illustration of this point. As noted in Chapter 4, the UAW forced GM to end its "southern strategy" (opening nonunion plants in the South and resisting union-organizing attempts) in return for continued union commitment to quality-of-working-life and other workplace innovations in the existing union facilities. The joint union-company design of the Saturn plant is only one of the recent products of this "union acceptance" strategy.

On the other hand, in some industries that have been highly unionized the companies have become increasingly dissatisfied with their union contracts and have embarked on efforts to open new, nonunion operations or, alternatively, operations organized by different unions. The construction industry is an example of the former strategy. A number of large, traditionally union contractors have developed what has been described as a *double-breasted* strategy, that is, the running of separate union and nonunion divisions.[11] Firms in the bituminous coal industry are examples of the latter strategy. A number of operators that have opened new mines in recent years have strongly resisted organizing drives by the United Mine Workers (UMW) even though they have contracts with the union in their other mines. In addition, some firms that have opened surface (strip) mines in the West have strongly opposed organizing efforts by the UMW and have managed either to remain nonunion or to be organized by the Union of Operating Engineers instead of the UMW.[12]

Both the construction and the mining examples suggest that the performance of the existing union-management relationship will influence the intensity of opposition by highly unionized companies to the extension of organization to new operations. The experience in the construction, trucking, and printing industries implies that the greater the difference between labor costs in union and nonunion firms in an industry, the more aggressively management will oppose any new union organizing. The coal industry example in particular suggests that the more strike prone or hostile the union-management relationship is (and again the greater the differences between the productivity of the firm's union and nonunion operations), the more opposed management will be to any new union organizing.

These examples all involve firms that already have unions representing some of their employees. It should also be noted, however, that neither the Conference Board interviews nor any other case-study evidence provides illustrations of unorganized firms that would not strongly oppose union-organizing drives given the resources to do so.

Overall, then, we can summarize the current state of management policies toward union organizing as follows:

1. In the majority of firms that are highly organized, avoiding new union organizing ranks as only a middle-range priority among the other labor relations goals of the firm;
2. In the majority of nonunion or weakly unionized firms, avoiding new union organizing is given top priority;
3. Highly organized firms in highly organized industries tend to be less strongly opposed to unionization of new plants, provided their economic

and labor relations experiences with their present unions have been relatively favorable; and

4. In general, firms of all types are strongly opposed to organization of white-collar employees, regardless of the firm's experiences with unions of its blue-collar workers.

Finally, beyond all of these relatively objective factors that influence the intensity of management opposition to unionization lie two critical factors that are difficult to identify or measure. The first is the philosophy of the top corporate executives. It is these individuals who make the ultimate decisions on how hard a line to pursue against unions. Although their decisions are based in part on the potential economic costs and benefits of avoiding unionization, they are also based on the executives' personal views of unions. Second, shifts in the social climate and the political power of unions may lead to corresponding shifts in the willingness of top management to resist unions aggressively, shifts reflected in the calculus top management uses to develop a policy toward any new union organizing.

All of the above points suggest that at this point in history, the U.S. industrial relations system is experiencing a reinforcing cycle of increasing managerial resistance to unions, one that is being fostered by a declining rate of union membership, by declining union power, and by the further decentralization of bargaining structures. If the union-nonunion gap in labor costs, the hostile political climate, and the weaknesses of U.S. labor law continue in force, they will serve further to reinforce the organizational and structural factors contributing to management's incentives and ability to avoid any unionization. In other words, unless something changes in the environment or in the strategies of the parties to break this self-reinforcing cycle, management resistance to unions and the erosion of union membership will continue.

MANAGEMENT STRUCTURES FOR COLLECTIVE BARGAINING

In this section we will first describe the general pattern of the management organization for collective bargaining and then go on to explore the variations in the structure across different firms. In its most general form the management structure exhibits three basic characteristics: the *size* of the labor relations staff in relation to the number of employees in the organization; the degree of *centralization* in decision making on labor relations issues; and the degree of *specialization* in decision making on labor relations, that is, the extent to which decision-making power is placed in the hands of the labor relations staff instead of in the hands of the operating, or line, managers. The term *labor relations staff* as used here refers to staff with responsibility for handling union-organizing attempts, negotiations, contract administration, and litigation with regard to union activity. The term does not refer to personnel staff who handle, for example, recruitment, staffing, equal employment opportunity, safety and health, and wage and salary administration, although an increasing number of firms now integrate these personnel and labor relations activities within a broad human resource management unit.

Before beginning, a word is in order to explain the role that management structure plays in our analysis of management as a bargaining organization. The function of an organizational structure is to provide a mechanism for establishing and implementing organizational strategies, goals, and policies.[13] The growth of a bureaucratic structure is viewed as a rational organizational response to the limited or bounded rationality of any individual decision maker.[14] That is, no individual has sufficient information or expertise to make effective decisions on all matters. Furthermore, once basic strategic decisions or long-term policies are established, they must be implemented on a day-to-day basis. Management therefore allocates responsibility for decisions in a manner that allows the organization to adapt to new problems and pressures from its environment and still maintain control over its economic destiny. In short, in the case of industrial relations functions, management develops a structure whose purpose is to bargain effectively with the union.

The presence of a union serves as one external pressure that induces a set of structural responses designed to allow management to bargain effectively. The three most important organizational responses are (1) to add labor relations staff and specialists to deal with union-management relations, (2) to reallocate power within the management structure by centralizing control over key strategic decisions affecting the economic performance of the firm, and (3) to reallocate power to labor relations specialists in areas where technical training, knowledge, and data are required to provide top executives with the information and advice necessary to make the key decisions. The stronger the union and the more centralized bargaining is, the more likely the organization is to make these structural adaptations.

But note, when a firm's business strategy changes, we would expect a corresponding change in its structure for bargaining to occur. This is exactly what we have been observing in labor relations in recent years. Shifts in strategy from those that valued labor peace to strategies requiring tighter cost controls and greater flexibility have shifted power from labor relations staff to line managers and human resource specialists. Moreover, the weaker the union, the greater the loss in power experienced by the traditional labor relations professionals.

The Size of the Labor Relations Staff

The majority of corporations included in the Conference Board surveys have labor relations staff at the plant, division, and corporate headquarters levels. About two-thirds of the firms have staff at the plant level; 60 percent have staff at the division level; and almost all of the firms (93 percent) have staff at the corporate level of the organization. The number of staff members employed by these corporations in relation to the number of unionized employees varies greatly. In 1977 the 601 firms responding to this question employed an average of 13.4 labor relations professionals each. This figure masks a very broad distribution, however. The data in Table 6–2 summarize the variations in the ratio of labor relations staff members to unionized employees. The most common ratio was one staff person per 201 to 400 union members; 28 percent of the firms fell into this category. At the higher extreme, however, 23 percent of the firms had one staff member for every 200 unionized employees or fewer. At the lower extreme 11 percent of the firms had more than 1,000 unionized employees for every labor relations staff member.

What accounts for this wide variation? Organizational theory suggests that a firm will invest more in specialized personnel as the importance of a functional area (such as labor relations) increases. The basic argument is that the more uncertain, volatile, or unpredictable events in a particular area of a firm's environment (such as union activity) become, the more likely the firm is to establish specialized units (often called *boundary-spanning units*) to manage this area of activity.[15] We would expect, therefore, that larger labor relations staffs will exist where unions are more able to impose significant costs on the firm.

To test this hypothesis we conducted a regression analysis of the Conference Board data and found consistent results. The ratio of the number of labor relations specialists to the number of union members was greater in the firms that were more highly unionized and in firms in industries with (1) high strike rates, (2) high ratios of labor costs to total costs, and (3) high rates of unionization. In addition, we found a considerable influence exerted by economies of scale. That is, the number of staff members per number of unionized employees decreased as the size of the firm increased. The results

TABLE 6–2

Distribution of the ratio of the number of labor relations staff members to the number of unionized employees in the firms responding to the 1977 Conference Board survey

Ratio	Number of firms	Percentage of firms
1/200 or fewer	138	23.0
1/201–400	169	28.1
1/401–600	120	20.0
1/601–800	57	9.5
1/801–1,000	45	7.5
1/1,000 +	68	11.3
No staff	4	0.7

then confirm the expectation that labor relations staffs are largest (holding constant the size of the firm) in firms where union activity is most likely to have its greatest effect on the economic performance of the firm and where it poses the greatest threat of a disruption to the firm's operations.

Centralization in Decision Making

One of the most highly controversial issues within any organization is who is going to make the key decisions on any given policy. The power to make decisions on bargaining is just as controversial an issue in management as we have found it to be in unions (Chapter 5). And any allocation of this power will have important implications not only for bargaining effectiveness, but also for the status, autonomy, and power of competing individuals and groups within the management organization.

Table 6–3 shows the locus of decision making for 11 typical labor relations activities within the firms responding to the 1977 Conference Board survey. The table data are based on responses to the question of who had primary responsibility for the activities shown in the table. Of particular interest here is the question of how centralized decision making on labor relations issues is within these large corporations.

The most striking pattern shown by these data is the high degree of centralization of the responsibility for labor relations policy in these firms. Almost 92 percent of the firms placed primary responsibility for developing overall union policy at the corporate level, either in the hands of the top labor relations executive (60 percent) or in the hands of the chief executive officer (32 percent). And in the majority of the firms the corporate labor relations executive also had primary responsibility for the following functions: developing union avoidance activities, responding to union-organizing campaigns, conducting contract negotiations or advising negotiators, drawing up the final contract language, costing union proposals, and doing the general background research for bargaining. Only the administration of the contract and general troubleshooting activities were decentralized to the division or the plant level in the majority of the firms surveyed.

The top level of the corporation also plays a very active role in reviewing and approving major policy decisions on bargaining. This can be seen more clearly by examining the data in Table 6–4. Here the firms were asked to report (1) who had primary responsibility for making the key decisions involved in negotiating an agreement with their major unions and (2) who reviewed and approved those decisions. The data demonstrate that the majority of the firms kept primary responsibility for key decisions at the corporate level, most often in the hands of the top labor relations executive. And in the majority of the firms the top executives of the corporation had to at least review and approve the key decisions. In about 25 percent to 30 percent of the firms the chief executive had primary responsibility for the crucial decisions establishing the limits of discretion for the management

TABLE 6–3
Location of primary responsibility for labor relations activities in the firms responding to the 1977 Conference Board survey
(in percentages)
(N = 668)

Activity	Corporate level		Division level		Plant level		Other	
	Chief executive	Labor relations vice president	General manager	Labor relations manager	Plant manager	Labor relations manager	Legal staff	Industry association staff
Developing overall policy toward unions	31.8%	60.0%	2.6%	3.6%	0.8%	1.2%	—	—
Directing union avoidance activities	5.1	72.2	3.9	11.9	2.4	3.5	1.0%	—
Directly dealing with an organizing campaign	3.5	61.1	4.0	17.0	5.4	7.8	1.3	—
General background research for bargaining	1.7	54.2	1.5	22.4	2.3	15.4	0.9	1.7%
Costing demands and proposals	2.6	55.9	3.3	20.9	4.2	12.0	1.1	—
Advising the contract negotiating team	13.7	59.5	4.1	10.2	2.1	3.5	6.0	0.8
Conducting contract negotiations	2.6	61.4	3.3	18.0	5.7	7.0	1.4	0.6
Developing language of the final agreement	1.8	63.1	2.0	16.0	1.4	7.7	6.8	1.2
Monitoring operations to anticipate problems	1.2	43.4	5.3	22.2	11.6	16.2	—	0.2
General administration of the contract	0.8	16.0	5.1	19.9	22.5	35.7	—	—
Handling grievances and arbitration	0.6	39.9	3.3	20.5	10.5	24.4	0.8	—

Note: The percentages across the rows do not total to 100 because of rounding.

TABLE 6–4

Locus of decision making in negotiations with major bargaining units, Conference Board respondents, 1977

(N = 668)

Decision	Corporate level		Division level		Plant level		Other	
	Chief executive	Labor relations vice president	General manager	Labor relations manager	Plant manager	Labor relations manager	Legal staff	Industry association staff
The company's initial proposals for wage items								
Primary responsibility	4.4%	55.9%	6.7%	18.7%	6.6%	6.7%	0.2%	0.6%
Reviews and approves	56.0	19.7	17.2	3.2	3.2	0.2	0.2	0.4
The company's initial proposals for benefits								
Primary responsibility	5.0	60.8	5.0	18.2	4.5	5.4	0.2	0.9
Reviews and approves	58.1	19.4	16.3	2.9	2.5	0.2	0.2	0.4
Outside limits								
Primary responsibility	27.3	44.8	13.7	9.7	2.0	1.7	0.2	0.6
Reviews and approves	61.7	18.3	17.6	0.2	2.0	—	—	0.2
"Strike issues"								
Primary responsibility	25.1	46.5	13.3	8.9	2.5	2.9	0.2	0.6
Reviews and approves	61.5	18.6	15.8	0.9	2.1	0.2	0.6	0.2
The final package								
Primary responsibility	30.1	41.4	15.1	7.8	3.0	1.6	0.3	0.8
Reviews and approves	59.5	19.1	15.7	1.6	2.3	0.2	1.1	0.5

Note: The percentages across the rows do not total to 100 because of rounding.

negotiators, determining the issues over which the firm should take a strike, and approving the final package. The data in these two tables depict a very centralized decision-making structure indeed and provide vivid evidence of the importance modern corporate management attaches to labor relations policy. The data also serve to bolster the hypothesis that the growth of centralized national unions is a response to the centralization of power within management (see Chapter 4).

Although the predominant pattern exhibits a high degree of centralization, there is some variation in the locus of decision-making power in these firms. Why do some firms centralize decision making more than others? The theories of organizational behavior that helped explain the labor relations staff ratios do not provide a clear-cut set of hypotheses to predict the degree of centralization. On the one hand, the more important the labor relations function, the more one would expect the firm to maintain central control in the hands of the top executives. Yet, on the other hand, the more volatile the labor situation, the more the firm could be expected to decentralize its decision making to allow more concentrated attention to the issues at hand. Apparently, corporations have resolved this strategic quandary by adding more professionals to their local labor relations staffs while maintaining centralized control over the key bargaining decisions.

The collective bargaining literature offers another explanation for variations in the degree of centralization. As in the case of the union structure, it suggests that the distribution of decision-making power within management will adapt to the nature of the bargaining structure: The more centralized the structure of bargaining, the more centralized management decision making will be. Some would go one step farther and argue that for the bargaining process to be stable and effective, management decision-making power should be concentrated at the level where bargaining takes place.[16]

The data presented in Table 6–5 allow us to examine this hypothesis. In this table the information on where the primary responsibility and the authority to review and approve decisions lie is classified by whether bargaining is done on a single-plant or a multiplant basis. The data show, as the bargaining theory suggests, that the primary responsibility for decisions is somewhat more decentralized in single-plant units than in multiplant units. Still, a surprising amount of centralized management decision making exists even in decentralized bargaining structures. For example, only 20 percent of the firms with single-plant bargaining structures gave the plant-level staff primary responsibility for developing wage proposals. Only 15 percent in single-plant structures gave plant staff primary responsibility for developing fringe benefit proposals. Fewer than 10 percent gave plant staff the responsibility for making such key strategic decisions as establishing the bargaining limits, determining strike issues, and approving the final settlement package. Corporate management controlled the key decisions in at least two-thirds of the firms, even when bargaining was done on a plant-by-plant basis. Thus, we can expect recent trends toward more decentralized

TABLE 6–5

Locus of management decision-making power in single-plant and multiplant bargaining structures, 1977 (N = 668)

	Single-plant structures			Multiplant structures		
	Corporation	Division	Plant	Corporation	Division	Plant
Primary responsibility for						
Developing wage proposals	54.4%	25.1%	20.6%	69.9%	25.4%	4.7%
Developing fringe proposals	61.0	23.6	15.4	75.1	21.6	3.3
Establishing bargaining limits	68.6	25.5	5.9	78.8	20.1	1.1
Determining strike issues	68.2	24.3	7.5	77.3	19.8	2.9
Approving final package	66.2	26.9	6.9	79.1	19.1	1.8
Reviews and approves						
Wage proposals	70.1	25.3	4.5	83.3	14.5	2.2
Fringe proposals	71.4	24.4	4.2	85.6	13.5	0.9
Bargaining "limits"	75.6	21.2	3.2	85.5	13.8	0.5
"Strike issues"	74.9	21.6	3.5	88.3	10.7	1.0
Final package	73.9	22.4	3.7	87.8	11.0	1.1

Note: The percentages across the rows do not total to 100 because of rounding.

bargaining structures to have only limited effects on the degree to which power is decentralized within the management hierarchy.

We dwell on these data here because they contradict one of the most commonly stated observations about the U.S. collective bargaining system, namely, it is highly decentralized. These data suggest, instead, that although the formal structure of bargaining in this country still exhibits a high degree of decentralization, especially in comparison with that in some Western European countries, control over the key strategic decisions within large corporations is highly centralized.

Specialization of the Labor Relations Function

Although there is little evidence to suggest that the power to set labor relations policy is shifting downward within management organizations, there is ample evidence to suggest that power has shifted *laterally* within management structures in recent years. Labor relations specialists have been losing power to line managers and, to a somewhat lesser degree, to human resource specialists. As suggested earlier, the main reason for this is that the business and labor relations strategies of many employers have shifted from needing the traditional expertise of the labor relations specialist—in achieving stability, labor peace, and predictability—to needing expertise in union avoidance, cost control, and flexibility in work rules and organization.

We will review the evidence on this shift in management goals in Chapter 7. For our present purposes, it is sufficient to note that other data from the 1983 Conference Board survey showed that the power of line managers in the companies surveyed was increasing over a broad array of human resource and labor relations functions. Moreover, this shift from labor relations specialists to line managers was most pronounced in those firms that espoused a union avoidance policy and in those firms that made the greatest use of innovative personnel practices in both their union and their nonunion facilities. Thus, we might conclude that when a shift in human resource and labor relations strategies was called for, either the labor relations professionals adapted quickly or, more commonly, management shifted responsibility for achieving and managing the innovation to some other group or individual.

This does not mean, however, that labor relations specialists are no longer necessary. Indeed, in a number of case studies we recently conducted, *lower level* labor relations managers secretly delighted in the "mistakes" some of the line managers and human resource management specialists made as they took greater control over critical labor relations decisions. In one large firm a career labor relations manager related the story of how the new vice president of labor relations who was brought over from another functional area had to call in the "old hands" to find out how the contract ratification procedures worked. Because of the need for this type of technical expertise, most firms continue to depend on teams of labor relations specialists to conduct negotiations and implement policies and agreements. But a number of major firms have established strategic planning groups for labor relations, and others have used cross-functional teams to develop new bargaining proposals. Finally, the majority of firms in the 1983 Conference Board survey assigned primary authority for human resource planning and introduction of employee participation programs to either human resource executives or line managers, not to labor relations specialists.

One implication of these trends is that the careers of labor relations professionals are changing dramatically and thus pose new educational and training requirements for current and future professionals. If these trends are indicative, the industrial relations professionals of the future will be expected to have (1) greater business, analytical, and planning skills; (2) expertise in both traditional labor relations activities and personnel or human resource management activities; (3) a more thorough understanding of operating management issues; and (4) an ability to work as a member of a multidisciplinary team in implementing labor relations strategies and policies. Labor relations is no longer the powerful fiefdom of the management hierarchy it was in the earlier days of strong unions and stable collective bargaining.

THE DYNAMICS OF MANAGEMENT'S DECISION-MAKING PROCESS

So far we have painted a rather static picture of management's decision-making structure. Yet the actual process of establishing policies and making key decisions over the course of the complete bargaining cycle (from the prenegotiation planning stage to the signing of the final agreement) is a dynamic one, replete with ambiguities over who has the authority to set and modify policies, conflicts among decision makers over the appropriate weight to be attached to different goals, and power struggles among competing decision makers seeking to gain greater influence and control over decision making within the management structure.

A number of theoretical works and empirical studies have well demonstrated that the process of establishing basic bargaining strategies and goals can be viewed as a form of intraorganizational bargaining.[17] Often this intraorganizational bargaining is every bit as intense as the bargaining between the union and management. Because the successful resolution of internal differences is normally viewed as a prerequisite to a smoothly functioning bargaining process (in Chapter 8 we will argue that the existence of unresolved intraorganizational conflicts is one major cause of impasses and strikes in bargaining), it is important that we understand the ways in which firms make these internal decisions.

Preparing for Negotiations: A Typical Case

To provide a more complete picture of how the management structure actually works, let us observe a typical firm's preparation for negotiations and the methods by which it establishes wage and fringe benefit targets for the negotiations process. We will also describe how this process has changed in recent years. Traditionally, the firm described here has negotiated a contract with the major bargaining unit in its largest manufacturing facility. This contract then sets the pattern for the economic settlements with several smaller units at other locations. (The following case study is based on our own research at a large, multiplant firm in manufacturing.)

The first step in the process of preparing for negotiations takes place at the plant level. The plant labor relations staff holds meetings with plant supervisors to discuss problems experienced in administering the existing contract. From these discussions the staff puts together a list of suggested contract changes. At the same time, the staff also conducts a systematic review of the grievances that have arisen under the current contract and collects information on local labor market conditions and on wages in other firms in the community. The staff then holds a meeting with the plant manager. Here the concerns raised by the supervisors are classified into two groups: those that are contractual problems, and those that should be addressed outside the negotiating process. In addition, the staff asks the plant manager to rank the suggested contract changes in order of their potential for making a significant improvement in plant operations.

Next a series of meetings are held at the division level involving the local labor relations staff, operations management at the division level, and the corporate labor relations director and staff. From time to time outside industrial relations consultants also sit in on these division-level meetings. Here the concerns of the various plants are evaluated against two criteria: (1) the operational benefits expected from proposed contract changes, and (2) the likelihood the changes desired can be achieved in the negotiations process.

The corporate labor relations staff plays a vital role in these division-level discussions, since the expected benefits of different contractual changes can be a matter of some dispute across the various plants. In addition, the division labor relations staff is responsible for carefully examining the contract language that exists in the various local agreements for differences and inconsistencies that could be replaced by clauses that reflect corporate labor relations goals or preferences. Often the plant labor relations representatives object to any such changes suggested at the division level because they do not correspond to the priorities of the plant officials and because the existing "discrepancies" may be serving a useful purpose in the plant. Thus, the division and the corporate labor relations staffs often serve a conflict resolution role in these deliberations among the local representatives. The outcome of these deliberations is a report, addressed to the labor relations staff at the corporate level, listing priorities for changes in the master agreement.

While these plant-level and division-level analyses and discussions are taking place, the corporate labor relations staff is conducting research to formulate the company's economic proposals. Local labor market and wage data from the plant level are analyzed along with company earnings, the wages of competitors in the industry, and national economic trends. The corporate labor relations director is responsible for keeping up with major contract developments in other industries and in other unions.

The corporate labor relations staff works closely with the vice president for finance to develop the economic targets for the wage settlement. Information on plant labor costs and corporate earnings, as well as on the longer term financial prospects of the company and the industry, are built into the wage target the corporate staff ultimately recommends.

The final step in the preparation process is a meeting with the chief executive officer and the board of directors, at which the corporate labor relations director presents for board approval the proposed wage target or maximum settlement on the economic terms, along with other proposed contract changes and a statement of the reasons for seeking the proposed changes. Sometimes this meeting does not take place until after the first negotiations session with the union. In our interviews with the labor relations director he stated he prefers waiting until then because it is useful to hear from the union before making his recommendation to top management. This helps him identify both the relative importance the union is likely to place on different wage and fringe benefit issues and the intensity of the union's concern about other areas of the contract. He also gave an interesting description of how he presents his recommendation to top management.

> I always number my proposed target settlements as proposed settlement target number 1. Someone once asked me what that meant. I said that this is what I think it will take to get a settlement but I number it because I may have to come back to you at some point with my proposed settlement number 2 or even my proposed settlement number 3, etcetera.

This is an apt characterization of the tenuous nature of the decision-making process not only in this corporation but in the negotiations process in general. Before negotiations (or very early in negotiations) the labor relations staff tries to predict as closely as possible what it will take to get a settlement. But ultimately the staff is at all times ready to revise its carefully arrived at estimates based on new or better information about the union's position as the negotiations proceed.

Preparing for Negotiations in the 1980s: The Case Revisited

This description of the way one firm prepared for bargaining is representative of the relatively stable bargaining of the 1970s. Since 1980, however, several things have changed within this firm that are illustrative of other firms as well. First, in 1980 a quality-of-working-life (QWL) program was introduced in the collective bargaining agreement at the "request" of the chief executive officer. In anticipation of his request the top labor relations executive invited the top union officers to visit several companies and unions with ongoing QWL programs to learn about them firsthand—before the start of negotiations. Once the new contract was signed and the program implemented, the union became a joint partner in the management of the program, which represented a significant change in the management of industrial relations at the firm. In particular, in the years since, union officers have been privy to more and more information previously held only by management.

In a second important change, as the company came to face increasing competitive pressures in the early 1980s, line managers began demanding significant changes in subcontracting rights and other work rules specified in the contract. As a result these managers became part of the initial contract planning team for the 1983 negotiations. In fact, in interviews with us union representatives indicated that they saw the line managers "calling the shots" within management for the 1983 negotiations. This was most apparent when at a critical point in negotiations, the industrial relations director brought the chief executive officer of the corporation to the bargaining table to state his own views on a number of the bargaining issues. His presence signaled to the union that top management was serious in its intentions to continue the QWL process *and* to support the line managers' demands for work rule changes. By personally clarifying where the corporation stood on these key issues, the CEO paved the way for a peaceful settlement of the contract.

In the years since 1983 union representatives, line managers, organizational development specialists, and industrial relations professionals in this firm have worked together on a number of joint long-range planning projects, including a study team that examined the question of introducing a productivity gains–sharing policy—a proposal that only a decade earlier would never have been discussed with union representatives (or even line managers) until it had been thoroughly researched by the industrial relations staff and was ready to be proposed at the bargaining table.

Many other examples of a greater diffusion of policymaking authority and of greater information sharing can be found throughout other U.S. companies that have begun to change their labor relations policies and practices in recent years. In the most successful firms information and power sharing is not limited to contract negotiations but is a continual process of education and communication over the life of the contract as well. Box 6–2 illustrates the language used to establish this type of ongoing process, here under the name of "mutual growth forums" at the Ford Motor Company.

The case study presented above illustrates the diversity of goals and interests that exists in the different functional levels within any modern organization. It shows that the development of a company strategy for negotiations is a highly political process, one in which the different goals and

---

BOX 6–2
UAW–Ford Motor Company mutual growth forums

"Both parties recognize that the need for change continues . . . and they must explore new methods of resolving their honest differences in orderly rational ways. . . .To provide such a new approach, to facilitate the process of continuing evolution and change, and to move the parties forward to new thresholds, Ford and the UAW have agreed to establish a Mutual Growth Forum that is intended to function—at both the local and national levels—as a highly visible new adjunct to the collective bargaining process.

"The forum does not replace collective bargaining, nor does it interfere in any way with the parties' grievance procedure. Rather, it provides a new framework designed to promote better Management-Union relations through better communications, systematic fact finding, and advance discussions of certain business developments that are of material interest and significance to the Union, the employees, and the Company."

Source: Letter of Understanding appended to the 1982 collective bargaining agreement between Ford Motor Company and the United Automobile, Aerospace and Agricultural Implement Workers of America.

preferences of various groups must ultimately be resolved and accommo-dated *before* meeting with the union. Although the labor relations staff still serves as a key participant in the development of the strategy, the concerns of operating management, financial staff, and other interest groups within the corporation are also integral to any final decision. Ultimately, the top-level executives, as in the case described above, serve as the court of appeals when internal differences are insoluble at lower levels of the organization.

RESEARCH ACTIVITIES OF THE LABOR RELATIONS STAFF

Both the survey data and the case description outlined above point to the important research function served by the labor relations staff in the corporation. In fact, it is also one of the most time-consuming roles played by labor relations specialists. To provide a better picture of the extent of this research function, we will describe one company's industrial relations research and planning department. (As in the previous case, we base our description on our own research, this time on a large, durable goods man-ufacturing firm that also bargains on a centralized basis with a single union. Each plant then has local, supplemental agreements as well.)

Created by the company in the mid-1950s, the labor relations research and planning department was originally staffed by labor economists. Since then the company has expanded the unit by adding specialists in indus-trial and organizational psychology, computer science, data processing, and econometrics. The basic functions of this department today are to maintain a comprehensive data file on the demographic characteristics of the compa-ny's work force; to develop and use an econometric model for analyzing union and management proposals and costing out final settlements; and to conduct specific studies of critical problems in the firm's relations with its unions. The research staff also participates in negotiations with the major unions. One of the staff members is either constantly present in negotiations or on call to provide cost estimates of alternative proposals. In addition, the research staff has responsibility for negotiating specific technical provisions of the contract, such as language dealing with cost-of-living allowances and other economic benefits. Finally, these researchers analyze and assess macroeconomic research developments bearing on the labor relations objec-tives of the firm.

At least a year and a half before the opening of formal negotiations with the large bargaining units in this firm, the research staff begins to pre-pare the background information necessary for developing the company's proposals. To do this, the researchers update their data base on employee demographic characteristics and analyze such personnel statistics as turn-over, absenteeism, and grievance rates at the plant level. They also carefully monitor internal union developments, specifically, union convention reso-lutions, union publications, and union leaders' statements concerning the upcoming negotiations. In addition, they survey plant managers for their views on their relations with the union and on the problems they would like to see addressed in the negotiations. The staff also works with labor relations staff members at the lower levels of the corporation to obtain their ideas and suggestions for negotiations. The research staff is ultimately responsible for putting together a summary report that goes to the vice president of industrial relations and the corporate director of wages and benefits. These executives then work with the manager of the research and planning department to develop a recommended set of targets for bargaining, which in turn they present to the president and the chairman of the board for approval.

This example is obviously one of a highly developed research staff; the firm probably invests more resources and assigns more authority for bargaining preparation to the research staff than most corporations do. The example does illustrate, however, given the necessary resources, the importance a firm will attach to the collection and analysis of information before bargaining and the sophisticated labor relations information and data management systems available within today's corporations.

SUMMARY

Over the past decade industrial relations strategies and structures have undergone considerable change within U.S. management organizations. Given predictions of ever-increasing rates of change in the economic and technological environments that lie ahead, we can expect that the pace of change and the expectations for even broader and deeper expertise on the part of industrial relations professionals will likewise continue. The lesson for industrial relations professionals is quite clear: Either adopt a strategy of helping to shape and manage these changes, or lose considerable power, status, and opportunities for career advancement.

Our analysis of contemporary values and strategies for managing labor relations demonstrates that the two sides of management strategy observable in U.S. history are still with us today. Although most managers can accept in the abstract the principle that unions have a legitimate role to play in a democratic society, in practice managers continue to act on the belief that unions are neither necessary nor desirable within their own organization. Yet management also continues to be as pragmatic as ever. If the costs of union avoidance are too high, that is, if unions are too powerful to avoid, management will work with union leaders to develop the strategies needed to be competitive. And in the current environment the top executives of many firms have been able to pursue the two strategies simultaneously, that is, avoiding further unionization in one location in the firm, while cooperating with the existing union at another. The question is whether management will continue to enjoy such discretion and power in the years ahead.

Suggested Readings

References on the philosophies, goals, structures, and functions in the management of labor relations and human resources include:

Bendix, Reinhard. *Work and Authority in Industry*. New York: John Wiley, 1956.

Chandler, Alfred D., Jr. *Strategy and Structure*. New York: Anchor Books, 1966.

Flanagan, Robert J., Robert S. Smith, and Ronald E. Ehrenberg. *Labor Economics and Labor Relations*. Glenview, Ill.: Scott, Foresman, 1984.

Foulkes, Fred. *Personnel Policies of Large Nonunion Companies*. Englewood Cliffs, N.J.: Prentice-Hall, 1979.

Freedman, Audrey. *A New Look in Wage Bargaining*. New York: Conference Board, 1985.

Harris, Howell. *The Right to Manage*. Madison: University of Wisconsin Press, 1982.

Heneman, Herbert G., III, Donald P. Schwab, John A. Fossum, and Lee Dyer. *Personnel/Human Resource Management,* 3d ed. Homewood Ill.: Richard D. Irwin, 1986.

Milkovich, George T., and Jerry Newman. *Compensation* (Plano, Tex.: Business Publications, 1984).

Simon, Herbert A. *Administrative Behavior,* 2d ed. New York: Free Press, 1957.

Slichter, Sumner, James J. Healy, and E. Robert Livernash, *The Impact of Collective Bargaining on Management*. Washington, D.C.: Brookings Institution, 1960.

Thompson, James D. *Organizations in Action*. New York: McGraw-Hill, 1967.

Walton, Richard E., and Robert B. McKersie. *A Behavioral Theory of Labor Negotiations*. New York: McGraw-Hill, 1965.

Witte, Edwin E. *The Evolution of Managerial Ideas in Industrial Relations,* bulletin no. 27. Ithaca, N.Y.: New York State School of Industrial and Labor Relations, Cornell University, 1954.

Notes

1. For a complete report of the 1978 survey, see Audrey Freedman, *Managing Labor Relations: Organization, Objectives, and Results* (New York: Conference Board, 1979); for the 1983 survey, see Audrey Freedman, *A New Look in Wage Bargaining* (New York: Conference Board, 1985). We wish to thank Audrey Freedman and the Conference Board for their permission to use the data in this book. Any conclusions drawn from these data are our own and do not represent the official position of the Conference Board.

2. Herbert A. Simon, *Administrative Behavior*, 2d ed. (New York: Free Press, 1957), 61–109.

3. Douglas V. Brown and Charles A. Myers, "The Changing Industrial Relations Philosophy of American Management," in *Proceedings of the Ninth Annual Winter Meetings of the Industrial Relations Research Association* (Madison, Wis.: IRRA, 1957), 92.

4. Harry Millis and Royal Montgomery, *Organized Labor* (New York: McGraw-Hill, 1945), 835.

5. For a description of the tactics used by southern textile firms to avoid unionization in the 1940s and 1950s, see Solomon Barkin, "Organization of the Unorganized," in *Proceedings of the Ninth Annual Winter Meetings of the Industrial Relations Research Association* (Madison, Wis.: IRRA, 1957), 232–37. For a review of union efforts to organize J.P. Stevens and the company's response, see Kenneth A. Kovach, "J.P. Stevens and the Struggle for Union Organization," *Labor Law Journal* 29 (May 1979): 300–308.

6. Richard B. Freeman and James L. Medoff, *What Do Unions Do?* (New York: Basic Books, 1984), 232.

7. For a discussion of contemporary personnel practices in nonunion companies, see Fred Foulkes, *Positive Employee Relations: Personnel Policies and Practices of the Large Nonunion Company* (Englewood Cliffs, N.J.: Prentice-Hall, 1980); M. Scott Myers, *Managing Without Unions* (Reading, Mass.: Addison-Wesley, 1976); or Daniel Quinn Mills, *Labor-Management Relations* (New York: McGraw-Hill, 1978), 48–66. See also Thomas A. Kochan, Harry C. Katz, and Robert B. McKersie, *The Transformation of American Industrial Relations* (New York: Basic Books, 1986), 93–100.

8. Thomas A. Kochan, Robert B. McKersie, and John Chalykoff, "The Effects of Corporate Strategy and Workplace Innovations on Union Representation," *Industrial and Labor Relations Review* 39 (July 1986): 487–501.

9. Kochan, Katz, and McKersie, *The Transformation*, 247.

10. For a history of the personnel policies followed by Sears, see Sanford M. Jacoby, "Employee Attitude Testing at Sears, Roebuck and Company, 1938–1960," Working Paper Series 112 (Los Angeles: Institute of Industrial Relations, University of California, June 1986).

11. "Open Shop Construction Picks Up Momentum," *Business Week*, 12 December 1977, 108–9.

12. "The UMW's Turf Slowly Erodes," *Business Week*, 19 December 1977, 75.

13. Alfred D. Chandler, Jr., *Strategy and Structure* (New York: Anchor Books, 1966), 15.

14. Simon, *Administrative Behavior*.

15. See James D. Thompson, *Organizations in Action* (New York: McGraw-Hill, 1967), for an early theoretical statement of this hypothesis.

16. John T. Dunlop, "The Function of the Strike," in *Frontiers of Collective Bargaining*, ed. John T. Dunlop and Neil W. Chamberlain (New York: Harper and Row, 1967), 109.

17. Richard E. Walton and Robert B. McKersie, *A Behavioral Theory of Labor Negotiations* (New York: McGraw-Hill, 1965), 281–339. For a good case study of intraorganizational bargaining, see Fred Goldner, "The Division of Labor," in *Power in Organizations*, ed. Meyer Zald, 97–143 (Nashville: Vanderbilt University Press, 1970).

CHAPTER 7

<hr style="height:4px; background:black; border:none;" />

Management's
Bargaining Objectives
and Performance

We will now shift our attention from management's broad labor relations goals, strategies, and structures to the more specific objectives and criteria used to guide management behavior in negotiations and to evaluate management's labor relations performance. In the first part of this chapter, we introduce the general concept of a wage target and discuss the role of target setting in bargaining theory and practice. We then analyze the criteria used by firms to establish their wage and benefit targets. These criteria are important not only to an understanding of management's approach to bargaining, but also in the discussion of bargaining power in Chapter 8. The third section of the chapter briefly reviews the nonwage objectives of concern to management in bargaining. The final section summarizes the criteria firms use to evaluate their labor relations performance and also presents Conference Board data on firms' actual evaluation of their bargaining performance in recent years.

MANAGEMENT'S WAGE TARGETS

Most collective bargaining theories, and especially behavioral models of collective bargaining,[1] assume that both the union and the employer establish specific targets, objectives, or expectations for a settlement. What researchers call *targets* or *resistance points* are often referred to by negotiators as the *limits* for bargaining, or the "bottom line" terms the parties would accept short of either calling or taking a strike or going to an impasse. The Conference Board surveys we drew on in Chapter 6, and public sector research as well, confirm that the majority of negotiators have some implicit or explicit target figure in mind either going into negotiations or after the early stages of negotiations are completed. For example, 82 percent of the respondents to the 1977 Conference Board survey indicated that their firms establish a wage target before going to the bargaining table. In the public sector study between 70 and 80 percent of the management and union negotiators surveyed indicated that it was also their practice to establish a wage target ahead of time.[2]

The development of these wage targets or limits is the heart of the internal management planning and decision-making process that takes place before or during the early stages of negotiations. As noted in the previous chapter, developing targets can also involve a good deal of intraorganizational bargaining and conflict as the diverse goals and preferences of the different departments and organizational levels within the firm are molded into a single package. Establishing targets—the central device used by negotiators on both sides of the table—helps clarify the limits of their discretion, commit decision makers within their organizations to these targets, and provide information to top executives that makes the process of negotiations appear more predictable. These are important functions for any agent with responsibility for negotiating with a group that is outside the control of the organization.[3]

Since, as shown in Chapter 6, top management is responsible for approving or authorizing any target positions in bargaining, the negotiating team must recommend targets that reflect top management's overarching goals for the organization. To recommend too high a wage target risks rejection of the recommendations and the loss of political influence and esteem that results from such a rejection. On the other hand, these targets play a pivotal role in the negotiations process once they are established, since they indicate the negotiator's latitude for compromising short of an impasse or a strike. Thus, the staff has some incentive to develop bargaining targets that are realistic and achievable. Above all, in presenting their requests or recommendations, the staff must be able to estimate the probability of achieving alternative targets in bargaining without a strike or an impasse or, otherwise, to estimate the costs and benefits of taking a strike to achieve the target.

Thus, a broad range of different criteria must be considered in selecting wage goals or targets. Some criteria reflect the desirability or utility of alternative wage and benefit increases. Some reflect the probability of being able to achieve the target.[4] The range of criteria that go into this decision-making process will be discussed briefly below. Data from the Conference Board surveys will then be presented to illustrate the relative importance of different criteria in contemporary firms and recent changes in the relative importance of these criteria.

Local Labor Market Comparisons

Economic theory predicts that in the absence of unionization, the rational employer will set wages at a level necessary to attract the desired number and quality of employees, given the prevailing wage level in the relevant labor market. For blue-collar workers this is usually the local labor market, that is, the geographic area within which workers are willing to commute to work for the employer. To allow wages to fall too low relative to wages at the other employment sites in the local area is to invite high turnover, a dissatisfied work force, and difficulty in recruiting workers with the requisite ability, training, and motivation to perform effectively. To set wages too high relative to the local labor market invites an excess of qualified job applicants and a very low voluntary turnover rate. Both of these sets of personnel indicators signal to the employer that wages have been fixed at a level inappropriate to the local labor market; they also serve to measure the costs of doing so.

Thus, local labor market wage comparisons, along with information on recruitment, selection, performance, and turnover, provide the most useful information for employers seeking to set wages in a way to minimize unit labor costs. Note that the use of this labor market criterion does not imply that the employer necessarily seeks to minimize wage rates or wage increases by paying the lowest wage possible that will attract workers to a given job. Given a particular local labor market, the employer must choose the quality of employees it wishes to hire. The basic decision for the employer is whether increasing the wage level will attract employees of sufficiently high quality and job performance and will lower indirect personnel costs (such as training, turnover, and supervision) sufficiently to lower unit labor costs.[5]

A variety of surveys of employers' compensation practices document the importance of local labor market comparisons. One survey of 184 firms found that competitive wages in the area was the most important criterion considered by firms in setting the wage level of their blue-collar workers; 54 percent of the companies ranked local comparisons as their top criterion. Nash and Carroll reviewed a number of other studies in addition to this survey and concluded that the most commonly identified compensation strategy is for firms to pay wages that are approximately equal to other rates in the community.[6] The authors also noted, however, that the local wage comparison is only one of a variety of factors that influence employer wage policies. Thus, even the scanty empirical evidence available to date tells us that firms consider more than the economic and personnel management signals outlined above in developing their wage preferences.

Labor market comparisons are more likely to be used in bargaining relationships where the union is weak than in ones where the union is strong or bargaining is centralized. Union negotiators have little incentive to consider labor market comparisons, since unions have traditionally rejected the normative premise underlying the economic theory upon which this criterion is based. According to that premise, workers of comparable quality should be paid comparable wages. Unions modify the premise to argue for *equal pay for equal work*. That is, workers employed in comparable jobs (regardless of differences in worker quality or performance on the job) should be paid the same. Furthermore, unions are more interested in obtaining a *"living wage"* than they are in obtaining a locally comparable wage.

The Firm's Ability to Pay

While the local labor market serves as the most common external determinant of employers' wage policies, the potential effects of wage adjustments on the profits and productivity (unit labor costs) of the firm are crucial internal determinants. In simplest terms employers approaching the wage decision examine their *ability to pay* alternative wage increases. Again, since authority for the final approval of the wage targets is vested in the hands of the chief executives in most firms, labor relations specialists must pay special attention to the nature of the current economic position of the firm and be able to justify any possible effects of the proposed wage on future labor costs, productivity, and profits.

Ability-to-pay considerations are likely to be especially salient in small firms and in firms facing a weak union, since the ability to pay reflects the specific short-run problems of the employer. Recall from Chapter 4 that the union is generally reluctant to break a pattern settlement unless the firm can demonstrate that a serious economic crisis would result if the firm were forced to meet the pattern. Union leaders and members often must be convinced that there would be sizable employment loss before they will agree to a below-pattern settlement. It was also pointed out that the larger the employer, the less willing unions will be to allow deviations from a pattern settlement. For example, throughout the 1960s and 1970s the UAW agreed to "off pattern" settlements with American Motors in order to keep that company in business. But it took the imminent threat of bankruptcy, along with government pressure on the UAW to agree to concessions for Chrysler, to break the auto pattern in 1979.

Thus, the ability to pay is an important criterion to employers, but one that traditionally has met strong union opposition, except in severe financial crises and in smaller firms that are less likely to pose a serious threat to a union-negotiated wage pattern. But, as we will see, ability-to-pay considerations have become more important in recent years, especially in companies experiencing severe competitive pressures.

Internal Comparisons

No major negotiations round in any company or public sector organization takes place in a vacuum. Every major set of negotiations is carefully watched by the employer's other workers, who hope that the settlement with one unit will set the pattern for the wage and fringe benefit adjustments of other units. This is especially true in organizations in which the white-collar work force is not unionized and in which (as is almost always the case) management wishes to minimize the incentives for white-collar workers to organize.

Consequently, in setting wage and fringe benefit targets, management negotiators are likely to consider the effects of any resulting settlement on the other employees in the firm. This is probably truer for fringe benefits than wages. In fact, authorization of fringe benefit improvements is one of the most highly centralized decisions within modern corporations. In particular, top management tries to guard against differentials in fringe benefit packages across groups, differentials that not only pose difficult problems of internal equity, but also increase the administrative burden on management.

Industry Comparisons

Under certain conditions employers may look beyond these local or firm-specific criteria to the wages paid by competitors in the broader product market, even in the absence of union pressure to do so. (It will be argued below that product market or industry comparisons are even more important to unions, and unions therefore attempt to force employers to consider them.) Whereas the labor market and personnel management criteria constrain wages on the low end, product market and industry comparisons constrain them on the high end. Obviously, employers need to keep their labor costs per unit of output from exceeding the labor costs of their competitors. Thus, product market comparisons set the upper limit on employer wage and benefit proposals. Nevertheless, if unions are absent or if the union is weak, the employer facing competitive conditions has no clear economic incentive to voluntarily set wages equal to the wages of the competitors. Under certain oligopolistic conditions, however, employers have been shown to see an advantage to using industry comparisons: By equalizing wage rates and labor costs, the firm can avoid price competition.[7]

In summary, in the absence of a union or in the presence of a very weak union, the following criteria are likely to dominate employer preferences in setting targets: (1) local labor market comparisons and internal personnel data, (2) the potential impact of the proposed target on labor costs and profits, (3) potential spillover or equity effects within the firm, and to a lesser extent (4) wage comparisons within the industry or product market.

The Union's Targets

Management must also take the union's preferences into account when setting targets for bargaining. Unless management is powerful enough to totally dominate bargaining, the management team will have to consider the potential *acceptability* of its targets to the union; that is, can the firm expect to achieve its targets in collective bargaining?

As we noted in Chapters 4 and 5, although unions definitely want to achieve substantial wage increases for their members, they will usually establish their own limits, or targets, for wage bargaining. In setting those limits, union leaders employ two basic criteria for evaluating a proposed settlement: (1) the potential effects of the settlement on the *real wages* of the membership (the wage adjustment minus any increase in the cost of living), and (2) a comparison between the proposed settlement and settlements with other bargaining units or with other employees. Comparisons with other units are important to unions for both economic and political reasons. Remember, unions' economic goal is to take wages out of competition. Their political goal is to respond to what have been termed *coercive comparisons* to the settlements achieved by other unions.[8] This term refers to the tendency of rank-and-file union members to evaluate their leaders by comparing their own settlement to settlements achieved by leaders of other unions or granted by other employers. These considerations come into play while the union's negotiating committee prepares for bargaining (see Chapter 5) as well as during the negotiations themselves.

Thus, the major effects of union preferences on management targets are to force the firm to consider comparisons among bargaining units; to consider the importance of cost-of-living increases to the employee; and in some cases to consider more seriously comparisons within the entire industry. Finally, the ability of the union to impose its preferences on the firm by striking (that is, the union's bargaining power) will determine the extent to which management *does* take the union's preferences into account. The union-preference criterion will therefore be among the most foremost factors determining management targets in a firm that simply cannot undergo a strike at the time of negotiations.

The Relative Importance of the Criteria

Let us now examine empirically how much weight firms actually gave to these different criteria for bargaining targets in recent years. The data presented in Table 7–1, based on the 1977 and 1983 Conference Board surveys, summarize the relative importance respondents assigned to the different criteria we have discussed. In both years the respondents were asked to rank their firm's top three criteria in setting targets for bargaining with their major union, to indicate any criteria considered but not among the top three, and to indicate any criteria not considered at all.

In 1977 the wage criterion most commonly ranked first by the respondents was the comparison to wages in the industry; approximately 37 percent ranked this as the most important criterion in setting their firm's targets, and over 56 percent ranked it among the top three criteria considered by their firm. The local labor market comparison was the second most commonly cited criterion; over 29 percent of the respondents ranked this as the top factor, and almost 44 percent ranked it among the top three. The expected profits of the company came in a distant third, with only 11 percent identifying it as their firm's most important criterion, and 23 percent ranking it among the top three criteria. Interestingly, no other criterion was given the top rank by more than 6 percent of the firms; in other words, there

TABLE 7–1

The relative importance of criteria for management's wage targets, 1977 and 1983 (in percentages)

	1983		1977	
Criterion	Ranked most important	Ranked among top three	Ranked most important	Ranked among top three
Local labor market conditions and wage rates	21.3%	43.8%	29.3%	43.9%
National labor market conditions and wage rates	5.0	15.7	2.5	16.7
Industry patterns	20.2	44.9	36.8	56.5
Major union settlements in other industries	2.5	11.5	2.9	18.1
Increases in the consumer price index	4.0	24.0	2.5	19.2
Productivity or labor cost trends in the company	20.2	54.4	5.0	24.3
The expected profits of the company	20.2	43.9	11.2	23.3
Potential losses from a strike	4.0	12.9	3.8	19.8
The potential influence of this settlement on other wage settlements or union wage levels	3.0	21.2	5.8	23.7

Sources: Conference Board surveys, 1977 and 1983.

was a great consistency in practice among the firms surveyed. Following in descending order of importance after the three criteria noted above were the potential influence of the wage settlement on the wages of other employees, productivity or labor cost trends, potential losses from strikes, settlements with major unions in other industries, consumer price increases, and national labor market conditions and wage rates.

The finding that industry patterns served as the most important criterion affecting management targets implies that during the relatively stable bargaining years of the 1970s, the union goals of taking wages out of competition and achieving equal pay for equal work were of greater importance to the firm than its own economic motivation to follow wage trends in the local labor market. Thus, we can view the use of industry comparisons for setting wages in the 1970s as part and parcel of the stability of the New Deal bargaining system during that period.

In turn, we can view the scant attention paid to the settlements with major unions in other industries as consistent with the evidence reviewed in Chapter 4 regarding the lack of any stable national or interindustry wage pattern during the 1970s. In only 2.9 percent of the firms was this the dominant factor in setting wage and benefit targets, and fewer than 20 percent considered it among their three most important factors. We can conclude that settlements in the highly publicized negotiations in steel, autos, and trucking, for example, did not have as great an impact outside their industries as within.

A comparison of the results for the 1977 survey with the 1983 survey results is most illuminating of the recent changes in industrial relations and bargaining. The one thing that stayed constant was the importance of local labor market comparisons. But in 1983, among the same firms, industry comparisons lost influence and ability-to-pay factors—productivity or labor cost trends and profits—gained. Specifically, if we focus on the top three rankings, productivity or labor cost trends gained 30 percentage points and expected profits gained 20 percentage points between 1977 and 1983. Intraindustry comparisons, on the other hand, dropped approximately 11 percentage points. Other criteria that lost in importance were precisely those of primary interest to unions: management's fear of losses a strike would impose and major union settlements in other industries. Thus, the shift in the wage criteria employed in these two decades is a useful barometer measuring the increased competitive pressures on these unionized firms. Moreover, the drop in the importance of intra- and interindustry wage comparisons reflects the greater difficulty unions experienced in taking wages out of competition, the key to the stability of the New Deal collective bargaining system.

In Chapter 12 we will present more evidence of the recent shift in the wage determination process under collective bargaining. For now, we will simply note that the seeming stability of collective bargaining in the 1970s was shattered as firms facing increased foreign and domestic nonunion competition shifted their wage criteria from external comparative standards to their specific ability—or inability—to pay.

MANAGEMENT'S NONWAGE OBJECTIVES

Most negotiations are not limited to seeking adjustments in the basic wage package; they also involve proposals and counterproposals on a variety of the other terms of the contract. In this section we will examine the extent to which firms establish targets or objectives for these nonwage subjects of negotiations, as well as the nature of their objectives on these issues. Table 7–2 presents the data used as the basis for this analysis. We will find further evidence in those data of management's growing aggressiveness in bargaining in this decade.

TABLE 7–2

A comparison of management's nonwage objectives in collective bargaining, 1977 and 1983

	1983 Nature of the goal				1977 Nature of the goal			
Subjects of negotiation	Number with the goal (1)	Tighten existing provision (2)	Keep status quo (3)	Trade improvement for other items (4)	Number with the goal (5)	Tighten existing provision (6)	Keep status quo (7)	Trade improvement for other items (8)
Pensions	166	15.1%	55.4%	29.5%	199	7.5%	45.2%	47.2%
Life insurance	154	17.5	53.9	28.6	178	7.9	50.0	42.1
Health insurance	204	59.3	32.8	7.8	191	14.7	43.5	41.9
Dental insurance	143	18.2	64.3	17.5	174	4.6	67.2	28.2
Time off with pay	186	31.7	61.3	7.0	209	12.0	52.6	35.4
Subcontracting	126	23.8	74.6	1.6	168	16.7	83.3	0
Layoff and recall procedures	121	39.7	50.4	9.9	164	29.4	63.2	7.4
Flexibility in assigning employees	170	68.2	30.6	1.2	201	54.7	42.8	2.5
Income security	80	8.8	76.3	15.0	116	5.2	87.1	7.8
Cost-of-living clause	135	52.6	42.2	5.2	194	13.4	76.8	9.8
Length of the agreement	133	31.6	59.4	9.0	196	23.9	61.9	14.2
Union security	90	13.3	81.1	5.6	124	10.5	85.5	4.0

Sources: Conference Board surveys, 1977 and 1983.

As shown in the table, the predominant objective of the firms in the 1977 survey was to maintain the status quo in almost all the nonwage areas of the agreement. With the exception of only two issues, pensions and flexibility in the assignment of employees, maintaining the status quo was the most frequently cited response.

In contrast, the 1983 survey data show an increase for all but three of the bargaining subjects in the percentage of respondents reporting that their firm wanted to achieve a more favorable bargain. More than two-thirds of the firms reportedly hoped to achieve greater flexibility in job assignments, over 59 percent wanted to tighten health insurance provisions, and almost 53 percent wanted to tighten cost-of-living adjustments. The firms also reported a greater reluctance to *improve* fringe benefits—such as pensions, life and health insurance, and time off with pay—as a trade-off for other goals in bargaining (columns 4 and 8 in the table). The only items management appeared slightly more willing to use as trade-offs were subcontracting, income security, layoff, and union security provisions. These data again demonstrate that the status quo orientation that characterized management bargaining agendas in the 1970s was replaced in the 1980s by a more assertive, demanding approach.

EVALUATING LABOR RELATIONS PERFORMANCE

We conclude our discussion of management in bargaining by discussing the priorities firms assign to their broader labor relations goals and the extent to which management evaluates its own labor relations performance in light of those goals. Again, our conclusions are based on information from the Conference Board surveys.

Specifically, the surveys asked respondents to rank the priority they assigned to different labor relations outcomes in assessing the overall labor relations performance of their firm. Those outcomes included the economic results of bargaining; strikes during bargaining and during the term of the agreement; the behavioral aspects of the bargaining relationship (such as conflict or cooperation), especially their effects on individual employees' attitudes and morale; and union avoidance. If we view organizational goals as the values or criteria used to order preferences in organizational decision making,[9] we can interpret the priorities assigned to these different outcomes as operational indicators of the broad labor relations goals of the organization.

As noted in Chapter 6, over the past decade or so managers have become considerably more sophisticated in the use of information systems and quantitative measures to evaluate the performance of specific components of their organizations. The Conference Board data suggest, however, that most corporations have not gone very far in applying these tools to evaluate their labor relations functions. In 1977 only 20 percent of the survey respondents said their company had a formal procedure for evaluating labor relations

TABLE 7–3
The relative importance of different labor relations outcomes, 1977 and 1983

	1983		1977	
Outcome	*Most important*	*Among top three most important*	*Most important*	*Among top three most important*
Effects of negotiations on labor costs	55.8%	79.1%	50.6%	68.0%
Size of settlements compared to industry settlements	11.2	55.7	19.0	50.2
Wildcat strikes during contract	0.7	5.2	0.8	6.2
New union organizing	9.1	29.3	8.0	24.4
Employee attitudes and morale	12.6	55.3	11.7	44.6
Cooperative relations with union	6.7	36.6	6.9	35.8
Unexpected strikes during negotiations	3.8	15.0	2.8	19.0

Sources: Conference Board surveys, 1977 and 1983.

performance. Another 60 percent of the respondents indicated that an informal evaluation was conducted periodically, but 20 percent indicated that no evaluation of labor relations ever took place in their firm. Corporate executives interviewed for that survey were asked the extent to which their organizations had formal systems or procedures for assessing the performance of their labor relations functions. It was clear that most of those interviewed considered *evaluation* to be a foreign term. When pressed about why more systematic or formal evaluations are not found in more corporations, most of them indicated that labor relations could be assessed only by more subjective criteria than those used to evaluate other management functions. These executives stressed, for example, the importance of the "quality" of the labor-management relationship and tended to equate quality with the degree of rapport between the management and union representatives in different divisions of their organizations. In short, the interview data suggested that most executives give relatively little systematic thought or effort to the evaluation of their labor relations functions.

On the other hand, those firms that did engage in some type of informal or formal evaluation seemed to have come to a relatively precise definition of what was important to them.[10] Table 7–3 shows the relative importance the survey respondents assigned to different aspects of their firm's labor relations performance. In this case there are few differences between the 1977 and 1983 rankings. In both years the effects of negotiations on labor costs ranked as the most important consideration. In fact, between 1977 and 1983 concern for labor costs increased relative to the other items in the survey. Consistent with the data in Tables 7–1 and 7–2, concern for the size of the firm's wage settlements relative to concern for the size of other settlements in the industry declined from second to third most frequently cited between 1977 and 1983. Concern for employee attitudes and morale, on the other hand, increased somewhat over this time period. This result is consistent with the view that in recent years workplace-level issues that management believes affect productivity and product quality have generally increased in their importance to management, a point to which we will return in later chapters. In this set of questions, avoiding further unionization and maintaining cooperative relations with union leaders remained unchanged in their relative importance, as did the two items least frequently cited— avoiding unexpected strikes during negotiations and coping with wildcat strikes during the term of a contract.

TOP MANAGEMENT'S VIEWS OF THE EFFECTIVENESS OF LABOR RELATIONS

So far we have presented information on the importance of different objectives or targets for negotiations and information on the degree to which the firms assess their wage and nonwage outcomes in collective bargaining. But the management of labor relations involves many activities in addition to the negotiation of contracts. In this section, therefore, we will discuss the effectiveness of the broader range of labor relations activities. The data used here are analagous to the data presented in Chapter 5 measuring individual union member perceptions of the effectiveness of unions, since they are based on the assessments of individuals, in this case the top labor relations executives in these firms. These self-assessments provide a snapshot of the current levels of satisfaction among top labor relations executives with the labor relations performance of their firm in their major bargaining units.

The labor relations outcomes included in the list and their respective ratings are presented in Table 7–4. All the ratings refer to the relationship between the firm and its largest bargaining unit.

The biggest difference in the ratings reported across these two surveys is that the managers in 1983 were more satisfied with their firm's labor relations performance on most of these dimensions than the managers in 1977 were. For example, managers reported high and improved satisfaction with their ability to achieve their bargaining goals (69 percent), ability to adjust to technological change (almost 68 percent), and the ability to work cooperatively with their unions (almost 74 percent). In both years a high percentage of managers reported satisfaction with their ability to avoid legalistic maneuvering and the performance of their grievance procedures. Increased but moderate levels of satisfaction were reported in 1983 with the productivity of the work force (almost 52 percent), employee attitudes

TABLE 7–4
Management's assessment of labor relations performance, 1977 and 1983

	1983		1977	
Outcome	*Very Good*	*Good*	*Very Good*	*Good*
Ability to achieve bargaining goals	31.4%	37.6%	19.5%	36.2%
Ability to work cooperatively with union	30.0	43.9	15.3	51.6
Ability to adjust to technological change	22.0	45.6	14.6	45.6
Productivity of workers	7.7	44.9	4.9	33.4
Management's ability to take a strike	21.3	26.5	17.1	30.0
Attitudes of employees	5.6	43.9	3.8	43.2
Performance of grievance procedure	14.3	47.7	10.1	54.0
Avoidance of legalistic maneuvering	28.2	41.5	23.3	47.4

Sources: Conference Board surveys, 1977 and 1983.

(almost 49 percent), and management's ability to take a strike (almost 48 percent). The responses to the productivity and attitude items suggest that these managers still saw room for improvement at the individual employee level of the employment relationship.

SUMMARY

The data reported in this chapter and the previous one provide a reasonably comprehensive overview of the current policies, structures, and objectives of modern corporations. In this summary we also offer some general conclusions based on this material.

Management in the United States has historically been, and continues to be, a reluctant participant in collective bargaining. Nonunion firms place their top labor relations priority on remaining nonunion, and firms only partially unionized place a high priority on avoiding further unionization. As the degree of unionization increases, firms balance their goal of avoiding further unionization against their need to work effectively with the unions in their existing bargaining relationships. Only firms that are highly organized and relatively satisfied with their performance in existing bargaining relationships reported putting little effort into avoiding unionization when they expand their operations. But dissatisfaction with an existing bargaining relationship will lead even the highly organized firms to seek a nonunion workplace in their new locations.

The most important goal of firms engaged in bargaining is to control labor costs. In the 1970s, when unions were strong, this objective was defined in terms of meeting, but not exceeding, industry patterns. When unions are weaker, as in the 1980s, management is able to give greater weight to local labor market comparisons. In this decade some firms have also shifted to a more absolute internal standard by tying wages to profitability or productivity.

Over two-thirds of the respondents in the 1983 Conference Board survey reported being satisfied with their firm's ability to achieve its goals in bargaining. Overall, management has taken advantage of the shift in bargaining power away from unions in recent years and has become more aggressive on wage and nonwage issues. Yet only half of the respondents indicated that they were satisfied with the productivity of their unionized work forces. As we will see, management has paid a great deal of attention to this problem recently, and productivity continues to be a central concern at the workplace level of industrial relations.

The set of labor relations goals second most important to contemporary managers involves the behavioral side of their bargaining relationship. Although fewer than half the firms place a high priority on developing cooperative relationships with their unions, a majority of them are concerned about the attitudes and morale of their employees. Some of this concern, again, stems from the motivation to avoid further unionization, but roughly one-third of the firms noted that they were engaged in efforts to improve the attitudes of employees covered under bargaining agreements. Together with the concern for worker productivity, this suggests that increasingly managers will try to motivate individual workers even within the context of a collective bargaining relationship.

As we saw in Chapter 6, the labor relations function within large U.S. firms continues to be highly centralized, but it has become less specialized in recent years. Key labor relations policies and bargaining decisions are established in deliberations among top executives, corporate-level labor relations specialists, human resource specialists, and line managers. Although the priorities attached to different labor relations goals may vary across functional areas and between hierarchical levels, the management structure is designed either to suppress many of these differences or to push them to the top of the organization for final resolution.

Many large firms have sophisticated models for costing out the economic terms of their labor agreements. But only a minority of firms have gone beyond this to apply modern management techniques in systematically assessing other aspects of their labor relations performance. The application of behavioral science methods to assess the attitudes and performance of individual workers has only recently been attempted with unionized workers. Firms will have to continue to explore the usefulness of these techniques in unionized settings if they are to make significant progress in improving the morale and productivity of their unionized employees.

In general, the data presented in this chapter paint a picture of two diametrically opposite types of management policies. One group of firms aggressively pursues a policy of avoiding unions or containing their expansion. Managers choosing this strategy apparently see union containment as the best means of controlling labor costs, promoting the firm's economic objectives, and protecting their own status and power as organizational decision makers. These firms apply a double standard to their employees. They seek to meet as many of the expectations and needs of the nonunion employees as possible to maintain their commitment, loyalty, job satisfaction—and their disinterest in unions. Once a group of employees organizes, however, top priority shifts from nurturing favorable attitudes to concern for minimizing labor costs, limiting union influence and power, and preserving management prerogatives through hard bargaining.

The other group of firms protects their economic interests by pursuing a policy of adaptation to collective bargaining through development of cooperative relationships with their unions. The majority of these firms do not appear to be interested in provoking any major confrontations with their unions to change the balance of power in their bargaining relationship. Instead, they are searching for ways of improving the productivity of their unionized employees.

The central question still remains: Which strategy in the long run is in the best interest of U.S. employers, workers, and the larger society?

Suggested Readings

See the listings for Chapter 6.

Notes

1. See Richard E. Walton and Robert B. McKersie, *A Behavioral Theory of Labor Negotiations* (New York: McGraw-Hill, 1965), 41–46.

2. Thomas A. Kochan, Mordechai Mironi, Ronald G. Ehrenberg, Jean Baderschneider, and Todd Jick, *Dispute Resolution Under Factfinding and Arbitration: An Empirical Analysis* (New York: American Arbitration Association, 1979), 40–49.

3. For a discussion of how organizations attempt to reduce uncertainty, see James D. Thompson, *Organizations in Action* (New York: McGraw-Hill, 1967), 117–31.

4. See Walton and McKersie, *A Behavioral Theory,* 24–40.

5. For a good discussion of the factors that influence a company's choice of a particular position in a local wage hierarchy, see Lloyd G. Reynolds, *Labor Economics and Labor Relations,* 7th ed. (Englewood Cliffs, N.J.: Prentice-

Hall, 1978), 187–90. For a more recent formulation of many of these same ideas under the concept of efficiency wages, see Lawrence F. Katz, "Efficiency Wage Theories: A Partial Evaluation," in *NBER Macroeconomics Annual,* ed. S. Fischer (Cambridge: MIT Press, 1986).

6. See Allan N. Nash and Stephen J. Carroll, Jr. *The Management of Compensation* (Belmont, Calif.: Wadsworth, 1975), 63–67.

7. See Robert J. Flanagan, "Wage Interdependence in Unions and Labor Markets," *Brookings Papers on Economic Activity* 3 (1976): 635–81.

8. Arthur M. Ross, *Trade Union Wage Policy* (Berkeley: University of California Press, 1948), 45–74.

9. Herbert A. Simon, "On the Concept of Organizational Goals," *Administrative Science Quarterly* 9 (1964), 1–22.

10. For several examples of the procedures used by some firms to "audit" or evaluate their labor relations performance, see Audrey Freedman, *Managing Labor Relations: Organization, Objectives, and Results* (New York: Conference Board, 1979), chap. 5.

CHAPTER 8

The Negotiations Process, Impasses, and Strikes

This chapter and the next, on dispute resolution, will examine the process by which unions and employers negotiate collective bargaining agreements. In this chapter we describe and explain the dynamics of negotiations and strikes. Together the material in these two chapters should provide an understanding of the conditions under which the negotiations process works well and the viable alternatives for dealing with impasses that arise in negotiations.

As noted in Chapter 1, the negotiations process is one of the central topics of interest to researchers, policymakers, and practitioners of industrial relations. More has been written about the negotiations process, strikes, and dispute resolution procedures than any other set of topics discussed in this book. In fact, it is difficult to think of any study of collective bargaining that does not, in some way, touch on at least one aspect of the process by which the parties arrive at a contract settlement.

Much of the reason for the centrality of this topic is obvious. Negotiations and strikes are the most visible parts of a collective bargaining system. Strikes provide the headlines for popular press coverage of collective bargaining. This visibility also makes the study of negotiations, strikes, and dispute resolution procedures interesting to students and researchers and makes participation in the process attractive to practitioners and neutrals.

THE VALUES OF FREE COLLECTIVE BARGAINING

The negotiations process is central to the study of collective bargaining for more important reasons than simply the fact that it catches the public's eye. The fundamental reason is the value that U.S. industrial relations scholars and practitioners have traditionally placed on the process of "free" collective bargaining, that is, the right to negotiate a labor agreement without interference from the government or any other outside force. To understand the exalted and protected status free collective bargaining has enjoyed in industrial relations, we must trace its derivation from the principles at the core of our political, legal, and economic system.

The political rationale for *free collective bargaining* can be stated simply: The right to form unions and carry out strikes is an essential component of political democracy. Oberer and Hanslowe stated this premise succinctly:

> One way of defining a free society may indeed be: a society the members of which are free to assert their individual interests collectively.[1]

This principle has its roots in the Jeffersonian view of political freedom: The essence of freedom is the ability to *effectively* influence one's affairs. In general, the less governmental interference with the performance of private institutions and the behavior of private individuals, the better. In industrial relations this view has often been interpreted to mean the freedom to negotiate a contract defining the terms and conditions under which one works. When the ability to effectively exercise the freedom to enter a contract requires negotiating collectively with the union as a bargaining agent, it is the collective negotiations process that must be protected.

The legal and economic doctrines underlying collective bargaining can be traced to the right to acquire property, again through the freedom to enter into contracts. The link between these legal principles and the collective bargaining process was clearly drawn in the judicial opinions of Louis Brandeis and Oliver Wendell Holmes. In 1896, Justice Holmes stated,

> One of the external conflicts out of which life is made up is that between the effort of every man to get the most he can for his services, and that of society, disguised under the name of capital, to get his services for the least possible return. Combination on the one side is patent and powerful. Combination on the other is the necessary desirable counterpart, if the battle is to be carried on in a fair and equal way.[2]

In a later case Justice Brandeis further stated that workers have a legitimate right to take concerted action to promote their self-interests even though doing so might harm an employer:

> As to the rights at common law: Defendants' justification is that of self-interest. . . . May not all with a common interest join in refusing to expend their labor upon articles whose very production constitutes an attack upon their standard of living and the institution which they are convinced supports it? Applying common-law principles the answer should, in my opinion, be: Yes, if as a matter of fact those who so cooperate have a common interest.[3]

Since the freedom to enter a contract also requires the freedom to reject a contract offer, the right to negotiate and the right to strike are closely related. Milton Konvitz stated this well in an article that explored the philosophical bases for the right to strike:

Without the power to affect the course of events, a person or a group lacks the responsibility to reach decisions. Power is the source of responsibility. Without the right to strike, unions will lack the foundation for voluntary negotiation and agreement. If a free labor agreement—free collective bargaining in a free enterprise system—is in the public interest, so is the right to strike, which makes the free labor agreement possible.[4]

Thus, free collective bargaining has its philosophical roots in values that are important to our democratic political system as well as to our economic system.

Free collective bargaining can also be justified on the basis of one of the fundamental assumptions of industrial relations outlined in Chapter 1 of this book. By espousing free collective bargaining, we acknowledge the legitimacy of the inherent conflict of interest that separates workers and employers. It is in the negotiations process that the conflicting interests and goals of the parties are acted out and directly confronted. The existence of the right to strike, or the right to pursue one's claims through some strike alternative, serves as an expression of the normative premise that employees and employers have a legitimate right to pursue their goals in collective bargaining and to express their conflicts of interest openly. The labor movement has traditionally viewed the strike as its ultimate source of power and industrial conflict as an important mechanism of social change.[5]

Two additional justifications have been offered by industrial relations scholars for promoting and protecting free collective bargaining. First, it is often argued that employees and employers have a better understanding of their needs, priorities, and problems than do outsiders—and an especially better understanding than does the government! This suggests that more effective solutions to problems, or compromises that are more workable and acceptable to the parties, will be found in a bargaining process free of outside interference than in one in which third parties constrain the participants from pursuing their own interests. Second, and perhaps more important, it has often been argued that the ability of the parties to deal effectively with their own problems declines once the employers and employees begin to rely on outsiders for resolving their differences (see Chapter 9).

Yet we must be careful not to view the right to form unions and strike as unconditional rights, since the exercise of these rights can conflict with other interests of the larger society. In addition to having an interest in the free expression of interests, the public has an interest in industrial peace and social stability. At times these objectives come into conflict. Society has an interest in limiting conflicts that create social costs and social inconvenience. At the same time, the mere existence of public inconvenience is not in and of itself sufficient grounds to limit labor and management's right to negotiate and engage in a strike if they cannot agree. Thus, much of public policy on strikes is an attempt to balance these competing interests.

The public often tends to be impatient with, if not intolerant of, strikes that cause inconvenience or that appear to have been caused by irrational behavior on the part of unions or employers. Furthermore, some people are skeptical of the value of strikes and unimpeded negotiations. As a result of this only tenuous approval by society, scholars and advocates of collective bargaining have traditionally sought to protect the negotiations process from societal pressures for intervention. While the public might often prefer to suppress conflicts in the short run because strikes impose economic and social costs on innocent bystanders, supporters of collective bargaining defend employers' and unions' ability to impose costs on each other as a necessary ingredient of effective negotiations. The strike threat is a powerful motivation for inducing compromises and bringing about agreement in bargaining. Thus, if we value collective bargaining and a free expression of conflict, we must see strikes and impasses as natural and necessary components of a collective bargaining system, and we cannot view any single strike or impasse as a pathological symptom or malfunction of the system. Nonetheless, frequent strikes or frequent impasses in a given bargaining setting suggest that the strike and the negotiations process are not effectively performing their functions. And reliance on strikes where public interests, health, and safety are jeopardized may justify some form of intervention. But deciding when intervention is appropriate and what form of intervention protects both private and public interests is often a complex task indeed.

Given the important roles the negotiations process and the strike play in a collective bargaining system, on the one hand, and the potentially harmful impact a strike may exert on the public, on the other, it is not surprising that industrial relations scholars and social critics often disagree on how well the process is performing. Archibald Cox, for example, once described the negotiations process as the "ideal of informed persuasion" because of the effective way the strike threat forces negotiators to face reality and make compromises.[6] Compare his view with the following of Abe Raskin, longtime labor reporter and editor for the *New York Times:*

> The more ludicrous the whole performance of [collective bargaining] becomes, the more insistently learned scholars explain why it all makes sense and why any community action to protect itself by substituting reasons for the unrestrained exercise of force in settling labor disputes represents a stab in the back toward Nathan Hale, Paul Revere and all the other apostles of American liberty.
>
> It is past time to arise and proclaim that the Emperor has no clothes. It is my conviction that, when all the people have to suffer because of the willfulness or ineptitude of economic power blocks, it is an affirmation—not a denial—of democracy to provide effective government machinery for breaking deadlocks.
>
> The question, in my estimation, is not whether to do it but simply how. I see no reason why in this institution alone, of all the facets of our society, we should exalt the right to make war as the hallmark of industrial civilization when we seek to exorcise it everywhere else, even in the global relations of sovereign powers.[7]

Thus, while the traditional supporters of the institution of collective bargaining seek to place walls around the process to promote and protect "free" collective bargaining, those most concerned with protecting society's interests against the social and economic costs of strikes argue for governmental intervention to resolve disputes before strikes impose those costs on the public. That this debate still goes on suggests that not everyone agrees with the way the collective bargaining system in the United States arrives at a compromise between the parties' total control of their own affairs and overzealous governmental intervention—a compromise that must be achieved if collective bargaining is to survive as an *effective* guarantor of the parties' right to address their own issues at the workplace.

APPROACHES TO THE STUDY OF THE NEGOTIATIONS PROCESS

As in other areas of collective bargaining research, three disparate approaches have been used to study the negotiations process. The traditional approach has been through institutional analyses that simply describe the dynamics of negotiations, strikes, and dispute resolution. More elaborate theoretical models of the negotiations process, on the other hand, have been developed by economists, political scientists, or game theorists. This research tradition often attempts to determine, through deductive models, how rational bargainers would behave under different bargaining conditions. More recently, behavioral scientists have attempted to develop their own models of the negotiations process using a more inductive, experimental approach.

Deductive Bargaining Models

The formal, deductive models of bargaining concentrate on either predicting whether an agreement will be reached in negotiations or predicting the point of agreement, that is, the outcomes of bargaining. The independent variables used to generate those predictions most often focus on the "rational" aspects of the negotiations process, such as the utility attached to alternative outcomes. These models attempt to develop general predictions about how bargainers would behave if they (and their opponents) acted as rational decision makers. This is why they are often referred to as *normative bargaining theories*.[8]

One of the most famous of these theories is the model of strikes developed by John R. Hicks.[9] Figure 8–1 diagrams the Hicks model. To describe this model, we will take the case where the parties are negotiating only over wages (or assume that all items in dispute can be reduced to monetary terms and represented by a simple wage). Bargainers are each assumed to have some expectation of what they would eventually agree to if there was a strike. In case A both parties expect a strike wage outcome of $w(es)$. If a strike occurs, however, both labor and management will have to absorb income losses. Workers will forgo earnings during the strike,

FIGURE 8–1
The Hicks model of strikes

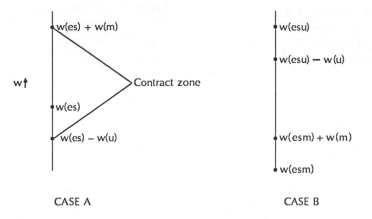

CASE A   CASE B

and management will lose profits because of the stoppage in production. Thus, cognizant of these potential income losses, during the negotiations the parties should be able to find a wage settlement that they prefer to the strike outcome.

To simplify, let us assume that the hourly cost to management of the strike would be $w(m)$ and the hourly cost to labor of the strike would be $w(u)$. Given the expected strike outcome, $w(es)$, management should be willing during negotiations to agree to a wage as high as the expected strike outcome plus the cost to management of the potential strike, or $w(es) + w(m)$. Labor, on the other hand, if it also expects a strike outcome of $w(es)$, during negotiations should be willing to accept a wage as low as the expected strike outcome minus the hourly cost of the strike to labor, or $w(es) - w(u)$. The difference between what management is willing to pay to avoid the strike and what labor is willing to accept creates a *contract zone* of potential settlements that both sides prefer to the strike outcome.

It is, of course, possible for there *not* to be such a contract zone. Case B in Figure 8–1 diagrams such a situation. In this case management expects a very low strike outcome of $w(esm)$, while the union expects a very high strike outcome of $w(esu)$. Even in the face of the expected strike costs, $w(m)$ and $w(u)$, there is no contract zone because $w(esu) - w(u)$ is greater than $w(esm) + w(m)$. The important point that Hicks noted is that, in this framework, there is no contract zone *only* if the parties have very different expectations of the strike outcome. The fact is that there is some true strike outcome. For labor and management to have divergent expectations regarding the strike outcome requires that one or both of the parties be *miscalculating* in their prediction of the strike outcome. Hicks therefore was led to the conclusion that strikes occur *only* in the presence of miscalculation. Strikes could also occur even if there is a contract zone, but in the Hicks framework this also requires miscalculation. Hicks argued that there may be situations where even though a contract zone exists, the parties cannot locate a settlement within the zone because—either through previous bluffing or intransigence—the parties are unable to find the settlements they both would prefer over the strike outcome.

In the Hicks model negotiators have great latitude to further their side's interests. Given a particular contract zone it is in management's interest to reach a settlement at the lowest wage in the contract zone, and it is in labor's interest to reach the highest wage settlement in the contract zone. Furthermore, during negotiations it is in each side's interests to attempt to change the other side's expectation of the strike outcome. Management would like to convince labor that the potential strike outcome is in fact a very low wage, and labor has an interest in convincing management that the potential strike outcome is a very high wage. The risk the parties face is that in their efforts to change the other side's view of the potential strike outcome, they might engage in tactics, such as bluffing or threats, that result in miscalculations and thereby the occurrence of a strike.

Hicks's model is a very useful starting point for analyzing the negotiations process. To build on his approach requires that we understand the factors that influence the willingness and ability of either side to engage in a strike, factors discussed in Chapter 3. These factors determine the position of the expected *strike outcome*. Furthermore, the Hicks framework suggests the need to uncover those factors that lead either side to be overly optimistic about the potential strike outcome or in other ways to miscalculate during negotiations. Nonetheless, because negotiations involve a large number of issues, because what would actually occur in a strike is highly uncertain, and because labor negotiations typically occur repeatedly between the same parties, even with the Hicks framework it is extremely difficult to predict the settlement point or causes of an impasse in any given negotiations.

Inductive, Behavioral Models

The most recent newcomers to the subject of bargaining theory are the behavioral scientists. Most behavioral models of negotiations build on the concepts of game theorists and economists, but they also incorporate a number of the strategic, interpersonal, structural, and psychological factors that come into play during negotiations. In addition, the behavioralists often use a different research methodology to test the validity of their models. Most of their models, for example, use laboratory experiments to test for the effects of different strategies such as bluffing, risk taking or risk avoiding, hard versus soft bargaining, framing, and open versus restricted communications.[10] Some behavioral studies have also built a variety of structural, organizational, and interpersonal variables into their experiments, such as time pressures, the intensity of the conflict, the incompatibility of the parties' goals, constituency pressures and intraorganizational conflicts, and the degree of trust between the parties.[11] In recent years a number of laboratory experiments have been designed to simulate bargaining problems that test the performance of alternative dispute resolution procedures such as mediation, conventional arbitration, and final-offer arbitration. These last analyses are discussed in the next chapter.

Most empirical tests of the behavioral models have, in fact, been limited to laboratory experiments, usually using college students as the negotiators. Although the controls built into these kinds of experiments allow the researcher to make more precise statements about cause and effect, the *external validity* of the simulations (allowing generalizations about the results to actual labor negotiations) may be somewhat suspect. Yet many of the variables that have been studied in the laboratories have direct applicability to the collective bargaining process. Thus, our analysis of the bargaining process will draw on a number of the findings from these laboratory studies.

The Behavioral Cycle of Negotiations

It is useful to think of the process of negotiations as a cycle with several qualitatively different stages.[12] In the initial stage the parties present their opening proposals. This stage often involves a larger number of people than will be involved in the negotiations of the final agreement. The union, for example, may bring in representatives of the various interest groups and levels of the union hierarchy who participated in developing the initial proposals and who will later be involved in securing ratification of the agreement. The union presents proposals that cover its entire range of interest and concerns. Some of the proposals will be of critical importance and will be at the heart of the discussions as the strike deadline approaches. Some are important but may be traded off at the last minute. Some may be translated into more specific demands at a later stage of bargaining or may be issues to which the union will assign a high priority in some future round of negotiations. Other issues are obviously of low priority and will be dropped as negotiations proceed into the serious decision-making stages. The presentation of a "laundry list" of issues serves several purposes. First, it allows union leaders to recognize different interest groups by at least mentioning their proposals. It is easier simply to include some unrealistic, or even unwarranted, demands in the initial proposals, air them at the table, explore the problems underlying them, and, if necessary, allow the employer (rather than the union) to reject them in bargaining than to seem to have arbitrarily nixed some group's pet proposal. Second, presenting a long list of proposals and inflated initial demands on some or all of the issues camouflages the real priorities and bottom-line position of the union.

Employer behavior at the outset of bargaining varies considerably. At times the employer will present a set of management proposals to counterbalance the union demands. At others the employer will simply receive the union demands and promise a response at a future negotiating session. In fact, some management representatives prefer to delay making any specific proposal on wages or other economic issues until well into the negotiations process. Management, too, will try to camouflage its bottom-line position, and it, too, may have unresolved internal differences at the start of negotiations. Recall from Chapter 6 that in some firms a decision on the bottom line is not made until after the union proffers its initial proposals and gives some preliminary indication of its priorities and real positions.

In the early stages the speakers for each side will argue strongly and often emotionally for the objectives of their constituents, both to carry out their representational obligations and to determine how strongly the opponent feels about the issues at stake. It should be no surprise that these initial stages are the forum for a good deal of grandstanding by both parties.

The middle stages of negotiations involve more serious consideration of the various proposals of the parties and the search for a framework for resolving the differences. The most important tasks performed in the middle stages of bargaining are (1) to develop an estimate of the relative priorities each party attaches to the outstanding issues, (2) to estimate the likelihood that an agreement can be reached without an impasse or a strike, and (3) to signal to the other side those issues that might be the subject of compromise at a later stage of the process. Sometimes the parties choose to divide the issues into economic and noneconomic issues; often the noneconomic issues are taken up first. There is no universal pattern, however. It is at these intermediate stages that the behavioral and political obstacles to a settlement begin to surface.

The final stages of bargaining begin as the contract or the strike deadline approaches. At this point the process both heats up and speeds up. Off-the-record discussions of the issues may take place between two individuals or small groups of representatives from either side, perhaps in conjunction with a mediator. These discussions serve several purposes: to escape the "audience effect," that is, the need to save face in front of one's constituents; to allow a fuller clarification of each party's stated position and needs; and to explore possible compromises. The bargaining taking place at the table, in many cases, is only the formal or public presentation of proposals and counterproposals, because by now the negotiators have a better idea of their opponent's bottom-line positions and they may have had private discussions of what it will take to reach a settlement.

Whether the real bargaining occurs at the table or in the back room is less important to our understanding of the process than are the factors that determine whether, in fact, a settlement will be reached without an impasse. In these final stages before a strike deadline each party is seeking to convince the other of the credibility of its threats to strike or take a strike and is trying to get the other party to change its bottom line to prevent a strike. Each is also careful to try to predict accurately what the other's real positions on the issues are, to avoid backing into an unnecessary strike (one where a positive contract zone exists). At this stage, therefore, usually only a small number of decision makers are involved in the process. Although these *individuals* may agree on how a bargaining settlement could be reached, should be reached, or at some later point, in fact, will be reached, the agreement is not yet in the bag. Because of their inability to sell it to their constituents at that point, or because of some other political constraint or strategic difficulty, the agreement might still not be reached without actually calling an impasse.

An Integrated Model

Let us try to mesh this behavioral description of negotiating stages with the contract zone model of the bargaining process. The first stage of negotiations centers on the opening offers of the parties. Differences between the stated demands or positions of the parties and their actual expectations of the strike outcome are a measure of the amount of bluffing that occurs. In the middle stages of bargaining the parties are trying both to influence and identify each other's expectations of the strike outcomes and to decide whether a positive or negative contract zone exists, in other words, the potential for an agreement. The parties will step back from their initial positions when they expect that movement will produce reciprocal movement and eventually lead to an agreement. Movement slows down, stops, or never gets started if either party decides that even if it granted further concessions, an agreement would not be achieved, or if some political, procedural, or other obstacle precludes further concessions. Thus, an impasse can occur either because there is no contract zone or because a positive zone exists but the negotiations process failed to uncover it.

The pressures to settle are the greatest in the final stages, when the parties are therefore most inclined to put their best effort forward to reach an agreement. Both parties are now trying to make sure they understand each other's position and are trying to pressure each other into reconsidering their bottom-line stands on the basis of the costs a strike would impose. Here is where the bargaining power associated with the strike threat plays its most important role in collective bargaining. Here the negotiators must decide how much they must modify their bottom-line positions to reach an agreement.

The negotiators must always consider whether the major political interests or decision makers within their organizations will accept the settlement. The negotiators may hold expectations of the potential strike outcome that are different from those held by their constituents. Following this line of argument, Ashenfelter and Johnson posited that strikes occur because union members have unrealistic expectations.[13] In their model of strikes they assumed management has accurate expectations of the strike outcome and workers' expectations, and so may union leaders, but union members are overly optimistic about what can be achieved in a strike. Under these assumptions, strikes are viewed as a device to lower union members' expectations. Although it is difficult to justify why, of the three parties, union members alone carry unrealistic expectations or why worker-union tensions are the only source of strikes, the Ashenfelter and Johnson framework highlights the important fact that strikes may occur where members and leaders have diverging expectations of the strike outcome.

The pressures affecting labor and management in recent years have led to a number of efforts to deviate from the stylized process of negotiations outlined above. Box 8–1 quotes from a summary of one such case. Whether

---

BOX 8–1
A new approach to contract negotiations

In the past, new contract negotiations between construction workers and contractors in Philadelphia have been marked by angry, bitter disputes that have often led to stalemates, job actions, and costly strikes.

This year, with literally millions of dollars worth of construction projects at stake, the Philadelphia Area Labor-Management Committee (PALM) decided it was time to try a new approach. PALM, which was jointly founded in 1982 by the Philadelphia Chamber of Commerce and the Philadelphia Council AFL–CIO, sought assistance from PON [Program on Negotiation] Director Lawrence Susskind, who developed and led a two-day negotiation training program for labor and business leaders in the construction industry.

Some 80 experienced union and management negotiators completed the intensive seminar, during which they learned how to move from positional bargaining to more effective communication, exploration of joint gains, collaborative development of options, and improved relationships. In addition, Susskind used an elaborate negotiation "game," or simulation, to illustrate how the theoretical concepts he presented could be put into practice. The game, called "Contract Negotiation in the Building Trades," is a nine-party, multi-issue negotiation involving three coalitions. During the simulation, seminar participants reversed their usual negotiation roles, and learned how "the other side" perceives issues. This simulation is among the teaching materials available from the Program on Negotiation's Clearinghouse.

Following the negotiation training—in sharp contrast to the negotiations of previous years—the construction unions and management reached a new settlement three months before their old contract expired. Among other provisions, the two-year agreement calls for an established figure for wage and benefit increases (in a formula to be determined by the unions) and changes in some restrictive work rules, such as allowing foremen to work as well as supervise in certain instances.

The PALM-sponsored negotiation training "did have a substantial effect on me," according to David Marconi, business agent for the Millwrights and Machinery Erectors Union, Local 1906. "I gave it a try, and I'm satisfied with the outcome."

Source: Reprinted, with permission, from "Negotiation Training Speeds Contract Settlement," *Program on Negotiation Newsletter,* December 1986, 6.

Note: The Program on Negotiation is a research and education project in Cambridge, Massachusetts, involving faculty members and students from local universities who are interested in negotiations and dispute resolution.

new approaches such as this will become commonplace in the years ahead and whether such changes will open the way to improvements in day-to-day relations after the contract is signed are questions well worth exploring through further experimentation and research.

STRIKE ACTIVITY

Strike activity can be measured in a variety of ways, depending on the purpose of the analysis. In a review of the research on strikes Stern concluded that a comprehensive theory of strikes should incorporate three dimensions: (1) their frequency, (2) their duration, and (3) their breadth or size.[14] In an earlier study Britt and Galle suggested measuring *frequency* as the number of strikes per 1,000 workers; *duration* as the number of worker days lost per worker; and *size* as the number of workers per strike.[15] They further proposed that the product of these three measures serve as a starting point for describing patterns of strikes in the United States.

The Historical Record

Table 8–1 presents the record of strikes called in the United States by more than 1,000 workers since 1929. As shown, the number of strikes annually between 1975 and 1985 ranged from 54 to 298, although the total number of strikes annually— including those involving fewer than 1,000 workers— averaged around 5,000 over that period. Approximately two-thirds of all strikes are over negotiations of a new contract; the remaining one-third are (generally shorter) strikes called over other issues during the term of an agreement.[16] The total work time lost due to strikes, a measure of the impact of strikes on the economy, has averaged well below one-half of one percent per year. The percentage of work time lost in strikes involving 1,000 workers or more was only .03 in 1985, as shown in Table 8–1.

For our purposes a prime measure of strike activity is the probability of a strike in a given round of contract negotiations. Although BLS data do not allow direct calculation of the percentage of contract negotiations that involve a strike (because the exact number of contract expirations in a given year is unknown), several indirect estimates are available. The Federal Mediation and Conciliation Service (FMCS) receives 30-day notice of all expirations of contracts covered by the National Labor Relations Act. FMCS annual reports show that strikes occur in only about 2 to 3 percent of the units for which these notices are filed.[17] This national average is rather misleading, however, because the probability of a strike is much higher in large bargaining units than in small units. In her analysis of a large sample of negotiations that involved 1,000 or more manufacturing workers between 1971 and 1980, Gramm found that 13.8 percent of the negotiations involved a strike.[18] This percentage is consistent with the data collected in the Conference Board surveys of bargaining in large firms discussed in Chapters 6 and 7.

TABLE 8–1
U.S. work stoppages involving 1,000 workers or more

Year	Number of work stoppages[a]	Number of workers involved (000)	Days idle during month	
			Number (000)	% work time lost
1929	52[b]	—	—	.07[b]
1950	424	1,698	30,390	.26
1960	222	896	13,260	.09
1965	268	999	15,140	.10
1966	321	1,300	16,000	.10
1967	381	2,192	31,320	.18
1968	392	1,855	35,567	.20
1969	412	1,576	29,397	.16
1970	381	2,468	52,761	.29
1971	298	2,516	35,538	.19
1972	250	975	16,764	.09
1973	317	1,400	16,260	.08
1974	424	1,796	31,809	.16
1975	235	965	17,563	.09
1976	231	1,519	23,962	.12
1977	298	1,212	21,258	.10
1978	219	1,006	23,774	.11
1979	235	1,021	20,409	.09
1980	187	795	20,844	.09
1981	145	729	16,908	.07
1982	96	656	9,061	.04
1983	81	909	17,461	.08
1984	62	376	8,499	.04
1985	54	323	7,174	.03

Sources: Monthly Labor Review 108 (December 1985): 74. The 1929 data are from *Monthly Labor Review,* various issues (March 1929–February 1930).

[a]Includes strikes and lockouts lasting a full shift or longer.

[b]Estimates.

Recent Strike Activity

The early 1980s marked a change in U.S. strike activity, for three reasons. First, strike frequency was lower than at any other time since World War II. As Table 8–1 shows, the percentage of work time lost because of strikes stayed below .10 from 1979 on and dropped to a record low of .03 in 1985. In contrast, the 1950s and 1960s witnessed highs of .26 and .29 percent of total work time. Second, whereas strikes in the 1970s in general seemed to net a positive return to union members, strikes in the 1980s frequently appeared to be defensive weapons used only as a last resort by unions fighting for their continued existence. Third, those strikes that did take place in the early 1980s often were more hostile, violent, and emotional than the earlier strikes.

In some cases in these years pay and work rule improvements came only after bitter strikes that, in turn, occasionally ended with the elimination of union representation. Wilson Meatpacking and Continental Airlines underwent bitter strikes and used bankruptcy protection to impose substantially lower pay and less costly work rules after their unions refused to agree to those terms in negotiations. Other meat-packing and some trucking firms also used reorganizations in ownership to gain lower labor costs. Some of those firms closed their unionized operations and then reopened them on a nonunion basis, hiring the same workers back on significantly less favorable terms.[19]

Employers used their victories in strikes over this period to radically alter work rules and work organization, as illustrated by one manufacturing plant included in our field research. In this firm workers went on strike after having refused management's demands for major changes in work practices. After a long strike, during which supervisors were able to keep the plant in operation, the workers returned to work on management's terms. A team system of work organization replaced a highly detailed job classification system and ended a tradition whereby shop stewards continually negotiated work rule practices with individual supervisors. Management instituted a pay-for-knowledge system, and all workers received higher hourly pay. In return, workers were required to learn and move across a variety of jobs. The traditional codification (and continual amendment) of formal rules gave way under the flexibility inherent in the team structure and under expanded informal communications between workers and their supervisors.

The early 1980s, generally, were characterized by employers' increasing willingness to hire worker replacements in an attempt to break strikes—if not the union itself. In firms such as Phelps Dodge management succeeded in those efforts; the existing union was dislodged in a decertification vote held among the ranks of the now-permanent replacements.[20] Figure 8–2 summarizes the events at Phelps Dodge in more detail.

FIGURE 8–2
A chronology of events at Phelps Dodge copper facilities

1967–80

In 1967 the International Union of Mine, Mill and Smelter Workers merged with the United Steelworkers of America (USW). Along with other unions in the copper industry the USW then pressed for coordinated bargaining over contracts in an effort to standardize wages and other contract terms across plants and companies in the industry. Those efforts met with some, although not complete, success.

Phelps Dodge opened a smelter in New Mexico in the early 1970s and was successful in keeping it nonunion.

FIGURE 8–2 (*continued*)

At Phelps Dodge's unionized copper facilities in Arizona and its refining operations in El Paso, Texas, strikes occurred during contract negotiations in 1971, 1974, 1977, and 1980.

1982

Facing sharp declines in the price of and demand for copper, Phelps Dodge temporarily closed its Arizona and New Mexico mining facilities and instituted a number of cost-reduction policies, including executive pay cuts and layoffs of salaried employees.

April 1983

A contract settlement was reached at Kennecot Copper Corporation and was approved by the unions' coordinated bargaining committees as the pattern settlement they hoped to negotiate elsewhere in the copper industry.

1 July 1983

A strike started at Phelps Dodge's Arizona and El Paso, Texas, operations after the company refused to agree to follow the Kennecot pattern in new contracts.

August 1983

Phelps Dodge began hiring permanent replacements for the striking employees.

August 1984

A 13-union coalition, led by the USW, launched a "corporate campaign" against Phelps Dodge and its executives. At stockholder meetings, including those of Manufacturers Hanover Trust (a major creditor of Phelps Dodge), the coalition pressed its campaign.

October 1984

An election was held to decertify all unions at Phelps Dodge's Arizona and El Paso operations. The employees voted to decertify, and subsequent challenges by the unions in the NLRB and the courts were unsuccessful.

Indeed, the declining utility of strikes has led a number of unions to search for alternative ways to bring pressure on employers without risking the costs of a full-scale work stoppage. Box 8–2 excerpts a *Wall Street Journal* story that summarized the return to one strategy from the past: the work slowdown.

MODELS OF STRIKE ACTIVITY

The causes of strikes have been studied from numerous perspectives, including international comparisons, aggregate time-series analyses of strike rates within single countries, interindustry comparisons, and comparisons across specific bargaining relationships.

Almost all statistical analyses of strikes find that strike frequency is positively associated with movements in the business cycle and negatively associated with movements in real wages.[21] Nevertheless, the theoretical

---

BOX 8–2
"Finding Strikes Harder to Win, More Unions Turn to Slowdowns"

The union hall at the sprawling McDonnell Douglas Corp. plant resembles an Army field office. Union officials plot strategy on three huge maps hanging on a wall, and lookouts on the roof keep score on the union's efforts by counting airplanes rolling off the assembly line.

The United Auto Workers local here is orchestrating a work slowdown—an increasingly popular weapon among labor unions. In a contract dispute, union employees are refusing to install parts without blueprints, and they are working to the minimums of their job requirements. The union also is weighing a plan to stage mass grievances by having hundreds of workers blow whistles whenever a member has a complaint against a foreman. . . .

The fight at McDonnell Douglas suggests that the battleground between union and management may be shifting to the assembly line from the picket line. As managements have become more adept at fighting strikes, labor unions are dredging up old-time alternatives such as the slowdown. If the strategy proves out, it could reshape union-management confrontations.

Such tactics are being taken up by unions as diverse as the flight attendants at AMR Corp's American Airlines and the Brotherhood of Boilermakers. The AFL–CIO's Industrial Union Department recently published a booklet teaching such techniques to its member groups. The manual, called, "The Inside Game: Winning with Workplace Strategies," has been so popular that the initial press run of 5,000 copies has been quadrupled.

"If management is going to launch a broadside against us, then we're going to fight back. They won't know what to expect from one day to the next," says Joseph Uehlein, the department's director of special projects.

Source: Alex Kotlowitz, *Wall Street Journal*, 22 May 1987, 1.

---

basis underlying the positive relationship between strikes and the business cycle is not as clear. Hicks's model predicts that strikes occur as a product of miscalculation and should occur randomly, rather than in association with the business cycle. The model predicts that higher *wage settlements* will occur when the economy is growing rapidly because labor will be more willing and able to sustain strikes during these periods and the expected strike outcome should then be higher. But it is not clear why the *strike rate* should rise when labor has greater bargaining power.

One could argue that worker militance and expectations rise along with the economy, and as workers press their demands, strikes increase in frequency—what might be called a *bargaining power model of strikes*. Although this is a plausible assertion, it is a model of strikes and militance very different from that postulated by Hicks. The bargaining power model focuses on the fact that strikes are typically initiated by the union and the work force. Thus, during periods when the union's bargaining power is relatively weak the union is less likely to press its demands and less likely to resort to a strike in seeking more favorable contract terms. The bargaining power thesis also recognizes that strikes frequently are initiated by workers on the shop floor who are upset by management's actions or by official union policy (these sorts of strikes often would be counted as unauthorized, or *wildcat,* strikes). Workers are less likely to engage in this sort of shop-floor action when labor markets are slack and workers fear the possibility of layoff.[22]

There is also little consensus on the theoretical reasons for the negative correlation observed between real wage growth and strikes. Some analysts adopt a variant of the *Ashenfelter-Johnson model* to explain this relationship. They argue that while declines in real wages will increase worker expectations, the function of the strike is to lower those expectations to the point at which an economically rational employer is willing to settle. Hibbs, on the other hand, adopted a variant of the bargaining power model when he argued that real wage movements prompt and therefore are a proxy for workers' wage expectations and militancy (that is, their willingness to strike to achieve their expectations).[23] The strike, by this explanation, serves as a means of inducing employers to raise their wage offers.

International Comparative Models

Comparisons of strike activity across national boundaries are precarious because the role strikes play as instruments of industrial protest and conflict varies considerably by country. In the United States strikes are tactical weapons wielded to induce employers to change their bargaining positions. Unions tend to remain on strike until a settlement is reached. Strikes in some Western European, South American, and Asian countries, however, may have mixed political and economic motives and often are only short protests that end before the settlement of a dispute. Given these caveats, however, several comparisons of strike activity in the United States with that in other nations are worth examining, as they have suggested several reasons for international variations in strike activity.

The United States stands at or near the top of rankings of workdays lost because of strikes and workdays lost per 1,000 workers (duration) but is consistently outranked by Great Britain, Canada, France, and Australia in the number of strikes per 1,000 workers (frequency).[24] Thus, strikes in the United States are longer and larger than in most other countries but somewhat less frequent than in at least several other nations.

Explanations for cross-national variations in strike patterns often start with differences in the nations' political systems. Of central importance is the degree of freedom that the trade union movement has within the legal-political system. One obvious way to limit strikes is through a totalitarian government that suppresses any form of organized dissent in society or through a government-dominated and government-controlled trade union movement. It is not surprising, therefore, that strike rates are extremely low in the communist countries of Eastern Europe and Asia and have also been so when dictatorships have been in power in such countries as Argentina, Brazil, Chile, South Korea, Taiwan, and the Philippines. Consider, for example, the history of Solidarity, a union movement that struggled to be independent from the government of Poland starting in the early 1980s. Its rise and fall is briefly documented in Box 8–3. Furthermore, many developing countries constrain the rights of trade unions and the right to strike, based on both political (control) and economic (development) objectives.

An international comparison of strikes undertaken in the 1950s tested two other popular hypotheses regarding strikes and the political system. The first is whether strikes are less frequent when a labor-socialist party is in power. This hypothesis reflects the belief that labor parties require industrial peace to retain the support of the middle class and thereby achieve or maintain their power. The evidence, however, did not support this first hypothesis. The second, which was supported by the evidence, is that strike activity varies directly with the strength of the Communist party in the society.[25]

Further hypotheses in the international context have addressed the connection between the industrial relations system and strike rates. Among those that have been tested are: the more decentralized the bargaining structure, the higher the incidence of strikes; the higher the percentage of the labor force organized, the higher the strike activity; and the more the trade union movement is integrated into society and accepted as a legitimate partner in economic decision making and planning, both at the enterprise and at the national government levels, the lower the strike activity. Hibbs found a strong positive relationship between decentralized bargaining and strike rates, for example.[26] These three hypotheses are all tests of the simple proposition that the more bargaining units that exist, the more opportunities there are to strike.

In a classic study Kerr and Siegel analyzed strike data across countries and industries, finding that strike rates were consistently higher in certain industries, such as mining and longshoring.[27] The authors therefore proposed that behavioral factors peculiar to certain industries were at least partly responsible for the higher strike rates. In their view, because longshoring and mining are distant from major population centers and involve harsh physical labor, the workers in the industries are comparatively poorly integrated into society and take out their frustrations and isolation by instigating relatively frequent strikes. In Hicks's terminology Kerr and Siegel identified a set of factors—social and geographic isolation—that contribute to the likelihood of miscalculation in bargaining. This interpretation, however, may misconstrue the spirit of their argument, since Kerr and Siegel also stated that strike occurrence may have very little to do with the issues on the bargaining table.

BOX 8–3
Solidarity

In July of 1980 the Polish government announced increases of 40 percent to 60 percent in the price of certain meats that are considered to be staples in the Polish diet. The price increase set off a wave of protest and worker dissent and solidified what had been a fragmented series of underground worker organizations under the banner of a single union: Solidarity.

The leadership of the union emerged under Lech Wałęsa during a severe conflict and sit-in strike at the Lenin Shipyard in Gdansk. Wałęsa and his fellow unionists pressed on the government a list of 21 demands, including the nonnegotiable demand for recognition of Solidarity as an independent trade union with the right to strike. After a two-week strike in Gdansk, followed by waves of strikes throughout the surrounding region, Wałęsa achieved his demand and the Solidarity movement began.

Throughout the rest of 1980 and into 1981 Solidarity staged periodic strikes to reinforce its demands. Wałęsa gained enormous popularity and fame in Poland and throughout the world, making frequent visits to other countries and meeting often with foreign and religious leaders and potentates.

By early February 1981 Soviet officials had become visibly unhappy with the growing influence of Solidarity; and at the same time General Wojciech Jaruzelski became prime minister, signaling an increasingly hard line by the government. In mid-March the government's hard line began to take the form of arrests of Solidarity members. Three months later, in an increasingly tense national atmosphere, meat prices were raised again and widespread popular protests followed.

In August 1981 Solidarity leaders called for widespread economic reforms, while the Soviet government appeared increasingly antagonistic to their cause. The autumn saw a further heightening of tensions and sporadic strikes.

On 13 December Jaruzelski imposed martial law, placed a military council in charge of the nation, jailed many of Solidarity's top leaders, and arranged for an effective news blackout, leaving foreign journalists with little knowledge of the ensuing events. Solidarity was outlawed in 1982.

Since the lifting of martial law in 1983 restrictions on Solidarity's activities have eased periodically. But as recently as early 1987 arrests were reported of intellectuals and others with close ties to Solidarity. Wałęsa has been under house arrest since martial law was imposed, and the movement, though still alive, has been forced back underground.

Sources: Lawrence Weschler, *Solidarity: Poland in the Season of its Passion* (New York: Simon and Schuster, 1982); Nicholas G. Andrews, *Poland 1980–81; Solidarity Versus the Party* (Washington, D.C.: National Defense University Press, 1985).

National Patterns

In 1960 a controversial study heralded the "withering away of the strike."[28] Most empirical studies of strike frequency in the United States over the post–World War II years have shown a declining trend, but the decline is modest enough to reject any notion of a "withering away." Furthermore, aggregate declines in strike frequency often cannot be generalized to more detailed levels of analysis. For example, the number of strikes in the construction and electrical machinery industries increased in the 1960s and 1970s over their frequency in the 1950s.[29] Nor is there much evidence of a withering in other countries. The Hibbs study, for example, found no consistent pattern in *strike volume* (frequency × duration × size) in any of the 11 western democracies he examined.

Other studies have suggested, however, that the causes and shapes of strikes in the United States have changed somewhat over time.[30] During the latter half of the nineteenth century and the first half of the twentieth century strikes tended to be (1) less frequent than now (because unions were less powerful and only small proportions of the labor force were organized), (2) smaller (because firms were smaller and bargaining was decentralized) and (3) longer (because employers in those years more vigorously resisted union organization and pressure than now). And although strikes in the years since World War II can be successfully explained by the business cycle and real wage loss, prewar strikes cannot. The earlier strikes are better explained by variations in political attitudes toward unions and the degree of organizational strength of unions.

In an analysis of strikes over the years 1900–1977, Kaufman found that the economic factors of unemployment, inflation, and union membership and various noneconomic factors, such as the outbreak of World War II and the enactment of New Deal legislation, explained variations in strike activity.[31] This analysis poses an interesting merger of both economic and political factors in search of an explanation for strike activity.

Interindustry Patterns

Interindustry studies of strikes often yield results in support of a bargaining power model of strikes. More specifically, these studies show that strikes are more frequent in industries with lower levels of unemployment, higher percentages of men in the work force, and a higher percentage of the work force organized.[32] An interindustry study of Great Britain also indicated that strikes were more frequent in larger plants but less frequent in larger firms if the analysis controlled for plant size.[33] This result helps explain the curvilinear findings on plant size and strike frequency in the United States. Eisele found that strike frequency increases as the size of the plant increases up to about 750 employees and then begins to drop off.[34] He suggested that these middle-sized, strike-prone plants were less likely than the larger plants to have a professional personnel or labor relations staff, who could intervene to help avoid strikes and other forms of industrial conflict. In the Hicksian framework this proposition could be interpreted as saying that professional staffs are more likely to avoid the miscalculations that cause strikes. Other studies have also found that strikes are more common in industries with a high proportion of multiplant bargaining units and in industries paying higher wages.[35] The connection between high wages and high strike rates may, however, simply reflect the success of previous strikes in increasing wages; high wages may therefore be as much a result as a cause of strikes.

Studies at the Micro Level

Two new strands of research on strikes appeared with the growing availability of micro-level data in the late 1960s. Gramm's research investigated employers' and unions' willingness to strike in an analysis of over 1,000 separate contract negotiations in U.S. manufacturing.[36] Other studies have used the micro-level data to analyze the effects strikes have on shareholder equity. Becker and Olson, for example, found that the stock market fairly accurately predicts whether a strike will occur, but it consistently underestimates the cost of a strike to shareholders.[37]

Studies of the Social and Political Context

Sociologists and political scientists have argued that social and political factors also affect strike activity. Although the various theoretical predictions about social and political influences on strike frequency are often hard to sort out, some empirical evidence suggests that strike rates are higher in communities whose members hold favorable political attitudes toward unions. Stern, for example, found community strike rates were higher in cities outside the South with higher per capita incomes, taxes, and government expenditures and higher rates of unionization. Lower strike rates were in southern cities and in states with right-to-work laws.[38] Although it is difficult to specify precisely which of these community characteristics are the key to strike behavior, together they provide a profile of a political and social community that is conducive to labor and less likely to look upon strikes as a revolt against the community itself.

The role of the political and social environment is especially important in public sector and quasi–public sector strikes, since these strikes can call any of a number of interest groups into the fray. In assessing the potential success of a strike, the public sector union also has to predict the reaction of political leaders, which, in turn, is determined in large part by the public's view of the strike and the strength and image of labor as one among many interest groups in the community. The importance of these political and social contexts will be examined in more detail in Chapter 14, which is devoted solely to the public sector.

The Public Policy Context

Strike activity is affected directly by laws regulating the collective bargaining process and indirectly through economic and social policies. Nonetheless, the law's effects on strikes are often misunderstood. Recall that the National Labor Relations Act (NLRA), in its preamble, cites promotion of industrial peace as one of its central goals. The preamble must be read in the context of the often violent nature of labor relations in the years before the act was signed. One of the major accomplishments of the NLRA, and of similar state statutes governing the public and private sectors, was that by institutionalizing the strike it reduced the degree of violence associated with strikes. And by establishing procedures for union recognition and certification, the law has also reduced the frequency of strikes over these issues.

It would be foolhardy, however, to suggest that legislation that institutionalizes and legitimates the right to bargain and to strike serves to reduce the *overall* frequency of strikes. Instead, by establishing procedural rights for employees wishing to organize and bargain, the legislation encourages union growth and thereby also increases the number of opportunities for a strike to occur. Furthermore, by protecting workers' right to strike, the law provides workers with security in exercising that right and also thereby increases the probability that in any given bargaining relationship a strike will occur. In short, once a law grants citizens a right and protects them in exercising that right, we can expect the citizens to exercise that right. Thus, we should be careful not to evaluate the effectiveness of a collective bargaining statute solely in terms of its effectiveness in deterring strikes unless the law specifically states that one of its objectives is to minimize strikes and establishes dispute resolution procedures as substitutes for strikes.

STRUCTURAL AND ORGANIZATIONAL SOURCES OF CONFLICT

Bargaining Structure

The structure of bargaining has a clear influence on the probability of conflict and strikes. Pattern followers are less likely to experience a strike than are pattern setters and other units negotiating outside of any accepted patterning arrangement, provided the pattern followers do not attempt to deviate from the pattern-setting agreement. This can be explained by the fact that pattern following provides a clear standard that both labor and management often find attractive. Furthermore, once the pattern leaders have settled, the rest of the parties in the pattern are less likely to miscalculate their bargaining power. The clearest example of this is the U.S. auto industry. The probability of a strike is higher for the target company than for the other two firms. Each of the five bargaining rounds between 1964 and 1976 resulted in a strike at the target company, and no companywide strikes over the terms of the master contract took place in the two firms not targeted in the round. Similarly, in the electrical products industry General Electric has traditionally served as pattern setter; and Westinghouse, the other main employer, and other, smaller firms in the industry have traditionally followed the GE agreement very closely. In the 20 years between 1956 and 1976 Westinghouse, for example, experienced only one, relatively short strike—a strike called when the company balked at accepting the pension provisions that were negotiated with GE in 1976.

Decision-making Power

Nothing is more frustrating to negotiators than to realize they are engaging in what is often called "shadow boxing" or *"surface bargaining,"* that is, bargaining opposite a representative who lacks the authority necessary to make commitments that will stick within his or her organization. Inadequate decision-making power or authority on the part of a negotiator greatly increases the probability of an impasse or a strike. The opponent will respond by resorting to the strike or some other form of pressure to force the real decision makers to the bargaining table or to force some kind of decision. This source of impasse is especially prevalent in the public sector, the quasi–public sector, such as not-for-profit hospitals, and in centralized firms or unions that bargain formally in a decentralized bargaining structure.

Intraorganizational Conflict

In Chapters 5 and 6 we stressed that the diversity of interests within both union and employer organizations creates a high potential for intraorganizational conflict. When power is dispersed or shared widely enough to allow the conflict to continue into the final stages of the negotiations process, these internal conflicts will spill over into the union-management negotiations processes and increase the probability of an impasse. Internal conflict, or intraorganizational bargaining, is such an important aspect of collective bargaining that Walton and McKersie and others have presented it as a dimension of the negotiations process in its own right.[39] Because of its importance we will examine its effects on the negotiations process in some detail.

Intraorganizational conflict often occurs when, as described in the previous section, one or both of the parties bring insufficient decision-making authority to the bargaining table. Unresolved conflicts internal to party A make it unclear to party B what A's actual resistance point is, and neither party is able to predict who will ultimately emerge as the winner in party A's internal power struggle over the policies to be advocated in bargaining. Thus, it is difficult for party A's negotiator to know what commitments can be made in negotiations that will be approved by the rest of the organization. Consider, for example, the case of severe intraorganizational conflict in a dispute between a teacher's union and a public school district, narrated in Box 8–4.

Clearly this impasse was caused primarily by the intramanagement conflicts. The union's only recourse was to call an impasse, bring in a

---

BOX 8–4
Intraorganizational conflict in a school district

Three years before the negotiations in question began, the teachers had engaged in a bitter strike opposed with hostility by both the community and the school board. The board president and two other members of the current board were members of the board at the time of that strike and still bore extreme hostility toward the teachers. The other four members of the board held less antagonistic attitudes toward the teachers.

The board's professional negotiator was also a carryover from the strike. The relationship between him and the union was one of mutual and extreme distrust and antagonism. Thus, as the new negotiations got under way, the board and the teachers were still locked in a hostile relationship.

Shortly before negotiations began, the board had hired a new superintendent of schools. Repelled by the animosity between the teachers and the board, he sought to take a more conciliatory stance toward the union. Before long, bitter confrontations developed between the board's negotiator and the new superintendent.

During the summer months the superintendent held informal talks with the union president, and together they worked out a tentative agreement on a contract settlement, subject to board and union membership approval. The board refused to approve the agreement, partly because of objections by the board's negotiator. Throughout the course of the negotiations the superintendent tried to persuade the board to dismiss the negotiator.

Since these events took several months to transpire, the teachers pressured their union leaders into calling an impasse and began to engage in slowdowns and other forms of job actions short of a strike. During the months the superintendent and the negotiator were at loggerheads, each arranged separate meetings with the union representatives, one trying to work through a mediator and the other trying to keep the mediator out of the process. Meanwhile both were lobbying members of the board to obtain the swing vote necessary to win the power struggle.

Obviously, no progress was made in negotiations until the internal dispute was resolved. The superintendent ultimately emerged as the victor in the power struggle, and the board dismissed its negotiator. The superintendent then brought in a new management negotiator with whom he could work and a contract was successfully negotiated.

---

mediator, and put pressure on the school board to resolve its internal differences and get on with the negotiations.

We use this example to avoid leaving the impression that intraorganizational conflicts are mainly a union phenomenon. It is true that the political structure of unions makes it more difficult for them than for most managements to resolve conflicting goals, priorities, and internal power struggles. Nonetheless, in firms where the locus of decision-making power is unclear or widely dispersed within management, open conflicts are also likely to occur and carry over into the negotiations process. These conflicts are common in the public sector because of its complex decision-making structures and numerous political constituencies.[40] Multiemployer bargaining structures in industries with heterogeneous employers are yet another likely environment for intramanagement conflicts.

Management Policies

Earlier in this book we argued that management is the driving force in U.S. industrial relations and that unions, on average, tend to be more defensive or reactive organizations. If this is true, management policies and strategies should have a major effect on the negotiations process and on the strike record. Indeed, a good deal of variation in the rate of strikes exists across firms within the same industries. Within the airline industry, for example, Northwest Airlines' strike rate was considerably higher than that of any other domestic carrier in the 1970s. This firm has a reputation for bargaining hard over issues of management rights.

The most widely publicized management strategy affecting the negotiations process was General Electric's policy of the 1950s and 1960s known as *Boulwarism,* mentioned earlier, in Chapter 2.[41] Boulwarism comprised a variety of strategies, the most visible and most troubling to the unions representing GE employees being the company's insistence on bypassing the initial and middle stages of the negotiations process and presenting to all the companies' unions one firm and final offer on wages. The offer was the product of considerable research and direct communication with employees regarding their preferences and complaints. The unions at GE opposed the single-offer strategy because it effectively forced them into either accepting the company's offer or rejecting it and going on strike. They filed an unfair labor practice charge with the NLRB, and in 1964 the board ruled in their favor (a decision later upheld in the courts).

But beyond this highly visible aspect of Boulwarism lay a number of other management practices, such as extensive direct communications with the employees (through newsletters, mass media, letters to employees' homes), opposition to coordinated bargaining by the unions, and reliance on community-based wage comparisons—all of which lingered after the NLRB decision. The unions' efforts in counteracting these practices coalesced in the formation of a Coordinated Bargaining Committee of all the GE unions in 1966. After a 122-day strike held in the 1969 negotiations, the company came to adopt a more conventional approach toward labor relations in the 1970s and completed the three subsequent rounds of bargaining without a strike.

Although it would be a mistake to attribute the 1969 strike and the conflicts between the unions and GE in the 1950s and 1960s solely to

Boulwarism, and the more peaceful relationship evident since then solely to the more accommodative policies, the change in management policy is indubitably part of the explanation for the turnabout in GE's strike record.[42]

Interviews conducted for the Conference Board surveys discussed in Chapters 6 and 7 further illustrate the link between management policies and strike activity. One company experienced only one strike in its 40 years under union contracts. Its peaceful history was in large measure attributed to the labor relations philosophy of its initial owner and chief executive. The only strike occurred after the chief executive had retired and when the union's leaders believed the new top management was backing away from that philosophy. In turn, the company's labor relations staff interpreted the strike as a signal from the union to top management that any shift from the previous philosophy would produce a militant reaction.

A labor relations executive at another company reported how the firm's strike record reflected the strategic position of the company and its willingness to take a strike. This company is in a highly competitive consumer goods market that depends greatly on brand-name loyalty. The company's chief labor relations executive reviewed the swings in his company's willingness to take a strike as follows:

> During the 1960s the company placed a very high premium on avoiding strikes. The company was expanding rapidly during this time and opened five new plants. It was engaged in a drive to displace the number one competitor in the industry and therefore wanted very badly to avoid strikes. In the 1970s the economic prospects of the company deteriorated. The company did not achieve the leadership position in the industry it had striven for in the 1960s. The period of rapid growth ended, and its changed financial conditions forced it to take a much harder line on productivity issues in bargaining. It made it clear that it was willing to take a strike if necessary to achieve the productivity adjustments it felt were needed to remain competitive. The company recently cracked down hard on wildcat strikers in one of its plants—something it would not have done in the growth environment and labor relations policies of the 1960s.

A number of general statements can be culled from these examples. First, management policy will exert a strong effect on the likelihood of strikes if management adopts an extreme approach—either cooperative or antagonistic—to labor relations. Second, employer policy exerts a more important independent effect during periods of economic prosperity than during periods of economic decline. This is consistent with a more general proposition: The tighter the economic constraints on the parties, the less discretion the organizational decision makers have in influencing events. This proposition implies that the procedural policies management adopts toward collective bargaining should have a greater net effect on the course of negotiations in less competitive economic environments, since in those environments management has the greatest amount of discretion.

Union Policies

Given the linkage between management policies and strike rates, it is only logical to ask whether there are also similar union organizational characteristics that affect the probability of strikes in negotiations. This question has not received much attention in the literature. One study found some weak support for the proposition that the more decentralized the control within the union, the greater the propensity to strike.[43] Interestingly, the construction unions' efforts in the 1970s to introduce more centralization in their decision making were based on this proposition. Beyond this, however, most discussions of union organizational determinants of strikes return to the political aspects of union decision making, which have already been discussed as one case of intraorganizational conflict.

Interpersonal and Personal Sources of Conflict

Negotiations are an intensely emotional process. The parties' attitudes in negotiating with each other are tightly intertwined with the substantive issues under discussion. The stakes involved are usually high, and the tactics used—threats, bluffs, grandstanding for one's constituents, exaggerated anger—are hardly conducive to building rapport among the parties to the process.[44] Add to these the fact that any single round of negotiations is part of a larger and longer term power struggle between parties separated by an inherent conflict of interests, and one can readily see why hostile attitudes can, and sometimes do, develop in a bargaining relationship and why they can constrain effective negotiations. Thus, we cannot overlook the attitudinal climate as a source of conflict that can lead to a strike or an impasse.

Interpersonal hostility can make it difficult indeed to move from initial or intermediate bargaining positions to the bottom line of a resistance point. Hostility hampers communications between the parties and can lead both parties to hold back on concessions they might otherwise be willing to make. Obviously, intense hostility can get in the way of serious discussion of the substantive merits of the issues.

One empirical study found negotiator hostility to be a very strong predictor of public sector impasses, although it was not a strong predictor of strikes.[45] The higher costs of disagreement associated with a strike may therefore induce negotiators to overcome their interpersonal conflicts more effectively than do the lesser costs of impasse procedures.

Personal attitudes, values, philosophies, and personality traits also influence negotiating behavior. Some personality traits, such as excessive authoritarianism, have been found to hinder the compromising necessary to bring about negotiated settlements.[46] A recent study showed that the negotiators' "perspective-taking ability," that is, their ability to see the other party's point of view, enhances the likelihood of a negotiated agreement.[47] Those who are philosophically opposed to unions, on the one hand, and those who are opposed to the role managers play in a capitalistic society, on the other, may see bargaining issues as matters of great principle and thus find compromising a difficult and painful task. Acceptance of the legitimacy of the other side's point of view is a necessary precondition for conflict resolution in any circumstance. Its absence in negotiations obviously increases the probability of an impasse.

Procedural Sources of Conflict

All of the sources of conflict discussed in the previous sections can lead to procedural breakdowns in the negotiations process and, in turn, to what Hicks referred to as strikes caused by miscalculation. The most commonly discussed forms of procedural breakdowns that can lead to these "unnecessary" strikes are (1) holding on to unrealistic expectations for the settlement, (2) being overcommitted to a bargaining position so that it is difficult to back off without losing face, (3) holding back concessions from one's resistance points, (4) miscalculating the opponent's resistance points, and (5) achieving tacit agreement between the negotiators but on terms unacceptable to those who must ratify or approve the agreement.[48]

Although these procedural breakdowns can be caused by other sources of conflict, they can also be autonomous problems that arise on their own during the course of negotiations. One or another of these problems inevitably arise to some degree during the early to middle stages of the process. They become serious obstacles to a settlement only if they persist and are not overcome in the final stages, when the pressure of the strike helps negotiators face reality and make the difficult compromises necessary on the substantive issues.

Bargaining History

Since the parties to labor-management negotiations often remain the same from one round of bargaining to the next, we must ask, finally, whether negotiations fall into relatively stable patterns of high or low impasse or strike rates. Or does an occasional strike serve simply to clear the air and encourage more peaceful negotiations in subsequent rounds of bargaining? Data from the 1977 Conference Board survey suggest that a positive correlation exists between the probability of a strike across multiple bargaining rounds. Card found that the occurrence of a *short* strike in a given bargaining round increased the likelihood of a strike in subsequent bargaining rounds; he also found that the occurrence of a *long* strike reduced the likelihood of a strike in subsequent rounds.[49] There is also some evidence that patterns of high and continual dependence on impasse procedures exist in some public sector jurisdictions. Specifically, the use of impasse procedures in one round of negotiations increases the likelihood that the parties will rely on them again in future rounds of bargaining. (A more complete discussion of this appears in the next chapter.) The largest and most politically complex municipal governments, for example, tend to turn to whatever impasse procedure is available as a normal part of bargaining.

SUMMARY

We have suggested some of the ways economic, organizational, and behavioral factors play a role in the negotiations process and how they can contribute to the incidence of impasses and strikes. These factors serve as more detailed explanatory variables within the broader framework of the collective bargaining process illustrated in Figure 1–1 and developed in the earlier chapters. Unfortunately, the empirical evidence is too meager to judge which of the various factors are the most significant contributors to strikes, but we can nonetheless see how these variables interact to exert an influence on the bargaining system.

Note that as the discussion moved from the external to the internal components of the system, each source of conflict was caused in part by the factors that preceded it in the discussion. More specifically, the structural and organizational sources of conflict are partly a function of their external environment; the attitudinal relationship between the parties partly reflects the intensity of the pressures on the negotiators coming from the other internal and external components of the bargaining system; and the probability of procedural breakdowns increases as the pressures from any or all of the other sources increase. Yet at the same time, each variable introduces to a settlement a particular source of conflict or obstacle that must be overcome if a negotiated agreement is to be reached. Thus, each of the variables can be the cause of an impasse or a strike, and jointly they will further increase the probability of an impasse.

Because of the interrelated nature of these sources of conflict, a change in any one (particularly a change in the external environment) can set off a chain reaction throughout the system that ultimately affects the negotiations process. We therefore need to understand and conceptualize collective bargaining events as linked together in a complex system of interrelated parts.

We can also now see how the different models of strike activity are interrelated. Cross-national variations in aggregate strike activity can be explained reasonably well by comparing the characteristics of respective political and industrial relations systems. To explain strikes at an aggregate level over time within a single country, we can use business-cycle and real-wage variables, a time trend, and measures of changes in government policy (such as incomes policies or passage of collective bargaining legislation). To compare strikes across industries, we must add measures of differences in union bargaining power to capture the value of the strike as a tactical weapon. To explain variations in strikes or impasses at the level of the bargaining relationship, we need to add organizational, structural, interpersonal, procedural, and historical variables to the economic, political, legal, and bargaining power components of the more aggregate models.[50]

Each of these levels of analysis helps to explain different aspects of strike activity and serves different purposes for researchers, policymakers, and practitioners. The macro models provide researchers a parsimonious set of concepts for describing differences across industrial relations systems and summarizing changes in these systems over time. They are not very useful, however, for making predictions at sufficiently disaggregated levels to be useful to policymakers or practitioners. Moving from the macro to the micro level increases the accuracy of predictions, but only at the expense of increased theoretical complexity. Yet it is just this complex set of factors that third parties and negotiators must recognize and manage to resolve as the negotiations process unfolds. Thus, each level of analysis offers its own contribution to a thorough understanding of the role and causes of strikes in collective bargaining.

Suggested Readings

Some of the classic bargaining models are presented in:

Hicks, John R. *The Theory of Wages*. New York: Macmillan, 1932.

Walton, Richard E., and Robert B. McKersie. *A Behavioral Theory of Labor Negotiations*. New York: McGraw-Hill, 1965.

Young, Oran R. *Bargaining: Formal Theories of Negotiations*. Urbana: University of Illinois Press, 1975.

Practical information concerning the conduct of negotiations is provided in:

Fisher, Roger, and William Ury, *Getting to Yes: Negotiating Agreement Without Giving In*. New York: Penguin Books, 1981.

Morse, Bruce. *How to Negotiate the Labor Agreement*, 10th ed. Southfield, Mich.: Trends Publishing, 1984.

Strike activity is the subject of a preponderance of the research on negotiations. For an extensive bibliography and a good discussion of the methodology of strike analysis, see:

Stern, Robert N. "Methodological Issues in Quantitative Strike Analysis." *Industrial Relations* 17 (February 1978): 32–42.

For a lively account of a strike, see:

Brecher, Jeremy. *Strike!* Boston, Mass.: South End Press, 1972.

Notes

1. Walter E. Oberer and Kurt L. Hanslowe, *Labor Law: Collective Bargaining in a Free Society* (St. Paul, Minn.: West Publishing, 1972), 42.

2. In *Vegalahn* v. *Guntner,* Supreme Court of Massachusetts, 167 (1896), quoted in Oberer and Hanslowe, *Labor Law*, 41.

3. In *Duplex Printing Press Co.* v. *Deering,* U.S. Supreme Court, 254 (1921), quoted in Oberer and Hanslowe, *Labor Law*, 68.

4. Milton R. Konvitz, "An Empirical Theory of the Labor Movement: W. Stanley Jevons," *Philosophical Review* 62 (January 1948): 75.

5. Neil W. Chamberlain and James W. Kuhn, *Collective Bargaining*, 2d ed. (New York: McGraw-Hill, 1965), 391; Robert Dubin, "Constructive Aspects of Industrial Conflict," in *Industrial Conflict,* ed. Arthur Kornhauser, Robert Dubin, and Arthur M. Ross (New York: McGraw-Hill, 1954), 37–47.

6. Archibald Cox, "The Duty to Bargain in Good Faith," *Harvard Law Review* 71 (1958): 1409.

7. A.H. Raskin, "Collective Bargaining and the Public Interest," in *Challenges to Collective Bargaining*, ed. Lloyd Ulman (Englewood Cliffs, N.J.: Prentice-Hall, 1967), 156.

8. See Oran R. Young, ed., *Bargaining: Formal Theories of Negotiations* (Urbana: University of Illinois Press, 1975).

9. John R. Hicks, *The Theory of Wages* (New York: Macmillan, 1932), chap. 2.

10. Max Bazerman, *Judgement in Managerial Decision Making* (New York: John Wiley, 1986).

11. Two recent reviews of these studies are John M. Magenau and Dean G. Pruitt, "The Social Psychology of Bargaining: A Theoretical Synthesis," in *Industrial Relations: A Social Psychological Approach*, ed. G.M. Stephenson and C.J. Brotherton (London: Wiley, 1978); and W. Clay Hamner, "The Influence of Structural, Individual, and Strategic Differences in Bargaining Outcomes: A Review," in *Bargaining and Personality: An International Perspective*, ed. D.L. Harnett and L.L. Cummings (Houston: Dame Publications, 1979). See also Daniel Druckman, *Social Psychological Perspectives* (New York: Sage, 1977); and A. Strauss, *Negotiations: Varieties, Contents, Processes, and Social Order* (San Francisco: Jossey-Bass, 1978).

12. This concept is most fully developed and employed in Carl M. Stevens, *Strategy and Collective Bargaining Negotiations* (New York: McGraw-Hill, 1963), 41–46.

13. Orley Ashenfelter and George E. Johnson, "Bargaining Theory, Trade Unions, and Industrial Strike Activity," *American Economic Review* 59 (March 1969): 35–49.

14. Robert N. Stern, "Methodological Issues in Quantitative Strike Analysis," *Industrial Relations* 17 (February 1978): 32–42.

15. David Britt and Omer Galle, "Structural Antecedents of the Shape of Strikes: A Comparative Analysis," *American Sociological Review* 39 (October 1974): 642–51.

16. Data on the total number of strikes and the number of strikes during negotiations and between contracts (not shown in Table 8–1) can be found in *Handbook of Labor Statistics* (Washington, D.C.: Bureau of Labor Statistics, U.S. Department of Labor, various years). For a discussion of the procedures and difficulties involved in collecting and compiling statistics on work stoppages, see *BLS Handbook of Methods for Survey Studies,* bulletin 1910 (Washington, D.C.: Bureau of Labor Statistics, U.S. Department of Labor, 1976), chap. 27.

17. Calculated from FMCS annual reports for the years 1968–75.

18. Cynthia L. Gramm, "The Determinants of Strike Incidence and Severity: A Micro-Level Study," *Industrial and Labor Relations Review* 39 (April 1986): 361–76.

19. See "The Pork Workers' Beef: Pay Cuts Persist," *Business Week,* 15 April 1985, 75–76.

20. The decertification vote and the United Steelworkers' efforts to challenge that vote are discussed in "Steelworkers to Challenge Vote Results," *AFL-CIO News,* 16 February 1985, 2.

21. Albert Rees, "Industrial Conflict and the Business Cycle," *Journal of Political Economy* 60 (October 1952): 37–82; Orley Ashenfelter and George Johnson, "Bargaining Theory, Trade Unions, and Industrial Strike Activity," *American Economic Review* 59 (March 1969): 35–49; Douglas A. Hibbs, Jr., "Industrial Conflict in Advanced Industrial Societies," *American Political Science Review* 70 (December 1976): 1033–58.

22. For an interesting analysis of both contract strikes and strikes between contract negotiations that is consistent with a bargaining power model of strikes, see Sean Flaherty, "Contract Status and the Economic Determinants of Strike Activity," *Industrial Relations* 22 (Winter 1983): 20–33.

23. Hibbs, "Industrial Conflict."

24. Hugh Clegg, *Trade Unionism Under Collective Bargaining: A Theory Based on Comparisons of Six Countries* (Oxford: Basil Blackwell, 1976), 69.

25. Hibbs, "Industrial Conflict."

26. Ibid.

27. Clark Kerr and Abraham Siegel, "The Interindustry Propensity to Strike," in *Industrial Conflict,* ed. Arthur Kornhauser, Robert Dubin, and Arthur M. Ross (New York: McGraw-Hill, 1954), 189–212.

28. Arthur M. Ross and Paul T. Hartman, *Changing Patterns of Industrial Conflict* (New York: John Wiley, 1960).

29. David B. Lipsky and Henry S. Farber, "The Composition of Strike Activity in the Construction Industry," *Industrial and Labor Relations Review* 29 (April

1976): 388–404; Robert A. McLean, "Coalition Bargaining and Strike Activity in the Electrical Equipment Industry, 1950–1974," *Industrial and Labor Relations Review* 30 (April 1977): 356–63.

30. Britt and Galle, "Structural Antecedents"; David Snyder, "Early North American Strikes: A Reinterpretation," *Industrial and Labor Relations Review* 30 (April 1977): 325–41.

31. Bruce E. Kaufman, "The Determinants of Strikes in the United States, 1900–1977," *Industrial and Labor Relations Review* 35 (July 1982): 474–90.

32. Britt and Galle, "Structural Antecedents."

33. John Shorey, "The Size of the Work Unit and Strike Incidence," *Journal of Industrial Economics* 23 (March 1975): 175–88.

34. C. Frederick Eisele, "Plant Size and Frequency of Strikes," *Labor Law Journal* 21 (December 1970): 779–86; Eisele, "Organization, Size, Technology, and Frequency of Strikes," *Industrial and Labor Relations Review* 27 (July 1974): 560–71.

35. Richard N. Block, "The Theory of the Allocation of Union Resources and the Supply of Union Services," photocopy (East Lansing: Michigan State University, 1979).

36. Gramm, "The Determinants of Strike Incidence."

37. Brian E. Becker and Craig A. Olson, "The Impact of Strikes on Shareholder Equity," *Industrial and Labor Relations Review* 39 (April 1986): 425–38; see also George R. Neumann, "The Predictability of Strikes: Evidence from the Stock Market," *Industrial and Labor Relations Review* 33 (July 1980): 525–35.

38. Robert N. Stern, "Intermetropolitan Patterns of Strike Frequency," *Industrial and Labor Relations Review* 29 (January 1976): 218–35. For an earlier study of the social context for collective bargaining, see Robert S. Lynd and Helen M. Lynd, *Middletown* (New York: Harcourt, Brace, 1969).

39. Richard E. Walton and Robert B. McKersie, *A Behavioral Theory of Labor Negotiations* (New York: McGraw-Hill, 1965).

40. Thomas A. Kochan, George P. Huber, and L.L. Cummings, "Determinants of Intraorganizational Conflict in Collective Bargaining in the Public Sector," *Administrative Science Quarterly* 20 (March 1975): 10–23.

41. Herbert N. Northrup, *Boulwarism* (Ann Arbor: Graduate School of Business, University of Michigan, 1964).

42. For historical studies that document the effects of company policies on strike activity in two firms, see Robert Ozanne, *A Century of Union Management Relations* (Madison, Wis.: University of Wisconsin Press, 1967); Walter H. Uphoff, *Kohler on Strike* (Boston: Beacon Press, 1966).

43. Myron Roomkin, "Union Structure, Internal Control, and Strike Activity," *Industrial and Labor Relations Review* 20 (January 1976): 198–217.

44. See Roger Fisher and William Ury, *Getting to Yes: Negotiating Agreement Without Giving In* (New York: Penguin Books, 1981).

45. Thomas A. Kochan and Jean Baderschneider, "Dependence on Impasse Procedures: Police and Firefighters in New York State," *Industrial and Labor Relations Review* 31 (July 1978): 431–49.

46. For an extensive review of evidence on the role of personality traits in bargaining, see Jeffrey Z. Rubin and Bert R. Brown, *The Social Psychology of Bargaining and Negotiations* (New York: Academic Press, 1975), 1583–96. See also Bazerman, *Judgement in Managerial Decision Making*.

47. Margaret A. Neale and Max H. Bazerman, "The Role of Perspective-Taking Ability in Negotiating Under Different Forms of Arbitration," *Industrial and Labor Relations Review* 36 (April 1983): 378–88.

48. The best discussion of these procedural aspects of the negotiations process is in Thomas Schelling, *The Strategy of Conflict* (Cambridge: Harvard University Press, 1960); see especially, chap. 1, "An Essay on Bargaining." See also Stevens, *Strategy*; Walton and McKersie, *A Behavioral Theory*.

49. David Card, "Longitudinal Analysis of Strike Activity," photocopy (Princeton: Industrial Relations Section, Princeton University, July 1986).

50. A comprehensive theory of strikes should not focus on only one dimension of strike activity, such as strike frequency, but should also help explain variations in the shape of strikes. To do this the theory must take into account the changing role of the strike in society and the power of the actors in the bargaining system.

CHAPTER 9

Dispute Resolution Procedures

$\mathbf{W}$e can now turn to the analysis of the major procedural techniques for resolving impasses, namely, mediation, factfinding, and various forms of interest arbitration. The primary purpose of this chapter is to show how these techniques affect the negotiations process and to assess how well they perform in dealing with the different causes of conflict or sources of impasse identified in Chapter 8.

A secondary purpose of this chapter is to note a number of new third-party roles that are emerging in industrial relations, those designed to achieve longer run changes in labor-management relations. The parties on both sides of the bargaining table are beginning to demand the services of third parties who have comprehensive knowledge of and experience in industrial relations, as well as the skills needed to help design and lead the community-based labor-management committees, in-plant quality-of-working-life and employee involvement processes, and joint committees for designing new work systems or new human resource systems that have become increasingly prevalent in recent years.

No single procedure is ideally suited for resolving all sources of conflicts or causes of impasses in collective bargaining. We therefore need to appreciate how these different procedures work, how effectively they deal with different types of impasses, and how they can be adjusted to improve their effectiveness. Much of the literature on dispute resolution has come from the experience in public sector bargaining, where, because strikes are often prohibited, dispute resolution procedures are of crucial importance. Our discussion of this literature starts with mediation, the most voluntary and least coercive dispute resolution technique, then moves on to a hybrid procedure called factfinding, and finally turns to what is usually a decisive form of dispute resolution, binding arbitration.

MEDIATION

Mediation is the most widely used, yet the most informal, type of third-party intervention into collective bargaining. In *mediation* a neutral party assists the union and management negotiators in reaching a voluntary agreement. A mediator has no power to impose a settlement, but rather acts as a facilitator for the parties. Unlike factfinding and arbitration, mediation is a well-accepted supplement to the negotiations process in both the private and public sectors.

The National Labor Relations Act (NLRA) specifies that a union must notify the Federal Mediation and Conciliation Service (FMCS) 30 days before calling a strike. The 1974 amendments to the NLRA, which extended the act's coverage to private, nonprofit hospitals, specify that in those hospitals mediation has to take place before a legal strike can occur. The Railway Labor Act also contains provisions for a mediation phase before a dispute can go to the next step of the impasse process. Almost all of the bargaining statutes covering state and local government employees call for mediation as the first phase of the impasse resolution process, and in the federal sector mediation as the first phase of the process is universal.

FMCS annual reports estimate that approximately 15 percent to 20 percent of all cases in which 30-day strike notices are filed require at least some informal (by telephone) type of mediation, and between 8 percent and 10 percent require a formal mediation effort. Mediation is more common in the public sector than in the private, as noted earlier, because strikes are illegal in the vast majority of public sector jurisdictions. In the state of New York, for example, between 30 percent and 50 percent of all negotiations reached an impasse and required mediation during the first 25 years of public sector bargaining. Other states have reported somewhat lower rates of reliance on mediation, but all states report rates that exceed the FMCS reported average for the private sector.

Most of the mediation in private sector disputes is done by the approximately 300 staff members of the FMCS or the staff mediators of the National Mediation Board, the administrative agency for the Railway Labor Act. Private mediators are usually hired only when the parties specifically request their assistance, either because of their familiarity with the industry or some other pertinent qualities. The FMCS, the U.S. Secretary of Labor, other members of the President's cabinet, or the President himself is sometimes brought into the mediation process in important disputes or those designated as national emergencies, as defined by Title II of the Taft-Hartley Act. In the public sector mediation is the province of staff mediators employed by the various state agencies that administer the public employment bargaining statutes and in some states the province of ad hoc, part-time mediators. These ad hoc mediators generally hold full-time posts as college professors, lawyers, or members of the clergy or in some occupation related to labor-management relations.

The Objectives of Mediation

The ultimate objective of the mediator is to help the parties reach a settlement. The ultimate measure of the effectiveness of mediation is therefore whether it brings about a settlement. For three reasons, however, we need to go beyond this single measure in assessing the performance of mediation as a conflict resolution process. First, almost all collective bargaining disputes are resolved at one point or another. The mere fact that mediation was involved in the process, or even was in progress at the time the settlement was achieved, is not a sufficient indication that the mediation was itself the cause of the settlement. Second, there is more to mediation than the final step that settles the contract. Mediation follows a continuously narrowing course as the mediator seeks to whittle away at the number of issues in the dispute. Third, progress toward a settlement is possible without necessarily completely resolving any of the issues. In other words, we can say that progress has been made if the parties have succeeded in narrowing their differences over the open issues.

Mediation is also a device designed to help the parties "come clean without prejudice," that is, to explore informally or off the record what would happen if they were to move away from their bottom-line positions. Mediators undertake this exploratory effort to prevent the "positive contract zone" type of strike from occurring, without formally jeopardizing the bargaining position the negotiators must take if a strike or continued impasse is inevitable. Thus, one major function of mediation is to allow this form of tacit bargaining and information sharing to take place, either directly between the parties or indirectly by both parties' sharing confidential bargaining information (their resistance points) with the mediator.[1]

Finally, the mediator also tries to prevent the parties from holding back concessions they would be willing to make to avoid a strike. It is by no means an easy task for the mediator to identify what the resistance points of the parties are, since in most instances the negotiators are extremely wary of sharing this information openly with the mediator. Instead, the mediator must guess at the parties' positions from the statements they make and then must try to get the parties to put forward their best offer in negotiations if it appears that by doing so a settlement can likely be reached.

Thus, although the ultimate measure of the effectiveness of mediation is its success in achieving a settlement, these intermediate indicators should also be considered as partial measures of success, since not every dispute is amenable to resolution via the mediation process.

Determinants of the Effectiveness of Mediation

Many observers believe mediation is an art that is difficult to learn and impossible to study. Practitioners often claim that no two mediation situations are alike and no two mediators would handle the same situation in the same way. Although there is a good deal of truth to these beliefs, theoretical and empirical research has identified some systematic patterns in the mediation process. In this section we will explore some of these patterns to clarify the conditions under which mediation can be a useful tool in dispute resolution.

We will use a model of the mediation process, developed and tested using a sample of public sector disputes, to organize our discussion of the conditions under which mediation is effective.[2] The model groups the determinants of mediation effectiveness under the following four categories: (1) the characteristics of the mediators, (2) the sources or nature of the conflict or impasse, (3) the situational characteristics of the dispute, (4) the strategies of the mediators, and (5) the parties.

Characteristics of the mediator. Perhaps the most general principle of the mediation process is that the mediator must be *acceptable* to the parties if the process is to succeed. Because of the voluntary nature of this form of intervention, no mediator can function without the trust, cooperation, and acceptance of the parties.

Acceptability is also important because the mediator must obtain from the parties confidential bargaining information, information which, if used indiscriminately, could destroy a party's bargaining strategy and leverage. Although acceptability can be achieved by reputation, most experienced negotiators will be hesitant to divulge confidential bargaining information merely because the mediator has a good reputation. Thus, the early stages of most mediation efforts (when the mediator is not personally known to the parties) will be taken up with the mediator's attempts to establish his or her credibility and gain the trust and confidence of the parties. Once gained, acceptability can also be lost as the process unfolds. When this occurs, a mediator may voluntarily withdraw from the case or the parties may seek other means of resolving the dispute.

Evidence suggests that *experience* is another personal quality important to successful mediation. This criterion is consistent with the view that mediation is an art that one must learn by trial and error through on-the-job training. An obvious catch-22 arises here, however: To gain experience, a mediator must work on some cases without having much experience. In any event, an empirical study of mediation in the public sector did find a positive relationship between mediator experience (measured as the number of previous mediation cases) and the effectiveness of mediation, especially effectiveness in inducing movement toward settlement and in narrowing the number of issues open in the dispute.[3]

Thus, the catch-22 is a real one that plagues not only the mediation process, but all forms of dispute resolution. The novice mediator has a very difficult time breaking into the occupation. Fortunately, not every collective bargaining dispute constitutes a national emergency, and so novice mediators do obtain on-the-job training and experience in some of the smaller and less complex disputes before taking on the challenge of major cases.

Beyond these two central personal characteristics, the personal attributes that arguably lead to success in other occupations have also been shown to be important to the success of the mediation process.[4] In fact, the litany of desirable mediator traits often reads like a modified Boy Scout oath: A good mediator is trustworthy, helpful, friendly, intelligent, funny, knowledgeable about the substantive issues in question, and so on. Undoubtedly these traits are just as important in mediation as they are in other walks of life.

Sources of impasse. Figure 9–1 lists the main sources of impasse; these parallel the causes of strikes discussed in Chapter 8. A central proposition underlying our discussion of the mediation process is that mediation is more suitable for addressing some of the sources of impasse than others. The results of the public sector study mentioned earlier indicated, for example,

FIGURE 9–1
Typology of sources of impasse in mediation

---

1. Economic characteristics
    Employer's inability to pay
    Erosion of employees' wage position
2. Structural characteristics of the relationship
    Pattern-breaking relationship
3. Organizational characteristics of the parties
    Inadequate negotiator authority to bargain
    Internal conflicts within one or both of the parties
4. Interpersonal characteristics
    Hostility between the parties
5. Personal characteristics
    Inadequate negotiator skill and experience
6. Nature of the issues
    "Matters of principle" at stake
7. Bargaining behavior of the parties
    Unrealistic expectations
    Overcommitment to a position
    Lack of desire to settle

Source: Taken from Thomas A. Kochan and Todd Jick, "The Public Sector Mediation Process: A Theory and Empirical Examination," *Journal of Conflict Resolution* 22 (June 1978): 214.

that mediation was most successful in addressing conflicts that reflected a breakdown in the negotiations process, caused, for instance, by one party or both becoming overcommitted to their bargaining positions or by a lack of experience on the part of the negotiators. Mediation was least successful, on the other hand, in resolving conflicts caused by the economic context of the dispute, such as the employer's inability to pay or major differences in the parties' expectations for settlement.

These results imply that the mediation process is more successful in positive contract zone disputes than in negative ones. That is, it is most effective in resolving conflicts in which the substantive preferences, or bottom-line positions, of the two parties overlap but impasse has occurred because of some attitudinal problems or because of a breakdown in the negotiations process. Where a negative contract zone exists, the mediation process is limited because here some form of outside pressure (such as the threat or imposition of a strike) is necessary to induce the parties to make major changes in their bottom-line positions. Thus, the mediation process is best suited to helping the parties move to (or perhaps marginally beyond) their resistance points. Only in conjunction with some external pressure can mediation be expected to succeed in getting the parties to adjust their bottom lines and reach agreement when a real gap exists between them.

Mediation is also ill-suited to impasses that involve structural or intra-organizational conflicts. Consider again the example of the teacher dispute described in Box 8–4 (Chapter 8), which involved major internal conflicts within the school board's management. In that case one mediation session was held before the internal split was resolved, but little progress was made. After the session ended the mediator was informed that the superintendent was going to try to get the board negotiator dismissed. For the next two months an internal power struggle ensued. The mediator kept in touch by telephone with all the parties (including, much to the dismay and shock of the board's negotiator, the school superintendent), but no formal mediation session took place until the superintendent emerged as the victor of the internal battle and the board negotiator was replaced. Obviously, the mediator in this case had to walk a fine line in trying to convince management to resolve its internal conflicts so that negotiations could proceed. This is a very different type of dispute for the mediation process to resolve. The more the mediator becomes involved in trying to mediate disputes within one of the parties' organization, the more the mediator risks losing acceptability with one faction or another. Yet failure to resolve the internal dispute insures that no progress will be made in resolving the union-management dispute.

In addition to being differentially successful in resolving different types of impasses, mediation is definitely less effective in cases of the most intense conflicts, that is, in disputes characterized by multiple sources of conflict.

This was one of the strongest findings in the public sector study and is also consistent with laboratory studies of dispute resolution procedures.[5]

Situational factors. The major situational factor influencing the success of mediation is the degree of pressure on the parties, or their motivation, to settle. Normally, the threat of a strike is the major force pressuring a settlement in the negotiations and mediation processes. Observers generally agree, therefore, that mediation works best when operating under a real and immediate strike threat, namely, at the final stages of the contract negotiations process, or at the point during a strike where both parties are under the greatest pressure to settle. Two separate empirical studies of dispute resolution in Canadian municipal and federal governments have supported this observation. In both studies some bargaining units participated in mediation where the right to strike existed, while others were involved in mediation under an arbitration system. Both studies found a significantly higher settlement rate in mediation under the strike system than under the arbitration system. In the municipal sector 60 percent of the mediation cases were settled without a strike, whereas only 20 percent were settled without going to arbitration. The comparable figures in the federal sector over four rounds of bargaining ranged between 38 percent and 70 percent (with a median of 67 percent) under the strike system and between 10 percent and 23 percent (with a median of 12 percent) under the arbitration system.[6] Similar results have been obtained in more recent studies of mediation in states where public employees have the right to strike: A higher percentage of mediation cases are settled in environments where the parties have the right to strike than where mediation is followed by factfinding or arbitration.[7]

Mediator strategies during the stages of mediation. While the success of the mediation process depends in part on the personal traits of the mediator, those traits are not the only mediator-specific factors that influence mediation effectiveness. Perhaps the most difficult determinant to study is the very heart of the process itself: what a mediator does to help produce a settlement.[8]

The strategies and behavior of the mediator vary at different stages of the intervention. During the initial stages of mediation the mediator is primarily concerned with achieving acceptability and identifying the issues in the dispute, the underlying obstacles to a settlement (the sources of the conflict or impasse), the attitudinal climate between the parties, and the distribution of power within each negotiating team. The initial stages of mediation call for a relatively passive, questioning and listening role on the part of the mediator. Normally this role takes the form of meeting with the two negotiating teams and shuttling between them to explore ways of pulling the negotiations away from the stalemate. In these stages the parties will often lash out at each other, exaggerate their differences and the intensity of their resolve to stand firm on their obviously reasonable positions, and try to convince the mediator of their own rationality and the stupidity or unreasonableness of their opponent. It is in these early, separate sessions that the bonds of trust, acceptability, and credibility are either being established between the mediator and the parties or not.

In short, the parties are testing the mediator. Some of the same grandstanding that occurs in the early stages of the negotiating cycle is repeated at this point in mediation for the benefit of the newest entrant into the process. The separate sessions with the mediator also give the parties an outlet for their pent-up emotions and frustrations. The biggest challenges for the mediator at this stage are (1) to diagnose accurately the nature of the dispute and the obstacles to a settlement and (2) to get something started that will produce movement toward a final resolution. Both parties may be reluctant to take the first step; a mediator is often faced with the unhappy statement of one party that "we made the last move so the next move is up to them," only to proceed to the other side and hear the same thing. The mediator cannot let either party's hesitance to move first stop the process before it is given a chance. Neither party, in all likelihood, wants this to happen, or the mediator would not have been called in the first place.

Once the mediator overcomes this stalemate, the next step is to begin an exchange of proposals and counterproposals and test for potential areas of compromise. At this point it is crucial that the mediator have made an accurate diagnosis of the underlying sources of conflict. The mediator is now beginning to intervene more actively by trying to establish a framework or procedure for moving toward a settlement. If the mediator has misjudged the underlying difficulties and tries to push the parties toward a settlement prematurely, or in a way that does not overcome some of the major obstacles, his or her credibility and acceptability will be lost and the process will break down. For example, a retired mediator once told the following story about one of his early experiences in mediating, in a strike on the West Coast between the International Longshoremen's and Warehousemen's Union and the Pacific Maritime Association.

> The mediator started the intervention in the normal way and the parties responded by discussing their differences in a serious fashion. The mediator then broke the parties into separate caucuses. When he went to talk with the union team he found them playing cards. To his dismay, he could not convince them to stop playing cards and get down to the business of settling the strike. Instead, he was told to go back to his hotel room and that they would call him when they needed him. Later the mediator learned that the major obstacle to a settlement in this case was a structural one—the longshoremen on the West Coast were waiting for the longshoremen on the East Coast to settle their contract so that they could then use it as a pattern for their own settlement.

During this second stage of the mediation process the mediator continues to probe to identify the priorities and bottom-line positions of the two parties and find possible acceptable solutions to the outstanding issues. Once the parties have begun to exchange and discuss specific proposals and counterproposals, the mediator attempts to determine whether their bottom-line positions overlap or are close enough to try to press for modifications that would yield an agreement.

Just as the mediator's accuracy in estimating the parties' bottom-line positions is crucial at this stage, so too is the mediator's timing. It is when the mediator judges the bottom-line positions to be close enough to push toward a settlement that he or she begins to take a more active, assertive, or aggressive role in suggesting actual compromises, pushing the parties to make compromises they earlier stated they would be unwilling to make and in general trying very hard to close the gap between the parties. Engaging in such active tactics prematurely (that is, when the parties are still too far apart, when the pressure to settle does not exist, or when some political constraint stands in the way of a settlement at that time), however, damages the mediator's credibility and acceptability. The more experienced the negotiators are, the less willing they will be to allow the mediator to "push them around" in this way. The mediator will get the message quickly, unambiguously, and directly—the negotiators may simply walk out! When conditions are not ripe for settlement, the mediator must hold back, for the time being, from overly aggressive tactics. When the situation is ripe, however, the mediator must take action or risk losing the opportunity to forge a settlement. Now we can begin to see why experience pays off. Or, put differently, here is where the art in mediation becomes obvious to even the most theoretically inclined model builders.

As the pressure to reach a settlement builds and the mediator senses that the time for the final push toward resolution is at hand, the mediator becomes ever more aggressive. No longer passively listening to the parties' arguments and rationalizations or to exhortations about problems with the other side, the mediator is negotiating hard with both parties, trying to get them to face reality and adjust their expectations and bottom-line positions. The mediator may be actively suggesting compromise solutions, while at the same time being as careful as possible to avoid seeming overidentified with a specific compromise or settlement point. Overidentification with a solution that one or both parties reject may lead to rejection of the mediator or limit his or her continued usefulness. Thus, any compromises are proposed merely as ideas to consider or as counterproposals the mediator believes he or she can persuade one side to accept if they would also be acceptable to the other side.

The dynamics within each of the negotiating teams often change at this point as well. Frequently, team members will differ on the substantive issues, on the degree of militancy to follow, and in their attitudes toward the other party. At this stage the mediator will often look to the professional negotiators on each team for help in dealing with the more militant of the team's members. Sometimes, the reverse is true as well: The negotiator will look to the mediator for help in assuaging the militant faction. In any event, these final-hour sessions often require that someone—the mediator, the professional negotiator, or both—convince the hard-liners that the best deal is at hand and that the final compromises necessary to reach a settlement should now be made. Again, trust and confidence in the mediator are critical to the success of these final dynamics. The professional negotiator will want assurances that the best deal is in fact at hand, before attempting to convince the rest of the team that they should settle. Similarly, the mediator will want assurances that the parties have indeed put their last, best offers on the table, before pressing hard for the settlement.

Sometimes the mediator is called upon in these final stages to make what are called "mediator proposals." Mediator proposals are riskier and more formal ventures than the many other suggestions a mediator will make during the course of an intervention. A mediator proposal is normally made only when both parties are close to a settlement and the mediator believes that by making the proposal the parties will come to agreement. In some cases the mediator may make a proposal that the parties have already tacitly agreed to, but, for political or other reasons, they prefer not to offer themselves. Some mediators believe that a proposal should never be made unless the mediator is sure it will be acceptable to both parties. Obviously, this tactic is used only as a final effort to close a dispute.

The preceding description of the dynamics of the various stages of the mediation process and the strategies used by mediators points out that mediators must be aggressive in pushing the parties toward a settlement—when the climate, timing, and pressures on the parties are right. We were not surprised, therefore, to find in our public sector study that the parties preferred aggressive mediators and that the aggressiveness of the mediator was significantly related to measures of the effectiveness of the mediation process, particularly to those that gauge movement in bargaining and a narrowing of the issues in the dispute. A study by Gerhart and Drotning reported a similar positive effect for mediator aggressiveness and further noted that the more intense or difficult the dispute, the more aggressive the mediator tended to be.[9] Let us stress yet again, however, that aggressiveness out of context, or at the wrong time, or based on a mistaken diagnosis of the nature of the conflicts holding up the settlement can be costly in terms of mediator credibility, trust, and ultimately acceptability.

The parties. Because of the risks to the parties themselves of their involvement in mediation, negotiators will not always welcome the mediator with open arms. The following advice one negotiator offers to other negotiators in mediation serves to exemplify negotiators' skepticism, as well as the important role they too play in the ultimate success of a mediation effort:

1. Understand which contract items are essential and which are not. Mediators will be tempted to impose additional pressure on the side that cannot see the forest for the trees. Remember that all your demands will not be achieved and that compromise is inevitable in collective bargaining.
2. Be careful in revealing your final position on the remaining issues too quickly to the mediator. Negotiators should keep something in reserve for the mediator. The mediator expects both sides to bargain with him.
3. Control the flow of information from the negotiating team to the mediator. It is preferable to have a single spokesman in sessions with the mediator. Otherwise, members of your team might accidentally reveal your final positions in an informal, free-flowing discussion.
4. Be wary of pressure from the mediator. It may be mediator-generated pressure. Do not be rushed or panicked into unnecessary concessions.
5. Demand a meeting with the other side if unusual pressure or confusion results from separate meetings with the mediator. The other side is not a party to mediator-generated pressure or deception. A joint meeting will reveal the independent activities of the mediator.
6. Maintain informal, friendly contacts with your opponents. Private conversations between the chief negotiators or the lawyers will provide additional information and limit possible distortion or pressure by the mediator.[10]

Toward a Model of Mediation

We can derive several basic propositions about the mediation process from the discussion presented above. First, mediation is more successful in resolving some types of impasses than others. It should work best in resolving positive contract zone impasses or disputes, those that arise because of some breakdown in negotiations procedures or because of attitudinal or personal sources of conflict. Mediation is not as effective in resolving negative contract zone disputes, those that arise from incompatible expectations, intraorganizational conflicts, or structural sources of conflict. Mediation is also more effective in resolving less intensive conflicts: disputes in which the number and magnitude of the obstacles to a settlement are relatively small. The greater the intensity of the conflict, the less effective mediation will be and the more other forms of dispute resolution, such as the strike or arbitration, will be required to settle the dispute.

Second, mediators must be acceptable to the parties. Unless the parties judge the mediator to be acceptable and trustworthy, they will not share confidential bargaining information with the mediator and will not be willing to accept the mediator's judgments and suggestions about how to proceed in trying to arrive at a settlement.

Third, mediation works best when the parties are highly motivated or under strong pressure to resolve their differences. Thus, the timing of mediation is critical to its success. It normally works best if the strongest push for a settlement is reserved for the final strike deadline stage of the process or for the point during the strike when the parties are under strong pressure to settle.

Fourth, the strategies mediators employ will vary over the course of the intervention process and over the different stages of the negotiations cycle. In the early stages of intervention the mediator will adopt a relatively passive role and simply listen to the comments of the parties to gain information and build rapport and trust with the parties. As the process moves along toward a climax, the mediator may become more assertive and directive to change the parties' expectations and generate the substantive compromises necessary to achieve a settlement.

Finally, to be successful, mediators must ultimately become aggressive in pushing the parties toward agreement, making suggestions for compromise or persuading the parties to change their expectations or bottom-line positions. But mediators must time their aggressiveness to avoid losing their acceptability and the confidence or trust of the parties.

The Future of Mediation

Before leaving this topic we must ask whether the role of the mediator and the mediation process is likely to change much in the future. We begin by questioning one of the most sacred and time-honored principles within the mediation profession, the principle that the mediator's primary responsibility is to help the parties achieve a settlement of the dispute.

In theory the mediator is not supposed to be concerned with the substance of the outcome. Instead, the traditional view is that mediation works because the job of the mediator is simply to bring the parties to agreement. Yet there are definitely times when mediators have trouble accepting this principle. Consider, for example, the mediator in the case told in Box 9–1.

All mediators must struggle from time to time with the moral question of how far to compromise their personal values and perceptions of equity in attempting to fashion a contract settlement. The traditional answer to this question has been: The mediator's primary responsibility is to help the parties reach an agreement and to keep his or her values and preferences, or the values and preferences of the larger society, out of the process; the mediator should not attempt to create a settlement that would be most consistent with "the public interest." The traditional view holds that the way the mediator best represents the public interest is by helping prevent or end a strike or

---

BOX 9–1
Report of a frustrated mediator

This dispute was resolved after one long night of mediation. The parties had been negotiating for over a year. A factfinding report had been issued, and considerable progress had been made on economic issues. The major remaining unresolved issue was whether these employees [janitors, bus drivers, and cafeteria workers in a school district] would have binding grievance arbitration in their contract. . . . It was clear that the [school] Board was adamantly opposed to binding arbitration. . . . The [mediation] process was made more frustrating by the condescending attitude that the district administrators took toward the members of the bargaining unit. Unfortunately, my role at this final step of the process was simply to get the union negotiators to face the reality that there was no way they could get an agreement containing binding arbitration. . . .

If I had let my own feelings toward the Board negotiating team surface during mediation, the process would have not only broken down but made it even harder for the parties to put this long and frustrating case behind them. Consequently, one walks away from this type of dispute with a lot of pent-up anger and frustration.

---

prolonged impasse.[11] To state that the job of the mediator is to achieve peace at any price, however, obviously goes too far. The moral dilemma is even more difficult to resolve if questions of individual rights are part of the settlement package preferred by one of the parties. Mediators of the future will continue to struggle with this moral dilemma and at some point may have to decide how high a priority they are willing to put on the singular goal of achieving a settlement.[12]

FACTFINDING AND ARBITRATION

Factfinding and arbitration are treated differently from mediation, both in practice and in the literature, because they represent more formal third-party interventions into the negotiations process. Most of the research on these processes, therefore, seeks to evaluate their effects on the negotiations process. Before the emergence of public sector bargaining in the 1960s the prevailing view was that collective bargaining could not survive in peacetime without the right to strike. This view is still deeply ingrained in observers of collective bargaining in the private sector. More specifically, the traditional and still-prevailing belief is that these formal dispute resolution procedures should be limited to cases of dire national emergency or to disputes in which the parties themselves decide it is in their interest to submit their dispute voluntarily to a procedural substitute for the strike.

Arbitration has traditionally been held in special disfavor because some view it as anathema to free collective bargaining. As one scholar put it, over 20 years ago:

> In the case against compulsory arbitration there are distinguished prosecutors galore, and the catalog of inevitable disasters runs the gamut from simple bad decisions to dislocation of the economic foundations of free enterprise. The division is not liberal/conservative, nor labor/management—there is no division. All the principal authorities are in agreement.[13]

Consequently, the private sector experience with factfinding and arbitration of new contract disputes has largely been limited to national emergency disputes under the Taft-Hartley Act or the Railway Labor Act or to isolated industries and cases in which the parties voluntarily submit their disputes to arbitration on an ad hoc basis.

As the demand for public sector bargaining became more vocal, however, policymakers had to make a difficult choice: Unions were calling for collective bargaining rights, while elected officials were reluctant to grant public employees the right to strike. Because of the general disfavor accorded arbitration, most states initially turned to factfinding as a pragmatic compromise between the "dual evils" of the right to strike and compulsory arbitration. Later, about half the states that had endorsed collective bargaining for public employees turned to some form of arbitration for resolving disputes between city governments and their police and firefighters.

Because of the considerable experience with arbitration and factfinding gained in the public sector over the last decade, we will draw heavily on the public sector record in making inferences about the performance and potential of these formal dispute resolution procedures. Wherever possible we will also bring to bear the scant experience with these procedures in the private sector as well.

We must offer a word of caution before we summarize the evidence on these procedures. No other topic of collective bargaining is more burdened with confusing labels and jargon. Factfinding, for example, is sometimes also described as "advisory arbitration," something of a contradiction in terms. *Webster's Third New International Dictionary* defines the act of arbitrating as submitting a dispute to an arbiter for a *decision*. The term *arbitration* should therefore be applied only to a process that ends in a decision, not a recommendation.

Beyond this confusion, however, the differences in labels correspond to real differences in the forms of arbitration. Figure 9–2 should help clarify the differences among the various forms of arbitration. It starts by differentiating between voluntary and compulsory arbitration. *Voluntary arbitration* is a dispute resolution system in which the parties agree to submit their differences to arbitration. *Compulsory arbitration* is a system in which law requires the parties to submit their unresolved differences to arbitration if they cannot reach a negotiated settlement on their own.

FIGURE 9–2
The terminology of alternative forms of interest arbitration

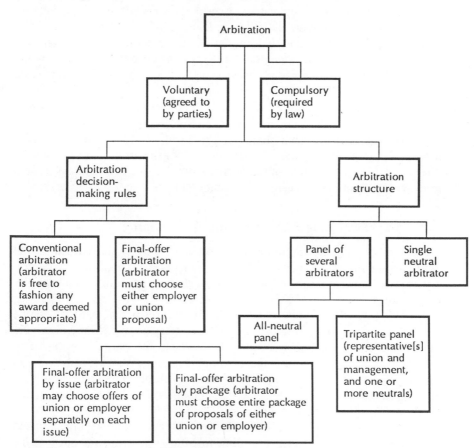

Another source of confusion is the difference between conventional arbitration and final-offer arbitration. *Conventional arbitration* (which can be
either voluntary or compulsory) is a dispute resolution process in which the
arbitrator is free to fashion any award he or she deems appropriate. Although
the conventional arbitration award is usually a compromise between the
proposals of the employer and those of the union, the arbitrator is also free
to accept either party's proposals or for that matter go below the employer's offer or above the union's (although that rarely happens). In *final-offer
arbitration* the arbitrator must choose either the employer's proposal or the
union's; the arbitrator may not fashion his or her own compromise. As a
further distinction, final-offer arbitration may be handled on a *total package*
basis—that is, the arbitrator must choose the complete offer of the employer
or of the union on all issues—or on an *issue-by-issue* basis, for example,

the arbitrator might choose the employer's wage offer, the union's offer on health insurance, and the employer's offer on vacation days.

There is yet another complication. Arbitration structures vary in a number of ways (discussed in more detail later). The arbitrator can be an *individual* or a *panel* of several. Panels, in turn, can either be composed of *all neutrals* or be *tripartite*, that is, composed of one or more representatives of the employer, one or more representatives of the union, and one or more neutrals.

Finally, we should mention that we are talking about interest as opposed to rights arbitration in all of the discussions in this chapter. *Interest arbitration* is the British term for arbitration over the terms of a new contract; *rights arbitration* is the British term for arbitration of grievances arising from the interpretation or application of the contract. In North America this is termed grievance arbitration (discussed in Chapter 10).

Criteria for Evaluating Factfinding and Arbitration

Since factfinding and arbitration are employed only if the parties or the public (through public policy) has preferred to prevent a strike, the central criterion for evaluating the effectiveness of these procedures is their ability to prevent a strike or a prolonged impasse.

A secondary criterion in evaluating the procedures is whether they can be employed without becoming overused or self-perpetuating. Many observers of the procedures fear their availability reduces the parties' incentive to bargain—a *chilling effect* on the negotiations process. The parties avoid making compromises they might otherwise be willing to make because they fear the factfinder or arbitrator will *split the difference* between their stated positions. A management negotiator, for example, may believe that it is better to go into factfinding or arbitration offering only 4 percent when management would actually be willing to offer 6 percent to avoid a strike or impasse; that is, by going in at 4 percent, the negotiator will increase the probability that the arbitrator (factfinder) will award (recommend) 6 percent. Put differently, if the negotiator goes into the procedure offering 6 percent, chances are that the recommendation or award will be for something greater than this amount. The same rationale, it is argued, drives the union negotiator. Thus, the bargaining process is chilled; each party tends to hold back concessions when bargaining under these procedures, rather than lay its best offer or bottom-line position on the table.

These procedures may suffer from overuse even in the absence of a chilling effect since they are not as politically or economically costly as the strike. Parties faced with difficult internal conflicts and political pressures may prefer to pass the buck to the factfinder or arbitrator and let themselves off the hook. Presumably, the incentive for passing the buck exists whether or not strikes are allowed. One study comparing the causes of impasses under arbitration and the causes of strikes found, for example, that internal political and attitudinal sources of conflict were more important in causing impasses than in causing strikes. The costs of a strike presumably induce settlements of the political and attitudinal disputes more effectively than does the threat of arbitration.[14] The chilling effect and the lack of costs of disagreement associated with these procedures have led some scholars to hypothesize that over time they may lead to a pattern of reusage or overdependence on them, also sometimes referred to as a *narcotic effect*.

Another important criterion in evaluating these procedures is their effect on the results or outcomes of bargaining. This criterion raises two main concerns. First, the procedures should not inherently favor the employer or the union. Sometimes this concern is expressed as the goal of achieving the same outcomes under arbitration as those that would have been achieved in the absence of arbitration. Although this is an important concern conceptually, it is difficult to choose a comparison group or standard against which to assess the performance of the procedure. Do we compare outcomes under these procedures against the outcomes in the absence of unions, in the presence of unions under the right to strike, or in the presence of unions working under some other form of dispute resolution?

Second, observers generally assume that these procedures are inherently conservative and that they favor the party that seeks the fewest deviations from the status quo. Thus, some fear that the presence of these procedures stifles innovation in bargaining or new breakthroughs in contract terms.

Finally, those concerned with the value of free collective bargaining and those who take a longer range view of the system note that these procedures should be judged in terms of their acceptability to the parties. In a bargaining system in which conflict is not totally suppressed, these procedures must be acceptable to the parties if they are to be successful and survive over any extended period of time.

In summary, along with their acceptability to the parties, the effectiveness of factfinding and arbitration should be assessed by their ability to prevent or avoid (1) strikes, (2) the chilling effect, (3) the narcotic effect, (4) systematically biasing the results of bargaining in favor of one party or the other, and (5) stifling innovation in collective bargaining and in contract terms.

The Performance of Factfinding

One of the original justifications for factfinding was that by making public the recommendations of the neutral, sufficient pressure would be brought to bear on the parties to force them to accept the recommendations or use them as the basis for a negotiated settlement. Every study of factfinding in the public sector has concluded, however, that it has not had this result. In most cases factfinding recommendations do not arouse sufficient interest and concern in the public to generate the pressure needed to produce a settlement. Public interest is apparently aroused only when a strike threatens or actually imposes direct hardships.

A recent review of the experience with factfinding suggested that its effectiveness declined over time on most of the criteria listed above.[15] For example, (1) the strike rate under factfinding was consistently higher than the strike rate under arbitration; (2) the rate of settlement without reliance on impasse procedures declined over time; (3) as the parties became more experienced with the process, they were more likely to accept the factfinder's recommendations as the basis for their contract settlements; and (4) over time factfinding became less acceptable to trade unions in a number of jurisdictions. By the middle of the 1970s the deterioration of bargaining systems under factfinding led about half of the states with laws governing police and firefighters to turn instead to some form of compulsory arbitration.

Factfinding continues, however, to be the most common form of dispute resolution among other occupations in the public sector. The reason for the greater reliance on arbitration among police and firefighters, and the greater reliance on factfinding among other public employees, is twofold. First, policymakers place a higher premium on preventing strikes by police and firefighters than strikes by teachers, transit workers, or other local and state government employees. Second, police and firefighters, more effective political lobbyists than the other occupational groups, have increasingly demanded some form of compulsory arbitration. Ultimately, it was the lack of finality in factfinding that led police and firefighter unions to reject the procedure and turn to arbitration.

Factfinding has survived more than 60 years under the Railway Labor Act (RLA) and more than 40 years under the Taft-Hartley emergency dispute procedures. The record under the RLA is mixed, however. Factfinding boards were highly successful in inducing settlements and avoided overuse over the years 1926–40; that record deteriorated somewhat during the 1940s, 1950s, and 1960s on both those measures and then improved again in the 1970s and 1980s. At present there is little interest in reforming the procedures.[16] Factfinding survives in the private sector laws partly because its record in helping resolve disputes has been more favorable than in the public sector but mostly because both unions and employers strongly oppose compulsory arbitration, for the traditional reasons noted at the beginning of this section.

Although the overall record of factfinding in the public sector has been less than spectacular, the procedure can make contributions to resolving certain types of disputes. It seems to be most useful as a supplement to mediation when one party is faced with internal differences and needs the recommendations of an expert neutral to overcome the internal opposition to a settlement. Recall that the existence of internal differences was noted as a particularly difficult type of dispute for mediation to resolve. Factfinding can work where either a positive contract zone exists or the gap between the parties' resistance points is not large.

Factfinding also appears to work better with inexperienced negotiators than with experienced negotiators. This helps explain why the effectiveness of factfinding in the public sector seems to have declined over time. As the parties become more familiar with factfinding and learn that the consequences of rejecting a factfinding recommendation are not politically or economically costly, they become less apt to place great weight on the expert opinion of an outsider.

Factfinding is less effective in overcoming serious disputes caused by a real gap between the expectations of one party and the bottom-line position of the other. The more experienced the parties, the less effective factfinding will be in changing these expectations. On the other hand, as just noted, it can be a very useful device for one of the negotiators in convincing the rest of his or her organization or constituents to face reality and reduce their expectations.

Consider, for example, the following case of factfinding in a dispute between a teachers' union and a school district:

> A neutral first attempted to mediate the dispute but was discouraged by both the professional negotiators for each side. They explained that they knew what their differences were and that if it was up to them alone they could settle the dispute without the help of a neutral. The problem was that the school board was unwilling to accept what both negotiators agreed was a reasonable salary settlement, and one faction within the union was unwilling to compromise on a contract-language issue. The mediator therefore agreed to proceed directly to factfinding. In the course of the hearing, the two negotiators presented their cases in ways that made it clear to the factfinder what they tacitly agreed to, and therefore, what they wanted the factfinder to recommend. The factfinder's recommendations closely followed these tacit resolutions. Both negotiators used the "neutral's recommendations" in selling the tacit agreement to their constituents.

The Performance of Arbitration

As noted above, arbitration in the public sector has had a better record of preventing strikes than has factfinding or bargaining without any impasse procedure. Although, obviously, no dispute resolution procedure, including arbitration, can prevent all strikes, arbitration appears to reduce the probability of strikes more than does factfinding.

To evaluate arbitration against the other effectiveness criteria requires drawing a distinction between conventional and final-offer arbitration. In theory final-offer arbitration should provide a stronger inducement to settle than conventional arbitration because it removes the incentive to hold back concessions in anticipation of an arbitrator's splitting the difference.[17] This should lessen the chilling effect and increase the rate of settlement short of invoking the procedure. The cumulative results of studies on conventional and final-offer arbitration support this theory. The median rate of reliance on final-offer arbitration in the jurisdictions that have been studied is 10 percent to 15 percent. The median rate of dependence on conventional arbitration reported in studies to date is 25 percent to 30 percent.[18] Furthermore, at least one laboratory experiment has supported the hypothesis that the chilling effect of final-offer arbitration is less than that of conventional arbitration.[19] Another experimental study found that the chilling effect of final-offer arbitration by the entire package was less than that of final-offer arbitration by issue; however, the differences between the two final-offer systems and conventional arbitration were not significant.[20]

Evidence on the narcotic effect of arbitration systems is mixed. The vast majority of disputes tend to be settled without resort to arbitration or factfinding, that is, without overreliance on the procedures, in almost all jurisdictions that have been studied. Even in systems that have been followed for as long as 30 years, the rate of cases going to arbitration rarely exceeded 50 percent.[21] Evidence supporting the narcotic effect hypothesis has been found, however, in studies that have traced the experience of the individual bargaining units over successive rounds of negotiations.

Studies using this latter approach have concluded that (1) a pattern of dependence on impasse procedures does evolve over time, and in some kinds of units but not others, and (2) the reliance on a particular procedure in one round of bargaining increases the probability that the same procedure will be invoked again in subsequent rounds. The second result is viewed as direct evidence of a narcotic effect. High rates of dependence on the procedures are most prevalent in the largest bargaining units, the most complex political and economic environments, where unions are militant, and where the parties are represented by skilled professionals. These data suggest that the existence of arbitration does not erode bargaining to the point that all or even a substantial majority of bargaining units become dependent on the procedure. But larger units with the most complex bargaining relationships are more likely to rely heavily on the procedures.

These findings are tentative at this point because they all come from public sector cases (mostly from police and firefighter disputes). Consequently, we should be cautious about assuming from these conclusions what would happen if arbitration were transferred to the private sector. Since the opposition to any form of *compulsory* arbitration in the private sector is still nearly unanimous, the possibility of this being attempted is remote.

Voluntary Arbitration in the Private Sector

A number of voluntary arbitration schemes have been used in the private sector in electrical construction, large construction projects (such as the Cape Canaveral space center and the Alaska pipeline projects), newspapers, and, most recently, the basic steel industry.

The Experimental Negotiations Agreement (ENA) was a voluntary arbitration plan first negotiated in 1972 between the United Steelworkers of America (USW) and the companies participating in the major industry association in steel. As mentioned in Chapter 2, the parties gave up both the right to strike and the right to lock out for their 1974 contract negotiations. A three-person panel of arbitrators was to decide on the contract if the parties could not reach an agreement through negotiations.

The major impetus to this experiment came from the high costs associated not only with an actual strike, but also with steel customers' anticipation of a strike. Although no industrywide strike had occurred since the bitter, 116-day strike of 1959, steel customers during each succeeding round of negotiations up to 1974 had stockpiled huge inventories as a hedge against a possible strike. That action reinforced what was already a boom-and-bust cycle of activity in the industry. Moreover, by 1974 the industry was struggling to maintain its share of the domestic market as foreign competition increased. To meet the demand for stockpiles, the companies had been forced to pay out large amounts of overtime and reactivate obsolete equipment before strike deadlines, which in turn resulted in higher, and less competitive, unit costs. In addition, after strike deadlines passed and new contracts were signed, large numbers of steelworkers were laid off until the steel customers depleted their inventories. It was estimated, for example, that 90,000 employees were laid off for six months after the 1971 contract negotiations ended.[22] Thus, both parties lost because of a strike threat, without a strike ever taking place.

The parties were able to settle their 1974 contract without invoking arbitration. They then renewed the ENA for both the 1977 and 1980 negotiations, but again each time the parties settled without actually invoking the arbitration process.

The deteriorating economic conditions in the steel industry in the 1980s brought an end to the ENA. In 1982 the industry's negotiators decided that significant wage and work rule concessions would be needed from the union, concessions they would be unlikely to exact under the ENA ground rules. In retrospect the top industry negotiators believed the ENA was partly responsible for the rapid escalation of steelworker wages from 1974 through 1981.[23] Thus, although the ENA did overcome the short-term problems posed by the strike threat, it may have delayed the reaction of the parties to their mounting problems of international competition.

The key to the negotiation of voluntary arbitration plans such as the ENA is that *both* parties must perceive benefits in agreeing to set aside the right to strike or the right to lock out for a specified period of time; that is, both the strike costs experienced in the past and the expected costs of future strikes must be high. Note, however, that in the steel case either the union or the employer could cancel the agreement to arbitrate at the end of each negotiating round. The ENA was not an agreement to arbitrate in perpetuity, but rather a limited truce for a specific period of time. Note also that the ENA became a major issue of internal dispute, pitting the USW's leadership against a group of union activists who charged that the leaders were giving up control of the union, as well as its major source of bargaining power—the strike. As will be discussed in more detail in Chapter 13, this is precisely the political risk associated with any experiment in union-management cooperation. Similarly, some management officials contended the ENA limited management's ability to make significant changes in the wage formulas or work rules carried over from prior contracts.

In voluntary arbitration schemes the parties normally limit the discretion of the arbitrator so that the existing balance of power between the parties is not disturbed. The ENA, for example, prohibited the arbitrator from modifying the union security, management rights, cost-of-living, or local working conditions clauses of the contract. Moreover, local unions retained their right to strike over local issues.

Voluntary arbitration has also been used on an ad hoc basis as a conflict resolution device of last resort. From time to time difficult strikes in the quasi-public sector (such as the 1975 dispute in New York City between the League of Voluntary Hospitals and Local 1199 of the National Union of Hospital and Health Care Employees and various disputes between the U.S. Postal Service and postal worker unions) have been resolved with an agreement to arbitrate.

In summary, voluntary arbitration is most likely to be used on a temporary or ad hoc basis in situations (1) where both parties perceive high costs of the strike and the strike threat; (2) where the strike threat has not worked well in the past in producing settlements without recourse to a strike; (3) where neither party seeks to upset the established balance of power in the bargaining relationship by either rolling back existing benefits or seeking major innovations in bargaining; or (4) where the leadership on both sides is politically secure enough to manage the internal opposition and the political pressures that accompany any union-management cooperation program.

Arbitration Structure and Process

A wide array of choices is available for designing the structure of arbitration systems. These structural options determine the nature of the decision-making process in arbitration in important ways. In fact, the parties' choice of a particular structure reflects their fundamental views on the appropriate functions of an interest arbitration system. In this section we will describe two divergent types of decision-making processes in arbitration and suggest how these are influenced by the structural design of the system.

The two decision-making processes commonly contrasted are (1) a mediation-arbitration process and (2) a judicial decision-making process. Advocates of the *mediation-arbitration* process view arbitration as an extension of the collective bargaining process in which the neutral arbitrator seeks to shape an award that is acceptable to the parties. Mediation-arbitration places a premium on using the arbitration proceeding as a forum for continued negotiations or mediation, albeit with the arbitrator holding the ultimate authority to decide on the contract. Those advocating this approach claim that no system of interest arbitration can hope to survive for long unless it produces outcomes that are acceptable to the parties. They also argue that the parties should maintain maximum control over the discretion of the arbitrator and should participate in the decision-making process as much as possible in order to maximize the amount and accuracy of the information used by the arbitrator in making the final decision.

The countervailing view of interest arbitration holds that the arbitrator should focus on the "facts" of the case and issue a rational award that adheres strictly to predetermined criteria or standards and is not influenced by the bargaining power or preferences of the parties. This is the *judicial* approach.

One can easily see how the structure of an arbitration system will determine which of these two types of decision-making processes will prevail. The following structural features all favor a mediation-arbitration process: (1) selection of the arbitrator by the parties, (2) use of a tripartite structure, (3) use of ad hoc arbitrators appointed on a case-by-case basis or arbitrators who serve as long as they remain mutually acceptable to both parties, (4) use of decision-making criteria or standards that are flexible and can be assigned whatever weights are deemed appropriate to a given case, and (5) forms of judicial review of the arbitration award that scrutinize only the procedural aspects of the process, not the substantive merits of the arbitrator's decision. The structural features favoring a judicial decision-making process, on the other hand, include selecting a single arbitrator (1) whose tenure for future cases is determd by someone other than the parties to the dispute, (2) who is required to apply predetermined weights to specified standards, and (3) whose decision can be reviewed by a court to determine whether the standards were appropriately applied in a given case.

Most students and practitioners of arbitration prefer the mediation-arbitration process because they believe it is more likely to survive and fulfills more of the traditional functions required of collective bargaining. They find the judicial approach too rigid, and they reject the claim that interest disputes can be decided by strict adherence to simple criteria or a priori standards.[24] For this reason most public sector arbitration systems have been designed with more of the features of the mediation-arbitration approach than those of the judicial model, and the process of decision making under the former has been found to conform quite closely to what is expected under this model.[25] Whether the mediation-arbitration structure produces the outcomes predicted by its advocates—the greater acceptability of results and therefore its greater durability—remains a question for future research.

PROCEDURAL DESIGN: BALANCING MULTIPLE OBJECTIVES

The design of a procedural system for resolving interest disputes requires balancing multiple objectives. The record of the various forms of dispute resolution that have been employed in both the public and the private sectors since the 1930s suggests that no one best way to achieve all of these objectives yet exists. Thus, in this section we will interpret the results discussed in the earlier sections in hopes of clarifying the pros and cons and the trade-offs associated with the alternative systems.

Although no system yet devised can provide an ironclad guarantee against strikes, the record recommends that parties searching to minimize the probability of a strike adopt some form of arbitration. Of the two forms of arbitration voluntary arbitration, because it demands the commitment of the parties, is likely to result in fewer strikes and fare better than compulsory arbitration will. At this point final-offer and conventional arbitration do not appear to differ in their potential to prevent strikes.

For those concerned about the chilling effect of arbitration the best choice is a system providing for mediation as the first form of intervention, followed closely by final-offer arbitration with a single arbitrator who is prevented from mediating at the arbitration state. Although a relatively high proportion of disputes will likely go to mediation under this system, the mediation process should result in fewer cases passing on to arbitration than would under an arbitration-only system. The mediation process, therefore, is the focal point of this type of impasse resolution system.

A variant on this system, one that provides for a tripartite arbitration structure, is called for in cases where the parties wish to increase the acceptability of the system by giving themselves greater control over the process and the outcome. Still greater control can be imposed by using the issue-by-issue method of final-offer determination. This system builds the potential for further mediation in the arbitration stage of the procedure and should result in a relatively high percentage of negotiations reaching impasse, a lower settlement rate in mediation prior to arbitration, and a higher rate of settlement in arbitration short of an award being handed down. Another variant on this system, appropriate for those who are opposed to final-offer arbitration, would be to use conventional arbitration with a tripartite structure. This system should have similar effects, except the rate of settlements by awards might be higher than the rate of settlements reached short of an award.

All of our preceding comments on the options assume the parties, or the public, place a high priority on preventing strikes. If this priority is slightly less important vis-à-vis the other objectives, a wide array of other options presents itself. For example, if the parties are especially concerned that arbitration stifles innovation or the ability to make major breakthroughs in collective bargaining, they can choose the right to strike or systems that provide an option to negotiate under arbitration. In either type of system we can expect that over time (1) weak bargaining units lacking an effective strike threat will turn to arbitration as long as they can obtain greater benefits from arbitration than from striking; (2) bargaining units with an ability and willingness to strike will prefer the strike option; (3) the rate of impasse will be relatively high because the parties must reach the critical pressure point in the procedure to reach agreement; and (4) the parties might switch from one of the two options to the other over time as they grow dissatisfied with the results under the one.[26]

A more liberal system might adopt the approach (used in the health care industry and for public employees in several states) of allowing strikes, subject to a prohibition in cases affecting public health and safety, after mediation, factfinding, or both have been exhausted. The number of strikes under this type of system is likely to vary considerably, depending on the nature of the economic and political environments and the characteristics of the relationships between the parties. Relationships with strong, militant unions in complex political environments may experience a higher strike rate than they would in the absence of the limited right to strike.

Finally, those who are philosophically opposed to both the right to strike and any form of compulsory arbitration can still rely on the most commonly used alternative to the full right to strike in both the private and public sectors—mediation followed by factfinding. Although it might be difficult, if not impossible, to return to this system once arbitration or the right to strike has been provided, this approach may nevertheless be useful as a first step in establishing bargaining rights in jurisdictions where the parties are unfamiliar with collective bargaining and dispute resolution.

NEW ROLES FOR THIRD PARTIES

The need for skilled third parties in conflict resolution and problem solving is not limited to the formal negotiations process. Indeed, in recent years a variety of new roles and processes have emerged in settings where labor and management have been attempting to achieve more fundamental changes and innovations in their bargaining relationships. Although their newness makes it difficult to evaluate these roles at this juncture, we will briefly review a number of their common features here to illustrate the growing range of conflict resolution and problem-solving mechanisms being used by contemporary labor and management representatives.

Neutrals are increasingly being called upon to chair or facilitate labor-management committees, serve as consultants to labor and management in quality-of-working-life programs, facilitate the joint planning or design of a new plant or work system, or work on other experimental projects designed to solve long-standing problems in a bargaining relationship.

All of these roles require the skills of a traditional labor mediator discussed earlier in this chapter. In addition, however, these roles differ from traditional mediation or arbitration roles in several important ways. First, most require what several authors have described as *metamediation*, that is, designing a new system or process for solving problems or resolving conflicts on an ongoing basis.[27] Often this requires that the parties first undergo an organizational development or team-building effort to change their attitudes and increase the level of trust they place in each other. Second, these third parties must possess more specialized knowledge of the substantive problems facing the parties than a typical mediator or arbitrator has. Thus, the third party is expected to be a consultant who brings technical expertise to bear on the problem and also is sensitive to the needs and interests of both labor and management. Third, the time horizon of the third party and the process tends to be longer. Whereas the traditional mediator is mainly concerned with achieving a settlement of the immediate impasse and less concerned with the specific merits of the settlement itself, third parties involved in these new roles must focus on the effects of any short-run decision on the quality of the longer term relationship.

The behavior of the parties to these new processes is also significantly different from traditional labor-management behavior. For example, to be successful, long-term problem solving requires the parties to share information more readily than they do in traditional collective bargaining. We will discuss the nature of this behavior and the change efforts themselves in Chapter 13. For now it is sufficient simply to note that the ability to solve complex problems on an ongoing basis is of pressing importance in collective bargaining today and therefore is creating the demand for new roles for third parties. At the same time, however, the parties still need to turn to the traditional mediation and arbitration processes. In short, effective conflict resolution and longer term problem solving are both critical to the success of contemporary collective bargaining relationships.

SUMMARY

The many years of experience with mediation, factfinding, and arbitration in the United States have given us a great deal of knowledge about how these processes work and of their contributions and limitations in improving the performance of a bargaining relationship. In recent years this knowledge and experience has also been used to develop an increasingly rich array of alternative dispute resolution procedures suitable for resolving marital, environmental, legal, commercial, and community disputes. At the same time, problem-solving principles from the social and behavioral sciences are being applied with increasing frequency in labor-management relationships. These developments reflect the ongoing need for social and economic institutions that maintain and enhance the society's capacity to resolve conflicts and solve problems of common concern.

Suggested Readings

The following bibliography represents a sampling of work on factfinding, mediation, and arbitration as dispute resolution procedures.

Cullen, Donald E. *National Emergency Disputes*. Ithaca, N.Y.: New York State School of Industrial and Labor Relations, Cornell University, 1968.

Goldberg, Stephen B., Eric D. Green, and Frank E.A. Sander. *Dispute Resolution*. Boston: Little, Brown, 1985.

Kochan, Thomas A., Mordechai Mironi, Ronald G. Ehrenberg, Jean Baderschneider, and Todd Jick. *Dispute Resolution Under Factfinding and Arbitration*. New
York: American Arbitration Association, 1979.

Kolb, Deborah. *The Mediators*. Cambridge: MIT Press, 1982.

Northrup, Herbert R. *Compulsory Arbitration and Government Intervention in
Labor Disputes*. Washington, D.C.: Labor Policy Association, 1966.

Pruitt, Dean G., and Jeffrey Z. Rubin. *Social Conflict: Escalation, Stalemate, and
Settlement*. New York: Random House, 1986.

Rubin, Jeffrey Z. *Dynamics of Third-Party Intervention*. New York: Praeger, 1981.

Simkin, William E. *Mediation and the Dynamics of Collective Bargaining*. Washington, D.C.: Bureau of National Affairs, 1971.

Stern, James L., Charles M. Rehmus, J. Joseph Lowenberg, Hirschel Kasper, and
Barbara D. Dennis. *Final-Offer Arbitration*. Lexington, Mass.: D.C. Heath,
1975.

Notes

1. Carl M. Stevens, *Strategy and Collective Bargaining Negotiation* (New York:
   McGraw-Hill, 1963), 142–46.

2. Thomas A. Kochan and Todd Jick, "The Public Sector Mediation Process: A
   Theory and Empirical Examination," *Journal of Conflict Resolution* 22 (June
   1978): 209–40.

3. Ibid., 224–35.

4. Henry A. Landsberger, "Final Report on a Research Project in Mediation,"
   Labor Law Journal (August 1956): 501–10.

5. See J. Thibaut and L. Walker, *Procedural Justice: A Psychological Analysis*
   (New York: Halstead Press, 1975).

6. John C. Anderson and Thomas A. Kochan, "Impasse Procedures in the Canadian
   Federal Service: Effects on the Bargaining Process," *Industrial and Labor
   Relations Review* 30 (April 1977): 291; John C. Anderson, "The Right to Strike
   Versus Compulsory Arbitration: Effects on the Use of Impasse Procedures in
   Canadian Local Government Negotiations," photocopy (Los Angeles: Graduate
   School of Management, University of California, 1978).

7. See Craig A. Olson, "The Dynamics of Dispute Resolution," in *Public Sector
   Bargaining*, 2d ed., ed. Benjamin Aaron, James L. Stern, and Joyce M. Najita
   (Washington, D.C.: Bureau of National Affairs, forthcoming).

8. For a discussion of mediation strategies, see Kenneth Kressel, *Mediation: An
   Exploratory Survey* (Albany, N.Y.: Association of Labor Mediation Agencies,
   1972). For an analysis of two contrasting mediator strategies, see Deborah Kolb,
   The Mediators (Cambridge: MIT Press, 1982).

9. Paul F. Gerhart and John E. Drotning, "Dispute Settlement and the Intensity of
   the Mediator," *Industrial Relations* 19 (1980): 352–59.

10. Joseph F. Byrnes, "Mediator-Generated Pressure Tactics," *Journal of Collective
    Negotiations in the Public Sector* 7 (1978): 108.

11. Eva Robbins, *A Guide for Labor Mediators* (Honolulu: Industrial Relations Center, University of Hawaii, 1976), 4.

12. For a good discussion of this dilemma, see William E. Simkin, *Mediation and the Dynamics of Collective Bargaining* (Washington, D.C.: Bureau of National Affairs, 1971), 34–40.

13. Orme Phelps, "Compulsory Arbitration: Some Perspectives," *Industrial and Labor Relations Review* 18 (October 1964): 8.

14. Anderson, "The Right to Strike."

15. Olson, "The Dynamics of Dispute Resolution."

16. Donald E. Cullen, "Emergency Boards Under the Railway Labor Act," in *The Railway Labor Act at Fifty* (Washington, D.C.: National Mediation Board, 1978), 151–86.

17. Carl M. Stevens, "Is Compulsory Arbitration Compatible with Collective Bargaining?" *Industrial Relations* 5 (February 1966): 38–52.

18. The specific studies that serve as the basis for the conclusions presented in this section are reviewed in Olson, "The Dynamics of Dispute Resolution."

19. See William W. Notz and Frederick A. Starke, "Final Offer Versus Conventional Arbitration as Means of Conflict Management," *Administrative Science Quarterly* 23 (June 1978): 189–203.

20. A.V. Subbarao, "The Impact of Binding Interest Arbitration on Negotiation and Process Outcome," *Journal of Conflict Resolution* 22 (March 1978): 79–103.

21. Mark Thompson and James Cairnie, "Compulsory Arbitration: The Case of British Columbia Teachers," *Industrial and Labor Relations Review* 27 (October 1973): 3–17.

22. John Hoerr, "The Steel Experiment," *Atlantic*, December 1973, 20.

23. For a history of the ENA, see John Hoerr, *And the Wolf Finally Came* (New York: Praeger, forthcoming).

24. See Irving Bernstein, *The Arbitration of Wages* (Berkeley: University of California Press, 1954); Alfred Kuhn, *Arbitration in Transit: An Evaluation of Wage Criteria* (Philadelphia: University of Pennsylvania Press, 1952); Robert R. France and Richard A. Lester, *Compulsory Arbitration in Utility Disputes in New Jersey and Pennsylvania* (Princeton: Industrial Relations Section, Princeton University, 1951).

25. Thomas A. Kochan et al. *Dispute Resolution Under Factfinding and Arbitration* (New York: American Arbitration Association, 1979), 99–111.

26. Anderson and Kochan, "Impasse Procedures in the Canadian Federal Service."

27. Stephen B. Goldberg, Jeanne M. Brett, and William Ury, "A Study in Metamediation," photocopy (Evanston, Ill.: School of Law, Northwestern University, 1987).

CHAPTER 10

Administering
the Employment
Relationship under
Collective Bargaining

In this chapter we will look below the level of formal contract negotiations to examine the administration of the day-to-day employment relationship under collective bargaining—the third level of industrial relations activities illustrated back in Figure 1–1. As in most other treatments of this aspect of collective bargaining, we will devote our primary attention to formal grievance and grievance arbitration procedures. In doing so, however, we will take a broader perspective, since the formal procedures are only two among the wider range of activities the parties engage in as they administer the employment relationship under a union contract. In Chapter 13 we will go one step further by examining how organizational change is introduced in union-management settings. Just as the early need to transform collective bargaining from a periodic negotiations process to a continuous relationship gave rise to grievance procedures and arbitration, today's competitive environmental conditions and the increasingly complex needs of the labor force are now giving rise to efforts to supplement the formal contract administration procedures with more flexible and continuous mechanisms for adapting to change.

Our view of the activities that take place at the workplace level of the employment relationship derives from a broad conception of what we have found to be the three generic functions of any workplace industrial relations system: conflict resolution and the assurance of due process; the supervision, motivation, and participation of individual workers; and the organization of work. Figure 10–1 models the interrelationships among these three functions of workplace industrial relations and their effects on the performance of the firm and the fulfillment of workers' goals.

FIGURE 10–1
The functions of a workplace industrial relations system:
Interrelationships and outcomes

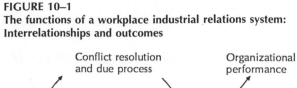

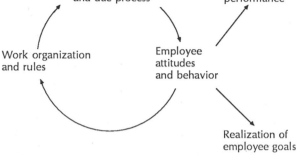

A critical factor shaping workplace industrial relations systems is whether, or the extent to which, a *high conflict–low trust syndrome* develops between labor and management. This syndrome can lead management and workers to institute detailed formal rules outlining their rights and job responsibilities. In turn those rules lead to further conflicts over their interpretation and enforcement. The resulting mistrust between the parties then perpetuates the cycle.[1] Conversely, a *high trust–low conflict syndrome* should open the way to greater flexibility in the parties' behavior and in the management of the workplace.

As we will demonstrate in Chapter 11, either one of these behavioral syndromes can have a major effect on organizational performance. Translated into the subject of this chapter, this means that a high level of grievance activity will be interrelated (both as a cause and as an effect) with low levels of employee trust and morale and with a heavy reliance on detailed contractual work rules. Research on the auto industry has shown that where it exists, this self-reinforcing cycle in turn impairs both productivity and product quality.[2]

Because the principle "management acts and workers and unions react" is so deeply engrained in the U.S. collective bargaining system, grievance and arbitration procedures have traditionally served as the primary focus of workplace administration under union contracts. But as noted at the start of this chapter, a number of new ways of carrying out the three functions of workplace administration have recently been emerging in both union and nonunion organizations. Many large firms have established grievance procedures and other communication, problem-solving, and complaint-handling processes for their nonunion employees, and increasingly they are instituting these last three for their unionized employees as well. In these organizations grievance procedures serve as the formal skeleton around which the more informal and flexible communication, problem-solving, and conflict resolution mechanisms are built. In the sections that follow we will review the functions grievance procedures are expected to perform, their historical evolution and current use, criteria for evaluating them, and the range of supplementary or alternative workplace administration processes that are being used in work organizations.

THE FUNCTIONS OF GRIEVANCE PROCEDURES AND ARBITRATION

The *formal grievance procedure* specifies a series of steps through which the parties can resolve any charges of failure to follow the terms of the collective bargaining agreement. The steps found in a typical procedure are outlined in Box 10–1. As shown, each succeeding step in the decision-making process involves a higher level of the union and management organizations.

BOX 10–1
Steps in a typical grievance procedure

A. Employee-initiated grievance
  Step 1
    Employee discusses grievance or problem orally with supervisor.
    Union steward and employee may discuss problem orally with supervisor.
    Union steward and employee decide if (1) problem has been resolved or (2) if not resolved, whether a contract violation has occurred.
  Step 2
    Grievance is put in writing and submitted to production superintendent or other designated line manager.
    Steward and management representative meet and discuss grievance. Management's response is put in writing. A member of the industrial relations staff may be consulted at this stage.
  Step 3
    Grievance is appealed to top line management and industrial relations staff representatives. Additional local or international union officers may become involved in discussions. Decision is put in writing.
  Step 4
    Union decides on whether to appeal unresolved grievance to arbitration according to procedures specified in its constitution and/or bylaws.
    Grievance is appealed to arbitration for binding decision.
B. Discharge grievance
    Procedure may begin at Step 2 or Step 3.
    Time limits between steps may be shorter so as to expedite the process.
C. Union or group grievance
    Union representative initiates grievance at Step 1 or Step 2 on behalf of affected class of workers or union representatives.

Modern grievance and grievance arbitration procedures must meet the needs of three separate constituencies. First, they should serve the interests of workers by delivering industrial justice, by protecting their individual job rights and enforcing their responsibilities, and by protecting workers who use the procedure from any retaliation or recrimination for having exercised their rights. If workers lose confidence in the efficacy of the procedures, the procedures will not only fail to carry out their original purpose, they will actually become impediments to effective workplace industrial relations.

Second, these procedures must serve the collective interests of labor unions and employers. As Chamberlain and Kuhn have noted, labor and management have a mutual interest in means to provide continuity and uniformity in the interpretation of the terms of the contract and conditions of employment, means that at the same time allow flexibility in addressing unforeseen developments and the unique needs of different groups and individuals.[3] Thus, finding the appropriate balance between uniformity and flexibility is a key challenge in administering the employment relationship. It is a particular challenge for grievance procedures and arbitration, as we will see.

Third, grievance and arbitration procedures must serve the interests of society by preserving industrial peace during the term of the contract, by keeping industrial disputes from overloading the courts or regulatory agencies, and by insuring that unions and employers comply with public policies governing employment. As we will show, this set of public functions is becoming increasingly complex and difficult to carry out. Some observers have even gone so far as to suggest that the growth in employment law has brought an end to the "Golden Age" of grievance arbitration.[4] To understand the rise of grievance and grievance arbitration procedures to their current, but threatened, position of centrality in workplace industrial relations, we first need to review their historical evolution.

THE HISTORICAL EVOLUTION OF GRIEVANCE ARBITRATION

Grievance arbitration followed on the heels of collective bargaining developments in this country. Arbitration of minor disputes over the interpretation of agreements was mentioned in the Industrial Commission Report of 1902. Before World War II grievance procedures ending in binding arbitration were common in the clothing and anthracite coal mining industries. But it took the strong advocacy of the National War Labor Board (WLB) for grievance arbitration to become a common practice across unionized industries. In many of the thousands of disputes it handled, the board encouraged the parties to include an arbitration clause in their bargaining agreement, and in some cases the board required it. Within a few years the Taft-Hartley Act was to embed grievance arbitration in national labor policy. Section 203(d) of the act states: "Final adjustment by a method agreed upon by the parties is hereby declared to be the desirable method for settlement of grievance disputes arising out of the application or interpretation of an existing collective bargaining agreement." It was a series of Supreme Court decisions known as the *Steelworkers' trilogy*, however, that gave grievance arbitration its protected status and exalted image.[5]

These three court decisions (see Box 10–2, at "1960") provided that (1) the courts should rule only on questions whether a dispute can be arbitrated, they should resolve any doubts about such questions by ruling in favor of arbitration, and they should not consider the *merits* of the grievance when deciding whether the case can be arbitrated; (2) the parties should view arbitration as the quid pro quo for giving up the right to strike; and except for issues that are specifically excluded from the arbitration clause, all disputes arising out of contract administration should be resolved by arbitration; and (3) the courts should not review the substantive merits of an arbitration decision but should confine their review to whether due process procedures were followed or whether the arbitrator exceeded his or her authority. The effects of these decisions were twofold. They encouraged the use of arbitration and insulated arbitration awards from judicial review, except in cases of procedural questions.[6] Although the courts still follow the basic principles stated in the trilogy, recent court and National Labor Relations Board decisions have modified the principles in a number of ways. Box 10–2 summarizes the most important of those decisions.

Thus, although grievance arbitration has become widespread since World War II, the nature of the process has been gradually shifting. Killingsworth and Wallen suggested that grievance arbitration evolved from the clinical approach that was advocated by the WLB and applied frequently during the early postwar years to become what is today a more judicial and legalistic approach.[7] The *clinical approach* emphasized mediation of disputes, informality of procedure, and arbitrator discretion in helping the parties develop a working relationship and consistent policies for interpreting and administering the contract. As Killingsworth and Wallen described it, these were the distinguishing roles played by the impartial chairmen who developed arbitration systems in the auto industry during the 1940s. The authors also cited the clothing and hosiery industries as ones that required strong arbitrators who were able and willing to serve as impartial chairmen to bring stability to an otherwise fiercely competitive environment.

Over the years, as the environment for collective bargaining became more structured and a body of past decisions, practices, and policies evolved as precedents, the arbitrator's scope of discretion narrowed. As the parties themselves became more professional, they came to demand a more *judicial approach* to arbitration. Killingsworth and Wallen explained this trend by observing that the discretionary, problem-solving model of arbitration had filled a void in an otherwise unstructured environment for dispute resolution and contract administration; but as the parties formalized their internal policies, they turned to arbitrators only in disputes in which their differences were clearly defined by the contract and the precedents that had arisen. The

BOX 10–2
**Key court and administrative decisions affecting
the conduct of grievance arbitration**

Year	Case	Decision
1957	*Textile Workers* v. *Lincoln Mills*	Provided for court enforcement of arbitration awards.
1960	"Steelworkers' trilogy"	
	1. *Steelworkers* v. *American Manufacturing Co.*, 363 US 564 (1960)	Court should determine only arbitrability, i.e., whether issue is covered by the contract, and should not decide the merits of a case. Doubts about arbitrability should be decided in favor of sending the case to arbitration.
	2. *Steelworkers* v. *Warrior Gulf and Navigation Co.*, 363 US 574 (1960)	Disputes over contract terms are assumed to be arbitrable unless they are specifically excluded. Arbitration is viewed as the quid pro quo for giving up the right to strike during the term of the contract.
	3. *Steelworkers* v. *Enterprise Wheel and Car Corp.*, 363 US 593 (1960)	Courts should not review the substantive merits of the arbitrator's decision as long as the arbitrator's award is based on the content of the agreement.
1970	*Boys Markets, Inc.* v. *Retail Clerks, Local 770*, 389 US 235 (1970)	Courts may issue an injunction against a union forcing it to refrain from violating a no-strike clause or where an issue is covered by an arbitration clause in the contract.
1971	*Collyer Insulated Wire* and *Local Union 1098*, 192 NLRB 837 (1971)	NLRB will defer to arbitration disputes in which the issue could be decided either through arbitration (because it is covered by a clause in the bargaining agreement) or by NLRB ruling (because it alleges an unfair labor practice).
1974	*Alexander* v. *Gardner-Denver*, 415 US 36 (1974)	Arbitrator's decision on a claim involving discrimination covered under Title VII of the Civil Rights Act does not preclude judicial review of the award, nor does it prevent the

BOX 10–2 *(continued)*

Year	Case	Decision
		employee from pursuing legal remedies through federal agencies or the federal court. Courts will hear the case de novo and decide it on its merits and will give the arbitrator's decision whatever weight the court deems appropriate.
1976	*Hines* v. *Anchor Motor Freight, Inc.* (preceded by several other key cases, especially *Steele* v. *Louisville & Nashville R.R.,* 1944; and *Vaca* v. *Sipes,* 1967), 424 US 554 (1976)	An arbitration award should not be sustained by the court when the union has violated its duty to represent the grievant fairly. Federal courts will entertain suits of this nature on the basis of Section 301 of Taft-Hartley.
1983	*Bowen* v. *United States Postal Service,* 103 US (1983)	A union may be held liable for a portion of an award to an employee if the union has violated its duty of fair representation.
1984	*Olin Corporation,* 268 NLRB 86 (1984)	The NLRB expanded the *Collyer* doctrine of deferral to arbitration of disputes involving unfair labor practices. The NLRB will defer to an arbitrator's decision unless the arbitrator's award is "clearly repugnant" to the law. The NLRB retains the right to decide whether an arbitrator adequately considered the facts that would constitute an unfair labor practice.
1984	*United Technologies,* 268 NLRB 83 (1984)	The NLRB further expanded the *Collyer* doctrine of deferral to arbitration of disputes brought to the board prior to arbitration that both involve statutory rights and are covered by a collective bargaining contract.
1986	*AT&T Technologies* v. *Communications Workers,* Docket no. 84-1913, 7 April 1986	Courts, not arbitrators, should resolve disputes over arbitrability by examining the language found in the agreement giving rise to the issue.

parties therefore preferred to limit the role of the arbitrator to that of a final judge rather than that of a mediator seeking to explore alternative ways of resolving a problem.

Thus, modern grievance arbitration, though still considerably more informal than court proceedings, has become more dependent on the use of formal rules of evidence, examination and cross-examination of witnesses, submission of written briefs and posthearing briefs, and written transcripts. Although Killingsworth and Wallen viewed these developments as a natural adaptation to a maturing collective bargaining system, they also proposed that as grievance procedures and arbitration become more formalized and judicial, the parties may find the need to develop informal problem-solving systems parallel to the formal procedures. The difference between the current and the earlier period, they stated, is that now the parties may be sophisticated enough either to establish these informal mechanisms without the aid of an outside neutral or to allow an arbitrator to mediate a settlement only when the parties are interested in settling a case at this final stage of the process.[8]

GRIEVANCE PROCEDURES AND THE BARGAINING SYSTEM

The administration of a collective bargaining agreement does not operate in isolation from the events that take place in the negotiations process. The behavior and attitudes of the parties during negotiations are a reflection of their stance toward each other during the life of the contract (as noted in Chapter 8), and vice versa.

A number of studies have identified the importance of bargaining system characteristics in the contract administration process. Most of these studies have focused on the determinants of (1) the grievance rate (usually defined as the number of grievances filed per 100 employees over a given period) or (2) the percentage of grievances going to arbitration. Figure 10–2 summarizes the major explanatory variables examined in these studies. Note that these variables are quite similar to those in our model, presented in Chapter 8, of the determinants of impasses and strikes in negotiations. This similarity is not surprising, since as noted above we can expect that the same factors that increase the level of conflict and reduce the ability of the parties to settle without an impasse in negotiations also increase the level of antagonistic behavior during the course of administering the contract.

The attitudinal climate or level of trust between the parties is one of the characteristics that is most likely to carry over from one to the other of these two phases of the bargaining relationship. When a large backlog of unresolved grievances piles up and adds to a hostile atmosphere between the parties during the term of the agreement, the negotiations process becomes a convenient forum for venting these hostilities. Similarly, when the grievance procedure or an arbitration decision has failed to resolve a problem, one party or the other can be expected to place a demand on the negotiation table to remedy the situation. On the other hand, vague or inconsistent

FIGURE 10–2
Determinants of grievance activity

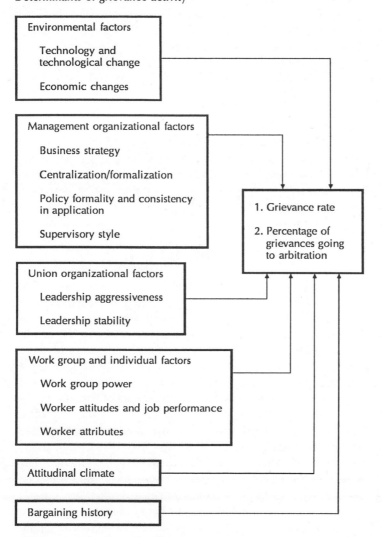

language in a contract that was negotiated in a climate of distrust and conflict is likely to set the stage for conflict during the administration of the agreement. Thomson and Murray have concluded, for example, that high levels of distrust and conflict in the overall bargaining relationship require more formal grievance procedures and a more judicial approach to grievance handling.[9]

A study by Turner and Robinson found that cooperative attitudes between union and management officials increased the likelihood that grievances would be settled at the lower steps in the procedure.[10] Their study, along with Thomson and Murray's evidence, therefore documents the importance of the attitudinal climate of the relationship as a determinant of grievance activity. The data we have collected on auto plants demonstrate a positive and significant correlation between the rate of grievances filed and two indicators of the intensity of conflict in local contract bargaining, namely, the number of issues introduced into the negotiations and the length of time taken to reach a contract settlement.[11] In a comparative study of the dynamics of grievance settlements in two auto plants, Mower found that in one, exhibiting a highly adversarial relationship, grievance rates and rates of appeal to higher steps in the procedure followed the cycle of bargaining. That is, the union in this plant would save up grievances and file them just before the start of contract negotiations to use this stockpile as a lever in negotiations and to rally the rank-and-file in support of the union's contract demands. In contrast, Mower observed no such politicization of the grievance process in a comparable auto plant that had a history of cooperative labor-management relations.[12]

The attitudes of the parties and the level of conflict in negotiations are not the only links between the overall bargaining system and the grievance process. Research by Thomson and Murray and by Peach and Livernash has stressed the importance of relating grievance activity to the nature of the environment and the organizational characteristics of the parties.[13] This line of research has found technology to be a particularly important environmental influence. The central proposition offered by Peach and Livernash is that the greater the rate of technological change, the higher the grievance rate. They further observed that technologies requiring high levels of worker responsibility and close supervision are likely to have higher rates of grievance activity than others. Thomson and Murray also presented evidence that the type of technology influences the types of grievances that are filed. Two more recent studies lend further support to the hypothesis that periods of changing technology or retooling of machinery are associated with higher rates of grievances.[14]

In pointing to the role of technology in grievances, these authors have built on the classic studies of the effects of technology on work group behavior.[15] Kuhn, for example, proposed that the more strategically the work group is located in the production process, the greater its bargaining power is during the term of an agreement. And in turn, the greater the group's bargaining power, the more grievances the group files, or alternatively the more the group can engage in *fractional bargaining*, that is, informal bargaining with the supervisor to modify or even to ignore provisions of the agreement that do not suit the group's particular needs.

A fundamentally different argument concerning the relationship between technology and grievance activity or workplace conflict has been offered by Shimada in a study of Japanese auto plants operating in the United States. He suggested that the essence of the Japanese system is to build a high degree of labor-management cooperation and worker trust, flexibility, and skill into the production process. Thus, in this type of production (or service) technology, the high degree of workers' control and influence over the cost and quality of the product or service requires management to take steps to insure that a high trust–low conflict cycle is sustained at the workplace. [16] If new technologies require high trust, motivation, and flexibility on the part of workers, we should expect to see more efforts by firms and unions to reduce grievance rates and seek more informal means of solving their problems, improving communication, and resolving conflicts as advanced technology diffuses to more and more workplaces.

Note, however, that managers in the Japanese production system have an incentive to maintain the trust and cooperation they have achieved because the production system is based on a high skill content and on employee control of the work. In production systems in which managers have chosen to engineer as much skill content and worker control out of the production process as is possible—a process that routinizes and specializes the job structure—this incentive is much weaker. Under these circumstances the counterincentive for employees is to use whatever leverage the technology affords them to engage in the fractional bargaining described by Kuhn and Sayles. Thus, the way in which firms (and union representatives) choose to *use* advanced technology will have a great bearing on whether new technologies reduce or increase mistrust and formal grievance activity.

A recent study of the differences in arbitration rates between Bethlehem Steel and the U.S. Steel Corporation (since renamed USX) brings home the effects of different industrial relations and business strategies on the nature and volume of grievances. Both of those firms experienced employment declines of approximately 70 percent between 1966 and 1985. Over those years, while the number of grievance arbitration cases at Bethlehem declined in rough proportion to the decline in employment, the caseload at U.S. Steel remained stable even in the face of the employment decline. The difference in the experiences of the two companies can be traced to their different labor relations philosophies and relationships—and even deeper to the different business strategies of the companies.[17] Bethlehem Steel not only has had a relatively cooperative relationship with the Steelworkers union, but also has followed a business strategy of trying to remain active and competitive in the steel industry. U.S. Steel/USX on the other hand, has historically had highly adversarial relations with the Steelworkers and more recently has taken steps to diversify its investments outside of steel and to seek greater bargaining leverage over the union by contracting out as much work as possible, even if doing so risks violating its labor agreements and thereby generating additional grievance arbitration cases.[18] Thus, again we see how workplace-level activities are driven by, or at least highly interdependent with, activities and policies decided at higher levels of the industrial relations system and policymaking within the firm.

Other management organizational variables that have been identified with grievance activity are the centralization of management decision making, the degree to which management policies are formalized and applied in a consistent fashion, and the leadership styles of first-line supervisors. Peach and Livernash found that the greater the centralization of management decision making, the higher the grievance rate and the more grievances are pushed up the steps in the procedure to higher levels where the authority to make decisions is vested. They also observed that the less consistently management policies are applied (or the less formalized the policies), the higher the grievance rate. In a study of supervisory leadership style and grievance rates, Fleishman and Harris found that supervisors who relied on a leadership style labeled "consideration"—a style that heavily emphasizes communication, high respect for subordinates' ideas, and high mutual trust between supervisor and workers—and who scored low on a style labeled "initiating structure"—a style that emphasizes defining the role of the subordinate clearly and giving close direction to the work group—had lower grievance rates in their departments.[19]

On the union side the aggressiveness of union leaders, political stability within the union, and the aggressiveness of rank-and-file workers have been associated with grievance activity. Although several studies have attempted to identify other characteristics of individual workers that affect grievance activity, the evidence they have uncovered is sketchy and difficult to interpret. One study found, for example, that poor performers were more apt to file grievances than good performers. It is difficult to determine the cause-and-effect sequence here, however, since poor performers may be more closely supervised and supervisory efforts to change their behavior may lead to grievances. Alternatively, managers may base their assessments of workers' performance in part on whether or not the worker has filed a grievance. Indeed, Lewin and Peterson's recent study of workers who file grievances and those who do not found that in the year before they filed a grievance, grievance filers had received significantly higher job performance evaluations than those who did not file.[20]

The Lewin and Peterson study also documented a number of demographic and work history characteristics that distinguished between grievants and nongrievants. Those who filed grievances tended to be more highly educated, male, blue-collar, and in the middle of the tenure distributions of their firms. These findings are generally consistent with those of earlier studies of this topic.[21]

Knight has criticized most previous studies for their failure to consider the effects of the history of the bargaining relationship. In comparing two plants in the same firm—one with a high grievance rate and one with a low one—he found that this difference could be traced back to the history of the union-management relationships at the two sites. The high-grievance plant had had a stormy episode during the initial union recognition process, whereas the low-grievance plant had recognized the union in a much less highly charged atmosphere.[22] Thus, as in studying any aspect of bargaining, we must be careful to trace the causes of grievance activity back to their origins.

The results of these empirical studies, as illustrated in Figure 10–2, provide the basis for a model of grievance rates and perhaps for a model of the parties' reliance on grievance arbitration. A complete theory of the grievance process would need to go beyond this, however, to describe and explain the dynamics of grievance handling and the arbitration decision-making process.

CRITERIA FOR EVALUATING GRIEVANCE PROCEDURES

Grievance and Settlement Rates

Just as one important question about the effectiveness of the negotiations process is whether the parties can avoid strikes and impasses, an important criterion for evaluating grievance and arbitration procedures is whether the parties can avoid a heavy caseload. The advantages of settling disputes informally or at the step closest to the site where the problems arise are self-evident.

Students of the arbitration process have always stressed, for example, that most employee complaints are resolved informally before they become formal grievances. Lewin and Peterson's study provides empirical support for this opinion. Between 16 and 40 percent of the employees in the organizations they studied reported having discussed (and resolved) with their supervisors a problem concerning their contractual rights.[23]

Yet high settlement rates or the absence of high grievance rates can come about for reasons other than the fact that the parties are effectively resolving their problems at the lowest levels or through informal mechanisms. These rates may be obscuring the fact that the union is not aggressively enforcing the terms of the contract or that the workers have become disillusioned with the formal grievance procedure and are either suppressing their problems or using other means to voice their claims. For example, one recent study reported that 18 percent of a sample of teachers indicated they would not file a grievance for fear of management retaliation. Another 10 percent believed filing a grievance would be futile because management would not change its behavior. For these reasons, the use of these rates as criteria should be accompanied by an analysis of the causes or reasons for the rates before making any judgment on the effectiveness of the procedures.

Wildcat Strikes

It almost goes without saying that any conflict resolution system that has as its purpose the avoidance of wildcat strikes should be evaluated against this objective. By this measure grievance procedures in the United States are doing quite well. Wildcat strikes are not problems of major proportions, at least in the eyes of management in the majority of industries. The Conference Board surveys reported in Chapter 7 found that in evaluating its labor relations effectiveness top management assigns the lowest priority to avoiding wildcat strikes. This again may be a tribute to the effectiveness of grievance procedures in minimizing the need for strikes during the term of the contract.

The percentage of strikes that occur during the course of an agreement has been declining in all industries in recent years. In 1976 only 14 percent of all strikes outside of coal mining took place during the term of the agreement; in 1963 that figure was 34 percent.[24] The story in coal mining is quite different, however. Wildcats increased in coal mining during the 1970s after having declined somewhat throughout the 1960s. Between 1970 and 1974 some 1,500 wildcat strikes were called annually in mines covered under the national agreement between the United Mine Workers (UMW) and the Bituminous Coal Operators Association (BCOA).[25]

Studies of the causes of wildcat strikes have focused on the same set of environmental, organizational, and personal characteristics as is used to explain grievance activity.[26] But often added to this set are the individual worker's loss of confidence in the grievance procedure and the inherent bargaining power or militancy of the workers. It is the combination of pent-up frustrations along with the willingness and ability to take direct action that is expected to produce wildcat strikes. For example, Brett and Goldberg investigated variations in the frequency of wildcat strikes in mines covered under the UMW-BCOA contract and interviewed miners in two strike-prone mines and two mines not prone to strikes. They found the strike-prone mines were larger and had numerous wildcat strikes in previous years, less favorable foreman-worker relationships, a less cooperative labor relations climate, workers who believed it was necessary to strike to get management to talk about problems, workers who perceived arbitrators to be unfair and biased, and managers who met only infrequently with union officials and spent little time on labor relations activities.[27] The authors also found that frustration with delays in the grievance procedure and perceptions that the procedure was unfair were common among coal miners in all four mines. In addition, the tradition of not crossing picket lines and of supporting wildcat strikes, even when the worker did not believe the issue involved warranted a strike, was found to be prevalent among coal miners. Thus, because of that tradition (and perhaps for fear of the consequences of trying to cross picket lines), a small group of workers calling a strike could expect to garner the support of the vast majority of the miners.

These studies, along with the economywide data on the decline of wildcats and the low level of concern managers have for this problem, all suggest that a smoothly functioning grievance procedure—one that is speedy and perceived as fair—can effectively minimize the incidence of wildcats. It is only in cases of severe frustration and wholesale breakdown of the formal procedures that workers turn to wildcat strikes as an outlet for their problems.

Delays and Costs

The two criteria most commonly employed to evaluate grievance procedures are the time taken to settle claims and the costs associated with processing them through to arbitration. These are reasonable criteria, since the original purpose in developing the procedures was to find an expeditious and inexpensive substitute for court procedures. The parties themselves are increasingly concerned, however, over both the delays and costs involved in following the procedures. Consider, for example, the following critique by John Zalusky, a staff member of the AFL–CIO:

> The traditional labor arbitration procedure has grown in complexity until today it is taking on the appearance of a courtroom procedure. The presence of lawyers, use of transcripts, swearing in of witnesses, pre- and post-hearing briefs, and long delays throughout—in setting hearing dates, extending deadlines for the filing of briefs, and waiting for the decision—are all too common. The arbitration process is so large and cumbersome it is beginning to discourage industrial justice for two very basic reasons: cost and delay.[28]

Zalusky went on to report that the average time required to process a case through arbitration in 1975 was 223 days, or over seven months. The estimated average cost to the union in a case involving a lawyer, transcripts, and posthearing briefs was estimated to be $2,220.

In recent years, therefore, the parties have developed a number of innovative alternative procedures to cut down on excessive delays and costs. Among these alternatives are several minor modifications of existing practices, such as keeping grievances oral as far into the procedure as possible to promote informal resolution, tightening time allowances at various steps of the procedure, and agreeing that oral settlements or settlements at intermediate steps of the procedure will not serve in any way as precedential. Box 10–3 presents the text of a well-known and successfully implemented agreement that exemplifies these alternatives.

Expedited arbitration is a more radical alternative that has also garnered much attention in the past 15 years; Table 10–1 illustrates the key features of five expedited arbitration schemes in practice. A six-year review of one of these—the Steelworkers' system, begun in 1971—found that (1) it cut the cost of the average grievance arbitration case to roughly $55 per party; (2) more than half the cases initiated were resolved short of arbitration; (3) the awards almost always conformed to the time limits specified (see Table 10–1); and (4) the procedure has spread to other Steelworkers' contracts in the aluminum, can, copper, and metals industries.[29] Expedited arbitration appears to be one viable strategy for reducing the costs and delays involved in many, merely routine cases.

Another innovation that has recently gained in popularity is *grievance mediation*. A pioneering effort to use mediation to resolve grievances before they go to arbitration has been developed and applied in the coal industry by Stephen Goldberg, Jeanne Brett, and their associates.[30] Their analysis of five years of experience with this process showed that of 634 cases that were referred to mediation 83 percent were resolved without resort to arbitration. Goldberg and Brett calculated the average cost per arbitration case in the

---

BOX 10–3
International Harvester–UAW procedure for the oral resolution of grievances

Both parties agree that avoiding written grievances and the handling of oral grievances are dependent on the understanding and the continuing cooperation of management and union representatives and employees.

In this connection the parties encourage the expeditious consideration of complaints at the point of origin by bringing together people with the special talents and skills required for full exploration of the problem involved and by . . . joint investigation and resolution of differences within the framework of the labor contract.

The Company and the Union have established the following objectives:

1. Avoidance of grievances and misunderstandings.

2. Oral handling of grievances within the framework of our agreements.

3. Expeditious investigation and quick disposition of such grievances or problems.

4. In connection with the oral handling of grievances the parties further agree that since the retroactive provisions of the contract relating to grievance settlement are tied to dates on which written grievances are presented and processed through the procedure, that another form of control must be used. Although we believe that the new program should work to minimize problems of effective dates of the disposition of cases, it is agreed that reliance on recollection or memos should be adequate to avoid subsequent misunderstandings as to the date on which the problems were raised.

5. Procedure for disposition of unresolved Step 2 grievances.

Source: 1971 Agreement between International Harvester and the International Union, United Automobile, Aerospace and Agricultural Implement Workers of America, pp. 19–22.

Note: Although we cite the 1971 agreement, the practice was in existence for a number of years. For a description of the background and performance of this program, see Robert B. McKersie and William W. Skrapshire, Jr., "Avoiding Written Grievances: A Successful Program," *Journal of Business* 35 (April 1962): 135–52.

---

industry in 1985 was $1,300, whereas the average cost per mediation case was $309—a savings of roughly $1,000 per case.[31] In addition, over the five-year period the average time lapse between the request for mediation and the resolution of the case was 19 days, a period considerably shorter than the average of 52 days required to schedule an arbitration hearing and receive a written award. But even further testimony to the value of grievance mediation can be found in the high levels of satisfaction with the procedure itself reported by the management and union representatives and the miners who took part in it.[32] Despite the fact that it is more highly formalized and more carefully managed than the ad hoc use of grievance mediation in other industries, it still demonstrates considerable savings over the use of more traditional grievance arbitration procedures. Thus, grievance mediation has spread beyond its popularity in the coal industry to other industries as well.

Contributing to the delays in grievance arbitration systems is the persistent shortage of arbitrators acceptable to both parties. The parties' trust in the third party is just as critical an issue in grievance arbitration as we have seen it is in contract disputes (Chapter 9). Because of the high stakes in many grievance cases (potential back pay settlements and precedent-setting decisions, to name but two), the parties are reluctant to call on an inexperienced or unfamiliar arbitrator. As a result, a relatively small number of highly experienced and well-known arbitrators are overemployed and booked well in advance, while a large number of less experienced or lesser known arbitrators eagerly await their next case. This demand for experience creates the familiar catch-22: Only an arbitrator with experience is acceptable, but an arbitrator can gain experience only by being accepted.

Some progress has been made in resolving this catch by using less experienced arbitrators in the expedited arbitration system. And on another front various private agencies and universities in recent years have developed formal arbitration training programs. Some arbitrators have also taken on "apprentices," teaching them the basic skills involved in drafting awards, holding hearings, and ruling on evidence. Thus, the supply of arbitrators is expanding. It is now up to the parties to take greater advantage of the growing cadre of younger, more formally trained arbitrators.[33]

The Effects of Arbitration Decisions

Another important question in evaluating the effectiveness of grievance and arbitration procedures is what happens *after* an arbitrator has reinstated a discharged employee. If the grievance procedure is effective in carrying out industrial justice, a worker unjustly discharged should be able to return to work and both perform well in the job and progress satisfactorily within the organization. The procedure itself may, however, work against these results, in several ways. First, the delays involved in processing a case through arbitration may lead a grievant who has been discharged to seek alternative employment; some reinstated employees therefore do not return to their former jobs. Second, reinstated employees are put back on their jobs against the will of their employers, often to the dismay of their immediate supervisors, and sometimes to the dismay of their fellow workers. Simply stated, not a few reinstated workers face hostility upon their return to work. Even if management, supervisors, and fellow workers make a good faith effort to treat the reinstated employee fairly, he is likely to distrust their intentions or to lack confidence in his ability to perform effectively.

A number of studies of reinstatement provide a mixed picture of post-arbitration success. A study of 207 reinstated employees from 38 different unions at 123 different employers found that 10 percent of the discharged employees never returned to their former jobs and another 20 percent left the

TABLE 10–1
Key features of five expedited arbitration systems

Feature	United Steelworkers— Basic steel industry	American Arbitration Association Service	Allied Industrial Workers Local 562— Rusco, Inc.	American Postal Workers— U.S. Postal Service	Mini- Arbitration Columbus, Ohio
Source of arbitrators	Recent law school graduates and other sources	Special panel from AAA roster	FMCS roster	AAA, FMCS rosters	Its own Joint Selection and Orientation Committee from FMCS roster
Method of selecting	Preselected regional panels. Administrator notifies in rotation	Appointed by AAA regional administrators	Preselected panel by rotating FMCS contacts	Appointed by AAA regional administrators	FMCS regional representative, by rotation
Lawyers	No limitation, but understanding that lawyers will not be used	No limitation	No lawyers	No limitation, but normally not used	No limitation

Transcript	No	No	No	No	May be used
Briefs	No	Permitted	No	No	May be used
Written discription of issue	Last-step grievance report	Joint submission permitted	No	Position paper	Grievance record expected
Time from request to hearing date	Ten days	Approximately three days depending on arbitrator availability	Ten days	Approximately seven days depending on arbitrator availability	Not specified
Time from hearing to award	Bench decision or 48 hours	Five days	48 hours	Bench decision written award 48 hours	48 hours
Fees (plus expenses)	$100/1/2 day; $150/day	$100 filing fee; arbitrator's normal fee	$100/1/2 day; $150/day	$100 filing fee; $100 per case	$100/1/2 day, 1 or 2 cases; $150/full day, 1 or 2 cases; $200/day, 3 or 4 cases

Source: John Zalusky, "Arbitration: Updating a Vital Process," *American Federationist* 83 (November 1976): 4.

employer within one year of reinstatement. The author concluded that only half of the reinstatements worked out to the satisfaction of both parties.[34] Another study found that of the 53 reinstated employees examined, three were subsequently discharged for a second time; approximately 10 percent did not return to work; and, in a follow-up survey, about 40 percent of those reinstated were rated by their employers as unsatisfactory performers. In particular, those who had been poor performers before their discharge continued to be poor performers after reinstatement. Workers with more seniority and workers in larger organizations were more likely to be given satisfactory performance ratings after reinstatement than were shorter term employees and employees in smaller establishments.[35]

A third study, one on public sector teachers, reported even less favorable results. Of 35 teachers reinstated in New York State between 1973 and 1976, 12, or roughly 35 percent, failed to return to their former jobs (7, because the arbitrator's award was still in court at the time of the study). Of the 23 who did return, only 8 were still employed by their school districts at the time the research was conducted; 6 of these had received tenure, and 2 were awaiting a tenure decision. Half of the arbitration decisions were challenged by the employers in the court; and the majority of the employers that reinstated teachers reported that the performance ratings of the teachers did not change after their reinstatement.[36]

A recent review of six different studies of reinstatement found that approximately 60 percent of reinstated employees who returned to work were judged to be satisfactory workers after reinstatement.[37] An interesting new finding uncovered by reanalyzing the data from these studies was that satisfactory job performance was *positively* correlated with seniority for workers who were exonerated by an arbitrator but negatively correlated with seniority among workers the arbitrator had found guilty of the offense that gave rise to the grievance. (Apparently nonexonerated workers who were reinstated were relatively high seniority employees whom arbitrators gave "another chance.") This led the authors to conclude that arbitration seldom changes poor performers into good performers. Taken together these studies point out the need to look beyond the arbitration decision itself as the final outcome of the grievance arbitration system.

The findings of the Lewin and Peterson study are not encouraging on this score. Their analysis of the later experience of grievants in four firms showed that, relative to a comparison group of employees who had not used the grievance procedure, grievants later received lower job performance ratings, had lower probabilities of promotion, and were more likely to experience voluntary or involuntary turnover. Moreover, those grievants who had appealed their cases to the higher steps of the procedure later had more negative performance and promotion experiences than those who had settled at the lower steps. And those employees who had won their grievances — that is, whose grievances were found meritorious by either management or an arbitrator—had lower subsequent performance ratings than those whose grievances had been denied by management or an arbitrator. Even more surprising, the same negative profile of aftereffects fit the *supervisors* of grievance filers. Relative to a comparison group, supervisors of grievance filers received lower performance ratings, were less likely to get promoted, and were more likely to experience involuntary turnover. Lewin and Peterson's results suggest that grievance filers and their supervisors in the organizations studied faced considerable risk of retribution for using the procedure.[38]

The obvious implication of all this evidence is that both management and union representatives need to pay careful attention to what happens *after* a grievance is resolved. Although most of the attention on grievance arbitration has focused on insuring that the procedures used to file and resolve complaints are fair and equitable, it may be that the more fundamental challenge lies in assuring that employees' careers are not jeopardized by the visibility (or notoriety) they find they achieve when exercising their right to process a grievance to its conclusion.

Another piece of the folklore surrounding grievance procedures is that they serve as a *common law of the shop*. Management and union representatives are said to *learn* from grievance settlements and arbitration awards the appropriate interpretation of contract clauses and then adapt their behavior accordingly. The one empirical study of this learning or "feedback" function suggests that there is a great deal of variability in the extent to which this learning occurs.[39]

In sum, these studies suggest that the grievance and arbitration processes can have positive, learning effects or negative, retribution effects, depending on whether the management and labor representatives are committed to the goals and values the process was designed to foster. The positive results do not occur automatically, however. Instead, top management and labor leaders must foster commitment to the values of due process and effective conflict resolution throughout the work organization, and they must make a concerted effort to train and educate the supervisors and lower-level union representatives who administer and enforce workplace industrial relations on a day-to-day basis.

The Centrality of the Grievance Arbitration Process

Most discussions of the effectiveness of the grievance arbitration process focus on its usefulness in resolving issues once they have been introduced into the procedure. Implicit in this discussion is the assumption that the grievance procedure is the forum to which workers naturally turn when they experience problems on the job. Because of its visibility, the grievance procedure tends to be viewed as the centerpiece of the contract administration process. Yet this assumption is seldom questioned, much less tested.

One study that did address this question found that the most important problems workers faced on their jobs were in fact only seldom introduced into the formal grievance procedure.[40] A rank-order correlation between the relative importance of workplace problems experienced by the workers studied (retail clerks in supermarkets) and the frequency with which the workers used the grievance procedure to resolve those problems was −.51. That is, the more important the problem to the worker, the less likely the worker was to take the issue to the grievance procedure. Although this strong, negative correlation may have been unique to the particular work force and geographic dispersion of the retail food industry (which is predominantly female, with a high proportion of part-time workers, high turnover rates, and very geographically dispersed local union members and business agents), it strongly suggests that in the future we must take a closer look at this question.

More specifically, have grievance procedures and arbitration become so cumbersome, legalistic, and slow that workers prefer to use other means to resolve their problems on the job? Has management become more sophisticated in resolving worker complaints through informal mechanisms so that the grievance procedure is no longer as important a mechanism for industrial justice as it was once believed to be? Do many of the issues of everyday concern to workers fall outside the scope of the collective bargaining agreement and, therefore, outside the scope of the grievance procedure? Is the formal procedure primarily but an insurance policy to be used only for major violations of individual rights, such as unjust discipline, discharge, or denial of promotions? Answers to these questions not only would help in evaluating the performance of modern grievance procedures as systems of industrial justice, but they would also broaden our understanding of the importance of the local union and the contract administration process in the daily lives of the workers covered under collective bargaining agreements.

The Duty of Fair Representation

One of the most prominent topics in discussions of grievance handling and the arbitration process is the *duty of fair representation*. As far back as 1944 the Supreme Court held that, in return for the rights of exclusive representation, the union has the duty to represent all members of the bargaining unit "without hostile discrimination, fairly, impartially, and in good faith."[41] Since then, the issue of the union's duty of fair representation has mushroomed in importance to the point that it is now one of the most frequently debated topics among union representatives, arbitrators, and advocates of individual worker rights and union democracy. Four related developments have brought this issue to the fore, especially in the 1970s: (1) the increasing stringency of the standards the courts have used to judge whether an employee has been fairly represented by the union, (2) the increasing willingness of individual workers to bring claims against unions for failure to represent them fairly, (3) the increasing reluctance of unions to drop grievances of questionable merit short of arbitration for fear of being sued for failure to represent the grievant fairly, and (4) the resulting rise in the number of court cases dealing with this issue.

There are few quantitative indicators of the magnitude of these trends, and there is little evidence to demonstrate without a doubt that expansion of this doctrine has increased the number of nonmeritorious grievances being processed. Nonetheless, in a study of duty of fair representation cases in British Columbia, Knight did show the cases increased between 1975 and 1983 by an annual rate of 23 percent, while the provincial labor board responsible for adjudicating those claims ruled in favor of the grievant's claim against his or her union in only 3 percent of the cases. Eighty-two percent of the claims were withdrawn or rejected, and the remainder were resolved by compromise, a case settlement, or a promise by the union either to investigate or to arbitrate the case. Knight further demonstrated that some of the cases arose out of the tactical or political use of the grievance procedure by individual members or factions within the union.[42] These data do not resolve the question whether the costs of enforcing a duty of fair representation doctrine outweigh the benefits, but they do offer some empirical confirmation to those who have argued that the numbers of these cases have grown and that many of them are of questionable merit.

In various decisions the U.S. Supreme Court has defined the duty of fair representation to prohibit "arbitrarily ignoring a meritorious grievance or processing it in a perfunctory manner";[43] fraud, deceit, or bad-faith conduct in the handling of a grievance; and refusal to handle a grievance out of personal hostility toward the grievant. In *Hines* v. *Anchor Motor Freight, Inc.* the court ruled that both the employer and the union were liable for failure to handle fairly an employee representation case.[44] The case involved an employee whose discharge had been upheld in arbitration. After the arbitration award was rendered, new evidence was discovered that proved the employee was not guilty of the offense. Both parties were charged with having failed to investigate fully the facts of the case in the original procedure. Essentially, a charge of negligence was applied to both the union and the employer in this case. In *Bowen* v. *United States Postal Service* the court went one step further by apportioning liability for back pay between a union and a company in a case where an employee was reinstated after the union refused to take the case to arbitration.[45]

Unfortunately, these various judicial efforts to clarify and specify the standards to be applied in duty of fair representation cases have not yielded unambiguous criteria for evaluating the union's performance. Summers has provided perhaps the most comprehensive summary of the principles of the duty of fair representation that have evolved over the years. These principles are listed in Box 10–4.

BOX 10–4
Union responsibilities under the duty of fair representation

First, the individual employee has a right to have the clear and unquestioned terms of the collective agreement which have been made for his benefit followed and enforced until the agreement is properly amended.

Second, the individual employee has no right to insist on any particular interpretation of an ambiguous provision in a collective agreement, for the union must be free to settle a grievance in accordance with any reasonable interpretation thereof. The individual has a right, however, to be guaranteed that ambiguous provisions be applied consistently and that the provision mean the same when applied to him as when applied to other employees. Settlement of similar grievances on different terms is discriminatory and violates the union's duty to represent all employees equally.

Third, the union has no duty to carry every grievance to arbitration: it can sift out grievances that are trivial or lacking in merit. But the individual's right to equal treatment includes the right of equal access to the grievance procedure and arbitration for similar grievances of equal merit.

Fourth, settlement of grievances for improper motives such as personal hostility, political opposition, or racial prejudice constitutes bad faith regardless of the merits of the grievance.

Fifth, the individual employee has a right to have his grievance decided on its own merits. The union violates its duty to represent fairly when it trades an individual's meritorious grievance for the benefit of another individual or of the group.

Sixth, the union can make good-faith judgments in determining the merits of a grievance, but it owes the employees it represents the use of reasonable care and diligence both in investigating grievances in order to make that judgment and in processing and presenting grievances in their behalf.

Source: Clyde W. Summers, "The Individual Employee's Rights under the Collective Bargaining Agreement: What Constitutes Fair Representation?" in *The Duty of Fair Representation*, ed. Jean T. McKelvey (Ithaca, N.Y.: New York State School of Industrial and Labor Relations, Cornell University, 1977), 82–83.

Responsiveness to Labor and Employment Laws

Events of the past two decades have raised an additional concern about grievance and arbitration procedures: whether they are effective mechanisms for protecting the individual rights granted by the many public policies governing employment conditions and standards. Of chief concern is whether arbitration is useful in resolving claims of discrimination raised under the protections of Title VII of the Civil Rights Act. But the same concern also rises in claims involving alleged violations of regulations on safety and health, wages and hours, pensions, disability benefits, workers' compensation, unemployment compensation, and many other regulations that may overlap or even conflict with the provisions of the collective bargaining agreement. In fact, concern over this question today ranks as a top item of debate among arbitrators and industrial relations practitioners.

The question is crucial because it has the potential to change the nature and functions of the arbitration procedure significantly or at least reduce the scope and status of arbitration as a conflict resolution procedure. Arbitration has traditionally been promoted as a private mechanism for resolving disputes arising out of the rights provided in *private agreements* between unions and employers. Arbitrators were accorded their high status by the Supreme Court in the Steelworkers' trilogy because they were presumed to have greater expertise in resolving these private disputes than do the courts and because their decisions were to be based specifically on the contents of the private agreement.

This view has eroded with the growth of governmental regulation of the workplace. The key Supreme Court decision in *Alexander* v. *Gardner-Denver* departed from the trilogy doctrine in cases of Title VII claims. [46] The Court ruled that an arbitrator's decision in a case involving a claim of discrimination does not preclude judicial review of the substantive merits of the claim, nor does it preclude the grievant from pursuing the claim with an appropriate administrative or judicial agency. Furthermore, the court will hear such cases de novo, that is, it will make its own independent judgment of the merits of the claim and will apply whatever weight it deems appropriate to the arbitrator's decision. This case thus rejected the trilogy doctrine of judicial review only of arbitrability and procedural questions, with the arbitrator solely responsible for judging the merits of the claim. The key difference in the *Gardner-Denver* case is that, unlike in a normal grievance—where the grievant achieves his or her rights from the terms of the contract and therefore the arbitrator need interpret only the language of the agreement and the past practices of the parties or the "common law of the shop" to reach a decision—the arbitrator now must also consider the rights accorded the grievant by public law as well.

The arbitration community is divided over the issue whether arbitrators should consider the requirements of external laws when deciding grievances or instead confine their decisions to interpretations of the rights accorded by the bargaining agreement. [47] Those advocating that the arbitrator stick to the bargaining agreement do so because they fear that considerations of external law will increase judicial scrutiny of arbitration decisions and that arbitrators may make erroneous interpretations of the law. They believe arbitration has not only been widely accepted as an institution by the parties but also assigned its protected status by the courts in the Steelworkers' trilogy precisely because arbitrators limit their decisions to issues and areas in which they have special expertise and jurisdiction. Thus, these advocates of minimal reference to external law are ready to trade off a reduced scope of jurisdiction in arbitration for protection of the institutional status and autonomy that has been afforded labor arbitration since 1960 (precisely because those disputes involving claims against external law or the collective bargaining agreement itself would have to be handled by public administrative agencies or the courts).

Those who argue that arbitrators should play a more active role in resolving claims involving public laws do so with full awareness that the arbitrator's role thereby shifts from one serving primarily the collective interests of the parties and the individual interests of the grievant (derived from a formal agreement) toward one serving public policies. The central arguments in favor of this new role are that arbitration is still cheaper, faster, and more efficient than the already overloaded administrative and judicial systems and that the new role simply serves to update the procedure to reflect the new environment of employment relations. In this new role, it is argued, arbitration thus remains an important and useful procedure for resolving disputes that arise under collective bargaining.

These advocates of an expanded role for arbitration also recognize that a number of concomitant changes in the administration and process of arbitration would be necessary.[48] First, arbitrators would probably need to have been certified in some way by a governmental or private agency as being qualified to handle claims involving the law. Second, employees would need to have the right to separate counsel at the arbitration hearing if they feared the union might not fairly represent their interests. Third, arbitrators would need to be empowered to deal with class action suits to handle claims of discrimination that involve an entire class. And finally, arbitrators would need to be more vocal and aggressive in conducting the arbitration hearing. They might need to request information that the parties do not voluntarily present when the dispute involves a potential conflict between the provisions of the private contract and public law.

Although the two alternative roles for arbitrators (along with numerous alternatives in between) have been actively debated, as yet only one empirical study has evaluated their respective merits in practice.[49] The debate could obviously benefit immensely from systematic experimentation. Whether arbitration can adapt to these challenges will have much to do with whether the "Golden Age" of this institution is at an end or whether it is merely opening the door to a new set of challenges.

CONFLICT RESOLUTION AND EMPLOYEE-MANAGEMENT COMMUNICATIONS IN NONUNION SETTINGS

The absence of a union does not eliminate the need for conflict resolution systems at the workplace. Instead, means other than the traditional union grievance procedure must be used to perform this generic industrial relations function. If such means are not employed, according to Hirschman's *theory of exit and voice*, employees who have no effective means to voice their discontent with any inequities they perceive will simply choose to exit the organization.[50]   Indeed, evidence is ample that employee turnover rates are higher in nonunion than union settings.[51]   Some of this higher turnover may be traced to the lack of effective grievance or appeal mechanisms in nonunion settings.

Yet over the past two decades an increasing number of employers have instituted complaint or appeal systems similar to grievance systems, as well as other communication and conflict resolution procedures for their nonunion employees.[52]   The more formal of these procedures parallel union grievance procedures, except that only a few of them end in binding arbitration by an outside, or third party, neutral. Profiles of three such nonunion procedures appear in Box 10–5. Supplementing these formal procedures is a host of processes such as ombudsman offices, "speak up" programs, employee-counseling services, and attitude surveys and related communications programs. Although the use of these various processes has expanded considerably in recent years, we are only beginning to accumulate empirical evidence on their performance as mechanisms for conflict resolution and due process.

Nonunion Grievance Procedures

Critics of nonunion grievance systems argue that employees seldom use these systems either because they have little faith in the fairness of the systems or because they fear reprisals. A study by Lewin of the performance of grievance procedures in three high-technology, nonunion firms provides some support for these claims.[53]   Grievance rates in these firms ranged from four to six per 100 employees, a rate well below the rates found in most union systems. Appeals to the higher steps of the procedures were also infrequent. Two cases per 100 employees went to the second step, one per 300 went to the third step, and only one per 500 went to the final step of the procedure. Moreover, Lewin found that compared to employees who did not file grievances, grievance filers (and their supervisors) had lower performance ratings, lower promotion rates, and higher rates of turnover in the year following their use of the procedure. Finally, survey responses from two of the firms indicated that approximately one-third of those who did not file grievances chose not to do so because they either feared reprisals or believed there was little chance their appeal would be successful.

Thus, it appears the grievants in these nonunion firms exercised their right to use these procedures at considerable risk. If this pattern is at all representative of experiences in other firms, it supports some of the critics' arguments. We must not forget, however, that the Lewin and Peterson study of users of *union* grievance procedures produced a very similar pattern of results.[54]   We therefore cannot yet conclude that nonunion grievance systems perform significantly worse in resolving conflict and guaranteeing due process than their union counterparts.

320

BOX 10–5
Profiles of nonunion grievance procedures in three firms

	Financial services firm	*Aerospace firm*	*Computing equipment firm*
Step 1	Informal discussion with immediate supervisor	Written appeal filed with immediate supervisor	Written appeal filed with personnel officer, who meets separately with employee and immediate supervisor
Step 2	Written appeal filed with functional or departmental manager, who gives written response	Written appeal filed with personnel officer; hearing officer appointed to meet with employee's immediate supervisor and employee's representative	Written appeal filed with functional or facility manager, who meets separately with employee and immediate supervisor
Step 3	Written appeal filed with facility or business unit manager, who gives written response	Written appeal filed with corporate vice president of employee relations; VP, another management official, and employee's representative constitute board of inquiry	Written appeal filed with divisional or corporate vice president of personnel, who chairs a management appeals committee
Step 4	Written appeal filed with management appeals committee, which gives written response	Written appeal filed with adjustment board composed of outside arbitrator, management official, and employee's representative; board decisions are binding	Written appeal filed with chief executive officer, who makes final decision
Step 5	Written appeal filed with company vice president of human resources, who makes final decision		

Source: David Lewin, "Conflict Resolution in High Technology Firms," in *Human Resources in High Technology*, ed. Archie Kleingartner and Cara Anderson (Lexington, Mass.: Lexington Books, 1986).

The Ombudsman

One alternative to the traditional grievance procedure is to employ an *ombudsman* to help resolve problems, complaints, or conflicts between or among employees, supervisors, and managers. Within the typical organization chart the ombudsman reports either directly to the office of the chief executive or to the head of the human resource management department. Since the ombudsman's mandate is more open-ended than the mandate for a grievance procedure, ombudsmen play a more varied role in resolving conflicts and also often handle a broader range of issues than does the typical grievance procedure. Box 10–6 lists a range of functions the typical ombudsman might perform. Indeed, the informality and flexibility with which the ombudsman can approach this role is commonly viewed as one of its distinct advantages. Although we know very little about the actual functioning of this service, it nonetheless holds out obvious benefits for both employees and employers—in both union and nonunion workplaces.

The Nonunion Systems and Union Avoidance

These various conflict resolution systems in nonunion settings may serve important generic functions for employees and employers, and therefore

---

BOX 10–6
Functions of an ombudsman

—To give a personal and confidential hearing, to defuse rage, to provide a caring presence to those in grief about a dispute.

—To provide (and sometimes to receive) information on a one-to-one basis.

—To counsel people (confidentially) on how to help themselves, by helping to develop new options, by problem solving, by role playing.

—To conciliate (that is, to go between parties without bringing them face-to-face).

—To mediate by bringing parties together face-to-face.

—To investigate formally or informally, either with or without presenting recommendations.

—To arbitrate or adjudicate, although this is a rare function.

—To facilitate systems or procedural changes by recommending "generic" solutions, by upward feedback, internal memos, and "management consulting" with institutions, by public reports, by recommendations to legislatures, by supporting education and training.

The classic phrase describing most ombuds practitioners is "They may not make, or change, or set aside any law or policy or management decision; theirs is the power of reason and persuasion."

Source: Mary P. Rowe, "Notes on the Ombudsman in the United States, 1986," photocopy (Cambridge: Massachusetts Institute of Technology, 1986).

represent constructive additions to a modern industrial relations system, but they can also serve as a means of managerial control and union avoidance. Indeed, many firms that use these systems and many professionals who administer them will openly acknowledge that one of their purposes is to discourage unionization. A former General Electric executive stressed this point when commenting on the reason GE had established a nonunion grievance procedure (one that ends with a peer-review panel): "We took away a major union issue." [55] Evidence from the Conference Board surveys discussed in Chapters 6 and 7 shows that this tactic has been very successful in avoiding unionization; that is, having a grievance procedure for nonunion employees significantly reduced the likelihood that new plants opened by a firm would be organized.

To the extent that the express purpose of having these procedures is one of union avoidance, the history of grievance procedures has taken an ironic twist: What started as a unique and highly acclaimed innovation designed to deliver due process to employees in a speedy, inexpensive, and informal fashion has been transformed into an employer strategy for reducing employees' chances of achieving the representation they need to make a truly independent grievance procedure and due process system operational. Thus, like all other human resource management innovations that are driven at least in part by union avoidance motives, nonunion conflict resolution systems are a double-edged sword. If the society values a strong and free labor movement and the right of employees to make independent choices about whether to be represented by a union, and if these nonunion systems provide less real power or less effective due process to employees than do union representation and union grievance procedures, policymakers and practitioners alike will have to come to grips with this issue sooner or later.

SUMMARY

Grievance procedures have historically served as the centerpiece of the day-to-day process of administering the collective bargaining agreement. They have also been hailed as one of the most innovative features of the U.S. industrial relations system. Their centrality to the system is due in part to the importance of the principle, embedded in the New Deal collective bargaining system, that it is management's job to manage and the union's job to grieve. Moreover, the detailed contracts that grew out of this model of industrial relations further intensified the need for an orderly means for sorting out conflicting interpretations of contract language and achieving uniformity in the enforcement of the provisions.

Yet the centrality of the formal grievance and arbitration procedures is now being challenged by a number of recent developments. First, the need for greater flexibility, adaptability, and labor-management cooperation in today's competitive organizations has led some unions and firms to simplify their work organizations and contract language and to attempt to break out of the high conflict–low trust cycle. Where successful, these experiments have significantly reduced the numbers of grievances filed and the parties' reliance on arbitration. Second, the need for earlier worker involvement in broad, strategic decisions that often lie outside the scope of the formal contract language has begun to challenge the management manages–unions grieve doctrine. Third, public laws governing a broad spectrum of employment conditions, such as discrimination, safety and health, employment at will, privacy, and drug testing, are challenging the exclusivity of the private arbitration system as *the* channel for resolving disputes over employment issues. And finally, the rise of alternative conflict resolution systems in the nonunion sector not only reflects and reinforces the growth of that sector, but also serves as an alternative to traditional grievance procedures and arbitration by a neutral third party.

All of these developments suggest that an effective industrial relations system in union settings must be more than simply a smoothly functioning grievance procedure. To keep in step with the times, the system must combine the strengths of a well-functioning grievance procedure with the more flexible and varied conflict resolution and communication processes that have developed in nonunion settings. Conversely, in nonunion settings, a truly effective workplace system must be one in which due process is delivered without later recriminations for its users, and one in which the primary function of the system is due process and not managerial control or union avoidance. Finally, no workplace system can be effective unless it is open to change and adaptation. In Chapter 13 we will explore how work organization and worker and union participation programs have meshed with and supplemented these formal procedures.

Suggested Readings

Some general works on grievance and arbitration procedures are:

Aaron, Benjamin, et al. *The Future of Labor Arbitration in America*. New York: American Arbitration Association, 1976.

Elkouri, Frank, and Edna Asper Elkouri. *How Arbitration Works*, 3d ed., Washington, D.C.: Bureau of National Affairs, 1984.

Fleming, Robben W. *The Labor Arbitration Process*. Urbana: University of Illinois Press, 1964.

Kuhn, James W. *Bargaining and Grievance Settlement*. New York: Columbia University Press, 1961.

McKelvey, Jean T., ed. *The Changing Law of Fair Representation*. Ithaca, N.Y.: ILR Press, 1985.

Thomson, Andrew J.W., and Victor V. Murray. *Grievance Procedures*. London: Saxon House, 1976.

324

Notes

1. Alan Fox, *Beyond Contract: Work, Power and Trust Relations* (London: Faber and Faber, 1974).

2. Harry C. Katz, Thomas A. Kochan, and Kenneth R. Gobeille, "Industrial Relations Performance, Economic Performance, and QWL Programs: An Interplant Analysis," *Industrial and Labor Relations Review* 37 (October 1983): 3–17.

3. Neil W. Chamberlain and James W. Kuhn, *Collective Bargaining*, 3d ed. (New York: McGraw-Hill, 1986), 151–53.

4. David E. Feller, "The Coming End of Arbitration's Golden Age," in *Arbitration 1976: Proceedings of the 29th Annual Meeting of the National Academy of Arbitrators*, ed. Barbara D. Dennis and Gerald G. Somers, 97–151, (Washington, D.C.: Bureau of National Affairs, 1977).

5. For a more thorough review of the development of grievance arbitration, see Robben W. Fleming, *The Labor Arbitration Process* (Urbana: University of Illinois Press, 1964).

6. For a good discussion of the historical development of rulings on grievance procedures and arbitration, see Chamberlain and Kuhn, *Collective Bargaining*, 141–53.

7. Charles C. Killingsworth and Saul Wallen, "Constraint and Variety in Arbitration Systems," in *Labor Arbitration—Perspectives and Problems: Proceedings of the National Academy of Arbitrators, 1964*, 56–81 (Washington, D.C.: Bureau of National Affairs, 1965.)

8. Ibid., 80.

9. Andrew J.W. Thomson and Victor V. Murray, *Grievance Procedures* (London: Saxon House, 1976), 124.

10. James T. Turner and James W. Robinson, "A Pilot Study of the Validity of Grievance Settlement Rates as a Predictor of Union Management Relationships," *Journal of Industrial Relations* 14 (September 1972): 314–22.

11. Katz, Kochan, and Gobeille, "Industrial Relations Performance," 8–9.

12. Nancy R. Mower, "The Labor-Management Relationship and Its Effects on Quality of Work Life," M.S. thesis (Cambridge: Massachusetts Institute of Technology, 1982).

13. Thomson and Murray, *Grievance Procedures*; David Peach and E. Robert Livernash, *Grievance Initiation and Resolution: A Study in Basic Steel* (Boston: Graduate School of Business, Harvard University, 1974).

14. David Meyer and William N. Cooke, "Determinants of Favorable Outcomes for Grievants in Formal Grievance Procedures," photocopy (Laramie: College of Commerce and Industry, University of Wyoming, 1986); Casey Ichniowski, "The Effects of Grievance Activity on Productivity," *Industrial and Labor Relations Review* 40 (October 1986): 75–89.

15. Leonard R. Sayles, *The Behavior of Industrial Work Groups* (New York: John

Wiley, 1958); James W. Kuhn, *Bargaining and Grievance Settlement* (New York: Columbia University Press, 1961).

16. Haruo Shimada, "Industrial Relations and 'Humanware': A Study of Japanese Investment in Automobile Manufacturing Industries in the U.S.," photocopy (Cambridge: Massachusetts Institute of Technology, 1986).

17. Jack Stieber, "The Future of Grievance Arbitration," *Labor Law Journal* (forthcoming).

18. "Bad Blood at Big Steel Could Lead to a Costly Strike," *Business Week*, 19 May 1986, 82–84.

19. Peach and Livernash, *Grievance Initiation*; E. A. Fleishman and E. F. Harris, "Patterns of Leadership Behavior Related to Employee Grievances and Turnover," *Personnel Psychology* 15 (1962): 43–56.

20. David Lewin and Richard Peterson, *The Modern Grievance Procedure in the American Economy* (Westport, Conn.: Quorum, forthcoming).

21. Ibid.; Howard Q. Sulkin and Robert W. Pranis, "Comparison of Grievants and Non-Grievants in a Heavy Machinery Company," *Personal Psychology* 20 (Summer 1967): 111–19.

22. Thomas R. Knight, "Factors Affecting Arbitration Submission Rates: A Comparative Case Study," M.S. thesis (Ithaca, N.Y.: Cornell University, 1978).

23. Lewin and Peterson, *The Modern Grievance Procedure*.

24. U.S. Department of Labor, Bureau of Labor Statistics, *Collective Bargaining in the Bituminous Coal Mining Industry*, BLS report 514 (Washington, D.C.: GPO, 1977).

25. Jeanne M. Brett and Stephen B. Goldberg, "Wildcat Strikes in Bituminous Coal Mining," *Industrial and Labor Relations Review* 32 (July 1979): 465–83.

26. See, for example, Alvin Gouldner, *Wildcat Strikes* (Yellow Springs, Ohio: Antioch Press, 1954).

27. Brett and Goldberg, "Wildcat Strikes."

28. John Zalusky, "Arbitration: Updating a Vital Process," *American Federationist* 83 (November 1976): 1.

29. Ibid., 5.

30. Stephen B. Goldberg and Jeanne M. Brett, "An Experiment in the Mediation of Grievances," report to the U.S. Department of Labor, September 1981.

31. "News Release," Mediation Research and Education Project Inc. (Evanston, Ill: Northwestern University, 26 November 1985).

32. Stephen B. Goldberg, "The Mediation of Grievances Under a Collective Bargaining Contract: An Alternative to Arbitration," *Northwestern University Law Review* 77 (October 1982): 270–315.

33. Interestingly, the arbitrator training programs have helped solve an additional problem in the profession—its previous dominance by white men. In fact, several training programs were expressly designed to bring minorities and women

into the arbitration profession. As of 1972 the National Academy of Arbitrators, an organization of the arbitration elite, had only four black and three female members among a total membership of 400; see William B. Gould, *Black Workers in White Unions* (Ithaca, N.Y.: Cornell University Press, 1977), 212. The number of women in the Academy has increased considerably since then.

34. Arthur M. Ross, "The Arbitration of Discharge Cases: What Happens After Reinstatement?" *Critical Issues in Arbitration: Proceedings of the Tenth Annual Meeting of the National Academy of Arbitrators, 1956* (Washington D.C.: Bureau of National Affairs, 1957), 21–56.

35. Thomas J. McDermott and Thomas H. Newhams, "Discharge-Reinstatement: What Happens Thereafter," *Industrial and Labor Relations Review* 24 (July 1971): 526–40.

36. Charlotte Gold, Rodney E. Dennis, and Joseph Graham III, "Reinstatement after Termination: Public School Teachers," *Industrial and Labor Relations Review* 31 (April 1978): 310–21.

37. Robert C. Rodgers, I.B. Helburn, and John E. Hunter, "The Relationship of Seniority to Job Performance Following Reinstatement," *Academy of Management Journal* 29 (March 1986): 101–14.

38. Lewin and Peterson, *The Modern Grievance Procedure*.

39. Thomas R. Knight, "Feedback and Grievance Resolution," *Industrial and Labor Relations Review* 39 (July 1986): 585–98.

40. Janice A. Radle, "A Cry for Justice: An Examination of Formal and Informal Grievance Settlement," M.S. thesis (Ithaca, N.Y.: Cornell University, 1978).

41. *Steel* v. *Louisville & Nashville R.R. Co.*, 323 US 192 (1944).

42. Thomas R. Knight, "Tactical Use of the Union's Duty of Fair Representation: An Empirical Analysis," photocopy (Vancouver: University of British Columbia, 1986).

43. *Vaca* v. *Sipes*, 386 US 171 (1967).

44. *Hines* v. *Anchor Motor Freight, Inc.*, 424 US 554 (1976).

45. *Bowen* v. *United States Postal Service*, 103 US (1983).

46. *Alexander* v. *Gardner-Denver*, 415 US 36 (1974).

47. For a review of the different approaches, see David E. Feller, "The Impact of External Law upon Labor Arbitration," in *The Future of Labor Arbitration in America* (New York: American Arbitration Association, 1976), 83–112.

48. See, for example, Gould, *Black Workers*, 240–41. See also Harry T. Edwards, "Arbitration as an Alternative in Equal Employment Disputes," *Arbitration Journal* 33 (December 1978): 23–27.

49. See Harry T. Edwards, "Arbitration of Employment Discrimination Cases: An Empirical Study," in *Arbitration 1975: Proceedings of the Twenty-eighth Annual Meeting of the National Academy of Arbitrators*, ed. Barbara D. Dennis and Gerald G. Somers (Washington, D.C.: Bureau of National Affairs, 1976).

50. Albert O. Hirschman, *Exit, Voice, and Loyalty: Responses to Decline in Firms, Organizations, and States* (Cambridge: Harvard University Press, 1971).

51. Richard B. Freeman and James L. Medoff, *What Do Unions Do?* (New York: Basic Books, 1984), 94–107. The authors point out (pp. 104–7) that seniority systems, as well as grievance arbitration systems, reduce quit rates in union settings.

52. See Alan Balfour, "Five Types of Non-Union Grievance Procedures," *Personnel* 61 (March-April 1984): 67–76.

53. David Lewin, "Conflict Resolution in High Technology Firms," in *Human Resources in High Technology*, ed. Archie Kleingartner and Cara Anderson (Lexington, Mass.: Lexington Books, 1987).

54. Lewin and Peterson, *The Modern Grievance Procedure.*

55. "Letting Workers Help Handle Workers' Gripes," *Business Week*, 15 September 1986, 82.

CHAPTER 11

Contract Terms and Job Outcomes

Our attention now turns to the effects collective bargaining has on wages, fringe benefits, job security, and other job outcomes. In addition to describing some of the key provisions in collective bargaining agreements that affect job outcomes, we compare the wages, working conditions, and other job outcomes of union and nonunion employees. It is through such comparisons that we can estimate the *average* effects of collective bargaining. Rather than provide an exhaustive analysis of all contract provisions, we will focus here on those that are either the most common or the most controversial. We put off until the next chapter analysis of the ways collective bargaining agreements have been changed in recent years as the parties have responded to the environmental and other pressures outlined in earlier chapters. As a result, our assessment in this chapter relies primarily on data from before 1980.

Handicapping any analysis of the impact of collective bargainings on job outcomes is the complexity of interrelationships across job outcomes and between unionization and job outcomes. Changes in wages, for example, set off a chain reaction in other job outcomes. Some of these second-order changes move in the same direction as the wage effects, while others move in the opposite direction. On the one hand, an increase in wages may result in a corresponding, automatic "roll up" in such fringe benefits as sick leave pay, vacation pay, pensions, and unemployment benefits. On the other hand, a wage or benefit increase may create pressures for the firm to hold down costs in other aspects of the employment relationship, as, for example, by explicitly trading off higher wages for lower benefits or less pleasant working conditions or by adjusting workplace practices to reduce the costs of the contract changes. These adjustments lead to compensating differentials—poorer or more difficult working conditions to compensate for a high wage. (Compensating differentials can work in the other direction, with better working conditions allowing a lower wage.)

Because of these complex interrelationships across job outcomes and because unions affect outcomes indirectly as well as directly, we must lay out a clear theoretical framework for understanding the effects of a union if we ever hope to make sense of these relationships.

THE THEORETICAL FRAMEWORK

Figure 11–1 diagrams the propositions in the framework used to trace these effects. The framework follows in three stages.

Stage 1: Primary Union Effects

Unions' primary effects are on the compensation received by their members—fringe benefits as well as wages, since a union's success in improving wages is likely to carry over to fringe benefits. Union members have always been concerned with the package or distribution of benefits as well as the level of wages. Thus, we expect a positive differential between union and nonunion benefits as well as a positive wage differential. Unions that have sufficient power to increase wages and benefits should also be able to achieve other goals that workers expect of them. Based on a "union power" hypothesis, therefore, we would expect positive relationships between unionization and wages, fringe benefits, and other terms and conditions of employment favorable to employees.

Stage 2: Management Adjustments

The next step in tracing a union's effects requires an analysis of management's response to changes in the labor contract. The central question here is: How does management adjust to the increases in labor costs that are likely to occur as a result of collective bargaining, or how, if at all, does the employer recoup the potential productivity losses associated with union-negotiated improvements in wages, benefits, and working conditions? Employers have two alternative responses: one based on standard neoclassical economic theory, and the second based on the "shock effect" hypothesis.

Neoclassical theory suggests that increases in labor costs result in some combination of the following responses: (1) a reduction in the scale of output and employment, (2) an increase in the price of the product, or (3) a substitution of capital for labor—all mechanisms for bringing the *marginal productivity* of labor and earnings back into equilibrium. According to neoclassical theory, all are dysfunctional from the standpoint of the firm

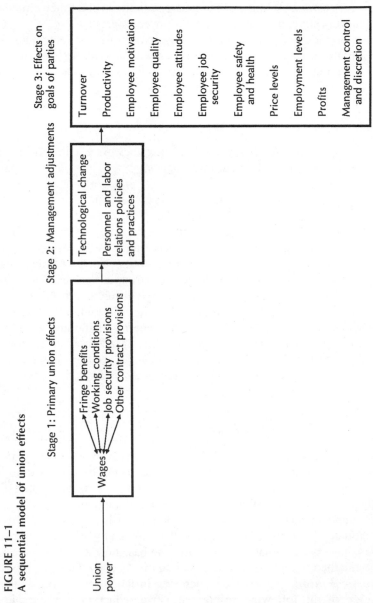

FIGURE 11–1
A sequential model of union effects

Stage 1: Primary union effects   Stage 2: Management adjustments   Stage 3: Effects on goals of parties

Union power

Wages
Fringe benefits
Working conditions
Job security provisions
Other contract provisions

Technological change
Personnel and labor relations policies and practices

Turnover

Productivity

Employee motivation

Employee quality

Employee attitudes

Employee job security

Employee safety and health

Price levels

Employment levels

Profits

Management control and discretion

and the society, however, since they result in higher prices or reduced employment opportunities, or both. The underlying assumption in this theory is that the system was, in fact, in equilibrium before unionization (or before the negotiated increase); that is, the employer had been operating at peak efficiency, and labor costs reflected labor productivity.

The *shock-effect proposition* was put forth in the 1940s by Sumner Slichter,[1] who argued that the presence of a union or the negotiation of a new contract forces management to search for more efficient means of running the firm. Furthermore, increases in wages and other improvements in the terms and conditions of employment may have offsetting effects on other personnel costs and thereby reduce the pressure on unit labor costs.

Figure 11-1 illustrates some of the paths these adjustments may take. Increases in wages, fringe benefits, or other terms of employment may reduce voluntary turnover and thereby reduce hiring and training costs, thus helping the firm retain highly productive employees. As time goes by, higher wages should attract better workers for positions in the bargaining unit. Employees may become more motivated and work harder because of the improved contract terms, while management may invest more in training to improve the ability or skill levels of the employees. The employer may also require that the supervisory and human resources planning functions become more efficient by formalizing policies, increasing the use of personnel and labor relations specialists, and so on.

The key assumption of the shock-effect theory is that the firm was not necessarily operating in the most efficient manner before unionization or before the negotiated increase. Thus, unionization may prompt management to respond in ways that lead to greater efficiency than would otherwise be the case.

Stage 3: Secondary Union Effects

Suppose a union is successful in increasing wages and fringe benefits and the employer reacts as either the neoclassical or the shock-effect theory would predict, or in some combination of the two. The employer's response, in turn, affects employee welfare because it may reduce the number of jobs in the bargaining unit, change the way the work is organized or the way technology is used to perform the work, speed up production, increase the amount of supervision, or reduce expenditures in other areas affecting the job environment, for example, investment in plant maintenance, new equipment, or health and safety devices. Any of these managerial responses is then likely to engender a countervailing union response to address the resulting problems of job security and working conditions.

The greater the wage and benefit premiums won by the union, the stronger management's motivation to reduce expenditures in these other areas, and the more concerned union members will become about their working conditions and job security. Moreover, once the workers have achieved higher wages and improved benefits, they will turn their attention to gaining improvements in other areas of employment, for both economic and psychological reasons. For example, since those other employment conditions are presumably positive economic goods, the majority of union members will want to purchase more of them as their wages rise. Behavioral theory and evidence amply explain and document the fact that employees' interest in the nonwage aspects of their jobs increases as wages increase.

This secondary response has traditionally taken the form of union demands for (1) job security protection, (2) work rules that limit management's ability to speed up the pace of work, (3) more time off with pay to ease job pressures and increase work opportunities as a means of protecting job security (that is, lunch or rest periods, shorter hours, added vacation and holiday time, higher overtime premiums), and (4) safety and health protections and procedures. Employers usually resist these union proposals because many of them further increase labor costs, reduce managerial discretion, and expand the scope of union influence. Whether the union can achieve these contract demands will again, therefore, depend on the union's bargaining power.

Recent economic pressures have led firms to seek greater flexibility in deploying their work force, and new technologies such as robotics have facilitated the shift to more flexible production methods. This has encouraged a movement toward more flexible systems of work organization and, in some cases, to greater worker and union involvement in decision making. Unions have therefore been challenged to go beyond their traditional concerns to become involved in quality-of-working-life programs, gaining workers more say over how their jobs are performed or redesigning job and work group structures. At the same time, unions have had to address worker concerns over uninteresting work, mental stress, job dissatisfaction, and related psychological reactions to their jobs.

We know very little about the aggregate effects of unions on these aspects of employment. Although a majority of union members apparently would like to see their unions improve these aspects of their jobs (see Chapter 5), evidence reviewed later, in Chapter 13, suggests that these issues are of primary concern to workers only when they are linked to the preservation of other, more traditional bread-and-butter issues of wages and employment security.

The central implication of this discussion is that the effects of unions on an array of job outcomes depend on the relative strength of two opposing forces: the union's power to achieve its objectives on the job outcomes of concern to its members; and the employer's ability to respond to union gains in one area by holding the line on improvements in others. As we move from the primary or traditional areas of union effects to those that, to date, have been less central to collective bargaining, the effects of union power should be less significant than the effects of managerial policies and practices.

Key Propositions

The sequential effects of unions in collective bargaining can be summarized by the following propositions.

1. The primary effect of unions is to increase wages and fringe benefits and to improve the working conditions of their members. Of these effects the initial and dominant one is that on wages.
2. The greater the union's power, the more the wages of the union's members will exceed those of nonunion workers in comparable jobs.
3. The more unions raise wages, the higher fringe benefits tied to wages will be.
4. The more unions raise wages, the higher the priority union members will assign to improving fringe benefits, working conditions, job security, and other provisions of the collective bargaining contract.
5. The greater the union's power, the more successful it will be in improving the fringe benefits, job security, working conditions, and other terms of the labor agreement, and the less the employer will be able to recoup the higher wages through trade-offs or compensating differentials in these other areas of the employment relationship.
6. The greater the union's power, the more the employer will formalize its personnel and labor relations policies and practices in an attempt to recoup the increased costs associated with the terms of the collective bargaining agreement.
7. The effect of unions on the attitudes and behavior of individual workers depends on the joint effects of the terms of the collective bargaining agreement and the ways the employer adapts its personnel and labor relations practices and policies.

These propositions summarize the series of events that are set in motion by unionization and that must be addressed if we are to trace the overall effects of collective bargaining on the goals of workers, employers, and society. In the following sections we review the empirical evidence of union effects on various job outcomes.

UNION WAGE EFFECTS

Theoretical Background

We compute *relative union effects* by calculating the union-nonunion differential. In contrast we assess *absolute union effects* by comparing unionized employment conditions to what would exist in the absence of unions: the union–no union differential. Since it is extremely difficult to estimate what employment conditions would have been in the absence of unions, most research has focused on assessing relative union effects.

H. Gregg Lewis provided the earliest and now-classic analysis of unions' relative wage effects.[2] In the research that followed Lewis, the technique most frequently used to measure unions' relative wage effects has been a regression analysis in which the wages of a pool of union and nonunion workers are used as the dependent variable, and the union status of each individual or group of workers is entered as an independent variable along with a series of controls for other determinants of wages.[3] The types of control variables normally included in these equations are (1) human capital or labor supply characteristics such as age, education, experience, and training; (2) the region of the country; (3) race and gender (as measures of the effects of discrimination); (4) the industry and occupation; and (5) the size of the firm. Since some of these are also correlated with the probability that a worker is unionized, including them in a regression equation as control variables increases the accuracy of the estimate of the independent union effect. Early studies focused on the industry or occupational levels of analysis. Many compared differences in average industry wages, using the percentage of the industry unionized or covered by a bargaining agreement as the measure of unionization. The later availability of micro-level data including individual or firm observations allowed a comparison of the wages of individual union members and those of comparable nonunion workers.

Several technical problems make it difficult to know if these estimates of the relative union effects provide a good approximation to the absolute effects of unions on employment conditions. The major problem in sorting out the net effects of unions is that union wages may spill over to the nonunion sector; nonunion employers may match union-negotiated wage increases to discourage their employees from unionizing. The nonunion wage is therefore higher than it would be otherwise because of the *threat effect* of unionization. Thus, estimates of unions' relative wage effect may understate the absolute effect of unions on wages, since they do not fully account for the extent that union wages have spilled over to the nonunion sector.

On the other hand, the presence of unions in one firm or industry may lower the wages of nonunion workers elsewhere because by raising wages, unions induce unionized firms to cut back on employment. The workers displaced then seek employment in nonunion firms and industries. This *supply effect* would then result in lower wages for the nonunion workers. Thus, estimates of the relative union wage effect may overstate the differential between union wages and the wages that would exist if there were no union.

Another highly technical problem is whether union membership should be treated as an exogenous variable (one that can be assumed to be determined outside the model being estimated) or as one that is caused by some combination of other job characteristics, such as the wage level, working conditions, and job security. A number of researchers have contended that *unionization* is a function of wages, selected working conditions, and individual worker or industry characteristics.[4] Estimates of unions' influence on wages may therefore be overstated or understated unless this simultaneous or reciprocal causality is eliminated from the estimates. Suppose, for example, unions tend to organize high-wage industries or workers. In this case the union coefficient in a single-stage regression equation captures both the effects of unions on wages (the true effect of interest here) and the effects of wages on unions (that is, higher wage jobs attract more unionization). Recognizing this problem, several researchers have used a set of simultaneous equations in which the first stage estimates the probability of being unionized and the second stage uses this probability as the "instrumental" variable for generating the estimate of the net effects of unions on wages. This type of analysis generally serves to lower the estimates of unions' wage effects.

The Empirical Evidence

The numerous empirical studies of union wage effects demonstrate the difficulty of trying to come up with a single aggregate estimate of the effects of unions on wages (or any other job outcome). Indeed, the results indicate that the wage effects of unions vary (1) over time, (2) over the course of the business cycle, (3) across occupations, (4) across industries, and (5) by workers' gender, race, education, and age.

Albert Rees used Lewis's findings to summarize the wage effects of unions up to 1962. Rees concluded that the average effect of unions on wages was between 10 and 15 percent.[5] Studies conducted after 1962 led him to revise his summary estimate to between 15 and 20 percent.[6] Lewis's analysis had shown unions to have their largest relative wage effects during periods of recession because unions set a floor on wages and resist wage cuts (or are successful in increasing wages at a faster rate than nonunion workers). Lewis had estimated, for example, that the union wage effect in the 1930s was perhaps 28 percent or more; by the end of that decade it had declined to between 10 and 20 percent. The decline continued throughout the 1940s until around 1947, when the effects of inflation reduced it to between zero and 5 percent. Between the late 1940s and 1960, Lewis estimated, unions increased the union-nonunion wage differential to between 10 and 15 percent.

Later studies that used individual data files further illustrated the variations in union effects. The results of those studies can be summarized as follows:

1. Unions have a greater positive effect on the wages of blacks, and particularly black men, than on whites. Ashenfelter's estimates were that the union-nonunion wage differential for black men in 1975 was approximately 22 percent. Duncan also found that obtaining a union job and remaining on that job paid off more for black than for white youths.[7]
2. Unions reduce the effects of age and education on earnings by flattening out the normal age-earnings profile that is observed in the nonunion

sector. That is, unions increase the earnings of younger workers by raising the entry-level salaries on union jobs above what an inexperienced worker would be paid in a comparable nonunion job. At the upper end of the wage distribution, the effects of seniority provisions in union contracts protect older workers from wage erosion after they pass their peak productivity years. Unions also reduce the effects of education by reducing intraoccupational and interoccupational wage dispersion through their advocacy of *equal pay for equal work* rather than *equal pay for equally endowed workers*.[8]

3. Union wage effects vary across occupations. One study estimated the following union-nonunion differentials: laborers, 42 percent; transportation equipment operators, 38 percent; crafts workers, 19 percent; operatives, 18 percent; service workers, 15 percent; managers, 2 percent; clerical employees, 2 percent; professionals, 0.58 percent; and sales workers, −4 percent.[9]

4. Union wage effects vary across industries. Ashenfelter estimated that union wage effects in 1975 for white male, blue-collar workers were 43 percent in construction; 16 percent in transportation, communications, and utilities; 12 percent in nondurable goods manufacturing; and 9 percent in durable goods manufacturing.[10]

5. Unions reduce the white-collar/blue-collar wage differential in firms where blue-collar workers are organized. Unions also reduce intraindustry wage differentials by promoting wage standardization. The reduction in wage dispersion within an industry due to the presence of unions more than offsets the increase in earnings dispersion across industries, so that the net effect of unions is to reduce wage inequality among workers.[11]

6. Unions produce larger relative wage effects in less concentrated industries,[12] most likely because, even in the absence of unionization, concentrated industries pay higher wages than do competitive industries.[13]

Over the years, in addition to increasing wages, collective bargaining has introduced a number of innovations in the administration of wage systems. Chief among these have been cost-of-living adjustments, deferred wage increases (sometimes referred to as "annual improvement factors"), red circle rates (stipulations that provide for rate retention to employees whose jobs are evaluated downward because of technological change), and wage reopener provisions (whereby the contract remains in force over several years, but wages are renegotiated at some specified point during the life of the agreement).[14] In some industries, such as steel, the union and the employers have jointly developed complex systems for evaluating jobs and establishing a more rational structure of wage rates. In other industries, such as apparel, the unions and the employers negotiate and administer complicated wage incentive systems. Because many apparel firms are small, the International Ladies' Garment Workers' Union, a major union in the industry, provides technical advice to employers on the layout of jobs and the setting and revising of incentive rates.[15] Thus, we can see that the setting, adjusting, and revising of wages and wage-payment systems under collective bargaining are complicated tasks—requiring not only an ability to exercise bargaining power, but also a good deal of technical expertise.

Concessionary bargaining in the 1980s produced wage outcomes that differed substantially from past patterns. As noted earlier, we will discuss these new patterns in the next chapter.

UNION EFFECTS ON FRINGE BENEFITS

Theoretical Background

In general, unionized workers receive both a wider variety of benefits and a higher level of benefits than nonunion workers—for a variety of reasons.[16] Since World War II, when the War Labor Board first sanctioned and then actively encouraged bargaining over fringe benefits as a means of holding down the size of the basic wage increase, unions have fought to broaden the scope of fringe benefits included among the mandatory subjects of bargaining. In the 1948 *Inland Steel* case the NLRB ruled that pension and retirement issues belonged on the mandatory list of subjects.[17] By the late 1950s the board had added to the list issues such as health insurance, sick leave, supplementary unemployment benefits, vacations, and holidays, and since then these have become standard provisions in almost all collective bargaining agreements. Thus, unions have led the battle to make fringe benefits a central component of the total compensation package.

Union members expect their leaders to place a high priority on fringe benefit bargaining. The data reported in Chapter 5 showed, for example, that dissatisfaction over fringe benefits is an important reason for unorganized workers to vote for unionization. The data also showed that unionized workers rated fringe benefits as the substantive bargaining issue to which they would have their union give top priority.

Older workers and workers with longer tenure are likely to place a higher priority on fringe benefits than on other issues, particularly straight-time wages. Freeman and Medoff noted that unions are likely to follow the preferences of their older members more than those of younger members because the older ones tend to have greater political influence within the union and tend to remain on the job, since the probability of quitting declines as seniority increases.[18] We later review evidence showing that unions reduce voluntary turnover. Union members are likely to stay on their jobs for a longer time than nonunion workers and therefore are likely to gain more from deferred benefits such as pension plans, vacation pay tied to seniority, early retirement, and disability retirement pay.

Fringe benefits are what economic theory defines as *normal goods*, that is, goods employees will purchase more of as their income rises. Thus, as unions increase wages, their members will prefer to purchase additional fringe benefits over additional wage increases. This effect is compounded by the tax advantages associated with fringe benefits. Employees pay no income taxes on deferred benefits until they receive the benefits (if received as income, as in the case of a pension) and never pay tax on some benefits (such as medical care). Thus, workers will value an additional expenditure on fringe benefits more highly than the same expenditure on wages. This preference should increase as the wage level increases. In addition, as unions increase wages, members become more conscious of the mix of benefits provided in the overall compensation package and will encourage their unions to place a high priority on improving the fringe benefit component of the overall contract.

The Empirical Evidence

The Freeman and Medoff study previously cited demonstrates that unions increase the probability that (1) a wider range of fringe benefits will be available and (2) the percentage of total compensation going to benefits will be greater. Among unionized firms within the manufacturing sector in the mid-1970s, 25 percent of the total wage bill was allocated to fringe benefits, while among nonunion firms the fringe benefit allocation was 19.6 percent. The comparable figures for all private sector firms were 22.7 percent in union firms and 17.4 percent in nonunion firms. Not surprisingly, the union-nonunion differences were larger for voluntary fringe benefits than for government-mandated benefits, since the former are subject to collective bargaining and employer discretion. Freeman and Medoff estimated that, on average, unions increased expenditures on voluntary fringe benefits by approximately 36 percent. They calculated that about half of that total effect was caused by a direct union effect on total compensation, while the other half was a function of the roll-up effects of unions on wages.

Our own analysis of the differences in wages and fringe benefits across 85 union and nonunion plants of the same large conglomerate reinforces these findings and extends them to the case of union and nonunion plants within the same firm. Table 11–1 reports the wage and fringe benefit premiums found in the firm's union plants in 1979, 1982, and 1983. Several patterns are reflected in these results. First, in all three years the union plants paid significantly higher entry-level wages and had higher fringe benefit costs and total labor costs than the nonunion plants. Second, in no year was there any significant wage premium for the most highly skilled workers. Third, although the magnitude of the estimates of wage and labor cost differentials varied somewhat from year to year, the differentials were quite persistent over the course of the business cycle in the years 1979–83.

Trends in Fringe Benefit Provisions

As noted above, the vast majority of unionized workers receive a comprehensive package of fringe benefits. The major breakthroughs in fringe ben-

TABLE 11–1
Union labor cost differentials across union and nonunion plants of the same firm, 1979–83

Type of Compensation	1979	1982	1983
Top wage rate	5%	1%	6%
Bottom wage rate	28	24	34
Average wage rate	6	12	20
Total benefit costs	24	23	30
Total labor costs	11	15	23
Skill differential	–39	–42	n.a.

Source: Unpublished data from our field research for 1983. Data for 1979 and 1982 are reported in Anil Verma and Thomas A. Kochan, "The Growth and Nature of the Nonunion Sector Within a Firm," in *Challenges and Choices Facing American Labor*, ed. Thomas A. Kochan (Cambridge: MIT Press, 1985), 89–118.

Note: All numbers are approximate precentage differentials based on regression equations that include control variables for plant age, size, region of the country, and industry. The 1983 equations also control for skill-mix differences across the plants. Sample size varies between 80 and 85 plants for the different years.

efit bargaining date back to the 1940s and early 1950s for such issues as pensions, vacations, sick leave, health and life insurance, and overtime. The 1960s and 1970s witnessed rapid escalations in benefit levels and the diffusion of these benefits across industries and workers. Survey research conducted by the U.S. Chamber of Commerce has documented the magnitude of the increase in fringe benefits. Employee benefits as a percentage of payroll for firms in the Chamber's surveys rose from 18.7 percent in 1951 to 36.6 percent in 1983.[19]

Governmental regulations have helped spur the increases in benefit expenditures. The Employee Retirement Income Security Act of 1974 (ERISA), for example, has had profound effects on pensions. The act (1) specifies minimum standards for vesting of pension contributions, (2) requires more detailed reporting and disclosure of information about the plan to both employees and the government, (3) requires all future liabilities be fully funded on an annual basis and all past unfunded liabilities be amortized over a number of years, and (4) establishes an insurance protection program for workers affected by plan terminations. The costs of the termination insurance are met by a tax on existing plans.

The major policy problem created by ERISA lies in the potential liabilities to the government if one or more of the major multiemployer plans were to terminate. Overall, ERISA is a good example of both the speed by which changes can be achieved through direct governmental regulation and the complex problems that result when the federal government attempts to establish uniform practices and standards in an area that previously was characterized by diversity.

UNION EFFECTS ON WORKER ATTITUDES

Do unions affect the job attitudes of workers? To date, the evidence on this question is mixed. Most of the studies on this subject have focused on the narrow, and somewhat controversial, question of the relationship between union membership and job satisfaction.[20] One study found unions had a significant positive effect on workers' attitudes toward compensation—the job outcome on which unions exert their greatest influence.[21] Two other studies, however, found unions to be a source of negative attitudes toward other aspects of the job, such as satisfaction with supervision or with job content, after controlling for demographic characteristics and wage level.[22]

The most straightforward interpretation of these results is that unions have their primary effects on wages and other bread-and-butter issues, and that carries over to members' evaluations of those aspects of their jobs. Unions have been less successful, however, in making substantive improvements on the other aspects of their members' jobs. The negative relationships between unionism and members' attitudes toward these other job aspects further suggest that employer adjustments to unionism may result in a worsening of some nonwage aspects of the work environment.

An alternative interpretation of these results can be found in earlier studies that suggested because unions are an instrument for voicing dissatisfaction on the job, they raise members' awareness of the problems associated with the job. Thus, union members may respond more negatively to job satisfaction questions than nonmembers do because of this "voice" effect of trade unions. Whatever the reason behind these findings, they suggest that unions and employers may wish to pay more attention to workers' attitudes toward these issues that have traditionally fallen outside the scope of the formal collective bargaining process.

UNION EFFECTS ON WORK RULES

Protection from Arbitrary Treatment

Perhaps one of the most important effects of unions has been the protections they have secured for their members from arbitrary discipline, discharge, or denial of benefits and promotions. Unions pioneered the development of (1) the principle of *just cause* for dismissal or discipline and (2) grievance procedures ending in arbitration for adjudicating disputes over actions that violate the just-cause principle or some other term of the labor agreement. Installing this system of *industrial jurisprudence* is often cited as one of the most distinct achievements of the U.S. collective bargaining system.

Grievance arbitration is now almost universal in private sector bargaining agreements, and it is rapidly spreading to a majority of public sector contracts as well. Although the number of nonunion grievance procedures has also swelled in recent years, most of these do not provide for binding arbitration by a neutral. It is only in such special cases as those of tenured teachers, college professors, and civil servants that similar types of just-cause principles and appeal procedures exist that end in a determination by someone other than the immediate employer. The primary statutory protections available to workers dismissed, denied benefits, or denied promotions are those prohibiting such actions on the basis of discrimination by race, gender, age, religion, or support for union activity.

As Jack Steiber writes, "The United States stands almost alone among industrialized nations in not providing statutory protection against unjust discharge or 'unfair dismissal' as it is commonly called in most countries." [23] Instead, U.S. courts have enforced the common doctrine of *employment at will*, although the doctrine has been somewhat less strictly applied in recent years. A few state courts have ordered that discharged employees be awarded back pay, reinstatement, or both on one of the following grounds: if an *implicit contract* existed between the employee and the firm that limited the employer's discretion in its dealings with employees; or if the employee was discharged after having refused to carry out illegal acts or after having performed acts (such as reporting the firm's environmental pollution to authorities) the employee believed served the public interest. In these latter cases the courts found that employees were entitled to protection when their actions served a public purpose.[24]

Clyde Summers has vigorously championed instituting a comprehensive arbitration system to protect nonunion workers from unjust discharge. He views the absence of any such protection as one of the more profound paradoxes of U.S. labor policy:

> The paradox becomes even more painful when we realize that employees in the United States protected by arbitration under collective agreements probably have more complete and sensitive protection against unjust dismissal, more efficient procedures, and more effective remedies than employees in any other country in the world. But employees in the United States who do not have arbitration available are almost alone in not having any general protection against dismissal without notice and without cause.[25]

Summers proposes for the nonunion sector building on the just-cause principle and the procedural guides that have developed in the union sector. He prefers to continue reliance on private arbitrators (who would need to be approved by state or federal agencies to have the force of law behind them) rather than to turn to a labor court or an administrative agency for adjudicating grievances by nonunion employees.

Support for extending this collective bargaining principle and practice to the nonunion sector remains primarily in academic circles. Before any effort is made to adopt an arbitration scheme, we must address several questions of scale. How serious is the problem? How many employees are unjustly discharged or disciplined by nonunion employers for reasons other than discrimination (where remedies exist)? Would an arbitration system work in the absence of an organization such as a union that can serve to screen out grievances clearly lacking in merit? Or would the threat of litigation discourage employers from disciplining workers even when they had just cause? Finally, are the personnel and human resource programs of private firms now providing effective safeguards against arbitrary managerial actions? If we find the scope of the problem is large and private practices are insufficient to deal with it, the paradox noted by Summers may warrant the attention of policymakers. It is unlikely, however, that this issue will gain much attention unless more visible signs of employee discontent and workplace injustice surface. Until then, arbitration will continue to be one of the key "premiums" provided to employees covered under collective bargaining contracts. (Chapter 10 provided an analysis of the effectiveness of grievance procedures.)

Seniority

Seniority plays a pivotal role in collective bargaining agreements. It is important to employees because it is used as a basis for allocating benefits and job opportunities to workers. It is important to employers because it restricts the discretion they have in carrying out their personnel and human resource management functions. And seniority is becoming increasingly important to public officials as they wrestle with such labor policy goals as equal employment opportunity, income security, and productivity.

Seniority is normally defined as the employee's length of service with the employer. In some cases, and for some purposes, it may be measured as the length of service in a particular department, job, or other subunit of the organization. Two types of seniority provisions can be distinguished: (1) benefit-status provisions, and (2) competitive-status provisions. The former tie increases in various economic benefits, such as vacations, pensions, supplementary unemployment pay, severance pay, and guaranteed annual wages, to the length of service with the employer. The latter make seniority a factor in personnel decisions, such as promotions, job assignments, layoffs, and transfers. Seniority also plays a role in grievance arbitration. Most arbitrators will take the grievant's length of service into account in considering whether any disciplinary action taken against the worker was equitable, especially in light of a previously good personnel record.

The prevalence of seniority provisions. Seniority provisions are mentioned as a factor to be used in promotion decisions in 82 percent of the manufacturing and 59 percent of the nonmanufacturing agreements in a 1986 contract data base compiled by the Bureau of National Affairs.[26] The lower percentage in the nonmanufacturing contracts is largely attributable to the relative absence of these provisions in the construction industry. The only two manufacturing industries where seniority tends to play a relatively minor role are apparel and leather goods—industries characterized by sharp skill differences, seasonality, high turnover, employer instability, and a tradition of work sharing. Of those contracts mentioning seniority in the BNA study only 5 percent specified that it be the sole criterion governing promotions within the bargaining unit. It served as a determining factor, provided the employee was qualified, in 41 percent of the contracts; as a secondary factor considered only when other qualifying factors were equal, in 26 percent of the contracts; and as a consideration equal to other factors in fewer than 17 percent of the contracts.[27]

Based on survey responses from about 400 firms Abraham and Medoff concluded that in 1981 over three-quarters of hourly unionized employees worked in settings in which seniority had an important independent role in the promotion process.[28] Interestingly, the authors also found that seniority was used frequently in the nonunion sector as well, though not to as great a degree as within unionized firms. Over half of both hourly, nonunion employees and salaried, nonunion employees worked in settings in which seniority had an independent role in the promotion process. In a related study Medoff and Abraham found evidence that the earnings of nonunion employees exhibited substantial within-job differentials that were associated with seniority and did not reflect employee productivity differences.[29]

As unionism developed in the United States, seniority emerged as an important bargaining goal of most unions, whose members viewed it as a means of curbing arbitrary treatment or favoritism in personnel decisions. Unions also came to support the notion that employees gain a *property right* to their jobs as their length of service increases. Accordingly, unions argued that those employees with the longest service should (1) be entitled to the most secure jobs, (2) have the first opportunity to bid for better jobs as they open up, and (3) be accorded some deference in scheduling vacations and accruing other benefits.

Although the labor movement has been the primary force in spreading these concepts of seniority rights throughout U.S. society, employers, too, have shown they believe in giving some weight to seniority in managing their work force and structuring their benefits. Indeed, the concept is now so commonly accepted as an advantageous, legitimate, and expected part of the industrial relations system that it is part of the personnel decisions of most nonunion as well as union employers, as revealed in the Medoff and Abraham studies discussed above.

The pros and cons of seniority provisions. Besides their income effects seniority provisions protect the security of workers' incomes and jobs by reducing the threat of layoff, increasing the chances of obtaining transfer or bumping rights (displacing a newer employee when a layoff occurs), abbreviating unemployment spells and expanding income supplements during temporary layoffs, and expanding severance payments in times of permanent job loss or economic dislocation. These protections obviously pay off most as employees pass their most productive years, especially in situations where technological or market developments change employee skill and ability requirements.

Seniority provisions also play an important role in shaping the career prospects of workers. Both the scope of the seniority unit and the weight assigned to seniority in promotions affect the range of possible paths for upward mobility and the probability that an individual worker will obtain a promotion. Together the scope of the seniority unit and the weight given seniority determine the expected length of time required to move up in the organization. We should recognize that strong seniority provisions improve the promotion chances of workers with average to below-average ability and motivation, while they may serve to slow the career advancement of younger employees possessing higher than average ability and motivation. Thus, seniority does not necessarily benefit all employees equally.

Seniority provisions offer employers both advantages and disadvantages. By increasing the economic and job security of workers as their tenure increases, seniority provisions should help stabilize the work force and reduce the number of valued workers who leave the firm. They also may reduce psychological stress and increase older workers' satisfaction with their jobs. If firm-specific training and experience contribute to improved job performance, the use of seniority should help to keep the most productive workers within the organization. Finally, seniority provisions reduce managers' and workers' uncertainty about the ongoing makeup of the work force and increase formalization of the personnel function. As a result, the employer can design jobs and training programs to insure that job performance does improve with length of service, thereby simplifying the personnel and human resource planning function. By definition seniority provisions allow the employer to compute the probable movement of individual workers through different jobs in the organization over time.

All these benefits are greatest to those firms having relatively routine and unchanging technologies in which individual differences in ability and motivation make little difference in job performance. The more variable the technology and skill requirements, or the more important individual discretion and motivation are to job performance, the greater the costs associated with strict adherence to seniority, and the more employers will seek to limit both the scope of the seniority unit and the weight assigned to seniority in promotion decisions. At the extreme are jobs that require great technical, professional, or artistic skill and jobs in which individual differences are the predominant determinant of job performance. It is hard to imagine, for example, seniority ever playing an important role in determining the starting lineup of a professional baseball team or the cast for a major motion picture.

Seniority and public policy goals. Seniority provisions in collective bargaining have come under fire in recent years from government agencies, individual workers, and courts involved in promoting or adjudicating equal employment opportunity laws and regulations. In the past seniority had served to discriminate against minorities and women primarily by establishing segregated seniority units or progression ladders. Some firms had set up departmentwide seniority units that systematically excluded blacks, women, or both from the most desirable jobs and progression ladders. Blacks, for example, may have been hired only as laborers, while whites were hired into the higher paying jobs in the maintenance department. Where this occurred, or where firms refused to hire minority or female workers at all, the effects of past discriminatory acts were perpetuated by the use of seniority criteria for either competitive- or benefit-status purposes.

The basic challenges recently facing courts, government agencies, and the parties to the bargaining process have been (1) to ensure that present practices and seniority rules do not discriminate against any individuals or groups, (2) to avoid perpetuating the effects of past discrimination, and (3) to protect the interests of nonminority workers who are not responsible for the past discrimination but may have indirectly benefited from it. The law is evolving day by day as various state and federal courts and administrative agencies enforce Title VII of the 1964 Civil Rights Act and related state fair-employment-practice laws. The following summary statements, however, represent the status, as of this writing, of seniority as a bona fide criterion for allocating job opportunities or economic benefits.

1. Job-based or departmental seniority units are legal as long as they are created and administered in a nondiscriminatory fashion. Before the Supreme Court announced this interpretation, however, virtually every lower federal court had held that a seniority system that perpetuated the effects of past discrimination was illegal. Federal agencies have therefore negotiated a number of consent decrees with firms and industries that had departmental seniority units that excluded minority workers from the most desirable jobs. The most important of those decrees was in the steel industry: Its effects were to change the seniority system from departmentwide to plantwide units and to provide a system of transfer rights to minority workers who had been discriminated against under the old system.[30]

2. Workers who have been discriminated against since the effective date of the Civil Rights Act (1965) may be entitled to both back pay and "constructive seniority" to make up for their losses. That is, a worker who was not hired in 1965 or beyond because of discrimination may receive both the back pay lost and the seniority credits he or she would have accrued since the date of the discriminatory act.[31]

3. Workers cannot be compensated (either through back pay or constructive seniority) for discrimination that occurred prior to the Civil Rights Act.[32]

4. Employers and unions may voluntarily agree to modify their employment practices to take affirmative steps toward eliminating the effects of past discrimination. In the central case where the Supreme Court reached this conclusion, for example, the company and the union agreed to admit to a training program more minority workers than would have been eligible under the previous seniority rules.[33]

5. Seniority systems may not be altered by a court for the benefit of workers who were not themselves victims of discrimination. An employer may follow the existing seniority system when making layoffs, even if the effect is disproportionately adverse to recently hired blacks and women, as long as the seniority system is bona fide.[34]

6. If an employer is found guilty of egregious discrimination, a court may order affirmative, "race-conscious" relief—such as minority hiring goals—even if those who will benefit from the affirmative action measures are not the actual victims of the employer's discriminatory practices.[35]

Unanswered questions.   This brief overview of the role of seniority provisions vividly illustrates why some see them as the heart of a collective bargaining agreement. Clearly, seniority provisions are among the most complex to negotiate and to modify as conditions change. More than any other kind of provision they serve to illustrate the value of the decentralized, bilateral approach to decision making that collective bargaining provides; they also serve to amply warn of the dangers in trying to develop a standard set of practices and rules through governmental regulation. The variations in the nature and strength of seniority provisions in union contracts attest to the ability of collective bargaining to fit a general principle to the specific circumstances of each bargaining pair.

Nonetheless, a number of questions regarding seniority warrant more intensive empirical research before we can make definitive statements about its value from the standpoint of individual workers, employers, and the public. Is seniority a barrier to eliminating the effects of past discrimination? How have seniority rules been revised since the passage of Title VII, and how are the parties now adjusting their rules in the aftermath of the most recent court decisions? Do these revisions have positive or negative effects on productivity? What have been their effects on employee attitudes and perceptions of fairness and equity in the workplace? Is seniority viewed as retarding the career prospects of younger workers? Do younger workers share the belief that access to opportunities and economic benefits should be determined primarily by length of service to the organization? These are all empirical questions that have yet to be addressed systematically by industrial relations researchers. Answering them would not only provide a better understanding of the current role that seniority plays in our society, but also of the role it is likely to play in the future.

Turnover

The proposition that unions reduce employee turnover has been around for three decades now. In a classic article published in 1958 Ross asked whether a new industrial feudalism was developing through the spread of seniority, pension, layoff, and other job security provisions in union contracts.[36] Early efforts to test this hypothesis used regression analyses with variations in interindustry turnover rates as the dependent variable and measures of the percentage of workers unionized or covered under bargaining agreements as the independent variable. The results were mixed, with some studies finding no significant differences.[37]

More recently, studies using measures of job security provisions in contracts and studies using observations of individual workers have found that the presence of a union and the presence of these provisions do significantly reduce turnover. Block found, for example, that the stronger the seniority provisions in bargaining agreements, the lower the quit rate in the industry.[38] Freeman and Medoff showed that even after controlling for the wage level and job satisfaction (each of which alone would produce lower turnover rates), union membership was associated with a significantly lower probability of a worker's voluntarily leaving the job.[39] This finding was especially strong for older workers: The probability of older union workers' voluntarily quitting their jobs was almost zero.

Although these studies provide ample evidence that (1) unions reduce turnover and (2) the stronger the job security provisions, the stronger the union effect, they do not furnish a good explanation for these findings. March and Simon's model of employee turnover offers some useful theoretical clues, however.[40]

March and Simon suggested that the probability of turnover is affected by (1) the ease of leaving the job and (2) the desirability of leaving. The ease of leaving is determined primarily by the alternative employment opportunities open to the employee. The more favorable the alternatives in the labor market, the greater the ease of leaving (and replacing the job with an equivalent or better job) and the higher the probability of turnover. The desirability of leaving is largely a function of the level of dissatisfaction with the current job. The greater the dissatisfaction, the greater the desirability of leaving.

We can integrate unionism into this model in two ways. First, the greater the impact of the union on wages, the lower the ease of leaving (replacing the job with an equivalent job in the external labor market). This is because the union increases wages above what the union worker's *human capital* (skills and education) could attract in the external labor market. Furthermore, the greater the fringe benefits, job security, and promotional opportunities the union has secured for the worker, the more difficult it is for him to replace his job in the external market. Thus, unions, and especially the more successful unions, should reduce turnover because they make it harder for workers to leave the organization.

This union effect is likely to be strongest among those workers who have the least attractive alternatives in the external labor market, such as those subject to age, sex, race, or other forms of discrimination and those who have the least marketable skills. The effect is also likely to be stronger among older workers with more seniority. The older the worker, the greater the value of his pension, sick leave, and job security protections and the more difficult it will be for him to find a new job with equivalent benefits and protections.

We have already reviewed evidence showing that the returns to a union job are likely to be greater for blacks than for whites and that blacks, at least young blacks, are highly unlikely to quit a union job voluntarily. Those findings serve as indirect evidence that unions reduce turnover the most among workers likely to have difficulty finding jobs of equal value; and they support the hypothesis that unions reduce turnover by lowering the ease of leaving.

The effects of a union can also operate through the desirability-of-leaving proposition in the March and Simon model. Hirschman's theory of "exit and voice" is helpful in making this integration.[41] In Freeman and Medoff's extension of Hirschman's theory to the labor market, voicing dissatisfaction on the job and acting to change job conditions serve as alternatives to leaving the job when the worker is dissatisfied.[42] If the union offers workers a viable alternative for voicing concerns on the job, union members may choose *voice*, rather than *exit*, as a means for addressing their dissatisfaction.

It is extremely difficult, however, to assess whether unions' grievance and voice procedures or unions' effects on wages and other employment conditions are the source of the lower quit rates among union members. Freeman and Medoff observed that quit rates among union workers are lower than those among nonunion workers, even after controlling for the effects of the higher wages earned by union workers. But is the lower quit rate among union members that remains after controlling for wage effects due to the exit-voice trade-off, as Freeman and Medoff hypothesized, or is it due to the other improved working conditions that unions provide? We might be able to answer this question if we had a measure of the pervasiveness or effectiveness of the grievance procedure across workers or workplaces and then could test whether more pervasive grievance procedures actually produce lower quit rates. Unfortunately, the data for such a test are not available. In this as in many cases, we know that unions have an impact on employment outcomes, but research has not identified precisely why and how they do.

Job and Income Security

Theoretical background. In addition to its inherent importance to all workers, job security is of special concern to them for a number of other reasons. Union workers demand job and income security for much the same reason they demand fringe benefits: Unions increase wages and other labor costs and thereby give employers reasons to make compensating adjustments in employment conditions. As unions increase labor costs, union workers are exposed to greater job security risks resulting from (1) employers' efforts to adjust to the higher labor costs, and (2) employers' reduced demand for union labor. The union response to these adjustments is to attempt to negotiate job and income security provisions that protect the workers from the adjustments. Some security provisions make it more difficult or costly for the employer to substitute either nonunion labor or capital inputs for union work covered under the contract. The union may also try to negotiate additional paid time off to reduce the employment losses or require the hiring of additional workers.

In addition to responding to economic adjustments by employers, unions seek to protect workers from arbitrary treatment. The data presented in Chapter 7 on management responses to unions suggest that this protection is of even greater importance to unionized than to nonunionized workers. Recall that nonunion employers and those with a minority of their workers unionized place a high priority on reducing the incentives for union organizing. In contrast, employers in the highly unionized workplaces are less concerned about employee attitudes than their counterparts in less unionized settings. These data suggest that once employers recognize they have lost the battle over unionization, their attention turns to coping with the economic consequences of collective bargaining. Employers whose employees are unionized may therefore adopt a more formalized or harder line toward employee supervision and discipline than employers of nonunionized workers. One study offers some empirical support for this hypothesis. Dimick found a strong correlation (.64) between the percentage of employees unionized in a firm and the number of areas of employee conduct covered by formal disciplinary rules and regulations.[43] Given this rules-based approach, and especially if the employer still harbors anti-union animus, the union will seek protection against arbitrary treatment of individual workers and against efforts to weaken the union.

Employers frequently oppose demands for job and income security provisions because they (1) increase labor costs, (2) reduce employers' ability to adjust labor costs to fluctuations in business conditions, and (3) limit managerial discretion and freedom. We can expect, therefore, that the comprehensiveness of the job and income security protections that unionized workers achieve is a function of the bargaining power of the union. Bargaining over these issues represents the classic conflict over the workers' need for security and the employer's need for efficiency and desire for autonomy and flexibility. Indeed, industry strike activity has been found to be an especially strong determinant of the comprehensiveness of job security and work rule provisions in contracts in manufacturing industries.[44] With this in mind we can now examine the types of security provisions in union contracts and the issues that are now at the frontier of bargaining agendas and public policy debates over job and income security.

Security from economic dislocation. One category of job security provisions is protection from the effects of either short-term and temporary or long-term and permanent job loss for economic reasons. This category includes (1) job preservation and (2) income and fringe benefit protection in the event of job loss.

One way for unions to protect jobs is by negotiating work rules that specify (1) who is to perform the work and (2) how many workers are required for given tasks. Work-sharing provisions cut the workweek during periods of slack demand rather than allow the layoff of employees. This practice is found in 18 percent of all union contracts and in almost all apparel industry contracts.[45] One major disincentive to work sharing is that unemployment benefits in most states do not cover workers on a shortened workweek; a complete layoff is necessary for unemployment eligibility, although a few states have begun to experiment with providing unemployment compensation to workers affected by a reduction in work hours. Most contractual work-sharing agreements limit the time period during which this alternative can be used to forestall layoffs. Most also limit the number of hours that will be reduced before commencing layoffs.

Other types of work rule provisions that affect employment levels and security are restrictions or limitations on supervisors' right to do bargaining-unit work, on transferring employees and filling vacancies, on the ratio of apprentices to journeymen, on management's rights to change the nature or speed of the work, and on the extent of subcontracting. Although many of these provisions were originally designed to protect workers' safety and health or to constrain management from eroding the jurisdiction of the union by substituting nonunion for union workers, some now have the effect of retaining more workers than are needed to perform the work, or what is referred to as *featherbedding*.

Short-term income security. The two major forms of income protection against short-term fluctuations in the demand for work are supplementary unemployment benefit (SUB) plans and guaranteed annual wage plans. The latter are found in only a handful of cases, such as plans covering East Coast and Gulf Coast dock workers. The BNA contract survey found that only about 3 percent of the workers covered under major contracts have any form of income guarantee. The vast majority of these provide a limited weekly income guarantee for those who begin a given workweek; they do not provide for long-term income maintenance in the absence of available work.

The first major SUB plan to be negotiated was in the auto industry in 1955. The United Auto Workers had originally sought a form of guaranteed annual income. Ford Motor Company, the target firm in that round of negotiations, countered with what has grown into the industry's SUB plan. The pattern set in the auto industry spread quickly to the can and steel industries by the end of the following year and to a number of other durable goods manufacturing industries that typically experience cyclical and seasonal fluctuations in employment (such as the tire and farm equipment industries). The BNA data show that 14 percent and 16 percent of the contracts sampled in 1962 and 1986, respectively, had SUB plans.[46] Thus, like wage guarantees, most of the major SUB plans were negotiated in the 1950s. Since then the eligibility rules and benefits under those plans have been liberalized, but they have not spread to a significant number of other contracts or workers in the past decade.[47]

Security from plant shutdowns. Another important set of collective bargaining clauses deals with permanent job loss caused by either technological change or a plant shutdown. Here the provisions address both job preservation and income protection. They include interplant transfer rights or transfer rights to other jobs within the plant or organization; early notice of technological change, a plant shutdown, or both; and relocation allowances. Plant shutdown or relocation provisions existed in 23 percent of the BNA's 1986 contract file, up from 18 percent in 1983. Early notice to, or discussion with, the union about these matters was required in one-half of the agreements that addressed these subjects. These provisions were most common in apparel, leather, and rubber industry agreements. [48]

In recent years a number of firms have guaranteed workers more extensive employment security in exchange for pay concessions. This development is discussed in more detail in the next chapter.

Safety and Health

Another important job outcome influenced by collective bargaining is the health and safety of the work force. Unions historically have used three interrelated strategies to improve safety and health conditions at the workplace: (1) supporting governmental regulations and safe practices and conditions, (2) negotiating safety provisions into bargaining agreements, and (3) encouraging the formation of joint union-management safety and health committees at the plant level. Union activity has increased on all three of these fronts in the past two decades. The labor movement was the driving force behind passage of the Occupational Safety and Health Act of 1970 (OSHA). The number of safety provisions in bargaining agreements has expanded considerably since then, as has the number of safety and health committees in unionized plants. Although this section will concentrate on collective bargaining provisions and the overall effects of unions on safety and health conditions, the interdependence of these three strategies should be kept in mind.

Theoretical background. To understand the nature of this interdependence, we need to look at the dilemma unions faced before 1970. Safety and health had always been an issue of middle-range importance to U.S. workers yet not an issue of high enough priority to a sufficient number of union members that they were consistently willing to strike to achieve demands for safety improvements. Their reticence to strike over the issue was partly a function of the high variance in the exposure of different workers in the same bargaining unit to unsafe or risky jobs or conditions.

A union's dilemma, therefore, was to find ways of responding to the health and safety problems of workers exposed to hazards, without relying on the threat of the strike to achieve its demands. Joint committees to study and monitor health and safety conditions in the plant became an attractive alternative to the strike because employees and employers share a common interest in promoting workplace safety and health. Of all issues safety and health should qualify as integrative issues. Many union officials, however, have historically been skeptical of the potential of union-management committees of any kind. Before passage of OSHA union leaders often contended that the majority of safety and health committees had little real influence because top management was not committed to them. And some employers rejected joint committees because of the potential costs of implementing committee recommendations. The committees further suffered from a lack of commitment from rank-and-file workers and local union officials.

Faced with these limitations of the negotiations process and joint committees, the labor movement turned to federal legislation as a third strategy. Although most states had statutes that set safety and health standards, union leaders viewed those laws as too variable in both quality and enforcement. Consequently, they supported OSHA in the belief that it would (1) provide adequate and consistent standards and enforcement, (2) serve as a source of increased union power in negotiations over safety and health issues, and (3) provide a stronger basis for influencing management through joint committees. Occupational safety and health is therefore an excellent example of an issue in which public policy plays an important role as a source of power in collective bargaining.

The economic *theory of compensating differentials* has been used by some to analyze employers' policies toward occupational safety and health policies and practices. The theory assumes that employers provide an optimal mix of higher compensation for risky jobs and investment in risk-reducing policies. The higher the job's risk, the higher the wage paid to compensate workers for exposure to hazards. Alternatively, the employer can invest in reducing the risks associated with the job and thereby reduce the need for the compensating differential.

This theory suggests that unions can affect safety and health at the workplace in two ways. First, they can demand a higher compensating wage differential for workers exposed to higher risks. Although the evidence is far from conclusive, there is some indication unions have been successful in obtaining a positive wage differential for risky jobs.[49] The differential, in turn, has both a direct effect and an indirect effect. The direct effect is obviously to compensate those workers who are exposed to risks. The indirect effect is to increase the employer's incentive to lower the risks on the job so that the union demand for the compensating differential is no longer justified. The second way unions can influence safety and health is to negotiate either protections against job hazards or changes in the work environment that will eliminate the hazards.

Whether either of these strategies is effective depends on whether the parties have accurate information on the causes of injuries and occupational illnesses. While the parties may be readily able to diagnose the causes of *injuries*, they have only recently begun to recognize the hidden, long-term development of *illnesses* resulting from exposure to such health hazards as excessive dust, dangerous chemicals, and the multitude of carcinogens that may be present in the workplace. Thus, national unions, with their centralized staffs and resources, have an important role to play in disseminating information on hazards present on different jobs to their local officials and rank-and-file members. Part of that role is to identify the relevant sources of risks on the job, inform workers of those risks, and provide information on how to reduce exposure to hazards.

Most behavioral theories of accidents distinguish between two basic sources of risk: (1) the job environment, and (2) worker behavior. Unions focus on means to reduce the risks associated with the job environment; they pay less attention to changing the worker behaviors that lead to accidents. The two major behavioral causes of accidents are workers' inadequate knowledge and their inadequate motivation to perform the work safely. The former can be dealt with through training, especially of new workers. The latter requires rewarding employee safety on the job and rewarding supervisors for good safety records.

The evidence. Table 11–2 illustrates the range of safety and health provisions commonly found in collective bargaining agreements in 1978. A comparison of the percentages listed in this table with comparable figures for 1970 shows that all of these provisions became increasingly common over the 1970s. For example, in 1970, 31 percent of the contracts in the BNA sample provided for safety and health committees; by 1978 that figure had risen to 43 percent, and by 1986, to 49 percent.

General provisions stating that the employer is responsible for making the work environment safe or that the employer agrees to comply with applicable safety laws (something employers presumably have to do whether the union contract requires it or not) allow the union to use the contractual grievance procedure to process safety complaints rather than being forced to rely solely on either a joint union-management committee or complaints to the Occupational Safety and Health Administration, which is responsible for administering and enforcing OSHA. Fewer than half the contracts in 1986 contained detailed clauses requiring the employer to provide first-aid services, removal of hazardous working conditions, safety equipment, or rights to refuse unsafe work, or for union participation in the inspection of plants. In general these provisions were more common in

354

TABLE 11–2
Collective bargaining provisions on safety and health

Type of provision	Percentage in all contracts	Percentage in mfg. industry contracts	Percentage in mining industry contracts
Some provision on safety	82%	87%	100%
General statement of responsibility	50	58	75
Employer to comply with laws	29	29	50
Employer to provide safety equipment	42	46	92
Employer to provide first aid	21	26	50
Physical examinations	30	30	75
Removal of hazardous working conditions	22	19	67
Accident investigations	18	24	58
Safety committees	43	55	92
Dissemination of safety information to employees	16	18	38
Dissemination of safety information to union	19	21	44
Employees to comply with safety rules	47	50	67
Right of inspection by union or employee safety committees	20	30	56
Wage differentials for hazardous work	15	6	6

Sources: First nine items, "Safety and Health Patterns in Union Contracts" *Daily Labor Report,* no. 178, 13 September 1978, E–1; last five items, *Major Collective Bargaining Agreements: Safety and Health Provisions,* bulletin 1425–16 (Washington, D.C.: Bureau of Labor Statistics, U.S. Department of Labor, 1976).

manufacturing than nonmanufacturing industries, and in all cases were much more common in high-risk industries such as mining. Thus, the probability that these provisions will be included in contracts depends partly on the magnitude of the risks found in the industry.

On the frontier of safety and health bargaining today are issues of occupational health. Unions and employers now must address the effects of years of heretofore undetected or unknown exposures to toxic substances. Only in the last several years have most unions and many employers begun to address the problem of exposure to carcinogens and other health hazards in the workplace. Two main strategies are emerging. One is to compensate for the accumulated effects of past exposures by moving workers to safer jobs without loss in pay and by reforming workers' compensation systems to provide benefits not only to those disabled by injuries but to those suffering from occupational diseases. The other approach is to reduce workplace exposures. Here efforts take a variety of directions such as (1) supporting new or stricter governmental standards for exposure to polluted air, dust, toxic chemicals, radiation, and other potential carcinogens; (2) promoting the dissemination of information on toxic substances found at the workplace; and (3) negotiating provisions for more industrial hygienists, examinations by physicians other than company doctors, and so on.

We must ask whether unions and employers have been successful in using these contract provisions and procedures to reduce exposure to job hazards and to cut the rate of injuries and illnesses. This is a very difficult question to answer without detailed data on injury and illness rates in union and nonunion firms and rates in work sites with different safety and health contract provisions. Without these data we have to rely on the data from surveys of individual workers. The Quality of Employment Survey, for example, elicited data on union and nonunion workers' perceptions of hazards on their jobs (such as excessive dust, noise, heat, dangerous chemicals, electrical hazards, and unsafe machinery) and their injury experiences. Although analysis of these data showed that the union members reported more serious problems with job hazards, no significant differences were found in the workers' injury experience. At the same time, the union members surveyed were significantly more likely than the nonunion respondents to work in industries with higher than average injury rates. Even after controlling for these locational effects, however, the results noted above did not change.[50]

Thus, although unions and employers have been expanding their efforts to improve safety and health conditions over the past several years, and although some evidence suggests that unionized workers receive a higher compensating wage differential for hazardous work than nonunion workers, as yet there is no conclusive evidence that their efforts have reduced the injury or illness rates of workers covered under bargaining agreements. One study has shown, however, that the safety record of a coal mine was significantly improved as a result of a broader union-management experiment to improve productivity and the quality of work.[51] Thus, significant improvements in workplace safety and health may require a more comprehensive program and effort than the average union and employer now have in place through their collective bargaining provisions and health and safety practices.

Productivity

A critical issue, perhaps the most critical issue, in assessing the impact of unions and collective bargaining is how these institutions affect productivity and efficiency. This issue has become salient in recent years as the aggregate annual rate of productivity growth declined from 3.2 percent during the 20 years following World War II to 1.1 percent from 1975 to 1985.[52]

Theoretical background. It is difficult to measure empirically the effects of union-negotiated work rules on productivity. Examples of feather-bedding have been highly visible in the railroad industry—where controversy over the number of workers on a train crew has been in the public eye for years—but no detailed studies have examined the costs associated with union work rules in different industries.

Some of the difficulty in assessing average union effects arises because such a high proportion of the new plants opened since 1960 are unorganized. As a result, the correlation between plant age and union status is strong: Nonunion plants tend to be younger. Furthermore, as a plant ages, its work rules tend to become more rigid and cause a reduction in its economic performance. Given the association between unionized status and plant age and the fact that both exert independent effects on plants' economic performance, it is difficult to distinguish between the effects of each.

The evidence. Recent research provides some evidence comparing work practices in union and nonunion plants of the same firm. Verma conducted an in-depth comparison of eight plants in a multidivisional manufacturing firm.[53] Three of the eight were union plants; the remaining five were nonunion. Table 11–3 summarizes some of the differences in the workplace industrial relations systems he found across those eight plants in 1982.

In approximately 1960 the company had begun experimenting with using behavioral science concepts in the design and management of its professional, managerial, and hourly work force—almost exclusively at the nonunion plants. At the three plants labeled "new, nonunion" in Table 11–3—those built after 1960—the company designed some or all of the workplace systems using the behavioral science innovations described in Verma's case study. The other two nonunion plants, labeled "old, nonunion" in the table, had been opened in the 1950s and the 1930s, respectively; and all three union plants were opened before 1960.

In fact, Verma's results showed the old, nonunion plants have more in common with the union plants than with the new, nonunion plants. First, the new plants were smaller than both the union and the old, nonunion plants. Second, in contrast to both of the older types of plants the new, nonunion plants made greater use of all-salaried compensation systems and

TABLE 11–3
A comparison of work practices in union and nonunion plants of the same firm

Work practices	Type of Plant		
	New, nonunion (N=3)	Old, nonunion (N=2)	Union (N=3)
Average number of job classifications	6	65	96
Average number of wage grades	7	11	14
Average number of maintenance job classifications	1	10	11
Percentage of maintenance workers in a "general maintenance" classification	75%	20%	1%
Supervisors prohibited from doing subordinates' work	No	No	Yes
Subcontracting occurs only after meeting with union/employees	0%	0%	100%

Source: Anil Verma, "Union and Nonunion Industrial Relations at the Plant Level," Ph.D. dissertation (Cambridge: Massachusetts Institute of Technology, 1983), 129.

less use of cost-of-living escalator payments (not shown in the table). Third, and similarly, three measures of the structure of the jobs and work practices showed the older, nonunion plants to be more closely matched to the union than to the new, nonunion plants. As shown in Table 11–3, the two types of older plants had many more job classifications, many more maintenance job classifications, and a much lower percentage of workers in a "general maintenance" job classification than the new, nonunion plants—although in all cases the old, nonunion plants scored in between the other two types of plants.

But on the other hand, both the old and the new nonunion plants reported fewer constraints on managerial flexibility to allocate workers than did the union plants. Issues that fit this pattern included restrictions on subcontracting and the rights of supervisors to fill in for or do the work of their subordinates.

Although these comparisons draw on a very limited sample and crude measures, a consistent pattern emerges that places the practices found in the old, nonunion plants in between the practices of the old, union plants and the newer, nonunion plants. In our own research we have observed the same pattern in the workplace practices of a number of other firms that have both union and nonunion plants. We can conclude, therefore, that both the union status and the age of a plant may exert independent effects on the design and operation of workplace industrial relations systems.

MANAGEMENT'S RESPONSE TO WORK RULES

Whatever the work rules provided in the labor contract—be they grievance procedures, seniority rights, or job security—all limit the amount of discretion management exercises at the workplace.

Management Rights Clauses

One strategy management employs to limit the effects of restrictive work rules is to negotiate a management rights clause. In 1986 management rights statements appeared in 84 percent of manufacturing contracts and in 74 percent of nonmanufacturing contracts.[54] Some of the provisions were simple, general statements such as, "The supervision, management, and control of the company's business, operations, and plants are exclusively the function of this company." The majority of the provisions, however, enumerated a specific list of rights reserved to management, as in the following example:

> The rights to hire, promote, discharge or discipline for cause, and maintain the discipline and efficiency of employees are the sole responsibility of the corporation except that union members shall not be discriminated against as such. In addition, the products to be manufactured, the location of plants, the schedules of production, and the methods, processes, and means of manufacturing are solely and exclusively the responsibility of the corporation.

The obvious purpose of management rights clauses is to limit the territory of union influence and retain for management the freedom to run the organization efficiently. The traditional labor relations literature has articulated two views of the management rights concept; these are used by arbitrators and the courts in resolving disputes over contract interpretation. The *reserved rights* or, as it is sometimes labeled, the *residual rights* doctrine takes the view that all rights not covered by a specific clause in the contract are retained by management. In contrast, the *implied obligations* doctrine assumes that the union recognition clause requires management to negotiate changes in terms and conditions of employment even in the absence of an express contract provision covering the issue involved.[55]

The residual rights doctrine has naturally been most popular among management practitioners. Those supporting this view argue that it derives logically from the property rights that stockholders (or the public, in a governmental organization) delegate to management. Since neither union members nor their representatives are directly accountable to the owners, they should not have a right to infringe on the ability of management to act on the owners' behalf, except in the case of an issue over which management has agreed to share its authority by way of specific contract language.

This doctrine has been challenged by labor relations scholars and arbitrators for both philosophical and practical reasons. The critics rely implicitly on the implied obligations doctrine to support their philosophical position and a theory of the employment contract that is gaining increasing popularity among behavioral scientists. Chamberlain and Kuhn, for example, proposed that while management may have a property right to allocate the resources needed to run the organization, the management of human resources requires the consent of the managed. They stated that workers are under no legal compulsion to cooperate with management.[56] Killingsworth made a similar argument, noting that management's "right" to assert discretion over any subject is limited in a very practical way by its power to impose its will on employees. He noted that the reserved rights doctrine is of little value as a legal principle because it ignores the power relationship between employer and employees.[57]

Holding a similar view are the organizational behavior theorists who have developed the concept of management's zone of acceptance or *zone of authority*. Chester Barnard and Herbert Simon averred, for example, that the authority of management depends on the employees' acceptance of management's right to direct employee behavior.[58] Workers and work groups are likely to vary widely in whether they accept a narrow or broad degree of managerial authority. In practice, therefore, the work force's acceptance and practical definition of management rights may deviate considerably from the specific rights provided in the labor agreement and from the philosophical arguments found in the management or the arbitration literature.

Productivity Bargaining

Where collective bargaining has produced work rules that inhibit labor efficiency, the parties can engage in *productivity bargaining* to eliminate those restrictions.[59] Productivity bargaining can take one of two forms: a one-shot buyout of outmoded practices; or a long-term, joint union-management program for adjusting to technological change. The latter approach will be discussed in Chapter 13.

The best example of the one-time buyout approach to productivity bargaining comes from the railroad industry. A breakthrough in the dispute over the so-called crew consist issue occurred with the negotiation of a pattern-setting agreement between the Milwaukee Railroad and the United Transportation Union (UTU) in 1978. The pattern was then adopted in the UTU agreement with Conrail and appears to be spreading to other carriers as well. The crew size controversy involved the number of brake operators assigned to a train crew.[60] Between 1960 and 1978 each crew included two brake operators, although the industry claimed during those years that technological changes made only one necessary. The 1978 agreement resolved this dispute with a prime example of the buyout approach to productivity bargaining. The Conrail agreement provided:

1. A freight train with fewer than 70 cars may operate with only one conductor. This is called a "short crew."
2. No employees will be laid off or fired because of the plan; the plan will be implemented by using attrition and job transfers.
3. Whenever a short crew is used, each member of the crew will receive $4 above the regular pay.
4. For each short crew used, Conrail will contribute $48.25 to an employee productivity fund to be divided up at the end of each year, with each employee receiving an amount based on the number of short-crew runs that person made.[61]

No quantitative estimates exist to assess how often productivity bargaining has been used to trade outmoded work rules for some form of job and income protection or security. There are, however, a number of visible and highly publicized examples in addition to the one just described. In 1960 the Pacific Maritime Association, representing the West Coast longshore industry, signed a Mechanization and Modernization Agreement with the International Longshoremen and Warehousemen's Union.[62] This agreement provided a $5 million productivity fund, wage and employment guarantees, and incentives for early retirement by high-seniority workers in return for an end to work rules requiring multiple handling of goods and employment of more workers than needed as containerization swept through the docks. In 1963 the United Steelworkers signed the Kaiser Steel Long-Range Sharing Plan, which provided job security and productivity bonuses in return for a freer hand to management to introduce new technology and revamp work rules. In 1974 the International Typographical Union and the New York City newspapers negotiated an 11-year agreement providing lifetime job security and early retirement incentives to typesetters in return for management's introduction of computerized technologies. Again, although these bargains were highly publicized at the time, we have no way of knowing how common they have been elsewhere.

As noted earlier, Chapter 12 will discuss more recent productivity and work rule changes.

THE IMPACT OF INDUSTRIAL RELATIONS PERFORMANCE ON ECONOMIC PERFORMANCE

General Economic Performance

Broader than all the questions of union effects discussed in this chapter is the question of how industrial relations performance affects economic performance. We have made an initial stab at answering this broader question in our research at the plant level. Specifically, we analyzed differences in annual plant-level data on industrial relations and economic performance at two divisions (43 plants) of the General Motors Corporation.[63] Our data show that the plants with relatively good industrial relations performance also have relatively higher labor efficiency (productivity) and product quality.

For example, the data show that higher rates of grievances and a higher degree of trust in the organizational climate (as measured by attitude surveys) are correlated with higher rates of labor efficiency and higher product quality. Regression analysis further shows that the overall variations in industrial relations performance across the plants explain a significant portion of the variance in both labor efficiency and product quality, after controlling for the size of the plant and other plant characteristics.

Norsworthy and Zabala found a similar pattern of effects for indicators of industrial relations performance in their analysis of aggregate industry-level data.[64] They went a step further than we did by converting their results into estimates of the economic losses experienced in the auto industry that were due to poor labor relations performance. The authors estimated that a 10 percent improvement in worker attitudes and behavior would have translated into a 3 to 5 percent reduction in the annual unit costs of production between 1959 and 1976. In turn, this reduction would have produced between $2.2 and $5.5 billion of annual savings in production costs over those years.

Ichniowski's analysis of variations in productivity at 11 highly capital-intensive paper mills demonstrated similar effects for variations in grievance and accident rates.[65] After controlling for the various factors of capital, materials, and energy that affect productivity in those plants, he found that productivity at the plants having the average number of grievances was 1.2 percent lower than productivity at plants with no grievances. Plants with average injury rates had 1.3 percent lower productivity rates than would have been the case if the injury rates were zero. Further analysis showed that the output losses associated with higher grievance and injury rates had substantial effects on profits. Moving from zero grievances to the average level of grievances was estimated to reduce profits in a mill by approximately 15 percent. Moving from no injuries to the average rate of injuries was estimated to result in 17 percent lower profits. Thus, even in highly capital-intensive settings, industrial relations performance at the plant level has significant effects on economic performance.

A study of productivity in the coal mining industry suggested that collective bargaining effects on productivity vary substantially over time as well as across workplaces.[66] In 1965 the bituminous coal mining industry exhibited a positive productivity differential associated with the presence of collective bargaining. In 1975, however, collective bargaining in the industry produced a negative productivity differential of 20 to 25 percent. The authors attributed this change to the effects of deteriorating industrial relations in the coal industry in the 1970s. They concluded that internal union instability, a rise in wildcat strikes, and a general deterioration of the climate between the United Mine Workers and the coal operators over that decade caused at least part, and perhaps most, of the productivity decline experienced in the industry's unionized sector. If these findings can be generalized to other contexts, we can tentatively propose that the effects of unions on productivity depend on the quality of the union-employer relationship.

The Net Effects of Unionization on Productivity

A number of recent econometric studies have estimated the differences in productivity associated with collective bargaining at the industry or firm level of analysis. Using cross-sectional, industry-by-state data, Brown and Medoff estimated that collective bargaining was associated with a 20 to 25 percent higher rate of productivity in the manufacturing sector.[67] Other studies applying the same basic methodology found positive productivity differentials attributable to collective bargaining in the wooden furniture and cement industries.[68]

A number of measurement and statistical problems plague these cross-sectional studies, however. It is extremely difficult to measure, for example, the quality of labor inputs and control for their effects. If the higher wages firms pay for union workers result in work forces of higher quality, and if this is not fully controlled for in the regression analysis, the union variable may mistakenly pick up some of this unmeasured labor quality effect.

An even more serious issue of causality clouds cross-sectional analyses of union productivity effects. Consider what unionization may imply for the long-run survival of firms and how this could affect cross-sectional analyses. Suppose firms vary substantially in their productivity because of various idiosyncratic factors, such as the special skills of the managers or work force in the firm or the locational advantages held by the firm. We know that unionization results in higher compensation. In the long run, therefore, we would expect that among firms that become unionized, those whose managers and workers have lower skills and productivity will be more apt to go out of business after unionization than those firms having highly skilled and productive employees. If we then compare the productivity of union and nonunion firms after this process has proceeded, we are likely to find that productivity is higher at the remaining union firms than at the nonunion firms. But this finding could result from the fact that the unionized firms that remained in business tended to have high productivity anyway and not because unionization raised productivity. This example illustrates how cross-sectional regression analysis ignores dynamic processes and effects.[69]

Whatever we conclude regarding union effects on productivity, we must bear in mind the difference between productivity in single organizations and the efficiency of the overall economy. Firms could raise their labor productivity by substituting capital for labor in response to higher union wages, that is, by increasing their capital-to-labor ratio. But this would lead to a lowering of the overall efficiency of the economy if the capital purchased by union firms in response to higher wage rates could have been put to better use elsewhere in the economy.

It is difficult to reconcile the cross-sectional evidence that Freeman and Medoff and others have provided with the evidence discussed earlier comparing the work rules in union and nonunion plants. We believe that the work rule flexibility found in many nonunion workplaces is of particularly high value to firms faced with economic pressures that require flexible and high-quality production, as is the case with many firms today. Although we also believe, as discussed earlier, that it is difficult to disentangle the effects of plant age from unionization, we are nevertheless willing to say that unionized workplaces are, on average, less productive than nonunion workplaces. Management certainly is acting as if that were so, as described in Chapter 6. But at the same time, hard and systematic evidence comparing the productivity of union and nonunion workers and workplaces is scarce. This is an extremely important topic for future research.

SUMMARY

The presence of a union sets off a chain reaction in a wide range of economic and behavioral job outcomes that affect the goals of employees and employers. This chapter presents a framework for tracing these effects and summarizes the existing empirical evidence. As noted in the previous chapters and at several points here, estimates of the "average" effects of collective bargaining must be interpreted with caution because there is much variation across union and nonunion workplaces. With this caveat in mind, we can now summarize our main conclusions.

1. Unions raise the wages of their members over those of comparable nonunion workers. The magnitude of this effect varies considerably over time and across occupations. The most recent studies suggest the average wage effect is between 15 and 20 percent and is somewhat higher for nonwhites than whites; for younger workers and for older workers than workers in their prime working years; and for blue-collar than white-collar workers.
2. Unions increase the range of fringe benefits available to workers and the level of benefits provided. Some of this effect is due to the built-in relationship between wages and those fringe benefits that are tied to the wage rate, while some is due to the direct effect that unions have on benefits.
3. Unions have negotiated a wide range of job security provisions. The most prominent union effect on job security lies in the protection against arbitrary discharge or discipline afforded union members through the grievance arbitration provisions found in most private sector labor agreements. Unions have also increased the security of long-service

employees through the seniority provisions in labor contracts. A minority of unions have been successful in negotiating income security provisions that supplement the state unemployment compensation system during short, temporary layoffs. A smaller minority of unions have negotiated provisions protecting the income and job security of employees affected by permanent job loss resulting from technological change or plant shutdowns. Again, the magnitude of these protections and benefits is a direct function of the worker's seniority. Recently, some bargaining agreements have provided enhanced employment security in association with pay concessions or work reorganization.

5. Unions have attempted to improve worker safety and health through a combination of negotiated provisions, labor-management committees, and federal legislation. Although contract provisions on safety and health have expanded over the past 15 or so years, we as yet have no conclusive evidence that the rate of injuries has declined in the union sector. Some comprehensive experiments with labor-management committees have, however, improved safety conditions in specific organizations. Unfortunately, there is no way to determine conclusively how these efforts will pay off over the lifetime of the workers covered under collective bargaining.

6. Unions reduce turnover, primarily by increasing the value of the jobs held by union members over the value of the alternative jobs available in the external labor market. This effect increases directly with the seniority of the worker.

7. Plant-level industrial relations performance has a substantial effect on economic performance, according to the existing evidence, but evidence on the net effect of unions on productivity is mixed. Cross-sectional econometric studies tend to show that unions raise productivity. Analysis of work rule flexibility across the union and nonunion plants of the same employer suggests that unionization is associated with less flexible and more costly work practices. The impact of unionization on productivity is mediated by age effects; unions tend to be in older plants. Ultimately, the effects of collective bargaining on productivity depend on the ability of management to adjust to higher union labor costs by modifying personnel practices, adopting technological innovations, and upgrading the quality of the work force.

Suggested Readings

For comprehensive assessments of union effects on wages, other employment conditions, productivity, and profits, see:

Freeman, Richard B., and James L. Medoff. *What Do Unions Do?* New York: Basic Books, 1984.

Lewis, H. Gregg. *Union Relative Wage Effects: A Survey*. Chicago: University of Chicago Press, 1986.

For analyses of how collective bargaining and workers have adjusted to technological change, see:

Hartman, Paul T. *Collective Bargaining and Productivity.* Berkeley: University of California Press, 1969.

Shultz, George P., and Arnold R. Weber. *Strategies for Displaced Workers.* Westport, Conn.: Greenwood Press, 1966.

Notes

1. Sumner Slichter, *Union Policies and Industrial Management* (Washington, D.C.: Brookings Institution, 1941).

2. H. Gregg Lewis, *Unionism and Relative Wages in the United States* (Chicago: University of Chicago Press, 1962).

3. See Richard B. Freeman and James L. Medoff, *What Do Unions Do?* (New York: Basic Books, 1984).

4. See, for example, Greg Duncan and Frank Stafford, "Do Union Members Receive Compensating Wage Differentials?" *American Economic Review* 70 (June 1980): 355–71; John Abowd and Henry S. Farber, "Job Queues and the Union Status of Workers," *Industrial and Labor Relations Review* 35 (April 1982): 354–67.

5. Albert Rees, *The Economics of Trade Unions* (Chicago: University of Chicago Press, 1962), 79.

6. Albert Rees, *The Economics of Trade Unions,* 2d ed. (Chicago: University of Chicago Press, 1977), 74.

7. Orley Ashenfelter, "Racial Discrimination and Trade Unionism," *Journal of Political Economy* 80 (May/June 1972): 435–64; and Greg Duncan, "A Model of Wage Growth," photocopy (Ann Arbor: University of Michigan, 1978).

8. See, for example, George E. Johnson and Kenneth Youmans, "Union Relative Wage Effects by Age and Education," *Industrial and Labor Relations Review* 24 (January 1971): 171–79.

9. Farrell E. Bloch and Mark S. Kuskin, "Wage Determination in the Union and Nonunion Sectors," *Industrial and Labor Relations Review* 31 (January 1978): 183–92.

10. Orley Ashenfelter, "Union Relative Wage Effects: New Evidence and a Survey of Their Implications for Wage Inflation," in *Econometric Contributions to Public Policy,* ed. Richard Stone and William Peterson (New York: St. Martin's Press, 1978), 31–60.

11. Richard B. Freeman, "Unionism and the Dispersion of Wages," *Industrial and Labor Relations Review* 34 (October 1980): 3–23; and Freeman, "Union Wage Practices and Wage Dispersion Within Establishments," *Industrial and Labor Relations Review* 36 (October 1982): 3–21.

12. Leonard Weiss, "Concentration and Labor Earnings," *American Economic Review* 56 (March 1966): 96–117.

13. James A. Dalton and E. J. Ford, Jr., "Concentration and Labor Earnings in

Manufacturing and Utilities," *Industrial and Labor Relations Review* 31 (October 1977): 45–60.

14. For a discussion of these and other wage administration provisions in union contracts, see U.S. Department of Labor, Bureau of Labor Statistics, *Major Collective Bargaining Agreements: Wage Administration Provisions,* Bulletin 1425-17 (Washington, D.C.: GPO, 1978).

15. Mitchell Lokiec, *Productivity and Incentives* (Columbia, S.C.: Bobbin Publishing, 1977).

16. The theoretical arguments and empirical evidence here draw heavily from Freeman and Medoff, *What Do Unions Do?*, 61–77.

17. 77 NLRB 1, 21 (1948).

18. Freeman and Medoff, *What Do Unions Do?*, 73.

19. See U.S. Chamber of Commerce, *Employee Benefits, 1983* (Washington, D.C.: U.S. Chamber of Commerce, 1984), 27.

20. A particular point of debate is whether job satisfaction is a meaningful measure of workers' evaluations of the quality of their jobs. For two recent critiques of the use of the concept, see Gerald R. Salancik and Jeffrey Pfeffer, "An Examination of Need-Satisfaction Models of Job Attitudes," *Administrative Science Quarterly* 22 (September 1977): 427–56; Daniel S. Hamermesh, "Economic Considerations in Job Satisfaction Trends," *Industrial Relations* 15 (February 1976): 111–14.

21. Tove Helland Hammer, "Relationships between Local Union Characteristics and Worker Behavior and Attitudes," *Academy of Management Journal* 21 (December 1978): 560–78.

22. Richard B. Freeman, "Job Satisfaction as an Economic Variable," *American Economic Review* 68 (May 1978): 135–41; George Borjas, "Unionism and Job Satisfaction," *Journal of Human Resources* 14 (Winter 1979): 21–40.

23. Jack Stieber, "The Case for Protection of Unorganized Employees Against Unjust Discharge," in *Proceedings of the Thirty-Second Annual Meeting, December 28–30, 1979,* ed. Barbara D. Dennis, 155–63 (Madison, Wis.: Industrial Relations Research Association, 1980).

24. The evolving law in this area is reviewed in "The Employment-At-Will Issue," BNA Special Report, part 2 (Washington, D.C.: Bureau of National Affairs, 1982).

25. Clyde W. Summers, "Arbitration of Unjust Dismissal: A Preliminary Proposal," in *The Future of Labor Arbitration in America*, ed. Benjamin Aaron et al. (New York: American Arbitration Association, 1976), 161.

26. Bureau of National Affairs, *Basic Patterns in Union Contracts, 1986* (Washington, D.C.: Bureau of National Affairs, 1986), 88.

27. Ibid., 88–89.

28. Katharine G. Abraham and James L. Medoff, "Length of Service and Promotions in Union and Nonunion Work Groups," *Industrial and Labor Relations Review* 38 (April 1985): 408–20.

29. James L. Medoff and Katharine G. Abraham, "Experience, Performance, and Earnings," *Quarterly Journal of Economics* 95 (December 1980): 703–36.

30. For a discussion of this agreement and a general treatment of the effects of equal employment opportunity laws and court rulings on collective bargaining, see Arthur B. Smith, Jr., "The Impact on Collective Bargaining of Equal Employment Opportunity Remedies," *Industrial and Labor Relations Review* 28 (April 1975): 376–94. See also Casey Ichniowski, "Have Angels Done More? The Steel Industry Consent Decree," *Industrial and Labor Relations Review* 36 (January 1983): 182–98.

31. *Franks* v. *Bowman Transportation Co.*, 424 US 747 (1976).

32. *International Brotherhood of Teamsters* v. *U.S.*, 431 US 324 (1977).

33. *United Steelworkers* v. *Weber*, 20 FEP 1 (1979).

34. *Firefighters Local Union 1784* v. *Stotts*, 34 FEP 1514 (1984).

35. *Sheet Metal Workers Local 28* v. *EEOC*, 41 FEP 107 (1986).

36. Arthur M. Ross, "Do We Have a New Industrial Feudalism?" *American Economic Review* 48 (December 1958): 903–20.

37. John F. Burton, Jr., and John E. Parker, "Interindustry Variations in Voluntary Labor Mobility," *Industrial and Labor Relations Review* 22 (January 1969): 199–216; Vladimir Stoikov and Robert L. Raimon, "Determinants of the Difference in Quit Rates Among Industries," *American Economic Review* 58 (November-December 1972): 1120–43.

38. Richard N. Block, "The Impact of Seniority Provisions on the Manufacturing Quit Rate," *Industrial and Labor Relations Review* 31 (July 1978): 474–81.

39. Freeman and Medoff, *What Do Unions Do?*

40. James G. March and Herbert A. Simon, *Organizations* (New York: Wiley, 1958).

41. Albert O. Hirschman, *Exit, Voice, and Loyalty: Responses to Decline in Firms, Organizations, and States* (Cambridge: Harvard University Press, 1970).

42. Freeman and Medoff, *What Do Unions Do?*, 94–110.

43. David E. Dimick, "Employer Control and Discipline," *Relations Industrielles* 33, no. 1 (1978): 23–27.

44. Thomas A. Kochan and Richard N. Block, "An Interindustry Analysis of Bargaining Outcomes: Preliminary Evidence from Two-Digit Industries," *Quarterly Journal of Economics* 91 (August 1977): 431–52.

45. Bureau of National Affairs, *Basic Patterns in Union Contracts, 1986,* 71.

46. Ibid., 41.

47. For a good description and analysis of SUB plans, see Audrey Freedman, *Security Bargains Reconsidered: SUB, Severance Pay, Guaranteed Work* (New York: Conference Board, 1978).

48. Ibid., 83. For an international perspective on plant closing limitations see Bennett Harrison, "The International Movement for Prenotification of Plant Closings," *Industrial Relations* 23 (Fall 1984): 387–409.

49. Craig A. Olson, "An Analysis of Wage Differentials Received by Workers on Dangerous Jobs," *Journal of Human Resources* 16 (Spring 1981): 167–85.

50. These results are reported in Thomas A. Kochan and David E. Helfman, *The Effects of Collective Bargaining on Economic and Behavioral Job Outcomes*, report to Assistant Secretary of Labor for Policy, Evaluation and Research, October 1979.

51. Paul S. Goodman, *Assessing Organizational Change* (New York: Wiley-Interscience, 1979).

52. *Economic Report of the President* (Washington, D.C.: GPO, 1986), 303.

53. Anil Verma, "Union and Nonunion Industrial Relations at the Plant Level," Ph.D. dissertation (Cambridge: Massachusetts Institute of Technology, 1983).

54. Bureau of National Affairs, *Basic Patterns in Union Contracts, 1986*, 86.

55. For a discussion of these two views, see Frank Elkouri and Edna Asper Elkouri, *How Arbitration Works*, 3d ed. (Washington, D.C.: Bureau of National Affairs, 1976), 412–35.

56. Neil W. Chamberlain and James W. Kuhn, *Collective Bargaining*, 2d ed. (New York: McGraw-Hill, 1965), 89–90.

57. Charles C. Killingsworth, "Management Rights Revisited," in *Arbitration and Social Change, Proceedings of the Twenty-Second Annual Meetings of the National Academy of Arbitrators*, ed. Gerald G. Somers (Washington, D.C.: Bureau of National Affairs, 1969), 3–13.

58. Chester I. Barnard, *The Functions of the Executive* (Cambridge: Harvard University Press, 1938); Herbert A. Simon, *Administrative Behavior* (New York: Macmillan, 1947). See also Edgar H. Schein, *Organizational Psychology* (Englewood Cliffs, N.J.: Prentice-Hall, 1965).

59. See Robert B. McKersie and Lawrence C. Hunter, *Pay, Productivity and Collective Bargaining* (London: Macmillan, 1973).

60. Douglas M. McCabe, *The Crew Size Dispute in the Railroad Industry* (Washington, D.C.: Federal Railroad Administration, U.S. Department of Transportation, 1977).

61. "Contrail-UTU Agree on Crew Consist, Wage Package, and Drafting One-Year Agreement," *Daily Labor Report*, no. 179, 14 September 1978, A-7.

62. Paul T. Hartman, *Collective Bargaining and Productivity: The Longshore Mechanization Agreement* (Berkeley: University of California Press, 1969).

63. Harry C. Katz, *Shifting Gears* (Cambridge: MIT Press, 1985), 105–32.

64. J. R. Norsworthy and Craig A. Zabala, "Worker Attitudes, Worker Behavior, and Productivity in the U.S. Automobile Industry, 1959–1976," *Industrial and Labor Relations Review* 38 (July 1985): 544–57.

65. Casey Ichniowski, "How Do Labor Relations Matter? A Study of Productivity in Eleven Manufacturing Plants," Ph.D. dissertation (Cambridge: Massachusetts Institute of Technology, 1983).

66. Marguarita Connerton, Richard B. Freeman, and James L. Medoff, "Productivity and Industrial Relations: The Case of U.S. Bituminous Coal," photocopy (Cambridge: Harvard University, 1983).

67. Charles Brown and James L. Medoff, "Trade Unions in the Production Process," *Journal of Political Economy* 86 (June 1978): 335–78.

68. Kim B. Clark, "The Impact of Unionization on Productivity: A Case Study," *Industrial and Labor Relations Review* 33 (July 1980): 451–69; J. Frantz, "The Impact of Trade Unions on Productivity in the Wood Household Furniture Industry," undergraduate thesis (Cambridge: Harvard University, 1976).

69. This also is another example of the potential effects of selection bias in econometric analysis.

CHAPTER 12

Diversity and Dynamism in Industrial Relations

$\mathbf{T}$he previous chapter reviewed evidence on the average effects of collective bargaining on various job outcomes. It would be a mistake if the reader came away from that analysis with the impression that there is little variation in the effects of collective bargaining. The opposite is very much the case. Collective bargaining yields diverse outcomes across plants, firms, and industries, at any one time and over time.

Collective bargaining outcomes negotiated in the 1980s have taken a markedly different path from the past, especially in those cases where unions have agreed to "concessionary" settlements. We analyze the most recent collective bargaining experience in detail in this chapter both because these developments are interesting in their own right and because they are particularly illustrative of the diverse and evolutionary nature of collective bargaining.

But before focusing on recent collective bargaining, we should first consider the factors that produce dynamism and diversity in collective bargaining. Our theoretical framework emphasizes the roles that environmental factors and strategic choice play in the evolution of industrial relations systems. To appreciate fully how the environment and strategic choice engender diversity in collective bargaining experiences, we need first to step back and view collective bargaining within the broader context of alternative industrial relations systems. We therefore begin this chapter by describing the diverse patterns of personnel policies that emerge across union and nonunion workplaces and the role that managerial and union strategic choice, as influenced by the environment, plays in the evolution of these various patterns of industrial relations.

THE ROLE OF STRATEGIC CHOICE

As described in earlier parts of this book, the evolution of industrial relations practices is influenced by environmental factors such as the economy, public policy, technology, demographics, and the law. Chapter 3 discussed how these environmental factors influence bargaining outcomes. Here we focus on the effects of the strategic choices made by labor and management in the face of those environmental constraints. First, let us review the basic ways strategic choice operates.

Management makes strategic choices in the design of personnel policies and through responses to employees' desires and expectations, including their demands for union representation. Management also makes other strategic choices regarding its business plans, choices that sometimes are heavily based on consideration of the linkages between human resource and business strategies.

If the employees become unionized, management will attempt to use its bargaining power to shape collective bargaining processes and outcomes within the context of its bilateral relationship with the union. Although management's need to negotiate with union representatives will add various constraints to its strategic options, the employer's preferences regarding personnel policies, as in nonunion environments, will nonetheless be heavily influenced by the linkages between human resource and business strategies. Managers may have to make decisions regarding, for example, whether to continue investing in a given product line, whether to try to operate nonunion plants to produce a given product, or whether to supply a product by relying more heavily on the outsourcing of parts or production to another plant or firm. These decisions all influence management's strike and bargaining leverage in any part of the firm covered by a labor contract.

Unions make a number of strategic choices concerning their collective bargaining strategy. At a very broad level, as discussed in Chapter 5, unions must choose how much to focus their resources and attention on collective bargaining as opposed to other means, such as political action, through which they could improve employment conditions. At the bargaining table unions make strategic choices between pushing hard for improvements in employment conditions and minimizing the trade-offs in employment that might follow from any resulting labor cost increases. Unions also make strategic choices concerning the mix within a collective bargaining settlement, such as the relative size of current compensation (wages) versus deferred compensation (pension benefits).

Many factors influence these strategic choices. For example, it appears that the more senior union members, in part because they are more likely to represent the median voter in the union, tend to have a strong influence on union wage policies. This explains why unions are often unconcerned about the employment displacement that may result from a settlement unless layoffs have already been substantial or a plant closing is threatened.

Nonetheless, the political dynamics within unions force consideration of numerous points of view. The course of concessionary bargaining, discussed in more detail later in this chapter, provides a number of examples of the diverse strategies unions have pursued when threatened by layoffs.

As described later in this chapter, a few unions have recently begun to experiment with an industrial relations pattern that is markedly different from the traditional system. Some unions have been willing to agree to contingent compensation and teamwork systems in exchange for management guarantees of more extensive employment security and worker and union participation. Other unions have rejected this restructuring of the traditional industrial relations system. Furthermore, virtually every union is now engaged in intense internal debate over whether the union should encourage and participate in work and labor relations restructuring.[1]

In nonunion settings, employees' choices, such as whether to stay with the employer and how vigorously to pursue training and promotion opportunities, often find expression through informal channels. These informal expressions can take the form of absenteeism or varying levels of job performance. Nonunion workers also make choices regarding union representation and how vigorously to press for it.

Workers, as individuals, also make a variety of career decisions and choices in unionized settings. The difference under unionization is that the union enables employees to act collectively in making their choices, to use their bargaining power to shape and express their individual career goals and decisions through collective bargaining. Let us now discuss more specifically how the strategic choices made by individual employers and unions have led to the diversity that exists across industrial relations systems in the United States. The basic patterns of these choices, as discussed in the following two sections, are outlined in Figure 12–1.

NONUNION INDUSTRIAL RELATIONS SYSTEMS

Even within the nonunion sector there is wide diversity in personnel, or what we prefer to call industrial relations, practices. In broad terms nonunion industrial relations systems exhibit three basic patterns.[2] It should be remembered that these patterns are only ideal types and that some firms contain elements of one or more patterns.

The Paternalistic Pattern

In what can be called the *paternalistic pattern* of industrial relations, personnel policies tend to be informally administered, and their administration involves substantial discretion by operating managers. A paternalistic firm would, for example, offer no formal leave and sickness policies, and its supervisors would grant paid leaves on a case-by-case basis. Supervisors and

FIGURE 12–1
Patterns of industrial relations

	Nonunion			Union		
	Paternalistic	Bureaucratic	Human resource management	Conflict	New Deal	Participatory
Characteristics of basic personnel policies	Informal	Formal	Company identification	Distrust	Stability	Flexible
	Managerial discretion	Standardized	Strong corporate culture	Instability	Job control	Informal
	High variation	Rule bound			Formal and written rules	
Characteristics of specific personnel policies	Piece rates	Job evaluation	Employment stabilization	Strikes	Detailed job classifications	Employment security
	Temporary work	Deferred compensation	Pay-for-knowledge	Decertifications	Wage formulas	Contingent compensation
			Work teams		Seniority-based layoffs	Work teams
			Elaborate complaint procedures		Standardized wages	Labor-management committees
					Elaborate contracts	All employees salaried

other managers in these firms similarly exercise a high degree of discretion over other discipline and pay policies—with the result that the employment conditions of employees differ substantially across work groups, plants, and firms. This pattern is common among small retail stores, such as grocery stores and gas stations, and in small manufacturing plants.[3]

The Bureaucratic Pattern

Larger firms find the diversity common to paternalistic firms too unsettling and costly. In their efforts to achieve economies of scale, larger firms find it advantageous to standardize and bureaucratize personnel policies, thereby creating a *bureaucratic pattern* of personnel administration. These firms have also come to realize that diversity can spur unionization if some employees believe other employees elsewhere in the firm are benefiting from more favorable policies than they are.

The bureaucratic pattern is characterized by highly formalized procedures, such as clear (and typically written) policies regarding pay, leaves, promotion, and discipline. Firms following the bureaucratic pattern also make use of highly detailed and formalized job classifications and use job evaluation schemes to determine pay levels and job duties. Examples of firms that follow this pattern include most of the large, nonunion corporations that expanded in the post–World War II period.

The Human Resource Management Pattern

As an outgrowth of their efforts to increase flexibility and cost competitiveness while maintaining their nonunion status, a number of firms began to adopt a new pattern of personnel policies in the 1970s.[4] This sophisticated *human resource management (HRM) pattern*, like the bureaucratic pattern, relies on formal policies, but the nature of those policies is different from that traditionally found in nonunion firms. The HRM pattern includes policies such as employment stabilization, team forms of work organization, skill (or knowledge) based pay, and elaborate communication and complaint procedures. Like the firms following the other nonunion patterns, the HRM firms vigilantly try to avoid unionization. Where they differ from the other nonunion firms is in the extent to which they consider union avoidance questions in decisions such as plant location and in the design and implementation of other personnel policies such as employment stabilization and communication policies. In their efforts at union avoidance, as in so many of their personnel policies, what distinguishes the sophisticated HRM firms is the extent to which they coordinate and plan their various policies and the resulting close linkages that result across their various personnel policies.

The HRM firms also are noteworthy for the extensive measures they take in trying to induce employees to identify their interests with the long-term interests of the firm. Those measures include publishing company newsletters, offering salaries to all employees, and nurturing strong corporate cultures. Here we can cite as examples such firms as IBM, Procter and Gamble, and Delta Airlines.[5]

A number of factors influence which of these patterns nonunion firms will follow. Management values and strategies play an important role. For instance, many of the sophisticated HRM firms had strong founding executives who helped initiate strong corporate cultures.[6] Business strategy also makes a difference. The sophisticated HRM pattern seems to provide the advantage of more flexible and adaptable work organization through the use of team systems and skill-based pay. These characteristics are particularly attractive to firms with rapidly changing technologies and markets. Thus, it is no surprise that many firms in high-technology industries follow the sophisticated HRM pattern.

Steel minimills also illustrate how business strategy is linked to personnel practices. Among nonunion minimills those producing a wide variety of products ("market" mills) and those concentrating on high-quality products tend to follow the sophisticated HRM pattern, while those pursuing a low-cost and high-volume product strategy tend to follow a variant of the bureaucratic pattern.[7]

UNION PATTERNS OF INDUSTRIAL RELATIONS

The dominant form of collective bargaining in the United States since World War II was characterized by highly detailed and formal contracts, grievance arbitration, seniority-based layoff procedures, numerous and detailed job classifications, and pay systems that relied heavily on pattern bargaining and formulaic wage criteria. In Chapter 2 we described this New Deal pattern of collective bargaining in detail. Here we will focus on the diversity of outcomes that existed across time and across plants even within the firms following the general New Deal model. We will also consider how economic pressures and strategic choices helped to produce this diversity. But before doing so, we define two other patterns of collective bargaining: the conflict pattern and the participatory pattern.

Under the *conflict pattern* labor and management are engaged in a serious struggle over their basic rights, and often over whether there will be union representation. Because of the high costs to both parties of engaging in this intense conflict, the pattern tends not to be stable but instead transitory, occurring during periods when the firm is moving either from a union to a nonunion pattern or from a nonunion pattern to a stable form of the traditional New Deal bargaining relationship. We later discuss some recent conflicts that ended with the loss of union representation.

A number of contemporary firms and unions have been experimenting with a *participatory pattern* of industrial relations, characterized by contingent compensation systems (linking firm or work group pay to economic performance), team forms of work organization, employment security programs, and more direct participation by workers and unions in business decision making. We postpone until the next chapter a more complete discussion of these participatory experiments, which have been an outgrowth of pressures for cost reduction and greater flexibility in the management of human resources.

Diversity across Bargaining Relationships

It is important to recognize that wide variation exists in the collective bargaining outcomes of firms following the New Deal collective bargaining model. Consider, for example, the variations in wage increases that are negotiated under collective bargaining in any given year.

In 1978 the average wage increase negotiated in major bargaining units (units covering 1,000 workers or more) was 7.6 percent for the first year of the agreement and 6.4 percent over the life of the contract (normally three years). But even in this year that preceded the recent wave of concessionary settlements, one-third of the workers in these large units settled for less than 6 percent in the first year, while 24 percent received increases of 10 percent or more.

In 1985 the average wage increase negotiated in major bargaining units was 2.3 percent for the first year of the agreement and 2.7 percent over the life of the contract. Reflecting the diversity of economic pressures, one-third of the workers covered under these agreements settled for no wage increase in the first year, while 25 percent received a raise between 4 and 6 percent, and 8 percent of the workers received increases over 6 percent.[8] Over time, variations in wage settlements translate into considerable wage differentials.

The difference between auto industry and apparel industry contracts is but one example of interindustry variations in collective bargaining outcomes. In 1986 the average autoworker earned $13.50 per hour, whereas the average apparel worker earned only $5.87 per hour. The average autoworker was also entitled to more vacation time, more holidays, and about $600 more in monthly pension benefits upon retirement than the average apparel worker.[9]

Collective bargaining also produces diverse outcomes across workplaces within the same industry and even within the same firm. The data in Table 12-1 illustrate this diversity among plants within one division of General Motors in the full calendar year 1979. Despite their common technology, union, and employer, the 18 plants observed exhibited a wide variety of grievance, discipline, and absenteeism rates, as well as diverse performance on other industrial relations and economic performance measures. Note, for example, that grievances per 100 workers varied from a low of 24 in one plant to a high of 450 in another plant. Absenteeism varied between 4.7 percent and 10.3 percent. The number of contract demands introduced in the negotiations for the 1979 local agreements in these plants varied from a low of 4 to a high of 1,163. In the case of the indices of economic performance, however, it is not as easy to interpret the significance of the reported

TABLE 12–1

Measures of industrial relations and economic performance in 18 GM plants, 1979

Performance indicators	Mean	Minimum	Maximum	Standard deviation
Grievances	124.3	24.5	450.2	133.1
Absenteeism	7.4	4.7	10.3	1.7
Discipline	44.5	20.0	86.8	17.5
Contract demands	364.6	4.0	1163.0	196.4
Negotiation time	76.8	−110.0	532.0	143.4
Climate	2.9	2.2	3.8	.5
Product quality	127.6	122.0	137.0	3.7
Direct-labor efficiency	87.4	57.1	103.7	13.2

Source: Harry C. Katz, Thomas A. Kochan, and Kenneth R. Gobeille, "Industrial Relations Performance, Economic Performance, and QWL Programs: An Interplant Analysis," *Industrial and Labor Relations Review* 37 (October 1983): 8.

Legend:

Grievances: the number of grievances filed per 100 workers.

Absenteeism: the absentee rate as a percentage of straight-time hours, excluding contractual days off.

Discipline: the number of oral warnings, disciplinary leaves, and discharges assessed per 100 workers.

Contract demands: the number of contract demands submitted by the local union in triannual local contract negotiations.

Negotiation time: the number of days taken to reach settlement in local contract negotiations before (negative) or after (positive) settlement of the master agreement between GM and the UAW international.

Climate: an average score (based on a one to five response format) on five survey questions measuring the state of labor-management relations in the plant. The survey was administered to all managerial and supervisory employees in the plant. The higher the average score, the more cooperative the relations.

Product quality: an index derived from a count of the number of faults and demerits that appear in inspections of the product adjusted for differences in product attributes.

Direct-labor efficiency: an index comparing the actual hours of direct labor input to standardized hours adjusted for differences in product attributes.

variations in the indices because they are the product of GM's particular accounting and quality-control systems. Nonetheless, these figures do show considerable variation around their means.

What explains this diversity in industrial relations performance across the plants, all of which were following the same basic New Deal pattern of industrial relations? In part, the diversity may stem from differences in the work forces and the managerial styles or personalities in each plant. Or it may stem from the volatile nature of labor-management relations. In some plants the two sides seemed to be caught in what Fox termed a low-trust dynamic, in which mistrust leads to ever-deteriorating industrial relations and economic performance and ever-deteriorating interpersonal relations.[10] Nonetheless, the exact source of interplant diversity in industrial relations performance within the same organization remains something of a mystery, and an important subject for future research.

Diversity over Time: Concessionary Bargaining

As Chapter 3 pointed out, the bargaining power of labor and management varies as a function of changes in the environment. When the environment puts unions in a strong bargaining position, they tend to win relatively favorable contracts, and the obverse. Changes in the environment—be they economic, public policy, demographic, or technological changes—thereby contribute to the diversity found within collective bargaining relationships over time.

The collective bargaining agreements signed during the "concessionary" period of the early 1980s differed strikingly from previous settlements. The settlements of the 1980s serve as a vivid example of how collective bargaining outcomes and processes can change substantially from one time to another. In this section we review some of the central features of agreements reached in the 1980s. Part of our objective is to summarize the common terms of those settlements and assess the extent to which the settlements amounted to labor givebacks on the one hand, versus labor gains through the negotiation of new issues such as employment security on the other— issues labor had long wanted to discuss at the bargaining table. Another analytic objective is to identify the factors that contributed to concessionary bargaining, both the environmental factors and the strategic choices made by labor and management.

Pay concessions. Many agreements negotiated in the early 1980s called for either pay cuts or pay freezes. In 1982, 1.5 million workers, or 44 percent of those covered by newly signed major collective bargaining agreements, received first-year wage cuts or freezes.[11] In 1983, 15 percent of workers covered by major agreements received first-year wage cuts, and another 22 percent received first-year wage freezes. In a summary of Bureau of Labor Statistics data on wage freezes and pay cuts in collective bargaining contracts covering 1,000 or more workers, Mitchell showed that between 1980 and 1984 about 50 percent of union members under those contracts experienced cuts or freezes lasting longer than one year.[12]

These wage concessions contributed to a nationwide drop in the rate of compensation increases, as illustrated in Table 12–2. Part of the decline in compensation increases reflected the diminishing contribution of cost-of-living adjustment (COLA) clauses in union contracts. Not only had the pace of inflation slowed, but, in a number of agreements, COLA payments were deferred or temporarily eliminated. Whereas COLA payments had accounted for 33.7 percent of the effective wage adjustments in major

TABLE 12–2

Percentage changes in compensation and prices in the United States, 1979–85

	1979	1980	1981	1982	1983	1984	1985
Compensation adjustments over the life of contracts covering 5,000 workers or more	6.6%	7.1%	8.3%	2.8%	3.0%	2.8%	2.8%
Employment costs (wages, salaries, and benefits):							
Union	9.0	10.9	9.6	6.5	4.6	3.4	2.6
Nonunion	8.5	8.0	8.5	6.1	5.2	4.5	4.6
Annual percentage increase in the consumer price index (December to December)	13.3	12.4	8.9	3.9	3.8	4.0	3.8

Sources: For compensation adjustments, *Current Wage Developments* 37, no. 2 (1986): table 15; for employment costs, *Current Wage Developments*, various issues; for annual increase in the CPI, *Economic Report of the President* (Washington, D.C.: GPO, 1987), table B-58.

collective bargaining agreements in 1981, in 1983 they accounted for only 15 percent of those adjustments.[13]

Although the growth of nonunion wages and salaries was also slowing in the early 1980s, by 1983 nonunion employment costs had begun to rise faster than union costs (see Table 12–2). This trend began to reverse the substantial widening of the union-nonunion wage gap that had taken place in the 1970s.

The slowdown in pay growth was particularly acute in the most heavily unionized firms, often the hardest hit by competitive pressures. Unions in those firms also suffered the greatest losses in bargaining power in the 1980s. For example, a regression analysis of data from the 1983 Conference Board survey found that the more highly unionized firms negotiated smaller wage increases than the less unionized firms.[14] This development was a conspicuous departure from the patterns of wage outcomes negotiated during the 1970s.

It is not clear whether the slowdown in union wage and fringe benefit advances represents a *structural* shift in the wage-setting process or only a temporary one. Some wage equations that accurately predicted wage settlements in the 1960s and 1970s overpredict the wages negotiated between 1980 and 1984, in some cases by as many as 3 percentage points annually.[15] But some researchers have concluded that wage setting in the early 1980s did not differ from what one would have expected given the economic changes under way at the time. Freeman, for example, using Current Population

Survey data, found only a slight drop in the union-nonunion wage differential from 1977 to 1984 across a number of industries.[16] He also found that the percentage of workers taking wage cuts or freezes in the early 1980s is well predicted by a simple equation using the inflation and unemployment rates from 1955 to the 1980s. We will need to see much more research into this question before we can conclude that a basic structural change in union wage setting has taken place, much less determine the nature and causes of any such change.

Whatever the future may tell us, there is no doubt that the wage settlements of the early and mid-1980s were extremely small. It also is clear that union bargaining power in the 1980s seriously eroded. This shift in the balance of power between labor and management was obvious in employers' aggressive requests for early contract openings, their demands for a decentralization of bargaining structures, and their shifting away from a strategy of promoting industrial peace to one of emphasizing control over labor costs, even at the risk of major disruptions in union-management relations. In the process, management often broke with traditional communications and other protocols of bargaining and demanded major changes in the noneconomic terms of the employment contract as well.

Unions responded to threatened deep cuts in employment by accepting wage and work rule concessions and, where they had the power to do so, by negotiating quid pro quos that gained them greater employment security and more influence in managerial decision making. Where quid pro quos were negotiated, unions essentially traded short-run cash-saving concessions for noncash benefits that would enhance their ability to represent their members in the future.

These developments were concentrated in those settings under the severest economic pressures and where employers sought industrial relations change as part of their overall business strategies or where unions sought change as part of their representational strategies. An intensified threat from either domestic nonunion or international competitors was the driving force behind labor and management decisions to make major modifications in their traditional bargaining approach. The growth in the union-nonunion wage differential over the 1970s had only served to increase the competitive pressure from the nonunion sector. In addition, in industries such as airlines, trucking, and communications, governmental deregulation opened the door to new entrants to their markets, abruptly escalating cost competition. Further exacerbating the pressures to cut costs in the union sector was the deep macroeconomic recession of the early 1980s.

As these competitive pressures mounted, union members faced large-scale layoffs and plant closings. Cappelli's analysis of concessionary agreements reached in 1982 revealed the important role played by actual or threatened employment loss to large numbers of union members.[17]

Figure 12–2 outlines the key concessionary events or agreements that emerged in the early 1980s and some of the strikes that surrounded their

FIGURE 12–2
Key events in concessionary bargaining

Case	Date	Significance
Chrysler–UAW	October 1979	Chrysler breaks from the historic patterns that had linked its contract with the UAW agreements at GM and Ford. COLA and other pay increases are postponed and later eliminated, and in exchange for these and other concessions Douglas Fraser, then president of the UAW, is put on the Chrysler board of directors.
Federal air traffic controllers (PATCO)	August 1981	President Reagan fires striking controllers, setting a significant example for other employers. (See chapter 14.)
GM–UAW, Ford–UAW	March 1982	Early renegotiation of contracts brings pay and work rule concessions. The UAW wins profit sharing, employment security, and other quid pro quos in exchange.
Continental Airlines	September 1983	Claiming bankruptcy protection, Continental abrogates its collective bargaining agreements and lowers employee pay and benefits by approximately one-fourth. Employees then go on strike, but Continental continues to fly.
American Airlines	November 1983	Introduction of a lower tier of pay (one-half of existing rates) for new pilot hires. Two-tier pay then spreads to many other airlines and industries.
Hormel–UFCW	October 1984	A strike by Local P-9 at Austin (began in protest against wage cuts) leads to a bitter dispute between the local and its national union (UFCW). The local union is eventually put into receivership by the national union, and a settlement is reached keeping the Austin plant's wages in line with other Hormel plants and meat-packing companies.

introduction. Like so many concessionary settlements, in all the cases outlined in the figure workers eventually accepted pay and benefits that involved either nominal pay cuts or pay increases that were significantly below the increases provided in previous contracts in these firms.

In addition to producing lower pay settlements, a number of recent agreements introduced or expanded the use of contingent compensation systems that link worker pay to company performance. In some cases this link was established through profit sharing or employee stock ownership plans

(ESOPs), the latter being an extreme version of this development. Profit sharing or stock ownership arose at firms such as Eastern Airlines and the LTV Steel Company as a quid pro quo for pay and work rule concessions and as part of desperate efforts to avoid bankruptcy. At other firms, such as the major automakers, contingent compensation in the form of profit sharing (in addition to being a quid pro quo for union concessions) was introduced in response to the growing volatility of product sales.

Again we must ask whether these changes in compensation systems represent a fundamental shift in industrial relations patterns, and a shift linked to other changes in industrial relations, or merely a temporary feature of concessionary bargaining. The experiences over the next few years, particularly in those firms whose economic status improves, will be revealing.

Recent work rule changes. In their efforts to slow the growth in unit labor costs and respond to environmental pressures, labor and management in the 1980s often made changes in work rules part of their concessionary labor agreements. In a number of trucking companies, work rule changes involved drivers' taking on some loading tasks. In steel plants the concessions included increases in the pace of work, often accomplished through reductions in staffing levels. Airline pilots and flight attendants were induced to agree to increases in their flight hours. Autoworkers made concessions that limited the frequency of intraplant transfers (bumps) that were allowed during layoffs. For many workers across industries, work rule concessions also brought reductions in the number of job classifications and a lessening of the role seniority plays in job transfers and job assignments. Figure 12–3 outlines how the National Steel Company reduced the number of job classifications for craft workers in one of its plants, as part of a concessionary contract signed in 1986.

In itself, the negotiation of work rule change was not unusual. The tendency for employers to question work rule provisions more aggressively during periods of slack demand or intensified competition has been well documented in the collective bargaining literature. Slichter described just such an effect resulting from the intensified competition between union and nonunion plants that took place historically during various recessions and the depression of the 1930s.[18] The 1958–59 recession also resulted in U.S. employers' taking a hard line on work rules and attempting to regain some of the prerogatives they had gradually lost during the business expansions of World War II and the early postwar years.[19] The productivity bargaining literature of the 1950s and early 1970s represented another installment in the saga of how work rules are subject to periodic buyouts during hard times.[20] Finally, the 1972 recession prompted Henle to document cases of "reverse collective bargaining" that came about under the downturn.[21] Nevertheless, although pay and work rule concessions were a part of collective bargain-

FIGURE 12–3
A draft of job unification of trades and crafts in a steel works

New job classification   *Existing job classification*

Electrician ———————————— Motor inspector
                                  Wireman
                                  Electrical repairman
                                  Wireman leader
                                  Power repairman
                                  Tack welding function

Electronic technician ————————— Instrument repairman
                                  Electronic repairman

Motor winder ———————————— Winder

Mechanic ——————————————— Millwright
                                  Maintenance repairman
                                  Pipe fitter
                                  Rigger
                                  Welder
                                  Fitting fabricator
                                  Pipe repairman
                                  Roll shop machine repairman
                                  Maintenance repair layout man
                                  Rigger shop layout man
                                  Sheeter
                                  Rigger leader
                                  Systems controller
                                  Rigger shop general layout man
                                  Weld shop equipment repairman
                                  General mechanic—rigger shop
                                  Layout man—dock

Crane repairman ———————————— Crane millwright
                                  Crane inspector

Refrigeration repairman ———————— Refrigeration repairman

Machinist ———————————————— Machinist
                                  Bearing repairman

Mobile equipment ————————————— Mobile equipment mechanic
  repairman   Tractor repairman

Blacksmith ———————————————— Blacksmith
                                  Forger

FIGURE 12–3 (*continued*)

Industrial carpenter ───────────── Carpenter
                                      Painter
                                       Decorative painter
                                       Plasterer
                                       Sign painter

Bricklayer ───────────────── Bricklayer

Turbine and boiler ───────── Turbine repairman
    repairman   Boiler repairman

Roll turner ──────────────── Roll turner

Electrical helper ─────────── Motor inspector helper
                                       Wireman helper
                                       Instrument repairman helper
                                       Electronic repairman helper
                                       Repairman helper (winder)
                                       Repairman helper (yard)
                                       Tractor repairman helper
                                       Crane millwright helper
                                       Power repairman helper

Mechanical helper ────────── Millwright helper
                                       Welder helper
                                       Maintenance repairman
                                         helper
                                       Pipe fitter helper
                                       Rigger helper
                                       Machinist helper
                                       Blacksmith helper

Service helper ───────────── Carpenter helper
                                       Painter helper
                                       Bricklayer helper
                                       Helper (roll shop)
                                       Turbine and machine
                                         repairman helper
                                       Turbine repair helper

Source: Takahara Yamagami, "The Survival Strategy for the U.S. Steel Industry," master's thesis (Cambridge: Sloan School of Management, Massachusetts Institute of Technology, 1987).

ing in the past, particularly during deep recessions, the recent depth and pervasiveness of these concessions is unprecedented in all the years since the Great Depression.

The general focus of management's recent demands for concessions has been to increase its flexibility in human resource management. This push has been particularly salient in management proposals for broader job classifications, greater managerial discretion in allocating overtime, more liberal subcontracting rights, and restrictions on voluntary transfers or other movements across jobs.

In some cases modifications in pay and work rules came about only after bitter strikes — strikes that occasionally ended with the elimination of union representation. Wilson Meatpacking and Continental Airlines underwent racking and prolonged strikes and used bankruptcy protection to impose substantially lower pay and less costly work rules after their unions had refused to agree to those terms in negotiations. Other meat-packing and some trucking firms also used reorganizations in ownership to achieve lower labor costs. Some of those firms closed their unionized operations and then reopened them on a nonunion basis, hiring the same workers back under much less favorable terms.

The early 1980s generally saw an increased willingness on management's part to hire replacements in an attempt to break strikes. In firms such as Phelps Dodge, management succeeded in those efforts and eventually the union was dislodged in a decertification vote held among the ranks of the now-permanent replacements.[22] Not all acrimonious strikes ended with the demise of union representation, however, as noted previously in the Greyhound case described in Box 2–8.

The role of management and union strategy.   The strategic choices of management and unions guided the course and consequences of concessionary bargaining. Managerial decisions, often taken long before contract negotiations, influenced the degree of economic pressure for union concessions. As Chapter 7 pointed out, management's investment and product decisions have direct effects on industrial relations. Whether management, for example, chooses a low-cost, high-volume product strategy rather than a high-quality, high-innovation strategy shapes the extent to which the employer is concerned with lowering wage costs.

Cappelli has provided an interesting example of the role of managerial business strategy in his analysis of the course of airline concessionary bargaining in the early 1980s.[23] The author points out that those airline carriers, such as USAir and Piedmont Airlines, that succeeded as regional carriers were under less pressure than the others to engage in concessionary bargaining because by servicing flights where they had monopoly power, these carriers managed to avoid intense price competition. Among the national carriers, by contrast, deregulation had led to intensified competition and pressure on the carriers to lower their labor costs. Cappelli also noted that it was the financially stronger national airlines, such as American and United, that first secured pay and work rule concessions; these carriers had the wherewithal to offer employment security in exchange for the concessions. Airlines such as Continental and later TWA, on the other hand, had to resort to more drastic measures to win concessions—namely, bitter strikes— because they faced the threat of bankruptcy, were under extreme pressure for immediate labor cost cuts, and found it difficult to trade any quid pro quos for the concessions.

Management's strategic initiatives altered the process of bargaining as well. As Chapter 4 pointed out, employers in the 1980s pressed to decentralize bargaining structures. To convince the work force that concessions were necessary, management also introduced new communication tactics, some of which bypassed the traditional role unions played as an intermediary between management and workers. At American Airlines, for example, direct mailings outlining management's position to the employees played a critical role in labor negotiations held in 1983. Auto companies continue to use news broadcasts and analyses shown on video monitors on the shop floor to apprise workers of industry developments.

Airline bargaining also reveals some of the varying union strategies at play in concessionary bargaining. As Cappelli demonstrated, the various unions representing pilots and flight attendants often were more willing to agree to concessions than was the International Association of Machinists (IAM), which represents airline maintenance workers. Part of the explanation for this divergence lies in ideology: The pilots and flight attendants were less opposed to concessions as a matter of principle than the IAM, whose national leader repeatedly condemned concession making over the course of the early 1980s. Labor market factors were also important, however; the pilots and flight attendants had a great deal of income to lose if their employer went bankrupt, unlike the airline maintenance workers, who could more easily find comparable employment elsewhere in the labor market. The dispute at George A. Hormel & Co. mentioned in Figure 12–2 is another example of the dissension and debate under way within unions concerning whether concessions are appropriate.

The course of collective bargaining in the steel industry in the mid-1980s further exemplifies the important role played by strategic choice. In 1986 bargaining for new national agreements at the major integrated steel mills took place on a company-by-company basis, in sharp contrast to the long tradition of coordinated national bargaining between the United Steelworkers (USW) and the major steel corporations. (This is also a further illustration of the recent erosion of centralized bargaining discussed in Chapter 4.) In 1986 the outcomes of this decentralized bargaining varied substantially across the major steel companies. Without taking a strike, the Wheeling-Pittsburgh,

National, and LTV steel companies all reached contract settlements that included wage and work rule concessions but provided USW members with profit sharing or stock payouts and with enhanced forms of participation in business decision making. Contracts at the three companies did vary somewhat, but together their negotiations stand in particularly sharp contrast to those at USX, formerly U.S. Steel. USX and the USW engaged in a 184-day strike in 1986 before reaching a settlement that did not differ substantially from the settlements reached at the steel companies that had peacefully negotiated agreements earlier in 1986.[24] Why the difference?

The most important factor appears to have been the history of poor relations between U.S. Steel and the USW, a history shaped in recent years by various strategic business decisions made by the company's management. U.S. Steel had antagonized the USW and its members when, after winning pay concessions in the 1982 steel negotiations, it purchased the Marathon Oil Company. The steelworkers had assumed, mistakenly, that the profits generated in large part through their concessions would be used for further investment in the company's steel operations. Furthermore, day-to-day relations between labor and management had become sorely strained at the plant level. To some extent this was a common feature of companies throughout the steel industry, intensified in recent years by the numerous plant closings and layoffs that were occurring. But relations were especially bitter at U.S. Steel. Management at a number of the other steel companies seemed to believe that gaining the confidence of the work force was critical to their recovery and therefore had devoted considerable resources to communication or participation programs geared toward that objective. U.S. Steel and later USX management, in contrast, seemed to focus on diversification or coproduction agreements (a form of outsourcing) as the focal point of their business strategy and discounted the value of worker and union participation.

Generally, as labor and management in unionized settings searched for an appropriate response to the growing competitive pressures of the 1980s, they often modified collective bargaining by introducing new subjects into their negotiations. This entailed creating linkages between changes at the middle tier of industrial relations and changes at the workplace or strategic levels of industrial relations.

In some firms the changes occurring across the various levels of industrial relations added up to a shift in industrial relations from the traditional New Deal pattern to what we earlier called the participatory pattern. In no case, however, had the participatory pattern fully matured to the point that it was well institutionalized into managerial and union operating practices. At this point, what the participatory pattern does involve is *experimentation* with an industrial relations system that encompasses contingent compensation, employment stabilization, team forms of work organization, and worker and union involvement in business decisions. As noted above, we will discuss the evolution of this participatory pattern in more detail in the next chapter. Here we focus on how various components of the participatory pattern emerged as a product of the expanding bargaining agenda of some firms and plants in the early 1980s.

One way the bargaining agenda expanded was through the gains or quid pro quos labor received in exchange for its concessions in pay or work rules. The most significant quid pro quos were participation programs and enhanced employment security, as these activities required unions to modify their representational roles.

Recent changes in employment security. A number of recent collective bargaining agreements provide enhanced employment security through a variety of mechanisms. For example, harking back to the type of productivity bargaining that occurred in the West Coast longshoring industry in the early 1960s, American Airlines introduced lifetime job guarantees to workers on the payroll as of 1982. (The American Airlines contract also substantially lowered the pay of new hires.) The 1982 agreements at Ford and GM created a guaranteed income stream program to compensate high-seniority autoworkers permanently laid off because of plant closings or other reasons. In 1984 the two automakers instituted a "job bank," guaranteeing six years of income support or redeployment to workers displaced by technological change, outsourcing, corporate restructuring, or negotiated productivity improvements.

The dominance of employment security as a quid pro quo for union concessions was hardly surprising in light of the extensive layoffs of the early 1980s. Over most of the post–World War II period employment insecurity had taken the form of layoffs that were temporary or occasionally of longer duration (when recessions were particularly severe); for most workers the periods of layoff were followed by recall. Thus, the union response had been to bargain for income maintenance via unemployment benefits supplemental to the state unemployment insurance programs. But faced with the extensive economic restructuring of industries that began in the late 1970s, workers with substantial seniority could no longer assume they would be called back; plant shutdowns and the worldwide consolidation and technological updating of manufacturing facilities made large-scale recalls a thing of the past. Thus, in the 1980s workers and their unions shifted the bargaining agenda to demand greater guarantees of employment security than they had demanded in the past.

The development of new work structures geared toward greater flexibility in the deployment of the work force has also spurred interest in employment security. Traditionally, plants were organized along the conventional lines of occupations commonly found in the external labor market, lessening the difficulties associated with layoffs by making alternative employment more easily available. But as firms pushed for fewer classifications and more firm-specific training, workers sought assurances of employment continuity. Without such assurances they feared their specialized training would make them ill-equipped for jobs elsewhere. Employment security programs also became attractive because the teamwork systems being simultaneously introduced in many settings worked best if employees were highly trained and committed to their work. Both of those attributes can be encouraged by enhancing workers' employment security.

Not all efforts to introduce greater employment security with more flexible production methods have succeeded. GM and Ford, along with the UAW, sought to link employment security and redesigned plant work rules, in a program called the pilot employment guarantee, in their 1982 national agreements. But only two sites (out of a contemplated eight sites) finalized an agreement to implement that program. Furthermore, employment guarantees or job banks like those at Ford and GM to date are included in only a few other collective bargaining agreements in this country. The interesting question here is whether these recent experiments with enhanced employment security will spread to other work sites in the future.

It also remains to be seen exactly how the new employment security programs are implemented and what their implications are. Some programs provide employment guarantees to only a subset of the work force, while others provide for the hiring of more temporary and part-time workers. As a result, these plans could engender intense political rivalries within unions — between those workers who have employment security and those who do not. Future research also needs to determine whether employment security results in greater worker acceptance of flexible work rules and a greater bond of commitment between the firm and its work force. We return to many of these issues in the next chapter when we discuss the worker and union participation programs that have been closely linked to these new employment security plans.

SUMMARY

At the theoretical level this chapter discussed the various patterns of industrial relations that exist in union and nonunion settings. It also outlined how environmental factors and strategic choice influence the evolution of these various industrial relations patterns.

Diversity reigns in collective bargaining outcomes and processes, both across bargaining units at any one time and within and across units over time. Some of this diversity is explained by environmental or organizational differences. Other important determinants are the differences in union and management strategies. Recent events have provided a vivid illustration of both the dynamics within bargaining and the role played by union and management strategies.

Concessionary bargaining has resulted in pay increases that are substantially below those of previous years. Debate is already under way over whether the low wage settlements and the bargaining process changes of the 1980s signal a fundamental shift in the nature of collective bargaining.

It is not surprising that a shift in bargaining power to the advantage of management explains some of the concessionary settlements of recent years. What is surprising, however, is the broadening of the bargaining agenda that has occurred within recent bargaining and contract settlements at some firms. Expanded employment security, worker and union participation programs, and contingent compensation are notable quid pro quos that some unions have negotiated in exchange for pay and work rule concessions. What this signals is an increase in the number of unionized firms following what we call a participatory pattern of industrial relations. But these developments are not universal. Numerous other labor-management relationships in recent years have turned to a more conflictual pattern.

Since domestic nonunion and international competition is likely to continue to grow, unions will continue to search for new strategies that provide new sources of power and influence in bargaining. In the absence of any shift in strategy, or if these new strategies fail, unions will find it difficult to maintain the status quo, much less achieve major gains for their membership. Will unions choose to extend the growth of participation programs, employment security, and contingent compensation? Or will they devise some other strategy? The potential strategies of future unions and employers will be the subject of the final chapter of this book.

Suggested Readings

The changes in bargaining outcomes and processes that took place in the early 1980s are analyzed in:

Kochan, Thomas A., Harry C. Katz, and Robert B. McKersie, *The Transformation of American Industrial Relations*. New York: Basic Books, 1986, especially chap. 5.

Mitchell, Daniel J. B. "Shifting Norms in Wage Setting." *Brookings Papers on Economic Activity* 2 (1985): 575–609.

A classic discussion of influences on the diversity of collective bargaining is:

Levinson, Harold. *Determining Forces in Collective Bargaining*. Berkeley: University of California Press, 1968.

Notes

1. See Harry C. Katz, "Policy Debates Within North American Trade Unions," in *New Technology and Industrial Relations: International Experience*, ed. R. Hyman and W. Streeck (London: Basil Blackwell, forthcoming).

2. Typologies of industrial relations patterns with some similarities to this scheme are provided in Richard C. Edwards, *Contested Terrain* (New York: Basic

Books, 1979); and in Alan Fox, *Beyond Contract: Work, Power and Trust Relations* (London: Faber and Faber, 1974).

3. See Peter Doeringer, "Internal Labor Markets and Paternalism in Rural Areas," in *Internal Labor Markets*, ed. Paul Osterman (Cambridge, Mass.: MIT Press, 1984).

4. As Chapter 6 pointed out, this sophisticated human resource management pattern developed in a few nonunion firms in the 1950s and had roots in earlier corporate policies of the 1920s (often labeled welfare capitalism; see Chapter 2).

5. Note that Delta Airlines is not a pure case of this nonunion pattern because its pilots are unionized.

6. For evidence on the role of founding executives see Fred Foulkes, *Personnel Policies in Large Non-union Companies* (Englewood Cliffs, N.J.: Prentice-Hall, 1980).

7. See Jeffrey Arthur, "Industrial Relations Practices in Steel Minimills in the United States," M.S. thesis (Ithaca, N.Y.: Cornell University, 1987).

8. These figures are from *Collective Bargaining Negotiations and Contracts: Techniques and Trends* (Washington, D.C.: Bureau of National Affairs, 1985), 839.

9. *Employment and Earnings* (Washington, D.C.: U.S. Department of Labor, 1986).

10. See Fox, *Beyond Contract*.

11. These figures are derived from *Current Wage Developments* (Washington, D.C.: Bureau of Labor Statistics, U.S. Department of Labor: various issues), and are reported in Robert S. Gay, "Union Settlements and Aggregate Wage Behavior in the 1980s," *Federal Reserve Bulletin* 70 (1984): 843–56. For similar calculations, see Robert J. Flanagan, "Wage Concessions and Long-Term Union Wage Flexibility," *Brookings Papers on Economic Activity*, vol. 1 (1984): 183–216.

12. Daniel J.B. Mitchell, "Shifting Norms in Wage Determination," *Brookings Papers on Economic Activity*, vol. 2 (1985): 575–609.

13. See Flanagan, "Wage Concessions," 189, table 2.

14. See John Chalykoff, "Industrial Relations at the Strategic Level: Indicators and Outcomes," photocopy (Cambridge: Sloan School of Management, Massachusetts Institute of Technology, 1985).

15. One example is the set of wage equations estimated by Mitchell, "Shifting Norms." For a more complete discussion of this evidence, see Thomas A. Kochan, Harry C. Katz, and Robert B. McKersie, *The Transformation of American Industrial Relations* (New York: Basic Books, 1986), 110–11.

16. Richard B. Freeman, "In Search of Union Wage Concessions in Standard Data Sets," *Industrial Relations* 25 (Spring 1986): 131–45.

17. Peter Cappelli, "Concession Bargaining and the National Economy," in *Proceedings of the Thirty-fifth Annual Meeting, December 27–30, 1982, San Francisco,* ed. Barbara D. Dennis, 362–71 (Madison, Wis.: Industrial Relations Research Association, 1983).

18. See Sumner Slichter, *Union Policies and Industrial Management* (Washington, D.C.: Brookings Institution, 1941).

19. See the symposium "The Employer Challenge and the Union Response" in *Industrial Relations* 1 (October 1961): 9–56. See also George Strauss, "The Shifting Balance of Power in the Plant," *Industrial Relations* 2 (May 1962): 65–96.

20. For a good summary of the productivity bargaining developments during this period, see George P. Shultz and Robert B. McKersie, "Stimulating Productivity: Choices, Problems and Shares," *British Journal of Industrial Relations* 5 (March 1967): 3–18.

21. Peter Henle, "Reverse Collective Bargaining: A Look at Some Union Concession Situations," *Industrial and Labor Relations Review* 26 (April 1973): 956–68.

22. Figure 8–2 provided a chronology of events at Phelps Dodge.

23. Peter Cappelli, "Competitive Pressures and Labor Relations in the Airline Industry," *Industrial Relations* 24 (1985): 316–38.

24. "USX Members in Nine States Approve Pact with Contracting Out Prohibitions, Profit Sharing," *Steelabor* 52 (January 1987): 12–13.

CHAPTER 13

The Dynamics of Change in Union-Management Relations

One important attribute of a viable collective bargaining system is its ability to adapt to changing pressures and problems. As the previous chapters demonstrated, collective bargaining in the United States has recently come under enormous pressure from heightened international competition, technological change, and the growing nonunion sector. The last poses a particular serious threat because of the innovations under way at a number of nonunion workplaces.

Yet the current challenge facing unionized workplaces is not unprecedented. The history of U.S. industrial relations has been characterized by an oscillation in primacy between union and nonunion systems. In the 1940s and 1950s it was the unionized workplaces that had the innovative lead, introducing such policies as supplementary unemployment benefits, sophisticated pension and health care benefits, and novel training programs. But, as discussed in Chapters 6 and 7, by the early 1960s the innovative edge had shifted back to the nonunion workplaces, some of which were introducing such sophisticated human resource management policies as employment security programs, more flexible systems of work organization, and new communication and complaint procedures.

Recent events point to the continuing dynamism of U.S. industrial relations as, once again, the mantel of innovation has begun to pass back to the union workplaces. In the early 1980s a number of unionized firms and plants began to make important innovations in their industrial relations systems. Some firms introduced new systems of work organization and new compensation and communication policies. Meanwhile, at other sites employees and unions became more involved in strategic business decisions. Many of these innovations were linked to the changes occurring at the middle level of the collective bargaining system, arising as they did within concessionary bargaining, as discussed in the previous chapter. At yet other sites innovations at the workplace and strategic levels were the driving force behind subsequent changes at the collective bargaining level.

Whether they started at the top, middle, or bottom levels of the union industrial relations system, the recent innovations in the union sector had varying degrees of success. Some experiments flourished, while others failed and were followed by a return to bitter labor-management relations. This chapter examines the many innovations evident in the union sector over the 1980s. Our review of these new practices and their effects is designed to help address two crucial questions: whether the experiments in selected settings are significant enough to help close the competitive gap between the union settings and the most innovative nonunion settings; and whether the changes are diffusing broadly enough and in ways that will lead to further adaptation and innovation to result in what we could call a "new industrial relations system." Before we look at the origins and implications of these recent innovations, let us first take a historical perspective.

PREVIOUS CALLS FOR REFORM

Calls for reform have been heard many times throughout the history of collective bargaining in the United States, most often following a long, bitter, and costly strike. For example, the 116-day steel industry strike of 1959, the 140-day rubber industry strike of 1976, and the 109-day coal industry strike of 1977–78 all led to public clamor for reexamination and reform of industrial relations in these industries. The result: a government-sponsored study of collective bargaining in the steel industry,[1] the promise (but no action) to create a top-level labor-management committee in the rubber industry, and the establishment of a national study commission in the coal industry. Long strikes at individual companies have also resulted in soul-searching and attempts at reform.[2] At other times the trigger to the call for change has been the development of some seemingly new industrial relations problem that collective bargaining, in its traditional form, has had trouble addressing. Concern over the effects of technological change played this role in the late 1950s and early 1960s, whereas concern over the quality of working life and declining productivity played a similar role in the 1970s and early 1980s.

Serious external threats to society—most notably in the form of a major war—have also served to prompt collective bargaining reform. This was clearly the case in the two World Wars and to a more limited extent during the Korean War, when wage and price controls were introduced. In the 1970s government officials attempted to rally public support for efforts to combat inflation with the same spirit that produced a climate for reform during the wars.

Finally, at times investigations of major scandals or highly publicized research efforts have served as the spark for reform of the collective bargaining system. The Industrial Relations Commission reports of 1915, the LaFollette Committee investigation of company labor relations behavior in the 1940s, and the McClellan Committee hearings on union corruption in the 1950s all served in this way.[3] The 1972 *Work in America* report also tried to spark interest in reform and to increase union leaders' and employers' concern for issues of the quality of working life.

Many public calls for change implicitly assumed that change could best be introduced through greater union-management cooperation and problem solving outside of normal collective bargaining processes. Although effective forms of ongoing interaction and discussion away from the crisis atmosphere of a strike deadline represent a laudable goal, the notion that they can occur independent of collective bargaining is misguided. The evidence discussed later in this chapter regarding recent experiments suggests that, in fact, the opposite is true. Collective bargaining reforms seem to work best when they are associated with consistent changes across all three levels of industrial relations activity; that is, workplace changes must be reinforced by changes at the collective bargaining and strategic levels, and the same is true for changes at the other two levels.

History also reveals that many important reforms were initiated through the collective bargaining process itself. Expanding the scope of bargaining, modifying work rules, introducing technological changes, and, indeed, securing the actual right to bargain itself—all these came out of unions' hard-fought struggles either in collective bargaining or in the arena of national politics. It would be a mistake, therefore, to attempt to make changes in human resource management in unionized settings without working through the collective bargaining process.

The history of union-management cooperation in this country has not been one of unparalleled success. We have witnessed many more failures than successes in cooperative efforts to introduce change. The critical question, therefore, is under what conditions *can* change be successfully introduced into collective bargaining.

A MODEL OF THE CHANGE PROCESS

Most models of social change adopt the thesis that to be successful, attempts at change must go through at least three distinct stages.[4] The first stage requires stimulating or motivating change by "unfreezing" current practices. That is, some stimulus must first spark the parties' interest in considering alternative strategies and practices. The second stage requires the negotiation, choice, and implementation of a course of action. The third stage of the process occurs when a new equilibrium is established in the relationship, that is, when new processes or interactions "refreeze" into a long-term pattern.[5] Let us examine this three-stage sequence and its implications in more detail.[6]

Stage 1: Stimulating Change

Unions and employers will generally be reluctant to embark on significant efforts to change their established practices unless they are experiencing strong external or internal pressures to do so. There is tremendous inertia in any collective bargaining relationship. Some of this inertia results from the success and stability achieved in following the traditional practices.

U.S. unions have historically promoted "free" collective bargaining and relied on their strike leverage as their primary instrument for effecting social and economic change. This strategy is too well entrenched and has been too successful to expect any major departure from its use—without some significant new development to force a change. Similarly, management has historically sought to limit expansion of union and worker involvement in managerial decision making, for both ideological and economic reasons. Both parties also recognize that they are separated by basic conflicts of interests and that power will always play an important role in the employment relationship. Consequently, change is seldom motivated by a simple desire to improve a relationship when that relationship is judged to be functioning smoothly or at an adequate level of effectiveness.

In short, the parties must see it as *in their self-interest* to make an adaptation in their traditional relationship. One or both parties must expect serious consequences to result from not participating before they will participate in a change effort. Each party, therefore, will base its decision on participating in the effort on its assessment of whether the change will contribute to *its own goals* and the goals of its constituencies.

These are the conditions necessary for unfreezing the existing practices and stimulating a consideration of any alternatives. The measure of success for this first phase is whether both parties *commit* themselves to participate in the change.

Stage 2: Implementing Change

Once the parties are committed to the change, they can then begin to implement the agreements they have reached. The second stage of the change process involves the implementation and maintenance of the agreed upon changes for what is usually a well-specified period of time.

The implementation of any change involves major political risks to both union and management representatives. To maintain the commitment to the change in the face of opposition therefore requires that the parties manage these political risks. The political conflicts that arise in this phase of the process are similar to the role conflicts any negotiator faces. Some individuals and groups are likely to oppose any type of change, since change normally entails some reallocation of power, some costs, and a good deal of uncertainty in the short run. Constituents' resistance to change has to be anticipated.[7] To prevent the effort's folding under that resistance, the negotiator must aggressively respond to constituents' fears, provide sufficient information to constituents about ongoing changes, and represent the constituents' concerns in deliberations over the change.

An obvious implication of these political concerns is that to gather political support, the parties to a change must demonstrate tangible evidence of achievement to their constituencies. Furthermore, the benefits of the change must accrue to enough members on each side so that the various interest groups see it in their own self-interest to be a part of the change process. Finally, to sustain the change effort through a cycle of negotiations, the parties must continue to grasp opportunities for further achievement of their goals.

The role of union leaders in this stage of the change process is fraught with problems. Union representatives walk a tightrope to be perceived as instrumental in achieving whatever benefits come from the change and yet also keep from being so closely identified with the change that they cannot withdraw if political opposition becomes too great or if the anticipated benefits do not materialize. In part as a consequence, often either management or a third party—such as a mediator, consultant, or government official— is the driving force behind efforts at changing union-management relations. It is simply too risky politically for most union leaders to be seen as the leading advocates for change.

Stage 3: Institutionalizing Change

Over the long run successful efforts to change workplace industrial relations must be integrated with the formal collective bargaining and contract administration processes and with other levels of the industrial relations system. As the examples discussed later in this chapter show, successful change efforts require a redesign of collective bargaining policies and processes. Typically, this redesign involves a broadening of the bargaining agenda and process.

We will now employ this model of the change process to analyze a number of different efforts at introducing change at various levels of the U.S. collective bargaining system in recent years. We start by examining efforts to introduce changes in national industrial relations policy and then examine changes at the strategic, bargaining, and workplace levels of the system.

CHANGE EFFORTS AT THE NATIONAL LEVEL

The highly decentralized nature of the U.S. collective bargaining system, the absence of a unified and centralized labor movement or a formal labor party, the diversity of interests within the management community, and the lack of consensus among labor, management, and political interest groups over national labor policy have all made it very difficult to introduce change through consultations and discussions at the national level.[8] But despite these inherent constraints, a number of national labor-management commissions, conferences, and committees have attempted to introduce change at the macro level of the bargaining system, and some of these efforts succeeded.

Before passage of the National Labor Relations Act in 1935 a number of presidential commissions and conferences attempted to investigate labor relations practices and working conditions in the United States. Those commissions were early efforts at investigative reporting and social action research designed to (1) change the political climate for trade unions, (2) promote labor legislation, and (3) reform the industrial relations practices of management.

The Hewitt Committee Report of 1880 was the first major national investigation of labor conditions in industry. This was followed by a similar report filed by the Industrial Commission in 1902. The highly publicized Industrial Relations Commission, whose report was filed in 1915, was formed in response to the growing incidence of radical discontent and violence in industrial settings throughout the country at the time, not the least example of which was the bombing of a *Los Angeles Times* office during a union-organizing drive in 1910.[9] The commission's report cited the absence of industrial democracy and inadequate working conditions as two of the most serious social problems facing the nation at that time. This document served as a background paper for those who were later to support the New Deal legislation in the 1930s, as well as for industrialists who turned to welfare capitalism and employee representation plans as devices for forestalling the growth of independent trade unions.

A more urgent mission faced the presidential labor-management conference called by President Woodrow Wilson at the outbreak of World War I: to insure sufficient labor-management cooperation to sustain the war effort. After considerable deliberation the labor and management representatives on the committee agreed to what in essence was a status quo armistice. Employers would not try to break the existing unions and would promote cooperative relations in collective bargaining in return for union promises to restrict strikes and to make no major moves to expand union influence.

After the war President Wilson once again called labor and management representatives together to continue the cooperative spirit and to reach a consensus on general principles for the conduct of labor relations. This effort broke down, however, over the issue whether workers should be allowed to join national trade unions or only unions of company employees.[10] Thus, no longer facing the threat of war, the parties returned to their previous power struggles and conflicts.

The parties again made limited pledges to cooperate and maintain the status quo during World War II. The National War Labor Board and the agencies that preceded it actively sought the support and involvement of representatives of organized labor and management. Again, following the war a national labor-management conference was called, this time by President Harry S. Truman in 1945, to try to establish some general principles governing the conduct of collective bargaining and labor-management relations. This conference broke down because the labor representatives were unwilling to limit union interest in collective bargaining to a tightly defined range of issues.[11]

The effort to develop a national dialogue and consensus on labor issues did not end there, however. Instead, every president since John F. Kennedy, except Ronald Reagan, has established some formal or informal labor-management committee at the national level to discuss labor policy issues. The topics considered by those committees have varied from technological change to labor market policies and means to combat inflation. All the committees lasted but a short time.

As a general rule the more those top-level committees took up issues over which unions and employers most often quarrel, the more quickly they met their demise. For example, the early committees after World War I broke down over the question of union security. The World War II labor board's efforts also broke down over this issue. The labor members of a national-level labor-management committee for the construction industry that functioned during the administration of President Gerald Ford walked out in protest of the President's veto of the common-situs picketing bill. In 1978 one of the labor members of an informal national labor-management committee, chaired by former Secretary of Labor John Dunlop, left the group in protest over management representatives' aggressive lobbying against the labor law reform bill. The Dunlop committee has since then been reconstituted, although it has chosen to discuss broad issues that are *outside the labor policy arena*. The group's members recognize that given the differences that separate them on labor law issues, efforts to reach consensus would be futile at this time and might jeopardize the possibility of making progress on other issues.

Several other top-level labor-management committees and conferences have been initiated in recent years to discuss the future of labor relations in the United States.[12] The question remains, however, whether these top-level discussions can lay the foundation for any significant changes in either public policy or private practices. We return to a discussion of this issue in Chapter 15 when we outline the challenges facing national labor and human resource policymakers.

Although these national commissions and committees have served as useful devices for investigating working conditions in industry and for calling attention to industrial relations problems, they typically have had little direct effect on collective bargaining practices or public policies. Two reasons stand out as explanations for their limited impact. First, except in the case of the wartime commissions, these groups seldom have the political power to turn their findings and recommendations into specific public policies. Second, they have been unable to make commitments on behalf of management and union officials who control the practice of industrial relations.

On the other hand, the fact that national-level consultative bodies have been formed so often throughout U.S. history suggests that officials at the top levels of government, labor, and management see them as serving some useful function. Indeed, in a political democracy some dialogue between the labor and management communities and with the top levels of government is essential. It is especially important given the nation's two-party governmental structure, since neither the labor movement nor employers have formal representation within either party, in the President's cabinet, or in Congress.

Top-level mechanisms for interaction provide an opportunity for labor and management leaders, governmental officials, and academicians to discuss their views and ideas on long-term labor issues. National bodies can also encourage experimentation and research into new ways of dealing with industrial relations problems. They can also help generate some of the external pressure needed to stimulate changes at the lower levels of the system. In times of extreme social, political, or economic crisis, they may be able to make binding commitments and thus set the scene for moving to the second stage of the change process. They are limited, however, in their ability to instigate *specific* changes in the practices, policies, or behavior of union and management officials at the level of the bargaining relationship. To instigate specific changes at lower levels, the national efforts must be supplemented by corresponding efforts at those other levels of the bargaining system.

CHANGE EFFORTS AT THE INDUSTRY LEVEL

In many highly competitive industries comprising numerous employers and a single union or a small number of unions, industrywide labor-management committees have historically been formed to discuss problems of mutual interest. Those committees represented early efforts by unions and employers to discuss broad issues of mutual concern outside of the formal structure and process of collective bargaining. Although industrywide committees rarely led to extensive union or worker involvement in strategic business issues, they are a good place to start in our review of specific cases.

One example was a committee started in 1974 as part of the federal government's wage and price control program. The initial stimulus to form the Joint Labor-Management Committee of the retail food industry (JLMC) came from the federal government in the early 1970s.[13] The federal government also sponsored the formation of a retail industry subcommittee of the National Pay Board as part of its efforts to control wage and price inflation. (The federal government tried to persuade other industries to form joint committees at that time but was rebuffed by either labor or management in each case.) The parties in the industry agreed to continue the committee as a privately funded and constituted entity after federal regulators discussed the possibility of greatly reducing federal regulations in the industry if the parties did so. The JLMC has succeeded in supporting or conducting several major long-term research projects investigating industry problems, including a study of the effects of new technology in stores and warehouses and a study of the occupational safety and health standards governing warehouses.

In the men's clothing industry the Tailored Clothing Technology Corporation (TC^2) program has been under way since 1980.[14] This project represents a dramatic example of a union's (the Amalgamated Clothing and Textile Workers Union [ACTWU]) becoming involved at a very early and basic stage in an R&D effort to mechanize production to help stem the flow of imported goods. By contrast, most unions in the United States limit their involvement with new technology to its consequences; that is, they seek to address technology only after management has made the strategic decision to introduce it. A few unions have been involved with the initial decision if management was willing to discuss the projected development it had in mind. In this instance, however, the ACTWU is helping to develop machinery not yet available on the market.

The ACTWU and the International Ladies' Garment Workers' Union (ILGWU) have been involved in strategic matters throughout the history of the garment and textile industries. These industries are characterized by having many small employers and substantial ease of market entry (and also substantial involuntary exit). The union, therefore, has historically served as a stabilizing force in the organized portions of these industries. During the early 1900s, for example, the unions provided technical assistance in running many of the small shops on a modern basis.[15] By doing so they were able to transform what otherwise would have been a proliferation of sweatshops into enterprises capable of providing a living wage and acceptable working conditions.

In terms of the three-stage change model introduced earlier, industrywide committees, like the national committees, have the potential for stimulating change and perhaps for making the initial commitments needed to introduce a specific innovation. They are not very effective, however, in carrying the change process through its middle stage, where political resistance and conflicts are most likely to surface. Furthermore, the industrywide committees are often far removed from the attitudes and behaviors of individual employers, local union officials, and rank-and-file workers. Consequently, their efforts to introduce change must be supplemented with efforts at the level of the individual firm and plant. The committees can again be useful, however, in institutionalizing the changes by designing ways for integrating the new practices and policies into the formal collective bargaining relationship and agreements. Thus, any broadly based effort at changing collective bargaining practices, policies, or outcomes may benefit from having the advice of an industrywide component.

CHANGE EFFORTS AT THE COMMUNITY LEVEL

Area labor-management committees usually comprise labor and management representatives and key community politicians. Almost all were started under the active leadership of one individual in the community.[16] The Jamestown, New York, committee, for example, developed largely out of the efforts of the former mayor of the community.

Area committees have tended to grow out of a labor relations or economic crisis in the community, such as plant closings or other sources of employment losses. This was the dominant motivation in Jamestown. In a few communities, such as Toledo, Ohio, the initial stimulus stemmed from the high level of industrial conflicts and strikes in the area.[17]

Formal evaluation of the performance of these committees is difficult because their specific goals and scope of activity vary widely and because their supporters have actively publicized their successes. These committees might be viewed as analogous to a national committee operating in a more limited geographic area; they suffer from the same lack of authority to make commitments. Yet they do have the potential of building political and community support for change and innovation. They also provide a forum for dialogue and thereby may help change the general industrial relations climate in the region. Although some of the committees have claimed responsibility for attracting new industries and reducing the unemployment rate in their community, the causal link between committee activities and economic improvements is difficult to establish. Obviously, these committees cannot work economic miracles. They can, however, help mobilize community resources and support for attracting new business, examine the labor supply needs of new industries, and encourage local educational and training institutions to meet the needs of existing and incoming industries.

In terms of the change model, the major role of these committees is, again, in stimulating or motivating action. They can provide strong external leadership and community encouragement for changes within specific companies, plants, and local unions. They can also help support experimentation, by attracting federal and state funds and drawing on the expertise of third-party facilitators and the surrounding educational institutions. Their major limitation comes in implementing the change process, since, again, the representatives on the committees often lack the power to commit individual employers or local unions to specific changes or to manage the internal political opposition that arises during the second phase of the change process. Furthermore, since there is no direct tie between the community-based efforts and the collective bargaining structure, it is difficult for the committees to avoid interfering with the jurisdiction of the formal collective bargaining process.

In short, area committees are likely to encounter difficulties in institutionalizing changes. Nonetheless, by providing a forum for dialogue among labor, management, and political leaders at the community level, these groups can help stimulate improvements in the quality of labor-management relations.

CHANGE EFFORTS AT THE ORGANIZATIONAL LEVEL

As suggested throughout the earlier chapters of this book, unionized industrial relations systems now face intense environmental pressures, including those arising from the innovations and lower costs found in the newer nonunion organizations and workplace systems. In response to these pressures labor and management have been introducing a wide range of innovations in their workplace systems. Some of these changes have now gone beyond the workplace level and are introducing fundamental changes in strategic-level relationships and in collective bargaining itself. Most of these efforts started out with a focus on increasing the involvement of individual workers and informal work groups and thereby increasing employee motivation, commitment, and problem solving. Some efforts went on to alter the organization of work and thereby to simplify work rules, lower costs, and increase flexibility in the management of the work force. Finally, a smaller number of change efforts have altered the roles of labor and management at the strategic levels of decision making, in ways that represent fundamental departures from the New Deal industrial relations system.

In this section we review the fledgling efforts to introduce quality-of-working-life (QWL) programs into labor-management relations in the 1970s, the early 1980s experiences with narrow forms of QWL, and more recent experiments with broad-scaled efforts to transform industrial relations at all levels of the labor-management relationship.

Early QWL Efforts

Efforts in the 1970s to spark interest in QWL programs were largely unsuccessful, for several reasons. First, because these programs were largely initiated from outside the organizations, labor and management did not see a clear need to change. For example, the federal government's National Commission on Productivity and Quality of Working Life tried hard to stimulate interest and experimentation but managed only to generate pilot or demonstration projects in several manufacturing firms and one coal mine. The commission was eventually disbanded after it received a negative evaluation by the General Accounting Office and lost its political support.[18]

Second, many labor leaders and industrial relations managers resisted change because they believed the alternatives proposed questioned the basic assumptions of the traditional job control model of unionism and the process of collective bargaining. Professionals on both sides of the table were skeptical of claims by QWL advocates that increased problem solving and participation could replace contractual rules that had been carefully bargained over the years. Some labor and management representatives also feared that informal problem solving would threaten their roles and status. Many labor leaders believed that QWL was simply another in the long line of managerial tactics to undermine collective bargaining and further weaken unionism. Since most of the QWL experience before the 1970s had been in nonunion firms and few of the advocates of QWL had much appreciation or understanding of unions, those fears were not unfounded.

Third, few line managers or top executives saw the strategic or bottom-line relevance of QWL. Instead, they tended to view QWL as a behavioral science fad that at most promised to improve job satisfaction and perhaps employee motivation. As we will see, this perspective was to change dramatically in the 1980s as line managers and an increasing number of top executives began to see participation and workplace innovations as keys to addressing two bottom-line objectives they were under increasing pressure to meet: productivity and product quality.

The 1980s: A Broadening of QWL

QWL was reborn in the 1980s as economic pressures intensified and forced labor leaders and managers to find new ways to address their productivity, quality, and labor cost problems. The pace of innovation increased as line managers took more initiative in introducing change and as both industrial relations professionals and labor leaders came under pressure to find ways to improve workplace performance. In response, three types of QWL processes emerged. The first was a direct extension of the earlier efforts—a narrow program specifically designed to increase individual and group problem solving around task-related issues. Quality circles (QCs) are a good illustration of this narrow type of effort. The second type goes beyond this narrow focus to address work organization and work rules, such as the number of job classifications and the role of seniority. The third type of QWL process expands the principles and processes of worker and union participation to encompass such strategic business issues as the design of new plants, the introduction of new technology, and investment decisions.

Narrow QWL programs.　By far most QWL efforts started out as narrowly focused QC programs based on the premise that they be kept separate from collective bargaining issues and procedures. But in studying a number of these programs, we have come to the strong conclusion that the most successful ones eventually broadened the scope of problems they addressed and found ways to successfully integrate QWL and collective bargaining changes.[19] Unless this broadening occurred, the QWL change process was precluded from addressing the important issues affecting economic performance and long-run employment security.

Not all narrow QWL processes made that transition successfully. In fact, by the mid-1980s articles had begun appearing in management journals criticizing many firms for treating QCs as just another short-lived fad.[20] One QWL program that did succeed in broadening its focus was one that involved the Xerox Corporation and the Amalgamated Clothing and Textile Workers Union (ACTWU) in Rochester, New York. As summarized in Box 13–1, the pivotal events in this case between 1980 and 1987 illustrate the iterative nature of this broadening process. At each successive stage the parties had to reaffirm their commitment to expanding the problem-solving process while at the same time resolve conflicts that occurred in negotiations and in day-to-day contract administration. The parties' ability to manage the tensions between problem solving and conflictual events was critical in this case, as in so many others.

For example, less than two years into the QWL process the program came under fire from rank-and-file workers when management shifted to a business and manufacturing strategy based on greater concern for cost controls. But instead of abandoning QWL, the parties began to use it to search for ways to cut costs and save jobs. The study-action teams in the wiring harness area represented the first such effort. The study teams suggested changes in work organization that required contractual changes, and thereby they created the need for the QWL process to be integrated into the collective bargaining process. The parties did this in their 1983 negotiations by agreeing to use the wiring harness study team experience as a model for how to handle similar subcontracting decisions in the future. In return for this and several other work rule and pay changes, management in 1983 agreed to a no-layoff provision, thus providing the employment security protection the workers and the union needed to maintain their commitment to the now considerably broader workplace reform process. As Box 13–1 indicates, since 1983, Xerox and the ACTWU have broadened their joint efforts to allow autonomous work groups in some areas, to plan a new work system for a new plant, and to establish decentralized "business area work groups" (teams that manage their unit's own affairs and tailor their participation and problem-solving processes to meet their specific needs and preferences).[21]

Several features of labor-management relations at the strategic level of Xerox helped increase the success of joint problem-solving efforts. Recall, for example, that in Chapter 4 we cited Xerox as one of the few companies that has not resisted union organizing in its new facilities. In addition, top Xerox executives and ACTWU leaders meet periodically to share information and discuss long-range issues affecting the business. Thus, workplace QWL activities evolved in this case in an environment where strategic inter-

---

BOX 13–1
The evolution of a QWL program at Xerox

1980 QWL language put in collective bargaining agreement.
Four joint Plant Advisory Committees and departmental steering committees established to create and support employee problem-solving groups.

1981 Over 90 problem-solving groups established.
Outsourcing of 180 wiring harness jobs on hold pending analysis of joint Study-Action Team.

1982 Study-Action Team identifies over $3.2 million potential savings; jobs not subcontracted.
Over 150 problem-solving groups exist in seven facilities.
Massive layoffs of unionized and exempt personnel.
First semi-autonomous work groups established on their own initiative.

1983 Contract includes no-layoff clause and mandated use of Study-Action Teams in all potential outsourcing situations, along with first year wage freeze, co-payment medical changes, and a restrictive absenteeism control program.
Strategic Planning Teams include the union to assess the future of the reprographic business.
QWL training made mandatory, polarizing the work force.
Study-Action Teams established in two additional areas, with work kept in-house in each case.

1984 Operating engineers' union withdraws from QWL in protest over issues of medical benefit changes.
QWL groups decline in New Building Operations; informal pre-shift meetings emerge in their place.
Study-Action Teams established in three areas, with work kept in-house in two cases.
Employee attitude survey in Components Manufacturing (CMO) prompts top-level reexamination of QWL.

1985 Launch of Business Area Work Group concept at CMO.
New plant built in Webster, New York, based on joint analysis and design team.

1986 Union supports flexible work assignments for hourly workers involved in new product development.
Contract extends no-layoff guarantee; modifies restrictive absenteeism program; establishes classification for hourly group leaders; and contemplates pilot study of gains sharing—all with a mixture of hard bargaining and problem solving.
Autonomous work groups increasingly established, prompted by early retirement of supervisors.

Source: Joel Cutcher-Gershenfeld, "New Path Toward Organizational Effectiveness and Institutional Security: The Case of Xerox Corporation and the Amalgamated Clothing and Textile Workers Union," report to the Bureau of Labor Management Relations and Cooperative Programs, U.S. Department of Labor, 1987.

actions supported and reinforced labor-management trust, cooperation, and participation. We see this linkage of practices across the workplace, collective bargaining, and strategic levels of interactions as a key determinant of the successful institutionalization of organizational change efforts.

Work organization reforms. As illustrated by the Xerox case, work reorganization has begun to be a central part of union-management change efforts. Interest in this issue reflects the pressures for greater flexibility, higher quality, and lower costs demanded by today's volatile and highly competitive markets and changing technologies. Yet introducing more flexibility in work organization requires changing many of the practices that grew up under the traditional job control model of unionism. It is not surprising, therefore, that these changes do not come easily or without a great deal of internal debate within unions and companies. Although there are many cases where greater flexibility is being introduced incrementally within existing work sites, the most significant examples of work organization reform are in new plants or in plants that are being completely retrofitted with new technology or new products. In particular, these examples can be found in most auto, steel, and other basic manufacturing firms, as they upgrade their facilities in an effort to be competitive with the newest nonunion and foreign producers in their industry.

Following the 1987 contract negotiations with the major steel companies, for example, the United Steelworkers and seven of the top eight steel firms began a series of industrywide joint training programs designed to diffuse knowledge and support for teamwork systems throughout their operations.[22] An examination of what is involved in a move to these new systems illustrates the close links between work organization changes, collective bargaining, and strategic interactions.

Teamwork systems require a fundamental reorganization of workplace relations because they replace multiple and narrow job classifications with jobs that are broader in scope, have broader decision-making authority, and provide greater opportunities for training and advancement. Typically, work teams do their own inspections since they must take responsibility for quality performance. In some cases the teams also do their own scheduling, task assignment, certification of workers' skill levels, material handling, housekeeping, and routine repair work. Team meetings provide a forum for discussing problems and for sharing information on financial performance. Traditional supervisors are replaced with team leaders, who often but not always are members of the bargaining unit rather than members of the first line of management. Finally, some teamwork systems use a *pay for knowledge* system of compensation, in which individuals are paid according to their skills (often measured by how many jobs in the work area they can perform). In one auto plant workers under a pay-for-knowledge plan were paid $13.20 per hour and were required to be proficient at two different jobs in the work area. If the workers could perform five different jobs in their work area, they received 30 cents more per hour; they received another 30 cents more per hour if they could perform eight different jobs in their work area and another 30 cents per hour if they were proficient at all the jobs in their work area. Under pay-for-knowledge schemes workers are paid their skill rate each day regardless of whether they are actually assigned to a job that requires the use of their level of skill.

In some plants with teamwork systems the local union takes on a fundamentally new and different role. For example, in General Motors' Pontiac Fiero plant "operating teams" composed of 10 to 15 workers make up the lowest level of the organization.[23] Workers and union leaders at this level and higher share information and participate in solving production and quality problems as they arise. The top "administrative" team at the Fiero plant includes the plant manager and the chairman of the local UAW's bargaining committee, giving the union access to a broad array of financial and other strategic information as a matter of course and a significant role in the governance of the organization. A key to the success of this arrangement was that the local union participated in the initial design of this organizational structure. As we will see, this is a central feature of relationships that are moving toward what we have labeled elsewhere "strategic participation from the bottom up." [24]

Participation in strategic decisions. The most fundamental departures from the principles of the New Deal industrial relations model are found in those settings where union leaders participate in top-level managerial decisions that affect the long-run character of the enterprise. As we have noted earlier in this book, the "management manages–union reacts" principle has been closely adhered to and indeed favored over the years by both labor and management leaders. It is only in recent years that this principle has been challenged as more and more labor leaders have come to recognize that effective representation of their members' long-run interests requires influencing managerial decisions *before* they are made rather than trying to address the effects of these decisions after the fact through collective bargaining. The mildest form of strategic interaction is that of information sharing and prior consultation between management and labor, as illustrated by the periodic meetings described above between Xerox executives and union officials. More significant forms are represented by the Fiero case—the union leader is formally included in the plant manager's administrative staff and attends management staff meetings. An extension of this is a formal position on the board of directors. This is a rare and unique role, which we will discuss separately below. Another form of involvement comes in joint strategic planning of new facilities or in implementing other major organizational changes. The plan for Saturn Corporation, a subsidiary of General Motors, exhibits more of these features than any other example we know of in industrial relations today (see Box 13–2).

These forms of strategic involvement are still isolated cases, however, and we expect them to continue to diffuse only gradually. At this point there is no guarantee they will eventually become institutionalized as part

---

BOX 13–2
GM–UAW Saturn agreement

Organizational Structure of Saturn:

Strategic Advisory Committee
*Does long-range planning. Consists of Saturn president and
his staff and top UAW advisor*

Manufacturing Advisory Committee
*Oversees Saturn complex. Includes company and elected union
representatives and specialists in engineering, marketing, etc.*

Business Unit
*Coordinates plant-level operations. Made up of company
representatives, elected union adviser, and specialists*

Work Unit Module
Groups of three to six work units led by a company "work unit advisor"

Work Units
Teams of 6 to 15 workers led by an elected UAW "counselor"

Key Industrial Relations Principles:

— Team forms of work organization with few job classifications
— Performance-based bonuses with all employees paid normal
  earnings on a salaried basis
— 80 percent of the work force protected against layoffs
  except in case of "catastrophic" events
— Worker and union participation in decision making

Source: Memorandum of Agreement Between Saturn Corporation and UAW
(Detroit: General Motors Corporation, July 1985).

---

of a transformed industrial relations system in the United States. Significant internal debate and conflict within management and labor ranks still exists over the wisdom of taking on these new roles. Opponents within the labor movement cite fears that unions will be coopted into supporting managerially controlled and potentially unpopular decisions. These critics believe that union independence will be compromised and rank-and-file dissent will grow. And management critics may represent an even more formidable barrier to the diffusion of union participation at the strategic level. Only in crisis settings or settings where unions had both the strength and the desire to demand greater involvement in managerial issues have we seen this participation extend beyond a single issue or a short period of time. Thus, it is not surprising that union involvement at the strategic level is generally found only in settings where unions already represent a large percentage of the firm's work force and interact with top executives in a centralized bargaining structure.

Assessing the Effects of Organizational Changes

At this point, it is difficult to assess how well the various QWL programs or broader changes in industrial relations are meeting the goals of the parties. As illustrated in Box 13–3, General Motors management seems convinced that QWL and work organization reforms contribute significantly to improved productivity and product quality. In large part the company bases its judgment on GM's cumulative experiences with QWL programs, the success of GM's joint venture with Toyota (New United Motors Manufacturing Inc., or NUMMI) during its start-up phase, and the lack of success GM has experienced otherwise in some of its most highly automated new plants. Yet we must be extremely careful not to overgeneralize from the small number of cases where QWL effects are apparent.

In our own research we have found it a hard task indeed to isolate the net effects of specific QWL programs or other interventions at the workplace from other events and changes simultaneously occurring in the organization.[25] Our own work and research by Goodman show that the narrowly defined QC types of QWL programs have only small positive effects on product quality and negligible effects on productivity.[26] Goodman's study also reveals the political dynamics and conflicts that emerged within the United Mine Workers over the issue of QWL programs, conflicts that eventually led the union to withdraw its support for the programs. On the other hand, in assessing the longitudinal impact of Scanlon plans in a sample of plants, Schuster found varied but generally positive and significant productivity improvements from these plans.[27] Further research is needed to reach definitive conclusions on the effects of systematic transformations of industrial relations practices at the three levels of industrial relations activity.

THREE SPECIAL CASES OF UNION PARTICIPATION

Three forms of worker participation deserve special discussion, because of their importance and their visibility in contemporary discussions of labor-management relations: union representation on boards of directors, union participation in new technology decisions, and employee ownership and stock ownership plans.

Board Representation

Formal representation on the board of directors of a company is the most visible way unions have achieved involvement in strategic business decisions. Starting with the addition of a UAW representative to Chrysler's board as part of the federal government's loan guarantees in 1980, a number of firms—for example, Weirton Steel, several airlines (Eastern, Western, Pan American, Republic), a small number of trucking firms, and various manufacturing firms—have added union representatives to their boards in

BOX 13–3

HOW TO RUN A FACTORY WITHOUT ANY NECKTIES

LET THE PEOPLE PARTICIPATE IN MANAGING THE BUSINESS

When General Motors worked out its strategy for the Eighties, it was clear that the development of a new method of production would have to proceed along two lines: technology and people.

GM was able to work out the technology for most of the demands of the new method. But we still needed new talents, new skills. So we acquired EDS, and then Hughes Aircraft. These potent new resources are now working closely with GM scientists and engineers in putting technology to work.

But technology alone is not a new method of production. Our goal was to integrate new technology with new social systems in a human partnership that gives people authority over machines and responsibility for their work. And that isn't easy. There were major questions to be answered, questions really never asked before. Could old patterns be broken down? Did the Japanese or the Europeans have the answer in their management systems? Could we unleash the creativity and management skills of people? Was there something uniquely American that could supply the competitive edge?

Today, the answers can be seen. Take the new General Motors assembly plant in Fort Wayne, Indiana. Here we are building our new full-size pickup. There are no people known as supervisors or hourly workers. They are called advisors and associates.

At one time, in every GM plant, the managers wore neckties. Not at Fort Wayne. The necktie, long the symbol of the distinction between white-collar and blue-collar workers, has been banished.

Symbols aren't everything, of course, but the symbols of confrontation have been replaced by the symbols of cooperation. Everybody eats together, parks together, and works together.

The people who build vehicles decide a lot of what goes on in the plant. They're involved in choosing the lighting for their areas, because they're the ones who need the light. They help determine how jobs will be done, because they're the ones who do them. They even help decide which tools to use, right down to the grade of sandpaper that's best for a specific job.

The people who work in this new truck plant are learning how the plant runs, what things cost, how customers respond to their work. And they're smart enough to put that knowledge to good use.

Everyone in the plant knows about computers and is learning to use a terminal. Everyone knows how to work with associates in a team. Everyone understands that there is a high level of technology in the plant and is striving to get the most out of it.

The president of the local union in Fort Wayne says that there has been a change in the culture of the plant. People now consider their work a craft. They get involved and like being involved. They want even more involvement.

It took thousands of hours of education and the common sense to find the right mix of people and technology for this new method of production. The result of all of this work and thought and investment is in the products. Our customers will be getting world-class trucks. In fact, we expect the quality of these trucks to set the standard for the world.

Putting people in charge of technology in a new method of production is the competitive edge.

The vision is paying off.

This advertisement is part of our continuing effort to give customers useful information about their cars and trucks and the company that builds them.

Chevrolet • Pontiac
Oldsmobile • Buick
Cadillac • GMC Truck

---

return for union concessions in other areas of the contract. In all of these cases the union in question represented a significant number of the firm's employees at the time board representation was granted. Yet despite the visibility of this new role for unions, we have precious few case studies and no other empirical evidence on how these experiments work in practice.[28] Two of these cases are summarized in Boxes 13–4 and 13–5, respectively. Although the two experiments were quite different, one thing they had in common was their short duration. Rath went out of business, which ended the experiment, and Western's merger with Delta Airlines ended not only board representation but union representation as well.

BOX 13–4
Board representation at Rath Packing Company

The threat of bankruptcy at Rath Packing Company in Waterloo, Iowa, in 1978 led the local union to negotiate an employee buyout of the corporation, effected in 1980. Through an employee stock ownership plan the workers and managers gained 60 percent of the company's stock and 10 of 16 seats on its board of directors. Although leaders of the international union, the United Food and Commercial Workers, advised against this plan, the local union and rank-and-file workers viewed it as the only alternative to company bankruptcy and the loss of their jobs.

Subsequent relations between management and the union officials at Rath vacillated between highly cooperative and highly adversarial, leading researchers Tove Hammer and Robert Stern to compare them to a yo-yo. Specifically, the initially cooperative pattern first gave way, after two years under the new arrangements, to a more adversarial pattern. Political pressures had been building up within the union as economic losses continued, no significant changes in plant operations or management were observed, and workers began questioning what had happened to the $5 million in wage and benefit deferrals they had conceded in the original negotiations. As these pressures escalated, the union began demanding that its representatives on the board vote as a unified block and promote the union's list of proposals at board meetings. The parties later returned to a more cooperative relationship when the chief executive officer was replaced and several union officials moved into key managerial positions. Adversarial relations came to the fore again, however, when financial losses continued to accumulate, management demanded further wage concessions, and the workers called a wildcat strike over a work rule dispute. The company ultimately filed for protection under Chapter 11 of the bankruptcy code. The labor contract was set aside by the bankruptcy court, and the company was radically reorganized.

Source: This description draws heavily from Tove H. Hammer and Robert N. Stern, "A Yo-Yo Model of Cooperation: Union Participation in Management at the Rath Packing Company," *Industrial and Labor Relations Review* 39 (April 1986): 337–49.

BOX 13–5
Board representation at Western Airlines

The experience with formal board representation at Western Airlines was of an entirely different stripe from that at Rath. Here the union leaders had varying degrees of interest in taking a stronger role in strategic decisions, and the rank-and-file generally lacked any interest at all in the matter. Employee representation on the board at Western, like that at Rath, was the result of a series of crisis negotiations. Beginning in the fall of 1983, after extensive top management turnover and increasingly severe financial losses, those negotiations resulted in a package that included union concessions on wages and work rules and management concessions on board representation as well as profit sharing and stock ownership for members of all of Western's five unions. (Employees were given 32 percent of the company's common stock outstanding, at a value of 50 cents for each dollar in wages conceded.)

The various union leaders did indeed differ in their perceptions of their new roles. Three of the unions placed union members on Western's board of directors, while a fourth, the Teamsters, chose an outsider to represent them to minimize any potential conflict of interest. Further, one of the union leaders had years ago taken the initiative to have a workplace employee involvement program installed, whereas the leaders of the other four unions have exhibited no interest whatsoever in this form of worker participation.

Western employees demonstrated their lack of interest in their responses to a 1985 survey of employee attitudes. On average they much preferred profit sharing to board representation, stock ownership, or employee involvement. The average response, on a four-point scale ranging from "strongly agree" through "strongly disagree," to the statement "Now that we have CAP [the new stock ownership and board representation program], I have a greater chance to participate in the management of Wester Airlines" was "disagree." The average response to a similar question about board representation in particular fell between "agree" and "disagree" but closer to the latter.

From these results we can conclude that for many Western workers the developments at the strategic level have been very remote. The workers appeared to be primarily interested in the cash value of these changes, and the unions remained generally unenthusiastic or ambivalent about this form of high-level participation. In mid-1986 Western Airlines merged with Delta Airlines, and Western employees regained a significant share of their previous concessions through the appreciation of Western stock that followed the merger. Western's unions lost their representational status because Delta employees greatly outnumbered Western employees and only the pilots at Delta were unionized.

Source: This description draws heavily from Kirsten R. Wever, "Power, Weakness and Membership Support in Four U.S. Airline Unions," Ph.D. dissertation (Cambridge: Massachusetts Institute of Technology, 1986).

It would be wrong to conclude from these cases that board representation is doomed to fail. But we do know that union influence on the employer's board of directors ultimately will require new communication and managerial skills and technical knowledge on the part of the worker representatives. We would further propose that board membership alone will yield few tangible results for workers or employers. To have lasting, positive results, this initiative will need to be linked to the changes in collective bargaining and at the workplace that are discussed in other parts of this chapter. Thus, board representation is still highly experimental and deserves closer examination before any definitive evaluation can be made.

The Case of New Technology

The introduction of new technology has always served as an opportunity for unfreezing an organization and initiating a range of organizational and industrial relations changes that go far beyond the scope anticipated by the designers of the new machinery or processes. Yet not all organizations take advantage of this opportunity. For example, between 1980 and 1987 GM reports that it spent about $50 billion on new production machinery. In some cases (See Box 13–3) GM has followed a broad approach to integrating human resource and industrial relations reforms into its plan for the new technology. But in other cases GM's strategy appears to have been one of throwing money at robots with little systematic planning or actual change in its labor relations practices. As a result, studies are now beginning to show that the GM plants with the highest productivity and product quality are not those with the most advanced technology but rather those that integrate their human resource strategy with their production processes.[29] Data show that as of early 1987 the NUMMI plant had the best productivity and product quality of all auto plants not only within GM but in all of North America. This plant has older technology than GM's most modern plants but allegedly does link the "humanware" and the "hardware" components of technology tightly together.[30] The NUMMI plant also has many features of the participatory industrial relations pattern described in Chapter 12.

Employee Ownership

A more radical form of workplace reorganization is that which follows after employees purchase a business from their employer. Recent history holds several examples of employee buyouts in the face of impending plant shutdowns.

Several studies have examined the effects of employee ownership on workers' attitudes toward their union and on the union as a bargaining organization.[31] The major conclusions to emerge from these case studies are that (1) the majority of employees still believe there is a strong need for union representation; (2) the role of the union changes in that it becomes a quasi-partner in making some of the strategic decisions the union would not have made under its former status; (3) the collective bargaining process remains an important decision-making forum within the organization; (4) the majority of blue-collar workers still prefer to see the bargaining process handle the traditional issues of wages and fringe benefits; and (5) new forums for decision making outside of collective bargaining often arise.

As in the case of codetermination, the labor movement has for the most part been unenthusiastic about employee ownership as a means of averting threatened plant shutdowns. The objections raised typically mention both economic and organizational concerns. Union leaders' chief organizational concern is that their members' perceived need for the union will wither away under an employee-owned firm, since the employees would essentially be bargaining against themselves. The empirical evidence from the case studies reviewed above should at least partially allay these fears, since member support for the union has remained strong in all the cases reported to date. Yet labor leaders may still fear that over the longer run, workers will lose allegiance to the union and their militancy in collective bargaining will erode. This is a strategic question that can be answered conclusively only with the passage of time.

The major economic reasons for union leaders' opposition to employee takeovers are (1) the ventures create pressures to cut wages and fringe benefits in order to save jobs and (2) they encourage worker investments in the oldest, least profitable, and least-likely-to-succeed plants in private industry. Union leaders argue that if the plant could be made profitable, either the existing employer would not want to pull out or other forms of private capital could be attracted to take over the plant and save the jobs. Union leaders are also concerned with the effects any concessions at the plants would have on wage levels in other unionized firms in the industry. Again, the case study evidence should allay some of these fears since it shows that conglomerates may abandon profitable plants simply because they can achieve higher profits on an investment elsewhere. In other words, not all shutdowns involve unprofitable plants. Still, employee ownership is likely to work only in small firms where the work force is relatively stable and committed to the community and to the organization, and where the workers are skilled enough to be able to improve plant productivity and economic performance through higher motivation and higher levels of individual and group performance.

Thus, workers, managers, and the labor movement in the United States seem to view employee ownership as a strategy of last resort for saving jobs. Although some advocates of employee ownership also see it as a strategy for introducing industrial democracy and worker participation and for redistributing power within organizations, there is little evidence that these objectives either rate high in the minds of workers faced with this option or actually are achieved once the transfer of ownership takes place. Instead, the case studies to date have found that the predominant reason employees supported the ownership option was to save their jobs.[32] Furthermore, although more democratic decision-making methods and structures did develop in some of the cases studied, a traditional division of labor between managers and line workers still remained in all of the firms studied. And the workers continued to perceive this division as legitimate and necessary to the success of the enterprise. At the same time, however, the evidence shows the majority of blue-collar and white-collar workers wished they had more influence over decisions affecting their jobs than they were given under the employee-owned firms.[33]

Finally, an extremely interesting and important question is whether worker-owned firms outperform other firms. Again this is a question for future researchers. One of the difficulties in answering it is that worker-owned firms may tend to be those that were already in poor health when the employees bought them. Thus, to succeed in identifying the independent influence of worker ownership, researchers will need to control fully for the influence of other factors that influence organizational performance, but this, too, may be very hard to do. Interesting evidence on this issue appeared in a study by Conte and Tannenbaum, who examined 98 U.S. and Canadian firms whose employees held substantial amounts of their employer's stock shares. The authors found a strong relationship between the amount of equity held by nonmanagerial employees and company profit levels.[34]

As noted earlier, another response to threatened bankruptcy has been to take advantage of favorable tax treatment and create employee stock ownership plans (ESOPs). Proponents view ESOPs as a form of workers' capitalism, while opponents believe the plans put workers' pensions and assets at risk without providing any real increase in worker involvement in business or workplace decisions. The trucking industry illustrates how one union has wrestled with these issues.

Between 1983 and 1985, 16 trucking firms organized by the Teamsters negotiated ESOPs. They did so in response to a continuing shrinkage in firms' and union employment in the industry following deregulation and after Teamster rank-and-file members had rejected a concessionary bargaining agreement negotiated between industry and international union representatives. After this contract rejection the Teamsters adopted a company-by-company approach to financial crises. Where the company and union turned to an ESOP, the union demanded and achieved minority representation on the board of directors of the company and a mangement plan for how the 15 percent pay cut that served as the quid pro quo for the ESOP would be used to bolster the business. In all cases the Teamsters sought employee ownership up to a maximum of 49 percent of the company's stock. This approach followed the union's conventional philosophy of leaving management in control of the enterprise and responsible for making the basic decisions. Worker and union influence on the board was achieved indirectly through Teamster-*nominated* board members, but not through putting a union official on the board. Thus, the union followed what we have labeled elsewhere a "limited engagement strategy" toward its role in an ESOP plan or an employee-owned firm.[35] Our own observation of these trucking cases indicates that in none of them have there been significant changes in worker involvement at the workplace. Yet several of these firms have undergone mergers and further ownership changes, and, at least in one of these cases we are now studying, the representative of the workers and the union on the board played a key role in safeguarding the workers' jobs and financial interests in the acquisition negotiations.

As in the two previous cases discussed here, we must ask how the organizational performance of the firms with ESOPs compares with that of conventionally owned firms. One study compared 51 large firms that had had ESOPs for at least 10 years with 51 matched, conventional firms.[36] The ESOP firms showed poorer performance on several dimensions of profitability. Yet this and other studies can be criticized on the grounds that they inadequately controlled for the influence of other differences across the firms.[37] As with the other forms of industrial relations change, more research is needed here to assess the effects of ownership changes on organizational performance and on the work force.

SUMMARY

It is difficult to make predictions regarding the future course of increased union and worker involvement in strategic business decisions. Participation programs are so new that labor and mangement have yet to confront the tough economic and political problems that often led to the demise of the earlier joint initiatives at the national and industry levels. Furthermore, since most participation plans have not lasted long, it is impossible to know how U.S. workers would react to sustained involvement and whether the recent efforts are likely to evolve toward even greater union and worker engagement in strategic business decisions. Although cases like the Saturn project are still largely on the drawing board, their growing numbers indicate that labor and management in this country are moving through an important period of experimentation with new strategies in organizational governance—strategies that, if diffused and institutionalized, will represent a fundamental departure from the New Deal model of collective bargaining and industrial relations.

Yet even if these experiments were to develop into healthy institutions, the U.S. labor movement would still face severe problems in spreading the new approach to bargaining relationships where it lacks the power to gain or sustain a meaningful role in strategic managerial decision making. Sustained diffusion and institutionalization may therefore require the active support of public policy. We shall return to this point in Chapter 15 when we discuss the choices future public policymakers will face.

The ultimate success of QWL programs and other workplace reform efforts depends on the ability of the organization to reinforce and sustain high levels of trust. That trust, in turn, depends heavily on the extent to which the strategies and events unfolding at the higher levels of the industrial relations system are consistent with and linked to the development of greater trust at the workplace.

To achieve tangible rewards, the expansion of worker participation programs and the introduction of new forms of work organization have often been accompanied by changes in the contract terms negotiated in collective bargaining. The expansion of shop-floor worker participation has also been spurred by increased worker and union involvement in strategic issues. This involvement was critical because it both assured the union that worker participation was not a step toward the demise of union representation and helped convince workers and the union that enhanced employment security would follow. But expansion of the process to the strategic level of decision making does not occur easily or automatically. Indeed, we have observed this expansion only in cases where unions are strong and relatively secure to begin with. Management tends to closely guard its control over issues that have traditionally been viewed as its prerogatives. Thus, a strong union presence and active union support for the process are essential. Nonunion firms and firms with weak unions are unlikely to develop or sustain a full form of worker participation.

Suggested Readings

The experience with worker ownership and the issues raised by such practices are thoroughly surveyed in:

Stern, Robert N., and Sharon McCarthy, eds. *The Organizational Practice of Democracy*. New York: John Wiley, 1986.

Whyte, William Foote, Tove Helland Hammer, Christopher B. Meek, Reed Nelson, and Robert N. Stern. *Worker Participation and Ownership: Cooperative Strategies for Strengthening Local Economies*. Ithaca, N.Y.: ILR Press, Cornell University, 1983.

Worker participation programs are analyzed in:

Kochan, Thomas A., Harry C. Katz, and Nancy R. Mower. *Worker Participation and American Unions: Threat or Opportunity?* Kalamazoo, Mich.: W.E. Upjohn Institute for Employment Research, 1984.

Notes

1. E. Robert Livernash, *Collective Bargaining in the Basic Steel Industry* (Washington, D.C.: U.S. Department of Labor, 1961).

2. See E.J. Lewicki and C.P. Alderfer, "The Tensions between Research and Intervention in Intergroup Conflict," *Journal of Applied Behavioral Science* 9 (1973): 424–49.

3. Several examples of this are also found in Great Britain. Both the Donovan Commission Report of the mid-1960s on collective bargaining structures and practices and the more recent Bullock Report called for new forms of employee participation in decision making and stirred great debate among scholars, policy-makers, and leading industrial relations practitioners in that country.

4. Kurt Lewin, "Frontiers in Group Dynamics," *Human Relations* 1 (1947): 5–41.

5. James Q. Wilson, "Innovation in Organizations: Notes toward a Theory," in *Approaches to Organizational Design*, ed. James D. Thompson (Pittsburgh: University of Pittsburgh Press, 1966).

6. The change model outlined here is presented in more detail in Thomas A. Kochan and Lee Dyer, "A Model of Organizational Change in the Context of Union-Management Relations," *Journal of Applied Behavioral Science* 12 (January 1976): 59–78.

7. Lester Coch and John R.B. French, "Overcoming Resistance to Change," *Human Relations* 1 (1948): 512–32.

8. See Jack Barbash, *Trade Unions and National Economic Policy* (New York: St. Martin's Press, 1975).

9. James Weinstein, *The Corporate Ideal in the Liberal State, 1900–1918* (Boston: Beacon Press, 1968), 175.

10. Neil W. Chamberlain, *Sourcebook on Labor* (New York: McGraw-Hill, 1958), 18–19.

11. Neil W. Chamberlain and James W. Kuhn, *Collective Bargaining*, 2d ed. (New York: McGraw-Hill, 1965), 85.

12. One such committee is called the Collective Bargaining Forum and is chaired by former U.S. Undersecretary of Labor, Malcolm Lovell. For an example of the issues discussed by this committee, see "Report on the National Conference on Competitiveness and Human Values," sponsored by the U.S. Secretary of Labor, 5 March 1986, reprinted in *Daily Labor Report*, no. 45 (7 March 1986): F-1–F-6.

13. See Albert Rees, "Tripartite Wage Stabilization in the Food Industry," *Industrial Relations* 14 (May 1975): 250–58.

14. See Thomas A. Kochan, Harry C. Katz, and Robert B. McKersie, *The Transformation of American Industrial Relations* (New York: Basic Books, 1986): 187–89.

15. For a good discussion on this point, see Jesse Thomas Carpenter, *Competition and Collective Bargaining in the Needle Trades, 1960–1967* (Ithaca, N.Y.: New York State School of Industrial and Labor Relations, Cornell University, 1972); and Steven Fraser, "Dress Rehearsal for the New Deal: Shop Floor Insurgents, Political Elites, and Industrial Democracy," in *Working Class America,* ed. Michael A. Frisch and Daniel J. Walkowitz (Urbana, Ill.: University of Illinois Press, 1983), 212–55.

16. Joel Cutcher-Gershenfeld, "The Emergence of Community Labor Management Cooperatives," in *Industrial Democracy: Strategies for Community Revitalization,* ed. Warner Woodworth, Christopher Meek, and William Foote Whyte (Beverly Hills: Sage, 1985), 99–120.

17. Ibid., 81–92.

18. "GAO Report Finds Productivity Center's Accomplishments Limited," *Daily Labor Report,* no. 103 (26 May 1978): A5–A6.

19. Kochan, Katz, and McKersie, *The Transformation,* 62–65.

20. See, for example, Edward E. Lawler III and Susan Mohrman, "Quality Circles after the Fad," *Harvard Business Review* 63 (January-February 1985): 64–71.

21. See the source listed in Box 13–1 for the full case study.

22. "Steelmakers Want to Make Teamwork an Institution," *Business Week,* 11 May 1987, 84.

23. Harry C. Katz, *Shifting Gears: Changing Labor Relations in the U.S. Auto Industry* (Cambridge, Mass.: MIT Press, 1985), 92–104.

24. Kochan, Katz, and McKersie, *The Transformation,* 197.

25. Harry C. Katz, Thomas A. Kochan, and Kenneth R. Gobeille, "Industrial Relations Performance, Economic Performance, and QWL Programs: An Interplant Analysis," *Industrial and Labor Relations Review* 37 (October 1983): 3–17; Harry C. Katz, Thomas A. Kochan, and Mark Weber, "Assessing the Effects of Industrial Relations and Quality of Working Life Efforts on Organizational Effectiveness," *Academy of Management Journal* 28 (September 1985): 509–27.

26. Paul S. Goodman, *Assessing Organizational Change: The Rushton Quality of Work Experiment* (New York: Wiley-Interscience, 1979).

27. Michael Schuster, "The Impact of Union-Management Cooperation on Productivity and Employment," *Industrial and Labor Relations Review* 36 (April 1983): 415–30.

28. Kirsten R. Wever, "The Case of Western Airlines and Four Airline Unions," report to the Bureau of Labor Management Relations and Cooperative Programs, U.S. Department of Labor, 1987.

29. John Krafcik, "Learning from NUMMI," photocopy (Cambridge: Sloan School of Management, Massachusetts Institute of Technology, 1987).

30. Haruo Shimada and John Paul MacDuffie, "Industrial Relations and Humanware," Sloan School of Management Working Paper (Cambridge: Massachusetts Institute of Technology, 1987).

31. See, for example, Tove H. Hammer and Robert N. Stern, *Democracy in Work Organizations* (New York: Kent Publications, forthcoming); Joseph Blasi, *Employee Ownership: Revolution or Ripoff* (New York: Ballinger Press, forthcoming).

32. Hammer and Stern, *Democracy.*

33. Tove H. Hammer and Robert N. Stern, "Employee Ownership: Implications for

the Organizational Distribution of Power," *Academy of Management Journal* 23 (March 1980): 78–100.

34. Michael Conte and Arnold Tannenbaum, "Employee-owned Companies: Is the Difference Measurable?" *Monthly Labor Review* (July 1978): 23–28.

35. Kochan, Katz, and McKersie, *The Transformation*, 193.

36. P.T. Livingston and James B. Henry, "The Effects of Employee Stock Ownership Plans on Corporate Profits," *Journal of Risk and Insurance* 47 (September 1980): 491–505.

37. For a comprehensive review of the evidence on ESOPs, see Hammer and Stern, *Democracy*.

CHAPTER 14

Collective Bargaining in the Public Sector

Collective bargaining has spread rapidly in the public sector since the early 1960s, to the point that, today, 36 percent of federal, state, and local government employees are represented by either a union or an employee association (see Table 5–1). This fact alone makes the public sector experience worthy of a separate chapter in this book—especially at a time when fewer private sector employees have union representation each year.

In this chapter we will apply the general framework developed in the previous chapters to the public sector experience. It is important to recognize at the outset, however, that the public sector is a special case of bargaining and employment practice. Government is not just an employer and a provider of services, but a provider of *public* services, and as such the public sector bargaining system is particularly responsive to the third set of actors we outlined in Chapter 1: the public. The public sector system that has evolved within the constraints posed by the public's demands exhibits some unusual characteristics; and debate over the appropriate form of public employee representation is ongoing and intense. Some critics of the existing system have argued that the unique nature of government as an employer makes collective bargaining, as traditionally practiced in the private sector, inappropriate for the public sector. Other observers would allow the traditional type of collective bargaining, but in a shape and form adapted to meet the special circumstances of the public sector.

In the first section of this chapter we will review these normative arguments. We then use our framework of bargaining systems to examine the historical phases public sector bargaining has passed through—one of the major themes of this chapter. The 1960s witnessed rapid expansion in public sector union membership and militance. But in the mid-1970s a taxpayers revolt emerged and slowed or reversed that expansion. Then in the mid-1980s teachers and a few other public employee groups benefited from public concerns over the adequacy of public services and saw their bargaining power rebound.

Public employees and unions have felt the effects of changing environmental pressures, but the changes that emerged within public sector collective bargaining were different in some ways from events in the private sector. Public sector unions faced neither a growing domestic nonunion sector nor heightened international competition. In contrast to the private sector, continuity and stability in public sector collective bargaining *institutions* prevailed throughout the 1970s and 1980s.

NORMATIVE PREMISES

Let us first examine how the normative premises of industrial relations outlined in Chapter 1 apply to the public sector. There we stated that (1) an inherent conflict of interests exists between employees and employers, (2) workers should have the right to pursue their interests through a union if they so choose, and (3) collective bargaining is one means unions use to represent the interests of their members on the job. We also stated that these premises should apply to all employer-employee relationships. As we have just noted, however, government differs from a private sector employer because it is at the same time the elected representative of the public. The problem for public policy is how to maintain the rights of employees to influence their employment conditions, through collective bargaining if they so desire, while maintaining citizens' rights to influence governmental action and expenditures.

Wellington and Winter, and others, have taken the extreme position that government's primary responsibility—to represent the public interest—makes collective bargaining inappropriate for the public sector.[1] Critics of public sector bargaining also claim that if labor unions are granted rights to exclusive representation and negotiations, they achieve undue political power and access to the governmental decision-making process, effectively closing off that access to other interest groups in society.

We believe these positions ignore employee interests and inaccurately assess the actual effects of collective bargaining on public sector decision making. It is our view that public employees, like private sector employees, have an inherent right to participate in the determination of their working conditions. Why should the mere fact that an employee works for the government strip that employee of the right to influence his employment conditions through collective bargaining? The charge that collective bargaining leads to a perverse distortion of governmental decision making is

424

not supported by the facts. As we discuss in more detail later in this chapter, public sector unions have had a modest impact on employee pay and other working conditions. In fact, where they exist, public sector unions influence governmental decision making as but one among the many interest groups participating in this process. In fact, public employee representation seems to enhance rather than detract from the process of representative democracy.

Our argument does not necessarily imply that the process for providing these rights should be identical to the process in the private sector. Indeed, just as we should recognize the government's role as an employer, we also have an obligation to shape industrial relations policies in the public sector in a way that takes into account the unique role the government plays as a provider of public services. Since a variety of interest groups are affected by governmental decisions, their diverse interests must be taken into account in the collective bargaining process.

Public policy must therefore balance these objectives. Since interests and environmental constraints all change as economic and political conditions change, industrial relations institutions in the public sector are likely to require periodic modification as well. In the mid-1960s the growth of public sector unions and the rising expectations of public employees led to the extension of collective bargaining rights to these employees. We are now in a position to examine how these bargaining institutions have evolved and how well they have performed the functions that employees, employers, and the public expect from them.

THE CHANGING CONTEXT

The percentage of all federal, state, and local government employees who were members of unions rose from 12.8 in 1960 to 20.6 in 1974. Other public employees had joined associations, many of which also engaged in collective bargaining by the 1970s. In 1974, 37.7 percent of all public employees were members of a bargaining organization, and by 1980 that number had risen to around 40 percent.[2] Factors that contributed to that expansion included the growth in government budgets throughout the 1960s and early 1970s, the example of civil disobedience and protest being set by civil rights and other groups in the 1960s, and the passage of laws favorable to public sector collective bargaining. The economic environment for public sector bargaining, however, tightened sharply in the mid-1970s as a consequence of slowdowns in the economy and in response to a conservative political tide that questioned the value of many government expenditures. By that time a number of state and local governments, including New York City, had begun to face major fiscal problems. Taxpayer resistance to public expenditures then created a backlash against public employees and reduced the political influence of public sector employee organizations. As we document later, the wage increases received by public employees during this period fell significantly behind those received by private sector employees. In light of this series of events we can distinguish a period of public employee advances in the early 1960s through the early 1970s, and contrast that with a later period when the growth in public sector union membership slowed and public employees strove to protect their previous gains rather than seek new ones.

THE ENVIRONMENTAL CONTEXT

As we discussed in Chapters 3 and 11, the more bargaining power private sector employees have, the more they are able and willing to sustain a strike and the less employers are willing and able to withstand a strike. Furthermore, the more bargaining power private sector employees have, the less employment drops over the long run in response to an increase in labor costs. The same conditions apply in the public sector. But because the impact of changes in the environment on public employees' strike leverage is so complicated, we first consider public sector bargaining and its environment in light of Marshall's conditions regarding the trade-off between wages and employment.

Marshall's Conditions

Alfred Marshall's first condition states that employees have more bargaining power (face a smaller reduction in employment from an increase in wages) when it is difficult for management to substitute other factors of production, such as machinery, for employees. On this score public employees, on average, should have more bargaining power than private employees, since it is difficult to substitute machines for humans in the provision of many public services, such as education and police and fire protection. Some substitution of capital for labor is feasible even for these services, however; computers can be substituted for teachers, police can acquire more cars and other equipment, and firefighters can use more and better equipment to substitute for labor.

Marshall's second condition concerns the price elasticity of demand for the final good. Here again public employees, on average, should have an advantage over most private employees. Government is typically the sole provider of a public good or service. A public employer cannot typically go out of business or move to some other area to escape higher labor costs. As a result, the demand for public goods should be relatively price inelastic, another factor making public employment relatively insensitive to increases in wages.

Marshall's third condition concerns what happens to the price of substitute factors of production if the demand for them increases. Here there is no clear difference between the public and private sectors.

With regard to the fourth Marshallian condition, the importance of being unimportant, public employees are likely to be at a disadvantage. As discussed in Chapter 3, in most cases public employees and labor costs are a substantial share of total production costs. The ratio of labor to total costs varies in the public sector from a high of around 90 percent in police and fire departments to a low of between 60 and 70 percent in education and other public services. This means that wage increases have a significant effect on total increases in government budgets and that labor costs are a prime target for cost-cutting efforts when the public demands lower taxes and expenditure levels. In the long run the high percentage of labor costs to total costs may act as the major impediment to public employee union power; in other words it should help make public employers more resistant to employee or union demands.

On net Marshall's conditions predict that the demand for public services is relatively price-inelastic; increases in labor costs should lead to relatively small declines in employment. An early study of the inelasticity of demand concluded that, on average, the demand for labor in the public sector was more inelastic than the demand for labor in the private sector. Furthermore, the inelasticity estimates were greater in states with high population density than in the low-density states.[3]

It is important to note, however, that Marshall's conditions concern the responsiveness of employment to price (wage) changes when other things are held constant. The problem that public employees confronted after the mid-1970s was that other things were not constant. Instead, tax revenues were declining in some jurisdictions, and the public's demand for public expenditures was declining—both of which led to cutbacks in government expenditures. The changes in the public's demand for government services were, in part, a product of the public's reaction to the advance in relative earnings public employees had received over the late 1960s and early 1970s (described more fully later). In this way the taxpayers' revolt was in part a delayed "price effect": The public was reducing its demand for public services in response to the rising cost of those services. Thus, it may well be that the long-run demand for labor in the public sector is much more elastic than the short-run demand for labor.

It is therefore interesting to note that a more recent study, using data on the years after the start of the taxpayers' revolt, concluded that the elasticity of demand for teachers in the public sector was comparable to that for private sector employees.[4] Thus, although in the short run the demand for labor in the public sector is likely to be less responsive, on average, to wage increases than the demand in the private economy, recent evidence suggests that as wage costs increase over time public employees are no longer immune to employment cutbacks. It may be that it takes a crisis atmosphere for politicians to reduce employment levels by any significant amount.

Strike Leverage

In examining public employees' strike leverage we again return to the concepts outlined in our earlier discussion of the influence of environmental factors on bargaining power (in Chapters 3 and 8).

Public employees' strike leverage is influenced by their ability and willingness to sustain income losses as a result of a strike. Just as in the private sector, striking employees in the public sector rely on alternative sources of income such as temporary jobs or the earnings of other members of the household. The availability of temporary work depends on the state of the labor market; more jobs are likely to be available during prosperous times. And also as among private sector employees, public employees on strike often rely on accumulated assets, available public assistance programs, or union strike benefits to replace forgone income.

Although public and private sector employees may therefore have roughly the same *ability* to withstand a strike, they may be very different in their *willingness* to go on strike. In the private sector the employer's willingness to continue a strike is heavily influenced by the firm's ability and willingness to sustain the income losses that result from the shutdown in production and sales during the strike. But in the public sector income is not necessarily tied to sales and production. Public agencies typically collect revenue through taxes and do not charge explicitly for services.[5] Thus, during a strike the public employer typically continues to receive revenue and consequently is not under pressure to agree to the strikers' demands as a result of potential bankruptcy fears. Nor do public agencies typically face competitors who may continue to produce during a strike and thereby strip the struck employer of customers. This absence of a link between strikes and employer revenues clearly works in favor of public employers during strike situations.

Yet in another way the special nature of public services can work strongly against public employers. The public employer may not lose income during a strike, but a strike can certainly anger the employer's constituents, namely, the public. The public is sometimes hard pressed to do without certain public services such as police and fire protection, education, and hospital services. These can be called essential services. Few substitutes for these services can be made available quickly, and the absence of these services can create hardships and, in some cases, health risks to the public.

It is difficult to evaluate whether public employees do or do not have a power advantage because public services vary substantially in the degree to which they are deemed essential. Police and fire protection may well be classified as essential services, but do city clerks and engineers provide essential services? Parents may vocally complain when schools are closed by striking teachers, but when social workers strike do cities or states hear any public outcry?

Moreover, the essentiality of a given service seems to vary significantly over time. In the late 1960s and early 1970s public agencies found it difficult to resist the demands of striking public employees. Yet in the mid- and late 1970s taxpayers often seemed eager to berate striking public employees as part of their more general efforts to lower taxes and the cost of government. The public's willingness to sustain public sector strikes also seems to sway with political winds. During the more liberal years of the 1960s the public often seemed willing to sustain public sector strikes, but this trend reversed during the more conservative years of the mid- and late 1970s.

A final note on the willingness and ability to take a concerted strike action: Public employees are affected by public policies as well as by economic and political contexts. Public employees are not included in the coverage of the National Labor Relations Act (NLRA). Thus, regulation of their right to strike is in the hands of the states and historically has varied enormously across and sometimes within states. The bargaining leverage public employees have in strike situations is also affected by whether the courts impose penalties on striking unions or employees. Since the law and its administration varies so much over time and across states we discuss this issue more fully in a later section.

Financial Conditions of Governments

To appreciate fully the special pressures that arise in public sector bargaining, it is important to understand the sources of revenue on which public employers rely. Local governments obtain the greatest proportion of their revenue from state governments. In 1983, 29 percent of local government revenues came from that source. Property taxes and aid from the federal government provided, respectively, 25 percent and 6 percent of local government funds in 1983.[6] The amount of federal aid to states and local governments grew considerably in the 1970s, but its growth slowed markedly in the 1980s.

Beyond these direct tax-based sources of revenues, local and state officials can generate funds from user charges and short-term or long-term borrowing. In addition to the limits imposed by the credit and debt capital markets, the revenue-generating capacity of local government is constrained by (1) the size of the tax base in the community, (2) the willingness of the public to tax itself, and (3) constitutional or other legal limitations on the amount of taxes local governments raise. The key determinants of the tax base are the level and the composition of employment in the community.

By the mid-1970s employment in the public sector had stopped growing; and many of the large states—particularly in the Northeast, where bargaining had been going on the longest—experienced severe fiscal strain. New York City, the prime example of the fiscal crises of the cities in the 1970s, hovered on the brink of bankruptcy for several years. Eventually, it was forced into accepting an emergency financial control board composed of representatives of the state government, private sector, unions, and, indirectly, the federal government. Between 1974 and 1979 the number of employees on the city payroll declined through a combination of layoffs and attrition.[7]

New York City's financial problems received tremendous national attention and helped fuel the incipient taxpayer resistance to further growth in public budgets. As a result, nine states adopted new tax or spending limitations, regardless of their actual fiscal health. The most widely publicized example, California's Proposition 13, was approved by the voters in 1979. This constitutional amendment limits property taxes to 1 percent of real market value and tax increases to 2 percent per year.[8] A number of cities with constitutional tax and debt limitations came close to, or reached, their revenue-generating limit by the latter part of the decade.

By the mid-1980s the tide had begun to turn back, with some observers claiming the cutbacks in government spending had gone too far, particularly with regard to public education. The Carnegie Commission, among others, issued reports charging that public education was inadequate given the many economic challenges confronting the nation and that part of the solution lay in upgrading the salary and status of public school teachers.[9] Evidence in support of that charge came from the fact that school districts were having difficulty recruiting science and math teachers because of competition from the growing computer industry. All these factors added strength to the claims of public employee unions, especially the teachers' unions.

In summary, although the inelastic demand characteristic of the public sector may provide what appears to be a favorable economic environment for public employee unions, the high proportion of labor costs in public budgets and public resistance to those costs tend to offset some of the potential leverage public sector unions might gain from this structural characteristic.

THE SOCIOPOLITICAL CONTEXT

Early critics of the spread of collective bargaining to the public sector feared that public employees would be inherently powerful because elected officials would be politically vulnerable to union organizations. The main proposition underlying this argument is that the public employee unions would be able to contribute both money and votes to electoral candidates and thereby gain substantial political leverage. It was argued that collective bargaining would distort the normal political process by giving unions preferred access to decision makers at the expense of other interest groups in society.[10] In contrast, others argued that in the absence of special organizing rights and protections public employee interests would consistently lose out to the power of opposing interest groups and particularly to pressures by taxpayers resistant to increasing government expenditures.[11] These proponents suggested that although collective bargaining would increase the political strength of public employees and could result in larger wage increases, it would not necessarily result in a disproportionate amount of political influence for public employees.

Both arguments ignore the tremendous diversity that exists in the political context of public sector collective bargaining in various regions and localities, as well as the changes in the political environment that occur as economic and social conditions change. The response of employers to public sector unions ultimately depends on the relative political influence of public employees and other interest groups in the jurisdiction.

In communities where the private sector labor movement is powerful, public employee unions have a more favorable political base from which to begin. In the absence of a favorable political or social environment for unions, their task of building effective union organizations is more difficult. Thus, the political environment for public employee unions is affected by the larger social context, the strength of unions in general in the community, changes in the social climate and political activity of countervailing interest groups, and finally changes in the economic conditions of the community. As economic conditions tighten and other interest groups become more aggressive, the political base of support for public employee unions and collective bargaining begins to erode. In those communities where unions have historically been unwelcome, these economic and social changes create an extremely unfavorable political environment for unions of public sector workers.

THE PUBLIC POLICY CONTEXT

Federal Employees

Federal, state, and local government employees are all excluded from coverage under the NLRA. By passing a special act in 1970 as part of the overall reform of the postal service, however, Congress provided postal employees the right to engage in collective bargaining over wages, hours, and working conditions. Other federal employees had received rights to unionize and negotiate over nonwage or fringe benefit issues through Executive Order 10988, signed by President Kennedy in 1962. This order was subsequently extended by President Nixon in Executive Order 11491.

In 1978 Congress replaced those executive orders with the first comprehensive federal law providing collective bargaining rights for federal employees, as part of a much broader reform of civil service procedures and policies. Title VII of this law (Public Law 95-454) protects the right to organize and bargain collectively on conditions of employment; it continues to exclude pay and fringe benefits from the scope of bargaining. The law is administered by a newly created Federal Labor Relations Authority. Responsibility for impasse resolution is vested in the Federal Services Impasses Panel. The panel may use mediation, factfinding, or arbitration to resolve disputes. The right to strike is still prohibited.

State and Local Government Employees

As of 1986 all but ten states had passed legislation providing to at least some of their state or local government employees the right to organize and bargain collectively. Table 14–1 lists these states by the type of coverage provided. Of the 40 states 25 have passed comprehensive laws covering a

TABLE 14–1
State collective bargaining laws

Coverage	States
1. All-inclusive laws	District of Columbia, Florida, Hawaii, Iowa, Massachusetts, Minnesota,[a] New Hampshire, New Jersey, New York, Oregon, South Dakota
2. All employees, separate laws	Alaska, California, Connecticut, Delaware, Illinois, Kansas, Maine, Montana, Nebraska, North Dakota, Pennsylvania, Rhode Island, Vermont, Wisconsin
3. Some employees covered	
Teachers	Indiana
Teachers and noncertified public employees	Maryland
Police and firefighters	Kentucky,[b] Texas[c]
Firefighters	Alabama, Georgia, Wyoming
Police, firefighters, and public school employees	Oklahoma
All but state civil service	Michigan, Washington
Local employees, teachers, and nurses	Nevada
Firefighters and teachers	Idaho
All but teachers and police	Missouri
State classified service	New Mexico
Teachers and transit workers	Tennessee
All but judicial	Ohio
4. No laws	Arizona, Arkansas, Colorado, Louisiana, Mississippi, North Carolina, South Carolina, Utah, Virginia, West Virginia

Source: Government Employee Relations Report (Washington D.C.: Bureau of National Affairs, July 1986).

[a] Excludes employees at charitable hospitals.
[b] Qualified for certain cities.
[c] Conditional on municipal vote.

number of occupational groups. All of the states that have not yet enacted public sector bargaining laws are in the South or the West.

Public sector bargaining laws were passed earliest and are most comprehensive in those states with liberal political histories, high levels of expenditures per capita on governmental services, and above-average growth in personal income between 1960 and 1970.[12]   States with public sector laws also tend to be those with a high percentage of their private sector employees unionized. The pattern of legal enactment experienced in the public sector conforms more to the hypothesis, noted in Chapter 3, that public policy reflects the existing political balance of power and social norms than to the hypothesis that it serves to make up for power imbalances. That is, laws providing bargaining rights were passed where government expenditures and income were already relatively high and where labor had the greatest influence. Similar laws are yet to be passed in the states where wages tend to be lower and labor weaker.

Variations in the political effectiveness of occupational groups also influence the nature of the laws governing different groups within each state. Police and firefighters, for example, tend to have the most comprehensive statutes and to have impasse resolution procedures ending in arbitration rather than mediation or factfinding. Teachers also fare better than other local employees in the majority of states. State government employees tend to have the weakest or least comprehensive forms of collective bargaining rights and impasse procedures.[13]   Thus, the favorability of collective bargaining legislation to public employees in state and local governments depends not only on the state's political and economic environment, but also on the interest group effectiveness of different employee groups within the state and the essentiality of the service provided by the employee group.

The first collective bargaining laws for state and local employees were passed during the late 1960s and the early 1970s. In the 1980s to date, on the other hand, only one state, Illinois, has passed a comprehensive law extending bargaining rights to state and local government employees.[14]   Instead, the recent years have been witness to a number of revisions and amendments to the laws that were passed in the earlier years. Those amendments expanded the scope of collective bargaining to new issues, covered new employee groups, strengthened the agencies charged with administration of the laws, or modified the dispute resolution procedures.

Studies of public sector union growth suggest that the state bargaining laws exerted an important independent effect on unionization. States that enacted laws had relative increases in unionization in the ensuing years. Furthermore, the more favorable the laws were to unions, the greater the growth of unionization. At the same time, however, there are examples of sizable public sector union growth in some states, such as Ohio, that did not have laws favorable to public sector unions. Some evidence that the legal framework for bargaining does affect union growth comes from the effects of the Yeshiva decision, discussed in Chapter 4, which ruled that tenured faculty members in private colleges and universities performed managerial duties and therefore were not eligible for union representation. In the aftermath of that decision the previously rapid growth of unions representing such college and university teachers was reversed, suggesting that the law does make a difference. In sum, therefore, we can conclude that the laws did spur unionization.[15]

Federal Legislation Affecting State and Local Employees

The failure of the remaining states to provide collective bargaining rights for public employees has led to calls for federal legislation extending some form of bargaining rights to all public employees. Movement on this issue has been blocked by two obstacles. The most formidable is the constitutional question whether the federal government has the authority to mandate collective bargaining legislation covering state and local employees.[16] A second major obstacle has been the inability of various labor unions to agree on the form the legislation should take. Three different approaches have been advocated: (1) a simple extension of the National Labor Relations Act and the jurisdiction of the National Labor Relations Board to cover state and local employees; (2) special comprehensive legislation that takes into account the unique characteristics of public employees; and (3) a minimum-standards law of collective bargaining rights for state and local employees, with the specific form of the legislation left to the states. Given the constitutional questions raised by Supreme Court decisions, the minimum-standards option appears to be the least likely to be overturned. But the longer the separate state laws are in effect, the more difficult it will be to impose a uniform national law.

Like its private sector counterpart public sector collective bargaining is influenced not only by collective bargaining legislation, but also by a myriad of other economic and social policies and regulations imbedded in state and federal statutes. Chief among these are the laws outlined previously governing taxation and financial decisions in government. Also important are civil service laws and procedures and laws governing education. One of the more difficult issues that has arisen in the public sector, as collective bargaining has spread, is how to resolve conflict between the rights provided public employees by the collective bargaining statute and the provisions of other laws and regulations.

THE ENVIRONMENTAL CONTEXT: A SUMMARY

This brief overview helps us appreciate the diverse, interdependent, and dynamic environmental conditions under which public sector collective bargaining has developed. The early predictions that the economic and political context of public sector bargaining would inevitably tip the balance of power in favor of either the unions or the employers have proved to be overly simplistic. Bringing home this point are the different experiences of large cities such as New York, Los Angeles, Chicago, Memphis, New Orleans, and San Francisco—all of which developed different responses to public employee unions at different times, and all of which experienced major shifts in the political environment for bargaining over the last decade. And together these cities stand in even more marked contrast with the experiences and the political contexts of bargaining in small, rural, and conservative communities, where unions are actively resisted and viewed with a great deal of suspicion. The dangers of any broad generalizations about public sector bargaining are further demonstrated by the differences between the political and economic power of such occupational groups as police, firefighters, teachers, and sanitation workers and the power of librarians, clerks, and other white-collar professionals. The early critics of the potential power of public sector unions ignored these many sources of differences. Finally, none of the early forecasters foresaw the shift in the political and economic fortunes of public sector employees and employers that occurred as the political economy of public employee bargaining tightened in the mid-1970s.

Based on the dubious track record of the earlier forecasts, any efforts to generalize about the environment for collective bargaining should be viewed with extreme caution, if not skepticism. If predictions must be made, however, they should at least be based on the following propositions that emerge from past experiences with public sector bargaining.

1. The economic context of public sector bargaining is more conducive to public employee unions when:
   a. the wages of the public employees are low relative to other employees in the area;
   b. employer revenues are rising and the government can more easily pay additional wages and fringe benefits;
   c. the demand for public services is high and increasing and the public is willing to tax itself at a rate high enough to obtain additional services;
   d. employment in the community is stable or expanding;
   e. the credit rating of the governmental employer is sound;
   f. federal and state aid is increasing; and
   g. the inflation rate in the overall economy is low or moderate.
2. The political climate for public sector unions varies directly with the general social and political climate of the community and state. This, in turn, will partly depend on the rate of unionization of private sector employees in the community and the state.
3. The political climate is more congenial to public sector services in economic environments that are favorable to public employees.
4. Public policy toward collective bargaining will depend on how favorable the economic and political contexts are for bargaining and on how effective public employee unions are in promoting their concerns as interest groups.
5. Those states that have not yet passed collective bargaining statutes for state and local employees will continue to be slow to do so, as they continue to exhibit attitudes less supportive of public sector unions than do the states that have already passed such laws.
6. Future modifications in existing state collective bargaining laws will depend on the bargaining and lobbying power and effectiveness of the particular occupational groups involved.
7. Changes in federal legislation for state and local employees are unlikely to come about unless public sector employee organizations achieve

consensus about the type of legislation they prefer, unless the AFL–CIO puts this legislation higher on its list of political priorities than it is now, and unless the constitutional question is resolved.

PUBLIC SECTOR BARGAINING STRUCTURES

As outlined in Chapter 4 the major structural features of collective bargaining are (1) the degree of centralization in the formal bargaining structure, (2) the breadth or scope of employee interests included in bargaining units, (3) the role of supervisors in collective bargaining, and (4) the extent of informal pattern bargaining that occurs. These issues will be taken up in this order, with the exception of the discussion of supervisors, since this was dealt with in Chapter 4.

It should be recalled that the structure of collective bargaining in the private sector evolved relatively slowly and incrementally over its history. Since we have at most a 25-year history of bargaining in the public sector to review at this point, we should be careful not to conclude that the current state of affairs necessarily represents a plateau in the structure of public sector bargaining. Although we have reasons to believe that the current structure reflects the special characteristics of public employment and therefore will not move in the same direction as private sector structures, only time will test this assertion.

The Degree of Centralization

Collective bargaining in the public sector is highly decentralized. Almost all bargaining is done on a single-employer basis, that is, with a particular city, state, or federal government or agency. There are a few isolated examples of formal multiemployer bargaining, but there is little indication at this time that multiemployer bargaining will become an important feature of the public sector. The major *economic* constraint against formal multiemployer bargaining is that taxation and revenue-generating decisions are made by local governments. Unless pressures come from state or federal sources to centralize bargaining, and unless these pressures are tied to federal or state tax and revenue inducements to do so, the decentralized pattern of bargaining is likely to persist. The economic diversity across local employers and the variations in wages, fringe benefits, and terms and conditions of employment that have developed through decentralized bargaining also would make it difficult to consolidate bargaining units among employers. The major *political* constraint against centralizing bargaining in a multiemployer arrangement is that each political jurisdiction carefully guards against erosion of its political autonomy and decision-making power. The conflicts that arise any time a state or federal agency attempts to take power out of the hands of local school officials, for example, would very likely arise in any effort to centralize bargaining.

Nonetheless, information sharing and informal coordination do occur within and across state and local governments. As public sector bargaining has grown, so has the number of organizations of labor relations professionals in the public sector. These groups share information and conduct surveys to assist one another in the conduct of their separate negotiations.[17] In some states, such as New York, school districts are organized into area associations that often correspond to county or comparable regional subdivisions. Many of these associations pool the funds of member school districts and hire a single labor relations professional to represent them. This practice has an informal centralizing effect, since the professional negotiators can begin to develop consistent policies and contract provisions across the various school districts. And since the teachers' unions in these districts also normally rely on only a small number of business agents, the professional negotiators on both sides of the table in any given geographic region tend to be the same people. Although the power of these professionals to bring about standard practices and provisions in agreements is limited by their own political influence with school boards and local union organizations, over time they are beginning to bring more standardization across district lines.

A few of these districts in New York have engaged in experimental forms of coordinated bargaining. In one case where four districts attempted a form of coordinated bargaining, variations in the contracts that existed before the attempt, major differences in the districts' ability to pay, the unwillingness of member school districts to relinquish autonomy over bargaining decisions, and intense personal rivalries within the ranks of both the union negotiators and the employers all caused this experiment to fail. Of the districts that participated one withdrew from the coalition before impasse, the others went to impasse with no issues resolved and required the use of both mediation and factfinding, one district went on strike after factfinding, and the settlements in all the districts ended up being negotiated separately. Although the failure of this experiment does not mean that similar efforts will necessarily meet the same fate, substantial economic or legal pressure from either state or federal sources will obviously be necessary to bring about more centralized bargaining.[18]

An example of an instance where federal pressure did force a consolidation of bargaining units was in Wilmington, Delaware, where the suburban and central school districts were required to merge as part of a plan to desegregate the public schools. Also spurring consolidation are efforts to equalize spending for public education across districts, some mandated by the courts and others by taxpayer groups critical of a reliance on local property taxes to fund education.

The Scope of Bargaining Units

Bargaining in the public sector tends to follow occupational lines more than is the case in the private sector. A city government is likely to have separate bargaining units for police officers, firefighters, blue-collar workers (either in one citywide unit or separate departmentwide units), and various professional groups. If bargaining rights extend up the hierarchy to include supervisors, they, too, may have a separate bargaining unit. If the city funds or operates one or more hospitals, separate bargaining units along craft or occupational lines within these facilities are also likely to exist. Finally, the public schools are likely to have additional separate units for teachers, school administrators, clerical and secretarial employees, bus drivers and maintenance employees, and perhaps school principals. State governments also tend to have a relatively large number of occupational or departmental groups. The pattern here is more varied, however, and the trend has been to consolidate these units into large, statewide units. Some cities have also been attempting to consolidate their bargaining units. As mentioned in Chapter 4, between 1967 and 1977 New York City reduced the number of its bargaining units from 400 to just under 100.

Severe fiscal crises can raise strong demands to consolidate bargaining units. Consider the dilemmas facing cities like Buffalo and New York City in the mid-1970s when contracts expired with all of their city employees and they were faced with the problem of spreading extremely meager resources across groups that had traditionally bargained separately. In 1976, for example, the city of Buffalo reached separate impasses in bargaining with its teachers, police, firefighters, blue-collar employees, and white-collar employees—virtually all of the employees that negotiate with the city. The problem underlying each of the impasses was the same. The city had no money to pay increases and was under severe pressure to devise a financial plan for assuring its survival. The city of New York experienced similar pressures and, in 1977, agreed with its major public employee units to negotiate the economic package on a coordinated basis. Not all employee groups responded favorably to this approach, however. The police officers, in particular, refused to participate in the coalition, believing they could do better on their own. And when economic conditions stabilized in New York in the early 1980s, the coalition broke apart.

The rivalries that separate police and firefighters in many cities effectively limit the potential for coalition bargaining with these two groups, even though, in the vast majority of municipal governments, their wages and fringe benefits are intricately tied to each other in the form of parity or some established differential. If there is to be any coordination in bargaining with these groups in the future, it is likely to take external pressure and strong demands from the employer to bring it about.

Pattern Bargaining

There is no evidence that public sector jurisdictions conform to any national, interindustry type of pattern bargaining. The types of pattern bargaining that most frequently do exist in the public sector are (1) intraemployer, interunit pattern bargaining and (2) interemployer, intraoccupational pattern bargaining. The former tends to exist where the employer has attempted to develop a comprehensive wage policy and apply it to all bargaining units under its jurisdiction. Employers using this strategy seek comparable wage and fringe benefit increases rather than comparable wage levels. Obviously, occupational wage differentials between such groups as blue-collar and white-collar employees are likely to persist. Over time, however, if these employers continue to persist in their demands for a standardization of wage and fringe benefit increases, these differentials are likely to decline. The decline is more apt to be in fringe benefits and the nonwage provisions of the bargaining agreement than in wages.

Empirical evidence of this form of intraemployer, interunit pattern bargaining comes primarily from bargaining in the Canadian federal sector. Anderson showed that wage increases and the diffusion of other changes in bargaining agreements spread rapidly through bargaining units in the federal government of Canada.[19] All of these units were bargaining with a single employer, the Canadian federal government. We have little empirical evidence to determine how extensive this form of pattern bargaining is in any sector of the United States at this time. There is evidence, however, that the previous pattern of parity between police and firefighter wages and benefits that predated collective bargaining in the public sector continues to survive in most bargaining jurisdictions. Where the parity pattern has broken down, it has generally resulted in an unstable bargaining situation in future rounds of negotiations because the group that lost ground attempts to recapture its lost status, while the group that gained ground seeks to maintain its improved position. The employer then gets caught in the middle of this unhappy dispute.[20]

The major source of the interemployer, intraoccupational pattern is the importance factfinders and arbitrators attach to comparability as a wage-setting criterion in public sector disputes. Many of the statutes in the public sector include a set of wage criteria that arbitrators and factfinders are to consider in rendering their awards or recommendations. Every study of these procedures that has examined the relative importance of the various criteria has concluded that comparability is given the greatest weight. While comparability can be interpreted in a variety of ways, most of these studies also conclude that the most frequently cited comparisons are within occupational groups in different cities. For example, the wages of firefighters in a given city are normally compared to the wages and benefits of firefighters in similar cities. The same holds true for teachers, police officers, and other employees. There is also some evidence that the existence of arbitration tends to narrow occupational wage differentials because of the comparability criterion found in the arbitration statutes.[21]

MANAGEMENT CHARACTERISTICS

Because many of the unique characteristics of public sector bargaining stem from the dual functions performed by government as an employer and as a provider of public services, a great deal of attention has been paid to managerial behavior in public sector bargaining. In this section we will review what has been learned from research into management's goals, structure, internal decision making, and general policies toward unions and collective bargaining.

An understanding of managerial behavior in the public sector must start with a thorough understanding of the political and organizational characteristics of government agencies and the pressures that unions and collective bargaining bring to these organizations. An underlying assumption of our representative form of government is that the goals of elected leaders reflect the preferences of their constituents. Thus, the more diverse the interests within a political jurisdiction, the more diverse we can expect the interests of the elected leaders to be. The doctrine of separation of powers that underlies the organizational structures of local, state, and federal governments further accentuates that diversity among power holders, since elected officials share power with administrative officers such as department heads, personnel departments, and civil service commissions. Finally, the growth of unions in the public sector has, as in the private sector, added a new power center within the management hierarchy, namely, staff specialists assigned to the labor relations function.

A number of studies have documented the broad diversity of interests and the diffusion of power that exists among city management officials who have influence over collective bargaining issues. For example, one study found that the rankings of a variety of labor relations goals reported by city officials vary across managerial groups, and each group places its highest priority on maintaining its own power in decision making.[22] City labor negotiators place their highest priority on keeping elected officials out of the negotiations process. Mayors and city council members place their highest priority on protecting their own decision-making powers. Civil service commissioners place their highest priority on protecting the merit system from erosion through collective bargaining contract provisions. Overall, the concern for protecting one's own power far outweighs any other substantive differences that may exist across these groups of management officials.

Although internal differences in managerial goals exist in all organizations, they are more important in public sector organizations because these organizations usually lack a clear hierarchy of decision makers to facilitate internal conflict resolution. The major consequence of the diversity of interests or goals, and of the diffusion of decision-making power across a large number of officials, is that internal conflicts are likely to occur more often and to be more public in public sector organizations. Conflicts between the mayor and the city council, for example, are as likely to occur in collective bargaining as they are over other politically sensitive issues in the community. These conflicts are also more likely to be difficult to resolve before, or during, the early stages of negotiations, because the hierarchy for decision making is less clearly defined and, therefore, the power and authority of each of the decision makers are more ambiguous. The consequence of these aspects of public sector organizations is that the internal conflicts are likely to spill over into the formal negotiations process. It is this sequence of events that has been shown to be the predominant cause of multilateral bargaining in the public sector.[23]

The sequence of multilateral bargaining (defined further in the next section) is diagrammed in Figure 14–1. The more diverse the interests within the management structure, and the more power is shared among management officials with diverse interests, the more common and open conflict is likely to be. Internal conflicts, in turn, are likely to transform bargaining from a bilateral into a multilateral process. Union officials will have different degrees of political access to the various management officials in power and will try to use their access to influence those officials to play a more prominent role in collective bargaining. As negotiations approach impasse, the pressures on management groups or officials to respond to their constituencies increase accordingly. Thus, the ability of management to act in a coordinated or unified way tends to break down in the face of an impasse or a strike.

Given this complex array of interests and organizational diffusion of power, the role of the management negotiator in the public sector is a difficult one. Like the representative of any employer, the management negotiator must serve in the dual capacity of (1) coordinating internal organizational interests and (2) representing the organization in its dealings with the union. The more internal diversity there is and the more power is shared among different individuals or groups, the more difficult the internal coordination role becomes. The problem is further exacerbated by changes in the political climate for unions. When unions have considerable influence and access to

FIGURE 14–1
A two-stage model of multilateral bargaining in city governments

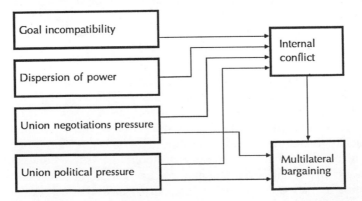

Source: Thomas A. Kochan, "City Government Bargaining: A Path Analysis," *Industrial Relations* 14 (February 1975): 100, figure 3.

elected officials, the management negotiator may find it difficult to hold elected officials together as a strong, united management team. In this context the management negotiator often needs to be a strong advocate of an arm's length approach to the unions. In contrast, when the political climate is more hostile to public sector unions, or when the elected officials are unfamiliar with and unsympathetic toward unions and collective bargaining, the management negotiator may have to convince the elected officials to be more realistic about what can be achieved in negotiations and to advocate a more accommodative approach to the collective bargaining process.

THE NEGOTIATIONS PROCESS

Our brief analysis of the political nature of public sector management serves as a useful backdrop for the following discussion of the negotiations process in the public sector. Because of this unique characteristic of management, public sector negotiations can best be conceptualized as a multilateral, rather than a purely bilateral, decision-making process.

Multilateral Bargaining

Multilateral bargaining is a negotiations process that includes more than two distinct parties or interest groups in such a way that no clear dichotomy between the union and the management organization exists. In contrast, bilateral negotiations usually involve formally designated negotiators or negotiating teams representing two groups: the employer and the employees. These teams negotiate to the point of reaching a tentative bargaining agreement, which they then take back to top management and the union rank-and-file for final approval or ratification. In viewing bilateral negotiations, it is assumed that all interactions between the union and the employer organizations are channeled through the formally designated negotiators and that the negotiators serve as the representatives for their organizations.

Although this description of bilateral negotiations is obviously an oversimplification of the way bargaining occurs in any context, it provides a useful contrast to the multilateral nature of negotiations in the public sector. For example, a frequently observed union tactic in public sector negotiations is the "end run." Here union officials calculate there is a sufficient diversity of interests or power bases within management to make it worthwhile to sidestep the formal management negotiating team and take their proposals before an alternative group—city council representatives, school board officials, or even the county or state legislature.

As illustrated in Box 14–1, another form of multilateral bargaining is intervention by individual elected officials who act on their own to try to influence the course of negotiations. They may do so in response to union pressures to change the formal bargaining stance of management or if the officials have become disenchanted with a position the union is taking in

---

BOX 14–1
Multilateral bargaining in the 1980s

The following excerpts from *Boston Globe* articles report a quintessential case of multilateral bargaining that occurred in 1986 in a strike involving Boston school bus drivers, the Boston superintendent of schools, and the mayor of Boston.

Laval S. Wilson, Boston's school superintendent, sharply criticized Mayor Flynn last night after receiving a letter from the mayor outlining proposals to end the 11-day-old strike by 600 school bus drivers. The letter also went to the drivers' union president.

"I believe we are now in a critical time in the negotiations, and feel that in the best interests of the schoolchildren of our city, both sides should seriously consider [the attached] proposals as options for breaking the current logjam and getting all of our kids back into the classrooms," Flynn wrote to Wilson and the union president James Barrett.

. . . Sounding angry and frustrated after receiving the letter . . . Wilson said in a telephone interview, "I think it's completely out of bounds for the mayor to put something in writing with proposals to both sides, and to make it public through the press as if these are the ways we can solve the strike. . . . It's unfortunate that the mayor is intruding directly on the negotiating process," said Wilson, adding that negotiations should only include the drivers, bus companies, and the School Department.

In a follow-up article the next day the political dialogue continued:

[Superintendent Wilson:] "I don't like someone undermining the negotiations process. We can't have two superintendents running Boston's public schools."

[Mayor Flynn:] "I could care less about the School Committee members whining about political turf. The Boston school system is not the private political domain of the superintendent and the School Committee."

The strike ended the following day with a negotiated agreement. The *Globe* article on the settlement stated:

Flynn took credit for bringing about negotiations that led to a proposed settlement. "A more harmonious relationship is in everybody's interest." . . . Asked if he was worried about Boston being labeled as a strikebreaker Flynn responded, "You bet I am. I'm not about to become another Calvin Coolidge." [In 1919 Calvin Coolidge broke a Boston police strike that is thought to have been the first strike by public employees in the United States.]

Source: Boston Globe, 17, 18, and 19 January 1986.

---

negotiations. Still another form of multilateral negotiations is the case of a decision-making group that rejects a negotiated agreement and refuses to implement it. Civil service commissions, school boards, or city councils, for example, often must ratify the final agreement. At that stage, again, constituent political pressures may come to bear on officials to change the terms and conditions of the bargain.

Yet another example is that of the community interest group that sees its concerns being affected by the negotiations process. As the scope of bargaining in teacher negotiations expands to deal, for example, with issues of student discipline, the curriculum, or the welfare of minority interests, community groups are likely to step up their involvement in negotiations. Finally, another manifestation of multilateral bargaining has been in jurisdictions where fiscal crisis has necessitated financial assistance from state and federal authorities, public employee pension managers, and private sector business leaders—all of whom usually demand some say in negotiated outcomes in return for their support.

Strikes and Impasses

Just as the political and organizational characteristics of public sector management and unions are helpful in explaining the development of multilateral bargaining, multilateral bargaining serves as a useful concept for analyzing the causes of impasses and strikes in public sector negotiations.[24] A basic premise underlying most models of strikes and impasses in the public sector is that they are heavily influenced by the political context of bargaining. Strikes and impasses are partially caused by the same factors that lead to open political conflict over other issues in the community. Conflict within collective bargaining, therefore, can be expected to occur most frequently in politically complex communities where diverse interest groups share power over decision making, and where unions are both militant and politically influential. A study of the determinants of impasses in police and fire-fighter negotiations found that the political and organizational factors in the multilateral bargaining model just reviewed were strongly correlated with the probability of an impasse.[25] A high level of hostility between negotiators and a history of previous dependence on impasse procedures further increased the probability of impasses in those bargaining relationships.

The strategic value or effectiveness of a strike in the public sector depends not only on the economic pressures that a group of employees can bring to bear on the employer, but also on the political pressures that can be brought to bear on elected officials to end the strike. In contrast, the more the public resists public employee strikes and the more elected officials can rely on an adverse climate for public employees, the more able they are to resist the pressures to settle quickly and at all costs.

The strike: A case study. The importance of the political context, as well as a number of the other sources of impasse outlined in the model, is nicely illustrated by the events surrounding a 1977 strike of state employees in Wisconsin. To understand the negotiations leading to this strike, we must review the events of the previous round of bargaining. The previous contract was settled through an end run around the management negotiators, in an agreement worked out in consultations between Wisconsin's governor and Jerry Wurf, then president of the American Federation of State, County and Municipal Employees (AFSCME). The memory of this end run carried over and conditioned the attitudes and expectations of the negotiators on both sides of the table in 1977.

The 1977 negotiations were further complicated by an agreement between the parties to open negotiations to the public. The early negotiations sessions were therefore characterized by much verbal sparring but little substantive negotiating. The union negotiators voiced repeated protests that the management negotiators lacked adequate authority to bargain.

In the background of the formal negotiations was a highly complex political situation. An interim governor took office at about the time the contract expired. Supervising the management negotiating team were the secretary of the Department of Administration, the governor, and a bipartisan committee of the state legislature. What this meant was the negotiators were reporting to a set of administrative and elected officials who were separated by a long history of interparty rivalry and differences over who should control the course of labor negotiations.

Most of the sources of impasse discussed in the model presented in Chapter 8 were factors in this dispute. The parties had a history of difficult bargaining, and the governor and other political officials who were not present in formal negotiations had a record of becoming involved as the negotiations process heated up. The decision-making structure on the management side was highly complex, with power shared among a number of competing political and administrative officials. As noted, intense political rivalries and differences existed among these management officials. The union and management negotiators distrusted each other, and the membership and union officers displayed a willingness to engage in militant action from the start of the negotiations. The fact that the bargaining unit covered employees in all parts of the state insured that this dispute would become a major political issue statewide. The presence of all these potential sources of impasse, in short, indicated that bargaining would indeed be difficult.

The dispute was settled only after the following sequence of events.

1. The union went on strike for 15 days, during which time the governor declared a state of emergency, called out the National Guard, and transferred physically and mentally handicapped patients from state to private institutions.
2. A court injunction was issued against the strikers.
3. An ad hoc, out-of-state mediator was brought in.
4. The governor and national officials from AFSCME entered the negotiations process.
5. The Joint Legislative Committee on Labor rejected a settlement that had brought the employees back to work.
6. Further negotiations and mediation efforts among the governor, representatives of the legislative committee, and the union took place.
7. The strike settlement was modified and approved by the legislature.

8. The state attorney general pursued contempt-of-court proceedings against the striking workers over the objections of the governor.

This case provides a good illustration of how the diverse political interests and pressures that lead to impasses or strikes are interrelated and together must be incorporated into any framework that seeks to explain the nature of public sector collective bargaining.

Empirical evidence on strikes.   The evidence on strikes in the public sector leads us to the following conclusions. First, the effectiveness of the strike as a tactic depends on the political power and influence of public employees. Strikes by unions in small, conservative, or rural communities have met with strong community resistance and have often been halted by a court injunction or some other means of weakening the union. Second, the likelihood of serious strike threats and the probability of a strike's occurring are greatest in the large, politically complex jurisdictions where unions have traditionally been politically active, powerful, and militant. Injunctions, on the other hand, have had little success in ending strikes by large, powerful unions in communities where the unions have considerable political influence. Third, employers in the public sector become more willing to resist strike pressures when economic conditions have deteriorated and the pendulum of public opinion has shifted against public employees.

There is conflicting evidence regarding whether passage of a public sector bargaining law affects the frequency of strikes. Burton and Krider found no effects of a law, whereas Stern and Olson found higher strike rates where local government employees were covered by a bargaining law.[26] There is substantial empirical evidence that the *availability* (not the *use*) of an arbitration procedure reduces the probability of public sector strikes.[27]

The nature of the environment in which bargaining occurs and the types of employees involved also appear to affect the propensity to strike. For example, teachers in large districts are more likely to strike than teachers in small districts, and strike propensities vary substantially across various public sector occupations.[28]

PUBLIC SECTOR BARGAINING: OUTCOMES AND EFFECTS

Wage and Other Compensation Outcomes

Studies of the results of collective bargaining in the public sector have generally followed the pattern of research on the private sector (see Chapter 10). The most common approach has been to estimate a union-nonunion wage differential. Two consistent findings have emerged from these studies. First, although the magnitudes of the estimates vary across the studies, the vast majority of the studies have found a significant wage differential between unionized and nonunion public employees.[29] Second, these estimates indicate that the wage effects of collective bargaining in the public sector are not greater than, and perhaps are slightly less than, the effects of collective bargaining in the private sector. The union-nonunion wage differentials are typically in the range of 5 percent to 15 percent. That is, unions do not, contrary to the Wellington and Winter hypothesis, appear to exert an inherently stronger effect on the wages of public employees than they do on the wages of private employees.

There also is evidence that collective bargaining has had a positive effect on selected fringe benefits of public employees, particularly in increasing pension benefits, reducing hours or days worked, and increasing time off with pay.[30] For some employees the substantial increases in pensions won by unions suggest that the simple wage differential seriously underestimates the compensation effects of bargaining. Did the increases in expenditures on employees' salaries and benefits result in major budgetary reallocations from other areas? Evidence comparing employment in union and nonunion cities suggests that public sector unionism raises or at least does not lower employment in the public sector. Apparently, public sector unions are able to lobby for greater government expenditures to eliminate any employment displacement caused by higher earnings.[31]

Historical (longitudinal) data also reveal that unions have raised relative earnings and point out some interesting dynamics in union wage effects. Table 14–2 reports ratios of the average annual earnings of public school teachers to the average annual earnings of production workers, and the same ratios for police and firefighter earnings to production worker earnings. The data show that from 1955 to 1975 teachers' relative earnings increased sizably (from 1.17 to 1.31), as did the relative earnings of police and firefighters (from 1.12 to 1.38).

These increases in relative earnings may at first glance not appear large, but it should be kept in mind that the U.S. earnings distribution typically shows a high degree of stability across occupations. In the face of that record these are indeed sizable changes. The important point to note here is that the period 1955 to 1975 was the one during which teacher, police, and firefighter unions increased both their memberships and their militance. The growth and militance of unions at the time may well have contributed to the relative earnings advances achieved by these public employees. At the same time, however, government expenditures were also growing over this 20-year period, and it is difficult to know how much of the increase in public employees' relative earnings should be attributed to their unions.

The data in Table 14–2 also indicate a sharp decline in teachers' and police and firefighters' relative earnings from 1975 to 1980. This was the era of the taxpayers' revolt, and it is difficult to quarrel with the suggestion by the table that the revolt had substantial effects on public sector earnings after 1975. Note that in five short years relative pay in these occupations

TABLE 14–2
Longitudinal evidence on the relative earnings of teachers and police and firefighters, 1955–84

Year	Teachers/ Production workers[a]	Police and firefighters/ Production workers[b]
1955	1.17%	1.12%
1960	1.20	1.15
1965	1.22	1.21
1970	1.28	1.32
1975	1.31	1.38
1980	1.05	1.13
1984	1.16	—

[a] Data in this column are ratios of the mean annual earnings of all public school teachers to the mean annual earnings of production and nonsupervisory workers in the private nonfarm sector. Teacher data for the years 1955–80 are from "Government Employee Salary Trends" (Washington, D.C.: Bureau of Labor Statistics, U.S. Department of Labor, various years). Teacher data for 1984 are from *Estimates of School Statistics* (Washington D.C.: National Education Association, 1985.). Production worker earnings data are from U.S. Department of Labor, Bureau of Labor Statistics, *Handbook of Labor Statistics* (Washington, D.C.: GPO, various years).

[b] Data in this column are ratios of the mean annual earnings of all local police and firefighters to the mean annual earnings of production and nonsupervisory workers (the latter are the same figures as those used to calculate the teacher earnings ratio). Police and firefighter earnings for 1955 through 1980 are from "Government Employee Salary Trends" (Washington, D.C.: Bureau of Labor Statistics, U.S. Department of Labor, various years.)

dropped to a point below the levels in 1955. Table 14–2 also indicates, however, that more recently relative pay in the public sector has again begun to rise. This most recent shift followed the shift in public concerns to issues of the adequacy of public education and public safety and protection. These concerns apparently led to a rise in relative earnings, though one that still kept public sector relative pay below the peaks achieved in the mid-1970s. The recent relative rise in public sector pay may also be a product of the slow growth in private sector pay, just as the fall in relative public sector earnings in the late 1970s likely was in part due to the rapid inflation in private sector pay rates in that period.

Further analysis of the course of collective bargaining in specific cities during the course of the taxpayers' revolt of the latter 1970s suggests that the revolt did indeed have substantial effects on public employees and the procedures that regulated their employment conditions. In the fall of 1975 voters in San Francisco altered municipal procedures in a number of ways to the detriment of city employees.[32] Wage and pension-setting procedures were modified, and city craft workers received pay cuts that averaged $2,000 and for some workers went as high as $4,500 annually. Those craft workers then went on strike but were resoundingly defeated, returning to work a month later under management's salary terms. Events in other cities at the time followed a similar course.

Membership Effects

Although public employees saw their pay gains slowed or reversed in the face of taxpayers' resistance, it is important to note that other events in the public sector did not follow the same course as in the private sector during the strains of the early 1980s. As we discussed earlier in this book, the percentage of the private sector labor force belonging to a union has been declining since 1953, and many unions lost sizable absolute numbers of members in the early 1980s. Furthermore, these unions in the 1980s were facing the difficult problem of responding to management's strategic initiatives and to intense pressures from the growth of domestic nonunion competition and heightened international competition. Public sector unions did face a decline in the public's support for governmental expenditures, but they did not face growing competition from nonunion or foreign producers. There were isolated examples of union members in state and local governments who were threatened during a strike by permanent replacement by strikebreakers. Nonetheless, although public sector employers may have grown more resistant to union demands after the mid-1970s, they did not aggressively try to remove their unions. As a result, the institutions of collective bargaining in the public sector have exhibited much more stability in recent years than their counterparts in the private sector.

The one important exception to these trends was the Professional Air Traffic Controllers Organization (PATCO). In August 1981 PATCO led its members out on strike to induce the federal government to increase the controllers' wages and benefits. President Reagan then fired the strikers on the grounds they had violated a no-strike clause in their employment contract. The government called in military controllers who, along with supervisors and some controllers who crossed picket lines, kept the air traffic system functioning (though limits were imposed on certain flights). The striking controllers were never rehired, and the Federal Labor Relations Authority decertified the union. (By 1987 the new controllers had voted in a new union.) Some analysts argue that the firing of the controllers had enormous ramifications by legitimizing a hard line in bargaining by other public and private sector employers. Management's resolve may have stiffened in both sectors, but, again, the course of collective bargaining has generally differed between the two sectors. Whether the private sector continues to face more serious environmental challenges and to exhibit greater instability than the public sector remains to be seen.

Other Outcomes and Effects

There is little doubt that collective bargaining has had a profound effect on both the process and the substance of personnel administration in public employment. As in the private sector, collective bargaining has increased the formalization of personnel practices and reduced the discretion of management in matters of discipline and discharge, promotions, transfers, and work assignments.[33] Unfortunately, however, there are still no broad-based studies of the effects of collective bargaining on the quality of services provided the public.

Case studies of both successful productivity improvement programs and of resistance by public sector unions to changes in work rules have been reported. A few cases of successful labor-management committees in the public sector have been cited (but not carefully evaluated), and at least two studies have suggested that the key to the effects of collective bargaining on the quality of public services is how well management adapts to the presence of the union.[34] These tentative findings echo an important conclusion we reached in Chapter 10, namely, the effects of unions and collective bargaining on the economic and organizational performance of the employer depend on the effectiveness of the working relationship the union and the employer develop. More concrete evidence is needed, however, before we can reach any reliable conclusions regarding the relationship between provisions in collective bargaining agreements (and their administration) and the quality and quantity of public services provided in a jurisdiction.

Characteristics of the economic, legal, and sociopolitical environments have all been found to be associated with variations in wages and other bargaining outcomes in the public sector. Three sets of economic variables have been found to be consistently related to the level of wages paid public employees: (1) the ability of the employer to pay, (2) community characteristics that reflect a high demand for public sector services, such as high rates of per capita expenditures for education, and (3) local labor market comparisons, as measured by the wages paid comparable private sector workers in the locality.[35] These economic factors provide a starting point for explaining variations in the wage levels of public employees in different communities.

Numerous analysts have studied the effects of arbitration on the bargaining process and outcomes. The evidence consistently shows that the availability of arbitration reduces the frequency of strikes. Of course, it would be surprising if the availability of this dispute resolution mechanism did not reduce the frequency of strikes. With regard to wage effects a number of studies have found that the availability of arbitration (not its use) has led to higher wage settlements and more favorable contract terms, but a few studies have concluded that arbitration has no effect on salaries.[36]

Another important question is whether the political environment has intervening effects on the outcomes of public sector bargaining, effects that are distinct from the effects exerted by favorable legislation. It is difficult to distinguish between the effects of these two components of the environment, since political environments favorable to unions also produce public sector laws that are supportive of collective bargaining. As we noted earlier, the existence of a public sector bargaining law has been found to increase union membership, and union membership in turn raises the wages paid police officers and firefighters.[37]   Another study found that the outcomes of firefighter bargaining were more favorable to the union in states with comprehensive collective bargaining laws and formal impasse procedures, such as factfinding or arbitration, than elsewhere.[38]   A similar finding was reported in a nationwide study of selected provisions in teacher contracts.[39]

One study using a similar methodology concluded, however, that the environmental conditions that produced these laws were more important determinants of bargaining outcomes than the laws themselves.[40]   More extensive qualitative evidence suggests that a strong collective bargaining law (such as a law providing for binding arbitration) has its greatest effects in political environments that are hostile toward unions or for employee groups that would have little bargaining leverage in the absence of a law. Thus, one interpretation of these findings is that the effects of a collective bargaining law in supportive political environments are only marginal, whereas the law serves as a significant source of union power in communities or for employee groups whose unions have a hard time building political influence and bargaining effectively in the absence of a law.

SUMMARY

The research literature has focused on three basic questions in its evaluation of the effects of collective bargaining in the public sector. Interestingly, each question reflects the fears of the early critics of public sector bargaining. (1) Has collective bargaining increased the political access and influence of public sector employees? (2) Has the strike proved to be a strong source of power in the public sector?   (3) Have dispute resolution procedures, particularly binding arbitration, led to outcomes injurious to the public welfare?   The preponderance of evidence suggests that these fears were overblown.

Although case studies have documented isolated examples of the importance of political influence and pressure, comparative studies that have included these variables have not found them to have played any more than a marginal role in explaining variations in wages and other bargaining outcomes across different jurisdictions.[41]   The evidence also suggests that the strike has not consistently proven to be a one-sided source of union power. Furthermore, analysis of wage effects finds that the union-nonunion wage differential does not appear to be larger in the public sector than in the private sector. Public sector unions do appear to have raised some fringe benefits substantially and to have increased the total amount of governmental expenditures and employment, but these effects are hardly significant enough to warrant any call for a dismantling of public sector bargaining. And finally, although the evidence on the effects of arbitration is mixed, there is no evidence that the presence of arbitration has seriously perverted the collective bargaining process in the public sector. These conclusions should not, however, be taken as final answers to the critics. Their questions will continue to be germane as the performance of the public sector bargaining system is monitored in future years.

THE FUTURE OF PUBLIC SECTOR BARGAINING

Early debates over public sector bargaining centered around the transferability of private sector policies and practices to this new environment. After more than a quarter-century of experimentation with a mixture of private sector and newly minted public sector policies, most debates now focus on the transferability of policies and experiences from one public sector jurisdiction to another. We are even beginning to reverse the original question by asking whether some of the policies experimented with in the public sector could be applied effectively in private sector contexts. This is especially true with respect to the various dispute resolution procedures that have been used as alternatives to the strike.

The public sector will continue to serve as a laboratory for monitoring the long-term consequences of a collective bargaining system that places a high priority on limiting the right to strike. What are the long-term consequences of a system that relies heavily on both third-party neutrals and outside advocates? What are the long-term effects of a system whose outcomes depend more on public choices and political decisions than on the direct constraints of the economic market? These are issues that will continue to be debated as experience unfolds.

At the very least the emergence of public sector bargaining has stimulated thought and analysis around these questions. In doing so it has opened the door to new ways of thinking about how collective bargaining can be adapted to new environments. The public sector has proven to be a valuable laboratory for experimentation and should continue to be so in future years.

Suggested Readings

Several general references on public sector bargaining are:

Aaron, Benjamin, Joyce Najita, and James L. Stern, eds. *Public-Sector Bargaining,* 2d ed. Washington, D.C.: Bureau of National Affairs, 1987.

Freeman, Richard B. "Unionism Comes to the Public Sector," *Journal of Economic Literature* 24 (March 1986): 41–86.

Lewin, David, Peter Feuille, Thomas A. Kochan, and John Thomas Delaney, *Public Sector Labor Relations: Analysis and Readings,* 3d ed. Lexington, Mass.: Lexington Books, 1987.

Notes

1. This argument can be found in Harry H. Wellington and Ralph K. Winter, Jr., *The Unions and the Cities* (Washington, D.C.: Brookings Institution, 1971).

2. Public employee union membership figures are traced in John F. Burton, Jr., and Terry Thomason, "The Extent of Collective Bargaining in the Public Sector," in *Public-Sector Bargaining*, ed. Benjamin Aaron, Joyce Najita, and James L. Stern (Washington, D.C.: Bureau of National Affairs, 1987); and Richard B. Freeman, "Unionism Comes to the Public Sector," *Journal of Economic Literature* 24 (March 1986): 41–86.

3. Orley Ashenfelter and Ronald G. Ehrenberg, "The Demand for Labor in the Public Sector," in *Labor in the Public and Non-Profit Sectors*, ed. Daniel S. Hamermesh, 55–78 (Princeton: Princeton University Press, 1975).

4. Robert J. Thornton, "The Elasticity of Demand for Public School Teachers," *Industrial Relations* 18 (Winter 1979): 86–91.

5. There are some exceptions to this, such as the tolls collected on roads and fees collected at parks.

6. *Facts and Figures on Government Finance* (Washington, D.C.: Tax Foundation, 1983).

7. See Joan P. Weitzman, "The Effect of Economic Restraints on Public Sector Collective Bargaining: The Lessons from New York City," in *Government Labor Relations: Trends and Information for the Future*, ed. Hugh D. Jascourt, 334–46 (Oak Park, Ill.: Moore, 1979).

8. For a description of Proposition 13 and the measures adopted in the other eight states, see "COPE Charts Impact of States' Spending and Tax Limitations," *Government Employee Relations Report* 812 (28 May 1979): 14–17.

9. See Carnegie Forum on Education and the Economy, *A Nation Prepared: Teachers for the Twenty-First Century* (Washington, D.C.: Carnegie Foundation, 1986).

10. Wellington and Winter, *The Unions and the Cities*.

11. Clyde Summers, "Public Employee Bargaining: A Political Perspective," *Yale Law Journal* 82 (1974): 1156–1200.

12. Thomas A. Kochan, "Correlates of State Public Employee Bargaining Laws," *Industrial Relations* 12 (October 1973): 322–37.

13. Ibid., 327.

14. *Government Employee Relations Report*, research volume (Washington, D.C.: Bureau of National Affairs, 1986).

15. See Gregory Saltzman, "Bargaining Laws as a Cause and Consequence of the Growth of Teacher Unionism," *Industrial and Labor Relations Review* 38 (April 1985): 335–51. Other studies are reviewed in Freeman, "Unionism." Even with the rigorous statistical techniques used in these studies, however, it is still not known if the passage of a law favorable to public sector unions was a reflection of factors that would have spurred the growth of unions even if the law had not been passed.

16. The issue of federal jurisdiction arose in *Joe G. Garcia* v. *San Antonio Metropolitan Transit Authority et al.*, 105 US 1005 (1985); and *National League of Cities* v. *Usery*, 426 US (1976).

17. Peter Feuille, Hervey Juris, Ralph Jones, and Michael Jay Jedel, "Multi-Employer Negotiations among Local Governments," in *Public Sector Labor*

Relations: Analysis and Readings, 2d ed., ed. David Lewin, Peter Feuille, and Thomas A. Kochan, 110–13 (Sun Lakes, Ariz.: Thomas Horton and Daughters, 1981).

18. The ups and downs of coordinated bargaining in New York City are traced in David Lewin and Mary McCormick, "Coalition Bargaining in Municipal Government: New York City in the 1970s," *Industrial and Labor Relations Review* 34 (July 1981): 175–90.

19. John C. Anderson, "Determinants of Bargaining Outcomes in the Federal Government of Canada," *Industrial and Labor Relations Review* 32 (January 1979): 224–41.

20. For an example of this pattern, see Thomas A. Kochan, Mordechai Mironi, Ronald G. Ehrenberg, Jean Baderschneider, and Todd Jick, *Dispute Resolution Under Factfinding and Arbitration: An Empirical Analysis* (New York: American Arbitration Association, 1979), 170–71.

21. Ibid., 70–71.

22. Thomas A. Kochan, L.L. Cummings, and George P. Huber, "Operationalizing the Concept of Goals and Goal Incompatibilities in Organizational Research," *Human Relations* 29 (June 1976): 537, table 3.

23. Thomas A. Kochan, "City Government Bargaining: A Path Analysis," *Industrial Relations* 14 (February 1975): 90–101.

24. The material in this section draws heavily from Thomas A. Kochan, "The Dynamics of Dispute Resolution in the Public Sector," in *Public-Sector Bargaining*, ed. Benjamin Aaron, Joseph R. Grodin, and James L. Stern, 150–90 (Washington, D.C.: Bureau of National Affairs, 1979).

25. Kochan et al., *Dispute Resolution*, 31–39.

26. John F. Burton, Jr., and Charles E. Krider, "The Incidence of Strikes in Public Employment," in *Labor in the Public and Non-Profit Sectors*, ed. Hamermesh, 161–70; James L. Stern and Craig A. Olson, "The Propensity to Strike of Local Government Employees," *Journal of Collective Negotiations in the Public Sector* 11, no. 3 (1982): 201–14.

27. Kochan, "Dynamics of Dispute Resolution," 160–63.

28. Stern and Olson, "The Propensity to Strike."

29. For a review of these studies see Freeman, "Unionism."

30. See ibid.

31. See ibid. These studies of union effects on expenditures had difficulty detecting whether higher government expenditures are caused by the same factors that cause public sector unions to grow or by the unions themselves.

32. The events in San Francisco are analyzed in Harry C. Katz, "Municipal Pay Determination: The Case of San Francisco," *Industrial Relations* 18 (Winter 1979): 44–59.

33. See David T. Stanley, *Managing Local Government Under Union Pressure* (Washington, D.C.: Brookings Institution, 1972); Hervey Juris and Peter Feuille, *Police Unionism* (Lexington, Mass.: D.C. Heath, 1973), 125–50; Lorraine McDonnell and Anthony Pascal, *Organized Teachers in American Schools* (Santa Monica, Calif.: Rand Corporation, 1978), 75–82; George

Sulzer, *The Impact of Labor-Management Relations upon Selected Federal Personnel Policies and Practices* (Washington, D.C.: Superintendent of Documents, 1979).

34. See McDonnell and Pascal, *Organized Teachers*, and Sulzer, *Impact of Labor-Management Relations*. For an analysis of the consequences of technological change see David Lewin, "Technological Service," in *Workers, Managers and Technological Change: Emerging Patterns of Labor Relations*, ed. Daniel B. Cornfield (New York: Plenum, 1986).

35. For a review of these studies see David Lewin et al., "The Impact of Unions on Public Sector Wages," in *Public Sector Labor Relations*, ed. Lewin, Feuille, and Kochan, 397–405.

36. For example, Craig A. Olson, in "The Impact of Arbitration on the Wages of Firefighters," *Industrial Relations* 19 (Fall 1980): 325–39, found that arbitration leads to higher firefighter compensation. Peter Feuille, John Thomas Delaney, and Wallace Hendricks, in "The Impact of Interest Arbitration on Police Contracts," *Industrial Relations* 24 (Spring 1985): 161–81, found that the availability of arbitration improves the earnings and other contract provisions of police. In contrast, David E. Bloom, in "Collective Bargaining, Compulsory Arbitration, and Salary Settlements in the Public Sector: The Case of New Jersey's Municipal Police Officers," *Journal of Labor Research* 2 (Fall 1981): 369–84, found no salary effects of arbitration in New Jersey.

37. Freeman ("Unionism") examined the evidence and concluded that legislation is the primary determinant of unionization, but Burton and Thomason came to a very different conclusion in "The Extent of Collective Bargaining in the Public Sector."

38. Thomas A. Kochan and Hoyt N. Wheeler, "Municipal Collective Bargaining: A Model and Analysis of Bargaining Outcomes," *Industrial and Labor Relations Review* 29 (October 1975): 53.

39. McDonnell and Pascal, *Organized Teachers*.

40. Paul F. Gerhardt, "Determinants of Bargaining Outcomes in Local Government Labor Negotiations," *Industrial and Labor Relations Review* 29 (April 1976): 331–51.

41. Ibid., 345.

CHAPTER 15

![band]

The Future of
U.S. Labor Policy
and Industrial Relations

T hroughout this book we have stressed how changes in the environment of collective bargaining are challenging many of the traditional principles and practices of labor and management in the United States. The events of the early 1980s signaled that in many settings the guiding principles of the New Deal industrial relations system were breaking down and no longer were adequately serving the interests of workers, unions, employers, or the public. The remainder of the 1980s has therefore been a period of experimentation and innovation in industrial relations practices among a significant number of companies and unions. At the same time, the decade has also seen a period of growing polarization and tension between many unions and employers and between the labor movement and federal policymakers.

The central question facing industrial relations professionals now is which of these two developments will dominate labor-management relations in the future. Will the innovations and experiments with new forms of cooperation and representation diffuse and become the foundation for a new model of U.S. industrial relations? Or will the pace and diffusion of innovation halt as union membership continues to decline and as labor and management lock horns in the struggle between unions' pursuit of survival and employers' pursuit of the nonunion option?

The purpose of this chapter is to explore the implications of these two potential developments for the future of U.S. labor policy and, more broadly, for the future of industrial relations practice.

Our concept of national labor policy is very broad in scope. It goes well beyond the specific content and administration of the National Labor

Relations Act and directly related statutes. By labor policy we mean the broad array of labor standards and regulations governing employment conditions, employment, training, and other labor market policies and programs. Since labor policies are part of a larger set of national economic and social policies, the effects of these broader policies must also be taken into account in any analysis of the impact of public policy on industrial relations. (A sampling of the broad array of policies affecting industrial relations is shown in Figure 15–1.) Moreover, labor policy involves not only statutes and regulatory rules but also the actions and leadership of the political and administrative officials who develop, implement, and enforce those policies.

We have chosen to link labor policy with a discussion of the future of industrial relations because we believe that public policy will play a key role in shaping the course of labor and management practice in the years ahead. The central hypothesis behind this view is that the pace of innovation will continue and diffuse to broader settings only if it is reinforced and supported by national labor, human resource, and economic policies. If national policies do not actively promote and reinforce these innovations, we believe labor-management relations will go through a prolonged period of unnecessary conflict and result in further deterioration in the competitiveness of unionized firms. This would produce a further decline in union membership and could eventually produce a void in worker representation in the United States.[1]

A critical factor in the course of the nation's future labor policies will be the challenge to the economy posed by the large and persistent trade deficits and sluggish productivity growth of the 1980s.[2] Concern for the competitiveness of the U.S. economy abounds, as illustrated by the number of highly publicized national, state, and university commissions seeking solutions to this problem.[3] The U.S. economy also has been plagued by persistently high rates of unemployment, a decade of decline in real wages for the average worker, and what appears to be a growing inequality in the distribution of income.[4] More coherent national labor and human resource policy will be necessary to insure that efforts to improve the competitiveness of the economy do not severely erode the standard of living of U.S. workers and do not impose severe hardships on those whose jobs will be either altered or eliminated as organizations adjust to new technologies and changing market circumstances.

In short we believe that, as in the 1930s, U.S. labor policy is now at a crossroads. How government responds will help shape the future of the labor movement and the types of collective bargaining relationships that evolve over the years ahead. Policymakers face a set of major political choices—whether to reaffirm their support for the basic principles of worker representation and participation that gave rise to the New Deal labor policies or allow union representation and collective bargaining to continue their decline in importance and effectiveness. If they select the former choice,

FIGURE 15–1
Selected components of national labor policies

A. General economic and social policies	B. Labor relations policies	C. Employment and human resource policies
1. Aggregate monetary and fiscal policies	1. Railway Labor Act	1. Wage and hour legislation (e.g., Fair Labor Standards Act, Davis-Bacon Act)
2. Incomes policies	2. Norris-LaGuardia Act	2. Equal employment opportunity laws, regulations, and enforcement efforts
3. Trade policies	3. Wagner Act	3. Occupational Safety and Health Act
4. Immigration policies	4. Taft-Hartley Act	4. Employee Retirement Income Security Act
5. Antitrust policies	5. Landrum-Griffin Act	5. Unemployment insurance system
6. Regulation of multinational corporations	6. Civil Service Reform Act of 1978, Title VII	6. Social security system
7. Environmental protection policies	7. Postal Reorganization Act of 1970, Public Law 91-375	7. Workers' compensation system
8. National health insurance proposals	8. "Little Wagner acts" at state level	8. Job Training Partnership Act and related employment adjustment programs
9. Energy policies	9. State employee bargaining laws and policies	9. Programs to improve labor-management cooperation
10. Productivity improvement and capital formation policies		
11. Industry regulatory policies (hospitals, transportation, etc.)		
12. Welfare policies		

policymakers will then need to choose between a conservative strategy aimed at reconstructing the New Deal model of collective bargaining through marginal adjustments and a reform strategy promoting new forms of labor-management relations that supplement traditional collective bargaining with new practices at the strategic and workplace levels of industrial relations. Even if the more sweeping reform strategy is pursued, it may not lead to an immediate reversal in the ongoing decline in union representation. If it does not, then a major issue likely to arise is whether more government regulations will be needed to fill the void in worker representation left by lower rates of unionization. As we noted in Chapter 1, ultimately it is the adequacy of worker representation and not the level of union membership that is the fundamental concern of public policy. This chapter therefore examines the alternative strategies that labor policy might follow in the future and explores the implications of these different choices.

ALTERNATIVE DIRECTIONS FOR NATIONAL LABOR POLICY

Three broad and very different strategic directions for national labor policy seem possible. The first is to continue the labor policies of the early 1980s, namely, to continue deregulating product markets and taking a generally laissez-faire approach to labor policy. This approach would focus on achieving the right mix of the policies shown in column A of Figure 15–1 and de-emphasize the policies in columns B and C. The second approach would focus on the column B policies by reasserting support for the basic principles that underlay the New Deal industrial relations system and reverse the laissez-faire labor policies of recent years by marginally reforming the National Labor Relations Act and related statutes. The third approach would be to focus on the interrelationships across the policies in the three columns by pursuing more substantial reforms and seek to integrate labor relations policies with broader economic and employment policies aimed at improving the competitiveness of the economy. Following this third approach would require initiating an exceedingly active labor policy, one that supported the diffusion of the recent reforms in industrial relations practice discussed earlier in this book.

Strategy 1: Laissez-Faire

In Chapter 1 we noted that the movement to deregulate the transportation and communications industries marked a subtle shift in national labor policy away from a gradual expansion of labor standards and regulations and toward an emphasis on greater competition. Although the specific objective of deregulation was to increase product market competition, its result was a chain reaction of unintended consequences in the labor market, in ownership structures, and in the employment terms and conditions of the workers in these industries. Thus, labor policy in this case was a derivative of this broader economic policy.

The ascendancy of competitive market strategies was also visible elsewhere in the employment arena. In contrast to the period of expanding employment regulations from 1960 to 1975, when the number of employment regulations administered by the U.S. Department of Labor tripled,[5] no major new labor standards or regulations were enacted by either the Carter or the Reagan administration. And although no major labor legislation has been repealed during the Reagan presidency to date, benefit levels were either frozen at existing levels or reduced, and a clear shift toward a more conservative enforcement strategy was adopted.[6] For example, the minimum wage has remained constant since 1981 even though increases in the cost of living eroded the purchasing power of the minimum by 28 percent between 1981 and 1987. The federal budget for employment and training activities was cut from a peak of approximately $11.2 billion in 1981 to under $5.6 billion in 1986. The number of Occupational Safety and Health Administration employees was reduced by 25 percent in the early 1980s.

The shift in labor policy administration was perhaps most visible in the decisions of the National Labor Relations Board. During the Ford and Carter administrations roughly 28 percent of the board's unfair labor practice decisions were in favor of employers. After President Reagan appointed two new members and a new chairman, the board decided 60 percent of its cases in favor of employers.[7]

Taken together these turns in labor policy and its administration do indeed reflect a laissez-faire philosophy. In actual administrative practice the effect was to scale back significantly, and in some cases reverse, the federal government's support for the labor policies of the New Deal.

Now that the government has adopted this laissez-faire approach, one might logically ask: Why not extend it and allow market forces full rein in employment relations? For the reasons outlined below we continue to believe there are strong normative, theoretical, and empirical reasons why *sole* reliance on competitive labor markets is not a sufficient strategy for national labor policy. At the same time, however, there are strong reasons why market forces should continue to play a *prominent* role in future labor policy.

The basic argument in favor of laissez-faire labor and human resource policies is twofold. First, market forces are extremely efficient in allocating labor and in pressuring labor and management to change practices that have become outmoded or inefficient. Protection from those forces encourages inertia and delay in adapting to change. The delay is only temporary, however, because no policy can restrain market pressures forever. And once a crisis finally forces adaptation, the costs of the adjustment are acute — much more acute than they would have been had the parties acted earlier. Society not only bears the cost of the output and productivity forgone while resources were misallocated but often is expected to help the parties absorb the costs of the transition. Some would argue that the decline in the competitiveness of the U.S. steel industry illustrates the inertia that can set in when management and labor believe that their actions will be protected from market forces because of their oligopolistic structure and the nation's interest in maintaining their industry.[8]

Second, even when market forces are proven inefficient, it is not clear that our theories and administrative abilities are strong enough to design and implement appropriate policy solutions. One of the reasons proposals for new industrial policies have as yet failed to generate much support is that no one has been able to demonstrate conclusively that any of them would yield more favorable economic and social consequences than do market forces.[9]

The normative arguments against a laissez-faire labor policy are essentially the same as those articulated in the early years of this century by the institutional economists (and reviewed in Chapter 2). Those arguments stress that labor is more than an economic commodity; the conflicts of interest between employees and employers are both inherent and enduring; and without effective government protection many workers will lack the bargaining power needed to assert their interests or secure their basic rights in modern employment relationships. Put most simply, competitive labor markets leave too many workers in a weak bargaining position vis-à-vis their employers and leave too many workers suspended in a state of permanent job insecurity.

For these reasons the early institutional economists supported policies designed to allow workers to accumulate "property rights" in their jobs as their tenure with the employer increased. In this view workers are not homogeneous or completely interchangeable commodities. Once hired, an employee should be entitled to greater rights to a job than competitors in the external labor market; and those rights should increase with the employee's tenure in the organization. The institutionalists believed that such a policy would reflect societal norms and expectations regarding what constitutes fairness and equity in employment relationships. Moreover, if the workplace is to reflect the democratic values of the broader society, it must allow employees a chance to participate in and influence managerial decisions affecting the terms and conditions of employment. Thus, unless we are willing to return to the view that labor is simply a commodity like any other, we must demand a labor and human resource policy that is attentive to the aspirations, expectations, and rights of workers.

Ultimately, then, the normative arguments against sole reliance on a laissez-faire approach to labor policy rest on the prediction that individual workers, employers, and the society as a whole would all suffer economic and political costs from a continued decline in union membership and worker representation. This view takes history as its guide in envisioning the scenario that is most likely to be played out if union representation should shrink to a point where unions in the private sector represented perhaps as little as 10 percent of the labor force. In this scenario the potential for management's abuse of its power and the void in worker representation would eventually produce pressures for both greater governmental intervention in employment relations and the emergence of new and more adversarial forms of unionism.

The theoretical arguments against the laissez-faire labor policy have been buttressed by more recent theoretical and empirical work. Essentially, the laissez-faire philosophy is grounded on the assumption that market mechanisms work through the preferences of the *marginal worker*. This assumes, in turn, high rates of labor mobility and the ready interchangeability of workers. Labor markets should clear (that is, provide the optimal allocation of labor) just as any other auction or single-transaction market does by bidding the price of labor down or up to the value of its marginal productivity.

The problems with this view are that (1) most employment relationships are long term in nature and (2) price (wage) and quantity (employment) adjustments made over the course of time affect not just workers at the margin but *all* workers within the *internal labor market(s)* of the organization. We also know that worker preferences are diverse and that the preferences of the junior, marginal workers are often quite different from those of the median or more senior worker. Time horizons also differ among workers with varying tenure in the organization. Those near retirement will have less interest in changing the existing conditions of employment or trading off short-run compensation gains for investments that will enhance workers' long-run competitiveness and future job opportunities. Moreover, improving the productivity and competitiveness of existing organizations involves changing the skills, motivation, and performance of the existing employees. It also requires initiating and sustaining organizational changes in settings where some individuals and groups perceive benefit in maintaining the status quo. Thus, market adjustments will not reflect the preferences of the average employee and may produce exceedingly costly social conflict.

It is necessary, therefore, to supplement market forces with a system of governance that encourages adaptability on the part of the majority of the existing workers and managers and also provides incentives for investments in long-run productivity gains and employment creation. Any such system requires moving away from policies that focus on the marginal worker or the new organizational entrant to policies that facilitate change and adaptation among workers and managers currently employed in existing organizations.

Collective bargaining is but one means of enhancing the influence of existing workers, resolving conflicting priorities, and mobilizing commitment to change within a given enterprise or organization. Nevertheless, the historical record suggests that collective bargaining can also be a very effective means for providing equity, due process, and adaptation.

Any future labor policy will have to address the fact that union membership is heavily concentrated in the oldest and most mature sectors of the economy. Those sectors will undoubtedly continue to experience a great deal of structural change and employment adjustment as management introduces new labor-saving technology, develops new products, adopts new business strategies and organization designs, and reallocates labor within and outside these organizations and industries. Labor policy will have to respond to the fact that many of the jobs being eliminated are high-wage jobs held by union members, while many of the new jobs being created are jobs those workers are not trained to perform or low-wage jobs in nonunion organizations—or both. If union leaders continue to believe they cannot organize and represent workers in these new jobs because of employer opposition and weaknesses in the existing labor law, and if workers see themselves as having no good labor market alternatives to their present jobs, we can expect considerable conflict over these structural adjustments. Market forces alone will not smooth out these adjustment processes and replace the wages of the workers affected by these changes.[10] Thus, a major public policy challenge lies in addressing the reason why workers and union leaders continue to resist these structural adjustments. The reason is clear: They bear the costs while others enjoy the benefits of the adjustments.

Experience with deregulation in mature industries such as airlines and trucking suggests that without any relevant labor or human resource policy, labor cannot, through the traditional forms of collective bargaining, force management to resist the resulting pressure to minimize labor costs. Once product market competition increased after deregulation, management found it easier to cut labor costs than to compete through managerial reforms, technological innovation, or product innovation. Deregulated industries have experienced widespread pay and work rule concessions, reduced employment security, reduced innovation in human resource management and labor-management relationships, and corporate restructuring and ownership shifts that have resulted in the expansion of those firms that are most aggressive in resisting unions or attempting to eliminate union representation.[11]

A national economic policy that seeks to foster competitiveness by encouraging greater product and labor market competition will lead to more developments such as these, especially in industries that are in mature (slow growth) stages of their life cycles. Yet in an economy that cannot compete with developing nations on the basis of labor costs, policies that encourage labor cost minimization may in the long run be self-defeating. Reducing labor costs may help save some jobs in the short run, but in the long run the U.S. economy cannot become more competitive and at the same time retain workers' standard of living without encouraging employers to invest in strategies that enhance the quality of their human resources.

Few dispute that the comparative advantage of the U.S. economy lies in its high-technology and high-quality products and in industry's ability to adapt rapidly and readily to change. That ability, in turn, demands skilled and adaptable employees who are strongly committed to their employers. But in mature product markets with labor markets experiencing high rates of unemployment and with some employers that compete on the basis of low wages, other employers in the market face intense pressures to match the low wages and low levels of human resource investments—unless they must also answer to an explicit public policy or strong resistance from their work force.

Strategy 2: A Return to New Deal Principles

A second alternative for future labor policy is to return to actively supporting the principles and policies of the New Deal industrial relations system. This would require, among other things, marginally reforming the NLRA and its administration to meet today's environment. Proposals for reform range from modest changes in NLRB procedures and improved administrative efficiency to legislative changes designed to restore a balance of power between labor and management. More specifically, new laws could make it more difficult for employers to oppose union-organizing efforts and make it easier for unions to achieve first contracts in units where the majority of the workers vote to unionize.[12]

This second strategy would require recommitting political support and economic resources to administering and enforcing the various labor standards and regulations that now govern employment relationships. Most importantly, we would see a return to the view that the appropriate role for government policy is to structure the rules of the game or the processes by which the parties pursue their interests at the workplace, but refrain as much as possible from intervening to affect the outcomes of the employment relationship. Following in the New Deal tradition, the focus of this strategy is on *procedural* rules that specify the rights of the parties and place limits on each party's rights to use its power. This marginal reform strategy also implies a strong belief that the parties, left to their own devices, can adapt their bargaining relationships in ways that promote their long-term interests without imposing undue costs on the broader society. Thus, a return to this model would amount to a reaffirmation of the adversarial principles and practices encouraged in the collective bargaining process. These are the underlying premises of the NLRA and the values that guided the efforts of the institutionalists who directed the efforts of the War Labor Board and the NLRB in the postwar period.

Recall that this basic policy was adopted in the 1930s as part of the broader New Deal economic reforms. As we noted in Chapter 2, even at that time, when concern for worker welfare and fear of labor unrest were probably at their peak, support for collective bargaining came only reluctantly from both the President and the Congress. Even then labor policy had to be rationalized as a part of a broader strategy for economic recovery and as necessary to avoid more radical forms of labor activity and violent labor-management conflicts. Since that time public support for unions has gradually declined.

These observations lead us to conclude that the marginal reform strategy is unlikely to take hold without a major shift in labor's political power and shifts in the nation's social climate. Without either one it is difficult to imagine wide popular support for strengthening the traditional forms of collective bargaining.

Nevertheless, minor changes in the administration of the existing law could come about if unions were able to help elect a President and a Congress more sympathetic to their objectives than those in the recent past. But if the analysis presented in the previous chapters is correct in suggesting that the principles of the New Deal model of collective bargaining no longer suit the needs of many firms and employees, neither small changes in current administrative practice nor a major reaffirmation of this model are likely to provide an adequate foundation for labor policy. Thus, although we concluded based on the empirical evidence reported in Chapter 4 that current procedures warrant improvement, any reforms that stay within the New Deal policy framework are not likely to be sufficient.

Strategy 3: An Integration of Labor, Economic, and Social Policies

A third strategy for labor policy would be to make it an integral part of the nation's economic and social policy agenda. In the 1930s labor policy was designed to meet the nation's needs for industrial peace and to overcome the weak purchasing power of consumers. Now, however, the needs of the economy and society center less on achieving labor peace and more on encouraging labor and management to adapt to international competition in ways that do not result in a deteriorating standard of living or become self-defeating. Thus, if labor policy is to make a significant contribution to meeting the economic and social challenges of contemporary society, a major restructuring in its underlying principles and scope may be in order. This restructuring would require that government leaders participate in and actively encourage a process of change and innovation in industrial relations. It would also require a clear view of which industrial relations innovations and changes are needed to improve both productivity and the standard of living.

The challenge of accomplishing any such restructuring of U.S. labor policy is twofold. First, how can collective bargaining and industrial relations contribute to the nation's current economic and social objectives? Second, what actions can government policymakers take to encourage labor and management to make the transition to new industrial relations practices?

A labor policy encouraging labor and management to adapt their practices in ways that both address their individual needs and contribute to national economic and social objectives is obviously consistent with the long-run functions of industrial relations analyzed throughout this book. We believe this strategy is definitely superior to either a strategy relying on market forces or a strategy attempting to return to the principles underlying the New Deal model. It is more consistent with both the needs of the economy and the basic interests of labor and management. We therefore devote the remainder of this chapter to outlining the roles that government, management, and labor leaders would need to adopt to make this approach to labor policy successful.

TOWARD A NEW INDUSTRIAL RELATIONS SYSTEM

Before discussing the necessary prerequisites of a new national labor policy, we need to clarify the desired features of a restructured model of industrial relations practice. Figure 15–2 summarizes the key features of a restructured model we and our colleagues developed after conducting a longitudinal study of the innovations in industrial relations practice introduced in a number of collective bargaining relationships over the past decade.[13] Although no single bargaining relationship we studied had institutionalized all of these features, each was working toward one or more of them. The model presented in Figure 15–2 should be viewed as an ideal type or stylized description of an industrial relations system whose features are better suited to the contemporary environment than the features of the New Deal collective bargaining system.

As shown in the figure, we organize the features of the new system within the three tiers of industrial relations activity introduced in Chapter 1. At the bottom level workplace industrial relations would feature employee participation in workplace decisions, flexibility in the organization of work and the deployment of human resources, and grievance procedures supple-

FIGURE 15–2
Elements in a new industrial relations system

Strategic level	Information sharing between management and workers Worker and union participation and representation Cross-functional consultations Integration of industrial relations with business and technology strategies
Collective bargaining and personnel policy level	Contingent compensation Employment continuity and security Strong commitment to training and development
Workplace level	Employee participation Flexible work organization Grievance procedures with communications and due process supplements

mented by other communications processes to achieve due process and conflict resolution. In Chapters 12 and 13 we stressed the interrelatedness of these workplace activities and their effects on organizational performance. The goal here is to promote a reinforcing set of activities that prevent the development of the low trust–high conflict cycle often found in traditional collective bargaining relationships. A major goal of the workplace system is to increase flexibility in the work organization by moving away from detailed and complex contractual provisions and narrow job descriptions.

The middle level of the model specifies the need for the parties to emphasize the employment and training side of the wage-employment trade-off. Various types of gains-sharing or profit-sharing arrangements are encouraged. The parties must be careful, however, not to let the shift to these contingent compensation policies erode wages to levels that lower workers' standard of living or serve to keep inefficient competitors in business. Thus, although the goal here would be to curb an overreliance on pattern bargaining and make wages more responsive to current economic conditions, a concern for industry and occupational norms and standards must also be maintained to avoid whipsawing by employers and an erosion of labor standards.

At the strategic level of the employment relationship the model makes a clear break with the principle that it is solely management's job to manage the enterprise and the union's job simply to negotiate over the effects of management actions already taken. Instead, a broader role for information sharing and consultation between management and worker representatives is encouraged. No single form of worker involvement or representation at the strategic level is anticipated, in keeping with the variety of informal and formal mechanisms that labor and management have already developed on their own. Moreover, the concept of exclusive representation of workers in a specific bargaining unit is modified in this model both at the workplace and at the strategic level. Thus, over time new cross-functional and mixed-occupational forums for consultation would supplement the formal negotiating units used to structure traditional bargaining relationships.

We should again stress that the complete features of this new model cannot yet be found in any bargaining relationship in the United States. Yet each of the separate features of the new model can trace its origins to recent experiments with new approaches to industrial relations. Our purpose in presenting this new model here is to build on these experiences and to bring together the separate proposals for reform that have been advocated in recent years. By making the new model more explicit we can now go on to examine the actions needed from leaders of government, management, and labor to diffuse and institutionalize it.

Diffusing and Institutionalizing the New System

Diffusing these types of changes in industrial relations and ensuring they will become ongoing practices will require both the active support of federal and state policymakers and significant shifts in the strategies of management and labor. Although it is hardly likely that any of these requirements will be met in the immediate future, we expect that debates over the future of labor policy and industrial relations practice in the years ahead will increasingly center on the issues discussed below. In keeping with the theme of strategic choice developed throughout this book, we believe that the future of industrial relations will in large part depend on the outcomes of these debates. In the long run it will be the strategic choices of the parties, along with the forces in their environment, that will determine the nature of industrial relations and its responsiveness to the changing needs of workers, employers, unions, and the society.

Government Strategies

Despite our earlier assertion that labor law reform is not likely to be achieved on its own, major reform of the principles and procedures underlying the NLRA is a necessary condition for achieving the type of industrial relations system envisioned in Figure 15–2. For unions to accept structural change and for low-wage workers to have the same opportunity to improve their standard of living through union representation and collective bargaining as did the generations before them, labor law must be restructured and enforced in ways that provide workers with an effective opportunity to achieve representation. The industrial relations record for the past decade is marked by high rates of employer unfair labor practice convictions, low rates of union successes in achieving first contracts, and long delays and weak remedies for unfair labor practice convictions. That record must be changed if respect for the law and the NLRB is to be reestablished. Moreover, ambiguities in the current law over the legality of voluntary recognition of a union by an employer need to be eliminated. Current policy encourages the parties to begin worker representation in an adversarial proceeding with the hope that eventually their relationship will mature and become more cooperative. A more affirmative policy of promoting cooperative and participative industrial relations is necessary in today's environment.

Other legal constraints on cooperation, consultation, and participation by employees, supervisors, and middle managers may also need to be removed. The Labor Department's discussion paper on labor law (see Chapter 4) has initiated debate over just this question. Supervisors must have greater opportunities for participation and representation in business and workplace decisions. Likewise, whereas constraints on the mandatory and permissible scope of bargaining may have made sense in an earlier era, we now know that strategic business decisions can have serious consequences for employment and income security. Effective representation in many contemporary settings therefore requires participation in strategic business decision making at an early stage of the process.

In addition to eliminating the legal barriers to industrial relations reform, government policymakers will need to promote actively the diffusion of innovations in private practice. Just as the Federal Mediation and Conciliation Service was charged with helping the parties avoid or resolve work stoppages and the NLRB was charged with enforcing the adversarial principles embodied in the NLRA, an equally visible and influential governmental role is needed to promote the diffusion of new industrial relations reforms. The War Labor Board may serve as a historical model for this role, since so many of the principles and practices common to collective bargaining in the postwar period can trace their existence to the support and encouragement given by the WLB.

A fundamental defining principle of the new industrial relations policy we call for is that it cannot stand apart from other federal human resource and economic policies. An extensive employment and training policy will be needed to assist workers who have to make the transition from one employment relationship or occupation to another. An unemployment compensation system that both covers a high percentage of the unemployed and encourages them to acquire the new skills needed to take advantage of new job opportunities would be another key part of this human resource policy. Also reinforcing the integrated policy would be regulatory policies that encourage the parties to take responsibility for monitoring and enforcing worker rights in the areas of safety and health, equal employment opportunity, and wage and hour laws.

Finally, this industrial relations policy cannot succeed over any extended period of time unless it is supported by broad macroeconomic policies that promote economic expansion, productivity growth, and long-term capital and human resource investments. Support for basic education, research and development, and the continued development of new sources of capital must go hand in hand with the labor policy reforms outlined above.

Government policy alone cannot spark the change, however. A new industrial relations model will not take shape without the active support of management and labor. To succeed in this, managers and unionists must overcome their own inclinations either to resist change or to favor alternative strategies that offer only short-run benefits.

Management Values and Strategies

U.S. managers will influence the diffusion of reforms in industrial relations through the key values they espouse and through the business and technological strategies that drive the basic goals and operations of the firm.

Management values. Innovation in unionized settings requires that management accept a broader role for unions and workers at the workplace and in strategic decision making than has been the case under traditional collective bargaining. Yet, as we have seen, opposition to unions and to expanded union influence is a deep-seated value of many U.S. managers and therefore serves as a significant barrier to the diffusion and institutionalization of this new model of industrial relations.

If managerial behavior continues to be dominated by this traditional value, most efforts to unionize new groups of employees will be highly adversarial. If current trends continue, unions will lose a majority of these contests and fail to achieve initial contracts in a significant number of the representation elections they do win. This will serve to further discredit NLRA procedures in the eyes of workers and their union representatives and will accentuate the level of hostility now prevalent in the labor-management climate nationwide. At the workplace level this hostile climate will strengthen the political positions of those union leaders favoring more traditional adversarial relationships with management—those who can hardly be expected to embrace reform and innovation at the same time. In cases where unions do achieve recognition through an adversarial proceeding, we can expect the adversarial relationship to carry over to their bargaining relationship and inhibit the development of the trust, flexibility, and participative relationship necessary for the new model of industrial relations.

Business strategies. Not all business strategies are equally compatible with diffusing and institutionalizing the industrial relations reforms proposed in Figure 15–2. Since unions today have difficulty in taking wages out of competition, many firms must now compete in markets where labor costs vary among the competitors. Yet competing through low labor costs is not a viable long-run strategy for most firms with international competition, and that strategy also undermines the worker trust, flexibility, and adaptability needed to make an alternative model of industrial relations work effectively.

Business and investment strategies that move work to different locations in response to short-run variations in labor costs are likewise incompatible with a new model of industrial relations. Any such strategy will leave U.S. workers perpetually lacking in both flexibility and job security. A low-cost production strategy will also divert management's attention away from the need to develop the comparative advantages U.S. firms can sustain in world markets—advantages built on advances in technology, highly skilled labor, and flexible production techniques. Thus, to sustain and diffuse major industrial relations reforms will require that U.S. managements adopt competitive strategies that meet the income and employment security expectations of the U.S. labor force.

Other business strategies that have the effect of limiting worker trust and flexibility also need to be challenged if industrial relations innovations are to take hold. The buying and selling of productive assets as mere short-run financial instruments without attending to the employment consequences borne by those affected by these actions has the same negative effects on employee trust and flexibility. Thus, corporate takeovers and other investment strategies that have only short-term or limited corporate objectives have deep, dysfunctional consequences for human resources and industrial relations. They should either be limited by public policy or be required to encompass labor policies that compensate and ease the adjustments demanded from the work force.

Technological strategies. One of the central lessons U.S. management has learned from Japanese firms operating in this country is that the
strategies used to design and implement new technology are key comple-
ments to human resource and industrial relations policies. Technological
strategies designed to embody all the production controls and labor-saving
features possible within the hardware itself serve to deskill and demotivate
workers, and they limit the opportunities for continued organizational learning and improvement. An alternative strategy is to take a *sociotechnical
approach* to technology in both its design and its implementation. This
approach uses technology to decentralize decision making in organizations
and upgrade worker skills by broadening job tasks and blurring the traditional distinctions between white- and blue-collar work. This approach also
has helped a number of the Japanese-managed auto plants in this country
to achieve very high levels of productivity and product quality—levels high
enough to set new standards that other U.S. plants must now try to meet.[14]
Thus, as with its business strategy, U.S. management will need to decide
whether its technological strategies will reinforce or inhibit the diffusion
and institutionalization of industrial relations reforms.

Should we expect a majority of U.S. managers to adopt the values and
strategies needed to support this model? If history is any guide, the answer
is quite clearly no, since these values and strategies require initiating and
institutionalizing significant changes in managerial practice that are unlikely
to occur in the absence of strong and sustained pressures to do so. Instead,
most managers are likely to prefer a more limited pattern of incremental
change and experimentation with new practices. Yet in environments where
international or domestic competitive pressures are strong, technology is
changing rapidly; and as worker expectations and aspirations for meaningful
jobs and careers are intensifying, the pressures for acceptance of the broad
features of this model are likely to continue to grow.

The central question therefore is: What role will unions or other forms
of worker representation play in responding to these pressures? Wherever
opportunities for achieving these changes without unions exist, we can
expect managers to take advantage of them. But wherever these opportunities do not exist, or the costs of pursuing them are high, we can expect
continued experimentation by management to introduce and institutionalize
elements of this new model into ongoing union-management relationships.

Labor Union Strategies

Labor leaders therefore face a parallel set of strategic choices in deciding
whether to support the diffusion and institutionalization of a new system
of industrial relations. At present the leaders of the U.S. labor movement
are deeply divided in their opinion of the recent reforms and innovations.
Unions' traditional opposition to participation in managerial decision making
stems not just from legal barriers and managerial resistance to the practice,
but also from union leaders' own fears that through participation they

will be coopted into supporting management's goals at the expense of their members' goals. Union leaders also fear that their support for participation and other industrial relations reforms will produce a backlash from the rank-and-file or from rival union leaders. They will have to reassess their views on these issues if industrial reforms are to diffuse.

Union leaders will also have to become more expert in communicating fully and frequently with their members about their participation in high-level management forums, and they will have to match workers' increased participation in business decisions with increases in union members' participation in internal union affairs. Increased participation in strategic and business decisions therefore poses new risks and challenges to union leaders.

Current and future union leaders thus will need to be trained in how to sustain a mixed-motive relationship with management. Their passive acceptance of these new strategies is unlikely to suffice. Strong, visible, and sustained support from union leaders at all levels of the labor movement is going to be necessary to convince managers, public policy officials, rank-and-file workers and union members, and the public that the U.S. labor movement is both willing and able to participate effectively in this new type of industrial relations system.

Why should labor leaders embrace this new model and adopt the new roles it requires of them? If the underlying conclusions of much of the current research and analysis of contemporary industrial relations are accurate, the answer to this question is quite simple: They must do so if they are to represent the interests of their current members effectively and organize new members. The central conclusion of the research reviewed in the various chapters of this book is that the scope of industrial relations activity has broadened in recent years to involve more activities above and below the level of traditional collective bargaining. Strategic decisions made at the top of corporations and day-to-day interactions at the workplace are now perhaps as important as the negotiations process. Union leaders must therefore acquire the ability to influence decisions and events at these levels as well as in collective bargaining negotiations. If they do not, their power and influence over the future of industrial relations will continue to decline.

SUMMARY

We began this book by presenting a normative perspective on industrial relations and a new and broader framework for analyzing current industrial relations practices. Throughout the book we have explored how the strategic choices of the parties interact with conditions in their environments to shape industrial relations policy and practice. It seems appropriate, therefore, that in this final chapter we have come full circle by posing the strategic choices that labor, management, and governmental decision makers now face if they are to participate actively in shaping the future of industrial relations. The field of industrial relations has a heritage of close connections between research, teaching, public policy, and private practice. This tradition must be fostered in the years ahead if our profession is to help address the challenges facing the actors in contemporary industrial relations.

Notes

1. For a discussion of these alternative scenarios for the future of industrial relations, see Thomas A. Kochan, Harry C. Katz, and Robert B. McKersie, *The Transformation of American Industrial Relations* (New York: Basic Books, 1986), 250–53.

2. For two different views of the consequences of U.S. trade deficits, see Robert Z. Lawrence, *Can America Compete?* (Washington, D.C.: Brookings Institution, 1984); and Otto Eckstein, Christopher Caton, Roger Brinner, and Peter Duprey, *The DRI Report on U.S. Manufacturing Industries* (New York: McGraw-Hill, 1984).

3. President Reagan established two such groups: the White House Conference on Productivity and the President's Commission on Industrial Competitiveness. By 1987 at least 14 other study groups had issued recommendations for restoring the nation's international competitiveness, and several additional university groups and others involving labor, management, government, and university representatives were working on this issue.

4. Christopher Tilly, Barry Bluestone, and Bennett Harrison, "What Is Making American Wages More Unequal?" in *Proceedings of the Thirty-Ninth Annual Meeting, December 28–30, 1986, New Orleans*, ed. Barbara D. Dennis (Madison, Wis.: Industrial Relations Research Association, 1987).

5. John T. Dunlop, "The Limits of Legal Compulsion," *Labor Law Journal* 27 (February 1976): 67.

6. Data on changes in the funding and administration of labor policies during the Reagan administration years are found in Sar A. Levitan, Peter E. Carlson, and Isaac Shapiro, *Protecting American Workers: An Assessment of Government Programs* (Washington, D.C.: Bureau of National Affairs, 1986).

7. F. Ray Marshall, "The Act's Impact on Employment, Society, and the National Economy," in *American Labor Policy: A Critical Appraisal of the National Labor Relations Act*, ed. Charles J. Morris (Washington, D.C.: Bureau of National Affairs, 1987), 33.

8. For a discussion of the decline of the steel industry, see Robert W. Crandall, *The U.S. Steel Industry in Recurrent Crisis* (Washington, D.C.: Brookings Institution, 1981). For a historical analysis of labor relations in the steel industry through the mid-1980s, see John Hoerr, *And the Wolf Finally Came* (New York: Praeger, 1987).

9. Paul Krugman, "Targeted Industrial Policies: Theory and Evidence," in *Industrial Change and Public Policy*, a symposium sponsored by the Federal Reserve Bank of Kansas City (Kansas City: Federal Reserve Bank, 1983), 125–26.

10. Paul Osterman, *Internal Labor Markets and Employment Policy* (New York: Oxford University Press, 1987).

11. Kirsten R. Wever, "Changing Union Structure and the Changing Structure of Unionization in the Post-Deregulation Era," in *Proceedings of the Thirty-Ninth*

Annual Meeting, December 28–30, 1986, New Orleans, ed. Barbara D. Dennis (Madison, Wis.: Industrial Relations Research Association, 1987).

12. See Morris, "Preface," *American Labor Policy,* for a discussion of a variety of different proposals for reform of the NLRA and the NLRB.

13. This model and the discussion that follows draw heavily on Thomas A. Kochan and Joel Cutcher-Gershenfeld, *Diffusing and Institutionalizing Innovations in Industrial Relations* (Washington, D.C.: Bureau of Labor Management Relations and Cooperative Programs, U.S. Department of Labor, 1987).

14. A description of this approach to technology and its relationship to industrial relations is contained in Haruo Shimada and John Paul MacDuffie, "Industrial Relations and Humanware," working paper no. 1855-87 (Cambridge: Sloan School of Management, Massachusetts Institute of Technology, 1987). See also Michael Cusumano, *The Japanese Automobile Industry* (Cambridge: Harvard University Press, 1986).

Author Index

475

Subject Index

O

P